PORTER AND IKE STOCKTON
COLORADO AND NEW MEXICO
BORDER OUTLAWS

IKE STOCKTON, THE SOUTHERN COLORADO AND NEW MEXICO OUTLAW AND DESPERADO — A REWARD OF $2000 FOR HIS CAPTURE.

PORTER AND IKE STOCKTON
COLORADO AND NEW MEXICO
BORDER OUTLAWS

Michael R. Maddox

Frontispiece: A woodcut from the *National Police Gazette*.
(Courtesy Frederick Nolan.)

Copyright © 2014 by Michael R. Maddox. All Rights Reserved.

No part of this publication may be reproduced, stored in a retrieval system, or transmitted in any form or by any means, electronic, mechanical, photocopying, recording, scanning, or otherwise, except by a reviewer who may quote brief passages in a review.

Cataloging information:

Maddox, Michael R.
Porter and Ike Stockton: Colorado and New Mexico Border Outlaws / by Michael R. Maddox
Includes bibliographical references and index.
ISBN-13: 978-0615964935
ISBN-10: 0615964931
1. Stockton, William Porter, 1850 – 1881. 2. Stockton, Isaac T., 1852 – 1881. 3. Outlaws – West (U.S.) – Biography. 4. Frontier and pioneer life – West (U.S.) 5. Cattle trade – West (U.S.) 6. West (U.S.) - History – 19th century. 7. Ute Indians - History.

*To my wife Pam,
the rock of my world*

One by one the roses fall; one by one the bad men die with their boots on.

Durango Herald, May 13, 1882

CONTENTS

ACKNOWLEDGMENTS ix

INTRODUCTION 1

1 – THE TEXANS 3

2 – CHAOS IN COLFAX COUNTY 23

3 – THE SAN JUAN COUNTRY 54

4 – IKE, THE KID AND THE COES 62

5 – TROUBLE IN OTERO 68

6 – THE ESKRIDGE BOYS 84

7 – MARSHAL STOCKTON 104

8 – HERE I AM, COME ON BOYS 122

9 – VIGILANTES AND RUFFIANS 146

10 – MURDER ON THE LA PLATA 167

11 – THE ADJUTANT GENERAL 188

12 – BAPTISM OF BLOOD 206

13 – DEATH OF A CATTLE KING 230

14 – COWBOYS AND INDIANS 257

15 – BATTLE IN THE LA SALS 268

16 – THE ALBUQUERQUE CAPTURE 284

17 – THE CALM BEFORE THE STORM 298

18 – BLOOD IN SILVERTON 310

19 – DURANGO'S JUDAS 327

CONTENTS

20 - REFLECTION	338
AFTERWORD – LOOSE ENDS AND LATER LIVES	340
APPENDIX	371
NOTES	373
BIBLIOGRAPHY	471
INDEX	489

A note on spelling: The spelling of personal names in 19th century America was creative and adventuresome. For many of the folks in this narrative, the spellings found in newspapers and other records were reliably inconsistent. For example, Big Dan Howland is shown as Howlan and even Howling and Lew Coe and Bert Wilkinson are equally referred to as Lou and Burt. I have attempted to use the name which evidence suggests is the family spelling. My apologies if I have chosen incorrectly. If the name is quoted from newspapers or other sources I have retained the spelling as it was in the original source.

Acknowledgments

Porter and Ike Stockton, gained enough notoriety during their time to be the subject of several articles and to be mentioned here and there in other articles and in a handful of books. Ike Stockton was the subject of the limited edition book, *Ike Stockton*, written by F. Stanley in 1959.

After making several trips to the New Mexico State Archives in Santa Fe and the Zimmerman Library at the University of New Mexico, I was hooked on the Stockton brothers. The assistance given to me by Al Regensberg, Barry Drucker and Felicia Lujan at New Mexico's State Archives was greatly appreciated. The Center of Southwest Studies and the Delaney Southwest Research Library at Fort Lewis College proved to be comprehensive sources of information about the Stocktons, their allies and their enemies. Nik Kendziorski and Elayne Silversmith maintain an amazing fountain of historical information on the mesa above Durango. Randy Vance provided valuable assistance with the Southwest Collection in the Special Collections Library at Texas Tech University in Lubbock. Another thank you goes to Jim Bradshaw at the Haley Memorial Library and History Center in Midland, Texas. District Clerk Wanda Pringle and her staff provided valuable assistance and access to information about the early history of Erath County. The Friends of the Stephenville Public Library provided initial assistance in researching the marriage records of Porter and Ike Stockton. Glenda Stone and others at the Dick Smith Library at Tarleton State University were most helpful. Information from the Center for Southwest Research and Special Collections at the University of New Mexico was also invaluable. The Colorado State Archives added information essential to my knowledge of events. The Durango Public Library and the San Juan College Library in Farmington proved to be crucial sources of material. The ample genealogy resources of the Special Collections Library of the Albuquerque/Bernalillo County Library System provided indispensable information about the Stockton family and others whose lives intersected with the Stocktons. Those collections were reincarnated as the Genealogy Center and moved to Albuquerque's Main Library during the course of my research. Debbie Stephenson of the Stewart Library at Weber State University was most helpful. Several internet sources allowed me to travel back in time and place without leaving my home. The extensive digitized United States census collections of the Genealogy Center of the Allen County (Indiana) Public Library were essential to my research and are available via the Internet Archive at archive.org. The Internet Archive's collection of 19th century and early 20th century publications were also invaluable. The *Colorado Historic Newspaper Collection* and the *Chronicling America* website of the Library of

Congress provided key information. There were other sources as well. They are mentioned elsewhere and no matter how small their contribution, all of them were important. Each source provided one or more stitches to complete the fabric of the story.

I also wish to acknowledge the support I received early on from author, James S. Peters and the encouragement provided by author, Marilu Waybourn. A special thanks to Les Sutton who provided little known information on the Cox family. I am indebted for the guidance provided on the Stockton family by Pam Birmingham and Gail Kaufmann. My thanks also goes to Lady E. Dalton who contributed her knowledge about the family of Hugh Martin Childress, Jr. Also, my appreciation goes to descendants of San Juan country pioneers; Melba Arnold, a descendant of William Locke and to my ninety-year-old cousin, Ella Ann Spargo. Ella Ann, who died before this book was finished, was a descendant of Mose Blancett. I am grateful to Frank and Sandra Pyle who shared photographs and their family's fascinating oral history. George W. Thompson and his cousin Lois Long and their families provided insights into the sometimes tumultuous history of the Thompson family. Siblings Wayne and Nona Dale and their cousin, Priscilla Trummel, graciously shared their family stories about George Lockhart. Randy Farrar, the descendant of Erath County pioneers was a valuable source of information on the early residents and early history of Erath County. Sandra Gwilliam provided her extensive knowledge about the family of Alf Graves and his wife Nancy Belle Cox. At the Aztec Museum I was delighted to unearth the late Joe Boettcher's well researched narrative of the killing of Port Stockton. Boettcher, a former principal of Aztec High School, was my father's closest childhood friend. Fifty years ago my father and "Betch" took me to the Middle Fork of the Piedra for my first fly fishing venture. To the Boettcher children, Jo Marie, Karen and Steve I say thanks. I also wish to thank Barry Cooper for sharing the family's memories of Lucy and Thomas Cooper. I also offer a special thank you to Mrs. Barbara Duke for allowing the use of her late husband's (Robert W. Duke) master's thesis. I am indebted to everyone who assisted me with this project.

I am fortunate to be able to provide a special thank you to my son-in-law Phil Shaw who provided his encouragement, editorial expertise and many other suggestions which were invaluable to the finished work.

To the families who have passed on their family history; to those who took time to record their history; to those who donated this information to archives, museums and libraries; to those institutions which store the information and to the people who care for the information I say, Thank You! Thank You! Thank You!

ACKNOWLEDGMENTS

Portions of the unpublished manuscript, "Who Killed Porter Stockton," by Joe E. Boettcher are used by permission of Joe E. Boettcher's children.

Portions of the Aztec (NM) Museum Association Newsletter article from September 1, 1988, "Coopers Were Early Pioneers Here," by Barry Cooper are used by permission of Barry Cooper.

Portions of the master's thesis completed for the University of New Mexico, "Political History of San Juan County, New Mexico 1876-1926," June 1947, by Robert W. Duke are used by permission of Mrs. Robert W. (Barbara) Duke.

Frederic Remington's "Driving to the Round-up," from Theodore Roosevelt's "The Round-up," The Century Illustrated Monthly Magazine, *Vol. 35, No. 6, April 1888. (Author's collection.)*

Frederic Remington's "In A Stampede," from Theodore Roosevelt's "The Round-up," The Century Illustrated Monthly Magazine, *Vol. 35, No. 6, April 1888. (Author's collection.)*

Introduction

Chasing down the original documents in an archive or library is like looking for one real nugget amongst overwhelming amounts of fool's gold. Every once in a while the glint is real. One day I came across a familiar name tucked in with others on a witness list for an 1879 murder in Colfax County, New Mexico Territory. Porter (also known as Port) Stockton was accused of shooting Ed Withers, and John Holliday was a witness.[1] As I looked at the record I wondered if this John Holliday was the same man better known as Doc. Was the itinerant gambler, part time dentist and legendary shootist in the burgeoning railroad town of Otero, New Mexico on June 11, 1879? As it turns out, he was.[2] Finding a connection to Doc Holliday, no matter how slight, encouraged me to learn even more about Porter Stockton and his younger brother Isaac, who was known to his friends and foes alike as Ike. Old west outlaws and men with tarnished reputations, like Doc Holliday, are often romanticized in latter day accounts. Porter Stockton is one man who resists such efforts. He was arrogant, hard-bitten and ready to kill with little provocation. Ike, on the other hand, had a way about him that won him friendship and respect. But in the end even Ike was deserted by most of his allies.

Living in the northwest corner of New Mexico, I had heard of the Stockton boys. They were outlaws of some kind was all I knew. On a sporadic basis the Aztec (New Mexico) Museum hosts a western shootout, which features locals acting as fanciful caricatures of the Stockton boys. Newspapers in Durango, Colorado and Farmington, New Mexico occasionally carry articles about Porter and Ike. Through osmosis I soaked up some of the Stockton facts and fables. In addition, there are several published accounts of their lives, but for the most part they offer little in the way of historical background and family history. The existing Stockton narratives provide a less than thorough examination of the explosion of violence which resulted in their brutal deaths nine months and forty miles apart in the Animas River valley. The turmoil involved the governors of New Mexico and Colorado, the U.S. Army and high ranking federal officials. Throughout their lives the Stocktons were surrounded by an intricate web of friends, family and enemies. Prominent among that group were two Texas cattlemen, Hiram Washington Cox and Irvin W. Lacy. The relationship between these two men and the Stocktons may have begun in friendship, but over time that relationship deteriorated. Very little has been published about Cox and Lacy, but like Charles Goodnight, who lived in a neighboring county, they drove thousands of cattle out of Texas. The saga of the Stockton brothers follows the churned up cattle trails out of the Cross Timbers of Texas and coincides with the establishment of the cattle industry all along the border separating Colorado and New Mexico. In an epic and deadly chase of livestock stealing Ute and Paiute Indians, Ike's story overflows into the southeast corner of Utah. Their tale is a microcosm encompassing all of the legends of the mythic American west. From cattle kings to cowboys, from cow towns to hell on wheels railroad camps, from shootouts to lynchings, their story twists and turns inevitably toward their grisly ends.

Thankfully some of those who lived through that era memorialized the events they witnessed. I hope I have been able to pull together those recollections in a manner which makes sense. Compounding the difficulty of discerning the truth are conflicting versions of the same event. In the thousands of facts researched and recorded here, I know I have made errors. Despite my best efforts I cannot find them, but I am sure others will let me know what and where they are. I can only offer an apology for my blunders and misinterpretations.

Now it's on to the cattle cradle of Texas and from there to the dusty and at times dangerous streets of Cimarron, New Mexico. The Stockton chronicle concludes with the roar of six-shooters, the specter of splinters exploding off a downtown boardwalk and the thud of bullets hitting their mark in a climactic noontime showdown.

Chapter One

The Texans

> *For a man is a man and a steer is a beast,*
> *And the man is the boss of the herd;*
> *And each of the bunch, from the biggest to least,*
> *Must come down when he says the word.*[1]

The horse thieves were in luck. Their stolen herd included Charles "Race Horse" Johnson's thoroughbred stallion, Selim, and his race mare, Blue Bird.[2] They trailed the herd south along the Florida Mesa in southwest Colorado. It looked like they might head down the Animas valley toward Farmington.[3] That was a ruse. They circled back to the southeast, crossed the line into New Mexico Territory and headed toward the Chama River country. Alf Graves, "Race Horse" Johnson, Porter Stockton and nine other determined men were on their trail. They overtook the thieves at dawn. A volley of shots and the pungent smell of gunpowder pierced the cold morning air. In total disarray and not fully dressed, the thieves returned fire and made a mad dash for their horses. Denny Gannon took a round from Stockton's gun.[4] After the smoke cleared, the posse men gathered around Gannon.[5] He was struggling to remove the one boot he wore. Finally, he asked one of the men to remove it, saying he didn't want his family to know that he had died with his boots on.[6] Not long afterwards he was gone, the last victim of killer Port Stockton.[7]

It may have been one of the few instances when Stockton's actions were justified. By 1880 Porter Stockton boasted that he had killed nineteen men.[8] We only have his word to support that claim, but there is no doubt that he was a remorseless, cold-hearted killer. He was supported in his misdeeds by his little brother, Ike. The Stockton brothers' heritage was southern. The family was typical of the many poor, uneducated, white settlers who had "Gone to Texas" after it entered the Union in 1845. William Porter Stockton was born in the summer of 1850 probably in Upshur County in the Piney Woods of northeast Texas. His parents, Samuel Stockton and Jane Hickey, were married in August 1843 in Itawamba County, Mississippi. Porter had three older sisters, Mary, Sarah and Emily and an older brother known only by his initials, G.H. It's likely that his first name was Guy.[9] Isaac Stockton was born less than two years later on the leap day of a leap year, 1852.[10] Two younger sisters and another brother, the namesake of his father, completed the family. About seventy-five miles north of the Stockton's Upshur County home was the Red River and across the Red was the chunk of land which served as the nation's Indian Territory. During the 1850s the Stockton family moved about fifty miles northwest to Sulphur Springs in Hopkins County. At the time, less than five hundred residents lived in the town. Samuel Tomlinson lived next door to the Stockton family and was probably their school teacher. The town was peopled with carpenters, blacksmiths and other tradesmen, including one saddler, one carriage maker and one shoemaker. It was also home to two minstrels. Outside of town, farming was the primary occupation. It was not cattle country and stock raisers were rare.[11] When the 1860 census was taken, father Samuel Stockton and the older brother were not shown as living with the family. They do not appear in subsequent census records and it seems likely that they died in the years prior to the Civil War. Eking out a living could not have been easy for the large family. Mother Jane Stockton, who could neither read nor write, made money by weaving.[12] To say the Stocktons were clannish is an understatement. Throughout their lives the Stockton boys, their sisters, uncles, aunts and their cousins contributed to a mutually supportive network. It is clear that during these early years Porter and Ike developed a bond that could only be broken by death.

The times became even harder with the outbreak of the Civil War. It was a period of insufferable hardship for Texans. The tumult brought an abrupt end to Port and Ike's childhood and this may have been when Porter Stockton's troubles began. Stockton reportedly killed his first man in about 1862. According to an 1881 article from the *Durango Record*, "He slew his first man when only twelve years of age – for calling him a liar – shooting the top of his head off."[13] The *Record's* account offers no other details about the killing. Despite the dearth of details, it may be a true tale. At the time, several residents who knew Stockton from an early age in Texas lived in the vicinity of Durango, Colorado. This was the first in a string of assaults in which Porter Stockton maimed and killed many men. In those raucous days, Stockton's manhood was bound to be challenged. With his father gone, he had no option but to fend for himself. Impulse control would never be Stockton's strong suit.

Compared to his older brother, Ike was, for the most part, mild-mannered and personable. He once told a newspaperman he was from Cleburne in Johnson County, Texas, about thirty miles south of Fort Worth.[14] During the Civil War the town was known as Camp Henderson and served as a gathering point for Confederate units before they were dispatched. It was renamed Cleburne in honor of Confederate General Patrick Cleburne in 1867.[15] That year marked the beginning of the Chisholm Trail and cattlemen and their herds passed close to Cleburne on their way north.[16] In 1881 the *Denver Republican* described Ike's time in Cleburne, "Stockton is a Texan, a man brought up on the plains among cattle and cattlemen, and in early years took part in several scrimmages with the Comanches." In the same interview the *Republican* reported Ike's assertion that, "He had never killed a man unless Ute or Comanche, and then in warfare."[17] At the very least, Ike can be given some credit for telling half of the truth.

It is evident that Ike and Port's mother died during the Civil War years or shortly afterwards. In 1868, sixteen-year-old Ike, his thirteen-year-old brother Samuel and his ten-year-old sister Amanda were living near the western boundary of Erath County in Eastland County, Texas. Residing with them was their twenty-two-year-old sister, Sallie (Sarah) Ivy. Ike and his siblings built a cabin in the shade of oak and elm trees near the village of Desdemona (originally known as Hogtown), about seventy-five miles west of Cleburne. There was a small spring near the cabin. They had no livestock to speak of, but game was plentiful and as he had done in the past, Ike put meat on the table. They stored their salt and flour in barrels. A little yarn about their time there was included in Mrs. George Langston's book *History of Eastland County Texas*. According to Langston, when Sallie told the family they were low on salt, Ike said, "Why, we can do without salt for two months." But after eating unsalted venison and unsalted mush, Ike changed his mind. He apprised his sister, "Red man, or no red man, this boy has got to be salted." He mounted up and rode the twenty miles east to Stephenville to buy or barter for salt.[18] Ike was not overstating the danger posed by raiding Indians. When the able-bodied young men left to fight Yankees, the Indians stepped into the void. Comanches and Kiowas swooped down on the rustic dugouts and mud-chinked cabins, and mutilated, raped, kidnapped and murdered the occupants at will. Many who lived along the western frontier of Texas abandoned their homes and moved eastward to safer areas. The danger presented by Indians was so great that even by 1870 population levels in many areas had not reached the levels recorded in 1860. When the Stocktons lived in Eastland County, few other families were foolhardy enough to live there. The 1870 census shows only eighty-eight brave souls residing in the entire county.[19] It is difficult to imagine placing wives, children and sisters in such a hostile environment, but Texas was filled with many who resisted retreat and pushed the frontier forward. Stephenville, the town closest to the Stocktons and the county seat of Erath County, was a metropolis compared to the microscopic population clusters in Eastland County. Tiny Stephenville was destined to play a pivotal role in Ike's life and in the life of his older brother. John M. Stephens settled in the area in 1854 and the following year he laid out the townsite which would become Stephenville.[20] The town lies on the eastern edge of the woodland region known as the Western Cross Timbers, about one hundred miles southwest of Dallas. Just north of Stephenville the South Fork unites with the North Fork of the North Bosque River. The tumult of the Civil War and the inevitable increase in Indian raids resulted in an exodus from Stephenville and Erath County. In 1860, almost 2500 people lived in the county. Ten years later, the census showed just over 1800 residents. Included in that number were Porter and Ike's grandmother and a substantial number of their uncles, aunts and cousins. Most of the men were farmers or cattlemen and they lived along the lush valleys of Duffau Creek, the Paluxy River and on the North Bosque River and its forks.[21]

Famed Texas author J. Frank Dobie provided a brief, undated description of Stephenville in his classic book, *The Longhorns*. Most residents lived in log cabins. There was one untamed saloon. For twenty-five cents customers twisted the barrel valve and filled their tin cup with what the proprietor unabashedly called whiskey.[22] Young cow herders from Erath, Palo Pinto and Eastland counties made sure the saloon was lively. Early resident W.H. Fooshee recalled that after drinking their fill they would mount up and beeline it out of town, whooping and yelling and firing off their pistols.[23] Stephenville provided a meager but essential trade center and the only post office for a large portion of the surrounding country. C.C. Painter carried the mail up from Meridian once a week.[24]

Ike and Port's residency near Stephenville placed them at a crossroads of the Texas cattle industry. That heritage runs deep and even today the town promotes itself as the "Cowboy Capital of the World." In the years after the Civil War thousands upon thousands of cattle rumbled north on the neighboring Chisholm Trail. The famed Goodnight-Loving trail also originated nearby. To the north, Erath County borders Palo Pinto County. One newspaper of the time trumpeted the burgeoning Texas cattle industry and named the thirteen "best grazing counties in Texas." Those counties included Erath and Palo Pinto, which sat squarely in the center of prime cattle country.[25] As the crow flies, the town of Palo Pinto is about forty miles north of Stephenville. Large numbers of wild cattle roamed the open range between the two towns and meandered throughout the region. The hardy animals could be found across the far reaches of Texas, but because of the determined entrepreneurial efforts of a handful of Palo Pinto cattlemen, this region shares a large portion of the credit for sparking the rise of the post-Civil War cattle industry. Trail driver Charles Goodnight and his early partner Oliver Loving were Palo Pinto cattlemen. Palo Pinto County was home to many other successful but now lesser known stockmen like, John Hittson and George Webb Slaughter.[26] Erath County also produced several prominent cattlemen, including Irvin W. Lacy, his partner Lewis G. "Luke" Coleman and Hiram Washington "Wash" Cox. From at least 1870 onward, the lives of the Stockton brothers would continually intertwine with the lives of Irvin Lacy and Wash Cox. By 1881 all four men could be found in the San Juan country along the border of Colorado and New Mexico. Only one of the four would survive the final outburst of violence which was fueled by the Stockton brothers.

Wash Cox was a native of Missouri, but became a Texas cattleman through and through. Cox was not one of those latecomers who are often identified as pioneers. He was undeniably a pioneer resident of Erath

County and he would later be a pioneering resident of the area that would become San Juan County, New Mexico. Wash Cox was strong-willed and civic minded and served in either appointed or elected positions wherever he resided. Newspaperman Frank Hartman, who was a reconciled former bitter enemy of Cox, described the trail driver this way: "He is one of those plain outspoken men who never means to be misunderstood. He never evades an issue. He tells you how he stands and you know by the faithful keeping of his word in the past, that he tells you the truth to-day and will keep his word to-morrow."[27] In 1849, twenty-four-year-old Wash Cox married fellow Missouri native Nancy Allard in Hopkins County, Texas.[28] It seems likely that Wash Cox first met the Stockton family in Hopkins County. In 1856 Wash and Nancy moved to Erath County.[29] At the time Stephenville was one of the very few isolated outposts of white settlers west of the Brazos River. Before 1860, many others moved from Hopkins County to Erath County, including the family of James Burleson (Jim) Allard, who was a brother to Nancy Allard Cox.[30] Wash Cox and his family resided on the upper end of Duffau Creek between the village of Duffau and Stephenville. They used the Stephenville post office, which was a dozen or so miles to the northwest. The family would spend at least fourteen years on Duffau Creek.[31] During those years Cox developed a reputation as a crack shot hunter and provided meat for many of his neighbors. Nancy Cox was also said to be able to shoot like a man, a skill that was a virtual requirement for women living on the Texas frontier.[32] One account of this time in Texas noted that it was not unusual for boys as young as eleven or twelve to carry real pistols and Bowie knives and even to play with the same weapons.[33]

Cox's arrival in 1856 gave him a head start in accumulating a large cattle herd. At that time the market was not strong and the cattle had little value. The grass was tall along Duffau Creek and elsewhere and the cattle would fatten with only a modicum of labor. During the winter, Texas cattle, like the buffalo herds, tended to drift south. Every spring the cowmen organized a cow hunt to gather up the unbranded calves and mark them with the brand their mama bore. Anytime women and children were left at home, there was the risk of a raid by hostile Indians. The most notorious instance of this type of attack in Erath County began eleven miles west of Stephenville in January 1861. The Lemley family had only recently moved there from Palo Pinto County. Indians raped and killed fourteen-year-old Liddie Lemley and her twenty-one-year-old recently married sister, Lucinda Wood. The two women were also scalped. Sixteen-year-old, Hulda Lemley and thirteen-year-old Nancy Lemley were abused and stripped of their clothing. The next day they were released by the Indians near Stephenville.[34] Incidents like these would have a decided influence on Ike Stockton.

Despite the danger, in 1860 several of Wash Cox's neighbors to the north sought new cattle markets. John B. Dawson and Joel W. Curtis from nearby Buchanan County (renamed Stephens County after the outbreak of the Civil War) accompanied forty-seven-year-old Oliver Loving and Syl Reed in driving several hundred cattle to the Rocky Mountains, which were then part of the western portion of the Kansas Territory. It was the first herd of Texas cattle driven to what would become Colorado.[35] That drive started near the upper Brazos and they drove north through Oklahoma and Kansas and up the Arkansas toward the Rockies. Loving wintered near the present town of Pueblo.[36] While Goodnight and Loving are among the most well-known of the trail driving Texans, it was thirty-year-old John Dawson who served as the guide for this drive.[37] The outbreak of the Civil War put an end to that market by restricting commerce between North and South, all but eliminating the flow of cattle between Texas and their neighbors to the north.

Wash Cox was one of the men who remained in Erath County during the Civil War. He was thirty-six-years-old when the hostilities broke out and he and Nancy had at least three young children.[38] As the Civil War progressed, the number of available herders became greatly outnumbered by the livestock, and the available market was severely restricted by the war. The result was a massive population boom for the cattle and horses. The animals became increasingly wild and large numbers escaped the branding iron. The Texans who remained along the frontier suffered greatly at the hands of Comanche and Kiowa raiding parties.[39] In 1861 or 1862 Cox and other men trailed a band of Indians who had stolen several horses. One Indian was caught and scalped at Motheral Gap. The remaining Indians rode toward Glen Rose and escaped.[40] Like Wash and Nancy Cox, Edward and Hannah Cox had moved from Missouri to Hopkins County, Texas in the 1840s and then to Erath County in the late 1850s. Ed Cox was born in Tennessee in 1810 and had been a farmer all his life. In Erath County he partnered with Nancy Cox's brother, Jim Allard, in the cattle business. Like Wash Cox, Ed Cox and Jim Allard lived on Duffau Creek. The Coxes and Allards endured frequent Indian raids on their cattle and horse herds. They pursued and battled the Indians on numerous occasions.[41] In 1865, Wash and Ed Cox were working on a cow hunt on Cowhouse Creek, thirty miles south of Stephenville. Ed Cox and others were attacked by over a dozen Indians. Fourteen-year-old Leonard F. Roberts and a cow hunter named Riley hunkered down in the brush and watched as the Indians scalped and murdered Ed Cox and fifteen-year-old John Durham "Bud" Hollis.[42] Families along Duffau Creek were devastated, as the Hollis family also lived there.[43] Shortly afterwards, Ed Cox's widow sold out to Jim Allard. Cox and Hollis were murdered in July.[44] Three months earlier, Robert E. Lee surrendered to General Grant in the village of Appomattox Courthouse and Texas soldiers who had survived the war began making their way home. The Texas cattle industry was about to erupt.

When the War of the Rebellion reached its end, the trade embargo with the North ended. In Palo Pinto County, G.W. Slaughter and his sons organized a herd and drove east to the wharves at Shreveport, Louisiana. They herd was delivered to a bayou just east of Jefferson, Texas. The Slaughter's Palo Pinto County neighbor, Charles Goodnight, was obsessed with developing northern markets. In 1866 Goodnight partnered with Oliver Loving to establish the trail which now bears their names. Their trail was destined to have a huge and long lasting impact on New Mexico, Colorado and the entire American west. It was probably while herding cattle up this trail that Porter and Ike Stockton first glimpsed New Mexico and Colorado. Goodnight and Loving's 1866 drive began on the upper Brazos, west of Palo Pinto. The cattlemen pointed their herd southwest, toward the Pecos River. When they struck the Pecos they followed the river on its northwesterly course. The headwaters of the Pecos are high up in the Sangre de Cristo Mountains of north central New Mexico, the southernmost range of the Rockies. South of the Sangre de Cristos, the herders broke away from the Pecos and pushed the cattle up the plains, close to the eastern slope of the mountains. The Texans passed through what is now Colfax County, New Mexico and into Colorado. They continued north along the front range of the Rockies toward Denver.[45] The steers had been sold earlier at Fort Sumner and after that Goodnight had returned to Texas to prepare for another drive. Near Denver, Loving sold the remaining stock to Colorado cattle king, John Wesley Iliff.[46]

Goodnight and Loving's trail drive had unforeseen consequences, some desirable and some not. Increasingly, developments in Erath County proved to be a microcosm of events in Texas as a whole, and the blossoming industry surrounding wild cattle was spawning multiple storms. At the center of these maelstroms were men: ambitious men, resourceful men, and in some cases violent men. Some had been tempered by the savagery of the Civil War, others by Indian battles along the Texas frontier. To be sure, the vast majority of Texas cowboys were not outlaws and many of them went on to be leading citizens in the Lone Star State and elsewhere. The same grittiness and determination that produced successful trail drivers produced other kinds of men as well. The trail that snaked through the Pecos River country was one of incredible hardship and danger. Driving cattle across large stretches of the arid portions of Texas and New Mexico, through territory inhabited by free roaming and combative Indians required men who would never back down from any challenge. Even Oliver Loving lost his life as the result of an Indian bullet received while hunkered down in the mud of the Pecos River.[47] Inevitably, some of the herders stepped over the line and became desperadoes. One of the tempests coming out of Texas would brew and build around

Stephenville before moving west and north along with the suffocating dust cloud stirred up by the hooves of thousands of Texas cattle. Erath County residents would figure prominently as the storm regained strength in Colfax County, New Mexico. The same Erathians would be present when the storm grew to reach its cyclonic and climactic outburst in the San Juan country of New Mexico and Colorado. Porter and Ike Stockton were at the epicenter of this final blast.

Frederic Remington's "Trailing Cattle," from Theodore Roosevelt's "The Round-up," The Century Illustrated Monthly Magazine, *Vol. 35, No. 6, April 1888.* (Author's collection.)

The trail drives of 1866 changed the dynamics of the cattle industry. Everyone now knew that the Texas cattle were money on the hoof. What had been a laid back industry moved into high gear. Cattlemen had been branding their herds for years, but the weak cattle market prior to Civil War resulted in weak statutes protecting stock owners. While their neighbors were off fighting Yankees, some could not resist temptation and began to scour the open range and put their brand on their neighbor's calves. A few thieves were even bolder. One account notes that in 1864 a herd of stolen Texas cattle were driven north and sold in Kansas.[48] With the success of Goodnight and others, cattle theft reached epidemic proportions. Putting one's own mark on yearling or older cattle who had avoided the branding iron became widespread. The men who owned the mother cows were not pleased, but since the calves were fully weaned, the owners had lost their opportunity to make a clear claim to the animals. Barefaced thieves risked indefensible blame and the wrath of the rightful owners by placing their brands on the not yet weaned youngest calves. Then there were thieves who did not care if the older brutes were branded or not. They gathered them up and drove them to buyers who were unconcerned with proof of ownership. The most brazen thieves utilized a selection of running irons to alter any brand into their own.[49]

The activities of horse and cattle thieves and heated disputes between livestock owners led authorities to take action. In January 1867 Erath County officials began to register brands for the first time. A.J. Gilbreath registered the first brand on January 16, 1867. Wash Cox rode into Stephenville from his home on Duffau Creek the next day. His brand was the ninth one registered in Erath County, a heart inside a circle. For good measure he branded his calves on the hip, side and shoulder. If a herder ran across an unbranded calf and had no branding iron, he marked the calf with the outfit's distinctive ear cuts. Calves ears were also cropped during the roundup and the earmarks were registered with the county. Cox cropped a shallow swallow fork on the tip of the right ear and made straight crop near the tip of the left ear.[50] Cox's small earmarks were problematic, since more severe cuts could easily obliterate the earlier marks.

In adjacent Palo Pinto County and nearby in Stephens County, cattlemen were looking for open land and taller grass. John Dawson was the leader of an interrelated army of friends and family who entered the cattle trade. His associates included Joel Curtis, brothers Tom and Mathias Stockton, the DeGraffenrieds, brothers Gad and Richard Miller, Taylor Maulding and Manley Chase.[51] On earlier trail drives the Texans saw an opportunity to develop large ranches along the Colorado and New Mexico border. In the summer the herds could graze in the cool high mountain meadows of the Sangre de Cristos. In the winter, they could move down to the high plains bordering the foothills. Dawson was able to negotiate the purchase of several thousand acres of land in the Vermejo River valley from Lucien Maxwell, the owner of the vast Maxwell Grant. He moved onto the land in 1867.[52] Dawson's partners were Joel W. Curtis, Richard D. Miller, and Taylor F. Maulding.[53] It was this deal that sparked the settlement of Texas cattlemen and marked the birth of an immense cattle industry in northeast New Mexico.

Even though some of the Texans set up ranches in New Mexico, the cowmen continued to drive cattle out of Texas. Many of their partners retained their homes in Texas, where they gathered up herds bound for distant ranges and distant markets. I.W. Lacy and Luke Coleman drove their first trail herd to New Mexico in 1868.[54] Like Lacy and Coleman, Wash Cox retained his home base in Erath County, even though Texas continued to be plagued by cattle thieves. After the Civil War Texas authorities operated under the restrictions of the federal Reconstruction Acts. Texas would not be fully restored to the Union until March 30, 1870, by an act of the United States Congress. On February 4, 1870, Brevet Lieutenant Colonel A.B. Beaumont issued Special Order No. 6 from his headquarters at Lampasas, Texas. The order's intent was to put some teeth into the fight against cattle rustlers. On February 28th the Erath County Commissioners Court passed the order into local ordinance. It said in part, "the marking and branding of calves, or cattle known as 'mavericks' Shall be and is hereby prohibited between the 1st day of December and the 1st day of April in each and every year." The Commissioners Court also said, "it is forbidden [by] all persons to drive, gather, head or pen any calf or 'maverick' for the purpose of marking and branding the same between the days aforesaid." Cattlemen were also forbidden to drive cattle out of the county without the written authority of the owner or his agent. Five men were appointed as inspectors and their responsibility was to "examine and inspect all droves of cattle collected and to be driven to market from Erath County, to carefully examine the bills of sale and list of marks and brands in the possession" of those in charge of the herd. Drovers were required to give five days advance notice to at least one of the inspectors. The inspectors were to report any violations to the nearest magistrate or peace officer. The substantial fine for failing to notify the inspector was at least one dollar per head in the drove. The five Erath County cattle inspectors were J.J. Keith, John S. Boucher, William G. Waller (who lived on Duffau Creek), West W. Hickey (Port and Ike Stockton's uncle) and Wash Cox. The order was well intentioned, but difficult to enforce. It also codified, by omission, the legality of mavericking for eight months of the year. The five men appointed to enforce the cattle regulations were some of the most respected men in Erath County.[55]

Cox, by his own assessment, was one of the two richest single stock raisers in the county. He valued his personal estate at $13,000. Most of his estimated value sported long horns, four hooves and a mean disposition. Robert Sloan, a neighboring stockman, gave his estate the same value. The assessment of Wash Cox as the richest stockman in the county discounts the claims of twenty-year-old John W. Middleton. The Texas native who lived on the Paluxy reported that his personal estate was worth $14,500. But Middleton was counting cattle which he had not yet stolen.[56] He would later flee Erath County after being indicted for cattle theft.[57] Middleton did not discriminate when it came to stealing livestock; he was also indicted in Erath County for the theft of four hogs.[58] Authorities in Stephenville were not the only ones with an interest in Middleton. During this same time period he was indicted in Palo Pinto County for an unspecified theft.[59] Given his penchant for finding trouble, he may be the

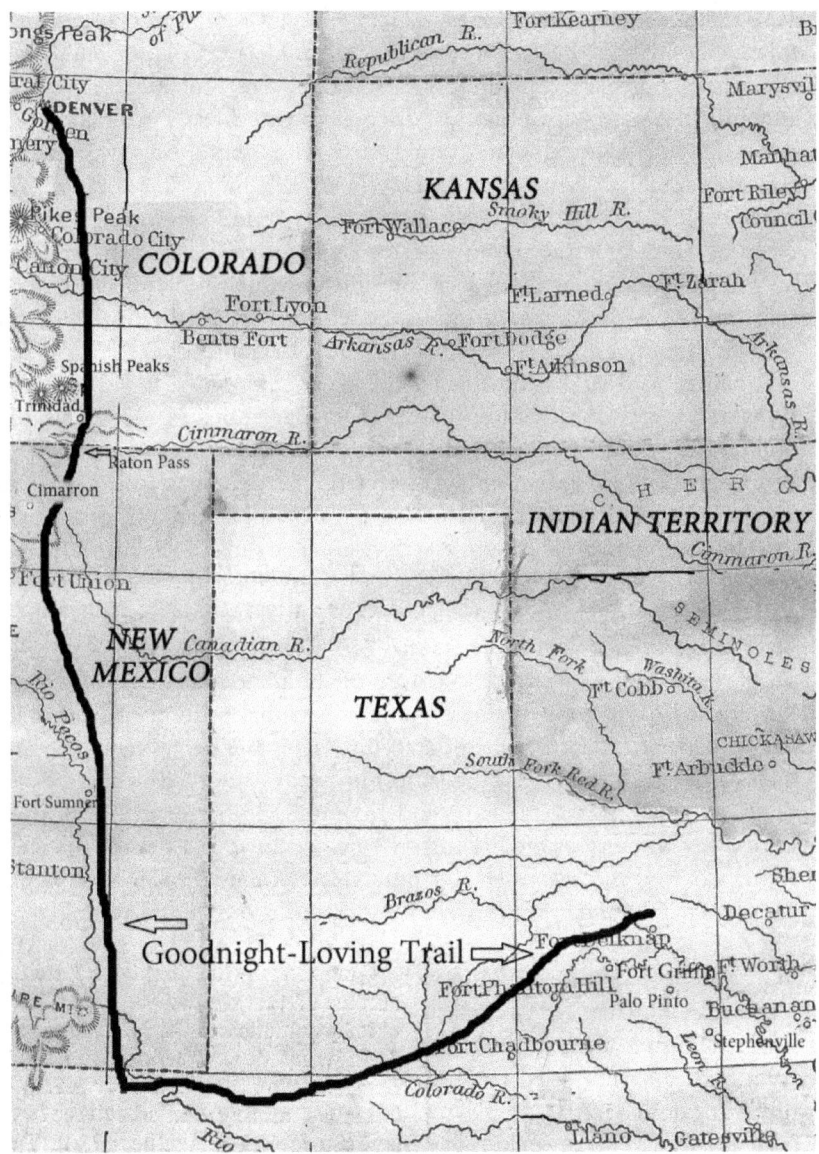

The path of the Goodnight-Loving Trail was added to a portion of J.H. Colton's Map No. 12, Section No. 5, from Colton's Common School Geography, *1868. Other minor additions were also made to the map. (Map is from the author's collection.)*

ephemeral John Middleton who turned up in New Mexico and fought in the Lincoln County War alongside Billy the Kid.

Like Wash Cox, Kentucky native Irvin Lacy would play a pivotal role in the lives of Ike and Porter Stockton. He was a close family friend and cattle trail partner with John Dawson.[60] Ike Stockton reported that 1866 was the first year of his close friendship with Lacy. Porter and Ike also had a family relationship to Irvin Lacy's wife, Sarah. She was their first cousin. Sarah Lacy's mother, Delila Hickey Brumley, was a sister to the Stockton boy's mom, Jane Hickey Stockton.[61] Irvin Lacy was born at Hazel Green, Kentucky in the summer of 1837. He moved to eastern Texas when he was eighteen and worked as an overseer. He later took up carpentry as a trade and by 1860 he was living near Stephenville. At the time he bunked with the family of fellow Kentuckian and blacksmith R.B. Skaggs. Lacy's occupation was listed as mechanic and the twenty-two-year-old had little to show for his efforts but high hopes. On December 31, 1862, his future brightened when he married fifteen-year-old Arkansas native Sarah Brumley. His new father-in-law, Jefferson C. Brumley, was a successful Stephenville cattleman. The Brumley family was apparently one of those who left Stephenville during the war years. They made Cleburne their new home.[62] Lacy stayed in Stephenville and throughout the 1860s was a man possessed. He began to accumulate a substantial herd of cattle. By the end of the decade he valued his personal estate at $12,000. His father-in-law's support may not explain the full story of the meteoric rise of his fortunes. Mavericked cattle probably made up a substantial portion of his holdings. Lacy's partner, L.G. Coleman, gave his estate the same value. Together, their cattle outfit was by far the largest in Erath County. Coleman, who was single in 1870, lived with Lacy and his family in Stephenville. Both men were thirty-three years old.[63] Unlike virtually every other brand registered in Erath County, the two men did not register brands under their separate names. Their brand was registered under the name "Lacy and Coleman." They seared their calves with an L on the hip and an LC on the side.[64] The LC outfit would soon become well known for the tough characters they hired as trail hands. They reflected the personality of Irvin Lacy.

During the late 1860s and into the early 1870s, I.W. Lacy became entangled in several legal battles. In the fall of 1867, he was charged with three separate counts of selling intoxicating liquors without a license; perhaps the cattleman held some personal animosity to the saloon keeper mentioned in Dobie's *The Longhorns*. In any case, witnesses alleged that Lacy had engaged in this activity in June and August of that year. Lacy fought all of the charges. In the fall of 1868 he was found not guilty on two of the counts by a jury of his peers. The third count was problematic. The witness knew he could buy a drink at Lacy's home. He reported that he went into Lacy's Stephenville house for that purpose and said, "Lacy, I want a good dram." Lacy fixed him a dram and the witness verified that it was intoxicating liquor by drinking the evidence. The witness noted that there were others coming in and out and there were several jugs of liquor in the house. After about a half hour he gave Lacy fifty cents and Lacy gave him a quarter. In the spring of 1869 Lacy was found guilty in this case and fined fifty dollars. Lacy was incensed with the judgment and kept this charge tied up with appeals all the way to the Texas Supreme Court. That august body affirmed the lower courts ruling. In February 1872 the Erath County District Court called Lacy to court to hear the final judgment and he failed to appear. The court ruled that he forfeit the three hundred dollars he had put up as an appeal bond. His sureties, E.B. Campbell and J.C. Brumley, who had put up an additional three hundred dollars were ordered to forfeit $150 each.[65] Campbell, who probably represented Lacy in this case, was a Cleburne attorney.[66]

As it turns out, bootlegging liquor was the least of Lacy's legal troubles. On January 8, 1870, he engaged in an argument with one of Stephenville's respected citizens, James D. Berry, who was a forty-nine-year-old attorney. What brought on this dispute is lost to history, but Lacy was charged with assault with intent to kill and murder. Berry claimed that Lacy beat and bruised him with a rock. Not satisfied with those results, he then fired a round into Berry with his pistol. The assault was witnessed by M.L. Keith, John Boucher, J.A. Frey and William Frey. For his part, Lacy said that attorney Berry first assaulted him with "a very large and dangerous stone" and attempted to kill him. Lacy's bond was set at five hundred dollars and his friend John R. O'Neal was surety in the matter. O'Neal was an illiterate but very successful farmer who lived on the Bosque River. Eighteen-year-old witness William Frey lived with the O'Neal family. Lacy, through his attorney E.B. Campbell, pleaded with the court to subpoena H.L. Ray as his witness in the matter. Mr. Ray was a Stephenville attorney who lived next door to Berry and was married to Berry's daughter, Rena. Not long after this incident Ray moved to Dallas County.[67] The case came to trial in August 1871 and Lacy argued self-defense. The jury found him guilty of the lesser charge of aggravated assault and he was assessed a fine of $125 plus costs.[68] It seems Lacy paid his fine and did not appeal the verdict. (Berry survived his wounds and his two story rock house is now the centerpiece exhibit at the Stephenville Museum.) At that time the Erath County District Court was held in a wooden building which stood on the east side of the public square.[69]

Two months after Lacy's assault on counselor Berry, Porter Stockton made his presence known in Erath County. This is the earliest known record of a criminal case involving Porter Stockton. On March 18, 1870, Stockton assaulted Taylor Avant, a nineteen-year-old former slave from North Carolina.[70] Court documents do not delve into the cause of this trouble, but as future events would tell, Porter Stockton was a bigoted bully. Stockton pulled his sidearm and used it to pistol whip Avant. In the aftermath of the Civil War, Texas was a dangerous and deadly locale for freedmen.[71] The rough treatment by Stockton did not cause Avant to leave the area and within months he married Martha Clark in Erath County.[72]

Despite his legal difficulties, Porter Stockton seemed unconcerned about the future and later in the year his courtship with Emily Jane Cowan, became serious. Emily was the daughter of William and Sarah Cowan. Sarah was known by the diminutive form of her name, Sally, and her maiden name was Hickey. Porter Stockton's future mother-in-law was also his aunt since she was the sister to his own mother. Porter's Aunt Sally and Uncle William and their six children came to Texas in about 1847. Shortly after the move, Sally gave birth to a daughter who they named Elizabeth. In 1850 or 1851, the ever-pregnant Sally gave birth to Emily Jane probably in Titus County. In Sally Hickey Cowan's time, it was often the child bearing wife who died early, but she was the exception. She outlived Mr. Cowan and then married a Virginia-born stock farmer named Isaac Robinson. In 1858 Sally Robinson, then forty-two years old, gave birth to another daughter whose fate was linked to the Stockton boys. The Robinsons named her Amanda Ellen. In 1860, the Robinson/Cowan family lived in Erath County next door to their Hickey grandmother, Sarah Meek Hickey Bibb. Mrs. Bibb lived with the family of her son, thirty-seven-year-old West Hickey. Family for the Stockton boys was indeed the tie that binds, and Porter Stockton re-cinched the family noose with a double knot. In the latter part of 1870 or in January 1871, he married his first cousin, Emily Jane Cowan. Perhaps a large contingent of the Bibb, Hickey, Stockton and Cowan clans and other friends witnessed the ceremony, which was performed by full-time Bosque River miller and part-time Justice of the Peace Dillon R. Burroughs. But Erath County marriage records present a mystery that is difficult to unravel. Those records say that W. Stockton married E.J. Marshall. There may be a good reason why the records show the bride's name as E.J. Marshall. Those reasons remain unclear, but it is certainly possible that twenty-year-old Emily Jane Cowan had previously married a man named Marshall. It was not long after the wedding, that Ike Stockton took a shine to Emily Jane's half-sister Amanda Ellen Robinson.[73]

In December 1870, Porter Stockton was indicted by the Erath County Grand Jury for aggravated assault and battery for his attack on Taylor Avant. Stockton evaded arrest on this charge until January 1875.[74] At that time Stockton enlisted the help of friends and relatives as sureties on the bail bond. John R. O'Neal, who had served as Irvin Lacy's surety, was one of Stockton's. It seems certain that the Stocktons were related to the O'Neal family. William C. Bibb and John Alsup also served as sureties. William Bibb was Porter's step-uncle. By 1870, seventy-two-year-old Grandma Bibb was one of the oldest residents in Erath County. She lived surrounded by members of her large family, not too far from Stephenville on the Bosque River with one of her grandsons. Other family members, John O'Neal, William Bibb and West Hickey lived nearby.[75]

The loss of his parents was one factor which contributed to the large chip Porter Stockton carried conspicuously on his shoulder, the one he dared men to knock off. Early on he developed a reputation as a man with a short fuse and an overly sensitive disposition. It was a lethal combination. Stockton's honeymoon period set the trend for what was to come. On January 2, 1871, Stockton was involved in another row. His victim this time was Perry Gravis. A dispute developed between the men and Stockton humiliated Gravis by forcing him to give up his pistol. There was sufficient evidence to believe that Stockton kept the pistol for his own use. In April 1871 the Erath County Grand Jury indicted Stockton for robbery of the fifteen dollar sidearm. As with the assault of Taylor Avant, Stockton evaded arrest on this charge for several years.[76]

Stockton was on a roll and about a month after his trouble with Perry Gravis he committed another assault. This resulted in an April 8, 1871 indictment for assault to kill and murder. Available records in this case do not shed much light on the incident. One of the summoned witnesses is shown as "Eugene Wood (col')." The parenthesized abbreviation indicates that Wood was colored. Given Porter Stockton's racist nature and considering that victims were routinely summoned to court, Mr. Wood may well have been the man Stockton intended to kill. He would never face trial for these charges.[77] As a result his name was entered into a list of names, offenses and physical descriptions which became known as the Texas Rangers' "Black Book."[78] The 1880 edition of the book contained over six thousand names and a thousand of those were wanted for murder. A Rangers' Black Book soon became as saddle worn as its owner.[79] The 1878 edition described Stockton as being five feet eight, 140 pounds with a light complexion, light hair and sandy moustache.[80] Porter was about twenty-seven when the book was published.

Many of the friendships which Porter and Ike Stockton formed in Erath County in the 1870s would endure until they met their untimely ends. Porter Stockton was a braggart who proudly crowed about his misdeeds. No one would mistake who or what he was. By contrast, Ike in his later years presented himself as an enterprising stockman and aspiring businessman. An astonishing number of upstanding citizens would be fooled by Ike's smooth-tongue. Those citizens did not have the benefit of judging him by those who were his friends in Erath County.

One of those friends came to the attention of Erath County authorities during the early months of 1871. Sandwiched between Porter Stockton's alleged January robbery of Perry Gravis and the attempted murder in February was a January 26th assault committed by George W. Morrison. Young Morrison would remain a close ally of the Stockton brothers for the next ten years. He was a twenty-three-year-old native of

Texas and in 1870 he described himself as a stock raiser and valued his personal estate at $3000. He lived on the Bosque River and his closest neighbors were Grandmother Bibb and John R. O'Neal. He had married the O'Neals' twenty-year-old daughter, Marinda a year earlier. Morrison's problems began when he put a bullet into James H. Carter, a twenty-four-year-old Stephenville stockman. Carter lived close to the family of farmer and mail carrier C.C. Painter. C.C's sixteen-year-old son William would soon be recognized as perhaps the most prolific yet inept cow thief in Erath County. The shooting of James Carter resulted in Morrison's April indictment for assault with intent to kill and murder. Witnesses to the assault were Stephenville merchant W.T. Mansker, James Carmack and William Keith.[81] Given that Morrison's father-in-law would later be Stockton's surety for bail, the fact that his closest neighbor was Stockton's grandmother, and the close time frame of the assaults involving the two men, it may be that Morrison and the Stocktons were allied in some continuing, but now lost to history, dispute. George Morrison was part of the storm that was headed to the San Juan country. Morrison's exodus from Erath County may have been hastened after he took a shot at Elijah E. Martin on May 17, 1873. Martin lived in Erath County near the village of Dublin. A few days later an Erath County grand jury indicted Morrison for aggravated assault. William Keith, one of the witnesses in Morrison's attempted murder case, was a witness in this case as well. David Martin and the victim were listed as the other witnesses for the state.[82] The sandy-bearded Morrison made the 1878 edition of the Rangers' Black Book, which said he was living in Colorado.[83]

Morrison's wild side was in direct opposition to his upbringing. His father William was described as "an active and worthy member of the Methodist church" and the family may have distanced themselves from George after his violent outbursts. His mother was the former Sallie O'Neal, so it seems apparent that George had married his cousin. The Morrison home in Erath County was in Dublin.[84]

Other Erath County outlaws and associates of the Stocktons would eventually make their way to southwest Colorado. Cattle rustler William (Bill) Painter was one of those men. During the fall of 1871, he was cutting a wide swath through the range, gathering and branding cattle. That would have been okay, except they were not his to drive or brand. On September 20, 1871, he stole a calf which belonged to J.U. Parr and marked it with the brand "JR." The use of that brand implicates the family of Leonard Roberts in Painter's rustling operation. The JR brand was registered to Leonard's father, John H. Roberts and to his brother, James H. Roberts. On November 15th Painter stole four calves from J.B. Blankenship. Witnesses in this case included J.B. and A.J. Blankenship and Bud Galbreath. Painter was accused of two other similar crimes. He branded a calf belonging to Stephenville merchant J.S. Hyatt. Hyatt lived in a crowded household, probably a boarding house, whose residents included two of Stephenville's physicians and the colorfully named deputy sheriff, Light Nowlin. Painter also attempted to steal a calf belonging to William Waller. Painter's rustling spree resulted in indictments for all four incidents during the December term of the Erath County District Court. In the Blankenship case the indictment accused Painter of the theft of "four calves (neat cattle) of the value of three dollars each." The term neat cattle distinguished domestic cattle from their wild brethren.[85] The witless Painter probably herded these four calves out of their pen near the Blankenship home. What role witness Bud Galbreath played in the latter theft is unclear. Galbreath's real name was Marion H. Galbreath. Eighteen-year-old Bud was a native Texan. His last name shows up with a variety of spellings, including Galbreth, Gilbreath, Gilbreth and others. In the latter part of the 1850s his father, James M. Galbreath, married Bud's stepmom, the former Elizabeth Ann Hickey. It was his third marriage.[86] Elizabeth Ann was yet one more of the sisters to the mother of Porter and Ike Stockton.[87] Galbreath had a wild side and he would soon be in serious trouble. While he was only a step-cousin to the Stockton boys, he developed an almost brotherly relationship with them. Galbreath was destined to join up with Ike Stockton along the Animas River valley of southwest Colorado.

Galbreath was consorting with cattle and horse thieves, but somehow he avoided being charged himself. He was a witness in at least one other case of Erath County stock thievery. The suspect in this case was Port and Ike's little brother, Samuel Stockton. On August 10, 1871, Samuel stole a gelding from Green Motheral. Witnesses in the case, besides Motheral and Galbreath, were James Frances and George Hill. Like William Painter, Sam Stockton was indicted during the December 1871 session of court. This case was continued on the court's docket as late as February 1874.[88] As for the witness George Hill, he would later turn up on the witness list for Porter Stockton's attempted murder charge.[89] The extent of the links between the Stockton brothers, Bud Galbreath, William Painter and George Hill are obscured by the passage of time, but it is clear that they were allied in various nefarious activities centered around rustling cattle and horses. The Erath County indictments may be just the tip of a much larger criminal iceberg. Like Porter, Samuel Stockton was headed down a dangerous path. Stealing horses was by far the most risky pursuit of stock thieves. Across Texas and throughout the West, courts were often not involved when it came to doling out justice to horse thieves. Only the most notorious cattle bandits were treated so harshly.

For cattle rustlers there were several methods to avoid detection. As it turns out, Marion Galbreath's older brother, Green, operated the only meat market in Stephenville in the early 1870s.[90] He used only a butcher knife, axe and scale for tools. W.H. Fooshee noted that Galbreath would drive his wagon out on the range, "shoot down a beef, skin it, cut it into quarters, throw them into his wagon, drive to town, to his market under the old shade tree," near the town square. In this open air market Galbreath charged two cents per pound for forequarter cuts and three cents per pound for all cuts from the hindquarter.[91] This put him in a position to quickly convert stolen cattle into a marketable and untraceable commodity. It seems likely that Galbreath's meat market was used in this fashion. It may also explain why William Painter brazenly stole cattle which were virtually his neighbor's pets. It would not be the last time that the Stocktons, stolen cattle and a butcher shop were connected in such a manner.

I.W. Lacy would learn this the hard way, but that was several years in the future. During the very busy December 1871 Erath District Court session, Lacy also faced charges of stealing a beef steer.[92] The details of this case are unknown, but it may have involved some hot blooded dispute over the ownership of an unbranded calf. Acquiescence in such a matter was not in Lacy's nature. Lacy was released on a one hundred dollar bail bond and summoned to appear before the court in February 1872. He had failed to appear at this same session on the charge of selling liquor without a license. As for this charge the court records noted, "the Defendant came not, but wholly made default." Lacy had three sureties in the matter: L.G. Coleman, Peter Burleson and Martin Van Buren Salyer, his brother-in-law. The court "ordered that the said judgment be made final and absolute against the said Lacy, but dismissed as to the said sureties." Lacy was left responsible for the one hundred dollar bail bond and the case was retired from the docket.[93] Lacy's bondsman, Pete Burleson, was fearless and hard-nosed. He would later serve as the sheriff of Colfax County, New Mexico. While in that position, Porter Stockton proved to be a perpetual and perilous problem.

Bill Painter was just one of the many herders who sought to enrich themselves with the cattle of others. He may have assisted Green Galbreath by providing cattle for the shade tree meat market, but that was not Painter's only method for making money.[94] His operation was clearly linked to the Roberts family, and in later years Leonard Roberts reminisced that in the early 1870s he drove cattle up the Chisholm Trail to Kansas for J.H. Edwards and Bill Painter. Edwards's role in Painter's illicit activities is unclear, but Uncle West Hickey may have sent a few cattle up the trail with this group. In 1870 his closest neighbor was J.H. Edwards. Roberts reported that they made only seven or eight miles a day. He noted, "We just grassed them through. We would be on the road two or three months at a time." At the end of the drive he said, "we would sell the cattle, then come home with several thousand dollars in our saddle bags."[95] It is a small wonder that some chose mavericking and others chose outright rustling as a means to success. The connections between Bill Painter, Bud Galbreath and the Stockton brothers strongly infer that the Stocktons trailed cattle up the Chisholm Trail with Painter. Porter Stockton almost certainly followed the cattle trails into Kansas.

Some accounts report that he killed a man in Dodge City.[96] Another source says Stockton shot a man in Ellsworth in August 1873.[97] Reliable sources provide no confirmation for these incidents. Of course, newspaper accounts often identified the perpetrators and victims of such episodes simply as a Texan or a Texas herder. Even though they were often nameless, the Texas boys, and most of them were indeed boys, left their mark on the cowtowns of Kansas and their end of the trail forays contributed substantially to the myths and legends of the American cowboy. Stockton's earlier crimes in Erath County and his later activities in New Mexico have a substantial factual basis. It would be the exception and not the rule, if he maintained a peaceable disposition while celebrating the end of a long trail drive.

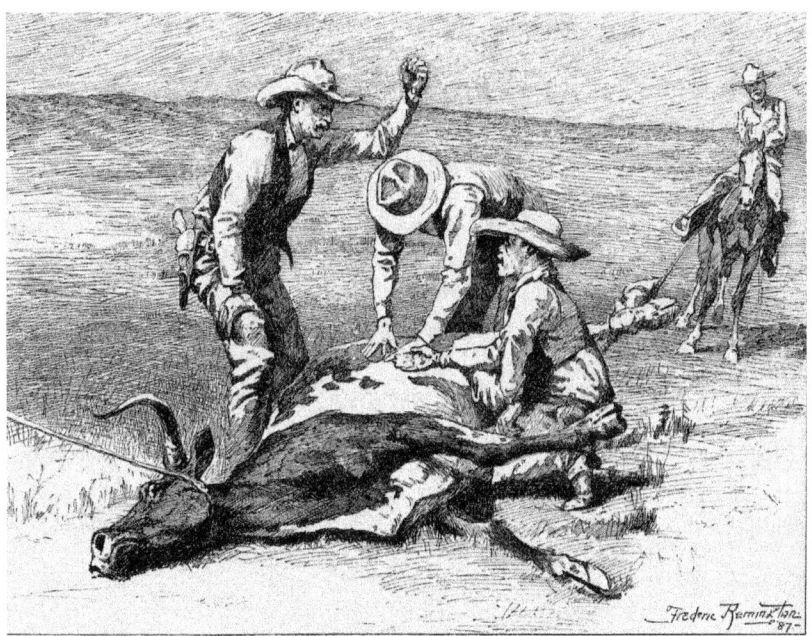

Frederic Remington's "A Dispute Over A Brand," from Theodore Roosevelt's "Ranch Life in the Far West," The Century Illustrated Monthly Magazine, *Vol. 35, No. 4, February 1888. (Author's collection.)*

Perhaps the northern drives encouraged Stockton to look for greener pastures. During at least a part of 1872 or during the early months of 1873, the Stocktons were living in Missouri. While there, Emily gave birth to their first child, a daughter who bore the most common female name in the family, Sarah.⁹⁸ Porter may not have been there for the joyous occasion. During the trail driving years men were often away from their families for months at a time. The Stockton's time in Missouri was suspiciously short-lived.

Inevitably, the future of Porter and Ike Stockton was tied to the trail used by Charles Goodnight, John Dawson, Joel Curtis and others. Throughout the early 1870s Dawson and his associates trailed herds out of Texas to stock their New Mexico range. Their success encouraged other cattlemen to pull up stakes and head west. The cattlemen employed a substantial number of cowboys to care for their livestock. Porter Stockton was the first brother to make the move west and he was just one of the many Texan herders who moved to the area. Given the timing of his arrival in Colfax County and the herders he was known to associate with, it is apparent that Porter Stockton worked as a drover for Lacy and Coleman. He would have also worked with and for their associates, like John Dawson, Joel Curtis, Tom Stockton and others who made their home in or near the Vermejo valley and on the Red (Canadian) River.

The Stockton family would spend the next few years in the border region that encompassed Colfax County, New Mexico and Las Animas County, Colorado. At the time, thousands of travelers passed through the region on the Santa Fe Trail. Many immigrants from Texas, Missouri and elsewhere were settling in the area. The influx of new residents, the arrival of cattle, cattlemen and their cowboys, the presence of a large and fiercely proud Hispanic population and the cloud of uncertainty hanging over the title claims of squatters residing on the Maxwell Grant created many powder kegs. The six-shooters and inflammatory tempers of Porter Stockton and other Texas cowboys would serve as fitful matches.

Chapter Two

Chaos in Colfax County

> *I think we can all remember when a Greaser hadn't no show*
> *In Palo Pinto particular,--it ain't very long ago;*
> *A powerful feelin' of hatred ag'in the whole Greaser race*
> *That murdered bold Crockett and Bowie pervaded all in the place.*
> *Why, the boys would draw on a Greaser as quick as they would on a steer;*
> *They was shot down without warnin' often, in the memory of many here.*[1]

The catalyst for a concussive wave of chaos in northeast New Mexico and adjacent portions of Colorado occurred in 1870, when Lucien Maxwell negotiated the sale of the bulk of his property to an English company. By July, local newspapers carried news of the change in ownership.[2] The sale of the grant to foreigners put the region in a state of anxiety. Soon after the initial sale a corporation known as the Maxwell Land Grant and Railway Company assumed control of the grant. The first immediate conflict occurred between the new owners and miners in the Moreno Valley.[3] The new company moved swiftly against squatters. Only months after the purchase their attorney, Stephen Benton Elkins, began ejectment proceedings. He was assisted in this effort by New Mexico's attorney general, Thomas Benton Catron.[4] Disputes about the grant persisted for many years, significantly contributing to the region's rugged growing pains.

Brutality and violence were never far away for those brought up on the frontier of Texas and throughout the 1870s a torrent of Texans surged into Colfax County. Many of them shared connections to Erath, Palo Pinto and nearby counties. The most notable of these men drove cattle for the same cowmen as Porter Stockton. The Texans immediately began gouging and scraping the wound that was Colfax County and when the wound began to scab over, they would yank it off and pour salt into it. The use of brute force as a means to an end was a natural course for the Texans. An examination of Colfax County's violence illuminates the abhorrent behavior and deeds which were run-of-the-mill for Porter Stockton. The Cimarron country would be tamed in spite of and because of the Texans, but the scar left by Porter Stockton, his fellow cow herders and the trail driving cattlemen is remembered to this day.

By 1873 the elder Stockton brother was living in Colfax County, but his presence is not certain until the latter months of that year. Despite possible perceptions to the contrary, a cryptic article in the *Cimarron News* from April 1873 does not refer to Porter Stockton. The article reported, "A

The eastern portion of New Mexico Territory. From an 1889 map of New Mexico and Arizona by L.B. Folger. (Author's collection.)

number of cases in the criminal docket go over till next term. Among others those of Territory vs. French, Territory vs. Stockton, and others for murder, the last named defendants not being yet indicted but held over to await the action of the next grand jury."[5] The puzzling notice did not to take into account that there was more than one man named Stockton living in Colfax County at the time. Thomas L. Stockton and his young brother Mathias "Thyke" Stockton were two of those men.[6] Their sister, Edwena, was John Dawson's first wife.[7] Like Dawson, Tom Stockton was one of the first Texas cattlemen to move to Colfax County. The Texans were not inclined to wait on territorial officials to handle problems they encountered. The *Santa Fe New Mexican* and other newspapers took note of the gunfire and death which accompanied their arrival. If Tom and Thyke were related to Porter Stockton, they did not brag about it. Considering the families lived close to each other in Texas and later in New Mexico, they may well have been related. Like Porter Stockton, Tom Stockton was known to employ violence when it suited his needs; unlike Porter Stockton, Thomas Stockton was a man of means.

Tom was born in Tennessee in 1832. Prior to the Civil War his family lived in Buchanan County, Texas. Census records for 1860 indicate that the closest post office was in the town of Palo Pinto. The Stockton family was logged on the census form in clear, crisp handwriting by enumerator and cattleman, John Hittson.[8] Stockton moved to Colfax County in 1867 and continued raising cattle as he had done in Texas.[9] He soon partnered with Frank Wilburn and established the Clifton House on the Red (Canadian) River northeast of Cimarron. Weary travelers who thought they had reached the end of the earth could not help but be impressed by the hostelry.[10] The walls were adobe, with two and half stories being above ground. The furnishings, lumber and windows had been freighted in by wagon over the Santa Fe Trail.[11] The Clifton House was strategically located on the mountain route of the Santa Fe Trail and it would play a pivotal role in the future of Porter Stockton. It was also used as a drover's inn, where cattlemen and cowboys could find board and lodging, conduct business, and tell lies to each other. Stockton's inn was said to cost $30,000, a stunning figure for the place and time. On the stage road it was about thirty-five miles northeast of Cimarron.[12] Stockton later leased the inn to the Barlow and Sanderson Stage Line.[13]

The April 1873 *Cimarron News* article about a potential murder indictment for a man named Stockton stemmed from events which occurred eight months earlier. On July 12, 1872, the bodies of two men who had been shot and killed were found on the Elizabethtown road. Further investigation revealed that the men had met their end at the hands of Tom Stockton, his brother-in-law and Confederate veteran, Finis (also known as Fine) Ernest, a man known as "Chuck" and two other men. The trouble began when the cattlemen noticed that about seventy head of cattle were missing from their Red River herd. They easily followed the cattle tracks up the Cimarron on the road leading to Elizabethtown, a bustling Colfax County mining camp, which in its early days was also known as Elizabeth City. At dusk the pursuers made camp on the Ute Creek trail. The next morning they traveled up Ute Creek and soon came upon George Cunningham and Leonidas Van Valser herding the cattle. Stockton and his men claimed they treated the thieves with kid gloves, disarming them and using them as herders for the trip back to Cimarron. The *Cimarron News* said, "where the road opens into the can[y]on, the two men, thinking, probably, that there was a chance to get away, made a dash, but were at once fired upon and both killed." We will never know the Van Valser and Cunningham version of events. The *News* said, "The general impression appears to be that the community are much indebted to the band from Red River for the courage and resolution with which the pursuit was kept up under such difficulties, and a blow struck at the lawless gang which has brought such trouble on our district." The paper also reported that an inquest was held the next day and the verdict "was practically one of 'justifiable homicide.' The bodies were buried the same day."[14] At the time of his death, Cunningham, a native of Ireland, was twenty-six-years-old. Van Valser, who was born in Canada, was twenty-seven. The two dead men were not newcomers to Colfax County. Like many others, they had been drawn to the mining activity around Elizabeth City, but had not made a big strike. In 1870, both men were stuck in jobs as laborers. When the Texans brought in thousands of cattle and turned them loose along the Sangre de Cristos, they could not resist temptation.[15]

Practically justifiable homicide was not quite the same as justifiable homicide and territorial officials took an interest in the incident. The two dead men had friends, including Robert H. Longwill, Medick E. Prevost, Samuel H. Irvin and William Irvin. The Texans did not care. Cattle thieves were cattle thieves and would be treated accordingly. The vigilante known as "Chuck" was a bit of a mystery man. He was later identified as Milton J. Arrington. In territorial court records it was Prevost who noted that "Arrington went by the name of Chuck." In September 1872, with the testimony of Longwill, Prevost and the Irvins, territorial officials succeeded in obtaining two indictments for larceny against Tom Stockton, Milton Arrington, Andrew Scott and William Parker. They were charged with stealing a horse, bridle and saddle from the dead men. Fine Ernest was not named in either indictment. The Longwills, Irvin and Prevost were not satisfied.[16] On April 5, 1873, Joseph G. Palen, the Chief Justice of the Territorial Supreme Court and District Judge of New Mexico's First Judicial District, heard evidence in the case. The testimony was not given before the sitting grand jury, but Justice Palen ruled "that there's probable cause to believe that Thomas Stockton, Milton J. Arrington, Fine Ernest, Andrew Scott and William Parker are guilty of the crime of murder." He ruled that Sheriff Orson K. Chittenden collect bail from the men "in the sum of ten thousand dollars." Two days later Thyke Stockton, Elihu Johnson and Sheriff Chittenden ponied up the $10,000 bail for Tom Stockton, Fine Ernest and Andrew Scott. Chittenden's loyalties in the matter explain why it was left to the judge to determine if probable cause existed. The men were advised that their case would be heard during the August session of court.[17] This was duly reported in the *Cimarron News* and in the *Santa Fe New Mexican*.

Milton J. "Chuck" Arrington was also indicted in a separate case involving a violent death during the same court session. This assault is often credited to future Porter Stockton enemy, Chunk Colbert. As it turns out, Colbert was not involved. A dispute with Arrington in the latter part of July 1872 culminated with the death of Charles Morris. Golden's *Colorado Transcript* identified the shooter as a man named "Harrington."[18] Prior to his death, Morris had his own legal troubles. In April 1872, Morris, Fred J. Ames and Charles Farrand were indicted by the Colfax County Grand Jury for the murder of John Fisher which took place on November 1, 1871.[19] Fisher was shot in the left temple, the bullet then exiting out the back of his skull. Because he had threatened the lives of several men, his murder was the common consequence of a preemptive vigilante mentality. His body was found about one mile north of Cimarron by the stage driver.[20] The following July, Morris encountered Arrington in Cimarron, near Edward F. Mezick's Store. The unarmed Morris could not avoid the confrontation. The *Rocky Mountain News* reported that, "Morris seized 'Chuck' and tried to hold his arms down, the latter resisted, seized his revolver, and firing over his shoulder shot Morris at the base of the left ear, through the brain. He leaves a widow and a young family." Arrington turned himself in to the sheriff. At the subsequent hearing, "The court room was filled with partisans of both sides armed to the teeth."[21] The *Colorado Chieftain* noted, "an examination was held before Justice Rinehart, who acquitted the prisoner on the ground of justifiable homicide. During the trial the court, prisoner and all adjourned to take a drink."[22] Once again the justifiable homicide verdict reported was not the end of the story. During the spring 1873 district court session, Justice Palen and the grand jury heard evidence in the case and Arrington was indicted on a charge of manslaughter. Records for this case are muddled and some are missing, but the case moved swiftly to a conclusion, on April 4, 1873 a Colfax County jury found Arrington not guilty.[23]

Some of the 1873 courtroom backlash against Tom Stockton and probably against Milton Arrington occurred because of Stockton's well documented activities immediately after the killing of Van Valser and Cunningham. During the remainder of the summer of 1872, Stockton became a trusted ally of cattleman John Hittson. According to one account, only a decade before Hittson "was a poor farmer in Tennessee." After moving to Palo Pinto County he amassed a fortune on the hoof and was said to drive "10,000 cattle to market annually."[24] Hittson would soon inflame the tensions between the Texans and the Hispanic residents of northern New Mexico. It is not known if Porter Stockton joined Hittson's group, but he may have because many tough Texans joined the cause. It was an activity he would have relished and it mirrored the conflict he would later have with at least one of the region's Hispanic residents.

For years, Texas cattlemen had suffered from the depredations of Comanche and Kiowa Indians. Thousands of cattle had been stolen from their home range and from trail drives. Many of those cattle were purchased from the Indians through middlemen, who were provided with trade goods by New Mexico businessmen. Those cattle were moved westward across the Llano Estacado and ended up on the ranches of native New Mexicans in the Pecos River valley and along the eastern side of the Sangre de Cristos. The Texans knew this was happening, but time, distance, logistics and jurisdictional concerns prevented them from taking action. As more Texas cattlemen moved to eastern New Mexico, they could not help but recognize the prevalence of Texas branded stock claimed by some of the local ranchers. The Texans now had a base of operations in Colfax County and John Hittson began to contemplate retrieving the stolen cattle. Hittson was a determined man with obvious prejudices. He gave an incendiary description of the middlemen to a newsman from Denver's *Rocky Mountain News,* saying, "Next, are what are termed Comancheros, a low, desperate class of Greasers, who are in the employ of these merchants to perform the dirty work and act as go-betweens." In the spring of 1872, Hittson went to Denver and gathered up about ninety men, split them into three groups, and made sure they were well-armed. The men headed south.[25]

In Colfax County, Hittson met with his former Texas neighbors. Tom Stockton played a prominent role in Hittson's venture.[26] Other conspicuous allies included James Patterson and Martin Childers, who was commonly known as Mart.[27] Childers was married to the former Hulda Ann Cox, who was the niece of Wash Cox.[28] Mart Childers is also known as Hugh Martin Childress, Jr., but the name Childers was invariably used in New Mexico's territorial records and in newspapers of the time. In 1866 he drove a herd into central Iowa and sold them for a whopping profit at thirty-five dollars a head.[29] By 1871 he was described as being "among the large cattle-raisers of Texas," with a herd of 10,000 cattle.[30] Childers had undoubtedly suffered losses he attributed to the Comanchero trade, which contributed to the deadly zeal he displayed with the native New Mexicans. He and his well-armed associates ran roughshod over the primarily Hispanic ranchers in the Pecos River valley and along the eastern foothills of the Sangre de Cristos. They rode into the ranchos and ranchitos, gathered up cattle and horses bearing Texas brands and moved out. As complaints about their methods mounted, Hittson adeptly advanced his case to anyone who would listen. Resistance was light until they rode into Loma Parda, about twenty-five miles north of Las Vegas. Violence erupted and two residents were shot and killed and another bullet tore through the thighs of the village *alcalde*.[31] Mart Childers was charged with murder for this incident and housed in the San Miguel County jail in Las Vegas. On December 28, 1872 he escaped and headed for Texas.[32]

John Hittson, Tom Stockton and Mart Childers managed to avoid any severe punishment for their actions during the summer, fall and winter of 1872. In fact, in Texas and elsewhere, they were viewed as righteous heroes.[33] That was not the case everywhere. The entire episode left a bitter taste in the mouths of many of New Mexico's Hispanic residents. It was said that for years afterwards mothers would invoke the fear of Hittson and his Texans, saying, "If you are not good, I'll give you to the Tejanos, who are coming back."[34]

More Texans were coming and they intended to stay. During the summer of Hittson's raid, I.W. Lacy and L.G. Coleman started the move out of Erath County to the Cimarron country.[35] H.W. Cox also pointed his herd toward the Sangre de Cristos.[36] The Coxes and others formed a long wagon train and headed for New Mexico. Family accounts report that on this single trip Cox brought 30,000 cattle, the largest herd to leave Texas up to that time.[37] That number is impossibly large for a single herd and the description provides a distorted view of the Erath County cattle exodus. The herd of 30,000 attributed to Wash Cox was no doubt an accumulation of cattle trailed out of Texas over the course of several years, probably in partnership with Lacy and Coleman, and others. Many of the tough herders who trailed cattle out of Erath County settled in Colfax County and some settled north of the border in Las Animas County, Colorado. The newly arrived Texans added to the violence which engulfed the region.

Trail drives and roundups for Lacy and Coleman, and Cox, mixed the Stockton brothers into a cast of characters destined for lasting notoriety, as well as with others for whom fame or infamy would be short-lived. Lacy and Coleman's trail boss in the early 1870s became one of the more well-known characters of his time and in the twentieth century he became the subject of several books.[38] Robert Clay Allison was born on September 2, 1841. He spent his early years in Tennessee and served with the Confederate Army during the Civil War. When the cause was lost he made his way to the Cross Timbers country of Texas.[39] He soon entered the cattle business. According to some accounts, Allison first entered the Cimarron area while working on cattle drives for Charles Goodnight.[40] He soon found his way to Erath County and joined Lacy and Coleman's outfit.[41] He was notorious for getting wildly drunk, but when sober he was chivalrous and personable. Six foot and two inches tall, Allison's blue eyes, wavy brown hair and manly frame made him popular with women, but he was deadly when riled.⁴² Even though he lived in Colfax County for only six years, his reputation as a shootist was firmly established by the time he returned to Texas.

Frederic Remington's "The Round-up," from Theodore Roosevelt's "The Round-up," The Century Illustrated Monthly Magazine, *Vol. 35, No. 6, April 1888. (Author's collection.)*

Clay Allison was no mere employee of Lacy and Coleman. He was their close friend and business partner. In 1871 Allison was in charge of driving a large herd of their cattle from Texas to Colfax County. Shortly after his arrival, Allison somehow managed to shoot himself in the instep with his pistol. The wound was serious and he had a lengthy recovery. He would suffer from this injury for the rest of his life. While Allison recuperated, Lacy and Coleman brought another herd up the trail and turned them loose on the plains near what is now the village of Maxwell. With his bullet injury on the mend, Allison was put in charge of the second herd and given 500 head of cattle on shares.⁴³ Irvin Lacy thought so highly of Allison he would later name his son Clay.⁴⁴ The three men registered their primary brand with the Colfax County Clerk under the name Lacy – Coleman – Allison. It was the brand Lacy and Coleman used in Erath County, an L on the right hip, and an LC on the right side. For earmarks they cropped the right ear and undersloped the left. Allison registered a brand in his own name. It was a C on the right hip and a 7 on the right side or shoulder. His brother John joined him. His cattle bore a JH on the right side. Lacy also registered a brand under his name, a 101 on the right side.[45] Allison's ranch was at the confluence of the Canadian and Vermejo Rivers. Lacy's ranch was fifteen miles to the northwest. Luke Coleman's place was eight miles up the road from Lacy's.[46]

Two of the infamous LC trail hands included Davy Crockett and Gus Heffron.[47] The Stockton brothers may have known Crockett for several years. Crockett claimed to be related to the original Davy Crockett of Alamo fame.[48] That was probably true. He was apparently the same David Crockett who was born in Texas in 1853 and in 1860 he was living with his family in Erath County.[49] After Davy Crockett's death at the Alamo, his son, Robert Crockett, settled near Granbury, which is thirty miles northeast of Stephenville. Old Davy's last wife, Elizabeth, is buried nearby in Acton.[50] At Cimarron, young Davy and Heffron teamed up to look for trouble and met with rousing success. Henry Goodman also drove cattle for Lacy and Coleman. Henry like the Stocktons and Gus Heffron, would eventually move to the San Juan country. The young South Carolinian came to Texas at the age of eleven in 1863 with his brother William. Both men eventually entered the cattle business. Goodman began driving herds to Denver for John Hittson. In 1873, William was killed by Indians near San Saba. About the same time Henry began working for Lacy and Coleman. He stayed with the LC outfit throughout the seventies and into the eighties, becoming their loyal and trusted top hand and a principal in the operation.[51]

Wash Cox would also do his part to populate Colfax County with herders who worked on his trail drives. Marion Littrell was one of those cowpunchers. Littrell would become a deputy sheriff in Colfax County and would later serve twelve years as the elected sheriff. On at least one occasion, Stockton incited violence would leave his life hanging in the balance. Littrell was born on February 1, 1855, near Eureka Springs, Arkansas. In the spring of 1871, at the age of sixteen, he left home looking for adventure. He ended up in Erath County and became a cow herder for Wash Cox.[52]

Cox sensed Littrell's high character and observed the care he gave his horse.[53] The trail driver had a rule for those who rode for him and wasn't afraid to let them know when they'd broken it. He made sure they knew, "The part of the horse from the cinch forward belonged to the outfit and from the cinch back belonged to the rider." Any rider who mistreated his mount was soon looking for new employment.[54] While driving cattle for Wash Cox, Littrell began a lifetime friendship with another young puncher named Zenas Curtis.[55] Zenas was born in 1857 in Parker County near Weatherford, Texas. He was the son of Buchanan County, Texas and Colfax County cattleman Joel W. Curtis, who trailed cattle to Denver in 1860 with Oliver Loving and others. The respect accorded Wash Cox is exemplified by the fact that Joel Curtis entrusted his teenaged son to work on several of Cox's trail drives.⁵⁶ As Littrell later recalled he and Curtis "kept going back and forth into Texas for more cattle for Cox" until 1877.⁵⁷ By that time Wash Cox had established his new home along the Animas River valley just south of the Colorado border. Littrell and Curtis trailed cattle for Cox on an almost constant basis for five years. After their time working for Wash Cox, Littrell and Zenas Curtis "took charge of outfits from the Clay Allison ranch." During their Colfax County years, the Cox family lived in a large house located near the confluence of Chicorica Creek and the Red (Canadian) River, at the base of Eagle Tail Mountain near where the town of Dorsey would later be formed.⁵⁸ In the wide open spaces of northeast New Mexico, this made him a neighbor to Joel Curtis, John Dawson, Clay Allison and I.W. Lacy.⁵⁹ While living on the Red River, two of the Cox boys became extremely ill after contracting smallpox. Zenas Curtis was a cowboy, but he later recalled helping nurse the Cox boys back to health.⁶⁰

A scene familiar to the cowboys of Colfax County. Frederic Remington's "Pulling A Cow Out of the Mud," from Theodore Roosevelt's "Ranch Life in the Far West," The Century Illustrated Monthly Magazine, *Vol. 35, No. 4, February 1888. (Modified, author's collection.)*

While Wash Cox and Irvin Lacy set up their ranches in New Mexico, Ike Stockton maintained his Texas residency and looked for a more domestic life. In the spring of 1873, Amanda Ellen Robinson, who was no older than fifteen, was united in marriage to Ike Stockton in Erath County. The Stockton boys were always close, and that relationship grew even stronger now that they were married to women who were not only their first cousins, but who were half-sisters as well.[61] Marriages between cousins were fairly common at the time because extended families often lived very close to each other, sometimes even in the same household, and it was a way to keep the family fortune in the family, even if the fortune was small.

With the early deaths of their parents, the Stockton children were left to make it on their own. The boys sought to do that anyway they could. Ike was not a hothead like his older brother, but he was not averse to enriching himself at the expense of others. Like both of his brothers and their associates, Ike soon faced criminal charges in Erath County. Just five months after his wedding, Ike went on trial as the result of two separate indictments for cattle theft. In the first case he was found guilty and fined $24 plus costs. In the second case he was found guilty of "willfully and illegally removing said animal from its accustomed range." For that he was fined $20 plus costs.[62] Those were stiff fines, but Ike avoided jail time. His punishment indicates that he was not seen as an unrepentant rustler. As time would tell, Ike was gregarious and well liked by many wherever he lived, but the guilty verdicts were an ill-fated beginning to the marriage; Ike's cattle thievery was now a matter of record. Ike and Porter Stockton were never separated for long and not long after this difficulty, Ike and Amanda Ellen began contemplating their move to New Mexico.

Life in Colfax County continued to be dangerous. The Lacy's had witnessed Comanche and Kiowa attacks in Texas. They soon found that New Mexico was not a safe haven. On September 25, 1873, a band of fifty Cheyennes invaded the Lacy's Vermejo home. The Indians were well-armed and traveling with two horses per man. For a short while they made themselves at home. The Lacy's astute and muted reaction to the home invasion prevented the situation from deteriorating. At the time I.W. and Sarah Lacy had a seven-year-old daughter, a five-year-old daughter and an infant boy, who was also named I.W. Lacy. The *Cimarron News* reported that "the Indians declared that they had no hostile intentions toward the whites, but were in search of the Apaches."[63]

As 1873 drew to a close, Porter Stockton made his presence known along the border of Colorado and New Mexico. Stockton's first verifiable scrape with New Mexico's territorial officials was memorialized by a legendary figure of the American west. Dick Wootton was a pioneer resident of Colorado and like others in the region, he soon knew Porter Stockton on sight. "Uncle Dick," as he was known, had a storied past as a frontiersman, freighter, scout and businessman who first traveled to Santa Fe by wagon train in the summer of 1836. Wootton was one of the men who stormed the church at the Taos Pueblo after the death of the first civilian American governor of New Mexico, Charles Bent, in the Taos Rebellion of 1847. Life moved on, and almost twenty years later, in 1865, Wootton sought and received charters from the legislatures of Colorado and New Mexico which authorized him to build a toll road over Raton Pass connecting Trinidad, Colorado and the area near present day Raton, New Mexico. The pass was part of the mountain route of the Santa Fe Trail. "Uncle Dick" operated a stage stop, hotel and eatery on the pass where he also lived.[64] It was early one day in late December 1873 that a man Wootton described as a half-breed Cherokee Indian stopped at his place. "Uncle Dick" knew the man by the sobriquet, Chunk.[65] Wootton may not have known it at the time, but Chunk was anxious to leave Colorado.

About 11:30 PM on Saturday, December 27th Chunk Colbert, Sam Doss, "Dutch Bill" Hoehne and George Waller were some of the many attending a fandango at the small Hispanic village of San Francisco fourteen miles east of Trinidad. Sam Doss was a local cattleman and a rabid racing aficionado. The crowd had gathered to see horse races the next day. Whiskey was lubricating the pre-race festivities.[66] According to the *Trinidad Enterprise* Waller became incensed when "Dutch Bill" brought a young negro boy into the dance. Waller said "that Dutch Bill was no gentleman to bring a negro in the room where white men were." (The typesetter or reporter probably erred and it was probably the introduction of a black youth into the presence of white women which was the point of contention.) Waller then made the mistake of taking a punch at "Dutch Bill." The *Enterprise* reported, "Race Dorse [Doss] stepped up and deliberately taking out his six-shooter, struck Waller two terrible blows over the head, knocking him down." Stunned and confused, Waller rose, glared at Chunk Colbert and said, "Who was that shot me?" When Colbert denied having any part in the affray, Waller called him a liar. Colbert needed no further provocation. "Hardly had he uttered the words," the *Enterprise* declared, "when Chunk commenced shooting at him, putting four balls in his body, killing him instantly."[67] The *Colorado Chieftain* described the shooting differently, saying, "Doss held Waller against the wall while Chunk fired six shots at him, five of them taking effect." Whatever the case, Waller was dead and Chunk Colbert was on the run. Chunk lived on the Red (Canadian) River in New Mexico as did Milton J. "Chuck" Arrington. This contributed to the latter day confusion between the two men.[68] After murdering Waller, Chunk sought safety south of the jurisdictional boundary separating Colorado from New Mexico.

Chances are very high that Porter Stockton and the deceased man had worked together on cattle drives and roundups. At the time of his death Waller was working as a cow herder for William J. Follis.[69] The year before Bill Follis had brought in a herd of cattle from Stephenville, Texas and had started a ranch near Trinidad.[70] Prior to that move, Follis had been one of the fewer than one hundred residents of Eastland County, when Ike Stockton and his siblings lived near the line separating Eastland from Erath.[71]

Porter Stockton soon took a personal interest in avenging Waller's death.[72] Early Sunday morning, both Colbert and Stockton stopped at Wootton's. "Uncle Dick" knew both men and their reputations. Everyone in the region utilized the hotel, stage station and eatery at Wootton's, including stage robbers, horse thieves and other outlaws. On one occasion the nation's vice president stopped there.[73] What Stockton knew at this point is open to question. Perhaps he was on Colbert's trail, but then had second thoughts about taking on Colbert one on one. However, it is just as likely that Stockton had ridden in from New Mexico and had no clue that Colbert had killed Waller. Given that Colbert lived near Tom Stockton's place on the Red River, Porter Stockton was almost certainly acquainted with him. Colbert was so notorious in the area that a headline later reporting his death did not even use his last name.[74] There was no confrontation between Colbert and Stockton and both men went on their way.[75] Colbert headed south to New Mexico, Stockton rode north.

His destination was Trinidad. At the time the town had a population of almost fifteen hundred people, mostly Hispanic. It had the appearance of towns found in north central New Mexico, with a preponderance of drab adobe buildings lining the narrow streets.[76] At some point Stockton joined the Trinidad posse which was after Colbert. He either met them on the road south of town or learned of Waller's death upon his arrival in Trinidad. Whatever the case, the posse headed for New Mexico. The well-armed search party included Patrick A. McBride, a hard drinking native of Ireland, who in a few short years would drink himself into an early grave.[77] His hail-fellow-well-met persona was essential to his political ambitions. At the time he was the Las Animas County Probate Judge and also served sporadically as an acting justice of the peace. Other members included two Las Animas County sheriff deputies, S.D. Hays and Nick Camblin. John Selles, a Trinidad constable, who worked at times as a deputy sheriff, also joined up, as did Thomas Charleton and William Welch. Charles "Tex" Bakewell (also identified as Beckwell and Blackwell) eagerly offered his services. Bakewell was a noted Trinidad ruffian and a close friend to Deputy Camblin.[78] The Trinidadians embarked on a determined effort to get their man. As they rode through the December chill, the tree shadows lengthened until pitch black engulfed the posse on Raton Pass.[79]

Upon reaching Wootton's place, Porter Stockton dismounted, entered the establishment, and at gunpoint demanded to know where he could find Chunk. A puzzled and perplexed Wootton told Stockton that Chunk had been there, but had left earlier in the day.[80] Stockton made a quick exit, the men mounted up, and with the loud pounding of hooves, they roared off into the night. Wootton's relieved patrons could now regale their friends and family with a wild west story of their own. After leaving Wootton's, the men traveled down the pass into New Mexico. They showed up at the Clifton House.[81] In the waning hours of Sunday, December 28th, Porter Stockton and the others were finishing a long, full day in the saddle.[82] Most of the guests at the inn were asleep and Chunk was ready for the taking. Inexplicably, the posse announced their arrival by clanging a bell until someone was aroused. They were directed to Chunk's room upstairs. Upon reaching the room one of the men inside raised up from his bed and a member of the posse fired a single shot.[83] The victim was not Colbert, but an innocent man by the name of John Canada. The single deadly shot burrowed deeply into the fleshy area on Canada's left side just below the ribs.[84] Now that everyone was awake, the men learned that Chunk was in another building forty yards away. The formerly determined Coloradoans sent the Clifton House cook to advise Chunk that a posse was there to arrest him. The cook advised Colbert and then turned to leave when, according to the *Colorado Chieftain*, Chunk said, "Wait a minute Bill, I would not go yet." Chunk's reputation and his six-shooter encouraged the cook's compliance. Colbert dressed and then said, "Good night Bill; you can go to bed now." Chunk made his escape. The Coloradoans, having lost their taste for gunplay and having done just about what Chunk had done on December 27th, left the scene and sought sanctuary north of the border.[85]

The incident was witnessed by many and New Mexico authorities pursued charges in the matter. The Colfax County indictment identified the murderers as "Noah Camblin, Patrick A. McBride, William Welch, Porter Stockton, Charles Beckwell and ---Hays whose first name is to the Grand Jurors aforesaid unknown."[86] John Selles and Thomas Charleton, who were also posse members, were not indicted.[87] Witnesses for the territory included Tom Stockton, Ed Mezick, Andrew Scott, Thomas Iman and the oddly named Balsty Bill.[88] Porter Stockton's indiscretions were beginning to erode his relationships with his fellow Texans, some who happened to be the most prominent cattlemen in the region, like Tom Stockton.

News of the March 1874 indictment reached Trinidad and those named were livid. On April 5th, Colfax County merchant and part time probate judge and grand jury witness Ed Mezick traveled to Trinidad. He then made the mistake of entering the saloon portion of the United States Hotel. The *Trinidad Enterprise* reported that Nick Camblin and Tex Bakewell entered the saloon and Deputy Camblin searched Mezick for weapons pursuant to a standing verbal order issued by acting Justice of the Peace Pat McBride. Mezick was not armed. Camblin stepped out of the way and Tex Bakewell pounced on Mezick and began pounding him with his fists while Deputy Camblin held the other patrons in check with his sidearm. Mezick had no choice but to submit to the beating.⁸⁹ Judge McBride held a longstanding grudge against Mezick. He had high political aspirations and was serving as a justice of the peace in Colfax County in October 1870 when he allegedly misused his position in a vote buying scheme. In April 1871, McBride was indicted for offering a bribe. In that case Judge McBride fined Samuel Cameron twenty-five dollars for an unspecified infraction and then offered to drop the fine if Cameron would promise to vote for Robert H. Longwill for the probate judge position in Colfax County. The foreman of the grand jury which indicted Patrick McBride was Ed Mezick.⁹⁰ With his political future besmirched in Colfax County, McBride soon moved to Trinidad and began rebuilding his political fortunes.

McBride's associate, Tex Bakewell, was clearly another Texan with a violent nature. In late September of 1874 he put three bullets into Fine Ernest's quarrelsome, thin skinned partner Alfred Jessup, Jr. Jessup survived.⁹¹ In July 1880, Bakewell shot and killed two Leadville police officers. He was sentenced to serve a life sentence in the Colorado Penitentiary.⁹² As for Chunk Colbert, he was fortunate to escape the wrath of Tex Bakewell and Porter Stockton, but in early January he would have a fateful meeting with Clay Allison.

Before that date with destiny, Allison had other pressing matters. For residents along the Colorado and New Mexico border, the last days of December 1873 and the first days of the new year were packed with action. On the same day that Colbert killed George Waller, a prominent cattleman, Michael Carney, was found murdered on the Vermejo.⁹³ Carney lived near Breckenridge, Colorado in Summit County.⁹⁴ He had traveled to the Vermejo on business and over $10,000 in money and drafts in his possession were missing.⁹⁵ About 10:00 AM on Sunday morning, Colfax County Sheriff John Charles (Jack) Turner and a posse captured the murderer, an army deserter named John Cowley, near the Red (Canadian) River. He was about twenty years old and had recently broken out of the Pueblo, Colorado jail. The *Pueblo Chieftain* said that a search of his pockets revealed that he carried "twelve hundred dollars in greenbacks."⁹⁶ French Canadian rancher Tony Meloche reported that Sheriff Turner and Clay Allison took the prisoner into a wooded area.⁹⁷ A rope was placed around his neck and looped over a limb. The terrified prisoner was hoisted up and then let down. Eventually he divulged where he had hidden the money and it was recovered.⁹⁸ At that point, one of Mr. Carney's cowhands, Hugh Helling, implored Turner that he be allowed to lynch Cowley. He unhitched the lariat from his saddle and lassoed the prisoner. Cowley clinched his saddle. Turner's interrogation tactics were rough, but that's where he drew the line. With the backing of Allison, Meloche and others, the lynching bee was quashed.⁹⁹ The posse rode out, but Sheriff Turner began to ponder the fate of John Cowley.

About 4:00 PM on Monday the posse rode into Cimarron.[100] Cowley was placed in the Cimarron jail on Elkins Avenue. On the ride Turner mulled over Helling's entreaties. He was disgusted with the cold-blooded nature of the murder. He sent an unmistakable message to the vigilantes by placing Cowley under the protective guard of one man, Robert Grigsby. The *Cimarron News* said, "Between nine and ten o'clock, Monday night, a crowd of heavily armed men assembled at the jail and commenced an attack upon the frail structure." Jailer Grigsby made a good showing of refusing to hand over the prisoner. He fired a shot through the door and threatened to shoot the first man that entered, but they were not to be denied. The mob advised Grigsby to not interfere or they would kill him. They threw kerosene on the roof and tried to burn it off. When that failed, they gathered crow bars and sledge hammers. With Cowley cowering in his cell, the vigilantes began to pound on the outer wall and soon wedged the tip of a crow bar inside. The excitement grew as some of the outer stone blocks were scraped back and forth. Slowly a hole began to open. Finally, the last stone obstacle was removed and the men grabbed Cowley. A rope was immediately placed around his neck like a leash. He was taken to a telegraph pole on Elkins Avenue about 150 yards from the jail. After hoisting the murderer, the vigilantes stayed long enough to be sure their mission was complete. Then they dispersed into the darkness, leaving Cowley dangling above a nearby church.[101] Before the arrival of the vigilantes, John B. McCullough, the Cimarron postmaster, had been allowed to interview Cowley. He learned that the doomed man was a native of Pennsylvania and had been hiding out in New Mexico for about three months. He also noted that the body loomed over the town until about 9:30 Tuesday morning.[102] The entire incident would be enough excitement to satisfy most men for a substantial period of time, but Clay Allison was not most men.

Chunk's recent murder of George Waller combined with his loutish and hostile behavior during their fateful January 7th meeting gave Allison all the righteous justification he needed to rid the world of Chunk Colbert. Chunk decided to remain in Colfax County, confident that his reputation would protect him from arrest. He made himself at home at a Red River saloon and "amused himself in shooting the eyes out of pictures and opening champagne bottles with pistol-bullets."[103] That was a mistake, but Chunk's next move was an even bigger error. He threatened "to shoot several persons against whom he had taken a dislike. His attention was finally drawn to Mr. [Clay] Allison, a stock man from the Canadian, with whom Chunk had some previous difficulty." The men were seated at a table and Colbert tried to distract Allison's attention by reaching for a cup of coffee with his left hand, while with his right he cautiously brought his pistol above the edge of the table top and fired. The *News* reported that just as Chunk pulled the trigger, Allison dove out of the way and returned fire, striking Colbert above the right eye.[104] Naturally, the *Trinidad Enterprise* provided a slightly different version. They said both men had been drinking and they were sitting at a table, playing cards. Chunk became angered and pulled his pistol, which struck the table and discharged. Chunk continued to raise the pistol and when it reached a deadly angle, Allison reached out and shoved it aside. Chunk's second shot roared into the wall. Now it was Allison's turn. Under the headline, "Shooting of Chunk" the *Enterprise* detailed Colbert's gory end, saying, "Allison shot him through the head, scattering his brains over the table, killing him instantly."[105] Pueblo's *Colorado Chieftain* noted, "Chunk was a desperate and dangerous character and Mr. Allison ran a narrow risk of his own life and only saved it by his coolness and courage." At the same time, Sheriff Turner was on his way to Trinidad to pick up a prisoner. He had learned of Chunk's presence and decided to arrest Colbert and deliver him to the Las Animas county sheriff. He arrived at the Clifton House about an hour after the shooting and found that Chunk had eluded authorities for the last time.[106]

The killing of Chunk Colbert may have not have been the only time that Porter Stockton and Clay Allison had the same goal. In an undated incident Allison and Stockton took exception to the slant of the news published in the *Cimarron News*. The two men and others entered the office of the *News* and Stockton used his knife to threaten the editor. Having made their point, the men mounted up and left town.[107] The newspaper continued to rankle some of the residents and in a later incident, on the evening of January 19, 1876, a mob forced their way into what was then called the *Cimarron News and Press*. They did their best to destroy the printing facilities and to make sure the newspaper would be shut down for a long while, they chunked portions of the equipment into the Cimarron River. Newspaper accounts identified the mob as being "outlaws and fugitives from justice."[108] In fact, Clay Allison led this mob as well. His chief assistant was Joel Curtis.[109]

Allison, Stockton and Curtis would not have been in Colfax County were it not for cattle, and events in 1873 and 1874 were harsh on the cattle trade. The Panic of 1873 led to the depression of 1874 and cattlemen suffered greatly from the economic downturn. Some operators were wiped out. The price of beef plummeted and in some instances cattle were slaughtered solely for the value of their hides and tallow. The Panic also resulted in what some Texas cattlemen called the "Big Steal." As the beef market weakened, thousands of cattle were driven out of state to far off ranges throughout the Rocky Mountain region and further west to California.[110] It was also in 1874 that the massive land claims of the Maxwell Land Grant were rejected by the federal government. Interior Secretary Zachariah Chandler declared that the bulk of the grant was open to settlement under the homestead and pre-emption laws.[111] The General Land Office's ruling that placed the Maxwell Land Grant in the public domain was met with disdain by the Maxwell Land Grant and Railway Company. They looked to the courts for relief and throughout 1874 they printed notices in the *Cimarron News* which notified squatters that "unless they quit and surrender the possession of said lands and premises, they will be treated as trespassers and proceeded against according to law."[112] Despite the growing conflict, settlers swarmed into Colfax County and began to stake their claims.

Those settlers included the Coe family. In 1875 four Coe brothers, Lew, Frank, Al and Jasper (Jap) were living in Colfax County.[113] They were joined by Jap's brother-in-law, Ab Saunders, and by their cousin, George Coe.[114] For eleven hundred dollars Lew Coe purchased property from Gad and Fount Miller at the junction of the forks of Sugarite Creek.[115] The Coe men hoped to establish successful lives in Colfax County, but that was not to be. Violence spawned by the Coes in 1879 and 1880 in the area that would become San Juan County, New Mexico was the precursor to the Stockton led havoc which followed. Before that George and Frank Coe would become energetic participants in the legendary frontier conflict known as the Lincoln County War.

Like the Coe family, Luke Coleman would eventually move out of Colfax County, but before that he sought a more domestic life on the Vermejo. In the mid-1870s Coleman tied the knot with Clay Allison's sister.[116] The move to New Mexico had a salutary effect on Irvin Lacy as well. While he was a successful stockman in Erath County, he also had his wild side. In Colfax County he became an influential and respected member of the community and he was soon known as one of the leading stockmen in the territory. In the late summer of 1874 he helped organize the Colfax County "Stock Association." According to the *Cimarron News*, its genesis was due "to the rapid settlement of this county and the vast increase in the number and size of the herds during the last two years." Lacy was selected as president of the organization. That same year he helped organize Colfax County's first county fair. The trail-driving Texan was chosen as chairman of the first fair board.[117] He also teamed up with Clay Allison to take on, through lawful channels, the always present cattle rustlers. One of them, James Kelly, made a particular nuisance of himself. Lacy and Allison are listed together with others as witnesses in territorial records in two separate instances of cattle theft involving Kelly.[118]

Rustlers were a fact of life for Wash Cox and I.W. Lacy and would be dealt with, one way or another. Wash Cox may have driven two herds out of Erath County in 1874. A herder on one of those drives was nineteen-year-old Solon A. Bull who lived near Stephenville. According to Bull, their destination was Dodge City. They pointed the herd toward Fort Worth after leaving Erath County and then crossed the Red River near Gainesville. In present day Garvin County, Oklahoma they passed by the recently abandoned Fort Arbuckle. They drove on through the vast emptiness that was then the vicinity of what would become Oklahoma City. After selling the herd, they spent several days in Dodge City.[119] This may have been the drive in which Cox sold 1500 head of cattle at Great Bend, Kansas and then trailed 250 horses and the 500 remaining cattle to Colfax County.[120] During August and September 1874 the *Cimarron News* announced that several large herds of Texas cattle had recently arrived on the Red (Canadian) River.[121] Ike Stockton may have joined one of these drives. In an 1881 interview, Ike dated his arrival in Colfax County to 1874.[122]

Ike's permanent exodus from Texas may have resulted from events in Bosque County, Texas in the spring of 1874. At the time, Bud Galbreath, Stockton's friend and associate in sketchy livestock activities in Erath County, was working on a cattle ranch west of Meridian, which is forty miles southeast of Stephenville. He and some of his fellow cowboys came into Meridian and trouble ensued. Allegations were made that Galbreath and others had raped one or more Swedish girls.[123] Galbreath was arrested, but escaped after gaining the upper hand on Bosque County Deputy Sheriff Jabez Pierson.[124] In the ensuing struggle, Pierson was killed. According to Texas authorities and others, Bud Galbreath committed the murder, but Galbreath claimed that a companion did the deed. After this incident, Galbreath says he and his friend moved to Colorado where they entered the cattle business.[125] Certain aspects of his story, which describe other events in Colorado, point to the possibility that the unidentified companion was Ike Stockton. Galbreath's account was made with the intent to absolve him of guilt, so it has to be taken with a grain of salt, if not a fifty pound salt lick. However, all credible alibis have some basis in fact, and as it turns out Galbreath's story meshes conveniently with Ike's arrival in New Mexico and his subsequent fate in southwest Colorado.

The same year that Ike Stockton moved to New Mexico, out on the plains of west Texas, the buffalo slaughter was in full swing. Wash Cox recalled encountering a particularly effective buffalo hunting camp on the Cimarron with a dozen men in charge of a fellow calling himself "Big Red." Cox later said that he could have walked a mile in any direction and stepped only on dead buffalo.[126] The Indians knew that their way of life was disappearing along with the buffalo herds. They did not accept their fate meekly and the danger faced by Wash Cox and his herders was ever present. Residents of Colfax County would pay a severe price. During the summer of 1874 the *Cimarron News* reported that, "large bodies [of] Cheyenne and Kiowa Indians had left their reservation in the Indian Territory for the purpose of making their annual raid through Eastern Colorado and New Mexico, but few were prepared for the sudden outbreak of these savages, in our midst." The *News* was busy gathering stories from recent arrivals and noted that from "parties just in from Rock Ranche crossing on Red River, we learn that a wagon train had stopped there

Thursday which reported three men killed and one wounded in a fight with the Indians."[127] Manley Chase's brother and Patrick Nicholson were riding near Tony Meloche's house when they saw what they thought was a group of friendly local Indians. The Indians were able ride close to the men and opened fire, killing Nicholson. Chase was wounded and as he bolted away he returned fire. Meloche, hearing the shots, ran toward the Indians and was grazed in the head. The Comanche and Kiowa band scalped Nicholson and escaped with twenty-seven horses.[128] The Indians were said to have killed two herders who were working for Rudolph Irminger and for "Uncle Dick" on the Red River. The newspaper said that after these attacks, "Word was immediately sent to the Ute and Apache camps and a large number of these Indians with some Americans started in pursuit, but the hostile Indians were too far in advance and they could not be overtaken." The *News* said, "A Mexican boy was captured by the Indians, who brutally cut his arms off above the elbows." It also claimed that, "eight Mexicans and three Americans, have been killed south of the Raton mountains, and over 150 head of horses driven off." A large number of cattle were reported shot and killed for no purpose other than the killing. A total of fourteen men were said to have been killed on Corrumpa Creek, east of present day Des Moines, including Mr. Conn, a sheepman, and James Roberts. The article concluded by noting, "A company of U.S. Troops eighty strong, passed through Dry Cimarron in pursuit of the Indians. At the present time, twenty-six men in all are known to have been killed in this county."[129]

If the Indians didn't get you, the Texans would, unless the law got them first. In several instances, that is indeed what happened. The years of 1875 and 1876 were characterized by sustained lawlessness in Colfax County. Herders, brought into the area by Lacy and Coleman and other Texas cattlemen, turned Cimarron into one of the wildest towns in the American west. In January 1875 the *Colorado Chieftain* carried correspondence from Cimarron which was signed "Eye Witness." The writer said, "For some weeks past it has been the habit of a number of Texans, living somewhere on Red river, to come into Cimarron in bands from four to eight in number, and when here, attempt to 'run the town.' " On Saturday, January 16th, the correspondent said, "four of these men came in armed to the teeth with rifles and pistols and proceeded to get drunk as usual."[130] The leader of the Texans was George W. Morrison.[131] The former Erath County resident and Stockton ally was accompanied by three men identified in newspaper accounts in a less than definitive manner as Alexander, Lieutenant Wallace and Spiller. The *Cimarron News and Press* noted that the hell raising cowboys were from the Vermejo. Whether they were from the Vermejo or the Red (Canadian) River, the cowboys were clearly linked to Colfax County's Texas cattlemen. Newspaper accounts leave do doubt that Morrison was the leader of the group. Upon learning of the disturbance, Sheriff John Turner tried to quietly defuse the situation.[132] The sheriff's entreaties were met with a tirade of alcohol induced profanities. The rowdies issued threats, pointed their firearms at Turner's face and advised him that he could not arrest them, even if he had the whole town by his side. Turner decided to take that dare and assembled a posse.[133] The cowboys were surprised when they realized that Turner was calling their bluff. They sought cover in Maurice Trauer's fortress like stone store, where they broke out the windows and waited for the sheriff and his men to walk directly into their field of fire. Turner had other plans and his men began a bilateral flanking action. The well-lubricated herders soon realized that they were outsmarted and outgunned. They flew out of Trauer's for their horses. Morrison led the exodus. He mounted up and rode toward Maxwell's grist mill. Alexander came out, cursed the posse members and mounted his horse. Turner approached him and demanded his surrender. Alexander took aim at the sheriff with his rifle, but before he could pull the trigger, a posse member opened fire. A load of buckshot drove into Alexander's right wrist and he bolted away in an unsteady gallop. Below Cimarron he and Spiller joined up. They were still in rifle range and bullets tore up the ground at their horse's hooves as they rode off. Alexander's horse took three rounds. Wallace headed for the ice encrusted Cimarron River. While crossing, his horse slipped and fell on the frozen surface. The animal struggled to regain its footing and Wallace took off on foot. Cimarron's aroused citizens riddled him with bullets. Morrison was only a mile from town, but out of view, when his horse gave out. Using his firearm and a ten dollar gold piece, he hired another horse from a sheepman on Ponil Creek. Spiller, Morrison and Alexander were not captured. Wallace was still alive, barely. He was taken to the St. James Hotel. That night, rumors flew that Morrison was gathering up allies along the Vermejo. It was feared that a large group Texans would raid the town. The citizens assembled at the courthouse, where ammunition was passed out and regular patrols were conducted throughout the night. On Monday the same rumors swirled, but up on the Vermejo cooler heads prevailed. It appears that the Lacy, Coleman and others stopped the cowboys in their tracks. On Tuesday, miners and others poured out of the mountains and into Cimarron to help defend the town. By then the danger had passed.[134] Sheriff Turner and the others did not believe that George Morrison had been injured, but that may not have been the case. In later years it was reported that Morrison had been involved in several dangerous skirmishes and that he had been shot more than once. Perhaps one of the bullets found the mark that day.[135] Lacy and Coleman, Wash Cox, and the other leading cattlemen did not need this kind of trouble; from then on, they saw to it that their toughest and clearest thinking men filled the sheriff and deputy slots in Colfax County. Apparently no charges were filed against the three surviving cowboys. Their crimes up until they piled out of Trauer's store consisted of making threats and property damage. There may have been some concern that Turner's posse could bear some culpability for the shooting of Wallace and the townspeople thought better about starting a war of attrition with the local cowboys. By early February the *New Mexican* noted that, "Wallace the wounded man is slowly improving."[136] It's likely that the Spiller in this incident was James Spiller. In the summer of 1875, he was indicted for defacing brands after a complaint was made by Henry Gray. Spiller's bondsmen in the case included Wash Cox, Clay Allison, David Crockett and Pete Burleson.[137]

Spiller's and Morrison's companion in the January incident was probably John Alexander. The same court session which delivered Spiller's indictment for defacing brands also resulted in John Alexander's indictment for burglarizing a coat valued at three dollars from the home of Richard Steele.[138] George Morrison stayed out of further difficulties, at least for a while.

Porter Stockton was not present when Morrison and his friends escaped Cimarron in a hail of bullets. That January he was in Erath County. He had no intention of dealing with the multiple criminal charges which were pending against him there, but on January 7th he was arrested, probably by Deputy Sheriff H. Tinley, who was serving under Sheriff William Waller.[139] That same day, John O'Neal, William Bibb and John Alsup went into Stephenville and secured his release. They were sureties for his $250 bail bond for the aggravated assault and battery of Taylor Avant. They were also sureties for $500 bail bond for the robbery of Perry Gravis and for the $500 bail bond for the assault with intent to murder charge.[140] No one could say that Stockton did not have friends in Erath County. Now that they were on the hook for $1250, they did their best to insure that Stockton stayed there. In early March he made his appearance in Erath County's District Court. He faced trial on the robbery charge and a jury found him not guilty. Besides Stockton and the victim, the only other witness was his uncle, West Hickey.[141] The Avant pistol whipping case was also scheduled for the March session of court. Stockton requested a continuance until his witnesses could be located and brought to court. Stockton said that Mart Hickey and Henry Dulaney were present during the assault and would testify that he was attacked first and that Avant used no weapon. Stockton claimed he repelled Avant's attack using only his hands. Stockton told the court that he believed Dulaney was living in Coleman County, Texas. Mart Hickey was probably his first cousin, William M. Hickey, who was the son of his Uncle West. At the time of the incident in March 1870, William was seventeen or eighteen years old. Thomas Keith and a thirty-one-year-old Bosque River miller named Willis Harris were also subpoenaed. Stockton's motion for a continuance noted "that he has not had the benefit of counsel having been too poor to pay an attorney and not being able to procure the services of one until the appointment at this term by the court." Attorneys J.M. Calhoun and J.D. Martin were appointed to represent Stockton. They had successfully defended him on the earlier robbery charge.[142] The records for the most serious charge for the 1871 attempted murder provide little insight into the events which led to the indictment. Port's step-uncle, William Bibb, and Eugene Wood, the probable victim, were summoned for Stockton's scheduled 1875 trial. Ben Crabtree was subpoenaed as a witness for the defense. Crabtree was about sixteen years old at the time of the incident and in 1870 he was a Bosque River neighbor to Bibb, John O'Neal and George Morrison. The judge also issued orders of attachment for three reluctant witnesses: George and Margaret Hill of Shackelford County, and Stockton's uncle, J.C. Brumley of Cleburne. Brumley was listed as a witness for the state. Brumley's daughter Sarah (Mrs I.W. Lacy) would play a pivotal role in the future of Ike Stockton and it may have been at this point that the Brumley and Lacy families began to hope that Porter Stockton would just go away. Stockton skipped out on his court appearance on this charge. His sureties were summoned to appear before the court in October 1875. The State of Texas received a judgment against them for the $500 bond. His stalwart bondsmen were most unhappy that they were now being held to their responsibilities. In November they filed a motion in arrest of judgment. Stockton would never face trial on this charge and would remain a fugitive from Texas justice.[143]

Back in Colfax County, some residents were fed up with the hell-raising Texas cowboys. The Morrison incident and desire to get an upper hand was perhaps the impetus for the March 16, 1875 requisition from the New Mexico governor's office to Colorado Governor Edward McCook for the arrest of Porter Stockton, "Tex" Bakewell and their Trinidad associates for the murder which occurred at the Clifton House in December 1873. Sheriff Turner was appointed as the agent of the territory of New Mexico to receive any of those arrested for the murder.[144] As evidenced by the Morrison incident, Turner was a man with some nerve. He not only served as the Colfax County sheriff, but later became the sheriff of La Plata County, Colorado. He first saw that region in 1860 when he was a member of the Charles Baker party which entered the Animas River valley in southwest Colorado on a prospecting expedition. The area was Indian country, and over the prior three hundred years even nearby Hispanic residents, most who lived in Santa Fe and along the Rio Grande valley, seldom ventured into the region. Like the plans of the Texas trail drivers, Baker's plans were cut short by the start of the Civil War. "Americans" did not re-enter the region in any numbers until the 1870s.[145]

Despite being the subject of a New Mexico arrest warrant and a requisition to Colorado, Porter Stockton soon made his way back from Erath County to the Cimarron country. Unrest over the Maxwell Land Grant reached its crescendo with the notorious murder of a circuit-riding preacher, Franklin J. Tolby, on September 14, 1875.[146] The Methodist minister was an outspoken critic of the politically powerful Santa Fe Ring. He was threatened and told his words might get him killed.[147] Many believed he was behind a string of letters which had appeared in the *New York Sun*, which criticized the Ring.[148] The Reverend O.P. McMains believed that a mail carrier named Cruz Vega was involved in Tolby's murder. McMains admitted that, "I had Cruz Vega, the mail carrier interviewed."[149] It turned out to be much more than an interview. On the night of Halloween Eve, Vega was terrorized into telling what he knew. Describing what happened next, the *Colorado Chieftain* said "Señor Vega had a visit from a few friends who played a practical joke of a serious nature upon him, by suspending him to a convenient telegraph pole." The lynching of Cruz Vega naturally incensed his friends and relatives. Two days later, on Monday November 1st, Francisco "Pancho" Griego, went looking for Clay Allison. Pancho believed that Allison had played an active role in the lynching of Vega and had determined to even the score. The two men with others met at the door of the St. James Hotel in Cimarron. They ordered drinks and then Allison and Griego took a corner table and engaged in conversation.[150] That was not unusual; the two men knew each other and probably shared a grudging mutual respect. Like Clay Allison, Francisco Griego is frequently characterized as a desperado. At times he was that, but that one-dimensional view does justice to neither man. In August and September of 1875, Griego served on the grand jury which indicted James Kelly for rustling Lacy and Coleman cattle. He was so well-respected by his colleagues they chose him as foreman of the grand jury.[151] Though Allison and Griego respected each other, circumstances required that only one of them would be leaving the table. According to the *Pueblo Chieftain*, "after some conversation, Allison drew his revolver and shot Griego three times." The *Chieftain* reported, "The light [sic] were immediately extinguished, and Griego lay where he fell until next morning when he was found." The newspaper offered their opinion of the dead man: "Griego was well-known in Santa Fe where his mother resides. He has killed many Americans and was considered a very dangerous man. His death occasions little regret."[152] Allison left for the Vermejo and was later captured at I.W. Lacy's house, but suffered no punishment for this killing.[153]

While Lacy and Cox were friends with many notorious residents, they also worked for the betterment of the region. Early the following year I.W. Lacy was serving as the chairman of the Colfax County Commission.[154] Wash Cox was also a commissioner.[155] Among other projects, the two men worked together for the construction of a bridge across the Vermejo River.[156] At the same time, Stockton was intent on burning bridges. On January 15, 1876, he started off the year by killing a man named Antonio Arcibia. Stockton shot Arcibia twice in the chest, killing him instantly.[157] Details about this murder are sparse. According to an account in the *Durango Record* published in January 1881, "At Cimarron, he [Stockton] shot a Mexican in his bed, because he was snoring – and it proved a very effectual means of stopping it."[158] If this was the same murder or another one is not known. Arcibia had been married about seventeen months at the time of his death.[159] He was a veteran of the Civil War, a Union private with the Battalion of New Mexico Volunteers, Company A and with the First Regiment, New Mexico Cavalry, Company G.[160] Arcibia's Hispanic heritage and his Yankee affiliation were possible contributing factors to Stockton's actions. Gus Heffron, one of Lacy and Coleman's cowboys, was a witness to the shooting. Others who were present were Albert Tesor, Harry Whigham and George A. Bushnell.[161]

Just over two months after Stockton's murder of Antonio Arcibia, two of his fellow LC herders, Gus Heffron and David Crockett, were the main players in one of the most notorious incidents in the stormy frontier history of Cimarron. On March 24th, Heffron and Crockett entered Lambert's Saloon. Several black soldiers of the Ninth Cavalry from nearby Fort Union were also in the saloon. The unreconstructed Heffron and Crockett were incensed that the Buffalo Soldiers had the gall to feel they were welcome at Lambert's simply because they put their own lives on the line protecting citizens from raiding Indian parties. A row soon erupted and three of the soldiers were killed. The *Pueblo Chieftain* said, "From what we could gather from the bar-tender, there was no provocation whatever." The *Chieftain* reported that, "The shooting is said to have been done by David Crocket and Gus Hefron, of the Texan outlaws, who have created so much disturbance in Colfax county of late."[162]

Port Stockton didn't join his fellow Texan cowboys in these violent antics. At the time he was still on the run from Colfax County authorities. After the Arcibia murder, he kept his boots out of New Mexico and was biding his time just across the border in Trinidad, where he lived openly. At the same time Colfax County records show that Ike was literally working as a horse trader. Colfax County records used the term "horse peddler." Given Samuel Stockton's preference for horse stealing, it is not hard to imagine that Samuel was the source for Ike's inventory. At any rate, Ike's business interests were about to change.[163] In late August, Porter crossed paths with the new sheriff of Las Animas County, Casimiro Barela. The sheriff was born in Embudo, New Mexico. As a young man he moved to Las Animas County, arriving in 1867. Barela was a shrewd, quick-thinking man with boundless energy and a genial nature and became a successful stockman and businessman. He later served Las Animas County in the Colorado state senate for many years and was noted for his eloquence in both Spanish and English.[164]

Stockton soon made a nuisance of himself and in mid-August Barela attempted to arrest the prickly Texan. As was his custom, Stockton refused to be arrested. After Stockton mounted his horse, Barela grabbed the bridle. Stockton pulled his pistol, cocked it, and pointed the barrel at the Sheriff.[165] Barela wisely retreated from the fray and Stockton rode out of town. The Sheriff gathered a posse and headed for Raton Pass. When they came within sight of Stockton, shots were fired and Stockton's startled horse plunged over a cliff, taking the outlaw along for the ride.[166] Barela and the others believed that Stockton had been killed, but they could not find him. As nighttime fell, they gave up and returned to Trinidad.[167]

The next morning Barela headed out of Trinidad with the undertaker and wagon to retrieve Stockton's body. Miraculously, Stockton had survived, but his horse did not. Bloodied, bruised and unable to walk, he spent the night nursing his wounds and bandaging himself with pieces of his shirt.[168] Stockton was in no condition to take on the sheriff. He was arrested and hauled back to Trinidad. Stockton had bulldozed and embarrassed the sheriff, but Barela was a man of high ethics. He made sure Stockton's injuries were treated properly. Incarcerating Stockton was a costly undertaking for Las Animas County. Due to his weak condition, he was not kept in the jail, but at the county's expense was provided room and board by Jacob W. "Wink" Winkfield. At considerable cost a constant guard was posted at Winkfield's. Dr. J.C. Rogers treated Stockton's injuries and submitted a bill to Las Animas County for fifty-five dollars for his services and medicines.[169]

On August 20th, Barela sent a Western Union Telegram to the governor's office in Santa Fe. "Porter W. Stockton has been arrested by me," Barela wrote, "and is now in confinement awaiting requisition of your excellency for murder committed in Colfax County NM for which an indictment has been found in Taos County." The news of Stockton's arrest traveled fast and the next day Colfax County Sheriff Isaiah Rinehart sent his own telegram to acting Governor William Gillet Ritch asking that he send a requisition to the governor of Colorado.[170]

It was during this same week that the *Albuquerque Review* relayed news that, "James B. Hickok, alias Wild Bill, a well known scout and desperado, died in his boots in Deadwood, on the 2 inst."[171] Stockton probably missed out on this bit of information while he recuperated at Winkfield's. It was a week before Governor John L. Routt of Colorado received the necessary paperwork from acting Governor Ritch. After its delivery, Sheriff Rinehart picked up Stockton and he was arraigned in a Taos courtroom about ten days later.[172] Normally, that proceeding would have been held in Cimarron. But in 1876 the legislature removed the courts from Colfax County and those cases were being heard in Taos County.[173] Stockton entered a plea of not guilty and was granted a continuance. He was represented by attorneys Lee, Springer and Mills. Even the *New Mexican* commented on the speedy arraignment, which was unheard of in the creaky sieve of the territorial criminal justice system. Meanwhile, Port was taken to the Cimarron jail to await the next court session, which was six months away.[174] Stockton found that the small Cimarron jail was nearing capacity as it also held Reverend McMains and William Lowe. Both had been arrested for their role in the murder of Cruz Vega.[175]

Stockton had no desire to see a hangman's noose or to face a lengthy prison term. Ike agreed. McMains and Lowe witnessed Stockton's bold escape on September 16, 1876. It was a Saturday night when Ike Stockton showed up at the jail. James Roberts (a different James Roberts had been killed by Cheyennes and Kiowas in the summer of 1874) was watching the jail and Ike convinced the jail guard that it would be in his best interests to see that Porter was furloughed that night.[176] According to the *Durango Record*, shortly after Porter murdered the "Mexican" snorer, he escaped from jail when Ike showed up with some pies for his brother. After the jailer opened the door, "Ike pulled a pop and invited him to exchange places with Port, which he did. Port escaped on a horse, with a Winchester as his protector."[177] One account says that Gus Heffron and Davy Crockett assisted with the escape.[178]

While the Stockton brothers made themselves scarce, Heffron and Crockett became the chief tormentors of Sheriff Rinehart. In early October a citizen from Cimarron wrote to the *New Mexican* and noted that Heffron and Crockett "have been 'running the town,' for the past week, poking six-shooters and shot-guns in the faces of whom they met."[179] The two men rode their horses into saloons, stores and offices and threatened the life of the Indian agent.[180] They entered the Post Office and pointed a double barreled shotgun at Joe Holbrook and Postmaster John McCullough, and then taunted them while they recklessly played with the hammers of their guns. Holbrook was probably a deputy sheriff at the time.[181] On September 30th the two outlaws even found the time to humiliate and threaten Sheriff Rinehart. A letter sent from Cimarron and published in the *New Mexican* noted, "On Saturday they halted the sheriff and with their shot guns, loaded, cocked and armed at his breast told him he only lived at their pleasure, and politely informed him that when he made any attempt to arrest them to be sure to have 'the drop' or his time on earth would be short."[182] That was the final provocation. Rinehart made plans to take down Crockett and Heffron.

In the past, Rinehart had found it difficult to recruit men willing to take on Crockett and Heffron and other desperadoes like Port Stockton, but now Holbrook and McCullough eagerly volunteered their services.[183] At 9:00 PM that same Saturday, the sheriff, Holbrook and McCullough set out on their deadly mission. They headed for Henry Schwenk's barn on the west end of Cimarron. The three determined men had armed themselves with double barreled shotguns. They found the two toughs on horseback headed out of town toward the Urraca Mesa. They refused to surrender and reached for their weapons. Rinehart and his men did not hesitate. They each fired a shell and when the desperadoes turned tail to make a run for the river, their second barrels roared. Crockett was mortally wounded and his body was found across the river a few hundred yards away. Heffron was wounded in the wrist and the head.[184] He was treated by a doctor and placed in jail.[185] On October 31, 1876, Gus Heffron and Bill Lowe followed Stockton's example and escaped over the wall of the Cimarron jail, with the help of a rope thrown over from the outside. The *Santa Fe New Mexican* expressed their opinion on jail security in Cimarron by saying, "It would seem that they could be made more secure by larieting to a stake outside."[186] Sometime after his escape, Heffron began calling himself Hefferman and made his way to the San Juan country.[187]

According to some, about the same time as Heffron's and Lowe's escape, Port Stockton killed Juan Gonzales in Lambert's Saloon.[188] Henri Lambert's St. James Hotel housed the saloon where wild cowboys often loosed their six-shooters on the ceiling. In 1902, when the tin ceiling was replaced, the jagged scars of over four hundred bullet holes bore mute testament to the rowdy past of Cimarron.[189] Port Stockton probably spent a lot of time in Mr. Lambert's saloon, but the killing of Juan Gonzales within the confines of Lambert's establishment is an event which is difficult to corroborate from available contemporary records. Like other desperadoes of his time, Port was the subject of wild rumors and credited with shootings and mayhem in which he had no involvement. Of course, given his touchy disposition and the lack of newspaper records or even government records in many locales, there are doubtless other assaults and likely deadly incidents which have gone totally unreported. Anecdotal stories gathered many years after the events often confuse names, places and the sequence of events. The killing of Gonzales fits that mold.

Oddly, there was a man named Juan Gonzales who was shot and killed in the town of Bernalillo, fifteen miles north of Albuquerque, almost exactly two months after Porter Stockton's escape from the Cimarron jail. The question is, did Porter Stockton kill *this* Juan Gonzales? The victim of the Bernalillo shooting has some connections to the Stockton brothers. Shortly after Ike broke his brother out of jail, he moved to the aptly-named town of Lincoln in Lincoln County. Gonzales also lived in this tiny southern New Mexico town with an "American" whore. He had brought the prostitute out on a bull train from Leavenworth, Kansas.[190] According to Frank Coe, "Juan was a good looking man, a Spaniard, and light complexioned."[191] Coe also noted that, "He was well dressed, wearing a big watch and a silver chain. He rode a fine horse and all of the Mexicans were afraid of him as he was a scrapper."[192] Perhaps the source of the Juan Gonzales story had the name right, the location wrong and was in the ballpark on the time. Chances are high that Porter Stockton had been to Leavenworth on a trail drive. Perhaps Stockton knew "Mrs. Gonzales" from Leavenworth. Her former occupation may have played into the dispute between the two men. The Stockton brothers may also have known Juan Gonzales, at least by reputation, from his horse stealing activities near Trinidad. The problem with definitively pinning this shooting on Porter Stockton is the astonishing number of men named Juan Gonzales living in the territory.

Whether Porter Stockton was the man who killed Juan Gonzales or not, the story of Gonzales's demise is illustrative of the character of the Coe family and eerily portends their subsequent activities along the lower Animas River in northwest New Mexico. In the San Juan country the Coes would become deadly enemies of Porter and Ike Stockton. When they finally rode out of southern New Mexico, they were justifiably viewed with both fear and respect.[193] Several months before Ike moved to Lincoln, Frank Coe and Ab Saunders left Colfax County and settled in Lincoln County. George Coe would join them in southern New Mexico.[194] Their troubles with Juan Gonzales began soon after their arrival.

Gonzales was one of three men who were the recognized leaders of a wide ranging band of horse thieves. The other leaders were Jesus Largo and Nicas Meras.[195] They did not limit their operations to New Mexico. In the summer of 1870 the *Colorado Chieftain* noted that Juan Gonzales, "a desperado and noted horse thief," had been convicted of horse stealing at the recent district court session in Las Animas County.[196] Gonzales was familiar with the area from his days as a freighter on the plains. At one time he owned his own train of pack mules. After that business failed he made his living as a horse thief.[197] Gonzales and his associates made the mistake of stealing five horses from the Coe/Saunders ranch. One of the horses was a valuable stallion. Frank Coe formed a posse with several others, including Charlie Bowdre and Doc Scurlock, both of whom would play prominent roles in the Lincoln County War. The posse caught Nicas Meras and frontier justice was administered. According to Frank Coe, "After Nicas Meres [sic] was killed they put a quietus on stealing. It continued a little but on a much smaller scale."[198]

For the next several weeks, the Coes, Saunders and others kept their eyes open for Largo and Gonzales. Upon hearing that Largo had been captured, Frank Coe, George Coe, Doc Scurlock and Charlie Bowdre headed to Lincoln. Before entering town they received word that Sheriff Saturnino Baca and a protective guard were preparing to transport Largo to Fort Stanton. Baca rightfully feared that the Lincoln jail was not secure from Largo's friends or his enemies. The Coe group took off cross country for the road leading to the Fort. Upon finding a suitable location, they secreted themselves and waited patiently. Finally they heard the sound of horses and the buggy which carried Largo. Frank Coe reported, "George Coe, a big husky boy, stepped out from behind the willows and threw his Winchester down on Baca and it scared those Mexicans to death."[199] Sheriff Baca gave Largo up and he and his men quickly departed, all of them suffering from the sudden onset of amnesia. Largo was made to walk several hundred yards from the road before the group finally stopped by a large piñon tree. Bowdre said, "This is all right, and if they want him let them walk up and carry him out." Frank Coe dismounted. Largo eyed the piñon and the riderless horse and knew his time had come. Largo and Scurlock had worked together as cowpunchers, but Largo's pleas of "Doc! Doc!" fell on deaf ears. Frank Coe later recalled that after the rope was tied to the piñon and around Largo's neck "the horse [was] lead out from under him and we rode off with Largo kicking the air." Coe recalled that after the lynching, "Men we did not suspect left the country."[200] It would not be the last time that the Coes used lynching as a method of intimidation.

After the death of his partners, Gonzales made secretive sporadic visits to his Lincoln home. In October 1876, Frank Coe and Ab Saunders learned he was in the area, so they laid in wait near his house. He showed up, but did not stay long. As he was leaving, Saunders took a shot at him, but missed. Gonzales returned fire and eluded Coe and Saunders. He rode out of southern New Mexico for the last time.[201] He was well known in the territory and it was difficult for him to hide. In mid-November of 1876, Doroteo Chavez crossed paths with Gonzales traveling with four well-armed companions near Chilili in the eastern foothills of the Manzano Mountains. The men told Chavez they were headed to Albuquerque. Chavez relayed the news to Valencia County resident Don Manuel A. Otero, who in turn told merchant John Becker of Belen. Shortly afterwards the *Albuquerque Review* informed its readers.[202] Not long after this sighting, Gonzales turned up in Bernalillo, where on Saturday, November 18, 1876 he proceeded to raise hell. According to the *Albuquerque Review*, "after drinking freely throughout the day [Gonzales] commenced insulting and challenging to combat all he met, whereupon a warrant for his arrest was finally made out and upon its being served he drew his pistol and was in the act of attempting to shoot the constable when a spectator, who had been watching the movement - fired - and laid the desperado low."[203] The *Santa Fe New Mexican* described him as a member of a "gang of murderers" and noted, "The territory is well rid of a very bad man and Bernalillo and Lincoln Counties are greatly benefited by his summary taking off."[204] The shooter was not named and it may just be a curious coincidence or purely a case of name confusion which links Port Stockton to the killing of a man named Juan Gonzales in the fall of 1876.[205] As for Frank and George Coe, their reputation as men to be feared was now firmly planted.

After Ike moved to Lincoln County, sightings of Porter Stockton became very rare. At one point he hooked up with a fellow desperado named Ben Sterritt, who was one of his childhood friends from Hopkins County, Texas.[206] According to the Silverton, Colorado newspaper the *La Plata Miner*, sometime in late 1876 or early 1877 the two outlaws committed an unspecified crime near Fort Garland, Colorado. Sterritt and Stockton fled the area. In January or February 1881, Sterritt showed up near Alamosa calling himself Charles Walters. On the evening of February 3rd the stage and mail coach was robbed near Del Norte. Three days later, Alamosa's Marshal Cicero Weidner and Colorado Postal Inspector Robert A. Cameron led a posse in pursuit of the thieves. They cornered Walters and his running mate, Marion Melvin, about thirty miles from Alamosa in a cabin in Cat Creek Canyon. Shots were exchanged and Walters was killed. Melvin, who was wanted for the murder of S.D. Kasserman, held off the posse for seventeen hours. After reinforcements arrived, Melvin negotiated his surrender. The prisoner and the body of Walters were brought into Alamosa, where early residents of the young town recognized that Walters was Stockton's friend, Ben Sterritt. Upon further investigation, it was believed that the men were not involved with the coach robbery.[207] That revelation came too late for Ben Sterritt. It seems likely that a suddenly very quiet Porter Stockton joined his brother in southern New Mexico during some portions of 1877 and 1878. While Ike sought his fortune in southern New Mexico, Wash Cox and other former Erath County and now Colfax County residents set their sights to the west.

In northwest New Mexico and southwest Colorado there was a large, almost unpopulated piece of land that presented new opportunities for those willing to take a risk. It was the area Sheriff Turner had first seen in 1860. In 1873 and 1874, newspapers in Colorado, New Mexico and elsewhere began to carry more and more articles about the frenzy of activity as prospectors stricken with gold fever poured into the mineralized mountains of southwest Colorado. Even Ike Stockton would catch the fever. By now Porter Stockton was notorious for his activities in Texas and in Colfax County, but Ike would gain his own notoriety among the mountain peaks and river valleys of the San Juan country.

Chapter Three

The San Juan Country

Here's to the passing cowboy, the plowman's pioneer;
His home, the boundless mesa, he of any man the peer;
Around his wide sombrero was stretched the rattler's hide,
His bridle sporting conchos, his lasso at his side.
All day he roamed the prairies, at night he, with the stars,
Kept vigil o'er thousands held by neither posts nor bars.[1]

The region encompassing southwest Colorado and northwest New Mexico was one of the last unsettled areas in the American west. As the 1870s progressed many residents of Colorado, New Mexico and elsewhere became intrigued with the possibilities which could be found in the area now known as the Four Corners. Others who became caught up in troubles that overwhelmed the region in 1880 and 1881 began moving there in the mid-1870s.

The San Juan country includes cactus and yucca bearing desert regions, the mesa country, with its scrubby piñons and junipers, and the rugged tundra-topped San Juan Mountains. The headwaters of several rivers are found high up in the fourteen-thousand-foot peaks along the San Juan portion of the Continental Divide. The Atlantic bound runoff forms the Rio Grande. The bulk of the Pacific bound runoff eventually flows into the San Juan River. The San Juan tumbles through Pagosa Springs and then cuts through northwest New Mexico and into the canyon country of southeastern Utah. The Animas River valley, which would become the primary scene of the Stockton turmoil, begins its journey in the mountains above Silverton, Colorado. It flows through present day Durango before crossing the border and joining with the San Juan and the La Plata Rivers near Farmington, New Mexico, the area the native Navajos called Totah.

All of the adjacent portions of Colorado, New Mexico and Utah rightfully identify themselves as being the "San Juan Country" and all three states have their own San Juan County. In Colorado, much of the area was set aside for the Ute tribe. As prospectors began combing the San Juans for precious metals, the agreement with the Utes became problematic. Pressure to open the area was intense. In March 1873 Charles Stollsteimer of Conejos, Colorado reported "that at least fifteen hundred men are assembled at Loma, Del Norte, and vicinity, waiting for weather to enable them to enter the mines."[2] That September, Felix Brunot met with the Utes at the Los Pinos Indian Agency to begin negotiations for the cession of the San Juan mining country. Brunot was pessimistic as the Utes were justifiably mystified that an order expelling miners from the reservation had been suspended and the government itself had three surveying parties busy at work within the reservation.[3] However, by the latter part of September, Brunot had successfully negotiated the Utes out of 3.5 million acres of prime real estate encompassing the San Juan Mountains.[4] The agreement opened the San Juans to settlement and full scale development of mining properties.

Each spring as the weather warmed prospectors swarmed into southwest Colorado. In the fall many of them spilled out of the mountains to obtain other work and secure a stake for the next summer's prospecting expeditions. The annual exodus was brought on by the climate which one pioneer resident described as, "nine months winter and three months late in the fall."[5] As those who live there know, those three summer months are nothing short of spectacular. The "Great San Juan Excitement" was attracting fortune seekers from all over the world.[6] Wash Cox and the Stockton brothers were intrigued by the increasing number of first-hand accounts coming out of the new mining region, but not all of them were glowing. In January 1874 the *Santa Fe New Mexican* noted, "Mr. [J.D.] Fink informs us that there are only about twenty five men at Animas City, and that they are snowed in and unable to do anything; provisions are very scarce." The same account said, "the Utes are not friendly disposed towards the miners and settlers, and are strongly opposed to the taking up of ranches along the valleys."[7]

At the same time, across the line in northwest New Mexico, a substantial section of land was declared off limits to settlement. The treaty of December 10, 1873 set aside a large triangular shaped area for the Jicarilla Apache tribe. The far eastern corner of the reservation was at the intersection of the San Juan River and the Colorado line (now part of Navajo Reservoir). From there the reservation spread westward between the ever widening area located between the San Juan River and the Colorado border until it ended at the eastern border of the Navajo reservation, downriver from present day Farmington.[8] The Jicarilla Apaches never moved onto this reservation. Those familiar with the Animas and San Juan River valleys in New Mexico petitioned federal officials to open this area to homesteaders.[9] Concurrent events may have played a critical role in President Grant's decision making. In the last week of June, 1876, Lieutenant Colonel George Armstrong Custer led his soldiers to their deaths in southeastern Montana's Little Bighorn valley. Shortly after this debacle President Grant issued an executive order which rescinded his March 1874 executive order. The Jicarilla Apache reservation was eliminated. The former reservation was now part of the public domain.[10] This was electrifying news for many. It opened up some of the best river valleys in New Mexico to public settlement. Wash Cox decided it was time to look the area over.[11]

As perhaps Wash Cox and Alf Graves appeared as they headed out on their journey to check out the San Juan country. Cox's cattle would soon roam up and down the Animas River valley. Frederic Remington's "An Exploring Outfit," from Theodore Roosevelt's "Ranch Life in the Far West," The Century Illustrated Monthly Magazine, *Vol. 35, No. 4, February 1888. (Author's collection.)*

Twenty-one-year-old Alf Graves, a native of Alabama, probably traveled with Cox to the see the lower Animas River valley. The fate of Porter and Ike Stockton was unalterably linked with that of Alf Graves. Alf's father, Bill Graves and Wash Cox, were among the first settlers of Erath County.[12] In 1863, just two years after the kidnapping and killing of the Lemley girls near Stephenville, ten-year-old Alf Graves had his own close call. He started over to visit a neighbor's home, riding his father's horse, when he was spotted and then chased for a distance of two miles by a party of Kiowa or Comanche Indians. With the sound of their excited whoops ringing in his ears, and their arrows zinging past him, Graves bent low and urged his horse to run faster. His saddle loosened and began sliding down his horse's flank, but he held on and finally made it to the safety of a neighbor's house.[13] In 1870, Graves lived on the North Fork of the Bosque River with the family of his older sister Leana and her husband William Mefferd.[14] As he grew older Alf caught the eye of Wash Cox's young daughter, who was known as Nancy Belle. Graves made the move to New Mexico and on November 5, 1874, he married Nancy Isabelle Cox. Colfax County records say the marriage took place at the home of the bride's father on the Red River.[15] Graves was twenty-one and his Texas-born wife was fourteen on their wedding day.[16] Alf Graves was a good man to have by your side. He was brave to a fault and, according to one story, had seen brief service with the Texas Rangers prior to arriving in the Vermejo country.[17] That may be overstating the facts. It is more likely that Graves's community service was, like that of many other Texans, on a voluntary basis against Indians and outlaws.

Other Cox cowboys and Cox's thirteen-year-old son, James Allard Cox, also traveled to the San Juan country.[18] In the San Luis Valley the group passed by Fort Garland, where only ten years before Kit Carson had commanded the garrison. About twelve miles south of the village of Conejos, the transplanted Texans and their pack string crossed back into New Mexico, the border being marked by a large pile of rocks.[19] After crossing over Cumbres Pass, the group dropped into the valley of the Rio Chama.

A correspondent for Pueblo's *Colorado Chieftain* described the Chama valley as he found it in July 1876, saying, "there is a wildness and freshness about it very delightful to experience. Here are broad ranches the bosom of which have never been profaned by the tread of the cow-puncher."[20] Wash Cox and others would soon change that. Perhaps they continued twenty miles south of the border to the tiny village of Tierra Amarilla. It would be their last opportunity to purchase supplies. Tierra Amarilla was the trade center for a wide area and Thomas (T.D.) Burns ran a large mercantile operation there. Burns was of Irish descent, genial, but an aggressive businessman and a political force. (He would later found the Burns National Bank in Durango.)[21] Everyone in the San Juan country from the Apaches and Utes, to the original Hispanic residents, to the new Anglo settlers knew Tom Burns and he, in turn, seemed to know everyone in the surrounding country. The *Chieftain's* correspondent described Tierra Amarilla as "a quaint Mexican town divided into two plazas about a mile apart and has a population of between three and four hundred."[22] There was an infant town just forming further west at Animas City, but even its early residents relied on Tierra Amarilla, Santa Fe, Pueblo and Trinidad for their supplies. Bob Dwyer, who established a ranch on Junction Creek, was one of the first Animas City residents and he would be one of the first men to enforce the law in La Plata County.[23] Animas City, which would figure prominently in the future of Porter Stockton, was located about two miles up the Animas River from what one day would be the Durango train depot. Though Durango and the train station would not exist for another four years, Animas City would eventually be swallowed up by its upstart neighbor.

The brand of Tierra Amarilla's leading businessman and stockman Thomas D. Burns, from the Northwest New Mexican (Bloomfield, NM), Feb. 8, 1887. (From the collection of Robert L. Maddox, Jr.)

Cox and the others were on the trail for the better part of a week before they reached the lower Animas River valley. The grass in this virgin range was stirrup high, and Cox and his cowboys were pleased to find that the Animas dwarfed the Pecos, the Canadian and the other rios and ritos that flowed out of the Sangre De Cristos. For the next several months the Cox clan made preparations to move their cattle the next summer. Teenager Jim Cox was having the adventure of a lifetime.[24] He and Bill Razier, and others, stayed on the Animas that winter. They lived in a cave in one of the nearby bluffs, surviving off game, as they built cabins and corrals near the river.[25] More importantly they kept their eyes open for interlopers. It's not known if they saw any, but if they did, the Cox cowboys encouraged them to move on.

By 1877 the Cox family had completed their move to the lower Animas River valley, driving their wagons and cattle over Cumbres Pass.[26] This was no small task and at the time there was a looming danger posed by the Apaches. That July, the *Cimarron News and Press* carried a dispatch which said, "A party of about 1,000 Apaches from the Terra [sic] Amarilla passed through the eastern part of the county last week, and their trail could easily be traced by the heads of the beeves they had slaughtered. So say the stock men. They have gone into the buffalo country on a big hunt, to be gone four moons."[27] If Wash Cox ran into this large band, he probably bought his way out of difficulty with a few steers from his herd. At least one San Juan County pioneer history says that in 1877 Cox trailed 4500 cattle and one hundred horses to northwest New Mexico.[28] It's likely that the 4500 number was too high for a single drive. By way of comparison, a typical Texas cattle drive at that time averaged around fifteen hundred to two thousand cattle and required about one dozen cowpunchers.[29] It was rough country for trailing cattle, but Cox and his cowboys were up to the challenge.

Frederic Remington's "In a Bog-Hole," from Theodore Roosevelt's "Ranch Life in the Far West," The Century Illustrated Monthly Magazine, Vol. 35, No. 4, February 1888. (Author's collection.)

Alf Graves and H.W.'s eldest son, George Washington Cox, who was about twenty-one years old at the time, were two of the cowboys. The entourage drove a freight wagon loaded with three tons of provisions pulled by seven teams of steers.[30] The hooves of Cox's cattle cut down and flattened much of the route and in a distance of sixteen miles the wagon forded the river six times. Cox cattle soon ranged across both sides of the Colorado/New Mexico border.[31] The Cox and Graves families settled in the area now known as Cedar Hill. The Graves family set up their home on the north bank and the Cox family on the south bank of the Animas. The skiff they had built and then used to ferry wagons across the Animas at the area known as Twin Crossings was anchored nearby and the two families operated it as a high water ferry for several years. Early residents called the area Cox's Crossing.[32] Wash Cox journeyed back to Colfax County after the move. He attended his last Colfax County Commission meeting in the middle of October 1877. By January 1878, he was no longer on the Commission.[33]

Like the Cox and Graves families, many others heading to the San Juan country would in a few short years find themselves caught up in turmoil that engulfed the region in 1880 and 1881. Two men who would feel the harsh impact of the violence were the Hendrickson brothers who had preceded even Wash Cox in looking the area over. In a letter written in 1892, William Hendrickson recalled his first trip to the lower Animas with his brother Simeon. The Hendricksons first entered the San Juan Mountains on a prospecting trip from their homes in present day Custer County, Colorado. On July 17, 1875, the two brothers left from the vicinity of Animas City and headed west to Parrott City, Colorado.[34] Parrott City was a bustling new mining town on the south slope of the La Plata Mountains near the headwaters of the La Plata River. The setting was impressive, with the rugged peaks of the La Plata Mountains soaring above the town. The townsite had been laid out by Captain John Moss and E.H. Cooper in 1874.[35] The genial and dashing Moss convinced Tiburcio Parrott of San Francisco's Parrott and Company to finance the prospecting expedition to the La Platas. Mr. Parrott was an easy touch for such speculative ventures.[36] The Hendrickson brothers spent several days in the mining camp, before proceeding onto the Mancos valley where they found only one white man, who they identified as thirty-three-year-old James Ratliff. He was not alone; there were many Ute Indians camped in the area, but he had somehow managed to retain his hair. They spent several days making a giant circle, going down the Mancos River and then up the San Juan and the Animas, finally returning to their starting point. One of their camps was made at the Indian ruins that now make up the Aztec Ruins National Monument. They had expected to find Navajos, but they saw none, nor did they see any Indian sign. As far as we know, they saw no white men while in New Mexico either.[37]

The following year Animas City was officially founded and there was a frantic rush to settle the town. As William Hendrickson recalled, it wasn't until October that definite word was received that the lower Animas in New Mexico was open to settlement. Later that month, to avoid detection and any competition, Hendrickson and several other men stole out of Animas City at dusk and headed south. They hoped to make the first land claims in northwest New Mexico. Accompanying Hendrickson were Thomas and Milton Virden, Al Puett and Henry Woods. They found they were the first to arrive on the scene. Within a few days Hendrickson and the others made claims, most of them near the confluence of the San Juan and Animas Rivers.[38] By February of 1877 the *Colorado Chieftain* reported that, "A town has been laid out two miles above the mouth of the Animas river, by the name of Farmington, its founders being T. Verden, Hendrickson and Pewet [sic], all of Wet Mountain Valley [in Colorado]."[39]

Many others were being drawn to the San Juan country. The mining areas were attracting a steady stream of prospectors, miners, stockmen and other immigrants. The lower areas in New Mexico attracted farmers as well as stockmen. Some of the new arrivals were highly successful before pulling up stakes and heading for the new country, others sought their first fortune. Ike Stockton would be the first brother to make his way to the Animas River valley, but before that happened he headed south. He was drawn by glowing stories coming out of Lincoln County.

As a good day on the Cox range might appear. Frederic Remington's "Cowboy Fun," from Theodore Roosevelt's "Ranch Life in the Far West," The Century Illustrated Monthly Magazine, *Vol. 35, No. 4, February 1888. (Author's collection.)*

Chapter Four

Ike, the Kid and the Coes

*The devil has opened his furnace door
And poked the coals with his tail,
But we must jog on and jog some more,
Along the outlaws' trail.*[1]

It was probably in the fall of 1876 when Ike Stockton arrived in the town of Lincoln with his family.[2] That same fall, an ambitious native of England, twenty-three-year-old John Henry Tunstall, also arrived in town. Tunstall had the financial support and guidance of his father, who was a successful London-based businessman.[3] Tunstall was a young man in a hurry and soon entered the mercantile trade and cattle business.[4]

Ike did not have the support of a wealthy father or even the guidance a father would provide. Consequently his opportunities were smaller.[5] He operated the saloon in Montaño's store. The Stocktons lived in a nearby house.[6] This business insured that Ike would become acquainted with many of the major players in the drama which was about to unfold. Frank Coe, George Coe and Ab Saunders were already well established in Lincoln County and Ike may have known them from Colfax County. If not, they soon became acquainted.

While living in southern New Mexico, the Stocktons suffered a great tragedy, when they lost an infant daughter to smallpox. She was buried behind the Tunstall Store.[7] Dr. Gordon was the attending physician for the Stocktons and when asked at a later date about the family, he spoke "well of the family's standing at that time."[8] Tunstall's store was at the center of the epidemic of violence which was beginning to brew in southern New Mexico. The after effects of this maelstrom would be carried to the San Juan country by members of the Coe family.

During this time, George Coe met a young, likable, bucktoothed cowboy. Coe's acquaintance would achieve everlasting fame for his role in the Lincoln County War and the encounter would seal Coe's allegiance during the hostilities. Billy the Kid and George Coe would pal around for only eighteen months, but those months would be action-packed and give birth to the Kid's legend. As George Coe recalled, "He was a great boy with plenty of principle with his friends but pretty bad with his enemies." It may have been through the Coes that Ike first met the Kid.[9] Pat Garrett, whose fame is inextricably linked to the Kid's, indicates that as the conflict grew, Ike became a "secret ally" of Billy the Kid and his compatriots.[10]

Ike's business interests precluded his open support of one faction over another.

The Montaño Store in Lincoln, New Mexico. Ike Stockton operated a saloon in the west end of the building during the late 1870s. (Author's collection.)

Billy Bonney's boss was the doomed leader of one of those factions. John Tunstall felt he had the money, and with that money, the power to take on the reigning business interests in Lincoln County. His deadly spiral began when he joined in several business ventures with attorney Alexander McSween. In addition to cattle herds and a large mercantile store, they also opened a bank. Leading the forces in opposition to Tunstall and McSween was an equally aggressive businessman named James J. Dolan. His mercantile operation had originally been started by L.G. Murphy with Dolan and John Riley as junior partners. Merchant Dolan proved to be a treacherous and tenacious adversary.[11] The firm eventually became J.J. Dolan and Company. Mr. Dolan aligned himself with attorney Thomas Catron, a leading member of the territory's ruling political alliance, the Santa Fe Ring. Dolan also had the ear of Governor Samuel Axtell, who was viewed as working hand in hand with the Ring. He was also effective in using the press for his purposes. Dolan's grandiose plans were threatened by the equally grandiose plans of Tunstall and

McSween. There was one sure way to deal with the ambitious Englishman and his attorney.[12] On February 18, 1878, John Tunstall was murdered.[13] His death ignited the orgy of violence now known as the Lincoln County War.

Frank Coe served on the coroner's jury, which identified Tunstall's killers.[14] Afterwards, Tunstall was laid to rest. The pallbearers were Dick Brewer, John Newcomb, and future lower Animas River residents George and Frank Coe.[15] Sheriff Brady seemed in no hurry to arrest Tunstall's killers. Supporters of the slain Englishmen banded together with the intent of avenging Tunstall. A supportive letter to the *New Mexican* in Santa Fe classified this group as "outraged prominent citizens" and "regulators." In response to this letter an incensed James Dolan wrote the *New Mexican* and asked, "Who are those regulators and prominent citizens?" He answered his own question and topping his list was "Wm. H. Antrim, 'alias the kid' a renegade from Arizona." Others mentioned in Dolan's letter include, R.M. (Richard) Brewer, Doc Scurlock and Charlie Bowdre.[16] In early March, some revenge was taken, when two of Tunstall's killers were shot and killed by the Regulators.[17] In the early stages, the Coe boys were not active members of the group, but they would soon be sucked into the deadly conflict.

The Kid was a possessed man when it came to avenging the death of Tunstall. His next target was Lincoln County Sheriff William Brady, a supporter of the Dolan faction. On April 1, 1878, Sheriff Brady, George Hindman, Dad Peppin and Billy Mathews were passing near Tunstall's store when they were ambushed by the Regulators. Brady took the brunt of the initial volley and a second volley finished him. The others ran for cover. Hindman, who had also been struck, eventually fell in the street. The fight was not over when Ike Stockton ventured forth from his saloon and approached the two fallen men.[18] Hindman asked for water. Stockton hustled over to the nearby Rio Bonito, dipped his hat in the little stream and returned to Hindman. At the same time, Billy the Kid emerged from the cover of an adobe wall and headed for Brady.[19] The Kid was after Brady's rifle, which he had reportedly taken from the Kid in February.[20] As Bonney approached, Stockton tried to warn him away.[21] The Kid didn't take the hint, and as he neared the rifle he entered Billy Mathews's field of view. Mathews was ready and fired a round. The shot wounded the Kid and he quickly retreated.[22]

Three days after the shooting of Sheriff Brady, on April 4th, the Coe boys entered the fray.[23] The Coe's first gun battle of the Lincoln County War is now legendary among the shootouts of the western frontier. A one man whirlwind known as "Buckshot" Roberts wreaked havoc when he was attacked by a large group of Regulators after he showed up at Blazer's mill. Before the hostilities began, Frank Coe spoke earnestly with Roberts, trying to obtain his peaceful surrender. That did not happen.[24] The

Mesilla Valley Independent reported that when Frank Coe sprang to one side, the gunfight began. In the ensuing shootout Roberts was mortally wounded, but he still had plenty of fight left. He quickly fired several rounds. Charlie Bowdre sustained a minor wound. Another round burrowed into the chest of Kid and Coe ally John Middleton, who may have been the former Erath County cattle and hog thief. One of Roberts's rounds found George Coe's right hand.[25] When George Coe later moved to the Animas River valley, his right hand bore the mark of battle inflicted by "Buckshot" Roberts; he was missing his trigger finger.[26] Roberts somehow managed to find the door to Dr. Blazer's room where he sought shelter. Shortly afterwards he killed Dick Brewer, shooting him in the head. Everyone knew that Buckshot was a dead man and with the death of Brewer, the Regulators lost their taste for combat. They left Brewer's body behind and fled the field. Roberts hung on before finally dying the next day.[27]

George Coe also participated in the decisive and most well-known skirmish of the Lincoln County War.[28] In July, the Tunstall and McSween forces met the Dolan men in a clash which lasted for several days. Billy the Kid and a large group of Regulators were trapped in the McSween house. The outcome was a total disaster for the McSween/Tunstall forces. McSween's house was burned down and Billy the Kid barely escaped with his life. As McSween ran from his burning house, he was shot and killed.[29] George Coe and other McSween partisans had been posted in other buildings throughout the town. As the situation deteriorated, Coe escaped to the hills in a hail of bullets.[30] Coe began to realize that his future survival was doubtful, if he continued on the same course.

After the debacle, Billy the Kid made it clear that he was going after his enemies assets. George Coe told him "when it came to stealing horses for a living," he was through.[31] Horse theft was a serious matter, but the Coes and the Kid had other concerns as well. In April, District Attorney William L. Rynerson charged several men with murder as a result of the death of "Buckshot" Roberts. Lincoln County criminal case no. 264 listed those men in the painful legalese of the era as being, "the said Frank McNab and the said George Coe and the said Frank Coe and the said Steve Stevens and the said Henry Brown and the said Dock Scurlock and the said Charles Bowdry and the said John Middleton and the said ----- Wayt and the said William Bonney alias Kid."[32]

Lew Coe ran a small cattle herd in Sugarite Canyon, and he encouraged Frank and George to get out of southern New Mexico before they were killed. He advised them that he needed their help to move his cattle to the lower San Juan country. In November, the Coe's rode out of Sugarite Canyon with all their possessions loaded in wagons and headed over the Continental Divide. George Coe later wrote, "I never had such a time in my life trying to move cattle across those snow covered mts."[33] The

Coes began farming on bottomland they rented from the Joseph Howe family, across the Animas from the Aztec Ruins.[34] Frank and George Coe hoped their problems had been left behind in the Ruidoso country, but that was not to be. About his time living on the Animas, George Coe later wrote, "I had a harder time up there than I ever did in Lincoln County and went through just as narrow escapes there."[35]

Lew Coe settled on the north side of the Animas, two miles east of what is now downtown Farmington.[36] Lew selected his claim where a home had been burned to the ground. He assumed the owners had abandoned the land, but had he asked local residents, he would have found that was not necessarily the case. The owners of the house were the Virden brothers, two of the founders of Farmington. While they were in the San Juans prospecting for mineral treasure, Indians torched their house. Lew had in fact jumped their claim. When the Virdens returned from Colorado, Coe made an offer for the property and the Virdens accepted. They relocated near the confluence of the San Juan and La Plata Rivers.[37] The land dispute was settled amicably, but Lew Coe's claim jumping insured that the Coe family got off on the wrong foot with some of the local residents.

After the Coes left southern New Mexico, Ike Stockton remained for several months and kept out of trouble. If Porter came to visit his little brother, he was surprisingly quiet.[38] Before Ike left Lincoln County, combatants from both sides of the hostilities met to negotiate a peace pact. The agreement was short-lived. According to George Curry, a future territorial governor, the men sealed the pact with several rounds of drinks, including a final round at Ike Stockton's saloon.[39] That same night an altercation occurred between Susan McSween's attorney, Huston Chapman, and the Dolan faction. Chapman was shot dead. Jimmy Dolan, Billy Mathews and Bill Campbell were implicated in the shooting, which was witnessed by their mortal enemy, Billy the Kid, who had participated in the peace pact discussions.[40] That occurred in late February 1879.[41] Chapman's remains were placed in the tiny graveyard behind the Tunstall store which also held the remains of John Tunstall, Alexander McSween and Frank McNab.[42] The attorney's death was the impetus for Governor Lew Wallace's visit to Lincoln where he would meet face to face with the Kid in an attempt to attain his testimony against those who had murdered Huston Chapman. Wallace feared that Chapman's death would reignite the hostilities, but that did not happen.[43] The governor left Santa Fe in the first week of March and stayed at the Montaño place during part of his stay. It's not known if he visited Ike's saloon.[44]

Governor Wallace and Ike Stockton may not have met in Lincoln County. About the time that Wallace departed Santa Fe, Stockton was preparing to travel north to Colfax County. Perhaps he wanted to see how he stood with the county's legal authorities and check out prospects as the

Santa Fe railroad first pierced the northern border of New Mexico. During the early months of 1879, Porter Stockton also turned up in the Cimarron country. Despite their outstanding warrants, both Porter and Ike had some reason to believe that they were safe from arrest in Colfax County.

Frederic Remington's "The Herd At Night," from Theodore Roosevelt's "The Round-up," The Century Illustrated Monthly Magazine, *Vol. 35, No. 6, April 1888. (Author's collection.)*

Chapter Five

Trouble in Otero

> *Though lead is your diet and fight is your fun,*
> *I simply can't give you the jolt;*
> *For I love you, you blessed old son-of-a-gun,---*
> *You forty-five caliber Colt!*[1]

The Stockton brothers hoped that Sheriff Peter Burleson was not inclined to arrest his fellow Texans. Still, for two years, they apparently avoided Colfax County. Burleson's reputation contributed to their hesitancy. Pete Burleson became sheriff not long after Porter Stockton's September 1876 escape from the Cimarron jail. The former Texan was a close friend to I.W. Lacy and Wash Cox, and the Stockton brothers and Burleson had probably known each other for several years.[2] Burleson, according to one account, was known for his harsh methods and explosive disposition.[3] Like others, Burleson had good reason to leave Texas. While testifying in one Colfax County criminal case, L. Bradford Prince, the Chief Justice of the territory's Supreme Court, innocently asked the sheriff why he had left Texas. Burleson, in his Texas twang, said, "Well, jedge, I had reason ter believe a change of climate would be good for my health." Judge Prince belatedly realized that he had hit a nerve when several cowboys broke the decorum of the courtroom by bursting into guffaws.[4] Burleson had been ranching and was not inclined to run for sheriff. He had been corralled by Clay Allison and his future father-in-law, Orson K. Chittenden, and told he should run for the office. After some thought, he entered the race.[5] The challenges facing the sheriff increased when the Santa Fe rail lines entered Colfax County and a working terminus camp sprang to life.

In May of 1878 the *Colorado Chieftain* noted that "the railroad company has changed the name of La Junta station to Otero."[6] Otero was the creation of the Santa Fe Railroad and was not officially established until 1879. It was named for prominent New Mexican Miguel Antonio Otero.[7] The town was located about six miles south of an older campsite and stage stop known as Willow Springs, which would by 1880 be re-christened, Raton.[8]

In mid-February 1879 a trainload of dignitary excursionists left Trinidad bound for the new town. Before reaching the summit of Raton Pass, the small engine was switched with a much larger fifty-nine ton locomotive, which had the power to pull eight cars up the steep switchback rail line (the much smaller engines could only pull one car up the same grade). The railroad had named the colossal locomotive "Uncle Dick."[9]

The *St. Louis Globe-Democrat* reported that "Uncle Dick" was "the largest locomotive on the continent."¹⁰ A *Colorado Chieftain* reporter on the excursion said, "On the day of our arrival, the town had reached the mature age of three days, and ten thousand dollars worth of lots had already been sold. Hundreds of people were camped in tents and board shanties, and the din of the saw and hammer resounded on all sides."¹¹ The *Chieftain*, gushed that, "Otero will be known through all time as the first station and the first town on the first railroad that ever laid a rail into New Mexico." The account blathered on, saying "there is no doubt but it will always be the most important town in northern New Mexico. The probabilities are that Otero will become a county seat before a great while."¹² If liquor sales were a sign of future greatness, Otero was on its way with seventeen establishments, in addition to seven stores of various types, five restaurants, one hotel, with another one being built, and two livery stables.¹³ By the summer of 1879 the town was doing an immense business in freight. The *Globe-Democrat* reported, "You can there see hundreds of large freighting teams encamped, coming and going as far as the eye can reach." The railroad was rapidly expanding southward toward Las Vegas, but for a while travelers had to take a dreadful stage road that took eighteen hours to traverse.¹⁴

One of Otero's bustling dance halls was superintended by an over-proportioned madam named Dolores Martinez. She was known as "Steamboat" to her patrons. Miguel Otero, the son of the town's namesake, who would one day be the governor of New Mexico, estimated her weight at 350 pounds.¹⁵ By November 1879 Steamboat had moved south to Las Vegas, and the *Daily News* (which may have underestimated her girth) said, "It is currently reported in Las Vegas that Madam Dolores, the two hundred and fifty pound sylph, is the belle of the dance house there this winter. She teeters on her toe, balances her partner on her thumb, and waltzes like a 'Steamboat.' "¹⁶

Steamboat was just one just one drop in the deluge of wild west characters that flooded the new railroad camp. Another was William Martin, the local deputy sheriff and essentially the town's marshal.¹⁷ Martin had been encouraged to come to Otero by his friend, Ed Withers.¹⁸ In Otero, Withers, a thirty-three-year-old Texas native, ran one of the local livery barns.¹⁹ As for Bill Martin, he was well known as a notorious horse thief and all around hell raiser. Everyone called him "Hurricane Bill."

Throughout 1874 and 1875 newspapers carried numerous accounts of Hurricane's criminal activities. In July 1874, he was arrested near Wichita, Kansas, after trying to scare homesteaders out of their houses with warnings of an imminent Indian attack. His plan was to then plunder the empty homesteads.²⁰ Ten days after that report, the *Washington (DC) Evening Star* said the agent for the Cheyenne and Arapaho Agency announced the arrest of the "notorious horse thief and whiskey trader" known as

Hurricane Bill in Oklahoma.[21] In January 1875, he stole two hundred head of cattle from Mr. Quinlan near Medicine Lodge, Kansas.[22] Despite his reputation, in 1875 he found employment as a scout with the U.S. Army. That fall his work took him to Fort Griffin, Texas in Shackelford County. Below the actual fort was a rough frontier town, commonly referred to as The Flat.[23] The Flat was wide open and soon after Shackelford County was organized in September 1874, the new authorities tried to clean it up. Many residents went by alias names. In one criminal case, Hanna Eizenstein was charged with murder, but her partner was identified as simply "Edward a Mexican.' "[24] A May 1876 indictment lists, "Molly McCabe, Jim Oglesby, Hurricane Bill, Long Kate, Helen, Etta, Liz, [and] Minnie" as being charged with operating a disorderly house.[25] An earlier case involving Minnie, Molly McCabe and Griffin Long Kate described the crime as "Keeping a disorderly house, to wit: a house where vagabonds and prostitutes resort for the purpose of public prostitution."[26]

In another instance, Hurricane and a then obscure, pasty-faced, cadaverous gambler named Doc Holliday were charged in the same case for playing cards in a liquor establishment.[27] Both men were drawn toward the wildest towns in the west, and it was probably in The Flat where Hurricane first met the part-time dentist. Holliday would also spend time in Otero, where he crossed paths with Port Stockton. As was his normal practice, Holliday left Shackelford County leaving his criminal charges open.[28]

Bill Martin stayed long enough to find himself housed in the Albany, Texas jail. In June 1878 he witnessed vigilantes enter the lockup and pour lead into the former sheriff and notorious cattle thief and killer John Larn. After his release, Bill Martin left Texas.[29] He was subsequently listed as a wanted man in the Rangers' Black Book.[30] Shortly after this trouble, Hurricane Bill blew into New Mexico.

By March 19, 1879 Hurricane was in Otero. The horse thief, gambler and whore house operator had his hands full with his deputy sheriff duties. For a while, Otero had no lockup, so Hurricane would lasso recalcitrant cowboys and tie them to telegraph poles.[31]

About the time that Hurricane Bill appeared in Colfax County, Ike Stockton also traveled back to his former home. Ike seemed to be able to wander at will and was not concerned about leaving his saloon in Lincoln in the care of others for significant periods of time. His carefree attitude was not shared by Colfax County authorities however, and as Otero grew into a raucous frontier town, they faced many challenges in keeping the peace. Illegal gambling was rampant in both Otero and Cimarron, and some attempts were made to curtail the activity. Ike Stockton and Deputy Sheriff William "Dutchy" Goodlet are shown as the only witnesses in two criminal cases. The charges against John McClelland said that on March 1, 1879, McClelland, "Did unlawfully then and there Keep a Gaming Table, called High ball poker, the same then and there being a Banking Game."

Henry L. Waldo, the attorney general for New Mexico, was the prosecutor.[32] The second violation was for the exact same offense on the same day. The gambler in that case was Frank Randal.[33] Ike Stockton was adept at ingratiating himself with law enforcement authorities wherever he lived. Perhaps Ike felt that Goodlet, a former Colfax County dry goods clerk, was in over his head or perhaps he simply thought it would be to his benefit to ingratiate himself with Goodlet and his boss, Pete Burleson.[34] Almost exactly two years earlier, Deputy Goodlet had been directed by Burleson to arrest Porter Stockton, Nick Camblin and others for the 1873 murder of John Canada.[35] The deputy had to know that Ike was wanted for breaking his brother out of the Cimarron jail, but chose to ignore that transgression. Ike was skilled at finding those who operated on only the edge of the law and exploited those relationships to avoid imprisonment or worse. Like Bill Martin and many other deputies and constables along the frontier, Bill Goodlet was not the epitome of an upright lawman. Goodlet later moved south to Las Vegas where he allied himself with a group of notorious outlaws known as the "Dodge City Gang" and their associates: Hyman G. Neill (also known as Hoodoo Brown), Doc Holliday, "Mysterious Dave" Mather, "Dirty Dave" Rudabaugh, J.J. Webb and others.[36]

While Ike was in Colfax County, he was being sought by Sheriff George Kimbrell in Lincoln County as a witness in the matter of the murder of Sheriff William Brady. Judge Warren Bristol issued a subpoena which commanded "Mr. Ellis (Sr) --- Stockton [and] J.B. Mathews" to testify in the matter. Kimbrell located and served Ellis and Mathews, but did not find Ike.[37]

As the weather warmed and road conditions improved, the territory's judicial system began to boil. In late March 1879, Cimarron hosted their session of the district court under the auspices of Chief Justice Prince. The sessions were normally held only twice a year in most counties. The arrival of the roving entourage, which included the judge, clerks, and the defense and prosecuting attorneys, was often the highlight of the social season in New Mexico's small towns.[38] Pete Burleson's efforts made for a busy spring session. His tough attitude was cramping the style of his fellow Texans, and while it is not totally clear, he may have been the target of a planned ambush. One of the rowdy cowboys in Colfax County was George Hill. That is a common name, but it seems likely that Mr. Hill was the former Erath County resident who was listed as a witness in one of Samuel Stockton's horse theft cases, as well as Porter Stockton's attempted murder charge. It seems likely that Hill and his allies intended to intimidate the officers of the court. As the *New Mexican* reported, the incident occurred "within a stones throw of where the Grand Jury was in session."[39] It was a Thursday evening, March 27th, when the sound of several gun shots rang out. Sheriff Burleson bolted toward the sound and called for Deputy Stokes to follow. In the corral directly behind the Masonic Hall, the sheriff was confronted by four armed men: George Hill, John Hill, Robert Leigh and Henry Gordon. Burleson began gathering up their weapons and thought he had the situation in hand, but as George Hill reached into his pocket, Burleson heard the menacing sound of Hill's gun being cocked. Before the sheriff could react, Gordon grabbed his hand which held one of the seized pistols. According to Burleson, "George Hill commenced firing at me with a small pocket pistol. About this time Stokes fell, exclaiming 'I'm killed.' " If the four men planned on outnumbering Burleson and his deputy, they were rudely surprised. Clay Allison's brother, John Allison, and Henry Hodding entered the fray and grabbed George Hill. At some point during the skirmish, a bullet ripped through Hill's hip inflicting a blood gushing wound and witnesses believed he couldn't survive the hemorrhage. Robert Leigh was shot in the hand. Deputy Stokes, true to his final assessment, was killed by the .45 round that entered his chest, passed through his spine, and lodged in the muscles of his back. Gordon and Leigh were immediately arrested and placed in the Cimarron jail. In the confusion, John Hill mounted his horse and headed north. Mason T. "Mace" Bowman and John Allison started in pursuit and captured Hill near the Ponil. He was tossed into jail.[40] Burleson was grazed in the arm by one of Hill's bullets. On Saturday, the district court adjourned for the funeral of Deputy Stokes.[41] John Hill, Henry Gordon and Robert Leigh were all charged with carrying a deadly weapon in the town of Cimarron.[42] George Hill was charged with assault with intent to murder and with carrying a deadly weapon. Witnesses for the territory on the attempted murder charge included Burleson and two men identified only as Arrington and Woodburn. Arrington was probably Milton J., the man known as Chuck, and Woodburn was probably local cattleman John K. Woodburn. Alvino Archuleta of the Ponil and Robert Leigh were listed as witnesses for the defense.[43] Oddly, it appears that no one was charged with the murder of Deputy Stokes. George Hill may have been the shooter in that case, but it is likely that a plea deal was in the works. Before the end of March, a not guilty plea was entered for Hill on the attempted murder charge. He recovered from his wounds and in late August he changed that plea to guilty. The court suspended sentencing Hill "until some future day."[44] Hill fled to Texas.[45]

  George Hill also certainly knew George Morrison from their days near Stephenville, and it appears that Morrison was present when Hill assaulted Sheriff Burleson. It is not known what role Morrison played in the hostilities, but sometime that same day Morrison had the bad luck of encountering territorial Attorney General Henry Waldo. The short-tempered Morrison seldom traveled anywhere without being armed. Even though carrying weapons in Cimarron had been illegal for at least two years, he habitually flouted the law. Waldo was fed up with Cimarron's lawless atmosphere. Morrison was not arrested on the day Hill tried to kill

Burleson, but the following day Chief Justice Prince signed an arrest warrant charging Morrison with carrying arms. The only witness listed in the Morrison case was Henry Waldo. Arresting George Morrison for carrying a pistol was one battle Pete Burleson chose not to fight, but Henry Waldo forced the issue. A day after the warrant was issued, Burleson and Deputy E.L. Hunt took Morrison into custody. With the court in session, justice was swift. Morrison was held for two days and on April 1st he was fined $15 plus other costs for a total of $38.75. In 1879 that was a substantial amount of money. ($100 from 1879 would be valued at over $2000 in 2010, accounting for inflation.) But Justice Prince and Attorney General Waldo were not through. Morrison had been charged on two previous occasions with the same offense. He had also chosen to ignore the summons of the court in these matters for the past two years. Prince was pleased to have Morrison in his court. He stopped short of incarcerating the Texan, but used Morrison to send a message to the more uncivilized residents of Colfax County. In the remaining cases Morrison was fined $25 plus $27.05 in costs. In the other he was fined $100 plus $25.25 in costs.[46] If George Hill and George Morrison sought to intimidate Burleson and the top law enforcement officers in the territory, their efforts fell flat. Morrison was lucky; had Prince and Waldo known about his outstanding arrest warrant in Texas, they would have surely held him and contacted Erath County authorities. Burleson chose his battles, but he was clearly not a coward. However, Porter Stockton was unimpressed by the sheriff's reputation, even though warrants for his arrest were for far more serious matters than carrying a deadly weapon.

Otero's cast of outlaws, gamblers, whores and assorted desperadoes suited Porter Stockton, and he viewed the town as a safe haven. He was confident that no lockup in Colfax County could hold him; even if he found himself in the Cimarron jail, it was still a sieve-like operation. In May of 1879, James Hunt, the town's jailer, resigned and Dr. Cummings was pressed into service by Sheriff Burleson. Not surprisingly one of the prisoners managed to get a hammer grip on the doctor. The *New Mexican* noted that the "two other prisoners relieved him of the small mountain howitzer he carried" and completed their release. Before leaving they bound the doctor, gagged him with a flour sack, placed him in the cell while, "apologizing for the necessity which occasioned such treatment, turned the key and bade the Doctor good night."[47]

At about this same time, the Stockton brothers received some good news. The *Trinidad Enterprise* reported that, "The indictments found in Taos county for offenses committed in Colfax county several years ago, were quashed by Chief Justice Prince at the recent term of district court in Taos county, on the ground [sic] that a Taos county grand jury had no jurisdiction to find them."[48] That would include the time period covering Port's murder of Antonio Arcibia and his subsequent escape from the

Cimarron jail with the able assistance of his little brother. The charges could be refiled in Colfax County, but there was always the chance that they would slip through the cracks or that reliable and willing witnesses might not be found. Charges for the murder of John Canada were apparently still outstanding.

While the Stockton brothers were running around free and clear, former Colfax County Deputy Sheriff Joe Holbrook was on trial for murder as a result of the shotgun death of notorious Cimarron desperado David Crockett back in September 1876. Crockett's partner, Gus Heffron, survived the shootout. Oddly, even though that incident occurred in 1876, Holbrook was not indicted until March 1, 1878. Sheriff Rinehart and John McCullough were indicted during the same session. Witnesses in the case included W.V. Marshall, Jack Caton, J.H. Kingman, Cornelius "Buck" Carey, Antonia Luna, Mace Bowman and Gus Heffron. The foreman of the grand jury was former Erath County resident Wilson L. South.[49] South effectively used his influence to secure the indictment in what appears to be a misguided attempt to avenge the death of Crockett, who had been a herder for Lacy and Coleman. When the case came to trial, Holbrook's attorney shrewdly requested a change of venue and the spring of 1879 proceeding was moved to Taos County, where chances were high that a primarily Hispanic jury would decide the verdict. The *New Mexican* noted that the testimony included stories of, "Crockett's actions in riding into hotels, stores, dining rooms, etc., forcing merchants to perform menial services, stirring up his drinks with a revolver, etc." Taos County jurors were familiar with the hell raised by Texas herders. Much of the violence was directed at native Hispanic residents. The jury was not inclined to punish those who rid the country of its bad men. Holbrook was acquitted.[50]

By June, Doc Holliday joined Hurricane Bill Martin in Otero. At the same time hostilities between the Atchison, Topeka and Santa Fe and the Denver and Rio Grande Railroads reached the boiling point over the extension of new rail lines.[51] Bat Masterson was leading the AT&SF forces. Doc Holliday and a host of ruffians joined the clash.[52] Doc soon returned to less confrontational pursuits in Otero. He probably frequented Henry and Robinson's Saloon. The owners of this popular establishment were well known for offering unlawful gambling opportunities and Sheriff Burleson, Deputy Goodlet and a witness identified as only Mr. Arrington were shown as witnesses in at least two illegal gambling cases against the saloon's owners.[53] Before Doc arrived in Otero he was beginning to show his predisposition toward violence. Bat Masterson reported that he left his Georgia home after an argument led him to shoot several "negro boys." Masterson said, "he finally killed a man in Jacksboro, [Texas]" and in Denver in 1876 he carved up Bud Ryan's face with a knife.[54] While Holliday had grown acquainted with drunken gun-toting cowboys shooting up the saloons he inhabited, as they terrorized the patrons, he developed a keen distaste for their antics. That feeling would explode with devastating results in Tombstone.[55] During his short stay in Otero, he would witness at least one murderous instance of cowboy mayhem.

On June 11, 1879, a group of Texas cowboys along with their leader, Porter Stockton, rode into Otero. Perhaps Stockton was there to celebrate the dismissal of some of his Colfax County charges. Perhaps he now had some chance to live a normal life, become a stockman and live the rest of his life with his family as a free man. But Stockton was not a normal man, and would continue to live his life like he always had. Stockton and his friends proceeded to tear up the town. Doc Holliday and "Uncle Dick's" wayward son, Bill Wootton, were two of the witnesses to their escapades. Six months earlier Wootton had been hauled to jail by his half-brother, Sheriff R.L. Wootton, Jr., after he shot and killed a man in Trinidad's Olympic Theatre.[56]

What Holliday and Wootton encountered that evening was par for the course. According to the *Otero Optic*, "A lot of Texans came into town [Otero], and after filling full of bad whiskey, they became boisterous."[57] The *Denver Daily Tribune* in a dispatch from the *Trinidad News* said "Stockton and other cow-boys were drunk and fighting in one of the saloons." Deputy Sheriff Hurricane Bill Martin had seen enough and decided to arrest Stockton. In the process, Port's pistol either fell from its holster or a well-meaning friend removed it. After the arrest, some of Stockton's friends asked Hurricane if the prisoner could be released. According to the *Trinidad News*, Martin told the cowboys, "that if they would put up $12 to cover fine and costs, and take him out of town, he would let him go."[58] This was agreed to and Stockton was freed.

There are two versions of how Ed Withers arrived on the scene. The *Otero Optic* reported that Withers was in bed, heard the commotion, got dressed, armed himself and headed out to check on the trouble. As he approached a crowd, "Withers threw down the lever of his gun, as if to load it, when one of the crowd fired upon him killing him almost instantly."[59] The most detailed account of the murder was published in the *Trinidad News*, which noted that a friend of Withers came to the livery barn and told him some cowboys had been stirring it up at one of the saloons. The *News* said, "Withers asked him if Bill (Martin) was in trouble, and on being assured that he had been, he said he would go and help him." (Parentheses are in the original article.) Withers apparently met up with some of the cowboys or with Hurricane Bill and took possession of Stockton's pistol. Shortly thereafter, Stockton approached Withers and asked, "Where is that pistol?" By that time, Withers thought that the difficulties had been settled and replied, "I have it in my pocket." He gave the pistol to Stockton, who used it to fire a fatal shot into Withers's chest. This shocking description of the murder of Ed Withers make it clear that Stockton's simmering rage was clearly matched by his soulless indifference.

Those acquainted with Stockton knew there was only one way to put an end to his growing arrogance, but they had not yet developed the steely-eyed determination required for that solution. Stockton was brash and brazen, but not stupid and knew that any hint of vigilante fever would cool over time, so he grabbed a horse and headed out of town. Even though he left Otero, he did not disappear. The *Trinidad News* concluded their article by saying, "He [Stockton] is said to be with the round up, and not more than 100 miles from Otero." Stockton was an able cowboy who could find employment, despite his reputation.[60] The town was in an uproar, but Hurricane Bill decided not to test an armed and sober Stockton. He bolted for the livery and hid in the hay until he deemed it safe to re-emerge.[61] The initial version carried in the *Trinidad Daily News* was sparse, noting only, "Mr. Ed. Withers, one of the former proprietors of the livery, was shot and killed. The murderer is unknown, but supposed to be a cowboy from the range."[62] The *New Mexican's* brief blurb said, "A livery man in Otero, named Withers, was killed last week by a cow boy, Porter Stockton."[63]

The same day of the murder, Justice of the Peace E.F. Lancaster held an inquest into the death of Edward Withers. A six man jury concluded that Stockton had fired the shots with the intent to kill Withers and they directed that he be arrested to be dealt with as the law directs.[64]

Typical work for "cow boy" Porter Stockton. Frederic Remington's "The Rope Corral," from Theodore Roosevelt's "The Round-up," The Century Illustrated Monthly Magazine, *Vol. 35, No. 6, April 1888. (Author's collection.)*

Hurricane Bill made the mistake of overestimating the character of Port Stockton, and Ed Withers paid the price. As for Doc Holliday, what he actually witnessed is subject to conjecture, but given his reputation and his relationship with Martin, it seems likely that he would take Hurricane Bill's side and seek justice for Ed Withers. At the time of this shooting, Holliday was known to some, but had not achieved the notoriety he would attain after the famous shootout in Tombstone. Though Port Stockton probably knew nothing about the emaciated looking gambler, it is certain that he did not care if his victims had friends who would take up their cause anyway. He rode out of town with no one in pursuit. In the days immediately following the shooting, Colfax County authorities seemed distinctly disinterested in arresting the killer of Ed Withers.

That changed later in the summer when Sheriff Pete Burleson and a posse did go out in search of Stockton. I.W. Lacy's longstanding friendship and support of Sheriff Burleson may have contributed to Stockton's growing disdain for Lacy. The posse did not find Stockton. The sheriff's subsequent reimbursement request said, "I was very reliably informed that he [Porter Stockton] had come into the county with an armed band of outlaws to do violence to certain peacible citizens and then I set out with a force of eight...men to capture said Stockton after traveling for 3 weeks in the mountains we were unable to find them as the out-laws managed to avoid us and shortly afterwards left the county." He requested the sizable sum of $354 for expenses.[65]

After the murder of Ed Withers, Hurricane sought solace in the bottle. Three months later he was fired.[66] He turned up a year later in southern New Mexico, working as an army scout for Colonel Benjamin Grierson in the campaign against Victorio's Apaches.[67] Doc Holliday departed Otero before Hurricane Bill. Court witness records for the Withers's murder include the notation "(Las Vegas)" beside Holliday's name.[68] Doc operated his last dental office in Las Vegas, New Mexico in 1879.[69] If he was reluctant to use his sidearm in Otero, that was not the case in Las Vegas, where he shot and killed Mike Gordon.[70] Understandably, he didn't tarry in Las Vegas; he cleared up his affairs and followed the Earp brothers to Arizona. He would never testify in the matter of the Territory of New Mexico v. Porter Stockton.

During the last days of August 1879, Cimarron was once again hosting the roving session of the district court. On August 30th, Stockton was indicted for the murder of Ed Withers. At the same time he was re-indicted for the murder of Antonio Arcibia. The grand jury that indicted Porter Stockton included two men who probably sporadically employed Stockton as a cow herder. Manley Chase was the foreman and John Dawson was a juror. As a Texan and a cowboy, Stockton had always enjoyed some support from the local cowmen, but after the contemptible murder of Ed Withers that began to crumble. The Territory's witness list for the Withers's murder was exceptionally long. Besides Holliday and William Wootton, it included J.A. Knowles, John Grey, J.J. Sellis [John J. Selles], D.C. Taylor, J.C. Hull, W. Dalton, D.B. Curtis, Frank Curtis, Andrew J. Armstrong and lastly, Harry Bassett, who was soon to regret knowing Stockton at all. John Selles was the unindicted Trinidad constable who had accompanied Porter Stockton and others as a member of the Trinidad posse when John Canada was murdered. Frank Curtis was the brother of former Wash Cox cowhand Zenas Curtis. It is unclear, but D.B. may have been his older brother Richard A. Curtis. In addition to Port's indictments, the grand jury made sure that Ike was re-indicted for "rescuing a prisoner" and "assault in a menacing manner" for his role in the escape of his imprisoned brother in September 1876.[71]

Over the next year, territorial officials seemed to take an active interest in Port Stockton's case. Twice a year, Chief Justice Prince issued witness subpoenas as well as a notice to the sheriff commanding him to arrest Stockton and produce him for the next session of the court. One has to wonder just how determined the sheriff was in his efforts to find Stockton when the sheriff invariably reported back that he had been unable to locate the wanted man.[72]

With the issuance of new arrest warrants in Colfax County, Ike Stockton knew that he could not return to his former home. In Lincoln County he was uncomfortably entangled as a witness to the murder of Sheriff Brady by Billy the Kid and others.[73] On November 6, 1879, Judge Bristol issued witness subpoenas for "Stockton, J.B. Mathews, Saturnino Baca and Benny Baca." Four days later, Special Deputy Sheriff Simon Andrette located and served Ike Stockton.[74] It appears that Ike chose to duck out on the pending legal proceedings. He had at least two reasons to avoid his civic duties. First, he was sympathetic toward the Tunstall/Billy the Kid faction and secondly, faced with his own criminal indictments in Colfax County, he had no desire to be associated with the notoriety which territorial newspaper coverage would bring to a trial involving Billy the Kid. Leaving his Lincoln saloon behind, Ike and his family traveled north and by the latter part of 1879 they were living in the Animas River valley of northwest New Mexico.[75] He was twenty-seven years old at the time. His wife, Ellen, was about twenty-one and they had a four or five-year-old daughter named Delilah.[76]

Along the Animas, Ike found many of the same families he knew in the Cimarron country and in Lincoln County, like Frank and George Coe. Across the river from their new home, the Stockton family could explore the remnants of the ancient Anasazi village that now comprise the Aztec Ruins National Monument. Out on the open range along the Animas Stockton saw cattle. Large numbers of them roamed along the river bottom and onto the piñon and juniper covered hills and mesas. Remnants of the herd probably carried the heart in a circle brand which Wash Cox had used in Erath County, and his horses still bore that brand on their left shoulder. Most of the Cox cattle wore a brand that was distinctly designed to send a message to potential rustlers, while it served as an obvious deterrent to brand artists utilizing a dotting iron. The brand left no doubt who owned the cattle; the name "COX" covered their entire side. The brand discouraged anyone from adding a slash or other mark and then registering that brand in their name. The size had the added benefit of making Cox cattle clearly identifiable from a great distance. Wash Cox placed his brand on the animal's right flank.[77]

From the Northwest New Mexican *(Bloomfield, NM), Feb. 8, 1887. "Range Rio Arriba county, horse brand heart on left shoulder. Post Office Aztec, New Mexico." (From the collection of Robert L. Maddox, Jr.)*

Ike's arrival in the San Juan country was quiet enough, but it wouldn't be long before he achieved national notoriety. Back in Colfax County, death and turbulence swirled around Porter Stockton. Despite Sheriff Burleson's labors, Stockton continued to frequent some parts of the county. In late October 1879, the *Colorado Weekly Chieftain* said, "Some rough doings are reported along the line of the New Mexico and Southern Pacific below Otero, and a vigilance committee is called for."[78] Newspaper accounts indicate that Stockton was somehow involved with the death of Harry Bassett on November 20, 1879 in Otero. Bassett was the successor to Hurricane Bill as the Colfax County deputy sheriff at Otero. Like Ed Withers, he also worked at one of Otero's livery stables. Bassett had witnessed the murder of Ed Withers. Being a witness does not necessarily make him an enemy of Stockton, and he may well have been part of

Stockton's crowd, at least partially explaining why Stockton felt safe in Otero. Stories from the newspapers are cryptic when it comes to explaining the relationship between the two men. The *Chieftain* carried news of the shooting, but danced around Stockton's involvement: "A fatal shooting affray occurred at Otero, New Mexico on Friday, in which one deputy sheriff was killed and another fatally wounded. The row was between the two men injured and several other officers of the law, regarding the arrest of certain parties. Further trouble is anticipated."[79] The *Cimarron News and Press* noted that Deputy Sheriff Marion Littrell along with Will South and Zencas [sic] Curtis went to Otero with the intent of serving arrest warrants on several wanted men.[80] They were also looking for stolen cattle which they believed were being taken to Colorado.[81] If Port Stockton was rounding up cattle in New Mexico and driving them to Colorado, it would not be the last time that one of the Stockton boys was implicated in such a scheme. Littrell had access to three murder warrants calling for Stockton's arrest. The three men heard the details of the murder of Ed Withers from eyewitnesses including Zenas's brother. They were familiar with Stockton's bad temper and quick trigger finger. Burleson's choice of former Texas trail hands as deputies clearly shows the powerful influence that local cattlemen exercised over the sheriff's office.

Littrell and his men did not go about their business half-cocked. In order to arrest Porter Stockton or any of his associates, they knew they needed a well-thought-out plan. However, when the appointed hour arrived, their carefully laid trap went awry. The *News and Press* reported, "The Sheriff's party had consulted Bassett, who was also a deputy sheriff, some hours previous in regard to making the arrests, and afterwards accused him of acting in bad faith to them; some unfriendly words were exchanged when Bassett pulled his pistol and shot Curtis in the side, and before Bassett could shoot again one of the other party fired at him with a rifle, shooting him through the lungs." Apparently Bassett sided with Stockton and his fellow outlaws and compounded that grievous error by taking on the three lawmen. He was knocked senseless by Curtis's shot. He regained consciousness, but died from his wounds the next day.[82] The *Santa Fe New Mexican* offered a vague explanation for the row, saying that Bassett was shot and killed by Curtis after Bassett shot Curtis from behind. The article said, "An old grudge was at the bottom of the matter. Curtis has since died of his wounds."[83] In fact, Zenas Curtis survived until 1957, dying at the age of one hundred.[84] (His life spanned from the era of cattle drives to the atomic age, and with the advent of television, he could even critique TV westerns.)

Eight days after the death of Harry Bassett, the *Las Vegas Daily Optic* carried an article from the *Trinidad Enterprise* which conclusively links Stockton to the shooting, although it fails to explain the nature of his role, saying, "Word comes up again that considerable excitement prevailed last night at Otero the cause being the Stockton-Bassett affair. Rumor says men are being stopped upon the streets by armed men and rigidly scrutinized, and that the excitement is liable to result in an outbreak. Evidently the Oteroites must have blood."[85]

I.W. Lacy passed through Otero just in time to learn about the trouble there. He had spent much of November on an excursion and tour of the Kansas City and Chicago stockyards along with other members of the Stockgrowers Association of Southern Colorado. The trip was sponsored by the Atchison, Topeka and Santa Fe Railroad, the Kansas City and Chicago Railroad, and other rail lines. Fred Harvey, who established the Harvey House chain of restaurants, personally rode with the cattlemen and saw to their every need. While Lacy was living the life of a well-to-do cattleman, Stockton was stealing, killing and fighting his way through life. But no matter how different the men were in station and character their fates were irrevocably bound together.[86]

After Harry Bassett's death, Stockton left Colfax County for good. He headed south to the area between Las Vegas and Santa Fe and settled in with his family at a place variously known as Baughl's Station and Baughl's Siding.[87] Baughl's was located on a spur off of the main rail line. It was the base of operations for a massive timber harvesting operation which centered near the impressive ruins of the ancient Spanish Colonial Pecos mission.[88] Timber was abundant and at times as many as eleven steam powered lumber mills were operating in the area.[89] Baughl's was the beehive, and throughout the immediate vicinity men were busy cutting down the area's plentiful ponderosa pines, piñons and junipers. Teamsters and their wagons were hauling logs and lumber to and from the mills to meet the needs of the NM&SP railroad and the surrounding area. The firm of Walsen and Levy of Walsenburg, Colorado planned on delivering one hundred thousand ties to the railroad and Major Woodworth contracted to deliver over fifteen hundred cedar telegraph poles to the Western Union Telegraph Company.[90] Almost a thousand men were harvesting, hauling and preparing the timber.[91] By March the town consisted of eighteen buildings, including two huge warehouses, and to meet the demand, a new hotel was under construction.[92]

The *Optic* noted, "there are quite a number of bad men in and about the town."[93] It also reported that as of March 3, 1880, Port Stockton was operating a saloon in the booming hamlet.[94] The *Optic's* circulation included readers in Colfax County, but the sheriff of that county had a limited desire to tempt fate. He was content to run Stockton out of his jurisdiction and Port operated his San Miguel County saloon with impunity. The town had a marshal, but in an April 18th letter to the *Optic* R.E. Lay wrote, "Since Marshal [J.T.] Brainard resigned the town has been overrun by drunken men shouting and yelling like fiends at nights."[95] Port's fuse was as short as ever and he was involved in yet another shooting scrape. An account of Port's travels at this time said the incident occurred at Glorieta (usually spelled Glorietta in the old newspapers), which was about ten miles down the main line toward Lamy. That account may be in error and it seems likely that Baughl's Station and perhaps even Port's saloon was the location of the shooting. Evidently, his aim was off and the victim survived. The *New Mexican* reported that not long after this shooting he turned up in Animas City.[96]

It was also in the spring of 1880 that the *Las Vegas Optic* carried news of the arrest of Porter and Ike's little brother, Samuel, after a chase of epic proportions. On March 13th, a herd of horses was stolen in Hardeman County, Texas, which at the time was attached to Clay County for judicial purposes.[97] Both counties border Oklahoma east of the Texas Panhandle. Samuel Stockton was about twenty-five years old and still plied his trade in Texas.[98] Sam was already a wanted man. In July or early August 1876 he and an associate robbed the stage that traveled the road between Fort Worth and Weatherford. Their take was sixty dollars cash and two horses belonging to W.R. Turner who owned the livery in Weatherford. In May 1877 he was captured and locked up in the Fort Worth jail.[99] He fled the area and his name soon appeared in the Texas Rangers' Black Book.[100] In the fall of 1879 he may have raided Eagle and Holstein's sheep ranch in Throckmorton County, stealing a gun and field glasses among other items. After stealing the herd of Hardeman County horses, Samuel and an accomplice headed west into the Texas Panhandle. They were later seen passing by the ranch of W.S. Curtis and J.C. Curtis near Clarendon. Shortly afterwards Stockton and the stolen horse herd passed through Charles Goodnight's JA Ranch near Amarillo. The stolen horses were the property of the Stevens and Worsham Ranch on the Pease River.[101] W.H. Smith, the ranch foreman, trailed the men across the Llano Estacado and into New Mexico.[102]

The horse thieves were finally cornered, apparently on the ranch owned by "Whiskey Jim" Greathouse and Fred Kuch.[103] The ranch was located about forty miles north of White Oaks on the road to Las Vegas, near the present day town of Corona. At the time, White Oaks was a mining boomtown and traffic was heavy between the two towns. During this period it seemed that every horse thief and desperado knew they could find food and a safe haven there. Billy the Kid, who was making good on his promise to live by stealing, used the services of Greathouse and his ranch.[104] The *Las Vegas Optic* reported that Smith came to Las Vegas and enlisted the aid of E.C. Taylor, J. Greathouse, Las Vegas Chief of Police Lloyd Jarrett, Frank Steward from the Texas Panhandle, and others. (The newspaper apparently misunderstood the role of J. Greathouse.) The men proceeded to what the newspaper cryptically called the *Oche de Mil Egre*. According to the *Optic*, they "arrested two of the gang - a brother of the Stockton boys, and Ike Stowe, who are now in jail and will be taken to

Texas." The *Optic* said, "Stockton upon being approached, opened fire upon his pursuers, but before doing any harm, was surrounded and caught."[105]

After a long delay in obtaining a requisition from Texas Governor Oran Milo Roberts, the prisoners finally left by train for Texas via rail lines that crossed Colorado, Kansas and Oklahoma. On June 10th, the *Optic* carried an article from the *Shield* of Henrietta, Texas, which said that Clay County Sheriff Craig and the two horse thieves had finally arrived from Las Vegas. The *Shield* identified the thieves as Ike Stowe and West Brown.[106] The article does not make it clear, but West Brown was evidently an alias of Samuel Stockton.

If Stockton and Brown were one in the same, young Samuel was an outlaw of the first order. According to the *Arkansas City Traveler*, West Brown was well known as a "hard character" in Kansas and the Indian Territory. He was involved in the murder of two stockmen named Stockstill and Henderson as well as committing a robbery in Chautauqua County, Kansas and was believed to have been involved in a bank robbery in 1878 in Cowley County, Kansas. After his return to Texas he was placed in the Clay County jail in Henrietta. On October 1, 1880 he broke jail and headed for the Indian Territory.[107]

The combination of Samuel Stockton's arrest and his most recent shooting scrape encouraged Port Stockton to look for a new safe haven. He didn't return to Otero. Not only was he most unpopular in Colfax County, but Otero's days were numbered. On May 30th, the *Las Vegas Optic* carried a dispatch from Otero which reported the community's impending doom, noting, "The town is moving away by degrees." Four businesses had already left town and the article announced the closure of Gentle Anna's Cottage: "Gentle Anna hies to Willow Springs, too [sic] look after the morals of that place." It pointed to the future saying, "There is a new town being laid out at Willow Springs. It is to be called Raton City."[108] Only two years after the railroad gave it a name, the wild and wooly town of Otero began to fade from existence.

It seems that Porter never returned to Colfax County after his move to Baughl's. His brother had found refuge along the Animas River. The Stockton brothers never parted ways for long, and Porter would inevitably join Ike in the San Juan country. At the time, northwest New Mexico was attracting stockmen and many others who had never been west of the Continental Divide. The D&RG Railroad had also set their sights on the high mountain mining country in southwest Colorado. The cattlemen saw what would become known as the Four Corners region as the last bastion of the open range. The influx of people, the extension of rail lines, and the rapid expansion of cattle herds was a surefire recipe for trouble.

Chapter Six

The Eskridge Boys

> *'Twas good to live when all the sod,*
> *Without no fence nor fuss,*
> *Belonged in partnership to God,*
> *The Government and us.*
> *With skyline bounds from east to west*
> *And room to go and come,*
> *I loved my fellowman the best*
> *When he was scattered some.*[1]

By 1879 the cattle industry was facing some major challenges. In the early days, Wash Cox, Irvin Lacy and other cattlemen could drive their herds from the shores of the Gulf of Mexico into Canada without seeing a fence. Closer to home they allowed their cattle to roam and let line riders limit grazing areas. As time went on, the uncontrolled use of open range created clashes between those who owned large herds and the small cattlemen, as well as between all of the cattlemen and farmers who sought to protect their crops. In August 1879, the *Cimarron News and Press* foretold the end of the open range. The article presciently noted,

> never since the first settlement of Colfax county has been such an exodus of cattle-raisers as there is likely to be this summer…The San Juan country which is not likely to have any railroad for years presents to the large cattle-growers of this country who immigrated from the vast prairies of Texas a more promising range for their favorite mode of grazing herds. The complaint they make against Colfax county is that the range is over stocked, with the prospect of becoming more so with each succeeding season. Men who have lived all their lives on the frontier, controlling for their long-horns an unlimited range, have no taste for the more systematic but equally remunerative mode of stock raising which the strong tide of immigration accompanying the railroad brings about.[2]

The article concluded by noting that stockmen in New Mexico are entering a new era when cattle will not be able to range "from one end of the country to the other" and "when stockmen must own their range and take care of their cattle."[3]

In June of 1879 the *Colorado Weekly Chieftain* gave another reason for the exodus from Colfax County, saying, "At last, after over nine years of ceaseless litigation the title to the famous Maxwell grant says the *Tribune* is settled." The owners of the grant were issued a patent for 1.7 million acres of prime real estate, which straddled the Colorado and New Mexico border.[4] Subsequent lawsuits would eventually be appealed all the way to the U.S. Supreme Court and their final decision in 1887 upheld the claims of the grant's owners. Some of the squatters who built homes on the grant obstinately refused to accept the 1879 land patent decision, but the writing was on the wall.[5] For those who took a realistic view, the San Juan country beckoned.

I.W. Lacy looked toward the west and followed the lead of his fellow cattleman and former Erath County and Colfax County neighbor, Wash Cox.[6] In 1877 Lacy and Luke Coleman opened a large slaughterhouse at El Moro near Trinidad. The D&RG shipped the dressed beeves to Denver where they were placed on new Anderson Refrigerator cars for shipment across the country.[7] In the fall of 1878 Lacy and Coleman parted company. Coleman moved to the Texas Panhandle and formed the Shoe Bar Ranch with Leigh Dyer, the brother-in-law of Charles Goodnight.[8] Goodnight was then operating the adjacent JA spread.[9] Goodnight had been ranching on the Arkansas River near Pueblo, Colorado, but sold out and moved to the Panhandle in 1876.[10] Some of Coleman's cattle still bore the legacy Lacy-Coleman brand with an LC on the side and an L on each hip, one right side up and one upside down. Coleman's Dutch cook described the brand as, "Hell up and Hell down and Hell C on the side."[11]

Like Coleman, Lacy preferred to operate in a partnership. He joined forces with Trinidad resident George W. Thompson. His new associate was well known in Colorado and New Mexico. Thompson was born in Hardin County, Tennessee on December 12, 1837 and was raised in Harrison County, Missouri. He came to Colorado in the wake of the Pike's Peak gold rush. His love of fast horses and horse trading resulted in a job training horses for Lucien Maxwell.[12] Lacy's new partner drew an inside straight when he married Guadalupe Bent, the widow of Alfred Bent, who was the son of Governor Charles Bent, the ill-fated first civilian American governor of the territory of New Mexico. Mrs. Bent-Thompson was appointed guardian to represent the interests of her minor children, the potential heirs to a substantial portion of the Maxwell Land Grant. The Bent heirs had a long running court battle with others who claimed their inheritance. The legal battle went all the way to the U.S. Supreme Court.[13] Not long after their marriage, the Thompsons moved to Trinidad and by 1873 George was serving a term as the sheriff of Las Animas County. It was a dicey occupation. A year earlier, Sheriff Juan Tafoya had been shot and killed in Trinidad's Exchange Saloon.[14] It was not long after Lacy and Coleman parted ways that forty-five-year-old Thompson joined forces with Lacy.

The men first moved their cattle to the San Juan country in the spring or summer of 1879 due to dry conditions around Cimarron and Trinidad.[15] The summer of 1879 was also exceedingly dry in Rio Arriba County. Streams around Tierra Amarilla dried up, as had most of the town's wells. Stockmen anticipated that they would lose many of their drought weakened livestock during the winter.[16] Range conditions were better on the Pacific side of the Continental Divide. Thompson and Lacy ran their cattle in the La Plata valley in both New Mexico and Colorado and their range extended into the Mancos and Dolores River valleys and across the line over to Blue Mountain in southeast Utah. In the terminology of the day, Lacy and Thompson were "heavy cattlemen." Their extensive herds required that they have several foremen. In the San Juan country their prime foreman was Henry Goodman.[17] The LC herd shared part of their range with John Reid, who had a substantial herd and owned the *Animas City Southwest*.[18] Despite Reid's extensive holdings, many believed that Lacy was the richest cattleman in the San Juan country.[19] Thompson and Lacy may have owned the largest herd of cattle in northwest New Mexico, although others gave that distinction to Wash Cox, who according to one report owned close to seven thousand head and who at one time refused an offer of $100,000 for his branded stock.[20]

Cattlemen from many areas cast covetous glances toward the Animas, San Juan and La Plata river drainages. One of those stock raisers was Lorenzo Dow Eskridge. Dow, as he was known, was a thirty-two-year-old stockman residing near Conejos, Colorado, just north of Cumbres Pass and south of present-day Alamosa. Dow's father, Jeremiah, fathered sixteen children, probably ten with his first wife Martha (also known as Mary) Marvel and six more with second wife Sarah. All of the children were born in Delaware. Fate would later lead two of Dow's young brothers to the San Juan country. Those two were Joshua Hargo, who was born in 1858, and Manlove Dison, who was born in the fall of 1859. Martha was their mother.[21] The names Stockton and Eskridge were fated to be forever linked as the younger Eskridge brothers and the Stockton brothers were destined to become the most notorious outlaws to trod the Animas River valley.

At the start of the Civil War, Dow Eskridge was about fifteen years old. In April 1865, the month that Lee surrendered to Grant, Dow joined Company F of the 215th Infantry Regiment of Pennsylvania. They were stationed at Fort Delaware. About three and a half months later, on July 31, 1865, the entire regiment was mustered out of the army.[22] Dow headed west and by 1870 was a farmer in Richland, Labette County, Kansas with assets valued at five hundred dollars.[23] By 1873 Dow had married a Missouri girl named Permelia Garrett. Shortly afterwards the recently wed couple set up their new home at the base of the Rockies in the southern end of the San Luis Valley. The rest of the Eskridge family stayed in

Delaware. In 1870 they lived in Broad Creek Hundred, Sussex County. During the 1870s Jeremiah fathered at least three children while he was in his sixties. It was most likely sometime after 1875 that Hargo and Dison (often spelled Dyson) decided it was time to leave Delaware. By the late 1870s they joined Dow in Colorado.[24] Dow and Permelia settled on the Conejos River, ten miles west of Conejos in 1874.[25] That same year, Permelia's father, Mancil Garrett, settled south of Alamosa in the La Jara meadows.[26] Traveling with the family was Permelia Eskridge's younger brother, James W. Garrett. Jim Garrett was born in Missouri on January 7, 1857.[27] When Dison and Hargo (who was sometimes known as Harg) arrived in the San Luis Valley, they found a steadfast friend when they met Jim Garrett. The young men hoped they might emulate the success of Dow Eskridge.

Dow had prospered as a cattleman and as he watched the dust of trail herds headed for Cumbres Pass, he developed a keen interest in the range land available in the San Juan country. By the summer of 1879 he made plans to send Dison and his brother-in-law, Jim Garrett, over the Great Divide. The plan was to establish another Eskridge herd in the vicinity of Farmington.[28]

Those plans were probably delayed due to trouble with the Ute Indians at the White River Agency in northern Colorado. On September 29, 1879 the Utes went on the warpath. Their wrath was brought on by the arrival of army troops onto their reservation and their testy relationship with the Indian agent, Nathan Meeker.[29] Ten agency employees and Meeker were killed.[30] Meeker's nude body was found with a log chain around his neck and a flour barrel stave driven through his mouth.[31] Major Thomas Thornburgh's forces were attacked on the same day at nearby Milk Creek and the Major himself was killed.[32] Mrs. Meeker, Mrs. Shadrick (Flora Ellen) Price and her two small children were taken away, along with the agent's twenty-three-year-old daughter, Josie Meeker.[33] The unknown fate of the captives made riveting headline news until they were finally rescued in the latter part of October.[34] Full details of the ordeal suffered by the women were not revealed until January 1880, when Mrs. Meeker disclosed that all of the women had been raped by their captors. This revelation would assure that bad blood between the Utes and white residents would not easily fade away.[35]

As citizens of the region learned of the incident, residents in towns throughout Colorado and the neighboring vicinity gathered to discuss the situation. Many communities formed safety committees. People living in the San Juan country, because of the substantial Ute population, were frantic. In early October, a dispatch to Colorado Governor Pitkin declared, "Bands of Utes out setting fires on the line between La Plata and San Juan. They say they will burn the entire country over." From the San Juan country Pitkin received this offer: "Silverton stands ready to furnish one hundred men at the call of the governor if the state will furnish arms and ammunition, to assist in moving every red cuss to the underground reservation. Timber is all a-fire for miles."[36] In Ouray the men spent several days cutting timber and erecting fortifications at Paff's toll gate one-half mile north of town.[37] The governor received an unconfirmed report from Alma, Colorado that the Utes had burned the town of Breckenridge to the ground.[38] Many of the dispatches coming into newspapers, the governor's office and military posts bore little resemblance to the truth. Nonetheless, the U.S. Army made a grand show of force to ward off any future problems. The army dispatched cavalry forces from New Mexico by train to Alamosa. Two separate trains arrived with men and supplies. Seven cars were needed to haul the horses.[39] A large force traveled onto the Animas River valley. On November 8th the *Dolores News* noted that, "Last week General Hatch was at Animas City...with his command of cavalry and infantry." The paper noted, "Col. [G.P.] Buell, from Fort Wingate, New Mexico, with three companies, has gone into camp at the mouth of Animas River, New Mexico."[40] Colonel Buell took command of six hundred soldiers at Animas City and oversaw the construction of Fort Flagler on lands just outside of town.[41] Nevertheless, it took several months for the Indian scare to subside. About four months after the Meeker Massacre, in January 1880, Dow Eskridge sent his brother, Dison, and Jim Garrett to Farmington.[42]

According to Dow, he provided the young men with close to five hundred head of cattle.[43] That was an impressive number, considering Dow's meager net worth only ten years before. Up until 1873 he had been eking out a living as a Kansas farmer. Dison and Jim Garrett were in all likelihood assisted with moving the cattle by several others, including Hargo and perhaps a young cowboy who called himself Tex Anderson. It is not totally clear if Tex was part of the group, but it is clear that he had the misfortune to arrive in the area at virtually the same time. If U.S. Census records accurately reflect the proximity of households in the area, their closest neighbor was Lew Coe on one side and W.H. Weatherwax on the other. What Weatherwax thought of the new arrivals is not known, but the sudden intrusion of Eskridge, Garrett and their cattle herd did not please Lew Coe. The Coes were loyal to their friends, but to cross them was to risk their vindictive wrath. Even if they had tried, Eskridge and Garrett could not have chosen a worse location to set up their ranch.[44] Two miles to the east was the nascent Farmington townsite. It was located on a flat low lying bench, well away from the green cottonwood lined river. The dusty, dry and treeless locale had two stores, a school house and seven or eight houses.[45] The Eskridge/Garrett ranch was on the Farmington side of the Coe place. Hargo probably stayed along the lower Animas for at least several weeks, helping Dison and Garrett to build their house, corral and other structures.

Jim Garrett's first cousin, Tom Fulcher, may have also driven cattle over the divide with Eskridge and Garrett. He moved from the San Luis Valley at very close to, if not the same time. Fulcher was a twenty-eight-year-old stockman and he settled in the San Juan River valley about four miles upstream from Farmington. His closest neighbor was Francis Marion Hamblet. Fulcher and Garrett had known each other since early childhood. In the 1860s both families lived close to each other in Salt River Township, Schuyler County, Missouri.[46] In 1873 Fulcher's family settled in Colorado, eight miles from Alamosa. The Garrett and Fulcher families were reunited when the Garrett family settled nearby in La Jara in 1874.[47]

The Garrett and Fulcher families were not the only lower Animas newcomers with ties to Schuyler County, Missouri. In the 1860s George Coe and his much older married cousin Lew Coe lived near the Garrett family in the Salt River Township. George Coe was two years older than Jim Garrett.[48] There is no evidence of ill will between the Coes and Tom Fulcher, but the enmity between the Coes and Jim Garrett appeared so suddenly that it may have originally germinated in Missouri. By association, the ill will between the Coes and Jim Garrett extended to the Eskridge brothers. Jap Coe, in a letter written about a year after Eskridge and Garrett appeared on the lower Animas, recalled their arrival this way; "About that time three or four noted cow thieves came from San Luis valley with a bunch of cattle, a portion of which they had stolen, and turned them loose on the range with others." According to Jap, of all the Coe men, only Lew Coe could be called a cattleman. He owned a modest herd of about 150 head, while the rest of "the Coe boys own but a few milch cows. They are farmers; what we have we have made by honest hard work, and can prove it by any man personally acquainted with us, except a thief." As for the Coes and cattle thieves he said, "I can say with impunity that we do not steal and will not countenance that class of men."[49]

Garrett and the Eskridge brothers were received with less than open arms along the lower Animas. Besides the perception that they were cow thieves, their cattle added to the competition for use of the fertile lands along the lower Animas. The open range was becoming crowded. The large, wide ranging cattle herds were also becoming an irritant to the Navajos, Utes and other Indian tribes. Thompson and Lacy did not help the situation. In 1880 they continued to move more cattle from the Trinidad area to the San Juan country. The *Santa Fe New Mexican* said, "Mr. Lacy has lately added about twenty-five hundred head of cattle to his already large herd, which are now grazing in the San Juan valley." The harsh winter had not materialized and Lacy reported that his cattle were "in splendid condition." The *New Mexican* advised its readers that, "the cattle of New Mexico came out fat and sleek." Lacy was trying to move the industry away from the open range. That spring he was in Santa Fe lobbying for a "lease law" which would require cattlemen to take up land

and fence it. As a cowman, Lacy was constantly striving for methods to improve his herd and effectively utilize the range. He believed frequent round-ups were "harassing and fat-destroying" and made the cattle "wild, lean and difficult to manage," which offset the advantages of New Mexico's mild climate.[50] In July 1880 the *Cimarron News and Press* noted, "Mr. I.W. Lacy made a ten strike by moving his cattle to the San Juan. The feed there has been luxuriant and cattle are now fat." Meanwhile in Colfax and Las Animas counties, the cattle range was deteriorating. Eastern slope ranchers like John Dawson, Manley Chase and Wilson South were contemplating moving their cattle due to lack of feed.[51] Later that summer South would serve as foreman of the Colfax County Grand Jury which indicted former Las Animas County Sheriff R.L. Wootton, Jr. for cattle theft. I.W. Lacy and his brother-in-law, M.V.B. Salyer, were the only witnesses against Wootton.[52]

Lacy would never find escape from cattle rustlers. Evidence suggests that he was considering a full time move to the San Juan country, but because of subsequent events we will never know his intentions. Along the Animas and elsewhere along the river bottoms of western Rio Arriba County there was increasing potential for conflict between the cattlemen and local farmers. By the summer of 1880, a large portion of the lands close to the Animas River were occupied. From the Cox Ranch near the Colorado line to the confluence of the Animas and San Juan Rivers, there were thirty-two ranches and farms on the east side of the Animas and thirty-four on the west side. Many of the farmers cultivated grain and some were raising a considerable amount of vegetables. A few set out fruit trees as well. The size of their cultivated areas varied from about fifteen to sixty acres.[53] The San Juan valley was seeing similar development. On a trip to Santa Fe, William Locke and W.C. (Bill) Parker of Farmington, and J. Schneider from Cañon Largo advised the *New Mexican* that sixty-seven families encompassing three hundred or more residents lived within a ten mile radius of the Animas and San Juan confluence.[54] It began to dawn on territorial officials that northwest New Mexico was becoming a population center. Hence, the legislature realigned the borders of Taos County and placed the area in Rio Arriba County. The county seat, Tierra Amarilla, was substantially closer than Taos. The transfer occurred on Feb. 10, 1880.[55] Two new precincts, designated as numbers nineteen and twenty, were formed in western Rio Arriba County. Wash Cox and William Locke were elected as the region's representatives to the territorial legislature.[56]

Like Wash Cox, William Locke was a highly respected resident of the area. Locke was a little older than many of the settlers pouring into northwest New Mexico. He was a thoughtful, caring man and an ardent community supporter. His mistreatment was critical to the outcome of the turmoil which would soon unfold in the San Juan country. Locke was born on October 20, 1839 in Michigan and raised in Indiana and Illinois. He came west during the Pike's Peak gold rush, reaching the Rocky Mountains in what was then Kansas Territory in 1860. Soon afterwards he settled near Cañon City in Fremont County.[57]

In September 1874, Locke married Henrietta (Nettie) Vaughan in Osage County, Missouri. Later that year he led a Vaughan family wagon train from Missouri to Florence, Colorado.[58] Like their new in-law, members of the Vaughan family were destined to become caught up in the San Juan country conflicts. Locke was elected to the Colorado Territorial legislature in 1867 and served as the probate judge for several years. Locke heard glowing reports coming from those who had moved to western Rio Arriba County. In the early autumn of 1878, the Lockes loaded their wagon and moved to Farmington, arriving on the 10th of October. He later purchased a squatter's claim from Wright Leggett for three ponies. (Locke is often credited as being the first resident to set out fruit trees on the lower Animas, thus starting what would become a huge part of the local economy until fruit growing began to wane in the 1950s.)[59] As a measure of respect, even after Locke moved to New Mexico, he was often referred to as Judge Locke.[60] While Locke and Wash Cox looked forward to serving in the territorial legislature, the two new Rio Arriba precincts were also designated to have a justice of the peace and a constable.[61] Justice of the peace was a misnomer, if ever there was one.

One of the JPs was Jimmy Carroll.[62] The Howe land claim, where George Coe was living, was directly across the Animas from James Carroll's place. Carroll's claim included the lands which now form the Aztec Ruins National Monument.[63] Mr. Carroll was a forty-six-year-old single farmer. The son of Irish immigrants was a native of New York.[64] He wasn't a blood relative to the Coes, but the family held him in high regard. They had first met Carroll in 1876 in Lincoln County. That meeting took place when Carroll was camped about two hundred yards from Frank's home on the Ruidoso. He was a recent arrival from California and his four horse team was resting and grazing nearby. Frank offered the use of his corral and warned him about Juan Gonzales and the horse thieves infesting the area. Carroll did not take Frank's advice and the next morning he found that he had only a two horse team.[65] The Coe men were gratified that Jimmy Carroll would represent the law in western Rio Arriba County.

John Cox would serve as constable for Uncle Jimmy.[66] John Shriver Cox was the twenty-two-year-old son of Wash Cox and he lived near his parent's place at Cedar Hill. The other justice of the peace was Hannibal H. Halford (sometimes spelled Holford and Hallford).[67] Halford was a native of Pennsylvania, born in about 1840. He lived in New Mexico during the Civil War and joined the Union forces. He was the first lieutenant and second in command in Captain William D. Simpson's Independent Company of Mounted Spies and Guides, an obscure outfit which consisted of forty-eight men. After the war he worked as a laborer in

Colfax County in the mining enclave of Elizabethtown.[68] Like many other Colfax County residents, Halford believed the San Juan country offered a better future. In the late 1870s he moved to the Animas River valley and settled about seven miles downstream from the Aztec Ruins, at Flora Vista. The area around his homestead was known as Halford Flats.[69] Halford's stormy tenure on the bench was destined to be short-lived.

As more newcomers settled in the river valleys, conflicts with the local cattlemen grew. Some residents began to file claims against the stockmen for damages to their crops caused by roaming cattle. The crop owners would not find relief in Jimmy Carroll's court, as he was firmly allied with the Coe family, but they soon found support from Justice of the Peace Halford. The farmers were taking advantage of the "herd law" in New Mexico which at that time, according to the *Dolores News*, "compels cattle men to keep their stock off of crops of grain etc."[70] The largest herd in western Rio Arriba County belonged to Wash Cox and Alf Graves. The claimants may have been ignorant about who they were taking on, but Justice Halford, who had spent most of the 1870s living in Colfax County, was not.

Halford's support of the farmer's scheme made him the focal point for the wrath of Cox, Graves and the smaller cattlemen like Lew Coe. Halford also allied himself with Hargo and Dison Eskridge and on at least one occasion they served as constables for his court. The alliance of the Eskridges and Halford sparked a smoldering fire and brisk winds were on the way.[71] Many of the cattlemen in northwest New Mexico believed the Eskridge brothers were gathering up cattle and driving them into Colorado.[72] A large number of the stolen cattle were bound for the burgeoning mining camps of southwest Colorado, foremost among those destinations was Rico in the Dolores River valley. Initially, the cattlemen planned to arrest the stock thieves and seek justice through the courts, but the stockmen's faith in the court system would prove to be weak. For a variety of reasons, the conditions in western Rio Arriba County were ripe for the birth of vigilantes. Geographically, the area was isolated; it was a three day ride to the county seat, and a five or six day journey to the territorial capital. In addition, the rapid influx of population, especially an increase of undesirable elements, added fuel to the fire. To make matters worse, the close proximity of Colorado's protective jurisdictional boundary exacerbated the situation as hostilities evolved into widespread lawlessness. In an 1881 letter, Jap Coe does not identify Tex Anderson by name, but describes him as "a bold, daring cow thief and murderer." Jap noted that Tex's arrival along the Animas occurred simultaneously with the appearance of the Eskridge brothers and Jim Garrett.[73] Coe does not firmly link Tex with the Eskridge boys, but given their concurrent arrival coupled with the sudden spate of missing cattle, it appears that Tex was part of their operation. While the Eskridge brothers had a large number of relatives in the San Luis Valley, Tex had no nearby relatives. He was a newcomer with few friends and on top of that he was already being sought for crimes committed in Colorado. Anderson's dearth of kith and kin did not bode well for the young cattle rustler.

According to George Coe "the local stockmen" decided to arrest the rustlers. However, he then says that only he and John Cox made the arrest.[74] In northwest New Mexico, the cattleman who had the most to lose from rustlers was Wash Cox and he was not one to send out just one of his sons and George Coe to arrest a group of cattle thieves. In a subsequent letter, Lew Coe clearly implicates himself as being one of the leaders of the group who were after the cattle thieves and it seems likely that his small herd had been raided.[75] Those who rode over to the La Plata probably included Wash Cox's oldest son George, as well as John and perhaps their teenaged brother Jim. If Wash Cox was not there, the de facto leader of the Cox faction was his son-in-law Alf Graves. There were probably four Coe men riding to the La Plata that day; Lew, Frank and Jap, as well as George. Some of Cox's hired hands and the neighboring cattlemen added additional firepower. After reaching the La Plata, the men scoured the valley and apprehended the rustler known as Tex Anderson. The men secured their prisoner and headed out for a long, tense ride over the divide to the Animas valley.[76]

The March 13, 1880 issue of the *Dolores News*, under a headline of "A Little Hell in New Mexico," and with a dateline of Flora Vista, N.M. reported, "A man called 'Tex' was arrested here a few days ago, on a charge of stealing horses."[77] Given the testy relationship between the Coes and Hannibal Halford, it is clear that Tex Anderson was arraigned before Justice of the Peace Jimmy Carroll.[78] There are two stories about what happened in court. According to the *News*, Anderson was "Unable to give bonds."[79] However, according to a letter written by C.H. McHenry, "Anderson (alias Fox) was proven guilty of stealing before a Bogus Court he offered good bail, but was refused."[80] McHenry was confused about Anderson's alias and whatever his actual name, his fate was sealed. The Coes' favorite jurist bound Anderson over to district court for trial and assigned three special officers to transport him to the jail in Taos. It seems likely that John Cox was one of those special officers. From their years living in the Cimarron country, the Cox and Coe families were familiar with the justice, or the lack thereof, delivered by the courts in Taos County. Their cattle were disappearing on a steady basis and they feared that a jury might not hear the matter for several months. In the end, it was the incessant impotence of the New Mexico judicial system which finally tipped the scales against Tex Anderson. As Tex and his guards rode out, a large group of men had already gathered on the route. The *Dolores News* reported, "When but a few miles on their road fifteen masked men halted them, took the officers' arms from them, and took the prisoner, whose whereabouts is not known at present writing." The print was still being set up when the paper learned from the *Animas City Southwest* that Tex, who was also known as W.M. Anderson, was now the victim of an "atrocious murder."[81]

Tex had been hung from a cedar tree south of the San Juan River. The lynching occurred across the river from where fifty-seven-year-old, Illinois native Joe Crouch ran his cattle on the mesa between the Animas and San Juan Rivers. The mesa now bears his name. Forty-five-year-old cow woman Mary Jane Adams, who would later marry Joseph Crouch, was searching for strays when she stumbled upon the vigilantes and their hapless victim. She hid from view and witnessed the lynching.[82] As the members of the lynching bee rode away, they followed normal frontier protocol and left Anderson's limp body dangling from the tree. C.H. McHenry in a letter dated spring 1881, reported that it was a few days later that the victim "was found hung by the neck." Either the men who decorated the cedar tree knew they were being watched or Jane Adams told the wrong person. McHenry noted that soon after the lynching, "Mr. Crouch and a Mrs. Adams were ordered to leave the County under pain of death."[83] While McHenry's letter supports the claim that Jane Adams witnessed the lynching, his other assertion appears to be incorrect. Census records from June of 1880 show that Crouch and Adams continued to live along the lower Animas a full three months after Tex was strung up.[84]

The specter of Anderson's body blowing in the breeze served its purpose as the vigilante's thundered message echoed its way through the mesas, valleys and mountains of the San Juan country. The *Dolores News* said that it had learned "Anderson was a man who kept a plurality of guns, and for the purpose of bulldozing and intimidation, and a man who made numerous, (as termed by himself) 'gun plays.' "[85] While the Coe family would absorb the brunt of the blame or the credit for the lynching, it may have never happened without the tacit approval of Wash Cox.

Shortly after Anderson's lynching, Lew Coe wrote a letter to the *Dolores News* which said, "It has lately become necessary to hang a man to create a sensation here. There was a cow thief hanged here a short time ago, for stealing a yoke of oxen." The owner of the yoke of oxen was Peter Fox, a thirty-one-year-old native of Germany. It is unclear why the first *Dolores News* article said Anderson was charged with stealing horses and no matter whether he was stealing range cattle, work cattle, horses or all three, Tex Anderson was dead. Prior to his death, some of the local residents recognized Anderson as an outlaw they knew as Charles Smith. Of course, that also sounds suspiciously like an alias name. Coe noted that Smith had stolen a horse in Fort Griffin, Texas and then showed up in the area around Chalk Creek in Chaffee County, Colorado where he murdered a man and this led to his exodus to the San Juan country. At the time, many former residents of the area around Chalk Creek and the Arkansas River valley lived along the lower Animas and San Juan Rivers. It's likely that Anderson traveled due south to Buena Vista, crossed over Poncha Pass and continued south to the Eskridge home country on the southern edge of the San Luis Valley before crossing the divide into the Chama River valley. Coe noted, "Had not some of our people apparently known something of his past record, he probably might have escaped the rope for his last and smallest criminal offense." Coe defended the lynching and then pointed the finger of blame at himself by providing the newspaper with a copy of a letter, which he said was "taken from the hanged man's pocket."[86] The letter was signed by Allie Anderson. Miss Anderson was about fourteen years old when she wrote the letter.[87] Tex may have been a murderer and cow thief, but he was not without feelings as he had been holding Allie's letter for over six months. Its heading says, "Chalk Creek, Chaffee, Co., Col., June 8, 1879."[88] Young Allie lived in Chalk Creek with her seventeen-year-old sister, who was named Bell, her thirteen-year-old brother, two step-siblings, her mother, stepfather, three German-born carpenters and her seventy-year-old widowed grandmother, Elizabeth Tull.[89] Her mother, Margaret Anderson, married Charles Nachtrieb in 1871, when Allie was seven years old. Mr. Nachtrieb was a mover and shaker in Chaffee County, and the village of Nathrop is the badly bungled version of his name.[90] Allie's boyfriend, whatever his real name was, had appropriated her last name as his alias. The school girl's missive is a heartfelt love letter written in the melodramatic style of the time and it supports Lew Coe's allegations. In part, Allie says:

> I have received two letters from you, but ma told me to-day that I should never write to you, but I can write you this letter without her knowing it...I just received your last letter-it is in my bosom now, next to my heart....O, I never, never suffered so in my mind in my life, as I have since you killed that man; to think the only man I ever loved, has the stain of a man's blood on his soul. O, Bill, I have prayed for you, have prayed that we may be happy as we were again; but it can never be...Everyone says around here it is nothing for you to kill a man, it hurts me awfully to hear them talk so about my darling...Bill, you know you done wrong to go in that saloon. I have no doubt but that the man you killed meant to rob you, for the Sheriff of Park Co. was after the very man. He and two other fellows robbed the coach three times. He was a coach-robber in Texas. There was a $1,500 reward for him, dead or alive. The Sheriff caught the others and found him dead in Granite. But there is more of them yet that would like to get you... I am glad to hear you have found a good place to work. I hope you will do well and learn to be a better boy...There was a letter came here for you some time ago; it is from some of your folks, I will send it to you

now. Bill you have one good friend up here, and that is Ed. He told me everything you told him to, and is very anxious to hear from you. I never told him I heard from you; no one knows it but ma and B...Bill try to be a better boy. You are so young you could do lots of good in this world if you try. You may think me very foolish giving you advice, when you are six years older than I am...Bill, when you have your picture taken send it to me. I went up to the cabin the other day. I saw your violin hanging upon the wall, and I said to E., I wonder if Bill will ever play his violin again...I measured and weighed, yesterday. I measure five feet three inches, and weigh 122 pounds...If I never see you again I will always think the same of you - you will always be the same little Billy to me. All alone you have gone and left me, and no other's bride I'll be, for tonight I am a widow,
  Allie Anderson[91]

 Young Allie was only projecting her widow status, since she felt she would never love again. It's not known if she ever found out what happened to "little Billy."
 Wash Cox clearly supported the arrest of Tex Anderson and he may have supported the lynching, but he was shrewd enough to not take credit for either act. He knew when to be quiet. The Coes on the other hand did not know when to shut up. By their continual verbose denunciations of cow thieves, public perception elected them as the leaders of the necktie social. The murder of Tex Anderson combined with Frank and George Coe's reputations from Lincoln County gave them a notoriety that was not beneficial to them or their families. The lynching of Tex Anderson pitted the Coe family and Eskridge family against one another and Hargo Eskridge's reputation would soon match that of George and Frank Coe as he would prove to be one of their most formidable enemies.
 Throughout much of 1880 Hargo lived in southern Colorado. One of his favored locales was the "Dolores carbonate camp," as Rico was called. Despite its distance from the scene of the action, Rico and several of its residents figure prominently in the chaos that stretched from the lower Animas to Silverton and beyond in 1880 and 1881. The mining town hangs on a narrow shelf, in a spectacular setting, high up in the Dolores River canyon at an elevation of 8800 feet. As the crow flies it was only about thirty-five miles from present day Durango. Travelers leaving Animas City went up the Animas about fifteen miles to the Rico House. From there they followed the Silverton wagon road for about ten miles to the Frank Williams's and Rees Riley's ranches where the Pinkerton trail began. This was the end of the line for wagons, and supplies were loaded onto pack animals for the trip to Rico. The trail eventually topped out on the Animas River/Dolores River divide and then dropped into Scotch Creek which

flows into the Dolores about four miles below Rico. The total distance between Animas City and Rico was forty-five miles.[92] Winter snow pack closed this trail from December to mid-May.[93] Rico could also be reached by skirting around the western end of the La Plata Mountains to the Big Bend of the Dolores and then upriver from there. The mining camp was 110 miles from Animas City via this route.[94] During the summer months many people from Farmington and nearby areas spent time prospecting in the Dolores Canyon. In the spring of 1880 Rico had a population of about nine hundred people, which was close to five times the population of Animas City.[95]

The brawling boomtown's growth was fueled by deposits of silver. In the early days the gambling houses ran twenty-four hours a day, a mighty feat considering supplies had to be hauled in on the backs of burros. D.J. Shaw, a well-known San Juan freighter, ran a pack train of sixty jacks between Cascade Hill and Rico. When the trails were open the arrival of pack trains was a daily occurrence.[96] The mountainsides of the trails leading to Rico echoed with the hee-haw of jackasses and the imaginative profanities of their masters. While crossing deep streams, a burro's ears had to be tied up or it would be drowned. The overloaded little animals were pulled across the creeks by rope and once safely on the other side their ears were untied and their relieved and exultant voices filled the air. The hardy beasts of burden were known to take nasty falls of two hundred feet or more and survive, often saved by a snow bank or a mountain marsh or stream. Reverend George Darley of Lake City, who traveled throughout the San Juan Mountains in the late 1870s said, "Where a burro and a 'burro-puncher' cannot go, no other creature need try."[97]

Some of Rico's desperadoes received rough treatment as well. The *Dolores News* reported in October of 1879 that a thief named "Scarfaced Dan" was tried before a citizen's committee and banished from the camp with a warning never to return. The next day, after an open air church service performed by Reverend Roberts of Silverton, "Scarfaced Dan's" possessions were auctioned off by Sheriff Reilly with the proceeds going to his victim. That was followed by a horse race, the purse having been gathered up during the preceding church service.[98]

The prospectors and miners were a rugged lot and Reverend Roberts was not the only preacher roaming the San Juan country trying to save souls. One of the most memorable characters rambling through the mining camps was a dedicated frontier parson named C. Montgomery Hoge. Reverend Hoge had traveled over the Rico trail in October 1879 with hopes of establishing an Episcopal Church.[99] In May 1880, friends of Hoge purchased a forty by sixty foot tent to be used to hold services.[100] The parson was a reformed gambler and comfortable in any setting.[101] He was well known for his frequent forays into the dens of iniquity: saloons, dance halls and gambling parlors. He was not a "militant crusader" and was welcome in the camp. One Sunday, Brownie Lee, a well-known gambler and supporter of the parson, lent his assistance by going up and down the street announcing the upcoming sermon and asking the immoral lairs to close up for the occasion. The idea caught on and soon residents streamed toward the meeting place. As Charles Jones recalled, "almost literally the whole population went to the tent, dance hall girls, faro dealers, poker players, miners, merchants, freighters, 'bull-whackers.' " The tent was too small to hold the crowd, so the sides were raised up and the citizenry sat inside and outside of the walls.[102] Lake City's Reverend Darley reported that often the rowdy crowds were more generous with their donations than his more refined congregations.[103] The method of collection had something to do with that. As Jones recalled, "Brownie took charge of the collection, appointing 'Broke-Nose Dick Simms' and 'Sourdough Sam' to help." Both voluntary and involuntary collections were made. Brownie took up the money in his large hat, carefully inspecting the amount given by each donor. If the amount did not meet with his approval he cajoled the recalcitrant contributor, pointedly telling them to "raise the ante, for Christ's sake."[104] When the service was over, the parishioners wished the preacher well and resumed their revelry. Reverend Hoge would later play a role in the saga of Ike Stockton as well as found the Episcopal Church in Durango.[105]

About a month before Hoge's first tent service, Frank Hartman and Charles Adam Jones became the owners of Rico's newspaper the *Dolores News*.[106] The neophyte newsmen would play prominent roles as events ramped up in the new towns that dotted the Animas River valley. Hartman was born in Decatur County, Iowa on October 24, 1858. He came to Del Norte, Colorado in 1873 with his parents, Mr. and Mrs. George W. Hartman. In Del Norte he apprenticed for John Cochran, owner of the *Del Norte Prospector*.[107] In 1876 the Hartman family moved to the lower Animas and lived about three miles east of what is now downtown Farmington. This location was within a mile of Lew Coe's place.[108] They may have lived near their relative, Ellen Louisa Wilkinson.[109]

Hartman's partner, Charles Jones, was born in Stamp Creek in Georgia, about twelve miles from Cartersville, on April 21, 1861. Just nine days before, the opening salvo of the Civil War was fired at Fort Sumter. His father joined the Confederacy and his mother died when he was not yet two years old. For the remainder of the war, he was cared for by his slave "mammy," whom he knew as Aunt Eliza. Jones and his two young siblings (none older than four at the time of their mother's death) ended up as refugees when General Sherman's army overran Georgia. Aunt Eliza, with the three Jones children in her care, made her way to Tuskegee, Alabama, where Jones's father finally found them. Aunt Eliza's sense of duty and dedication to the children of her enslaver is profound and a testament to her humanity, even as the dominating culture sought to take it away. In his early teens Jones worked at the *Rome Courier*, where he learned to set type. In 1875 the family moved to Kansas City, Missouri. Jones spent about two years in Missouri.[110]

In early 1878 he hauled cattle for Dave Mastin by train from Missouri to Colorado. At every stop Jones and three fellow cowboys would prod the animals with poles so they would not lay down. He was now a true cow poke. That spring and summer he worked on Mastin's T-Heart Ranch on Carrizo Creek in southeast Colorado for $15 a month. The low wages contributed to his decision to move to the San Juan country in September, 1878. He was then seventeen years old. Jones made his way to Wagon Wheel Gap and over the divide to Howardsville. He traveled onto Silverton, where he did odd jobs for the Silver Producing Mining Company for several months. Eventually he became a full-fledged miner, working the hammer and drill, with the double faced hammer weighing six and a half pounds. It was a dangerous proposition to hold the drill while breaking in a new man. At only 120 pounds soaking wet, Jones had to put everything into his swing. Somehow he managed to not mangle his partner's fingers, hands or wrists. Jones recalled that they loaded the holes with "Giant" powder, No. 1 or No. 2 depending on what strength was needed. In cold weather, the miners often kept the powder in their boots to keep it from freezing solid. Many dispensed with crimpers and used their teeth to secure the cap to the fuse. The pay was $3.50 per day, less $1.00 a day for board at the mine boarding house at the mouth of the tunnel.[111]

In the spring of 1879 the mine's owners were unable to pay wages and Jones found himself in a tight spot but found employment as a printer for Silverton's *La Plata Miner*. In the fall, John R. Curry, the owner of the *Miner*, started a new newspaper in Rico. He hired Jones and Hartman as printers for the new weekly. Their press was a primitive Washington hand press which could be disassembled for transport. It still required a fearless pioneering freighter to haul it in through the rugged mountainous terrain of the San Juans. In April 1880, Hartman and Jones purchased the operation from Curry.[112]

That spring, the fledgling newspapermen fudged their ages in the 1880 census; twenty-one-year-old Hartman claimed he was twenty-four, and nineteen-year-old Jones claimed to be twenty-three.[113] Jones characterized his education as "sketchy," but the contents of the newspaper indicate an education more than sufficient for success in life.[114] Hartman was enterprising and educated as well, but the pair lacked the seasoning and mature judgment that comes with age and experience. Their choice of friends led them astray and could have easily destroyed their lives. Ownership and total editorial control of a newspaper would prove to be a risky proposition. The peril developed because Hartman despised the Coe family.[115] The origins of the bad blood are unknown, but Hartman's ill will would remain fierce. The conflict may have begun soon after Lew Coe settled a mile below the Hartman place near Farmington.[116] Young Hartman was a fighting Irishman, with a quick and often violent temper.[117] He was not one to forgive and forget. He would use his newspaper position to vent his anger and to taunt the Coes and their allies. Hartman arrived in Rico with a deep animosity toward the Coe men and under his influence Jones eagerly took up the gauntlet. The two young newspapermen were not mere reporters of the facts; the *Dolores News* became the strident mouthpiece for a group of desperadoes led by Ike Stockton. Their articles and editorials contributed to the pandemonium that engulfed the San Juan country in 1880 and helped extend the turmoil that lasted until the fall of 1881. In later years, editions of the *News* were carefully preserved, making the writings of Hartman and Jones a major source of information on the early history of the San Juan country. However, when it comes to Ike Stockton and the Coe family, the accounts in the *News* must be viewed with more than a healthy dose of skepticism.

Charles Jones, co-editor of the pro-Stockton Dolores News, *ca. early 1880s. Jones operated the* News *until 1886. He later became the manager of the massive Spur Ranch in the Texas Panhandle. His son Clifford, who was born in Rico, became the president of Texas Tech College (now Texas Tech University.)*
(Photo courtesy of Southwest Collection, Special Collections Library, Texas Tech University, Lubbock, TX, Clifford B. Jones Collection, No. CAJ Charles A.)

Frank Hartman's relative, Ellen Wilkinson, was a widow who was among the first settlers on the lower Animas. Ellen and her family were destined to be at the center of the Stockton and Coe storm brewing in the San Juan country. Her brother, Al Puett, along with William Hendrickson and others, had been among the earliest settlers in the newly opened portion of northwest New Mexico.[118] Ellen came from a well-known Indiana family. Her mother's brother, Joseph Wright, was a former governor and U.S. senator from Indiana, as well as Minister to Berlin during the Lincoln administration. Her first husband Mahlon Wilkinson was a man with a promising future. In the early 1860s he was Indian agent on the upper Missouri at Fort Union. He was later Register of the U.S. Land Office in Vermillion, Dakota Territory. He was working as an attorney in Washington, DC when he died in about 1870. After Mahlon's death, Ellen moved to the Wet Mountain Valley (near present day Westcliffe, Colorado) with her father, who purchased a large stock ranch. Her brothers Al and Austin Puett probably also moved to the Wet Mountain Valley at the same time.[119] After moving to the lower Animas, Ellen did not stay long before moving upriver to Animas City. On March 16, 1877, Judge Amos Johnson presided over the marriage of the widow Wilkinson to Simeon Hendrickson at the residence of the bride in Animas City. It was one of the earliest recorded marriages in La Plata County.[120] Ellen brought at least two children to the marriage, including Bert Wilkinson who was then fifteen years old.[121] The lack of a father during his youth contributed to the development of Bert's wild side as he passed through his teen years. As is often the case, Bert and his new stepfather did not get along.[122] After the marriage, he continued to live on the lower Animas with his uncle, Austin Puett.[123] During this period, Bert made the acquaintance of the Eskridge brothers and Jim Garrett.[124] All of the young men would soon become caught up in events they could not control and that would exact a heavy toll on the Wilkinson and Puett families.

The establishment of an army post in the La Plata River valley and the subsequent demand for a large quantity of beef for the garrison was one of those events. It was in the spring or summer of 1880 that the U.S. Army finalized plans to establish a permanent facility in southwest Colorado. The fort's establishment was a huge economic boon to the area and residents on both sides of the border were thrilled. Frontier residents also turned to army forts for medical help, protection from Indians, and to help maintain law and order. Residents eagerly bid on the wide variety of contracts posted by the army. Providing beef to frontier army posts was generally viewed as a lucrative business. In the San Juan country, Fort Lewis became the prize. The first Fort Lewis was established at Pagosa Springs That location was shortlived.[125] In 1879 General Phil Sheridan inspected the region and ordered the fort to be moved closer to the Navajo Reservation.[126] The new location was on the west side of the La Plata River about eighteen miles north of the New Mexico border and about fifteen miles west of Animas City. The site was on a wide area of flat ground above but close to the river, and it featured a breathtaking view of the usually snowcapped La Plata Mountains. However, the establishment of this new fort was delayed by the Meeker Massacre and, even after the scare was over, the army abandoned Fort Flagler at Animas City and moved back to their fort at Pagosa.[127]

In the middle of August the *Animas City Southwest* reported, "Gen. Pope, Gen. Bingham, Dr. Wright, Col. Cappinger, Major Dunn, Capt. Valkmar, Lieut. Evans, Lieut. Guilfoyle, Capt. Ruffner and Gen. Pope's two sons, with an escort of soldiers passed through town last Monday on their way to inspect the site for the proposed new military post." The article said Lieutenant Colonel Robert E.A. Crofton and companies A, B, C, D, and E of the 13th Infantry had been "ordered to the Mancos to establish a cantonment on the site selected." However, after looking over the Mancos, General Pope decided on putting the new fort in the La Plata valley.[128] By September 25th the *Dolores News* noted that Crofton was on the La Plata and was "rapidly preparing for the erection of the buildings, and is accumulating his supplies for winter quarters."[129]

One of the Fort's first beef suppliers was George West.[130] Prior to that, John and Charles Pearson provided beef to the six hundred troops stationed at Fort Flagler.[131] The livestock business was profitable despite the paltry prices paid for cattle, which hovered around five cents per pound on the hoof.[132] West hired a herder he described as a light skinned "Texas Nigger" known as Kid Thomas.[133] Besides herding West's cattle, he also cut out the beeves to be slaughtered by the post's butcher.[134] Thomas's duties eventually led to his acquaintance with the Eskridge brothers, Bert Wilkinson and Ike Stockton.[135] Feeding the soldiers at Fort Lewis made it the largest user of cattle in the region and the source of beef for the army was the subject of much contention.[136] If stolen cattle were slaughtered at the Fort, then legally owned cattle were spared and could be sold elsewhere. Several cattlemen would hold the Fort's beef contract over the next few months, not all of them with questionable ethics. The contractor had to keep a large and steady supply of cattle in the La Plata valley. With its sparse population, those animals became the tempting target for thieves.[137] While Fort Lewis was the largest single user of beef, other markets were readily available. The thieves were well aware of mining camp butchers and others who were willing to pay a reduced price for stolen stock. The population boom associated with the extension of the Denver and Rio Grande Railroad would soon create a new and prodigious demand for beef. Looking back on this time from the 1930s, one New Mexico pioneer woman noted that some highly respected citizens "got their start fifty or more years ago by rustling."[138] The role of George West in the criminal cattle trade is unclear, but he would survive and thrive, despite suspect associations made during this time period. Some of his contemporaries were not so fortunate. The activities of Kid Thomas, the Eskridge brothers, Bert Wilkinson, and Ike Stockton would lead to the violent deaths of three of them before the end of 1881.

Before that happened, a newcomer well-acquainted with violent deaths would move into the San Juan country. While the Coes enjoyed their feared status after the lynching of Tex Anderson, they were about to be dethroned as the biggest bullies on the Animas. The new arrival, his notorious reputation already established in Texas and on both sides of the Colorado/New Mexico border, was familiar to many of the San Juan country's recent arrivals. For the rest, it wouldn't take long before William Porter Stockton introduced himself in his usual, brutish manner.

A familiar sight in the San Juan Mountains. "Colorado.- Incidents of a Trip To the Mining Town Durango," Frank Leslie's Illustrated Newspaper, *May 28, 1881, artist J.J. Reilly. (Author's collection.)*

Chapter Seven

Marshal Stockton

> *So the trail it led him southward all the day,*
> *Through the shinin' country of the thorn and snake,*
> *Where the heat had drove the lizards from their play*
> *To the shade of rock and bush and yucca stake.*
> *And the mountains heaved and rippled far away*
> *And the desert broiled as on the devil's prong,*
> *But he didn't mind the devil if his head kept clear and level*
> *And the hoofs beat out their clear and steady song.*[1]

About the time that Tex Anderson was being lynched, Porter Stockton was wearing out his welcome at Baughl's Siding after adding one more shooting victim to his name.[2] It was also close to this time, in March 1880, that Ike Stockton traveled to Colfax County. Ike may have detoured through the county on his way to help Port and his family move to the San Juan country. He may also have been on his way to pick up stolen horses from his brother Samuel Stockton, but those plans were derailed when Samuel was arrested. Whatever his intent, Ike's presence was soon relayed to I.W. Lacy's friend, Sheriff Pete Burleson, who still held two warrants for Ike's arrest. Once again Burleson rounded up a posse and set out in pursuit of one of the Stockton brothers, but Ike proved to be as elusive as Porter had been the year before. On March 26th Burleson requested reimbursement for expenses, advising territorial officials: "having been informed that said [Isaac] Stockton was in the county and one of the leaders of an armed band of outlaws threatening violence of peacible [sic] citizens, and that I found it necessary to take with me an armed force of eight men who traveled with me and under my direction 15 days at an average of 30 miles a day." He requested $315 to cover posse costs.[3] Ike was not welcome in Colfax County and soon returned to his home in the Animas valley. He was probably accompanied by Port, his wife, and their three daughters, Sarah, Mary and baby Carrie.[4]

The territorial press had a well-developed interest in the whereabouts of Porter and Ike Stockton, and the location of George Coe and his cousin, Frank Coe, elicited the same curiosity. Editors knew that where they went, trouble followed. Under the headline "Lincoln Refugees," the April 26, 1880 edition of the *Santa Fe New Mexican* noted:

> It now appears that the worst characters who flourished in the days of outrages in Lincoln and Colfax counties and who have been

driven out of those counties, have congregated in the extreme northwest of the Territory, in the San Juan country, in the new part of Rio Arriba county. Among them are Geo. W. Cole [sic], indicted for murder in Lincoln county, and his brothers; Porter Stockton, indicted for murder and other offenses in Colfax county, and his brother, and a number of other well known desperadoes. They are driving out the peaceful citizens who have been farming along the fertile valleys in that section, and attempt to overawe all officers of the law. Means are being taken which it is hoped will bring them to justice.[5]

The article indicates that Port first settled on the lower Animas. However, another *New Mexican* article said that after the shooting in Glorieta, "He then made his way to Animas City." Port may have stayed briefly with his brother on the lower Animas, but he and his family soon moved north of the border to Animas City.[6] The *New Mexican's* coverage of the San Juan country was hit or miss and much of the news they carried came from visitors to the capital city who dropped into the newspaper's offices. The Tex Anderson lynching, coupled with the arrival of Port Stockton, were probably the impetus for some local citizen to visit the *New Mexican*. Perhaps William Locke and Bill Parker, who had been in Santa Fe a month earlier, mentioned the arrival of the Stocktons and Coes during their visit.

Stockton's appearance in the San Juan country coincided with an alarming rise in tension between the Coe and Eskridge families. Proceedings in Judge Halford's court became the centerpiece of their dispute. There are several accounts of armed standoffs and looming violence during Halford's tenure on the bench. None of the accounts are definitively dated, so it is impossible to know whether they refer to the same event or to one or more other incidents. In one case the *Dolores News* reported that Judge Halford appointed Dison and Hargo Eskridge and a third man as special constables for one session of the court because on prior occasions the witnesses, claimants and the judge were bulldozed by armed men. Halford's alliance with the Eskridge brothers was just one more act which would bring his judicial career to an end. When the time for court arrived, the Eskridge boys stood at the entrance and disarmed all of the spectators. Several men refused and they were barred from entering the court. They remained outside but did not leave. After the proceedings, arms were returned to those who had given them up and everyone went outside. Those who had remained outside began to threaten the Eskridge brothers and the other constable.[7] Hargo Eskridge, in a letter to the *Animas City Southwest*, recalled "a party of fifteen men, including George Brown, undertook to release some prisoners which my brother Dison and myself were holding as officers attending on court. They failed, and finally put up their guns, shook hands and made it up - all except George Brown and a man named Myers."[8] "Myers" was Frank Meyers, who at the time was trying to hone his reputation as a tough customer and gunman. George Brown was the son of pioneering resident John W. "Doc" Brown and his wife Hattie.[9]

Friction between the Coe forces and the Eskridge forces reached the point of no return in late April or early May. The seizure of two mules proved to be the flashpoint event that caused violence to spiral out of control in the San Juan country. As the spring weather warmed, Halford's support of the farmer's claims against the cattlemen continued. He was either exceedingly brave or exceedingly dense. The two mules in question belonged to a nearby neighbor of Dison Eskridge and Jim Garrett named Otto Henry Hanson. Hanson was a twenty-eight-year-old native of Germany, who was commonly known by his middle name. Halford ordered the seizure of the mules to satisfy a $40 debt claimed by Bill Parker, who had probably only recently returned from his trip to Santa Fe with William Locke. According to a letter written by Hanson and printed in Silverton's *La Plata Miner*, the claimant was "a bosom friend" of Squire Halford. Hanson wrote that on "the day appointed for an 'Impartial Trial,' the jury assembled, also Parker, Hanson and friends, and after waiting a long time for the appearance of the so called Justice of the Peace Halford, information was received that Halford had left the country before daylight that morning, taking with him the Bonds and one of the Bonded mules, (having previously donated the other to his 'pard' Parker,) since which time he has had no desire to return and resume his duties."[10] (Parentheses are in original article.) The friends of Hanson included George, Frank and Jap Coe, Frank Meyers, and George Brown.

Hanson's letter also takes to task the *Dolores News,* and although Hanson doesn't mention him by name, he makes a veiled stab at Frank Hartman. Hanson noted that the anonymous letters in the *News* which blast the Coes and mob law along the lower Animas are "originated from the pen of one now residing at Rico who was for a time a sojourner in the land of the lower Animas." Hanson said this sojourner "left with feelings of prejudice against a community where to live well he must work well." Hanson also defended the lynching of Tex Anderson, who he said was hung for "cattle stealing."[11]

Hanson's account of the mule saga may not be entirely accurate. A second version said Frank Meyers and Hanson accosted the constable who picked up the mules and liberated them. The two men were later arrested and appeared before Judge Halford. The court was held, but the proceedings were cut short when the Coes and several others interrupted the proceedings. Judge Colt and Judge Winchester were pulled from their holsters, and Meyers and Hanson left the proceedings as free men. Whatever happened, the Hanson mule saga marked the end of Halford's career as a jurist and the Coe's thorn was plucked and tossed out of the country.[12] On May 8, 1880, the *Dolores News* carried an article from the *Animas City Southwest* which said, "We have received information that the reign of mob law on the Lower Animas has not ceased. An organized gang cleaned out a police court, the other day, in a summary manner. The particulars have not been obtained. It is about time that the law abiding citizens in that country put a stop to the brutal force of ruffianism."[13] New Mexico Territorial Adjutant General Max Frost, who would later investigate this incident, had a different take on the situation. Frost spoke to Hanson and his friends. He reported that, "Halford is universally described as an unscrupulous man who was appointed Justice of the Peace on a petition, to which he had forged about 60 names and who finally left taking one of the mules in question, while the defendant Parker, took the other, virtually stealing them from the plaintiff in the case."[14]

The seizure of Hanson's mules set in motion a string of events that would change the dynamics of power in the San Juan country. As a result, several men would lose their lives. The expulsion of Judge Halford and the near showdown with the Eskridge brothers generated a tremendous amount of hostility which fueled the region's already incendiary tempers. The anger growing inside the Eskridge brothers and the Coes was a flickering flame which; if left alone, might have died out. That was not to be. When Hartman and Jones received word that Halford had been expelled from the lower Animas, they had printed only the first issue of their newspaper. Now that they had total editorial control, they eagerly took on the Coes and their allies. For the next several months the editors of the *Dolores News* not only added fuel to the fire, they fanned the flames.

The expulsion of Halford did send a message to the Coe's enemies. At least one of the alleged rustlers didn't wait around for anymore fireworks. About a week after the clearing out of the police court, the *Dolores News* noted "Bert Wilkinson, of the Lower Animas country, came into Rico this week. Bert will try for his fortune among the carbonates."[15] The *Dolores News* was one of only a handful of newspapers in the San Juan country. Frontier newspapers were entertaining, opinionated and often not concerned with the facts. The disparity between truth and falsehood in the *Dolores News* reached epidemic levels when it came to their accounts of the Coes and their enemies. A virtual virus of lies engulfed Hartman and Jones and their newspaper. Their disregard for the truth increased after the newsmen displayed a monumental case of reckless judgment. In May 1880, Hartman and Jones invited Bert Wilkinson and Hargo Eskridge to live with them. Cattle thieves and newsmen, it was an odd combination, yet it would be a long lasting relationship. Louis Crotzer, a printer, and Thomas McCuiston, a barkeeper, lived in the same residence.[16] Congested living quarters were a common arrangement in a town where almost all of the men were "baching it." The *Dolores News* was a false-fronted building, built on a single lot. The combination newspaper operation and residence for six men had to be extremely crowded. In his memoirs, Charles Jones remembered those times fondly and said he enjoyed Wilkinson's company. He described Bert as "a big gawk of a boy."[17] That June, Wilkinson boldly proclaimed to the census enumerator that he was a "stock dealer." His housemate, Hargo Eskridge, unapologetically claimed the same occupation.

The offices of the Dolores News *in Rico, Colorado, ca. 1880. The building also served as the residence for co-editors Charles Jones and Frank Hartman. Hargo Eskridge and Bert Wilkinson lived with them in June 1880. Jones and Hartman would serve as the unapologetic public spokesmen for Ike Stockton and his allies. (Photo courtesy of Southwest Collection, Special Collections Library, Texas Tech University, Lubbock, TX, Clifford B. Jones Collection, No. 422 E4.)*

There was another self-proclaimed stock dealer living in Rico. The thirty-year-old native New Yorker called himself August Hefferman. That spring Hefferman's housemates conveniently included three butchers, Charles A. King, John Kemp and George Webb, as well as teamster Charles Ricard.[18] King traveled to Rico during the second week of June 1880. Only a few days before, he was living in Pagosa Springs with his wife and two children and told the census taker he was a stock raiser.[19] King ran a small herd of cattle in the Piedra and Pine River valleys. One of the cowboys who had worked that range was Gus Hefferman and that may be where he first met butcher and small-time cattleman Charles King.[20] As for Hefferman, he was the former Lacy/Coleman cowpuncher and Buffalo Soldier killer, Gus Heffron. He fled to Colorado after escaping from the

Cimarron jail back in 1876.²¹ Hefferman moved to southwest Colorado and continued working for Henry Goodman and the LC outfit.²² By the spring of 1880, Hefferman's employment herding and protecting Thompson and Lacy's cattle was over, as evidenced by his self-described occupation as a stock dealer. Hefferman was a long-time acquaintance of the Stockton brothers and had witnessed Porter Stockton murder Antonio Arcibia. Like Porter Stockton, Hefferman was still wanted for murder in New Mexico. With thousands of LC cattle filling the open range, it does not take too much imagination to explain how the wanted fugitive had evolved from a simple herder into a stock dealer. As a former Thompson and Lacy employee, he was in a perfect position to know when and where to safely steal his former employer's cattle. He probably put his brand on Lacy's mavericks and altered brands as well. In the thinly settled San Juan country, the mining metropolis was an ideal destination for purloined cattle. Rico was home to almost one thousand hungry residents; primarily miners, carpenters and other men who labored hard for their money. The town supported five meat markets and many of the cattle delivered to those markets, stolen or not, were quickly butchered and sold.²³

Bert Wilkinson was the most egregious, callow example of the so-called stock dealers who had gathered in Rico. For the eighteen-year-old, there was only one way he could become a dealer in stock; he hoped to prove the old adage that says the only things a cowboy needs to start a brand is "a rope, a runnin' iron and the nerve to use it."²⁴ Ropes and running irons were easy to come by, and as subsequent events would tell, young Bert had the nerve to go with them. However, the reputations of Frank and George Coe, the lynching of Tex Anderson and the forced departure of Judge Halford gave Bert second thoughts. Within days of telling the census taker that he was a stock dealer, he and Will Dudley began operating a packing business between Rico and Corral Springs.²⁵

At the time Wilkinson had other relatives living in Rico. His uncle Austin had also left the lower Animas, set up his wife and family in a house in Pagosa Springs, and then took up residence in Rico with his teenaged sons, Oscar and A.M. Puett, Jr. Austin's forty-seven-year-old brother Al was living with them. All four of the Puetts listed their occupation as ranchmen. The Puett fathers, Austin and Al, may not have been active participants in the illicit Rico-based cattle trade, but they had to be aware of its existence. Butcher Charlie King, who clearly benefitted from the proceeds of rustled stock, was probably encouraged to come to Rico by Austin Puett. Immediately prior to his arrival in the mining town, King had lived next door to Austin's wife Maria in Pagosa Springs.²⁶ In Rico, King's meat market was located directly across the street from the offices of the *Dolores News*.²⁷

Accommodations at the *Dolores News* were crowded, and when the weather warmed up, Bert Wilkinson moved out and set up a camp near

Rico. At the same time young Os Puett sought independence from his family and looked for some action. He made an ill-fated choice to join up with the Eskridge brothers and Jim Garrett. This decision pulled him out of the respectable world of ranchmen and ensnared him into less honorable, though more exciting, livestock activities. It may have also been about the same time that Charles Jones volunteered to help Wilkinson and either Os or Al Puett, attempt to kill a huge bear which raided their camp in Iron Gulch (also known as Iron Draw) near Rico. At the time grizzlies still roamed the San Juans and they'd wisely tied their meat from a tree limb, dangling up very high. The height of their meat cache helped them estimate the enormous size of the animal. The men baited the tree again and slept nearby. It was a dangerous proposition and when the bear came in the first night, Jones was too fearful to awaken Puett and Wilkinson and the bruin finally left. Jones went back to the camp one more night, resolved to kill the bear, but it did not return.[28]

Now that Hargo Eskridge was residing with Hartman and Jones, the *Dolores News* had even more reason to ramp up their condemnation of the Coe family. As spring turned to summer the two groups seethed with rage as they traded accusations. On June 5, 1880, the *Dolores News* printed a letter which once again implicated the Coe men as being accomplices to the hanging of Tex Anderson and with "bull-dozing" their neighbors. In early July the *News* printed a letter from Frank Coe answering the charges. They left Frank's original spelling intact, perhaps to embarrass him, since that was not their usual practice. The letter said in part, "I notice a dirty little communication sent in by some cowardly villain who faild to sign his name to his liing article." Coe doesn't use names, but he denied driving one justice [Hannibal Halford] out of the country and forcing the other justice [Jimmy Carroll] to join them. He also denied "driveing an old jentleman & lady out of the country." In the same denial he added, "But I did live in a place once where the people took it upon them selves to order an old Bageyed villain out of the country who had been living in prostitution with another man's wife."[29] Coe may be referring to Jane Adams, who witnessed the Anderson lynching, and Joseph Crouch. It's not clear that Adams was another man's wife, but census records indicate that she was living with Crouch. However, Frank Coe's reference may also have referred to a woman identified only as Mrs. Hubbard. According to C.H. McHenry, she received a letter which said, "Mrs. Hubbard we, the law-abiding citizens, have been watching you, you have prostituted yourself with old Halford and others. You are ordered to leave under penalty of Rope, Tar and Feathers."[30] Frank Coe, who was behind much of the turmoil along the lower Animas, proclaimed his innocence and asked Hartman and Jones for two favors: to not print any more letters which insult the Lincoln County mob, unless the author's name is included, and to publish his letter with his name included.³¹ Coe had grit, but his bullheaded manner was not always in his best interests.

While Frank Coe traded barbs with Hartman and Jones, Animas City was in the midst of a small boom caused in part by the approaching railroad. Lumber mills in the vicinity were gearing up to receive orders which would soon amount to half a million board feet of lumber to be used to construct new buildings in the proposed town of Durango. Army troops had wiped out the previous winter's store supplies and general merchandise of all types was selling for high prices.³²

That spring Port Stockton and his wife had new neighbors. Living next door was John Cowan, Port's brother-in-law, and his two teenage children, fifteen-year-old William and thirteen-year-old Elizabeth (Lizzie) Cowan. (In 1882, Lizzie was at the center of events which ended with Durango's first and only legal hanging.) While Port was upriver in Colorado, Ike and his family stayed in New Mexico, at least for a while. Ike's family now included not only his wife, Ellen, and daughter Delilah, but a four month old baby boy named Guy. John Cowan and his children moved during June and were counted in both the New Mexico and Colorado census. They were shown as Ike's next door neighbors as well. Ike's other neighbors included his sixty-three-year-old mother-in-law Sarah Robinson and forty-three-year-old sister-in-law, Polly. According to 1880 U.S. Census records, Sarah Robinson, who was a housewife back in Texas, was calling herself a doctor in 1880. Ike Stockton called himself a "stockman" while living on the lower Animas. In Animas City, Porter Stockton described his occupation as a "Stock Grower."³³

As was his usual practice, Port worked on roundups and did related work for the cattlemen living in the area. That would have included one of his closest neighbors in Animas City, thirty-eight-year-old stockman William J. Wilson.³⁴ Wilson and Stockton were in all likelihood acquainted with each other from their early days in Texas. Animas City's Billy Wilson at one time lived just north of Stephenville in Palo Pinto County.³⁵ Chances are high that the two men met each other on a cow hunt or during an early cattle drive coming out of Texas. Once met, Wilson was a man no one forgot. He was highly esteemed for his coolness under pressure and for his ability as a cowboy. That ability was all the more amazing considering he had only one arm. Stockton's neighbor was known as "One Armed" Billy Wilson. (The portion of the highway coming out of Durango toward Farmington, known commonly as Farmington Hill, climbs the side of Wilson Gulch, which is named for Billy Wilson.)³⁶ In the 1880s, Wilson's Gulch was the headquarter camp for month long roundups encompassing the Animas, Florida and Los Pinos valleys.³⁷

During his lifetime Wilson was a solid, unassuming citizen, but he has since achieved legendary status due to his actions during one of the most acclaimed, harrowing escapes from death on the western frontier.

(The real incident bears a striking resemblance to one of the fictional episodes in Larry McMurtry's classic western novel, *Lonesome Dove*.) It was during an 1867 trail drive with Charles Goodnight and Oliver Loving that Wilson and Loving outraced a band of Comanches, only to find they were trapped on the Pecos River. The men withstood a siege by the Indians and the older cattleman was wounded in the arm. Loving urged Wilson to escape and bring help. Wilson managed to elude the Comanches by swimming down the Pecos for some distance until he was out of their sight. He then walked barefoot for three days before his path intersected with the trail drive and he was found by Charles Goodnight. He was in miserable shape and his feet were horribly swollen. A rescue expedition was mounted and they discovered that Loving had also managed to escape. At Fort Sumner a physician amputated Loving's infected arm.[38] The *Fort Worth Gazette* said the attack took place on August 6th and Loving only made it to Fort Sumner after he was found by "Mexican salt traders." Loving's condition deteriorated and on September 25th he died. In December his remains were exhumed and his body was transported to Weatherford, Texas, where he is now buried.[39]

In 1872, Billy Wilson's brother George shot and killed Juan Tafoya in a Trinidad saloon. Because Tafoya was the sheriff of Las Animas County, this transgression was not easily overlooked by the Trinidadians in attendance. George and his brother Fayette made their way to the U.S. Livery to retrieve their horses. Three of their fellow herders aided their escape. After crossing the bridge which led to the livery, two of the men turned, pointed their Spencer rifles back toward town, and stopped the enraged mob in their tracks. The cowboys sent a clear message to those who had thoughts of pursuit, after mounting up the *Trinidad Enterprise* noted "the party, five in number, rode slowly out of town."[40] One of the Spencer-toting men was "One-Armed" Billy Wilson.[41]

By at least 1877 Billy Wilson was living in Animas City.[42] On April 22nd of that year George Wilson was apprehended in Deer Trail, Colorado. In June he escaped from the Pueblo jail and fled to Animas City. Texas authorities were also after Wilson for the murder of Montague County deputy sheriff Robert Broaddus. George Wilson soon moved to Arizona. In October 1877 he was killed in a shootout with Prescott constable Frank Murray, Yavapai County Sheriff Ed Bowers, U.S. deputy marshal Wiley Standefer and future Tombstone marshal Virgil Earp.[43] "One Armed" Billy Wilson and his family lived in Animas City for several years.[44]

Wilson's former Cross Timbers neighbor called himself a stock grower, but that was not a legitimate pursuit for Porter Stockton. Living on the run, moving from town to town made that difficult and he preferred to let others do the work while he reaped the harvest. The position of town marshal in Animas City was an ever revolving door and soon after his arrival the position was vacated. Unimaginably, the wanted murderer soon represented the long arm of the law in Animas City. For the most part, Porter found his duties as Marshal less than exciting. In all of La Plata County there were only about one thousand residents and they were spread out in the La Plata, Animas and Pine River valleys.[45]

As it would have looked at the Wilson Gulch roundup near Durango. Frederic Remington's "The Midday Meal," from Theodore Roosevelt's "Ranch Life in the Far West," The Century Illustrated Monthly Magazine, *Vol. 35, No. 4, February 1888. (Author's collection.)*

Animas City was pretty calm by frontier standards. The arrests Porter made were for run of the mill incidents: drunk and disorderly conduct, fighting, and carrying deadly weapons. The real danger in town was if some unsuspecting soul set off Stockton's short fuse. The *Santa Fe New Mexican* claimed that he killed two men while employed as town marshal.[46] The *New Mexican* was misinformed, but the wanted murderer was an overzealous horse's ass when it came to enforcing the town's ordinances. He brought Christian and Lizzie N. Hansen (records show various spellings, i.e. Henson, Hensen and Hanson) up on the heinous charge of keeping their pigpen in an offensive condition. They were not happy with the charge or the fine imposed by police magistrate C.C.

Gaines. The Hansens, who were represented by attorney James Russell, began a courtroom fracas with Gaines and evidently he had Stockton take them to the log jail. The next day they appeared in court again and faced charges of contempt of court. According to court records Judge Gaines "discharged them with a reprimand, and without costs" on the contempt charge. They did pay $25.95 in fines and fees for the pig sty caper.[47] The offensive pig sty was probably close to the Hansen's Elk Horn Club.[48]

Stockton once charged "French Frank" Chabran for driving his team over the Second Street bridge at a speed faster than a natural walking gait. Even though he didn't use a stagecoach, Chabran was following the time honored custom of virtually all stage drivers on the frontier. In between towns, the pace of the stage was fairly easy, but as they neared the outskirts of town the pace quickened, and before the stage stop was reached the team was at a full gallop, dust flying and the driver demonstrating his skill by bringing them to a sudden stop at the station. Besides hauling passengers and mail from Silverton, Chabran also owned a butcher shop in town. There was actually an ordinance that forbid excessive speed while crossing the bridge. Four witnesses and Stockton testified in the matter of this shocking crime: saloon owner Billy Wickline, recently pacified pig sty owner Christian Hansen, Baden-born barber Phil Webber and G.S. Flagler. Chabran was found guilty.[49]

Stockton received a small salary and augmented his wages by performing other job related duties. As marshal, he was paid $1.00 for each arrest, $.75 for serving a summons, $.50 cents for serving a subpoena, and $1.00 for attending a trial. Dogs were big business. He was paid $1.00 for killing any unlicensed dogs or any bitch that was allowed "to run at large while in heat." Animas City had saloons, but one ordinance said, "No bawdy house or house of ill-fame, house of assignation, or place for the practice of fornication" were allowed within the town.[50] Durango would soon meet the demand for such services and there cowboys, miners and others would practice fornication without restriction.

Port was bored with his new position. Inevitably, he created his own trouble. Cap Hart, whose given name was Thomas B. Hart was a forty-eight-year-old native of New York.[51] He was a prominent cattleman who lived north of Aztec near the canyon that now bears his name. During the summer, Hart often ran his cattle in the mountains north of Animas City.[52] Hart was well known and highly respected for his role during some trying times in 1878. At that time, a persistent rumor spread that the Utes were going to kill all of the settlers in a mass attack in the middle of March. In the area around Aztec, the residents organized a militia and Hart was appointed captain. A protective stockade and other works were built near the Aztec Ruins and Hart traveled to Santa Fe to ask for guns and ammunition.[53] It's not known if he was referred to as "Cap" before this, but in contemporary newspapers and pioneer stories he is often identified by this term of esteem. On April 30, 1879, the first post office was officially created in Aztec and Hart was the postmaster.[54] Considering the prestige he held in the area, Cap Hart's treatment by Port Stockton came as a great shock.

The Elk Horn Club and Restaurant operated by Christian and Lizzie Hansen in Animas City, ca. 1880. (Courtesy of La Plata County Historical Society No. 92.21.214)

On July 3, 1880, Hart headed toward Animas City on business. The little town had an ordinance that prohibited the carrying of "any pistol, bowie-knife, dagger, or other deadly weapon." Sheriffs, marshals and constables while performing their official duties were an exception to the rule.[55] Hart rode into town, minding his own business, when he was stopped by Marshal Stockton who told him he must give up his belt and pistol. Cap Hart wasn't known to be a drunken lout who might shoot up the town, but Stockton obviously enjoyed exerting his authority. Hart couldn't hack Stockton's overbearing attitude. Considering that Hart had just made a long hard ride and had yet to dismount, the request was a bit premature. The cattleman told Stockton he would disarm, just as soon as he took his horse to the livery. That was a common practice in the many frontier towns that had similar laws as Stockton well knew. The two men exchanged heated words. Hart's anger got the better of him and he began to dismount. He intended to teach the bully a lesson. Stockton was not a fan of fair fighting, especially if he could have the advantage. The process of dismounting distracted Hart's attention and Stockton took the coward's way out and fired a shot under the horse's neck. The bullet struck Hart in the cheek, and passed out under his nose. Several teeth were lost in the process.[56] Stockton's pistol was only two feet from Hart's head when he pulled the trigger, but a split second before that Hart had jerked his head back, saving his life. Despite his wound, Hart drew his pistol and according to the *New Mexican,* "Port turned and run [sic] like a quarter horse." Hart fired at Stockton, but missed. Then he spit and said, "I caught his damned ball in my mouth, anybody that wants it can have it." A bystander found one of Hart's teeth, but not the bullet, in the blood and sputum on the ground.[57] Even though he was almost twenty years older than his assailant, he chased the outlaw marshal to a nearby dugout. Unfortunately, he was almost blinded from smoke, his eyes were watering, and blood was pouring from his mouth. He soon gave up the pursuit.[58] At the time, if Hart had been able to finish off Stockton, his act might have been viewed as justified. Stockton's time was yet to come. Even the town fathers were afraid to deal with Port and he continued to serve as the town marshal. Hart recovered from his wounds, and in September he was running close to 450 head on Cascade Hill to supply mining camps in the area. Because the high mountain meadows could prove to be a dangerous locale for cattle during the late summer thunderstorms, Hart's animals were known as "lightning rod" cattle. The *Dolores News* said, "Mr. H. is a gentlemen in every sense of the word and has many friends in this region."[59]

Stockton came to Animas City with a reputation, and if some did not believe the stories they had heard, the shooting of Cap Hart erased their doubts. Stockton was the cock of the walk now and he was given a wide berth. The little town settled into an apprehensive summer. The shooting of Cap Hart made it clear that no one was safe. Residents wondered when Port would lose it again. That happened on the afternoon of Thursday, September 16, 1880, when Stockton's wrath focused on an Animas City barber. In contemporary accounts of the incident, the *Dolores News* said the barber's name was J.W. Allen and the *Animas City Southwest* said his name was Thomas Smith.[60] The victim in this case is variously described as being Negro, black, or colored, although he may not have been of African descent. The *Dolores News* said the barber "is a Maouri, a race of people in Australia, and is well-educated, intelligent and has traveled all over the world."[61] Given his background, and that black men were a rarity in the local mining camps, it seems unlikely that the *Dolores News* editors would mistake Allen for any other dark-skinned man in the San Juan country. James W. Allen was not born in New Zealand, home of the

Maori people, but in Australia. His mother was an Aboriginal Australian and his father was Scottish. Before moving to Animas City, he was managing a Rico restaurant and living with an Illinois-born black miner. Porter Stockton did not make any fine distinctions when it came to Mr. Allen's heritage. He saw a strange speaking black-skinned man who was not accustomed to putting on a subservient air as a means of self-preservation. Given his Scottish/Australian heritage it is easy to understand the confusion about James Allen's background and his unusual manner of speaking.[62] One account noted that he spoke with a clipped British accent and was well liked in the small community.[63] Animas City resident Eugene Engley, who identified the barber as Thomas Smith not J.W. Allen, provided a contemporary recounting of the event. Engley was not only the editor of the *Animas City Southwest*, but as the mayor of Animas City had been instrumental in hiring Porter Stockton as the town marshal. According to the *Southwest*, "It seems that Stockton entered the barber shop and asked Phil. Weber [Webber] to shave him, at the same time making the remark that the 'black son of a b---h' (Smith) could not lay a razor on his face."[64] According to Engley, Stockton was already sitting in Webber's chair when the "black" barber entered the room. Stockton, once again demonstrating his inherent prejudice and volatile disposition, jumped down from the chair and struck Smith in the head with his pistol. The newspaper said "Smith then ran into the street, pursued by Stockton, who fired a shot from his revolver, the bullet striking Smith on the skull and glancing off. Stockton followed up this dastardly treatment by again striking his victim over the head with his revolver, inflicting several severe gashes." Engley described the assault as being "entirely unprovoked." He also noted that Marshal Stockton was inebriated when he walked into the barber shop.[65] The *Dolores News* said "Stockton, who has been, by the way, extremely free with his pistol since he had a little authority, pulled his revolver and fired, the ball just grazing the back of the barber's head." The townspeople had seen enough. Stockton was arrested and taken to the town's log jail.[66]

Later that day, the mayor allowed him out for supper. According to the *Dolores News*, Stockton escaped out a side window while taking his meal at P.J. Cates's hotel. At the time, liveryman Frank West was conveniently riding down the street. Stockton, who had somehow armed himself with a pistol, forced West to dismount, mounted up, and bid adieu to Animas City.[67] In the *Southwest*, Engley said "Stockton was arrested, but escaped through the 'gates ajar' into New Mexico." The city fathers had little desire to hold Stockton and preferred that he skip town. The fact that he obtained his getaway horse from the livery owner may not have been coincidental.[68] Blacksmith Charles Naegelin believed Stockton may have headed to the O'Neal place.[69] They lived in the Pine River valley.[70] That same day rancher Tim McCluer saw Stockton riding away from town. He reported that Stockton spent his first night on the run at the home of

Florida Mesa cattleman Columbus Evans Hampton.[71] His stay with the Hampton family was short.

Stockton was not without longtime friends in the San Juan country and among them were George Morrison and the O'Neals.[72] Their place on the Pine River included John and James O'Neal and their two families and George Morrison and his wife, the former Marinda O'Neal.[73] Like Porter Stockton, George Morrison was hiding in plain sight in La Plata County. He was still wanted by Erath County authorities for attempted murder.[74] The Cox family had a clear opinion of Morrison. Wash Cox's son, Ike Cox, said, "Morrison was a bad man, not so nervy, but if he had the best of a man, he would kill him. But if the other fellow had an even break he would not draw." When the Cox's lived in Colfax County, Wash had gone to Missouri and purchased a few Durham cows and two bulls. Wash Cox gave the Durhams special treatment and branded them with a small "C," down low on the thigh. Cox cattle roamed up the Florida and Animas valleys and were sometimes found many miles from their home range. Jim Cox sometimes represented his father's outfit at roundups in areas adjacent to the Cox range. During one roundup near Bayfield he spotted a Durham cow. The brand was hard to see, but the Durham stuck out like a sore thumb. When the roundup foreman asked Jim to look through the gathered cattle, he confirmed the brand and cut it out of the herd. A blustering George Morrison wanted the Durham and reasoned that he could easily intimidate young Cox. He boldly turned the cow back into the herd. As Ike Cox explained, that was "a very insulting thing to do." An anticipatory tension spread through the roundup camp. The cowboys were well aware of Morrison's hair-trigger temper and their eyes followed Cox as he rode slowly toward the older man. Jim was cut out of the same cloth as his daddy. He crowded Morrison, and with a quiet, but steely firmness and in his thick Texas twang warned, "Don't turn that cow back again, please." Morrison seethed as Cox wheeled his horse, rode into the gather and retrieved the Durham, but as Ike Cox noted, "Mr. Morrison knew just what that meant and he never turned her back again."[75] Morrison's residence on the Pine River was at the present site of Bayfield and he was the original homesteader of the townsite.[76]

Porter Stockton did not go to the Morrison's, but he did leave Animas City on the run, leaving behind Emily and his three children. Eugene Engley was right; Stockton's destination was New Mexico. Since Port couldn't return to Animas City, it's likely that Ike or perhaps Emily's brother, John Cowan, helped her and the children move to Rio Arriba County. The former marshal had put himself in a desperate situation. The days were growing short and the mornings were turning cool. If it was an early frost, lower Animas farmers had already seen their vegetable plants turn black and shrivel. Stockton needed someplace to live and he needed it now. After living in the Maxwell Land Grant country, he was familiar with the status of New Mexico land claims and how nebulous they could be.

That was indeed the case in western Rio Arriba County. In the first few years of settlement, those who came to the river valleys of northwest New Mexico could only claim squatter's rights. Formal applications for homesteads and the ability to obtain a land patent were not possible until the General Land Office made an official survey of the area.[77] This created some conflicts because even temporarily unoccupied claims were sometimes claim jumped. Usually these situations were settled amicably, as it was with Lew Coe and the Virden brothers.[78] The surveyor general of New Mexico was charged with surveying public domain lands. Every newly settled area in the territory clamored to be given priority status by the surveyor general.[79] Most of the San Juan country in New Mexico was surveyed by 1884.[80] Stockton didn't concern himself with technicalities when it came to finding a place to live.

This branding camp scene would have been familiar to George Morrison and Jim Cox. Frederic Remington's "Branding a Calf," from Theodore Roosevelt's "The Round-up," The Century Illustrated Monthly Magazine, *Vol. 35, No. 6, April 1888. (Modified, author's collection.)*

The outlaw heralded his arrival on the lower Animas by jumping the claim of a recently widowed woman named Lucy Cooper. In early 1880 Lucy's husband, Thomas Cooper, traveled from Lake City, Colorado to the lower Animas, where he found property for his family. The land was near Flora Vista in the broad valley on the south side of the Animas River. Lucy was having some health problems and a move to a lower elevation was recommended. Cooper was an Englishman and a ship's carpenter by trade. In Lake City he applied his carpentry skills building houses and businesses. Along the lower Animas, he built a nice home and then stayed in the area building watertight homes for other families. After saving a sizable amount of cash he left for Lake City to bring his family over the range. He did not get far. While crossing the Animas on a ferry, he drowned. The Cooper family suspected foul play, since he was said to be carrying a large amount of money. His body was never recovered. Some of the residents were aware that Cooper's wife lived in Lake City and she soon received word of his death.[81]

Perhaps it was just a coincidence that Mr. Cooper met an unnatural death at almost exactly the same time that Port Stockton was desperately looking for a place to live. The Cooper family had good reason to be suspicious about the death of Thomas Cooper, but there are no pioneer accounts or other stories implicating Stockton in the matter. The carpenter may have simply lost his balance on the Cox's Crossing ferry. That said, Stockton somehow knew that Thomas Cooper's new, well-built house was his for the taking. True to his character, he had no qualms about moving in and making himself at home. If the neighbors told him the claim belonged to Thomas Cooper's widow, they were rebuffed and if Port Stockton wanted to be reviled in his new community, he had chosen the perfect method. In pioneer times there could be almost no more heinous act than taking advantage of a widow and her children. In October 1880, Mrs. Cooper and her three children joined a south-bound wagon train being organized by Johnny Leslie in Lake City. The trip took three weeks and lasted into November. Finally, Mrs. Cooper accompanied by Johnny Leslie reached her husband's claim.[82] They arrived late in the day and Port Stockton was home. Leslie, who was described as being quiet and unassuming, inquired if it was the Cooper place and Stockton said it had been, but now it was his. Leslie said they would camp the night and figure it out in the morning. Stockton felt no further discussion was necessary. When Leslie turned his back to unload the wagon, Stockton clubbed him from behind with the butt of his pistol. Leslie collapsed on the ground. Frantic and distraught, Mrs. Cooper ran to the farm owned by John and Henrietta Pore Milleson. John and their twenty-year-old-son Burr Hiram Milleson were probably the first ones to arrive on the scene and they were stunned by Stockton's action. Leslie was taken to the Milleson home. He had suffered severe brain trauma, was unconscious for two days and unable to travel for two weeks.[83] He managed to make it back to Colorado but reportedly died less than two months after being clubbed.[84] If that was the case, Leslie may have been the fourth man murdered by Port Stockton in New Mexico. It was not unheard of for respected citizens to be run out of a town if it was learned that they had unscrupulously taken advantage of a widow. Stockton may not have been respected, but he was feared. It was no secret that attempting to run Port Stockton out of the country could prove hazardous to one's health, so by unspoken agreement he stayed where he was.

As fall turned to winter, Port's actions left the widow and her three children virtually stranded with no means of support. She found work caring for the children of Joel Estes, Jr., a new arrival to the area.[85] Estes was the thirteenth and youngest child of Joel and Patsy Estes. In 1859, the elder Joel Estes had made the first land claim in Colorado's Big Thompson valley on the site now known as Estes Park. Shortly after their arrival in the San Juan country, Joel Jr.'s wife died suddenly while traveling by wagon between Pagosa Springs and Durango. The aspiring cattleman was left with six motherless children, including Mary Alverda who was born in New Mexico on May 1, 1879. (In an ironic twist of fate, Joel Estes, Jr. married Port Stockton's widow, Emily Jane, in March 1882.) The Estes family lived near Aztec, but would later move up the Animas valley to Animas City.[86] Mrs. Cooper found caring for the six Estes children and her own three children onerous. She then worked for an invalid, Mrs. Cole, and she also worked as a housekeeper for the Coe's favorite jurist, "Uncle Jimmy" Carroll.[87] In 1881 she found work as the teacher in the first school in Aztec. This position came with a two room log cabin, with one room being the classroom and the other serving as living quarters for the schoolmarm and her children.[88]

Stockton was unfazed by the enmity he had created and unconcerned with the fate of the Widow Cooper and her children. The neighbors were outraged, but the fear of Port Stockton was so great that no action was taken. As Stockton and his family settled into their cozy new home for the winter, big changes were taking place upriver that would bring both prosperity and tumultuous times to southwest Colorado.

Chapter Eight

Here I Am, Come On Boys

> *The "wimmin folks" looked lovely ---- the boys looked kinder treed,*
> *Till their leader commenced yellin': "Whoa, fellers, let's stampede."*
> *The music started sighin' and a-wailin' through the hall,*
> *As a kind of introduction to "The Cowboys' Christmas Ball."*[1]

Throughout the spring, summer and fall of 1880 the Denver and Rio Grande Railroad was reaching toward the heart of the mining country in the San Juan Mountains. The D&RG drove its first spike in Denver on July 28, 1871.[2] As the line advanced, each mile marker denoted the distance from Denver. In February 1876, the railroad company started building a branch running west from Walsenburg up the Cuchara valley toward La Veta Pass.[3] Alamosa, and the river that was the namesake of the railroad, were not reached until the summer of 1878.[4] The rails then headed south. The D&RG erected a small station on top of Cumbres Pass, which was then known as Alta. There the engines could rest after their arduous, steep climb and travelers could disembark to stretch their legs and take in the mountain scenery.[5] In June 1880 the *Del Norte Prospector* reported that James Luttrell, land agent for the D&RG at Animas City, had "proved up on 2000 acre [sic] of land in the vicinity of the coal banks south of town, for the company; but at what time the new town of Durango will be laid out and lots placed on the market is something which God Almighty and Governor Hunt only know -- and they won't tell."[6] Former Colorado governor, A.C. Hunt, was the managing director of the railroad.[7] The wait for Durango would be short, as the D&RG's newest town would explode into existence.

Even though winter was not completely over, the D&RG moved into high gear. By March of 1880 the rails were advancing at the rate of one mile per day.[8] While merchants and others in Animas City were making money because of the approaching rail line, they were nevertheless in an uproar at the prospect that their town would not be the railroad hub of the San Juan country. In August 1880 the *Animas City Southwest* bemoaned the D&RG's plans to start the new town: "The D. & R. G. company have been offered a large tract of land within the corporate limits of Animas City for depot grounds and other purposes, and if the company is generous and wise it will not seek to annihilate a town as large as Animas City."[9] D&RG officials were not moved and by the middle of September Luttrell began to sell lots in the new town. Only the four block business district had been surveyed and corner lots were valued at five hundred dollars, while interior lots went for half that amount. The purchase contract stipulated that the new owners must immediately erect two story buildings using only brick or stone, not lumber.[10]

The D&RG rolls toward the San Juan country. "Colorado.-Incidents of a Trip to the Mining Town of Durango," Frank Leslie's Illustrated Newspaper, *May 28, 1881, artist J.J. Reilly (Modified, author's collection.)*

Throughout the summer there was a frenzy of railroad building, but the D&RG could not find enough men to do the work. Even as the warm months waned they were advertising for three hundred "tie choppers" and another one thousand laborers to work on the New Mexico and San Juan extensions.[11] On December 18, 1880 the Georgetown *Colorado Miner* noted, "Durango, the new town at the end of the Denver & Rio Grande, in the San Juan country, is enjoying an era of prosperity. Lots are selling from $300 to $1000."[12] The large number of men and their money attracted an unsavory crowd. Gambling dens, saloons, establishments of ill fame and a lawless element invaded the railroad towns.

Along the northern border of New Mexico towns like Chama and Amargo became havens for an unruly rabble.[13] When it came to violence and depravity, Durango would take a backseat to no other town along the parallel rails of the D&RG. But destiny was on Durango's side, and the arrival of the railroad, along with the town's location, would assure that it had a unique place of prominence in the San Juan country.

Before the appearance of Durango's first train, Hargo Eskridge and Bert Wilkinson were trying to strike it rich in the aptly named Rico. In July they made a claim on what they called "The Lookout Mine" on Expectation Mountain. It was said to have a four and a half foot mineralized vein and the men began to sink a shaft.[14] That might have involved more work than they bargained for and Hargo thought there might be easier ways to hit the mother lode. Later that summer he probably traveled south to look over the new Durango townsite. He knew that a saloon or any establishment which catered to the lowest aspects of human nature would be a moneymaker and he contemplated those prospects. He then continued south to the Garrett/Eskridge ranch.[15]

Hargo had perhaps already reached the lower Animas when a party of Navajos broke into Jake Bohannon's house. Bohannon's place was four miles above Aztec, at the confluence of the Animas and what is now known as the Bohannon Arroyo.[16] Bohannon had formerly lived on the Vermejo in Colfax County. His new home was downriver from the home of Alf Graves, and his spread out neighbors included Jim Kiffen, Pete Hargis and George Coe. Bohannon was an unmarried stockman and spent much of his day out on the range with his hired hands, Nathan Roberson and former Erath County resident Jake Bull. Jake's brother, Solon, was a former Wash Cox trail hand.[17] On Thursday, August 19, 1880, Bohannon returned to his home and found some Indians in the process of stealing blankets and other items, which they had loaded onto a mule and pony. Jake attacked the Navajos in hopes that they'd abandon their loot, but the Indians gained the upper hand when one of their arrows struck him.[18] Jake was outnumbered three to one, and with the arrow hanging out of his wrist, he decided it was time to retreat. He was in a tremendous amount of pain and suffering from blood loss. While Bohannon sought shelter in the vegetation along the banks of the Animas, the Indians rode away. He soon found Frank, George and Jap Coe who ran to his assistance. They pulled the arrow through Bohannon's wrist and treated the wound. Leaving Bohannon to recuperate, they grabbed their firearms, mounted their horses and set out in pursuit of the thieves. After a chase of three miles they found their quarry and began shooting. The Indians tried to outrun them, but after traveling several more miles the Navajos abandoned their pack burro and the bulk of the stolen property. The Coes gathered up the burro and other items and rode for home. George Coe later said that his neighbors were worried "that the Indians would come down and kill them, but that little chase we had did more good than anything in the world."¹⁹ Shortly after the incident, a correspondent identified as L.W.C. (no doubt Lew W. Coe) wrote to the *Cimarron News and Press* and reported that Bohannon fortunately came across three men harvesting a field. He did not identify the harvesters, but said that they pursued the Indians for eight miles and recaptured the stolen property. He added, "It has since been reported that two Indians died; I hope they did."²⁰ Many years later Wash Cox's son, Ike, recalled that the Coe boys shot one of the Indians and threw him in the river. After they rode off, the Indian climbed out of the river, found a horse and rode away.²¹

About two weeks after this incident Hargo Eskridge left the lower Animas and returned to Rico. At about the same time Rico's town marshal, Jim Cart, left for Alamosa after learning that his wife had died there. Hargo Eskridge stepped into the marshal's slot until Cart returned. In early October Wilkinson and Eskridge made another Expectation Mountain mining claim, which they named the "Diamond Maid." Thomas McCuiston, one of their *Dolores News* housemates, was a partner in this venture. The new claim reportedly had a sixteen inch vein containing gray copper.²² While their mining claims were not the bonanza they'd dreamed of, Durango tugged at them like a magnet they were unable to resist.

Ike Stockton was also taking notice of the flurry of activity, and that summer or fall Ike and his family moved up the Animas River. Their new home was a cabin about one quarter mile north of the town limits of Animas City.²³ Now that businesses and residents were starting to pile into the area around the proposed Durango depot, Animas City was in a steady decline. Even existing businesses in Animas City were planning to move to Durango. Ike found a suitable property for his young family, probably at a fire sale price.

Down on the lower Animas, Porter Stockton began stealing other folk's cattle. There was no subtlety in his methods. According to La Plata valley resident George Lockhart, Stockton was known for "killing stock and selling both meat and hides, and even had the impudence to offer to give a bill of sale for the hides."²⁴ Selling stolen hides bearing the brand of the true owner was more than bold. It is clear that Stockton's arrogance knew no bounds. Normally, a rustler burned the hides, buried them or stashed them in some unusual, well hidden location.²⁵ Sometimes they cut the brand mark out for separate disposal.²⁶ But Stockton had reached the point of taking what he needed and did not care who knew it. As Port's gall increased, so grew his reputation as a man not to be crossed. One can imagine the discomfort of local residents when Stockton showed up at their door selling stolen beef and hides. Few probably refused Stockton's sales pitch.

Local merchants had their own difficulties with Stockton. Cattleman and merchant William Haines was a forty-year-old Englishman, who lived on the San Juan with his wife Mary and six children. His store was one of a handful to be found in northwest New Mexico and just about everyone, including Porter Stockton, frequented Haines's establishment at one time or another. Haines was a trained lawyer, but for reasons unknown his primary means of support was the mercantile trade.[27] He was a major promoter of the area, a cattle dealer and a community leader. The Englishman's partner was Levy A. Hughes, a twenty-five-year-old bookkeeper from Indiana, who had previously lived in Santa Fe and worked for the large New Mexico based mercantile operation, Ilfeld and Company.[28] Stockton's antics were certainly a topic of conversation at the Haines and Hughes store and the owners witnessed his intimidating tactics firsthand.[29]

Throughout the fall Stockton made a nuisance of himself. William Hendrickson noted that Port "made himself conspicuous and feared by many, by breathing threats of death and destruction, and by butchering cattle belonging to others." Hendrickson observed that, "There is ample proof that he was a very dangerous man." Like others in the Animas valley, Hendrickson knew of Stockton's bombastic claims about the nineteen men he had killed. Invariably, he'd conclude his little speech by noting that it was about time he killed one more.[30] Hendrickson was not the only one reporting Stockton's torrent of threats. Others reported that he had threatened the lives of at least six of his Animas valley neighbors.[31] After the shooting of Cap Hart and the Animas City barber, his threats could not be blown off as the idle chatter of a boastful braggart, although he was clearly that. Jap Coe said Stockton was "a notorious cow thief and murderer who boasted of killing eighteen men in his time." Coe also said that Stockton "threatened the lives of some of our best citizens."[32] Stockton's loud mouth and wicked ways were rapidly sowing the seeds of his own destruction.

At this same time storekeeper and stockman William Haines was haggling with the army over the contract to provide fresh beef to Fort Lewis. He hoped to make better use of his cattle than providing for the needs of Porter Stockton. Despite the allure, the beef contract would prove to be a major source of trouble for everyone who held it. Haines had been awarded the contract on August 14th for delivery of beef to troops on the Mancos. A short time later the army sought to amend the contract, pending Haines's agreement to provide beef to the Fort's new location in the La Plata valley. The contract price was 6.5 cents per pound. Until the contract could be amended, the army purchased cattle on the open market. George West may have stepped in as the informal supplier while Haines and the army dickered. On September 20th Haines began supplying beef to the Fort, but then at the end of September, he said he could no longer provide beef for the agreed upon price. The price of beef had spiked to 8 cents per pound and Haines hoped to renegotiate the contract before he signed the amendment. First Lieutenant Cavenaugh was not pleased with Haines and advised his superiors that the beef provided by the Bloomfield merchant was not of good quality. He recommended that "Mr. Pond" (La Plata valley resident Johnny Pond), who had also made a bid, be given the contract. Pond's home was in New Mexico, just a half mile south of the Colorado border. Cavenaugh then informed Haines that he would be held to the contract and would be liable to make up the difference between his bid price and the price paid on the open market. Haines wrote to General John Pope, commander of the Department of Missouri, about the situation, but he would eventually lose the contract.[33]

Marketing their cattle was only one difficulty facing Haines and other cattlemen. Many were not prepared to deal with Porter Stockton and they no doubt advised Lacy's herders that Stockton was making a living from the LC herd. Lacy and his partner employed a large force of cowboys and many of them split their time between Trinidad and the San Juan country. Some of them knew Port personally from his days living in Colfax County and others knew him by reputation. One of Thompson and Lacy's top hands was a thirty-four-year-old native of Missouri named Tom Nance. George Thompson's sister, Malinda, was Tom Nance's mother.[34] After Tom's birth the Nance family moved out of Missouri to Fannin County, Texas.[35] They were living there when events spiraled out of control and the Civil War broke out. Unlike many of their neighbors, the Nances were staunch supporters of Abraham Lincoln. In rebel Texas this was a courageous, but dangerous position. Their support of Lincoln and the Union cause ran deep in their family history. One of the Nance's antecedents, Dow Thompson, served in the Black Hawk War with Lincoln and often told of wrestling with the future president.[36] Tom Nance's aunt, Martha Jane Thompson, was born in Sangamon County, Illinois in 1829, near the town so connected with Lincoln's history, Springfield, Illinois.[37] The connection to Lincoln may be even deeper. Tom Nance's grandmother, Nancy Enloe, was a native of North Carolina and the daughter of Abraham Enloe. Family lore and a host of conspiracy theorists report that it may have been Abraham Enloe, and not Thomas Lincoln, who was the father of Abraham Lincoln.[38] George Thompson's nephew would play a pivotal role in the San Juan country turmoil.

With the death of Lincoln and the end of the Civil War, the Nance family faced the return of Confederate soldiers. The war was over, but many of the Texans were not chastened by the defeat of their comrades in arms, which had occurred far to the east. Reconstruction in Texas was, for some, simply a continuation of the hostilities. In northeast Texas those problems exploded with deadly force in a dispute between the Lee and Peacock families. The Lee-Peacock conflict is among the most well known of the post-Civil War Texas feuds.[39] The Nance family joined with Lewis Peacock, the Baldock family, and fellow Unionists. They were opposed by forces led by Confederate veteran Bob Lee. In May 1868, Lee's group rode to the Nance farm and in the ensuing melee Tom Nance's younger brother, Dow Nance, and James Baldock were killed.[40] One of Bob Lee's deadly allies was Mace Bowman. The Confederate veteran and close friend of Pete Burleson served as the elected sheriff of Colfax County in 1882 and 1883.[41] Tom Nance is not mentioned in accounts of the Lee-Peacock Feud, but the death of Dow served to harden his attitude toward Confederate sympathizers. By 1870 Tom Nance's parents and younger siblings left Texas and moved to Harrison County, Missouri.[42] Tom Nance soon made his way to Colorado.

In June of 1880, the census taker reported that Nance and a dozen other cowboys were residing at the Thompson and Lacy headquarters about five miles north of Trinidad. Other cowboys sharing living quarters with Nance included Reuben (Rube) Baldock, whose family had been caught up in the Lee-Peacock feud. Nineteen-year-old Ben Howlan was also listed as one of the herders.[43] Census records are often inaccurate and it's possible that the census enumerator misunderstood "Ben Howlan" and that the herder's real name was Dan Howland, better known as "Big Dan." Howland had a bad reputation in Trinidad and would soon add to that reputation in the San Juan country.[44] As he had done while confronting perilous journeys up the Goodnight-Loving Trail, Lacy continued to employ dangerous herders with short fuses. He viewed his wild-eyed cowboys as a necessary evil.

During the fall of 1880, Howland remained in Trinidad, while Tom Nance traveled to the La Plata valley to help with Thompson and Lacy's San Juan herd. As he entered his mid-thirties he was still an impressive representative of the wilder and woolier cowboys of his day. He was not fully tamed and he never would be. Nance was not one to back down from a fight, whether it involved fists, knives or pistols.[45] Dr. Bernard James Byrne, a surgeon at Fort Lewis, was an admirer of Tom Nance. He reported that Nance had "bright blue eyes, clean white teeth, and the face of an angel Gabriel." Byrne was astounded by Nance's impromptu spectacles "of trick riding that would send shudders down one's back." He described Nance as the leader of a band of men who protected the ranges from the depredations of rustlers and horse thieves. Nance, said Byrnes, was "thorough in his methods and as ruthless as Satan."[46] Like most cowboys, Nance had a streak of independence a mile wide. But once he hired on, he was loyal to the outfit. His allegiance was to Thompson and Lacy and his actions reflected their wishes. His loyalty to the brand was strengthened by his family relationship to George Thompson. Even with that in mind, if his relationship to his employers soured, he would simply quit and move on. Up the Dolores River at Rico, fledgling newspapermen Frank Hartman and Charles Jones had perhaps never heard of Tom Nance. That would soon change.

In the meantime, the unseasoned editors continued to twist their accounts to bolster their own causes and stir up strife. Printing incendiary anonymous letters often served this purpose. A September 30, 1880 letter was signed by "Zuni." The letter's author said they first entered the lower Animas area four years earlier. Perhaps the author was Frank Hartman or possibly his sister Lillie, who had written letters to the *Dolores News* even before her brother was its editor. Zuni noted that some of the difficulties in the lower country were brought on because the Coes and others believed, "a Colorado man had no right to supply the troops with beef while stationed in New Mexico," the inference being that while the troops were at Fort Lewis, the beef contractor rightfully supplied their beef. On the other hand, if the troops were afield in New Mexico, they should purchase local beef on the open market. The writer goes on to say that some residents were hoodwinked into thinking they were breaking up a gang of cow thieves and "the affair culminated in hanging poor Tex." Zuni then takes on the Coe's version of the Jake Bohannon incident. Calling the Coes and their allies a "mob clan," Zuni wrote that they stole a mule from a Navajo, then made up the Bohannon story to cover their theft. Zuni alleged that one of the Indians the Coes reportedly killed showed up in the valley with a letter from the Indian Agent asking all good citizens to assist him in recovering the stolen animal. According to the letter, when the mule was found, it had been branded "COE."[47] The fact that Lew Coe described the event in a letter to the *Cimarron News and Press*, whose readers had little vested interest in San Juan country affairs, lends credence to the Coe version of events. As for branding the mule, the Coes would be expected to do that, since they obviously viewed the beast of burden as being the spoils of war.

While Frank Hartman worked the bellows in Rico, both sides of the dispute stoked the fire in Farmington. Dison Eskridge and Jim Garrett faced increasing pressure from the Coe family. There were growing accusations that they were engaged in cattle rustling. Dison went to a dance that autumn, where he had the misfortune of encountering George Brown, who had refused to shake his hand at Halford's court. According to Hargo, "Brown, with his gang, met Dison at a dance - alone; they set upon him with their shooters and run him off; not, however, until they had assured each other that when they met again it would be a fight to the death."[48] It was not an idle threat. It is possible that Frank Coe was there. At the time he was living in Farmington and his closest neighbors were George Brown and his family.[49]

After Judge Halford was run out of the country, the Coes had free rein along the lower Animas. In October, those who opposed them held a meeting to nominate candidates for justice of the peace and constable for one of the two precincts that covered the western portion of Rio Arriba County. Charles Holliday McHenry was a member of that group.[50]

McHenry served with the Fifty-first Illinois Infantry during the Civil War, eventually rising to the rank of first sergeant. He was lucky to be alive. The Fifty-first saw action at the Battle of Stones River, the Battle of Chickamauga Creek and fought under General Grant at the Siege of Chattanooga.[51] Not long after the nomination meeting, McHenry said that members of the Coe faction approached him and forcefully expressed their dissatisfaction with his activities.[52]

The general election that followed was held on the appropriate date, but that is about the only procedure that followed protocol. According to merchant and stockman T.D. Burns, who was chairman of the Rio Arriba County Commission, the ballots did not reach Tierra Amarilla until a full month after the election. The election judges were unable to canvass the vote before the required deadline. The delay affected the ballot boxes for both precincts and left western Rio Arriba County with a law enforcement void.[53] In one precinct, Mr. Hendrickson (probably William) received the most votes for justice of the peace and Boyd Vaughan had the most votes for constable. (Vaughan later took up ranching in Routt County, Colorado, where he assisted in the arrest of outlaws Harry Tracy and David Lant in 1898. His sister, Nettie, was married to William Locke.) The anti-Coe forces alleged that William Haines, who also happened to be the Bloomfield postmaster, did not forward the election ballots on to Tierra Amarilla as required.[54] Whatever happened, the lack of constables and justices of the peace left the San Juan country teetering on a treacherous precipice.

The law enforcement chasm in western Rio Arriba County was augmented by the rapidly changing situation just north of the border, as the D&RG's hell on wheels railroad camp roared into southwest Colorado. Beginning in November and extending into December well over one thousand people descended on the patch of sagebrush that would become Durango. The population would quickly swell to over two thousand as an ever increasing throng of railroad workers pushed the twin rails toward Silverton.[55] The advancing rail lines drew laborers from Bavaria, Prussia, Ireland, Australia and other parts of the world as well as most of America's states and territories. Henry La Count was superintendent of the railroad's ties and timbers section for the San Juan extension. Each mile of track required 3100 ties. During 1881, La Count's forces produced over 750,000 ties.[56] Housing was scarce and along the banks of the Animas there were a large number of tents and dugouts. Pure spring drinking water was supplied by homesteader Peter Fassbinder for twenty-five cents a barrel.[57] Frame buildings were going up at a rapid pace. Brickyards were operating at full capacity. Six sawmills were providing lumber for the building boom. Across the Animas from Durango, Patrick "Cap" Stanley was supervising the stone and brick work for the erection of one of the largest smelters in Colorado for the New York and San Juan Mining and Smelting Company. Their kilns were producing bricks by the thousands.[58] Along with legitimate entrepreneurs and men needing work, came prostitutes, bunco steerers, gamblers and others looking for a quick buck. By late November the town had seven hotels and restaurants, eleven saloons with four more being built, several dance halls and assorted other businesses.[59] In Durango's early days, the willing could try their luck at the faro tables or try their hand at other games of chance. At Durango's Bank Exchange, Curly McBride ran the roulette wheel.[60] The sporting crowd also sought entertainment at a number of houses of ill repute. One reporter described those who frequented Durango's Railroad Street, which held many of the town's dance halls, saloons and variety theatres, saying, "Here the cow-boy disports himself in terrible suits and stunning hats; the gambler parades his fine clothes and airs his bad grammar and ogles the blear-eyed and paint-bedaubed prostitute."[61] The *La Plata Miner* noted that, "About one-half of Rico and a portion of Animas City have drifted to Durango."[62]

Joining the exodus from Rico were Bert Wilkinson and his cousin Oscar Puett, as well as Hargo Eskridge. Bert and Hargo were attracted to the wide open town and remained there. Os Puett did not linger but traveled down the Animas where he hooked up with Dison Eskridge and Jim Garrett. In November, Ike Stockton left Animas City for Texas. Reportedly, he was on a stock buying trip and expected to be gone all winter. As fall turned to winter, Durango kept up its rapid growth and rumor had it that the town's name would be changed to "Palmer City," in honor of General William Jackson Palmer, founder of the D&RG Railroad.[63] The town was lacking one important structure. According to the *Animas City Southwest*, "What Durango needs most just at the present is a good strong calaboose, as the town is filling up with professedly *ba-ad* men, who need to be tied down occasionally to keep them within bounds." Deputy Sheriff Jim Sullivan patrolled the unincorporated town. If he desired to incarcerate anyone he had to haul them to the log jail in Animas City. Normally he didn't bother. The *Southwest* noted his usual option was "to knock down and drag out, which he does successfully."[64] Jim Sullivan was badly outnumbered and Durango's first Christmas would witness the first of several murderous outbursts.

December 1880 was a violent month throughout the San Juan country. Trouble began on the Pine River near the Middle Bridge which was home to Charles Johnson's combination stage station, road house and store, about four miles upriver from what is now the town of Bayfield. Johnson's also served as the local post office.[65] Charles Johnson (also known as "Race Horse" Johnson) was renowned for his stable of thoroughbreds. At one time he owned Jim Douglas, one of the most well-known horses of his day. In the mid-1880s the native New Yorker took Jim Douglas and Red Girl east and raced them in Chicago. He also raced his horses in his state of birth at Saratoga Springs and Sheepshead Bay on

Coney Island. Prior to his move to the Pine River valley in the 1870s, he lived near Rye, Colorado at the base of the Greenhorn Mountains.[66] On the evening of December 9th several desperadoes called at the home of Johnson's neighbor Colonel Jacob A. Epperson. Epperson was greeted by cocked pistols and the demand for his keys. The men robbed him of $250 and a good watch and chain. The thieves weren't without humor, and told their victim that they were the "James Brothers." Near midnight, the colonel arrived at Johnson's store to report the robbery. There were guests at the stage stop and soon Epperson aroused the slumbering inhabitants, who included newspaperman Eugene Engley. After he told them about the theft, no other action was taken during the night. The next day it was discovered that the same men had stolen several of Johnson's horses. The thieves got away with Johnson's thoroughbred stallion Selim and Blue Bird his prized race mare.[67] Johnson rode over to the home of Al Nunn, who had recently married his daughter Nettie. The men had a rocky relationship, but Johnson put that aside and told Nunn he needed his help. Nunn noted that besides Selim and Blue Bird, the thieves also rode away with "Daylight, a trotting mare, another thoroughbred, and an old saddle horse."[68] The bandit's actions were foolhardy. The rough looking thieves would never be able to sell the race horses for anything close to their true value without a bill of sale. In fact, many people in New Mexico and Colorado would have recognized Johnson's racers on sight.[69] The *Animas City Southwest* reported that James Sutherland, who was staying nearby at the John Thompson place, "had his race-horse, the Billy Wilson colt, exchanged for an old plug." The *Southwest* said, "The thieves seem green in the business," and noted that they were known in the area. The newspaper received a later report which said "the thieves and the stolen property were seen recently on the mesa west of [Tim] McCluer's ranch, on the Florida, also that four white men and two Indians are in hot pursuit at present writing."[70]

Charles Johnson sent out a messenger, known now only as Slim, to spread the word. He headed down the Animas and about three miles above Bondad he fortuitously ran into several of Washington Cox's men, who were driving north with several wagons intending to pick up supplies. Alf Graves, George Cox and John Cox left the wagon train and joined the pursuit.[71] Eventually a dozen men trailed the horse thieves. Charles Johnson led the posse and he was out for blood. Other posse members included one of Johnson's sons, E.A. Clayton, Peter Knickerbocker, Chick Porter, Josh Hale, Dave Murray, and somewhere along the line Johnson picked up the deadliest man in the San Juan country, Porter Stockton.[72] The thoroughbreds were not accustomed to harsh treatment in rough country. Inevitably, Blue Bird fell and injured her leg. This put the thieves in a bind and they soon made camp, enabling their pursuers to gain ground. The posse also made camp, unaware that the thieves were within easy striking distance. As sunlight peered over the eastern horizon the thieves arose and started a campfire, to take the chill off the bitter cold. Johnson

The Pine River Store north of Bayfield, ca. 1890. Charles "Race Horse" Johnson owned the store in the 1880s. Only three people are identified, No. 1 is W.T. Helm, No. 2 is Buckskin Charley a Ute chief, and No. 3 is C.F. Wood. (Courtesy La Plata County Historical Society, No.89.38.048P.)

and the others were already mounted and headed their direction.[73] They were now within thirty miles of Tierra Amarilla and were likely on lands that are now part of the Jicarilla Apache Reservation.[74] It was still early in the morning when the posse had to dismount and switchback their way up a steep hillside. Porter Stockton and Al Nunn were in the lead. At the top of the hill they found clear tracks and mounted their horses. They had barely gone fifty yards when Stockton motioned for Nunn to stop. He dismounted and pulled his firearm. Port moved to his left and brought his weapon up to shoot, but before he could pull the trigger one of the thieves let loose a round which narrowly missed Stockton as it thudded into a tree branch sending bark and wood flying. As the thieves continued shooting, Stockton moved to get a better view and returned fire. His shot was answered immediately with an anguished cry from the thieves' camp. Stockton needlessly told Nunn that he thought he had hit one of them. A round whirred close to Nunn as he knelt on the ground. He returned fire and struck one of the thieves in the right shoulder.[75] About twenty shots were exchanged before the horse rustlers gave up the fight and ran pell-mell for their horses. According to the *Southwest*, the remaining thieves "got away leaving the stolen stock, their camp outfit, flour, revolvers and a Winchester rifle. One of the party left without his boots and another left one of his boots." The posse returned on Thursday and reported there were seven thieves in all. The *Southwest* identified three of them: Jim Hill, Denny Gammon and Jim Martin. (Gammon's name was actually Gannon.) All three men were well known in the area and the *Southwest* noted that Gannon and Martin had run "a saloon over at the Post."[76] It is unclear if their saloon was at the recently abandoned Fort Flagler or over on the La Plata at Fort Lewis. About three weeks after the incident the *Durango Record* reported that Port Stockton killed horse thief Den Gannon.[77] The *Denver Republican* said that one of the blooded horses died because of the hard usage. The *Republican* also indicated that more than one thief was killed, saying, "The thieves will steal no more, nor will a court be troubled with their trial."[78] Al Nunn reported that Blue Bird was crippled and had to be left behind at a ranch, but later died from her injuries. He also confirmed that the man Stockton killed was named Gannon. He said one of the thieves was known as Buckshot and identified the man he shot in the shoulder as Jack (not Jim) Hill.[79]

The Denver newspaper offered no other details about the summary justice meted out on the trail. At least one of the horse thieves lived long enough to talk with the posse men. The short-lived survivor was almost certainly Den Gannon.[80] As he faced the inevitable he told the posse members that, "I had just as good Father and Mother as any one."[81] He said they had raised him right and he did not want them to learn how he had died. Gannon was wearing some desirable rings. After he died, Stockton decided he needed them. When they would not come off, he hacked off several of the offending fingers and retrieved them. He also took the young man's money belt.[82] Another account said Stockton did not cut off any fingers. Stockton intended to do that, but Alf Graves told him he would kill him if he did. Graves's brother-in-law, Isaac Hiram (Ike) Cox, said that made Port "very sore." After the argument, the men buried Den Gannon where he fell.[83] The vigilantes had been fully prepared to shoot the horse thieves, but Stockton's greed and willingness to mutilate a corpse stepped over a line the others wouldn't cross. The full truth of what really happened that cold December morning is lost to history, but Stockton's actions continued to make him enemies in the San Juan country. After this incident Stockton had no bigger enemy than Alf Graves. Port Stockton decided right then that Alf Graves wouldn't get in his way again. But Graves, horrified by his readiness to dismember a dead man, resolved that the San Juan country would be better off without Port Stockton.

Christmas was rapidly approaching when the men returned to their homes. The farmers and stockmen on the lower Animas tried to put aside their differences and endeavored to celebrate the season with good cheer.

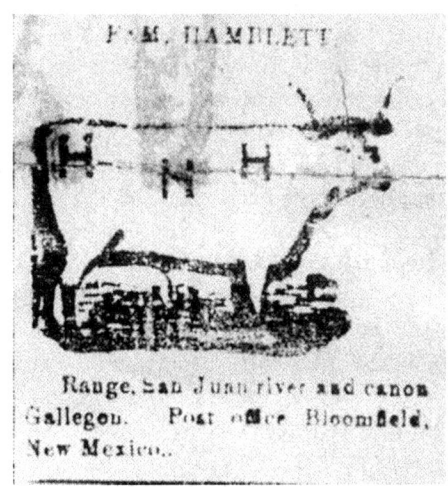

The brand of F. M. Hamblet, from the Northwest New Mexican *(Bloomfield, NM), Feb. 8, 1887. (From the collection of Robert L. Maddox, Jr.)*

Many of the residents attended at least one of two dances held on Christmas Eve. One of the parties was at the home of Francis Marion Hamblet, about four miles from Farmington on the Bloomfield road, near the confluence of the San Juan River and Gallegos Canyon.[84] Local fiddle players and other musicians provided the music. Polkas, waltzes, the schottische and square dances were common fare at local dances. People came from miles around by horseback and wagon to take part in the festivities. William Hendrickson and his housemate, Newlon Covert, rode over to a dance at Olio, near present day Kirtland. Hendrickson said later that he and Covert had a "jolly good time." That evening Covert returned home, but Hendrickson remained overnight. The next day as he was riding home, he ran into a stranger, who asked him if he knew the young men who had been killed at the dance. It was the first he had heard of the Christmas Eve tragedy. As he drew closer to home he saw people gathered at the community's small cemetery. He soon learned from Covert that Oscar Puett and George Brown had been killed at the dance at the Hamblet residence.[85] The threats of death that passed between Dison Eskridge and Brown at the earlier party had come to fruition. The other victim, Os Puett, had gone to the party accompanied by his friends, Dison Eskridge and Jim Garrett.[86] Puett was about eighteen-years-old and unmarried at the time of his death.[87] Brown was also single and about twenty-one years old.[88] Residents along the lower Animas referred to Puett as the "Coloradian" or the Colorado boy who was killed at the Hamblet's.[89]

Accounts vary as to the events at the Hamblet home, dependent upon who is telling the tale. In Durango there was a new newspaper called the *Durango Record*. The editor was a widow, Mrs. C.W. Romney. The shrewd businesswoman was gambling that Durango would boom, but not bust when the railroad arrived and passed on toward Silverton. The very first edition of the *Record* was published on December 29th. Heavy snowfall prevented the construction of the *Record's* permanent quarters, which when completed would house a large steam operated cylinder press.[90] The first issue of the *Durango Record* carried news of the incident at the Hamblet home.[91] Mrs. Romney reported that during the party the Hamblet residence "was visited by a party of three ruffians, Oscar Pruett [sic], Dison Eskridge and James Garrett, who conducted themselves in such an indecent and boisterous manner, using profane and obscene language in the presence of ladies that they were requested by the host to leave."[92] The group went outside, but remained boisterous and shot off their pistols. Hamblet, wishing to quiet them, went to the door and invited them to come back inside, behave themselves and enjoy the dance. George Brown also went outside "simply as a spectator, taking no part in the row." The three men greeted the invitation by firing toward the doorway and breaking away from the house at the same time. Several men rushed outside and returned fire. According to the article, Brown was standing by the door when he was shot in the chest. Young Puett fell behind as he and his two companions retreated and fired.

Puett's body was discovered some distance from the house about twenty minutes after the melee, with a bullet in his chest. In a dubious miracle of frontier forensics the reporting party deduced that he was "evidently shot by his own party, by accident, judging from the way he was running and the position he was in when found." The *Durango Record* concluded their article, noting, "The community are greatly enraged and seventeen of the best citizens are out in pursuit of the murderers, and a thousand dollars reward is offered for them, dead or alive. If caught short work will be made of them."[93] Along the lower Animas, Romney's account was heartily endorsed by the Coe faction. In the coming months, it would be one of the few times that happened.

After reading the *Record's* description of the shootout, Hargo Eskridge was outraged. As time would tell, young Hargo was articulate, venomous and fearless. The *Record's* second issue carried his response. In it, Hargo said the shooting of Brown "was a case of kill or be killed," although he offered few details about the incident. Oddly, considering two men were killed, Hargo was particularly upset that Dison and Jim Garrett were accused of using bad language. He said, "I do not know who your informant is, but I say that the obscene and profane part of it is a *big black villainous lie."* He challenged the informant and his friends saying "If any man or set of men – always provided it is not a mob – will tell me that, I will cram it down his infernol [sic] black throat."⁹⁴ On the same day Hargo's letter appeared in the *Weekly Record*, Jim Garrett's sixteen-year-old sister, Cora Garrett, penned a letter to the *Record* from her home in Conejos County. She demanded a retraction and apology. As for Jim Garrett's character she recommended the *Record* check with Field & Hill, a forwarding and commission firm in Alamosa and with Ed Schiffer and Company. Schiffer was a Durango grocer. Cora said she had known Dison for three years and had never heard him swear. Considering the growing wrath facing Garrett and Eskridge, the concern over allegations that they used foul language was misplaced effort. The *Record* defended their publication, saying they can't wait for an arrest and trial before publishing news of a murder. They noted that, "If injustice is done by this paper, its columns are open to the other side."⁹⁵ As the San Juan country turmoil progressed that promise would be tested.

Jap Coe recalled that night in a letter. He said that before the three men rode out to the Hamblet place, they "filled themselves with bad whiskey, fired into a store in town" and headed for the Hamblet home, where they knew they would find some of their worst enemies. He described George Brown as "an honest farmer's boy." That assessment was accurate, as far as it goes, but it fails to address all facets of Brown's character. Jap Coe also noted that the "farmer's boy" was equipped with a six-shooter. According to Coe, the three men provoked the row and then shot Brown. Coe reported that even though he was mortally wounded, Brown managed to inflict the wound which killed Puett and he winged Eskridge. Jap said that young Puett was not a cattle thief, but was staying with Eskridge and Garrett and was well aware of the bad blood between Brown and Eskridge. Puett accompanied his friends expecting, in fact hoping to find, trouble.⁹⁶

Hartman and Jones soon entered the war of words. The Rico newspapermen were more than willing to present the Garrett/Eskridge side of the fray and Hargo was not through venting his wrath. On January 15, 1881 the *Dolores News* carried his correspondence to Eugene Engley, the editor of the *Southwest*. Settlers along the lower Animas may not have been familiar with Hargo, but he was a force to be reckoned with, as they would soon find out. In the letter Eskridge said, "It is a very unpleasant task to answer such false and malignant communications as appeared in the first issue of the *Durango Record*, and again in your paper of January 1ˢᵗ."⁹⁷ Hargo then provided the *Southwest* with his secondhand version of events, which he had certainly heard from his brother, Dison. The *News* obliged Jim Garrett and printed his firsthand narrative. Piecing the two accounts together provides their side of the story.

Garrett said that both he and Dison were invited to the party by eighteen-year-old Lee Hamblet "in person," and they went there with no intent of causing a disturbance. His assertion that they had come to the party by invitation may be true. One of the Hamblet's friends was Tom Fulcher, who lived nearby. Fulcher was Garrett's cousin and it is certain that Eskridge and Garrett were acquainted with the Hamblet family through their association with Fulcher. The dance was in progress when Garrett, Eskridge and Puett arrived and upon entering the residence Garrett sat down and removed his spurs. Garrett does not describe Dison's reaction when he realized that George Brown was also at the party. He then went into the kitchen and talked with Fulcher and with the host, who he described as "old man Hamblet." While dancing continued in the other room, Os Puett came to the door and called Garrett. He had disturbing news. He told Garrett that, "we could not get numbers." As was common on the frontier, the men far outnumbered women at the party. The usual practice was to charge the men a nominal amount, usually one dollar for a ticket. The ticket had a number on it and before each dance the caller would yell out a sequence of numbers and only those holding the called numbers could dance. Refusing to sell numbered tickets to the three men was like a slap in the face. After hearing Puett's disturbing news, Garrett called to Eskridge, who headed toward Garrett. The instigators knew that the situation was about to erupt and as Eskridge walked toward Garrett, he was trailed by a group of men. Lee Hamblet's older brother, twenty-three-year-old John, took the lead and addressed Garrett, saying, "Jim I don't want you to think hard of me as I have always been a friend of yours, and if I was running it things would be different." Garrett, Eskridge and Puett were told to leave. George Brown and his allies were running things and now they had forced John Hamblet to eject the three men from his parent's home. Garrett told Hamblet that they had not been treated right, but if they were not wanted, that he was man enough to leave and he started for his horse. Eskridge seethed and looked for an opportunity to draw his weapon. Garrett was several feet outside the door when gunfire erupted inside the house, piercing the cold night air. With his adrenaline pumping, Garrett quickly ducked for cover behind a wagon. Inside the house, Fulcher grabbed Eskridge, perhaps to prevent more shooting, and Garrett heard Eskridge imploring Fulcher to turn him loose. He also heard Puett and Lee Hamblet speaking loudly.[98] Puett grabbed Hamblet around the neck and pleaded with him not to let the others kill him. Lee said, "Then God damn you, run; that's the only way I can save you." As Puett ran, he was shot in the back.[99] Puett screamed out, "Oh, I am shot!" Even though he was mortally wounded, he ran a few steps and fell. At that point, Fulcher loosened his grip and Eskridge ran for the door seeking the cover of darkness outside.[100] George Brown ran out the back door and sought to prevent Dison's escape. He hoped to catch Dison by surprise and came around the corner of the house with his gun drawn. But when Brown exposed himself, it was Eskridge who fired, killing Brown.[101] Someone came out of the cabin and yelled out, "Where is Dison?" Out of the pitch black came the chilling reply, "Here I am, come on boys." Shortly afterwards Eskridge dashed for his horse as blind shots whined toward the sound of his running. Then another person exited the house holding a gun and said, "God damn them, we will give them enough of it." Garrett was still hunkered down behind the wagon and decided not to wait to see if more men came outside. He quickly bolted for the tethered horses, where he found Dison. They leapt into their saddles and whipped their mounts into a dead run, quickly disappearing into the frigid darkness. Garrett later reported that he fired no shots during the incident.[102] Back at the Hamblet home, two men lay dead as others prepared to pursue Eskridge and Garrett. The fleeing fugitives rode over the San Juan/Animas divide and made their way to Port Stockton's house near Flora Vista. A few months later the *Durango Record* noted that "he [Stockton] was believed to have harbored Dyson Eskridge and Jim Garrett in their flight."[103]

Dison and Garrett knew their best hope was to head north and they soon made their way to Durango, where Hargo had opened a business. The Eclipse Hall, as Jap Coe described it, was "a man-trap and ten-pin alley."[104] Eskridge owned the business with a man named Haverty. Their advertisements in the *Durango Record* said, "Eclipse Saloon And 10-Pin Alley, Where you will always find the best brands of Wines, Liquors and Cigars. HAVERTY & ESKRIDGE."[105] Shortly after the Hamblet dance ruckus, Hargo described his situation, saying, "I am engaged in legitimate business, surrounded by a cosmopolitan population in a future great city."[106] Dison decided that discretion was the better part of valor. The *Record* reported that he had "fled the country and has not been heard of since."[107] He probably went to Conejos to seek advice and shelter from his older brother, Dow. Garrett may have also fled to the San Luis Valley to be with his family. Hargo wasn't going anywhere and if he was aware of the Coes' reputation from Lincoln County, he was decidedly unimpressed. He remained in Durango and defied the Coes and their allies. According to Hargo, not long after the fight at the Hamblet's, he received an anonymous threatening letter. He responded publicly in the *Record*, saying the threat of "a vigilance committee or mob of some kind does not scare me." In the same letter he called the *Durango Record's* informants "unmitigated liars and unprincipled villains." As to the charge that Garrett or Dison shot Puett by accident, he spewed, "They perjure themselves and poison the very air they breath." He throws down the gauntlet and taunts the cowboys of the lower valley, saying, "and, right here, before I 'bile' over, I will just add that my address is Durango, and I can be found at my place of business -- the Eclipse Hall, on F Street, day or night, awake or asleep."[108]

Some accounts say that Port Stockton accompanied Eskridge, Garrett and Puett to the party and joined in their insulting conduct and gunplay.[109] That was not the case. Stockton is not mentioned in letters written by Hargo Eskridge, Jim Garrett or Cora Garrett or in the first story about the shooting in the *Durango Record*. The first report carried in the *Animas City Southwest* also does not mention Port Stockton. Letters written by C.H. McHenry and George Lockhart a few months after the incident, both of which mention the shootout, do not mention Stockton.[110] Port Stockton was many things, but a shrinking violet was not one of them. It is just not possible that he was at the skirmish, yet left no impression on those who were there. The shootings at the Hamblet home unleashed a wave of violence that would spread like wildfire through the Animas valley and, even though neither Stockton brother was there, events of that night would have a decided impact on the two Texans.

The whole country around Farmington was in an uproar over the killings. The day after Christmas, William Hendrickson went into Farmington, where he found a large number of men gathered. For a town with only a few small buildings and a small population, the number of men was notable. Hendrickson saw George's father, Doc Brown, who at sixty years old, was one of the older residents of the area.[111] As was often common on the frontier, he was not a medical school graduate, his title being one of courtesy that reflected the high regard he held in the community.[112] Doc Brown earned his living as a farmer, but when it came to childbirth and the treatment of fractures, ailments and injuries common to the frontier, he was a natural. He was a godsend to the little community. Two days after the death of George Brown, Hendrickson recalled that, "The poor heartstricken father looked the very picture of desperation."[113] George Brown had received a Christian burial the day before, but for almost two full days the mortal remains of Oscar Puett remained unburied.

Even in death, Puett was the victim of his association with Eskridge and Garrett. The killings had a dramatic impact on Farmington, fracturing the community. The treatment of Puett's body foretold the troubles to come. Some residents began to take sides over the killings, but other residents wished to remain neutral. They feared taking sides, lest they offend one or the other. Both victims had friends and family in the area. Doc Brown was highly respected along the lower Animas. The Puetts, who had been among the area's earliest residents, were well known in northwest New Mexico and southwest Colorado. Almost immediately the side that favored the Brown family began to take precedence in New Mexico. That side was supported by the Coes. In Colorado, the side that backed the Puett family garnered the most support. That side was backed by the Eskridge brothers. With one notable exception, members of the Brown and Puett families stayed out of the way as the hostilities grew.

Eventually, Puett's remains were taken to Farmington's small adobe school house, which had been built in 1879 under the guidance of William Locke. No members of Puett's immediate family were nearby to take charge of the body. His parents were in Pagosa Springs and his uncle, Al Puett, was also out of the area. Flora Pyle was Puett's twenty-two or twenty-three-year-old first cousin and she and her husband Orville lived near the San Juan on the peninsula formed by the confluence of the Animas and San Juan Rivers. Because they feared retaliation, they would not allow the body onto their property.[114] Orville Pyle was born in Ohio into a Quaker family.[115] He shared the pacifist leanings common to his faith and was not inclined to confront the Coes or their allies. He was the first school teacher in Farmington and that may be the reason the remains were taken to the school house.[116] Threats may have come from their neighbor; while Frank Coe's closest neighbor on one side was the Brown family, his nearest neighbor on the other side was Flora Pyle and her family.[117]

William Hendrickson went to the school to view the body. Puett had, by then, been dead for two days and in an empathetic understatement Hendrickson observed, "It was evident, that the body should be buried." A one-armed Englishman named Seth Welfoot was one of the first to step forward. C.H. McHenry, a friend of the Puetts, also volunteered for the task.[118] In 1879 the McHenry family lived on Bob Dwyer's place in Animas City. In the early months of 1880 they moved to Rio Arriba County after McHenry purchased 160 acres on squatter's rights from Al Puett. His new home was a couple of miles below the Hamblet home.[119] Given his Civil War service, there is no question that he was a man with nerve. He lent his support to Hendrickson and Welfoot. The three men started to the cemetery with picks and shovels, but received advice that they should not go, because they might be fired upon. The group then tried to talk some disinterested strangers camped on the river into performing the task, but they refused. The men returned to the cemetery, but then walked a little ways away and marked off a grave, hoping the location might not offend anyone and under the belief that Puett's family might one day move the remains. Despite the obvious righteousness of their mission, they weakened and did not dig the grave. As the day progressed the crowd in town grew smaller. About twenty remained at W.G. Markley's adobe store, but no one would bury Puett. As the afternoon dragged on Hendrickson agonized over how to move the men, without offending anyone. Finally, he asked them a few questions to ponder in their own minds. He framed the questions around their duty as civilized men. He encouraged everyone to do what was right. He said there could be no harm in burying the boy, but if left unburied the body could cause much harm. At that, Bill Gannon, who had been living with William Locke and his family, stepped forward. Soon others volunteered.

It was the late afternoon, the shadows were long and there was a steady drizzle. Hendrickson reported that all of the men gathered in the store walked out and headed to the school house. They pulled their coats closed as the rain dampened their clothes and dripped from their hats. They retrieved the body, now bearing even more evidence of two days neglect. The sad but determined cortege trudged up the street, their boots

Frank Hartman as he appeared in his later years. In the early 1880s Hartman was co-editor of the pro-Stockton Dolores News *of Rico, Colorado. In the 1930s Hartman operated his last newspaper, the* Farmington Republican. *This photo was probably taken in front of the* Republican's *office, ca. 1930. Hartman and his family were among the very first families to settle in Farmington, arriving in 1876. He operated the* Republican *until his death on October 15, 1934.
(Photo courtesy of Southwest Collection, Special Collections Library, Texas Tech University, Lubbock, TX, Clifford B. Jones Collection, No. 422 E4.)*

Opposite Page: Farmington, New Mexico, 1884. This area is now downtown Farmington. (Courtesy Aztec Museum Association Historic Photo Collection.)

becoming weighted down with mud. Finally, poor Puett was lowered into his final resting place, apart from the main cemetery. Hendrickson was ill and did not wait. He walked over to the McGalliard home to lay down and rest. As the other men parted ways, a heavy gloom enveloped the valley.[120]

Christmas Eve 1880 was a rough day for the Puett family. At almost the exact time that Oscar Puett was being shot and killed, his young cousin, Bert Wilkinson, was shooting and killing a man in Durango.[121] Bert's mother, Ellen Puett Wilkinson Hendrickson, was at the epicenter of the family most drastically affected by the violence in the San Juan country. She was the sister of Al and Austin Puett and the aunt of Oscar Puett. Her second husband Simeon was the brother of William Hendrickson and she was the mother of Flora Pyle.[122] What was likely Bert Wilkinson's first murder took place in the saloon in the Coliseum Theater, which was owned by Miles B. "Jim" Marshall.[123] A gambler named Jerry Bartol had quarreled with Wilkinson over a year before. On Christmas Eve, Bartol renewed his fight with Wilkinson and then sought to stir up trouble between Wilkinson and Samuel Swinford, who was known as "Comanche Bill." Swinford was seeing visions of sugar plums when Bartol awakened him and shortly thereafter the men strode into the saloon.[124] The core of the dispute revolved around the favors of a Durango prostitute.[125] Bert had some hard edges, but was still young in the ways of the world. He had it bad for the lady of the evening and was willing to kill or die for her. Bartol's plan appeared to be working out as "Comanche Bill" and Wilkinson exchanged heated words. Wilkinson is often depicted as an overgrown kid, but his nerve that night contradicts that dismissive description. Swinford challenged Bert to a fight. Wilkinson eagerly took up the challenge and offered Swinford his choice of weapons. Guns were chosen and Swinford, ever the gentleman, asked Wilkinson to choose the distance. Young Wilkinson coolly replied, "Just as we stand."[126] Swinford evidently wasn't the gunman he thought he was; he fired and missed. Wilkinson returned fire, striking Swinford in the arm, the cheek and one fatal shot found his brain. Jim Sullivan, the marshal of Durango, was a few blocks away at the time of the shooting. Wilkinson was unscathed. He left Durango, but remained in the area. He was never arrested for the killing of Swinford. The *Dolores News* concluded their article about the shooting by saying, "He [Wilkinson] has many friends here who will regret to hear of his trouble."[127] As with other incidents in the region there was more than one version. The *Durango Record* described it as a general melee with Wilkinson and others on one side and Swinford and others on the other side, with at least a dozen shots being fired. They reported that Samuel Coon received a scalp wound. It was thought Wilkinson fired the fatal shots, but in the confusion no one could be certain. Wilkinson himself furthered that perception because, "He disappeared immediately after the shooting and has not been seen since."[128]

A few days after the killing, Jim Marshall asked the *Durango Record* to publish the following information, "M.B. Marshall & Co., wish it stated that they did all in their power at the time of the shooting of Swinford (known as Comanche), to prevent a quarrel, but to no effect. They aim to keep a quiet and orderly house at all times, where strangers can spend a pleasant evening."[129] That would soon prove to be an impossible task.

Frederic Remington's "A Row in a Cattle Town," from Theodore Roosevelt's "Ranch Life in the Far West," The Century Illustrated Monthly Magazine, *Vol. 35, No. 4, February 1888. (Author's collection.)*

For the Puett family, the sting of the lawless frontier was unimaginably harsh, yet their nightmare was not over. Down in Farmington well-armed cowboys were combing the countryside looking for Dison Eskridge and Jim Garrett. Most people in the area probably did not know that there was an interconnected web of family and personal relationships which bound the principal players involved in the Christmas Eve murders together. This volatile combination would soon result in a maelstrom of violence, which would encompass the Animas River valley from Farmington to Silverton.

Chapter Nine

Vigilantes and Ruffians

We are the whirlwinds that winnow the West---
We scatter the wicked like straw!
We are the Nemeses, never at rest---
We are Justice, and Right, and the Law! [1]

As the New Year began, the search for Eskridge and Garrett continued. Porter Stockton, who was always up for a manhunt, did not join the vigilantes. His lack of interest was no doubt viewed with suspicion. Rumors swirled that Port had hidden the fugitives and otherwise assisted with their escape to Colorado.[2] Ike Stockton reported that one day during the search the vigilantes passed by his brother's house. They informed him that they had not found Eskridge, who was number one on their list. Port retorted, "If you meant to lynch him I am glad you didn't get him. I believe every man should have a fair trial."[3] Ike was, no doubt, embellishing his brother's words or inventing them out of whole cloth. However, Port probably did openly express his support for Eskridge and Garrett in a less eloquent manner. Stockton's brazen cattle stealing had made him no friends. The stockmen accepted the fact that on the open range some loss was inevitable, but Stockton was stealing more than his share. The cattlemen had reached their limits of tolerance.

The plan to finally rid the San Juan country of Stockton's odious presence reached the point of no return in Bloomfield at the Haines and Hughes Store. According to Haines, Port Stockton and Alf Graves had an argument in his store in late December or early January. Few men had the nerve to stand up to Porter Stockton, but the bull-necked Graves backed down from no man. Their dispute over the removal of Den Gannon's rings hadn't cooled and while Stockton ranted, an unshaken Graves stood his ground. Stockton thought about immediately adding Graves to the list of men he had killed, but somehow he managed to control that impulse. Perhaps Stockton thought about Graves's steadfast and fearless in-laws: George, Jim and John Cox and their father, Wash Cox. Backing down in front of William Haines and other witnesses was the ultimate humiliation, and like the skulking bully he was, after Graves left, a blustering Stockton told William Haines that he would kill Graves the first chance he had. Haines dutifully sent word to the cattleman to watch out because Stockton intended to kill him on sight.[4] Graves had known Stockton's propensity for violence for a long time, going clear back to Erath County and later in Colfax County. He was more aware than most that Stockton had not received the justice he so richly deserved. Graves knew that Stockton needed to be killed and that someday someone would do that. Reluctantly, Graves realized that fate had chosen him to accept that daunting responsibility. Stockton had bitten the hand that fed him one too many times. He knew that large cattlemen, like Cap Hart, H.W. Cox and Alf Graves, were powerful and potentially deadly enemies. Yet throughout his time in the San Juan country he continually antagonized them. Then there was the region's other well-known cattleman, Irvin Lacy. He was in an odd position. His wife was a first cousin to Porter Stockton. It didn't matter. He and his partner, George Thompson, were fed up with Stockton's continual rustling and boastful threats. Graves's plan to kill Stockton moved forward with the full knowledge and support of the two largest cattle outfits in northwest New Mexico: Thompson and Lacy, and Wash Cox.

Graves had no intention of having a fair fight with Porter Stockton. He planned to overwhelm the outlaw with firepower. Stockton had always been his own worst enemy and several of the local men wanted to settle their differences with the swaggering brute. Perhaps others relished the opportunity to kill one of the most infamous desperadoes in the territory. At least six men were involved and there may have been ten or more. Only two of these men can be identified with absolute certainty: Alf Graves and Thomas Nance.[5] From the time he decided to kill Porter Stockton, Graves knew that if there was only one man who rode with him, it had to be Thompson and Lacy's herder and chief enforcer Tom Nance.[6] While Graves was stalwart and brave, he might have a split second hesitation upon finding a man in his gun sights. Nance would have no such compunction, no matter who was on the wrong end of his barrel. Among the papers of Governor Lew Wallace is an undated and unattributed, rough, scribbled notation which indicates that Tom Nance, Alf Graves, J. Raser and C. Raser were "willing to stand trial."[7] The scribbled note was probably made by Adjutant General Max Frost. As it happens that exact phrase was used in a letter about Stockton's killing from Frost to the governor. Frost's official report only names Graves and Nance.

James and Cal Raser were the sons of James and Jane Raser. (Their name was sometimes spelled Razor and Razier.) The Rasers were among the earliest settlers in western Rio Arriba County. In 1877 they lived on the La Plata, but they and several nearby families moved to the Animas valley after being harassed by Ute Indians.[8] On the Animas the Raser's were neighbors to John and Henrietta and Burr Milleson, which also made them neighbors to Port Stockton and his family. The elder James Raser was about sixty years old in 1880.[9] His son, James, was about twenty-five and he may have been working as a mail carrier in Ouray County, Colorado before returning to the lower Animas, where he began to look for trouble.[10] That December, Cal Raser was about nineteen years old.[11] The Raser family were known to be on friendly terms with Tom Nance, Alf Graves and the Coe family.[12] Some accounts include two young farmers in the group. One of them was Burr Milleson. The Milleson's were Port Stockton's close neighbors and it was the Milleson family who helped John Leslie after Port busted him over the head with his pistol.[13] The other farmer was twenty-seven or twenty-eight-year-old George Lockhart.[14] He lived over on the La Plata and was married to Edward Thomas's daughter Mary Ann. They had two children.[15] Lockhart was not averse to settling matters with gunfire. In June 1879 he had faced down a crowd of seven armed men who sought to collect a toll for passing over Cumbres Pass. In the ensuing struggle, Lockhart shot and killed José Marquez. Despite sustaining several bullet wounds, he fled south over the pass and made his way to his home in the La Plata valley.[16] The Lockhart and Thomas places were close to that of twenty-seven-year-old stockman and blacksmith Johnny Pond. Their families had witnessed local cattle rustlers in action, since the stolen animals were commonly driven up the lightly populated La Plata valley.[17] Some say that Al Dustin joined the vigilantes.[18] Almon E. (Al) Dustin was a native of Iowa and about twenty years old.[19] He would become the third man to serve as the sheriff of San Juan County, after it was carved out of the western part of Rio Arriba County.[20] Another cowboy, Joe Caldwell, is also mentioned as being one of the group.[21] Like Nance, Caldwell was riding the line for Thompson and Lacy.[22] According to George Coe, his cousin Frank Coe also participated.[23] At least one account, contemporary to the time, infers that the Coe men were members of the group who killed Port Stockton.[24] Perhaps others were there, while some of those shown above were not. The dense fogs of time make it difficult to come up with a definitive list.

The *New Mexican* reported that, while living on the Animas, Stockton continued to "make himself dreaded by all peace loving men." The newspaper also noted that, "He declared that he was absolutely desperate, a statement which those acquainted [with] his career readily believed."[25] George Coe wrote that eight to ten men rode to Stockton's home and that their intent was to give "Porter Stockton notice to leave [the] country."[26] That's doubtful. Given Stockton's character, that would have been a fool's errand. The only notice they intended to serve Stockton would issue from the barrels of their pistols and rifles. With the nooses from multiple murder warrants hanging over his head, why he continued to live openly in defiance of all the authorities is a question only he could answer. He was about thirty-one-years old, and one of the most infamous hooligans in the territory. Many outlaws, if they survived into their thirties, changed their ways, their name, and moved far away from the scenes of their crimes. Stockton's wife must have hoped and likely urged him to do just that. Often the reformed desperadoes lived to a ripe old age. But Stockton enjoyed the danger. He enjoyed being the biggest bully in the valley and held no fear of the future. Yet he had not lived that long by being careless, and any group of men approaching his home would have been met with suspicion and deadly intent. The vigilantes were equally ready. They knew Port Stockton had a penchant for shooting first and not even bothering to ask questions later. As the men gathered, they fully expected a deadly confrontation. They checked and re-checked their weapons, cinched their saddles tight and did all they could to give themselves an edge.

On prior occasions, Port moved on after sensing the wrath he engendered had reached the boiling point. Port had always outsmarted or outran his enemies, but for once his hubris was greater than his sense of self-preservation. The murder of George Brown galvanized the residents around Farmington. They felt they were on a righteous mission and they shared an absolute confidence that they would see no response from territorial and county officials. Since they now hoped to act without the color of law, they relied on the continued timid response from those in authority. They were fed up with wanton violence. They were disgusted and frustrated with their own impotence in the face of Stockton's menacing

Frederick Remington's "Saddling Fresh Horses," from Theodore Roosevelt's "The Round-up," The Century Illustrated Monthly Magazine, *Vol. 35, No. 6, April 1888. (Author's collection.)*

George Lockhart, ca. early 1880s. Lockhart was a vocal opponent of the Stockton-Eskridge crowd and may have ridden with the vigilantes on the mission to kill Porter Stockton. In February 1887 he was working as an Apache County, Arizona deputy sheriff when he was shot and killed by Navajo Indians. (Courtesy Wayne Dale.)

presence. The formation of vigilantes was a time-honored tradition on the frontier, but there was something starkly different in this case. Normally, the posse which formed to seek out Dison Eskridge and Jim Garrett would have faded away after their targets found safety in Colorado. If any man could fuel the vigilantes thirst for blood it was Porter Stockton, and now that he was allied with Eskridge and Garrett, his removal was of paramount importance. In one bold stroke they sought to kill three birds with one stone. By killing Stockton, they would not only rid the territory of one of its most infamous murderers, but they would remove their most deadly antagonist and send an unmistakable message to Eskridge, Garrett and their supporters. However, in their overwhelming desire to somehow strike a blow for justice, they neglected the icy calculation which made Ike Stockton and Hargo Eskridge formidable enemies.

Tuesday, January 4, 1881 dawned with typical bitter cold in the Animas River valley. For those who were there, it was a day long remembered. In later years, young awestruck boys would listen with rapt attention as men they viewed as old cowboys told their stories. Tales told around the campfire left an indelible impression on Burr Milleson's stepson, James A. (Harry) McWilliams. As an old cowboy himself Harry Mac, as he was known in later years, recalled those campfire stories with those who shared an interest in the region's early history. Harry reported that six men went out in search of Stockton. Four of the six named by Harry Mac were Alf Graves, Tom Nance, Al Dustin and Burr Milleson. The vigilantes heard a rumor that Stockton could be found over by Lew Coe's ranch on the outskirts of Farmington. They headed for Coe's place, but did not find Stockton. From there they proceeded up the old trail on the north bank of the Animas and forded the river where an arroyo enters the river just downstream from Stockton's place about six miles below Aztec. After crossing the river they headed east. The day was cold and Alf Graves was bundled in a huge mackinaw with his pistol buried inside. Graves was not a gunfighter, and it seems likely that the cattleman's weapon of choice was the one he knew best, his rifle. According to McWilliams, the men were riding in pairs with Graves and Dustin in the lead and Nance and Milleson riding drag. It is anybody's guess as to the identity of the men riding in the center. Perhaps it was the Raser brothers, or perhaps Frank Coe and George Lockhart were there. Harry Mac said that Milleson was riding to the right of Nance when Nance asked him to switch places. Nance's new position gave him a better field of fire as they approached the Stockton place. Graves's position in the lead made him the most likely first target. As the men neared the house, Stockton appeared at the door. He was not in the mood for conversation. He began to draw his rifle up into firing position. Tom Nance reacted swiftly, taking aim, he fired a round. His shot dropped Stockton in the doorway. The men thought the fight was over. They were wrong. Emily Stockton was true to her roots on the Texas frontier. She came outside, knelt by a wagon wheel and took aim with a shotgun. (Some versions say Emily was wielding a Winchester rifle.) Nance took no chances. He made a fortuitous shot, which shattered the stock of Emily's gun, inflicting a non-fatal wound. Besides Emily, her three children were also witness to the shootout and its gory aftermath. Linn Blancett, whose father and grandfather helped bury Stockton, told an almost identical account of the death of Port Stockton.[27]

This version of events is supported by the only official investigation of the shooting, which took place a full three months after the incident. Adjutant General Max Frost writing to Governor Lew Wallace reported that, "The killing of Porter Stockton was done by Thomas Nance and Alf Graves, out a party of 6. Stockton had threatened their lives and was in the act of draining his pistol." He also noted, "These men are willing to stand trial and are all here."[28]

On January 10th the *Durango Weekly Record* published a wildly different tale of Stockton's death. According to the *Record*,

> Porter Stockton, ex-marshal of Animas City, met his death at his ranch in New Mexico, thirty-five miles down the Animas on Tuesday, January 4th, at the hands of a party of eighteen, who called for the purpose of exterminating him. They surrounded his house, and Stockton and wife both came to the door, armed with rifles. Both sides opened fire, and Stockton fell pierced with eighteen bullets. His wife, who had fired one shot, was stuck in the abdomen by a splinter from the stock of her rifle which had received a bullet. At last accounts she was living, but no hopes are entertained of her recovery, as she was in a delicate state of health at the time of receiving the wound.

It is not known who provided the *Record* with this absurd tale, but it is clearly an impossibility that eighteen men could let loose a volley of fire at two figures in a doorway and hit one of them eighteen times, while the other was not struck by even one bullet.[29]

Several residents in Animas City, Durango and nearby communities had known Porter Stockton since his days in Texas. Those included Wash Cox, Alf Graves, George Morrison and "One-armed" Billy Wilson. There were certainly others. As news of the shooting made the rounds some of those men recalled Stockton's misdeeds and they were published in the *Record* alongside the story of his death. Port's last victim was identified as horse thief Den Gannon. The *Record* noted that Stockton "has been a terror to the community wherever he has lived, and lays claim to the killing of nineteen men, which is a fair average for a man of his years about thirty." The Durango weekly said the impetus for the deadly expedition was Port's threats "against the lives of a half dozen of the community."[30]

Alf Graves, who led the expedition to kill Porter Stockton, is the mustached man. Standing to his left is his wife Nancy Belle (Cox). Standing with them are their children, Laura, John and Bruce. Seated left to right are: Henry Wood, Mary (Graves) Wood Jim Taylor, Matilda (Graves) Taylor and Washington Graves. The Wood's children are Charles and Belle. The Taylor infant is Laura, ca. December 1896. (Courtesy Aztec Museum Association Historic Photo Collection.)

The death of Port Stockton was stunning news, but because telegraph wires had not yet reached Durango or Farmington, word of the killing was slow in traveling outside the San Juan country. On January 14, 1881, the *Santa Fe Daily New Mexican* carried an extensive article about the shooting. The headlines read, "Bullets. They Do Some Good on the Animas -- Death of a Noted Desperado -- A Woman Also Hurt." For some reason the *New Mexican* placed the day of the shooting as "Monday last." That would be January 10th, 1881. (Durango was much closer to the action and the *Record's* date of Tuesday January 4th is correct, but the erroneous *New Mexican* date has found its way into latter day accounts.) According to the Santa Fe daily, "Port is said to have made fourteen men bite the dust, and the announcement of his death to a crowd of San Juan men yesterday, made them throw up their hats with joy." The San Juan men described Port as "a man without a scruple of any kind and one who thought no more of taking the life of a human being than most men would think of shooting game or hooking fish." The Santa Fe newspaper said that Graves and three other men "had occasion" to ride by Stockton's place, "where the outlaw lived with a woman whom he called his wife." As they passed by, Stockton came out and renewed his quarrel with Graves and tried to draw his pistol. Seeing the action the three men with Graves opened fire and killed Stockton. "The woman" then fired at the men with a Winchester and the men returned fire, striking her and putting her out of action. The newspaper noted that, "at the store of Mr. Haines on Tuesday there was a general jollification." The *New Mexican* also recounted some of Port's most notorious misdeeds from the Cimarron to the San Juan. The shootings at F.M. Hamblet's house were a fresh memory, having occurred only three weeks before, but the incident is not mentioned in the article. The omission adds even more evidence that Port Stockton was not at the Hamblet home shootout.[31]

In northeast New Mexico, Port's death was welcomed. The *Las Vegas Daily Optic* said, "Porter Stockton, well and unfavorably known throughout New Mexico and later the terror of the San Juan country, is reported killed. The last man to fall a victim to his deadly aim in this Territory was poor Ed. Withers, at Otero. Stockton was afterwards in the saloon business at Baughl's station, but the officers preferred not to hunt him down; however, such fellows always go with their boots on."[32] The *Optic's* editor had never heard of horse thief Den Gannon. The Las Vegas newspaper later described Stockton as "one of the most hardened murderers and desperadoes that ever darkened the pages of history and annals of crime."[33]

Of course, as with every major event in the San Juan country, there had to be at least one alternate version. Two months after the shooting, Al Puett hand carried a letter from C.H. McHenry to Governor Wallace in Santa Fe. McHenry's letter contains a one sentence description of Stockton's killing, which says, "Porter recognized the party (some 6 men) as friends and was shot while his pipe in one hand and a match in the other."[34] One report, which may have come from Emily, says he had the pipe in one hand and a straw in the other.[35] If that is what happened, and it seems unlikely, the vigilantes had to be ecstatic. They could not have hoped for a better scenario. Considering that Al Puett was Oscar Puett's uncle and that both he and McHenry were virulent enemies of the Coe family, this simplistic version of events is of doubtful accuracy.

Up in Rico, Hartman and Jones didn't let the facts get in their way. They reported that Emily had been killed in the melee.[36] News of Stockton's death spread across the nation. In Missouri, the *Sedalia Weekly*

Bazoo carried the *Record's* eighteen assailant version of Port's death.[37] The shooting of Emily Stockton was the subject of much conjecture. Several months after the incident, Ike Stockton presented his version of events which was certainly based on Emily's recollection of that fateful day. Ike reported that Emily was inside the cabin when she heard the shots and realized Port was under attack. She grabbed a Winchester and ran for the door, hoping her husband could use it. According to Ike, when she appeared in the doorway, George Lockhart yelled out, "Shoot the damned bitch!" and the men opened fire. Hartman and Jones declared that after she fell, the vigilantes left her for dead, also leaving the three children to fend for themselves.[38] A few weeks after the shooting the *Dolores News* said, "It is reliably stated that the men who killed Port Stockton strictly forbade any of the neighboring women to go to the aid of Mrs. Stockton."[39]

As far as perception of right and wrong goes, shooting Emily Jane was a hard action to overcome. In the aftermath, the lower Animas vigilantes were mortified that they had felt it necessary to shoot a woman, even if she might have been shooting back. The narratives which came out of western Rio Arriba County went to extreme lengths to explain her wounds, justify her shooting, and assert that the vigilantes made sure she received proper care. The *New Mexican* reported that Emily was struck in the hand and, as for her more serious injury, they added an elaborate explanation, saying, "A splinter knocked from a post by a ball also struck her in the breast and inflicted another ugly wound."[40] George Lockhart's widow, Mary Ann, later recalled that Mrs. Stockton was taken to Fort Lewis, up the La Plata, and placed in the care of the Fort's physician.[41] Treatment of civilians by the post's doctors was a fairly common occurrence at the time. By early February the *Durango Record* advised their readers that "Mrs. Porter Stockton, who it will be remembered, was accidentally wounded by a splinter from the stock of a gun…is rapidly recovering."[42] Advising Gov. Wallace in a letter, Adjutant General Max Frost said that Mrs. Stockton did not wish to pursue charges "against the man who killed her husband."[43] Of course, as a criminal matter, territorial officials held that option, but evidently no charges were filed. The fact was that Graves, Nance and the other cowboys did what territorial officials should have done several years earlier. Unfortunately, Mrs. Stockton was injured and widowed in the process.

After the trouble encountered by William Hendrickson and others while trying to bury Os Puett, there was no doubt some trepidation when it came to burying Porter Stockton.[44] Members of the Cell Blancett and Clint Hubbard families took on the task. A grave was dug and Port's body was lowered into the ground. A brief religious service was conducted. A single cedar post was later placed at the gravesite.[45] Few mourned the death of William Porter Stockton. Justice had been delayed, but the steely fortitude of the lower Animas cowboys assured that it would not be denied.

The fact that Ike was in Texas probably played into the decision to finally rid the world of Porter Stockton, but the men reluctantly realized that sooner or later, they would have to deal with Ike.[46] Perhaps Ike intended to spend a relatively warm winter in the Texas sun. Word of Port's death traveled slowly to his ears and it seems that he did not travel by train on his return trip. It would take him over a month to return to Animas City. The delay may also have been caused by Ike's recruitment of some of his Texas friends to help him avenge his brother's death.[47]

Standing: Ollie Sharp and Burr Milleson. Seated: John and Henrietta Milleson, ca. 1890. The Millesons took care of Johnny Leslie after Porter Stockton struck him in the head with his pistol. Burr may have been one of the vigilantes who rode on the mission to kill Porter Stockton. (Courtesy Aztec Museum Association Historic Photo Collection, No. 83.37.02.)

The community fissure caused by the murders of George Brown and Os Puett grew even larger after Porter Stockton was gunned down. Seth Welfoot made the mistake of suggesting that, "the men who shot Mrs. Stockton were no better than Porter Stockton."[48] The Englishman's outspoken chivalry was commendable, but his comments make it clear that he had little understanding of the vigilante justice practiced on the frontier. He had already made himself a target when he helped bury Oscar Puett. The tenderfoot and had no idea of the wrath he would face for this perceived insult. As might be expected, Tom Nance took the comment personally. On about January 16th, Welfoot went out to gather wood. As he was headed back home he was accosted by Nance, James Raser and Frank Meyers. The three men hoorawed Welfoot mercilessly, surrounding the one-armed man, they taunted him and threatened him with their pistols. The *News* reported that he was taken into Farmington, where he was convicted by a kangaroo court for speaking badly of the vigilantes and given ten days to get out of the country, under penalty of death. The unrepentant, but suddenly clear thinking Englishman, abandoned his land claim and headed to southwest Colorado, where he would live for the next several months.[49]

After Welfoot's bullying, terror along the lower Animas was turned loose. Meyers's and Raser's next victim was a Navajo who made the mistake of trying to transact some business in Farmington. On Monday, January 24th, several Navajos came into town.[50] According to Bloomfield merchant, Levy Hughes, while the Navajo was shopping Raser decided he needed the man's lariat, which was tied to his saddle. It was probably an excellent quality, hand braided piece of Navajo handiwork. Upon leaving the store, the Navajo noticed the missing lariat. A boy who had been standing nearby told him that Raser had taken it. The Indian went looking for Raser, found him at a nearby house and demanded the return of the lariat. The *New Mexican* noted, "Razor, without denying the theft, began to curse the Indian and struck him with his fist." The Navajo gave as good as he got and struck Raser with his quirt. He then turned to leave the house. An enraged Raser drew his pistol and fired, but missed. Meyers, who had been observing the confrontation, then fired a shot and missed. A third shot was fired and the Navajo was reportedly struck in the right lung. After the shooting, some of the man's acquaintances hustled him away.[51] (The *New Mexican* may have been misinformed about the lung shot.) John McDermott of Farmington later advised the *Durango Record* that it was Meyers who fired the third shot.[52] Henry Page, the U.S. Indian Agent for the Southern Utes, received a report shortly after the incident. His account in the *Durango Record* said, "one of the young Navajo bucks was at a store in Farmington and two young men had been joking and 'skylarking' with him in a good natured manner, when some one turned the Indian's horse loose, taking and hiding his 'riata.'" The Navajo retrieved his horse and was told the so-called skylarkers had hidden his riata. He rode up to the men and asked for it. One of them grabbed the horse's bridle and tried to turn the animal. According to Page the Navajo man "raised his whip as though to strike." Raser drew his pistol and fired a shot over the Indian's head to scare him. The Navajo spurred away and at that point "Razor's companion, named Meyers, shot the Indian in the back. The Indian was leaning forward at the time, and the ball came out in front and near the shoulder."[53] An unattributed letter from Farmington to the *Record* declared that the shooting of the Navajo was the consequence of the merciless and unprovoked beating with quirts of a "Mr. Banks, a worthy stock-man, living on the La Plata" by a group of Utes. The sanctimonious letter writer affirms his own bigotry by noting, "The Indians have assumed the right to use their quirts (whips) on some of our citizens and, in turn, one Indian was shot and mortally wounded."[54] Condoning the attempted murder of a Navajo for acts reportedly committed earlier by a member of another tribe was a miserable rationale for the actions of Raser and Meyers. Accounts of

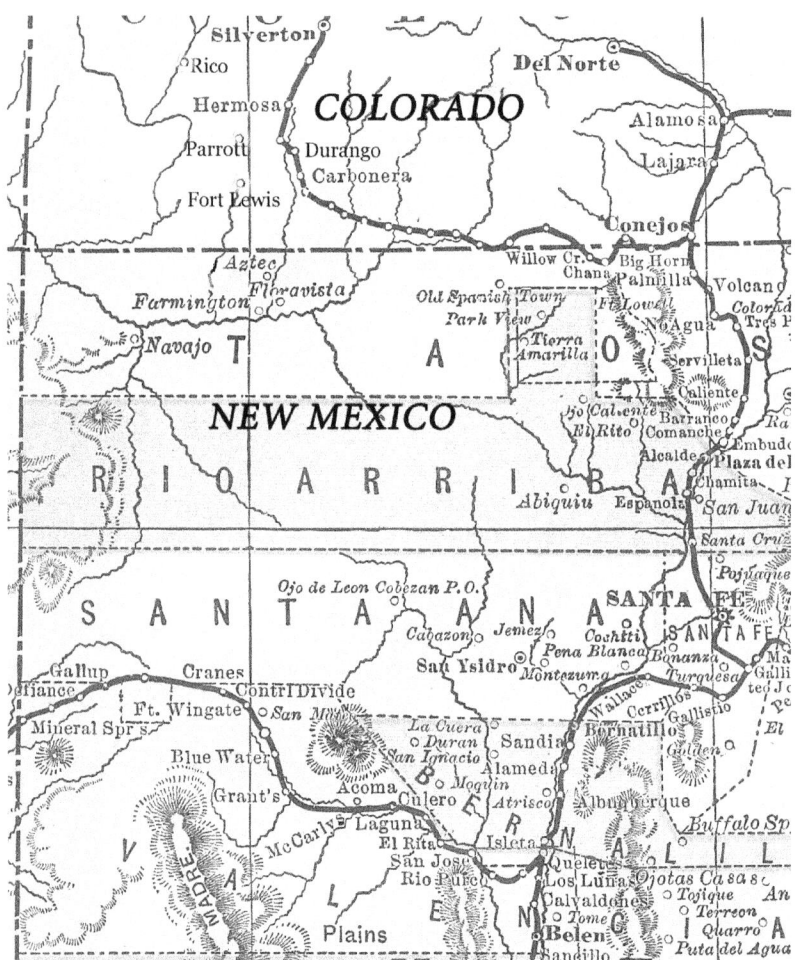

Northwest New Mexico and Southwest Colorado from L.B. Folger's 1889 map of New Mexico and Arizona. The depiction of Taos and Rio Arriba Counties is as it was prior to February 10, 1880. On that date portions of Rio Arriba County were extended northward to the Colorado border. In 1887 San Juan County, New Mexico was created out of the western portion Rio Arriba County. (Author's collection.)

Bank's quirting only appear after and connected to the Farmington attack.

Meyers's and Raser's reckless deed did not make them any friends in Farmington. Residents hunkered down and prepared for possible retaliation from the Navajos. It took them a few days to gather their forces, but three days later on January 28th a group of Indians appeared near town. They were armed and ready for battle. One of the Navajos named Gregorio came into town and warned the residents to not take part and they would not be bothered; they were only after the Tejanos, the name they used for all cowboys.[55] Farmington residents were stunned when Costiano (also known as Costiana) rode into town leading a group of about forty well-armed Navajos. Doc Brown went out to meet the group, with the hope of defusing the situation. The *Durango Record* reported that Brown asked the Navajos to wait until Captain Rogers from Fort Lewis could arrive and help sort out the problem.[56] The Indians said their injured man had died and according to the *New Mexican* they "demanded that Rasor be given up to them." (Perhaps they were unaware that Meyers had fired the damaging shot or the *New Mexican's* account was in error.) In the meantime, a group of about fifteen local men had armed themselves and were prepared to resist any attempt by the Indians to take Raser or Meyers.[57] Upon learning of the approaching white men, the Navajos sought cover and prepared to fight it out. Brown rode out and greeted the armed band. He warned them about the danger and they greeted Brown and his warning with insults, but told him to go ahead "get his Indians away." The Navajos left Brown and moved out, but stopped at the McGalliard home, where they were greeted by forty-five-year-old Mrs. Benjamin K. (Mary) McGalliard. The cool-headed mother of four shared a big pot of coffee with the Navajos.[58] She was well known by the Indians, and about two months before this incident, Second Lieutenant W. Davies, Thirteenth Infantry, Fort Lewis said of her, "Mrs. McGalliard [is] a great favorite with the Navajos and a good interpreter." Lieutenant Davies looked to Mrs. McGalliard as a valuable source of information about the local Navajos. As a caveat he noted, "she is evidently prejudiced in favor of the Navajoes."[59] Hendrickson happened to be at McGalliard's as the Navajos drank their coffee. He said they posted a lookout on the hill north of the Miller's store, in what is now downtown Farmington. The hill provided an excellent view up and down the valley. The sentinel believed the armed cowboys were again threatening and sent out a warning. Hendrickson recalled, "O what a flurry there was at Mrs. Mack's. I never saw any other human beings so excited, many of them left their coffee untouched, ran out and mounted their horses and up the hill they bounded." It was not fear that induced the rapid action. The Navajos were preparing for battle. Dr. Brown, seeing what was about to happen, mounted his horse and according to Hendrickson rode, "hither and thither and shouting at the top of his voice, trying to persuade the Indians to leave. This they finally did but said they were not afraid."[60] Residents later reported that the Navajos had a force estimated at a few hundred men surrounding the town.[61] (This is just one incident which earned Doc Brown his headstone epitaph which reads in part, "arbiter of frontier disputes.") While Doc Brown's role was crucial, it was the restraint of the incensed Navajos that prevented an epic massacre, the effects of which would have been devastating for both sides.

That same day a letter was written and hastily dispatched to Colonel Crofton at Fort Lewis. It was signed by William Hendrickson, Lew Coe, Franklin M. Pierce and several other Farmington men. The letter alleged that the Navajos were "continually, coming amongst us, and committing depredations such as stealing our horses and cattle and other violence." The writers tried to justify Meyers's cowardly shot in the back of the retreating Indian: "On Monday, 25, a party of armed Navajos came in town; using war like language, and finally ending up by one of the Indians attempting to quirt one of our citizens, and the Indian was shot in turn." They advised Crofton that thirty-six Indians came to town three days later and demanded the shooter, whom they refused to give up. Without troops the letter said, "it is certain there will be blood shed soon."[62] The letter may have been carried by Johnny Pond, who brought word of the shooting to Durango.[63] In response, Crofton sent Captain Rogers with about fifty cavalry troops to Farmington.[64]

The Indians held no fear for their safety and that night they camped near town. According to the *Durango Record*, after the troops arrived Dr. Brown and Judge S.T. Webster went to the camp to set up a meeting, but Costiano was not there. The *Record* reported that he had gone to meet with Ignacio, chief of the Southern Utes.[65] The local community had enough trouble and didn't need anymore. Meyers, in particular, had made himself very unpopular. According to Adjutant General Max Frost the two men were told to get out of town or they would be arrested and face trial. Frost reported that, "Frank Meyers and J.H. Raser, who shot and wounded a Navajo Indian, have left the country."[66] They had no desire to stand trial before a jury in Tierra Amarilla.

The northwest New Mexicans were operating in a law enforcement void. The sheriff of Rio Arriba County was too far away to do any good and the area had no local constables. Communities in southwest Colorado, like Rico, Silverton and Animas City, had town marshals and the sheriff was easily accessible to the population building up in Durango. Marshals and deputy sheriffs came and went at a rapid pace during this period in southwest Colorado. After Port Stockton abdicated his position, Animas City had at least three different marshals in three months.[67] Some of these men were reputable, like Bob Dwyer. However, some were of questionable character. Jim Sullivan fit the latter mold and the hard-fighting Irishman was destined play a key role as events in southwest Colorado intensified. The thirty-year-old floated in and out of numerous law enforcement positions during the early 1880s.[68] In the summer of 1880 he was a deputy sheriff for Ouray County and deputy marshal of Rico, working for Marshal Jim Cart.[69] According to one account, Sullivan was a brawler who needed Cart's steadying hand to keep him in line.[70] In October 1880 (about three weeks after Port Stockton lost his position), Sullivan became the marshal of Animas City.[71] A month later he was a La Plata County deputy sheriff.[72] By late January or early February of 1881 Sullivan was serving as the new marshal of Durango. It's not clear, but the marshal's law enforcement authority had to derive from a deputy sheriff's commission since Durango was not incorporated until later in 1881. Sullivan was a typical cop of the time. Hartman and Jones of the *Dolores News* were friends with the well-traveled lawman and gave this colorful description,

> Jim Sullivan, of Rico, has the marshalship of Durango, and has every wild and 'woolly' b-a-d-ee-bad man in Southern Colorado, to deal with. Semi-occasionally a brigade of 'whoop-a-la' fighters call around to see Jim. He receives them warmly, (pats their cranium lightly with a six-gun, and reads the riot act, then forms himself into a committee of one and 'fires' his visitors out of town.) Jim is one man among a thousand, and perhaps one alone, who could manage an unincorporated town, as completely thronged with devils as Durango.[73]

The presence of Jim Garrett and the Eskridge brothers added to Durango's bedlam. On February 1st an unnamed and out-of-work bullwhacker came up the Animas and into Durango looking for employment. He knew Garrett and took advantage of Garrett's hospitality at the expense of several meals. Despite that, the destitute bullwhacker conceived a plan to kill Garrett and take his body to New Mexico to collect reward money. He enlisted the aid of several other parties in his enterprise. Garrett soon received word of the treachery. He sought out the bullwhacker, hit him over the head with his pistol and told him to get out of town. "The last seen of him," the *Durango Record* said, "he was following Jim's advice."[74] For Marshal Sullivan, it was a non-event.

At close to the same time that Sullivan became Durango's marshal, Charles Jones found himself in a saloon fight in Rico. A man named Davis, who owned the Dolores House, took up the cause of his merchant brothers, Theodore and E.L. Davis, who claimed that Hartman and Jones owed them money. The innkeeper hit the saloons and began verbally abusing the *Dolores News* and its owners. As Jones passed by the Adobe Saloon, he heard Davis's ranting and decided to see what he would say to his face. A fight ensued and Davis sliced Jones on the right side of his upper forehead, producing the profuse amount of blood common to scalp wounds and leaving a large dangling flap of skin. Jones was taken to see Dr.

C.H. Ashmeade, who despite his occupation, fainted. The doctor soon recovered and with the help of his neighbor, Mrs. Charlie (Alice Snyder) Middaugh, stitched up the wound. Although Jones was not seriously injured, he suffered from loss of blood and had to stay in bed for a couple of days to recover. This resulted in a rumor that he would soon succumb to his wounds and, as a consequence, there was talk of lynching Davis. He left town, leaving his family and business behind and did not return to Rico. Jones did not tell his family about the incident, but it made the papers in Durango and Denver and his father soon learned of the attack. He wrote his son, saying, "we would like to know if you are much disfigured. Guess you had better send a photo."[75]

In the midst of all of the Animas and Dolores valley mayhem, Frank Coe and Helena Anne Tully announced that they would be married on February 7, 1881.[76] The dirt was still fresh on Port Stockton's grave, yet Frank and Helena Anne planned to be married in Durango. The newlyweds made arrangements to spend the night at the Shaw House, a hotel in Animas City. John W. Shaw operated the two story frame hotel, which also featured stables, sheds and corrals to accommodate a large number of visitors.[77] General Sheridan stayed at Shaw's Hotel during his 1879 inspection tour.[78] Inevitably, on the day of the wedding, Hargo Eskridge learned of the nuptials. The Durango correspondent for the *Ouray Times* noted, "Eskridge, on hearing of it, armed himself, and, in company with others of his gang, one of them marshal of Durango and a deputy sheriff of this county, went to the Shaw house about 1 o'clock at night."[79] The marshal was almost certainly Jim Sullivan.[80] He was known to be sympathetic with Eskridge and Stockton and both Eskridge and Sullivan had worked as deputy town marshals in Rico for Jim Cart.[81] On his mission to the Shaw House, Hargo was accompanied by his brother Dison and Jim Garrett. Only two days before the Coe wedding the *Dolores News* reported that both men were in Durango.[82] With Deputy Sheriff Sullivan at their side, the men could provoke a shootout with Coe and then justify it, under some pretense of performing a lawful act. According to the *Ouray Times's* correspondent, the men "gained an entrance up-stairs" and were trying to find Coe's room when they were met by John Shaw. Mr. Shaw was not impressed with Sullivan's credentials and he was not cowed by Hargo's reputation. He told the intruders that he would protect his guests at all costs. By now everyone was aroused and many of the guests had come out of their rooms to check on the commotion, except for Frank Coe and his bride. Shaw would not back down and now that the hallway was filled with witnesses, Hargo and his men gave up and left.[83]

Hargo stayed in Animas City all the next day, hoping to ambush Coe. He was still keyed up and looking for trouble. The correspondent for the *Ouray Times* was an eyewitness to Hargo's anger. While waiting for the newlyweds to make their exit from the hotel, Eskridge found a man who had spoken out for the Coes and beat him without mercy.[84] Despite Hargo's efforts, Frank Coe managed to leave Animas City unseen.

Eskridge reluctantly gave up his vigil and left Animas City in a hack accompanied by Jim Sullivan and the *Ouray Times* correspondent. Most likely the wagon was hired from the Myers and West Livery, who ran a line of hacks and sleighs between Durango and Animas City.[85] Eskridge and the others were unaware of what was likely an avocation for the correspondent, whose belated article describing the eventful trip was not credited by name. While traveling uphill on a narrow portion of the road they met a wagon coming downhill. The teamster stood up yelled out, "Wait and let me pass." In response, Eskridge drew his pistol and rested it on the shoulder of the man in front of him and said, "Yes, you son of a bitch, I have been waiting for you!" Sullivan shoved Hargo's gun to the side and said, "Hold! what are you doing!" An agitated Eskridge, said, "Let me alone; I want to kill that son of a bitch of a Johnnie Pond." Sullivan advised Eskridge that the driver was not Pond. Eskridge lowered his pistol and the startled wagon driver hurried down the road.[86] Hargo's intended victim was indeed Johnny Pond, who had just brought word to Durango about the shooting of the Navajo man in Farmington. For Hargo, anyone who sympathized with the men who killed Porter Stockton was his enemy, and Pond was a friend and neighbor of George Lockhart.[87] Sullivan's quick thinking saved Pond's life, or at least prevented him from being maimed. Before reaching Durango they ran into another man and Eskridge wanted to make him dance, but was stopped by Sullivan and the others. Finally, without any fatalities, the group arrived in Durango. They parked outside a saloon (probably the Eclipse) and even though Eskridge remained in the hack he ordered drinks for the crowd. While he waited for boardwalk service, he fired at a man on the street, just to see how close he could come without hitting him. The correspondent said that, "The Marshal and those in the wagon seemed to appreciate the joke."[88]

While Hargo was tearing up Durango, Frank and Anne Coe made it to the safety of the New Mexico border. The newlyweds would not be disturbed because ever since the killing of George Brown and Os Puett, the Farmington vigilantes had set up a travel blockade to and from Colorado. It was not a total blockade. In February 1881, Animas City resident, General James J. Heffernan, reported that Billy Boren's Largo Canyon toll road was lined with freight wagons heading toward Durango.[89] The vigilantes still hoped to catch Eskridge and Garrett when and if they came for their livestock. The armed men also believed that Ike Stockton, the Eskridge brothers and their associates would eventually make an attempt to kill those involved in the deaths of Port Stockton and Oscar Puett. In late February, the *Santa Fe New Mexican* reported that along the lower Animas some of the best citizens had formed a "vigilance committee." The *New Mexican* editorialized that the committee also included some bad elements, who were now running some families out of the country. The committee had become "as great an evil as the outrageous conduct of the 'roughs' had been." The paper further said that, "Several stores were closed on account of the absence of the proprietors."[90]

The *New Mexican* was not exaggerating. Durango, Animas City and Parrott City were becoming populated by families who had moved out of New Mexico because they were threatened by vigilantes or felt the situation there was unsafe for their families. Less than a week after Frank Coe's wedding, a Durango resident or perhaps a lower Animas expatriate penned a letter about the Farmington troubles and shipped it to the *New Mexican*. The letter was published unsigned. The writer speaks glowingly of the prospects for the area were it not "completely at the mercy of a mob of the most thorough and cowardly ruffians to be found in the United States. This mob, known as the vigilante committe [sic], comprises the entire population of the settlement, with but few exceptions, is organized and commanded by two brothers named Coe, who, it will be remembered, were prominent in like proceedings in Lincoln county some time ago." It's unclear to which Coes the writer is referring, since it was the cousins, Frank and George, who were the only Coes implicated in the Lincoln County turmoil. The letter noted that most of the members of the Coe gang are in the cattle business and "by a systematic course of plunder have become enriched." The writer claimed that not less than sixteen murders have been committed during the past year by the lawless band commanded by the Coe boys and he noted that a Colorado newspaper was calling Farmington, "the field of the cloth of gore."

The claim of sixteen murders was an outrageous assertion. Even in territorial New Mexico, that many killings in one place would have brought a response from officials in Santa Fe. As of February 1881, the governor and others were not actively concerned with events in western Rio Arriba County. The New Mexico expatriates had been treated badly and had no need for such exaggerations. In fact, overstatements were hurtful to their cause. The *New Mexican's* correspondent reported that a store owner named Percy was forced out and sought sanctuary in Parrott City. The merchant had to leave in the dark of night and later moved his family out of Farmington.[91] The Percy referred to in the letter was Franklin M. Pierce who was born in Tennessee in 1851. Pierce opened the second general store in Farmington in December 1879. He was a staunch Democrat, as well as a Masonic brother. He had moved to Colorado in 1875 for health reasons, settling in Florence. He was married to Sarah Vaughan, the sister to Mrs. William (Nettie) Locke. The Pierces first moved to Farmington in October 1879.[92]

The *New Mexican* was mistaken about one aspect of Pierce's move. He did not go to Parrott City. In early February the *Durango Record* noted that Pierce was staying at the Delmonico Hotel in Durango and that he was in the process of building a twenty-by-forty foot grocery and provision store in the Fassbinder addition on First Street.[93] Frank Pierce may have been the second man forced out of the lower Animas, after Seth Welfoot. As events began to spiral out of control, the Locke, Vaughan, and Pierce families became a target of the lower valley ruffians. Pierce was forced to close his store. The letter to the *New Mexican* said that shortly after "Percy" left, about $8000 worth of merchandise was looted from his abandoned store. The correspondent also mentioned the shooting of the Navajo by "Myers, Razor and Banks" and said, "These crimes are committed openly but no sheriff or peace officer can dare venture to make an arrest." The writer argued his case, saying, "The whole power of the Territory should be exerted to weed out this band."[94] The Coe men, rightly or wrongly, were being blamed for every bad act committed in western Rio Arriba County and even for some that had not occurred.

Frank and George Coe had nobody to blame but themselves for the wrath that was directed their way. Their active association with Billy the Kid and their actions in Lincoln County were only part of the problem. Upon their arrival in northwest New Mexico they insisted on drawing attention to themselves. They reacted to the law enforcement void, took advantage of the isolated conditions and became active vigilantes. Lew, Frank and Jap Coe insisted on defending themselves and their family by writing letters to newspapers in Colorado and New Mexico. Their correspondence only served to increase their notoriety. With no constables to deal with the likes of Raser and Meyers and the threat posed by the large population of Navajos, it is no wonder some residents pulled up stakes and left for Colorado. The exodus of some families from New Mexico began to earn the Coes, and those associated with them, powerful enemies on both sides of the border. From this point forward the self-absorbed Coe men began to realize that their actions were not beneficial to them and were in fact deleterious to their wives, families and hopes for the future.

On the other hand, Porter Stockton never changed his ways and reveled in his reputation as a killer. While alive, he bragged that he had killed nineteen men and that he would add to that total. If all nineteen victims existed, not all of them have been accounted for. His death in a roar of gunfire provided a fitting end to his violent life, but one cannot help feeling sorry for his wife and children as they gathered around his still warm but lifeless body, his blood oozing into the Animas valley dirt. His death avenged the murders of John Canada, Antonio Arcibia and Ed Withers. But did he kill nineteen men? The killing of Den Gannon brings the number to four. Some say his merciless beating resulted in the death of Johnny Leslie. Then there is the unnamed first victim, brought down by a twelve-year-old Stockton. Perhaps he killed two men in Kansas, one in Dodge City and one in Ellsworth. In the fall of 1876, he may have left New Mexico Territory with one less Juan Gonzales. That's nine victims. Arcibia,

Withers and Gannon can be said to have been killed by Porter Stockton with a high degree of certainty. The other six are less so, but he was at the very least an accessory to murder when John Canada was gunned down at the Clifton House. Considering his claim of nineteen victims, and the dearth of information about some of his reported victims, there are more than ten whose identities are unknown, have no place or time of death, and may have never existed in the first place. Like other desperadoes of his time, the number of men he killed is subject to conjecture. Did Billy the Kid kill the twenty-one of his legend? Probably not. As for the reasons behind the killings, many residents of Colfax County said Clay Allison never killed a man who did not deserve it.[95] The egomaniacal Stockton would doubtless make the same boast, although that was clearly not the case. He was a self-centered, bigoted and short-tempered scoundrel. In most cases he pulled the trigger because of some perceived slight or some pre-existing prejudice and could seldom plead self-defense. Despite his normally murderous intent, he left some survivors. At least two were in all likelihood former slaves, Taylor Avant and Eugene Wood. Then there was Perry Gravis and an unnamed victim near Glorieta. In Animas City there was Cap Hart and the Australian Aborigine barber, J.W. Allen. The number of verifiable murders and heinous assaults committed by Porter Stockton is by any measure a formidable total.

There are large gaps in the life of Porter Stockton. Given his penchant for violence, the lack of newspaper coverage and the state of law enforcement along the frontier, it is not hard to believe that his temper exploded with fatal results during some of those gaps. Alf Graves, Tom Nance and the others who rode out that cold January day certainly prevented Stockton from putting other victims in the ground. The men who dealt death to Stockton share part of the blame for what would follow, but it was those who took up the gauntlet for the wanton murderer and those who supported them who share the brunt of the blame. The New Mexicans had killed a despicable miscreant and at the time no one could conceive that his death would incite tumult along the New Mexico/Colorado border that would involve two governors and reach all the way to Washington, DC before it was over.

Chapter Ten

Murder on the La Plata

> *He wears a big hat and big spurs and all that,*
> *And leggins of fancy fringed leather;*
> *He takes pride in his boots and the pistol he shoots,*
> *And he's happy in all kinds of weather;*
> *He's fond of his horse, it's a broncho, of course,*
> *For oh, he can ride like the devil!*[1]

Ike Stockton left Texas with one goal in mind. There would be no turning the other cheek. He arrived in Animas City in late February. His friends, and there were many, offered condolences on the death of his brother. To some he did not openly express his thirst for revenge, but it was clear that Ike had steeled himself for the task at hand. Those who were acquainted with Ike knew that it was only a matter of time before he acted to avenge the death of his brother. Down the Animas in New Mexico, word of Ike's return soon reached the Cox Ranch and spread south from there. His arrival was an ominous sign for the men who killed Port Stockton. They knew he would come after them, they just didn't know when or how.[2] Ike was not an impetuous hothead, like his brother. However, when it came to family matters, his judgment was clouded. The 1876 Colfax County jail break is clear evidence of that.[3] If anyone knew how ineffective the territorial criminal justice system was, it was Ike Stockton, and he entertained no illusions that Port's killers would face retribution at the hands of a judge and jury. If he wanted to repay the debt he owed the lower Animas cowboys, he knew he would have to do it himself. Events in the twelve day period from Christmas Eve until January 4th united Ike and the Eskridge family in a single cause. The men began to recruit their friends to join them in a war on the cowboys of the lower valley. Ike may not have been prepared to go after I.W. Lacy or George Thompson directly, but he was prepared to go after Thompson's family. Ike's wishes took precedence and Tom Nance was placed on top of the target list. Reports said that Ike recruited allies from as far away as the Texas Panhandle.[4] Indeed, some of them came from even further east in Texas. Some of Ike's Erath County friends would soon make their presence known in the San Juan country.

Stockton, Hargo Eskridge and Jim Garrett assembled a sizable crowd of rowdies and prepared for action. Jap Coe may have had Bert Wilkinson in mind when he characterized Ike's allies saying, "They have all killed their man in some bawdy house or other place. They are bitter enemies to honest toil; that is out of their line. They are enemies to law and fugitives from justice."⁵ Despite Jap's obvious prejudice, there was truth to the broad brush he used to paint Ike's associates. Several of them were fugitives, some used alias names, and all of them seemed to be members of Durango's saloon crowd. Ike was their leader and a formidable enemy, though his appearance was deceiving. One reporter said, "He is a little smaller than the medium size of men, walks briskly, slightly stooped. Dresses well – wears a white shirt, black suit, stiff hat, and a neatly fitting boot." It was reported that, "He has no ruffian style." If one did not know him, they might assume he was just a local storekeeper. He carried with him his native Texas charm and in conversation he had "a clear, feminine, ringing voice, and when talking is quite sociable and entertaining."⁶ His face was "rather attractive" set off by a "neat goatee and moustache."⁷ His actual stature was about five foot four inches tall and he weighed about 160 pounds. In his shirt he wore gold round studs of plain design and he carried a silver pocket watch attached to a natty silver chain. His grayish blue eyes were small and piercing and, although he was only twenty-nine years old, he looked several years older. His hair was dark, cut short and he had a dark complexion.⁸ His personality had earned him many friends in Animas City and Durango, and many of them were respectable prominent citizens. Many local residents believed that he and the Eskridge brothers had been wronged and they supported the Stockton-Eskridge contingent. Ike continued to live in Animas City, but he and his allies made their headquarters a couple of miles down the road in Durango.

The Clayton brand. E.A. Clayton was one of several La Plata valley ranchers who were steadfast enemies of Ike Stockton and the Eskridge brothers. From the Northwest New Mexican *(Bloomfield, NM), Feb. 8, 1887. (From the collection of Robert L. Maddox, Jr.)*

On the afternoon of Sunday, February 27, 1881 Ike and at least seven other men armed themselves, left Durango and headed west.⁹ Upon striking the La Plata River they turned south and followed the broadening valley across the border into New Mexico. Ike and his men were familiar with the terrain normally covered by the local vigilance patrols and their entry into New Mexico went undiscovered. Their destination was the winter stock camp of Stockton's ally, George Morrison, which was about ten miles into New Mexico.[10] Morrison's rustic bivouac was the most likely location for Ike and his men to make camp and the Eskridge brothers had probably used it as part of their earlier rustling activities. Morrison, who lived on the Pine River, was wintering a large horse herd in the La Plata valley.[11] Tom Nance was their chief target, but the La Plata valley was home to several other men who held strong feelings against the Stockton-Eskridge crowd, including E.A. Clayton, Johnny Pond and William Shane. George Lockhart was one of the most vocal opponents of Ike Stockton and his allies. He also lived on the La Plata with his family and he was certainly high on Ike and Hargo's target list.

As a La Plata valley line camp would have appeared in 1881. Frederic Remington's "The Outlying Camp," from Theodore Roosevelt's "Ranch Life in the Far West," The Century Illustrated Monthly Magazine, *Vol. 35, No. 4, February 1888. (Author's collection.)*

Stockton knew that Nance could usually be found riding the line in the La Plata valley. In the days before fences, cowboys spent much of their time patrolling the edges of the range to prevent the outfit's cattle from straying. To the west of the La Plata valley was the Navajo Reservation and any animals that ranged too far west often turned up missing. Thompson and Lacy and others who had cattle in the La Plata valley had line camps set up at regular intervals along the edges of their range. The camps weren't much; often a crude dugout served the purpose. Stockton, Eskridge and Garrett were familiar with the normal pattern of work by Thompson and Lacy's punchers and with the location of the various line camps along the La Plata.

  According to the *Durango Record*, "The Garret, Stockton and Eskridge party, who have been forbidden by the Coe consolidation, to return to their homes near Farmington, took a trip down there the first of the week to look after their interests."[12] The members of this group bore witness to the accuracy of Jap Coe's disparaging description of the Stockton gang. They included Hargo Eskridge, Jim Garrett, Lark Reynolds, Wilson Hughes and Bill Hunter. Wilson Hughes was calling himself "Texas Jack" and Bill Hunter was known by the universal nickname, "Tex." A former Rico saloon keeper named Tommy Radigan also joined the band. The twenty-five-year-old New Jersey native was the son of Irish immigrants.[13] Reportedly, he had been a partner in a Trinidad dance hall with a fellow named Jack Williams and perhaps that is where he first met Ike.[14] Also joining the men on this trip was a former Conejos County deputy sheriff who called himself Charles Allison. The former deputy was a wanted man in Nevada.[15] Dison Eskridge did not make the trip. While Stockton had friends among the respectable citizens of Durango, Texas Jack and the other men did not exactly represent the upper echelons of Durango society.

  Two other men are also mentioned as joining the Stockton group, which would mean ten men, counting Stockton, made the trip. One was named Painter and the other was Gus Hefferman.[16] It seems highly likely that Painter was Bill Painter, Ike Stockton's friend and fellow cattle rustler from Erath County. "Texas Jack" and "Tex" and some of the others may have been from Erath County or nearby areas as well, but tracking them is difficult since chances are high that some of them were using alias names. Gus Hefferman should not be confused with the family of James Heffernan, who was the deputy U.S. marshal residing in Animas City. Considering Hefferman's Rico-based butchering operation had been stealing Thompson and Lacy's cattle since at least the spring of 1880, his friendship with Porter Stockton, and his history as a Lacy and Coleman herder, he was an obvious ally for Ike Stockton and would have eagerly joined the mission to get Thompson and Lacy's top enforcer Tom Nance.

  It was in the afternoon on March 1st that Stockton had his chance to kill Nance.[17] According to Al Dustin and Edward Thomas, Nance and Aaron Barker, who was working for "One-armed" Billy Wilson, were up the La Plata about ten miles from Farmington and headed downriver. Stockton and his men saw the two men and quickly prepared an ambush.[18]

In a letter, Jap Coe described what happened next: "concealing their horses behind the brush, hid themselves behind a brush corral and allowed two men to ride within ten yard of them when they opened fire on them, killing one man and his horse and missing the other."[19] Barker was killed, but Nance was saved by his cow horse. As shots rang out and puffs of dust arose, Nance wheeled his mount and bolted down the trail. In the ensuing chase Nance shot Tom Radigan in the leg.[20] After a running gun battle of several miles, Stockton and his men finally gave up. Nance was not injured, but one bullet passed through the shoulder of his coat. Even after he lost his pursuers he remained wary and carefully took a circuitous route before reaching Pete Winkle's ranch on the San Juan, about six miles below Farmington. Totally worn out, he spent the night at Winkle's place and then rode into Farmington bringing the sad tidings of Barker's death. Even though something like this was expected, the news was electrifying. A small party of men was quickly organized. Armed to the teeth, they rode out of town and headed up the La Plata. They were prepared for any eventuality, but did not intend to pursue Stockton because they felt they needed more men. In any case, Stockton's group was long gone. The Farmington men retrieved the body of Aaron Barker and returned to town.[21] Soon, word of the event spread up and down the valleys of northwest New Mexico. Their worst fears had been realized. For the foreseeable future, many of the residents along the lower Animas and San Juan Rivers would live in terror of Ike Stockton's next raid.

News of the frantic horseback chase and subsequent escape of Tom Nance would soon become the talk of the Animas River valley. Fifty years later, such scenes became standard fare at the Saturday matinee. As an experienced horse peddler, Stockton was an astute judge and ardent admirer of fine horses and was known to put up his own horses in local races. It's likely that he rode his racing mare, a bay named Nellie.[22] Nance was riding a horse with bottom known as Old Turp.[23] Stockton desperately wanted to catch Nance and believed no horse could outrace Nellie. Nance's horsemanship and Ol' Turp proved him wrong. The *Durango Record* reported that Stockton and his men gave Nance "a lively chase for six or seven miles, when their horses gave out and they returned to camp."[24]

After giving up their pursuit, Stockton and the others gathered up Radigan and headed north. The former saloon keeper was alive, but nearing death's door. The bullet had entered his left leg, near the knee. Blood gushed from the wound and his chances of survival were grim. Before they headed to Colorado they rifled through the clothing on Aaron Barker's lifeless body and took all of his money, as well as his saddle, bridle and firearms. According to Jap Coe, along the way they "stole three head of Lacy & Thomson's horses."[25] They rode up the La Plata toward Fort Lewis, looking over their shoulders and pushing their horses. For Radigan, it was an agonizing journey. The boys left their wounded friend in the care of the post surgeon, but did not wait around. They rode through much of the night arriving in Durango at about noon on Wednesday, March 2nd. After their return, Stockton and Eskridge visited Caroline Romney of the *Durango Record*, as well as the offices of the *Durango Southwest* to tell their story.[26] Back at Fort Lewis, Dr. Cochran, the Chief Surgeon at the post, amputated Tom Radigan's leg, saving his life.[27] He would wear a peg leg the rest of his life.[28]

The Brown family plot and Aaron Barker's grave are the only interments on a scenic, but lonely hilltop overlooking Farmington. Barker was killed in the La Plata Valley and Brown was killed at the Hamblet's Christmas Eve party. (Author's collection.)

The *Durango Record* obligingly reported the highly self-serving Stockton version of events. According to the *Record*, on Tuesday, March 1st, Stockton and his men were camped at the burned out remains of Garrett's cabin. The cabin was torched in the aftermath of the killing of George Brown. (The description of the location as being Garrett's cabin does not match census records, which clearly indicate that Garrett and Eskridge lived in the Animas River valley just east of Farmington.) The *Record* reported, "About 3 o'clock in the afternoon of the above day, when Stockton and his companions were in the tent, some of them asleep, and others having a chat with the cow-boys who had dropped in to see them, a couple of men rode towards the tent. Their names, as afterwards discovered, were Aaron Barker and Tom Vance [sic], and they were members of the opposition clique." The *Record* noted that the two men "had evidently stumbled into the camp accidentally." Barker was riding ahead of Nance by about a hundred yards. Too late he discovered that it was Stockton's camp. He dismounted and using his horse for protection, began firing. He managed to hit Tom Radigan in the knee. Naturally, Ike and his men had to protect themselves. Men poured out of the tent and returned fire, killing Barker's horse before dispatching its owner. Tom Nance also began shooting. The distance from his enemies hindered accurate fire, and being outnumbered he soon realized he stood no chance in a gun battle. He wheeled his horse and raced away.[29] The *Durango Southwest* offered a similar version. It reported that Ike and his men "were in camp about six miles from where his brother's wife lives, when they were fired upon by a man named Thos. Nance, the man who shot Porter Stockton, and some other desperado named Barker."[30] This was a mischaracterization of Barker, who was not an outlaw, had no known involvement in any of the hostile actions, and was simply one of Billy Wilson's herders. The location described in the *Southwest* matches that of the Garrett/Eskridge ranch near Lew Coe's place just east of Farmington.

The accounts carried in the *Durango Record* and the *Southwest* defy logic. There is no chance that Ike and his companions rode into the Animas valley within two miles of Farmington. It was too risky. There were too many residents along the Animas. A group of close to ten riders would have been noticed and the alarm sounded. Barker's actions, as described, make no sense. He was a cowboy who lived life in the saddle. It seems unlikely, that with no cover to protect him, he would choose to dismount, giving up his only means of escape and then open fire on a much larger group of men. It is also most difficult to swallow the assertion that Nance and Barker rode carelessly up on an obviously occupied camp at what the newspaper described as the burnt out remains of Jim Garrett's cabin, fortuitously giving Stockton the opportunity to avenge the death of his brother. It was the reason Stockton had returned from Texas. It was the very act he had sworn to do and which everyone in the country expected he would do. While the newspaper accounts had a false ring, the outcome was true; Barker was killed, Radigan lost his leg and a well-mounted Tom Nance outraced Stockton and his gang.

About a week after Barker's murder, the *Durango Record* received a letter from Tom Nance. In it, he described his version of the gun battle. Unfortunately, we will never know what it said. Editor Romney wrote a long-winded and somewhat tortured explanation of why she couldn't devote any space to the letter, especially since she "determined weeks ago, to remain neutral" in the matter. Romney explained that she preferred "to leave it to the courts to take the evidence in the case." She accurately characterized her earlier account as being "simply as the report of the boys just returned from there."[31] After reading Romney's comments the *Durango Southwest* weighed in on her refusal to publish Nance's letter, noting, "It must have been a fearful piece of literature if they refuse to give it to the public. It certainly could not have been very much worse than the editorial given upon the controversy. If the letter gave a true version of the affair the public should have the benefit."[32] The *Trinidad News* piled on Romney as well; "While the *Record* expresses a desire to keep out of the controversy, the position it has taken in effect makes it the organ of the desperadoes, who move out of Durango and murder the cattle men, and then go back and have their report of the affair published in the *Record*. The *News* repeats that the *Record* fails to get the right light on the situation; honest men, not outlaws, are entitled to consideration first." The assessment of the Trinidad newspaper is noteworthy since residents there were familiar with many of the principal players on both sides of the drama unfolding in the San Juan country. The Trinidad newspaper offered its opinion about those who opposed Ike Stockton; "On one side are Thompson and Lacey [sic], Wash Cox, ["One-armed"] Billy Wilson, Alf Graves, Coe Bros., James Dodson and others of like characters [sic], large stock owners, men of integrity and property, while on the other side are Ike Stockton, Eskridge, Garrett & Co., murderers and desperadoes, who have inaugurated the war on account of the killing of Porter Stockton a short time since, himself an outlaw."[33]

Up in Rico, Hartman and Jones did not claim neutrality and clearly expressed their opinion about the death of Aaron Barker and the narrow escape of Tom Nance; "That's about the size of it, we guess and a war of extermination it should be, against the Coe mob - for it is nothing more nor less than a cowardly mob of miserable cattle thieves." Continuing in the same vein, Hartman and Jones opined that those who oppose the Coes "are either killed or run out of the country. Then these self-styled 'vigilantes' burn their houses, confiscate their cattle and divide the stock between the members of this band of cutthroats, murderers and thieves."[34] The owners of the *Dolores News*, influenced by their friend Hargo Eskridge, and combined with Frank Hartman's hatred of the Coes, were totally committed to Stockton's cause. Jones and Hartman were young, impressionable, and totally enthralled by Ike Stockton. They viewed him as a tough but personable Texan, who had been wronged when vigilantes killed his brother. To them he was the magnetic and unquestioned leader of the pack. Unsurprisingly, the caustic rhetoric of the *Dolores News* would continue, unabated.

Newspapers in New Mexico offered their own versions of Barker's murder. The *Las Vegas Optic* said, "Some days ago a large posse of these villains attacked two herders, killing one and wounding the other, fleeing back to their hiding places."³⁵ The *Santa Fe New Mexican* said that Stockton and his men "went into camp at a spot near Stockton's former ranch the house itself having been burned in their absence by their enemies." The Durango and Santa Fe newspapers are a fountain of misinformation concerning the ambush location. Aaron Barker was without a doubt murdered about ten miles north of the San Juan River, up the La Plata. Events of that day and the name of Aaron Barker have been memorialized on maps of the area, as Ike's cowardly ambush took place very close to where the aptly named Barker Arroyo joins up with the La Plata River.³⁶ The capital city newspaper said that Ike Stockton shot Barker's horse and then killed Barker. The *New Mexican* noted, "The animosity between the Coe party and the Stockton gang is fiercer than ever and it is probable that the trouble will not be quieted until several more men have bitten the dust." The newspaper updated their readers on the latest alliance; "Stockton is now associated with young Garrett who was in the party which attacked a dance house in Farmington last Christmas and brought about the killing of two men. Both men are desperate characters and will injure the Rio San Juan country even more than they have done, before they are through with this fight."³⁷ Somehow the killing of George Brown and Oscar Puett at the neighborhood dance at F.M. Hamblet's family home was now being characterized as a "dance house" brawl.

Newspapers were having a heyday, so much so that one of them made space to callously skewer Aaron Barker and any future murder victims. The *Southwest* wrote, "We take great pleasure in writing obituary notices and all the request we have to make is that both parties will report promptly to this paper the name, age and complexion of the man killed, the color of his hair and eyes, his height and weight, and how much of a family he leaves, his usual avocation in life, how many men he has killed, and, if possible, the reason why the man was not killed sooner."³⁸ The next victim would provide the editors with a sobering reality check.

The approach of the D&RG rails was bringing a coarse crowd and Durango's violence was beginning to spiral out of control. Shootings and other mayhem associated with the town's saloons became a serious concern. A week after the killing of Aaron Barker, Durango had one of its most notorious shootings. The gravely wounded victim was a well liked, twenty-nine-year-old clerk named Thomas Greatorex. He was a native New Yorker, but had also lived in Charleston, South Carolina.³⁹ As a young man he worked in New York City for the Equitable Fire Insurance Company. In 1873 he moved to Denver and worked for Witter's Abstract Company as well as for General Dodge of the D&RG Railroad. In 1875 he moved to Rio Grande County, Colorado where he was a district court clerk. He had lived in Silverton for four years, where he worked on land and mining transactions and was the abstract clerk for San Juan County. His work made him widely known throughout the region. At one time he was a page in the U.S. House of Representatives. He was known for his southern gentility, outstanding personality and was respected for his business skills.[40]

That evening Greatorex attended the show at Jim Marshall's showplace variety theatre and dance hall, the Coliseum.[41] Prior to opening the Coliseum, Marshall operated a seedier Durango business known as the Palace of Pleasure. It was nestled amidst other wicked haunts on lower F Street.[42] Prior to his arrival in Durango he operated the Valentino Saloon in Rico.[43] However, in Rico the chief source of income for the forty-year-old Indiana native was as a card player.[44] Problems began soon after the show closed. The *Durango Record* reported that, "This morning, about 3 o'clock, Mabel Young and [Fat] Alice Haskell had a quarrel in the Coliseum auditorium, and in a short time were pulling each other's hair. Tom Lynch and Jack Roberts were present and took part in the affray, either with the intent of separating the parties, or for the purpose of aiding one of them."[45] The chivalrous Greatorex, seeing a woman (it is doubtful they could be called ladies) in trouble, tried to separate the combatants. Roberts struck him over the head with his pistol and Greatorex fell to the ground. While he was still on the ground, Jack Roberts shot him. Marshal Heathy was also injured in the melee, when he was struck over the head with a revolver. He was severely injured and did not know who struck him. In the pandemonium that followed, Roberts escaped out a side door. Greatorex was laid out on a table in the Coliseum. It was discovered that the bullet entered near the base of his spine. The pistol was discharged at close range and the clothes around the wound were singed from the blast. Dr. Plumb and Dr. Clay were summoned to the scene and moved the patient to the offices of the San Juan Lumber Company on Railroad Street. The newspaper fretted that "it is barely possible that he may live."[46] Prior to his arrival in Durango, Roberts had worked at a Rico sawmill and later was employed by butcher Charlie King who had benefitted from Gus Hefferman's illicit cattle trade in Rico. The *Dolores News* reported that Dr. Byrne, the assistant surgeon at Fort Lewis, arrived in Durango on Tuesday night to consult on the care of Greatorex.[47] Dr. James W. Brown from Silverton also traveled to Durango for consultation.[48]

A reward of $500 was quickly posted for Roberts. The wanted notice said,

> Roberts is 5 feet 8 inches, and sandy complected. When last seen he wore a light or scrubby moustache, rather redder than his hair, and which seemed to be cultivated to a point. Is somewhat freckled. Looks like an Irishman. Supposed to have left Durango on a bay horse. Above reward will be paid on the delivery of said Jack Roberts, dead or alive; to the sheriff of La Plata county, or

two hundred dollars will be paid for any information that will lead to his arrest.[49]

Word of the murder spread throughout the surrounding area and soon many men were looking for the dangerous Irishman. Meanwhile, Greatorex was clinging to life. A week after the shooting he rallied, but the following week his condition worsened and he died from his wounds.[50]

Like the cowman depicted here, Wash Cox wore a white beard. He saddled up for roundups well into his sixties. Frederick Remington's "Cutting Out A Steer," from Theodore Roosevelt's "The Round-up," The Century Illustrated Monthly Magazine, Vol. 35, No. 6, April 1888. (Author's collection.)

In the meantime, Jack Roberts had traveled south toward Farmington on foot. He probably kept near to but off the beaten roads, making camp in the piñons and junipers, using them for cover. Heading toward New Mexico was not the wisest choice, considering that many of the residents were keeping a watchful and wary eye out for Ike Stockton and his men. Among the lookouts were Tom Nance and a man described in the *Durango Record* as a German named Benning.[51] Nance's companion was twenty-year-old John H. Benning, the son of Henry Benning a Baden-born wheelwright. In 1880 the Benning family was living in the La Plata valley in Colorado. Nance was hoping to avenge the death of Aaron Barker when Roberts fell into his lap. Greatorex's killer had been on the run for a little over a week when Nance and Benning spotted the freckled-faced Irishman and quickly forced his surrender.[52] Word of the substantial reward offered for Roberts had reached the lower Animas and the two men took their prize to the Cox Ranch for safekeeping.[53] If Nance knew about Roberts's prior employment with Charlie King and Gus Hefferman, he decided that the certainty of Roberts's fate would meet his responsibilities as Thompson and Lacy's henchman and the reward was just a bonus.

It's not known what treatment Roberts received there, but under normal circumstances the Cox family was well known for their Texas-sized hospitality.[54] Their adobe ranch house was built in the Texas tradition, with a roof connecting two separate buildings. The space between was used for storing saddles, bridles and other ranch equipment.[55] With her black slat sunbonnet, Grandma Cox was said to be "the wonderful cook whom the cowboys dreamed about." Cowboys and others could depend on being fed a meal of beans, biscuits and beef.[56] Wash Cox was stern when the situation called for it, but he had a generous considerate side as well. During the winter out-of-work cowboys knew they could board at the Cox place and not be asked to pay anything.[57] Wash Cox saw to it that there would be no escape for Jack Roberts. Even if he was a murderer and cattle rustler, the doomed man was presumably treated with at least restrained courtesy during his short stay.

In the case of killer Jack Roberts, the intricacies of a requisition and extradition were not observed. A letter was sent up to Durango and an exchange for the reward money was set to take place at the Cox place. The *Dolores News* reported that, "No sooner had the news been circulated than forty men mounted and armed started for the place indicated with the money."[58] According to Ike Cox, only four men rode into the ranch. They were led by brick mason Cap Stanley and they were thoughtfully leading an "extry horse." Cox said the men asked Wash Cox for a spare rope. Jim Cox gave them his rope.[59] "The men have returned," noted the *News*, "but they had no prisoner. It is reasonably supposed that they got their man and 'lost' him on the road."[60] The *Record* said that it was only fifteen armed men who left Durango on Monday night, March 21st. They rode through the night and arrived at the Cox ranch house the next day. The exchange was made and the men started back toward Durango with Roberts. The *Record* confidently reported that about four miles outside of town they found a suitable tree and "Jack Roberts was launched into eternity." The next day a newsman from the *Record* and two officers rode up Wildcat Canyon, to the supposed scene, but were unable to find the killer's jerked remains.[61] That's because he was lynched before the men ever crossed into Colorado. Ike Cox reported that the next morning a badly shaken neighbor named Barrie came to their house looking for Wash Cox. Fifty-year-old tinsmith James Barrie told Wash that while he was out seeking his horses he had been rudely surprised to find a man hanging in a cottonwood grove in the area which was later known as Riverside, just below the state/territory line. Barrie's assessment that the old rancher would know best how to handle the situation was correct. Cox, aware that Roberts deserved his fate, did not dither. Riding upriver with his boys and some of his punchers, Cox saw to it that Roberts was quickly buried, without ceremony and more importantly without alerting others. Despite its ghoulish history, Jim Cox wanted his rope back, but Wash wisely insisted that it be buried as well.[62] Colorado's newspapers may not have known where Roberts met his fate, but that did not deter them from offering colorful tales of the grisly affair. Hartman and Jones speculated that, "His death resulted from unknown causes, probably from undertaking to balance on the ragged edge of thin air. Funeral services of the deceased will extend over a period of several days, Rev. Drs. Buzzard and Coyote officiating." The Rico newspaperman revealed no wrath for Durango's vigilantes.[63] The *La Plata Miner* said that Roberts had become lost on the return trip and speculated that, "He is thought to have gone to another climate via the limb of a tree."[64] The New Mexicans hoped to give Ike Stockton a similar sendoff, but Durango's residents were not as cooperative as Wash Cox and his ranch hands.

Down in Farmington, Stockton's attack on Nance and the killing of Aaron Barker resulted in some ill-conceived actions by the lower Animas vigilantes. Those who expressed any sympathy toward Ike Stockton or the Eskridge family were compelled to leave the country. The Coes or those associated with them made a strategic blunder when they forced the territorial representative, William Locke, to leave Farmington. Judge Locke was well liked and highly respected by many of the local citizens. Some of the wilder members of the Coe contingent stole his plow horse and threatened to steal his prize riding horse, which he valued at $500. To prevent that, Locke left town, riding that horse up the La Plata valley. At the time, some believed he intended to stay only briefly in Durango and then travel on to Santa Fe, to request that martial law be declared. Many of the respectable men on the lower Animas were beginning to see that as the best option to restore some semblance of order. The *Durango Record* reported that while Locke was away the Coe group threatened his family, shot out the windows of the school house, rubbed the food from their lunch baskets in their faces and told them "if their father ever came back there, they would fill him so full of shot, there would be room for no more." Locke reportedly sympathized with neither side, but as tensions mounted, that was not an option.[65]

While traveling up the La Plata, Locke was joined by Tom Fulcher's brother, John. The two men proceeded on to Fort Lewis, where they delivered a letter to Colonel Crofton. They advised Crofton "that our section of country is infested with two factions or parties, that are waging a war of extermination upon each other. Keeping the country in such an uproar, that a great many of our law abiding citizens have left in order that they might escape the bad results that must naturally follow." They went on to say that, "Others have been threatened with violence if they refused to join them." The letter noted that some men have left their families and possessions and were threatened with death if they returned. Some were given ten days' notice to get out of the country and they left, leaving "everything behind to the mercy of outlaws." They also reported that in one case armed men had entered a ranch house, threw the contents outside, pulled it down and then erected the house on another ranch. They said some of these men have appropriated other people's horses for their own use. Locke and Fulcher said, "Ruffians have come in and broken up our school." They concluded by noting, "if you can do anything to give our country relief, you will bestow a lasting favor upon all our law abiding citizens."[66]

Several others were forced out. Orange Phelps, who lived near Bloomfield, left after his son-in-law Josiah Starriett had a dispute with the Coe men.[67] Ike Stockton and the Coe family were not strangers to Orange Phelps. In 1876 he served as one of several Colfax County Justices of the Peace.[68] The conflict with the Coes pushed Joe Starriett to side with Ike Stockton and he was not inclined to switch sides.[69] Starriett lived near the Vaughan family and Seth Welfoot's place, but prudently sought safety elsewhere.[70] He moved to the D&RG camp at Amargo, where he opened a blacksmith shop.[71] Boyd Vaughan also moved out.[72] He had agitated the Coe men when he was elected as constable in the unrecorded election and his sisters were married to men who were viewed as enemies to the Coes: William Locke and Franklin Pierce.[73] The expatriates hoped that Colonel Crofton could provide relief.

Crofton, even if he wanted to help, was limited in his ability to intercede in the ongoing strife. The Posse Comitatus Act of 1878 severely restricted the use of the army to serve as enforcers of civilian law.[74] Most southerners despised the federal soldiers who performed this function in the aftermath of the Civil War, while those living on the frontier depended on their assistance.[75] When Reconstruction ended in 1877, southern congressmen led the way in pushing the Act through Congress.[76] After it took effect, it was up to civilian authorities to maintain order. Unfortunately, they were sometimes not up to the task and vigilante action was often the inevitable result. Even if Crofton was limited in his options, he continued to receive letters asking for his assistance. Crofton was not the only official receiving letters about the troubles in northwest New Mexico. Frederick W. Pitkin, the governor of Colorado, was also learning about the situation.

About three weeks after the killing of Aaron Barker, Pitkin received a letter from one of Ike Stockton's Animas City neighbors, James J. Heffernan. At the time the fifty-three-year-old Heffernan was serving as a Colorado deputy U.S. marshal.[77] The marshal was an advocate for his neighbor. Heffernan is often referred to as General Heffernan in newspaper accounts and local histories giving the impression that he had been a general for the Union during the Civil War. That was not the case. Heffernan served with the Fifty-fifth Regiment of the Illinois Volunteer Infantry. At the outset of the war he secured an appointment as captain of Company H, which was made up of men primarily from Carroll and Ogle Counties. His appointment engendered some ill will as the men had voted and elected another man to the post. He overcame the men's resentment and early on was characterized as one of the "best officers in the regiment." After rising to major his fortunes began to fall. On August 20, 1864, fourteen officers (all of the commissioned officers present with the regiment on that day) signed a document vilifying Heffernan and noting that his conduct had "rendered him wholly unworthy [of] the confidence of the officers and men of the 55th Illinois Infantry." He was mustered out as a major on November 19, 1864. The title of general evidently derived from his activities after he left the army. He served the Fenian Brotherhood with the title of "Brigadier-General in the service of the Irish Republic" during their May 1866 raid into Canada.[78] The American-based Brotherhood was attempting to win the independence of Ireland through their actions. After that adventure, Heffernan set his sights on the west. Before moving to Animas City, the Heffernan family spent several years in Utah, where the general tried his hand at prospecting.[79] Heffernan had a well developed sense of self-importance and full confidence in his own assessment of any situation.

One of the men who had been forced out of western Rio Arriba County was C.H. McHenry. Like Heffernan, McHenry had lived first on the Dwyer place at Animas City when he and his family arrived in the San Juan country.[80] The importance of McHenry's influence on Heffernan cannot be overstated, given that both men had shared the experience of serving with Illinois Infantry regiments during the Civil War. The two men became close friends. As had been the case with Orange Phelps, Josiah Starriett and others, McHenry had fled Farmington for his own safety. Shortly after his arrival, he told his story to Heffernan. Frank Pierce, who was busy preparing to open a new store in Durango, probably also had Heffernan's ear, but it was the plight of C.H. McHenry which most enraged Heffernan and drove him to pen his account of affairs to Governor Pitkin.

In his March 14th letter to Pitkin he described the roiling situation saying "good first class citizens of Colorado, stockmen and farmers, who are refugees from their homes – driven from homes by the men who made Lincoln Co. N.M. a synonym of blood and massacre." Heffernan advised Pitkin that these same men made Farmington their headquarters and eight good farmers had been "driven from their homes, leaving their homes in the night with their wives and children trembling and frightened to death behind them." He also reported that ruffians had taken the horses from the plow of William Locke, who he noted was a member elect of the New Mexico legislature from Rio Arriba County. Heffernan warned the Colorado governor that these same men were going to demand the surrender of certain citizens upon requisition to you "so that they can get them in their hands to murder them." Heffernan's knowledge of the conflict was unbalanced, obviously slanted by the accounts he heard from McHenry and others. Heffernan had known Ike Stockton for perhaps a little more than one year, on that basis he vehemently defended the Texan. He did not seek the opinion of Ike's fellow Texans, men like Wash Cox, I.W. Lacy, Alf Graves and others, who had known Stockton for ten years or longer. It's likely that he had never met the Coes and based his opinion about their character on information which came from their enemies and from articles in the *Dolores News*. He grandly informed Pitkin, "I, knowing all the facts of the trouble that has been serious enough to send a company of U.S. Soldiers to the scene of operations, ask that an investigation be held so that you [illegible] shall not be made a party to a scheme to murder good citizens and Coloradians."[81]

Heffernan's view was as one-sided as that of Frank Hartman and Charles Jones. His assessment of Ike's closest allies, men who would eventually be the subject of New Mexico arrest warrants, as "good citizens" was laughable. Somehow he had missed what was obvious. Ike and his associates were able to travel about the country for weeks at a time, indicating that they had no pressing responsibilities, yet somehow managed to support themselves. Many of Stockton's newest and closest allies were strangers to the area, who appeared to spend most of their time in Durango's hellish dives. They were not farmers, storekeepers or otherwise gainfully employed. Many of them used alias names. Most had no roots in the country, nor did they intend to plant any. General Heffernan was not the only one who had misjudged Ike Stockton. Many other prominent citizens in Durango, Animas City and Rico were charmed by the Texan.

One day after Heffernan wrote Governor Pitkin, Frank Coe wrote a letter to C.H. McHenry. Coe was doing his best to get on the right side of a looming public relations battle. After his experience in Lincoln County, he realized that the lower Animas country would soon be under the scrutiny of territorial officials. Lew Wallace was still the governor and was not inclined to ignore the continuing hostilities. On March 11th Coe received a letter from McHenry in which McHenry complained about being run out of the valley. Coe's reply was printed in the *Durango Record*.

> Farmington, N.M., March 15, 1881.
> C.H. McHenry, Esq:
> Dear Sir:--Am in receipt of yours of the 11th. This is the first notice I have had of your orders to leave the Valley. Now, Mc, you are a man of good common sense, and why do you fear to come back here? Here is your home and place of business, and now I will pledge you my word of honor as a man that you will not be molested. The unprincipled scoundrel that gave you that notice fully calculated to do you some injury - I have just shown your letter to Lew. He says for you to come back. Mc, you have no enemies here, and I will pledge you my life that you will not be molested. Nothing has surprised me more than this. I can only respect you for writing to me about it.
> Keep your teams there and bring your mill frames down. Mc, rely on what I have told you.
> Yours, &c, Frank Coe

The same day the *Record* also printed this letter from Farmington Postmaster and merchant, Alison F. Miller.

> Farmington, N.M., March 18, 1881.
> Mr. McHenry,
> Fort Lewis, Colo.
> Dear Sir: I understand by your hired man that you had received notice not to come back to Farmington; if you did, you would get killed. *Now I tell you [candidly]* that you have nothing to fear of any one by coming back; it is all a lie gotten up to keep you and a good many other *good men* out of the country. By all means come back, and that right away. I have seen a good many of the best men here, and they have told me to write to you at once, and to be sure and have you come back. If I thought there was the least danger in the world, I would be the last one to advise you to come back. Hoping to see you soon, I am fraternially [sic] yours,
> A.F. Miller

The *Record* praised the letters as "the beginning of a better era for that whole country," and added, "We hope to hear that other refugees, and indeed all of them receive similar invitation to return."[82]

About the same day that the Coe and Miller letters were sent up to Colorado, one of General Heffernan's "good citizens" and a recent "Coloradian" was involved in a shooting in Durango. The shooter was Charlie Allison, who had joined Ike Stockton's foray down the La Plata valley. Allison's victim was Andy Guinan, a carpenter who had recently trekked over the mountains from Gothic, Colorado in Gunnison County, where he was doing some prospecting. Allison and Guinan were at Larsh's dance hall on lower F Street when, according to Allison's dubious version of the affair, Guinan jumped over the stove and struck at Allison with his pistol. Allison pulled his pistol and clubbed Guinan on the head and then shot him in the wrist. As the shooting erupted Guinan's friends broke for the front door and according the *Record* the dance hall girls "made a rush for their rooms." Consequently, eyewitnesses were scarce. After Guinan was shot, he reportedly pleaded with Allison not to kill him. Durango's Marshal Heathy found Allison was armed with a revolver, but immediately after the gunfight, no revolver was found on Guinan and Guinan's friends confirmed that he never carried a weapon. Allison's victim ran outside after being shot and the *Durango Record* noted there was so much blood that F Street looked like a slaughterhouse yard. The *Record* speculated that somehow in the melee Allison had managed to shoot himself in the left thigh inflicting a serious flesh wound. Guinan was under the care of Dr. Plumb and was taken to Charles Hilliker's home on First Street to recuperate. Allison's recovery took place in a room in the dance hall where he was shot.[83] Guinan made a rapid recovery, but in early April Allison's condition was described as "very precarious." It was thought he might die from his wound and he also was placed under the care of Dr. Plumb.[84]

Deputy U.S. Marshal Heffernan was using his influence to protect some nefarious characters and one of those was Charlie Allison. In his speech and manner Allison purposely played up his role as a dangerous man, but at times his bluster was too much, and Ike disowned him.[85] Despite that, because of an unimaginable turn of events, Ike's fate was firmly knotted to the rambunctious desperado. Charlie Allison was not related to Cimarron's noted shootist, Clay Allison, although both men seemed to have a penchant for shooting themselves. Allison's real name may have been Charles Ennis or Annis.[86] His first known scrape with the law was a stage robbery which occurred on April 29, 1879 near Eureka, Nevada. Ennis, John Sullivan and a third masked man stopped the Ruby Hill stage and stole "about $400 in money and jewelry" from the passengers. A short time later, Ennis and John Sullivan stole "two of the finest horses" from the Stewart and Company livery in Eureka. They bolted down Main Street toward Elko. After a chase of forty miles, the thieves were overtaken at Railroad Canyon by the sheriff's posse. A gunfight ensued and John Sullivan was shot and killed. Ennis was taken into custody.[87] Within weeks Ennis was sentenced to serve seven and a half years in the Nevada state prison in Carson City.[88] In mid-June 1879 he leapt from the prison-bound train and escaped into the darkness. The one-time Virginia and Truckee Railroad brakeman was missing his right index finger.[89] Allison/Ennis left Nevada for good. After his escape he showed up in the San Luis Valley of Colorado where he hired out as a deputy for Sheriff Joseph Smith in Conejos County.[90]

Allison's bravado landed him the job, but as was his normal habit, he spent most of his time sampling the liquid refreshment in the local saloons. In late January or early February 1881, he shot Pat McCaffrey in San Antonio (Antonito), Colorado, in a saloon owned by Pat's brother, Tom McCaffrey.[91] The wounded man was struck in the upper leg, breaking the bone. He was taken to Denver by train for treatment. At the time Deputy Allison claimed he was trying to keep the peace between Tom McCaffrey and another man when he shot at Tom and hit Pat instead. Tom McCaffrey, who probably described the situation accurately, said Allison fired for no reason. Allison was arrested and taken to jail.[92] Recounting the shooting several months later, Allison reported that he and Tom McCaffrey had a row and that Tom shot at him with a shotgun. Allison said McCaffrey's aim was high and the pellets struck a chandelier. As Allison sought to return the favor, he alleged that Pat ran into his line of fire. He said, "The smoke was thick when I pulled, and I was excited, which accounts for the blindness of my shot." According to Allison he posted a $1000 bond and was set to appear before the next session of the district court.[93] His ability to post bond and gain temporary release was perhaps helped by Justice of the Peace George C. O'Connor, who was developing a reputation for supporting all the rough characters in Conejos County.[94] According to the *Denver Republican*, "McCaffrey survived, but, for the murderous intent of the act, Allison was driven from town by the citizens." Allison then moved only a short distance away to Conejos, where he may have first met members of the Eskridge family, but was shortly afterwards driven from that town as well.[95] Before the end of February he was living in Durango and had joined up with Ike Stockton and his gang.

Allison was an attractive man, about five feet eight inches tall, 160 pounds, and about thirty years old.[96] He wore a thick, sandy moustache and had dark blue eyes. He had a wicked sarcastic wit and displayed signs of having a good early education, although his talk was known to frequently contain the slang terms common to the frontier. In conversation he was fluent and animated.[97] Even though he sometimes fouled up, at other times he displayed a daring cool, but Ike's men were not impressed with his performance on the raid down the La Plata. In fact, he left such a bad taste in their mouths that they let Ike know that they would not go out if he was part of the band.[98] Allison was prone to making swaggering pronouncements about his bravery and his prowess with a pistol. His braggadocio soured some of Ike's tough, taciturn Texans. Despite his falling out with the Stockton gang, his future crimes would suck Ike Stockton into a deadly downward spiral.

Stockton put Allison out of his mind and retained his resolute focus on northwest New Mexico. Jap Coe reported that Stockton and his men issued "dire threats against" the men who had killed Os Puett and Porter Stockton. In response, Coe said the men of western Rio Arriba County went about "armed and on the alert as best they could."[99] People living along the Animas and San Juan Rivers had always felt ignored by county officials, first from Taos County and now from Rio Arriba. The county seat in Tierra Amarilla was a three day hard ride from the lower Animas. The high sheriff of the county, Juan Lucero, lived in the family's traditional home area at Los Luceros, which was even further away, seventy miles south of Tierra Amarilla.[100] The lower Animas men needed help. While Deputy U.S. Marshal Heffernan wrote Governor Pitkin seeking to protect Ike Stockton, they wrote New Mexico Governor Lew Wallace seeking protection from Ike Stockton. Residents of southwest Colorado and northwest New Mexico continued to have opposing views with regard to Ike. The New Mexicans sent a petition to Wallace. The *Las Vegas Optic* reported the petition said in part, "county officers are wholly unreliable, they do not and will not perform their duties as officers of the law." They asked Wallace to provide them with arms and ammunition, so they could form companies to protect themselves. According to the *Optic* the petition was "signed by over one hundred of the most prominent citizens of Taos and Rio Arriba counties."[101] While the men from western Rio Arriba County waited for the wheels of the territorial government to turn, they kept up their patrols along the Colorado border.

Governor Wallace would hear about the troubles from both sides. About a week after Marshal Heffernan sent his letter to Governor Pitkin in Denver, his ally C.H. McHenry wrote a similar letter to Governor Wallace in Santa Fe. Oscar Puett's uncle Al Puett delivered the confidential letter to Wallace on March 30th. The McHenry letter recounted the turmoil of the previous months. It advised the governor that the lower Animas vigilantes ordered that everyone take sides and fight Stockton and Eskridge. If they chose not to fight they were to be treated as enemies. The letter said about forty good citizens fled the country, rather than join up with the vigilantes. McHenry identified the following men as being the principal leaders:

Lew Coe	Frank Meyers	George Thomson
Frank Coe	John Brown	John Cox
Jasper Coe	George Lockhart	Henry Hanson
Thomas Nance	Ed Ray	Alf Graves
James Razor	Marion Hamblet	John Firbaugh
Cal Razor	John Hamblet	Wash Cox
J.H. Razor	Lee Hamblet	A.F. Stump

Fred Tully   N. Roberts   James Tully
Henry Benning

The former Union soldier alleged that about eighty men were associated with the vigilantes, but noted that most of those joined only because they felt they had no choice as they could not leave the country. McHenry had been badly treated before he fled to Colorado and that accounts for his skewed assessment. Sentiment in northwest New Mexico against Ike Stockton, Jim Garrett and the Eskridge brothers far outweighed any sentiment in their favor. McHenry wanted to paint his enemies as being outlaws and noted that the three Coes on his list were principal men in the late troubles in Colfax and Lincoln counties. McHenry was off target, since none of the Coes were principal players in the Colfax County problems and the only one on the list involved in the Lincoln County struggle was Frank Coe. George Coe, who was indicted for crimes in Lincoln County, does not appear on his list. The ill will generated by the Stockton-Eskridge group drew men of strength and high character who allied themselves with the Coes, like Wash Cox and John "Doc" Brown.[102] As more men joined the cause, the influence of the Coes began to wane. The personal and petty differences which resulted in good men being forced out of New Mexico would soon cede supremacy to clearly more important tasks as the New Mexicans focused their efforts on stopping the wholesale theft of cattle and avenging the murders of George Brown and Aaron Barker.[103] Governor Wallace would soon have to make sense out of the conflicting accounts. In the last days of March, the McHenry letter and the opposition petition reached his office.

"Colorado. - Incidents of a Trip to the Mining Town of Durango," Frank Leslie's Illustrated Newspaper, *May 28, 1881, artist J.J. Reilly. (Author's collection.)*

Chapter Eleven

The Adjutant General

> *He could hear the roar of the big six-wheel,*
> *And her driver's pound on the polished steel,*
> *And the screech of her flanges on the rail*
> *As she beat it west o'er the desert trail.*[1]

Lew Wallace was no political hack, but a man with extensive experience and education. Wallace himself may not have thought so, but if ever there was perfect fit of a man, a place and a time, it was Lew Wallace as governor of New Mexico during the waning days of the American frontier. The Rio Arriba troubles had been the subject of several articles in the *Santa Fe New Mexican* and other newspapers during the first months of 1881. Wallace was aware that problems were brewing in the northwest part of the territory. At the time he had served as governor for two and a half years.[2] His predecessor, Samuel B. Axtell, came under fire for his mishandling and even contribution to the troubles in Colfax and Lincoln Counties. Federal officials sent Frank Warner Angel to investigate. Not long after Angel submitted his report, Wallace was headed to New Mexico to replace Axtell.[3] Lew Wallace, because of his Civil War service, was well suited to serve as governor of a territory that was defined by its disorder.

When he became a major general during the Civil War, he was the youngest man to achieve that rank.[4] After the meteoric rise his war record was mixed, but he achieved accolades for stepping into the breach at the Battle of Monocacy in July 1864. At the time, Washington faced a serious threat of invasion by Confederate forces. Badly outnumbered, Wallace took on rebel soldiers serving under Confederate General Jubal Early. He was able to delay Early until Grant could send reinforcements. In all likelihood Wallace's action prevented the sacking of Washington. After the war he was the second highest ranking officer to serve on the military panel that judged the conspirators implicated in the assassination of President Lincoln. He later served as president of the commission that tried Confederate Captain Henry Wirz, who was commander of the notorious prison at Andersonville, Georgia. In 1876 he served as counsel to presidential candidate Rutherford B. Hayes in a dispute involving Florida's Electoral College vote. After Hayes became president in 1877, Wallace hoped for a plum diplomatic assignment. He was offered the position of Minister to Bolivia, but declined. In the latter part of August 1878 he accepted the position of Governor of the Territory of New Mexico. He traveled by rail to Trinidad and then by buckboard to Santa Fe.[5]

Wallace entered a territory that was in a state of disarray. The unrest in Colfax County remained a problem, but that was soon eclipsed by the situation in Lincoln County. The havoc in those counties was at times overshadowed by the territory's Indian difficulties. Apaches were running roughshod across the southern part of the territory, killing travelers and settlers and generally throwing fear into the populace. Over four hundred would be killed before the Apaches were finally contained in 1886, long after Wallace left the territory.[6] Wallace had his hands full, yet in his spare moments he was putting the finishing touches on what would become one of the best-selling novels of all time, *Ben-Hur*. Behind the governor's office, in the Palace of the Governors on Santa Fe's plaza, was what Wallace described as "an extensive room" with one small window, only an interior door and a "rough pine table." After business hours, Wallace would retreat to this hideaway, which was soundproofed by its thick adobe walls, and work late into the night completing his masterpiece. His wife Susan was advised that Billy the Kid had threatened "to ride into the plaza at Santa Fe, hitch my horse in front of the palace, and put a bullet through Lew Wallace." A friend advised her to close the shutters on the small window at night, so the student's lamp Wallace used for writing would not illuminate the Kid's target.[7]

After receiving the petition from Rio Arriba County, Wallace requested assistance from the territory's U.S. Marshal, John Sherman, Jr. They reluctantly concluded that no federal violations were involved and that U.S. marshals could not intervene.[8] Undeterred, Wallace then notified Judge L. Bradford Prince and requested that a grand jury be impaneled to investigate the Rio Arriba strife and bring indictments against the offenders using territorial statutes.[9] He then dispatched a letter to Denver to D.C. Dodge of the Denver and Rio Grande Railroad and advised him about the situation in northwest New Mexico. He asked Dodge to wire his agents and notify them to provide transportation for New Mexico Adjutant General Max Frost and provide him with subsistence stores and any facilities he might require. Wallace concluded the letter with the terse notation, "Territory pays expenses."[10]

Maximilian Frost was well known throughout the territory and, upon receiving his orders, he was tireless in dealing with the San Juan turmoil. Given the distances he had to travel, and the modes of transportation available, persistence and patience were more than virtues, they were job requirements. Colonel Frost, as he was known later in life, was born in New Orleans on New Year's Day 1852. His parents died when he was still a boy, his father being killed in battle.[11] As a young man he joined the U.S. Army and worked in the Signal Corps. In the fall of 1875 he was stationed in Colorado at the Pike's Peak signal station.[12] In April of 1876 the army sent him to Santa Fe. He became thoroughly acquainted with most of the territory while inspecting telegraph facilities, establishing telegraph offices and overseeing the construction of new telegraph lines. He was instrumental in installing lines that ran through areas where Apaches and other tribes were actively killing travelers and settlers. Out in New Mexico's wide open spaces, his work was like a gift from heaven, providing tiny communities with instant communication to the outside world for the first time. Acting Governor Ritch first appointed him as adjutant general. Both Governor Wallace and his successor, Governor Sheldon, reappointed him.[13] Under Lew Wallace, this was a key position in territorial government. Wallace was not hesitant in utilizing Frost to the fullest extent. For the Rio Arriba troubles, Frost would serve as the governor's eyes and ears.

With military crispness, Governor Wallace dispatched his adjutant general with these orders:

> You will proceed to Tierra Amarilla, Rio Arriba county, New Mexico, and make inquiry into the troubles reported as existing in valleys of the San Juan and Animas rivers; ascertain as certainly as you can the origin of the difficulty, the names of the persons engaged in it and their places of abode, whether in New Mexico or Colorado, and make full report to this office of your investigation and its result. Choose for informants the most disinterested. Take sixty muskets of the Territory from Fort Marcy, with one hundred and fifty cartridges per arm, proper calibre.

Frost was also instructed to form two militia companies, arm them and place them in the service of the sheriff or other reliable man. Wallace expressly forbid the pursuit of any outlaws into Colorado.[14] Portions of this dispatch flashed across the country. In Kansas, the *Iola Register* reported that Adjutant General Frost was proceeding to Rio Arriba County and that, "The desperadoes in that region are led by the notorious Ike Stockton, whose headquarters are on the Colorado line, at Durango, and have driven away fifty desirable settlers."[15]

While Ike and Hargo eagerly prepared to open a tent saloon, Max Frost made arrangements to travel to the San Juan country. At 2:00 in the morning on March 30, 1881 Frost boarded a stagecoach for a crisp early morning ride from Santa Fe to the recently completed end of the rail line at Española. At close to the same time the arms and nine thousand rounds of ammunition were freighted to Española utilizing a team hired from Swope and Cronk and kept under the guard of five soldiers provided by Colonel Edward Hatch, the commander of the Military District of New Mexico. From there he traveled on the Denver and Rio Grande rails bound for San Antonio, Colorado (a short time later it was renamed Antonito). Near the San Antonio station the rail line forked, the main line going to Denver and the west line headed back into New Mexico over Cumbres Pass. Given the growing animosity developing between the warring parties, Frost's quest to find disinterested parties would be difficult. Frost disembarked at the San Antonio station and traveled to nearby Conejos to meet with Dow Eskridge. While there he also spoke with the former lieutenant governor of Colorado, fifty-six-year-old Major Lafayette Head.[16]

"Colorado.- Incidents of a Trip to the Mining Town of Durango," Frank Leslie's Illustrated Newspaper, *May 28, 1881, artist J.J. Reilly. (Modified, author's collection.)*

It is likely that Frost was acquainted with Head based on his military background and wide travels in the region. Head had an erect bearing and wore a long gray beard. He was a keen observer who was known for clearly stating his opinion, but normally only did so when asked. His quiet understated tone added gravity to his opinions.[17] The hacienda of the Head family was a landmark remembered by many travelers. The one story home was made from one foot diameter peeled pine logs, closely fitted together and treated to exude a high sheen. It was almost two hundred feet long and fifty feet deep.[18] Head had lived in Colorado since 1854, when he gathered a group of about fifty New Mexico families and settled in the Conejos valley.[19] He was born near Boonville, Missouri at Head's Fort, a small stockade erected by his family for protection against Indians. In 1846 he was stationed in Santa Fe as a soldier under Colonel Sterling Price who is most renowned for his service as a Confederate general.[20] In January of 1847, Colonel Price was commanding the U.S. Army forces in New Mexico when the natives rebelled against the four month long United States occupation. Governor Charles Bent and several other Anglo residents were murdered. Head was probably among the 350 soldiers commanded by Price, who traveled from Santa Fe to Taos to suppress the rebellion.[21] Just two years later Head was a merchant in Abiquiu.[22] He married Martina Martinez, who was a member of an influential Hispanic family.[23] The Heads' hacienda featured traditional *mi casa es su casa* hospitality. One traveler who visited the major said, "We feasted on beans, fresh boiled eggs, bread, *carne, tole* and tea, all very good, and served up by a fair senorita in a yellow dress and a pullback, but whose dainty feet scorned shoes or stockings."[24] Among the Hispanic population, the major was the most esteemed local *patrón*. He had also served as Indian agent for the Tabeguache Utes.[25] He was highly respected by the Indians, Hispanics and Anglos and served as Colorado's first lieutenant governor after statehood was attained.[26] Head had known Eskridge for many years and vouched for Dow's good character. Max Frost could not help but be impressed by this endorsement.[27] Unfortunately, Dow's younger brothers were new arrivals and Major Head was unaware that they did not possess the same mature judgment and character as their older brother.

    The elder Eskridge's dreams of developing a San Juan herd had been blasted into nothingness with the murder of George Brown. His little brother was one step ahead of a lynch mob and he was certain that his cattle were being killed and stolen. He told Frost, "I intend to go down there and if I cannot get my stock peaceably, shall have to go with a strong enough force to take them anyhow." He told Frost he had been informed that he would not be allowed to take them peaceably.[28] The fate of Eskridge's cattle was one more situation that Frost would investigate. Frost laid over for 24 hours before boarding a train bound for Chama at 3:10 in the morning.[29]

    The 3:10 to Chama took six hours to make the approximately sixty mile journey from San Antonio. Frost found that the Rio Arriba problems were not confined to the Animas and San Juan River valleys. He described Chama as being "a very lawless and disorderly town; shooting all day and night. Consists of drinking and gambling places - boarding houses and a few stores & R.R. buildings."[30] At the time Chama was one of the wildest towns in all of America. One visitor who preceded Frost by two weeks described the town as consisting of 276 cloth tents and nineteen sparsely built wood frame buildings. The traveler said, "Out of the 295 tents and buildings, 266 are either saloons or sell liquors." Railroad laborers, freighters, travelers and others could slake their thirst at the Slab Box, Tontine, Old Judge, Health Office, Keg Saloon, Bank Exchange, Little Jim, Denver Sample Room, Palace Theater and the aptly named Hell Dive. Surprisingly, Cole's restaurant provided what was described as a "hearty first-class supper."[31] In March of 1881 it was said that holdups were everyday affairs and when shootings or murders occurred, few people paid any attention and such incidents normally went unreported.[32] The *New Mexican* said, "Chama is a good place for a man who is tired of life and has scruples about committing suicide."[33] Dr. A.L. Cole, formerly of Denver, kept busy caring for the wounded and was known to proudly display bullets pulled from his pocket, which he had previously extracted from the latest victim's body. Hundreds of tons of supplies shipped in from Denver and elsewhere were piled up near the depot, most of it awaiting freight wagons bound for Durango.[34] Freighter Jim McGee was overwhelmed with work, even though he kept several six mule teams on the road constantly.[35] The town had two stage lines, the Barlow and Sanderson and the Wall and Witter, both offering daily service to Durango, filling the gap between Chama and southwest Colorado. About Chama, the *Las Vegas Daily Optic* noted, "The soiled doves who do here congregate in numbers startlingly voluminous, are very much soiled indeed." Tinhorn gamblers were said to make up a large portion of the populace. While they were offensive, they were normally not considered to be a threat to life or limb.[36] With tongue in cheek, the *New Mexican* noted that Chama, "does a good deal of business of a certain kind, and is lively enough."[37]

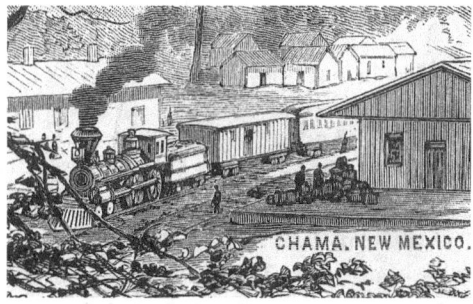

"Colorado. - Incidents of a Trip To the Mining Town of Durango," Frank Leslie's Illustrated Newspaper, *May 28, 1881, artist J.J. Reilly. (Author's collection.)*

Twenty miles west of Chama was another tent town by the name of Amargo. It too was a staging area for the D&RG railroad and conditions there were at least equal to those found in Chama. Amargo means "bitter" in Spanish and the town's spring provided a foul tasting source of water.[38] The *New Mexican* advised that in Amargo and Chama, "The law in regard to concealed weapons is openly defied, and in fact is a dead letter." It was said, "every man goes armed, and some are walking arsenals." It was reported that at night most of the residents spent their time "rioting, gambling, drinking, loafing, and [they] seem to take special delight in firing off six-shooters and Winchester rifles."[39] Railroad contractors operated numerous grading camps along the D&RG's right of way leading into and out of the town. They employed close to two thousand men, who looked to Amargo and Chama for entertainment.[40] Many in the two towns were not gainfully employed, but found other ways to make a living. The arrival of the licentious and lawless whirlwind associated with the leading edge of the D&RG rails in Durango would coincide with the final Stockton-Eskridge conflagration.

The evening of the same day Frost arrived in Chama, a large group of men rode out of Chama for Amargo. They were on a mission to rescue Rio Arriba County Deputy Sheriff Charles Johnson. It was feared that Johnson was about to be lynched.[41] Reports said that a thirty-year-old Kansan named Reuben Bertram had been shot and killed. The same round injured H.H. Lovell, when it struck him in the shin. The men were staying near La Count's railroad camp and Bertram worked for the water service of the D&RG construction contractor. The men had retired for the evening and were occupying the same bed when they were shot. The practice of sharing beds was borne of necessity and a common practice at the time. Bertram survived only ten minutes after a bullet severed the artery in his thigh.[42] The men were hit during a volley of indiscriminate gunfire at midnight in which fifty rounds were fired.[43]

According to the *New Mexican*, after the shooting, incensed railroaders "arrested" Deputy Johnson "and charged him with the shooting."[44] With Johnson's life hanging in the balance, a rider made a quick trip to Chama and a rescue party was organized. The unlikely leader of the rescue group was a notorious outlaw by the name of Jimmy Catron. The wayward Catron was twenty-seven years old and grew up in a family of eight children in Lafayette County, Missouri.[45] Catron was a close friend and dependable ally of Jim Garrett and the Eskridge brothers. He had lived for several years in Conejos County and at times lived close to the family of Dow Eskridge in the village of Conejos. Given his Missouri roots, he may well have been connected to Dow's wife and others in the Garrett family by blood or longtime friendship.[46] Catron was a dangerous man and doubly so if he had been drinking, which was the rule and not the exception.

Young Catron had a reputation as a man not afraid to use his pistol and the railroad men in Amargo were not prepared to stand up to him or his rescue party. An unattributed and sensational story of dubious accuracy in the *Chicago Inter Ocean* credits Catron with several murders. (The *Inter Ocean's* account was written in 1899. And while it may embellish his deeds, its publication over twenty years after the events described, buttresses the notion that Catron was a desperado of the first order.) The report notes that Catron killed his first man south of Alamosa in 1877. Catron and fellow cowboy Jim Mountz had a chuckwagon disagreement over flapjacks, and Catron killed Mountz in self-defense. A few days later, Jim Mountz's brother, George Mountz, caught up with Catron, who was driving cattle. Mountz took a shot at Catron with his rifle. The bullet passed under Catron's right leg, startling his horse as it severed a stirrup leather. Catron stayed in the saddle and returned fire, striking Mountz in the chest. Within a half hour George Mountz, as the pioneers often said, "crossed over the divide" and joined his brother. Catron's next trouble came in the Conejos dance hall. The victim was "a Mexican who made a thrust at him with a big knife and kept coming." The Conejos County sheriff was witness to the attack and refused to arrest Catron. Despite the blood and mayhem, Catron remained at the dance hall. As he was leaving at 3:00 AM he was fired on by two men. He returned fire and the newspaper reported that, "when lights were brought they disclosed two dead Mexicans." Two weeks later in Conejos he was fired upon by several assailants, but saved himself by finding cover in the Catholic Church.[47] Based on the large number of subsequent stories of mayhem associated with Jimmy Catron, it is clear that he held no scrupulous policy to only fire in self-defense as alleged in the *Inter Ocean*. The D&RG's railroad workers had enlivened the town of Conejos before extending the line over Cumbres Pass and Catron was no doubt well known to some of them.

In the summer of 1880, Catron worked as saloon keeper in Conejos. At that time Conejos had less than four hundred residents, but the town was wide open and its iniquitous dens serviced the ephemeral population of railroaders. The dance house frequented by Catron supported local prostitutes Sadie Tabor, Anne Doughty, Maria Romero and a motley assortment of full-time gamblers.[48] Before Charles Johnson became a Rio Arriba County deputy sheriff, he performed the same function in Conejos County and that may have been where he and Catron developed a convenient, if uneasy truce.[49] Johnson may have held that position when Catron was implicated for a murder which has a firm factual basis. On August 30, 1880, Catron, Cass Spore, Dave Rissler and James Nichols rode up in a wagon to the San Antonio (Antonito) rail station at 5:00 in the morning and fired off at least thirty careless shots. All of the men were inebriated at the time. One shot passed through a man's hat and another killed D&RG fireman James Bennett, who was standing on his engine, No. 19. Catron, Spore and Nichols were arrested and jailed in Conejos and it was thought the men might be lynched.[50]

Less than a year later Catron was no longer in jail and was intent on rescuing Deputy Johnson. Catron and his rowdy crowd were anxious to squash any efforts at vigilantism, knowing full well that once vigilantes got started, they might become the next victims of impromptu frontier justice.

The railroaders were rudely surprised when Jimmy Catron rode boldly into their camp and demanded Johnson's release. The leaders of the lynching party quickly caved, soon afterwards a very much relieved Johnson mounted his horse, and the rescue party roared out of town toward Chama.[51] Deputy Johnson made his case to Chama's Justice of the Peace Charles W. Marshall and convinced him of his innocence, although it was reported he would still have to face a judicial proceeding in Amargo.[52]

With the railroaders nascent vigilantism suppressed, and disorder fully restored, Catron went on a spree. Local businessman C.R. Fife described the mission to Amargo as a rescue, but adds to the confused situation by calling Catron the "Captain of the Vigilantes." (Catron was a one man crime wave who operated with complete impunity and it appears his best interests would be served by assisting Deputy Johnson.) In a letter to his partner, prominent merchant and stockman T.D. Burns, Fife said "The gang or mob that left here last night to rescue Johnson got back this morning." Their leader was in a celebratory mood and Fife noted, "Jim Catron, Captain of the Vigilantes was the party who was enjoying himself. Drunk as a Lord and going thro' town blazing away indiscriminately." Fife said he came very close to being struck by some recklessly fired rounds. As he was walking to an eating house he had to pass the entrance to the Board of Trade Saloon. When even with the door he heard Catron sing out, "Look out there." At the same time Catron fired several shots in Fife's direction. Fife said if the near miss had occurred at night, he might not have thought much of it, but as it was on a busy corner in broad daylight, he felt the whole situation was getting thoroughly out of control. Max Frost was duly impressed by the chaos he encountered and believed that even a justice of the peace with a force of four or five deputies could not bring law and order to the railroad towns. He believed that order could only be restored with the deployment of a strong and constant force of men. Despite the serious problems in Chama and down the line at Amargo, Frost had other priorities and at about noon on April 1st he set out for Tierra Amarilla.[53]

He was still traveling with a guard of soldiers and with the arsenal intended for the proposed militia forces, and after the rail trip he hired wagons in Chama from Levy Hughes of Bloomfield's Haines and Hughes Store. The fifteen mile journey to Tierra Amarilla took a mind-numbing and back-breaking nine hours over roads that Frost described as almost impassable.[54] Frost discussed the situation in western Rio Arriba County with Hughes, who informed him that in early March, H.W. Cox was "held up" by the Stockton crowd. Frost mistakenly identified Cox as J.H. Cox (one of H.W.'s sons), whom he described as "an old man, wealthy and a good Citizen." H.W. fit the description. Only one year before the prosperous stockman had been chosen to serve in the territorial legislature. The Stockton gang threatened Cox and told him not to get mixed up in the current problems or he would "fare badly." They let him know that they intended to kill his son-in-law Alf Graves, his son John Cox, three of the Coe men, and others.[55] Trying to intimidate Wash Cox was like poking a grizzly with a stick. Stockton and his men had committed a strategic error on a stunning scale. If Ike wanted a fight to the bitter end, he now had it. It was shortly after this that Cox and others raised "$2000 - in cash as a reward for the capture of the Ike Stockton crowd." Hughes told Frost confidentially about the reward and Frost dutifully sent the information on to Governor Wallace with a needless notation that "capture probably means death."[56]

Frost may not have been aware of it, but he soon found out that County Sheriff Juan Lucero lived at Los Luceros, about seventy miles south of Tierra Amarilla. The adjutant general had been only about ten miles south of Lucero's residence when he traveled to Española to board the train to the San Antonio station. Residents of Tierra Amarilla described Lucero "as a good and honest man," but Frost's dispatch to the governor said, "From all accounts I hardly believe he is a man of sufficient nerve and intelligence to deal in person with the troubles existing on the San Juan and Animas Rivers." Lucero was aware of the troubles and had offered to appoint as many deputies as the citizens desired and at their choosing. Frost also spoke with County Commissioner Juan Andres Quintana who he described as "a man of considerable intelligence and means." Quintana expressed his desire to do what he could to restore law and order in the section, but the commission had few options and little authority.[57]

Meanwhile, all of the attention by Governor Wallace was garnering Ike Stockton regional and national notice. On March 31st Denver's *Rocky Mountain News* devoted almost an entire page to the Stockton Gang. The long-winded recital was datelined, "Durango, Colo.," but the writer must have been a visitor. The author seemed to be knowledgeable about Ike and Port's activities in Colfax County. The article noted that after Port's escape from the Cimarron jail, it was not long before both men reappeared in Cimarron and "so great was the dread of the people and of the authorities that the sheriff could find no one hardy enough to attempt to arrest Port or his brother." As the article goes on to describe the Stocktons' activities in the San Juan country, the narrative becomes muddled and confused. It refers to the excitement around "Rio Arabia, New Mexico." It then describes how Port Stockton was gunned down by a dozen ranchmen in a saloon near Farmington, how Tom Nance's partner "Boxley" was killed, and offers other assorted misinformation as fact.[58] Newspapers from Los Angeles to New York City began to run articles about the Stockton Gang.[59] On April 2nd, the *New York Tribune* picked up bits of the *Rocky Mountain News* piece and carried a short front page article, which recounted the erroneous version of Port Stockton's death and then described the formation of Ike Stockton's gang.[60] In the nation's capital, the *National*

Republican declared that one reason the vigilance patrols were unable to corner Ike was because he and his gang of desperadoes had superior knowledge of the local terrain.[61] That was pure drivel, considering that many of those who opposed Ike Stockton were cowboys who rode the borderland range daily and were intimately familiar with every sandstone bluff, waterhole and back trail in the country. The *Dolores News* reported that *Frank Leslie's Illustrated Newspaper*, which had national distribution, was printing the artwork of J.J. Reilly, who was in Durango to document events in the region. According to the *News* one of his cartoons featured, "citizens with blood in their eyes and navy six shooters on their hips. Farmington is in the background with a pitched battle and skull and cross-bone border." They noted, "It will bring undertakers in abundance."[62]

Newspapers closer to home carried extensive coverage as events developed. On April 3rd, the *Santa Fe New Mexican* carried a letter sent by Chief Justice L. Bradford Prince calling attention to the grand jury, which was to convene on April 11th in Tierra Amarilla. Prince issued an urgent appeal for anyone with knowledge about the troubles in the San Juan country to come and they would be heard.[63] On April 6th Frost sent a letter by courier addressed to William B. Haines which began, "If you want any action taken, you must send men here to testify before Grand Jury. Be quick and send men, who know something, so Indictments can be found."[64] The very next day he sent a second letter addressed to W.B. Haines, A.F. Miller, J.H. Cox, "and all citizens of Bloomfield and Farmington, NM." Once again Frost has his Coxes mixed up and surely meant H.W. Cox and not his son. There is an urgency to Frost's letter as he requests that witnesses travel to Tierra Amarilla. He also notes that the governor hoped to make the trip up from Santa Fe and adds "Governor Wallace declares it of the utmost importance, that your citizens be here for the purpose named." Frost concludes the letter with a specific request, writing, "Thomas Nance should be one of the witnesses."[65]

In the meantime, across the Continental Divide in the Farmington area, mayhem was coming from several different sources. Max Frost received a report that horse and cattle thieves were operating in the Cañon Largo area east of Bloomfield. The robbers were identified as Manuel Gonzales, Epimenio Miera and an unnamed "American." In a letter to Wallace, Frost said, "They also say – that Gonzales has about 15 men, who are stealing cattle and making the Cañon Largo Country unsafe." Frost labeled Gonzales and his cohorts the "Cañon Largo Gang."[66] The reporting parties were shading the truth to their advantage. Nonetheless, the *New Mexican* said the gang might number as high as twenty-five men and said "they are evidently a hard crowd."[67] The apple didn't fall too far from the tree in the case of Miera, who was still in mourning over the death of his father, Pantaleon. The elder Miera was a former lieutenant with the notorious gang of horse thieves and murderers led by the noted desperado

Sostenes L'Archeveque. On the night of December 28, 1880, Pantaleon, who lived in the Rio Grande valley north of Albuquerque in Algodones, and Santos Benavides, who lived nearby in Bernalillo, were lynched from a cottonwood tree near Schuster's Store in the area known as Guache at the southern end of the town of Bernalillo. The *New Mexican* carried news of their demise under the headline, "A Stout Rope Sustains the Weight of Two Horse-Thieves."[68] The "American" outlaw in the "Cañon Largo Gang" was masquerading as a deputy U.S. marshal. The men told David Lobato they were looking for a horse which had been stolen in Nacimiento in Bernalillo County. When they could not find that horse, they took his best horse instead. Frost described Lobato as an "intelligent Mexican" and "a man of good reputation." Lobato operated a small store close to Cañon Largo, near present day Blanco, New Mexico. Gonzales and his two companions also took a mule and $150 from Guadalupe Arellano. After the thefts, the two victims rode to Moses Blancett's house near Bloomfield and asked for help to capture the outlaws. Blancett, who was known as Mose, advised them that since another Stockton raid was expected, men could not be spared for the undertaking. It was a wise decision by Blancett, as it turns out there were two sides to the story. Lobato and Arellano then proceeded directly to Tierra Amarilla to meet with Frost and await the convening of the grand jury.[69]

The so-called "Cañon Largo Gang" and Stockton's gang weren't the only problems in western Rio Arriba County. One of the Navajo headmen was still demanding reparations for the tribesman who had been shot by Frank Meyers. The Navajos reported that he was badly crippled and virtually helpless. No one was offering payment. The *New Mexican* commented on the standoff saying, "Up in the San Juan country if you kill an Indian you must pay for him, if not his tribe will resent the injustice done him, and trouble will ensue." The Navajos were threatening to raise a ruckus over the matter.[70]

The Farmington fracas, which had occurred in late January, earned the Navajos some powerful allies. The account of that incident, which had been investigated and written up by Fort Lewis's Captain Rogers, had been sent up the line by Colonel Crofton. Slowly, it found its way to General John Pope, commander of the Department of Missouri, and from there it reached the highest levels of the federal government. The attorney general, the secretary of war and the secretary of the interior received copies. Thomas H. Nichol, the acting commissioner of Indian Affairs to the secretary of the interior, reported that Colonel Hatch and General Pope urge "that immediate action be taken to bring to justice two white outlaws Raser and Myers, who recently made an attack upon and dangerously wounded a Navajo Indian without cause or provocation at said place." Commissioner Nichol feared that a Navajo outbreak could result if civil authorities failed to act and he concurred with Captain Rogers's recommendation that troops be temporarily stationed in Farmington to prevent such an occurrence. Colonel Crofton learned all of this in a letter from the Adjutant General of the Army, which he received in the latter part of April.[71] By then the Navajos had already taken some revenge.

On April 2nd a freighter, who had ventured into the Navajo country on the lower San Juan, was brutally slain.[72] The victim, F.J. Hoffman, hailed from Logansport, Indiana. The scene of the attack was about eight miles below the Hogback near Bowen's ferry on the San Juan River. Around 7:00 AM on April 3rd, Hoffman's body was discovered by two of his friends, H. Sanftenberg and Edward Proles, who had gone to meet him because they had received reports of possible problems with the Indians. The victim had been struck four times in the head and once in the shoulder with his own axe. All of the head wounds penetrated the skull. The only items missing, from a very full wagon, were a rifle and $30 in silver, which he was known to be carrying. The team was still hitched. Over $200 in cash was found on the body. Lower valley settlers John Deluche and W.M. Rambo believed that Costiano and his brother had something to do with the murder. It had only been a few weeks before that Costiano led the large Navajo group into Farmington and asked that Raser and Meyers either be arrested or given over to them for shooting their kinsman. Evidently, earlier on the day of Hoffman's murder, Costiano and his brother had been present when Matt Everett, who was apparently a local trader, paid $30 in silver to Hoffman. The freighter then placed the money in a mess box and headed toward the San Juan. Two days after the murder, Costiano's brother showed up at Bowen's landing carrying a rifle which matched the description of the one stolen. The rifle in question may have been a Sharps, Model 1853. When asked about it, Costiano volunteered that he had purchased it from a white man living on the La Plata River. He gave the price variously as $25 and $35.[73]

The Navajos were not the only Indian tribe threatening the region. By March of 1881 rumor had it that some of the Utes were in a surly mood. In Colorado there was some fear that even a minor incident could flare into a widespread war with the Utes.[74] Those fears would soon be partially realized along the Utah and Colorado border.

As the Navajos and Utes simmered, Max Frost was in Tierra Amarilla, preparing for the convening of the grand jury. After several days in the small hamlet, he was still having difficulty securing a sufficient number of wagons for the next leg of his journey, which would take him to Bloomfield. He kept busy sending a steady stream of correspondence to Governor Wallace. Frost sought accounts from those who had recently been to Durango, Farmington, and the nearby area.[75] He heard a rumor going through Chama that Ike Stockton was claiming he had killed six men in the San Juan country. The *New Mexican* commented, "Ike's six added to Port's fourteen makes quite a good showing for the two brothers." Frost reported that, "a great many men in that county are absolutely afraid to talk about him or his actions." The newspaper noted that Stockton "contemplates another expedition into Rio Arriba county when he hopes to kill more."[76] Frost advised Wallace that the Stockton gang continued to be welcome and supported in Durango, while down in New Mexico the ranchmen were "keeping up their Pickets and Patrols." The New Mexican vigilance patrols were armed, prepared for action, and had embargoed all of the livestock south of the Colorado line. At one point some work oxen belonging to a D&RG construction crew wandered downriver into New Mexico. A confrontation over the oxen between a D&RG work crew and the New Mexicans ensued and the railroaders returned to Colorado empty-handed. Up the Pine River, Stockton's Erath County compatriot, George Morrison, found one of the New Mexico cowboys riding his prize horse. The quick-tempered Morrison was livid. He retrieved the horse, but the situation almost resulted in gunplay until cooler heads prevailed. Evidently, La Plata County Sheriff Luke Hunter went over to Morrison's to investigate the matter. Frost also said that, "Two desperadoes killed at San Juan Junction three days ago."[77] Frost's telegraphed dispatch, which was signed simply "Frost," said the two men were killed at the "end of track."[78] He offered no more details about this incident.

The adjutant general was a powerful and influential figure and T.D. Burns was pleased to provide young Frost with complete use of his facilities. While in Tierra Amarilla, Frost used Burns's offices as his temporary headquarters. Several of the letters sent to Governor Wallace were copied for Frost's records on letterhead which read, "T.D. Burns - Dealer in General Merchandise - Cattle, Sheep, Wool, Hides and Pelts - Tierra Amarilla, N.M." Others were on letterhead which read, "Office of Burns & Co., - Forwarding and Commission Merchants, – And Dealers in General Merchandise. – Mark and Consign your goods care Burns & Co. end of track San Juan Extension Denver & Rio Grande R.R."[79] Frost discussed the situation fully with Burns and Bloomfield merchant Levy Hughes. Both men were in positions to know the participants in the San Juan saga and the details of past events. They also offered their opinions about possible options to deal with the difficulties facing Frost. In that vein Hughes told Frost, that, in his opinion, not only would Dow Eskridge be allowed to round up his stock in the San Juan country, but that local residents would actually help him. In late March cattleman I.W. Lacy passed through Tierra Amarilla on his way to Durango. He spoke with Burns about the situation and told Burns that he would gladly provide the elder Eskridge with herders to help him round up his cattle. Burns advised Frost that "Mr. Lacey's word can be relied upon."[80] Providing herders to help round up the Eskridge cattle seems like a farfetched idea in light of the bitter feelings held by the lower Animas men toward Dison and Hargo Eskridge. However, some knew that Dow had a legitimate claim to at least some of the cattle which Jim Garrett and Dison Eskridge had trailed to the lower Animas in January 1880. Returning the cattle was viewed as a method to defuse the situation and strip Stockton of his most valuable allies. While Lacy was willing to help Dow Eskridge, he was blunt and confident in his condemnation of Ike Stockton. He told Burns that Ike and his men had stolen fifteen of his horses and had taken a large number of his cattle, which they were selling to butcher shops in Durango. Lacy said Ike's acts were in response to Tom Nance's role in the killing of Port Stockton.[81]

The murder of Aaron Barker, the attempted murder of Tom Nance and the theft of his livestock spurred Lacy to take action. With that in mind, he sent one of his hired hands, Big Dan Howland, to Durango.[82] It appears that in 1880 Big Dan worked for Lacy as a herder in Las Animas County, where according to the *Trinidad Times,* he was "well and unfavorably known."[83] He set Howland up as a detective in Durango and covered his expenses.[84] The employment of a cattle detective or stockman's detective was a risky proposition for I.W. Lacy. It upped the ante in his dispute with Ike Stockton. The term cattle detective generally referred to a lone wolf hired gun. Part of their job was to gather information and relay that to their employer. That was only a small part of their duties, a cattle detective's chief goal was to intimidate rustlers and run them out of the country. If threats failed, they knew their employers expected them to use their firearms to finish the job. Detectives were effective against the isolated cowboy or small time rancher, who was known to throw a wide loop. In those instances, the mere rumor of their presence sometimes caused cattle thieves to move on. After his arrival in Durango an unwitting Bob Dwyer hired Howland as a constable. Howland had worked in a similar job in Trinidad.[85] This put Big Dan in close contact with Durango's saloon crowd and positioned him to pick up bits of information about the activities of the Eskridge brothers and Ike Stockton. He would also be working with constables and deputies who were friends and supporters of Ike and his men. If others in La Plata County's law enforcement community opposed Stockton, they did not take any action because of their fear of Stockton and Hargo Eskridge. Howland's new job put him in position to eliminate Stockton or the Eskridge brothers using some pretext and the color of the law for cover. If Howland hoped to intimidate Ike Stockton, Hargo Eskridge or others in the crowd, he quickly realized that he was outnumbered and outgunned. Whatever Lacy had in mind, it soon went to pieces. After only three days on the job, Bob Dwyer fired Howland. Perhaps Dwyer learned that Howland was already working as a cattle detective for Lacy and had no desire to put himself in danger from Stockton's crowd.[86] Lacy hoped that Big Dan would provide him with useful information in his war against the Stockton-Eskridge crowd. It may not have been explicitly stated, but Lacy almost certainly expected Howland to kill Stockton if necessary. After being fired, Big Dan rode for Lacy's La

Plata valley cattle range and with him rode Lacy's plans to eliminate Ike Stockton.

Lacy had other spies and sympathizers living in Durango. One of those was leather craftsman J.F. Bond. The saddler and harness maker had been a business associate of Lacy's for several years. As early as 1874 he was offering the same services and products out of his Commercial Street shop in Trinidad.[87] The Farmington cowboys knew it was not safe to enter Durango, but they needed the supplies which were available in the burgeoning town. Consequently, they sent their less well-known friends to Bond. The saddler did what he could to help Lacy's cause, providing the New Mexicans with ammunition as well as ordinary provisions.[88]

Back in Tierra Amarilla, Frost learned that Governor Wallace was stuck in Santa Fe. He had hoped to travel to Tierra Amarilla to meet with Frost and the men who would testify before the grand jury, but he advised Frost that he might be unable to do that because Secretary Ritch, who assumed the governor's mantle in his absence, was himself out of the capital.[89] Wallace had also just learned that the western portion of Rio Arriba County had no justices of the peace or constables due to improprieties with the fall of 1880 election. He advised Frost that the county commissioners had no authority to appoint justices of the peace, but they could appoint constables. He told Frost to request the commissioners to set up new elections to fill the justice of the peace vacancies.[90] As for the upcoming grand jury, Wallace made his wishes clear, writing Frost, "I must have indictments against the parties in Colorado before a stop can be put to the threatened raids from the vicinity of Durango. With certified indictments requisitions can be presented to Governor Pitkin [of Colorado]. Hence the importance of the court." Wallace had also just learned about the two indictments outstanding against Ike Stockton for old crimes committed in Colfax County. Judge Prince was carrying the indictments with him to Tierra Amarilla.[91]

Obviously, Wallace was a busy man. As he coordinated the efforts of Frost and Judge Prince, he wrote his boss Secretary of the Interior Samuel J. Kirkwood, and apprised him of the situation. Northwest New Mexico, despite its tiny population, continued to be the subject of concern at the highest levels of the federal government. In early April, Wallace received a reply from Kirkwood advising him that he had notified Secretary of War Robert Todd Lincoln and Attorney General Wayne MacVeagh about the situation. Kirkwood requested that the attorney general "direct the marshals of New Mexico and Colorado to use all means in their power to repress these disturbances."[92] Unfortunately, neither the Colorado nor New Mexico marshal's office ever took an active role to suppress the hostilities. In fact, Deputy Marshal Heffernan's championship of Ike Stockton served to prolong the situation as Ike continued to use the state line of Colorado as his personal protective barrier.

Safely ensconced in Durango, Stockton confidently counted on the support of many of the local residents. Ike's thirst for revenge was not satisfied by the death of Aaron Barker and not long after that incident the *Durango Southwest* reported, "The Stockton party now number about 35 men, who say they have stock down in that country and have resolved to 'round it up' if they have to kill all the thieves down there to do it."[93] The men who joined forces with Stockton were a rough crowd and Durango continued to feel the effects of their presence. "All the thieves down there" not only included the Coes, who had questionable reputations, but also men like Wash Cox, Alf Graves and other respectable cattlemen, who were now determined to see Stockton killed or run out of the country.

On about April 8th Stockton and his men lived up to their promise and traveled to New Mexico to round up cattle. A report in the *Denver Republican* on April 15th said, "It was only a few days ago that this gang drove into Durango thirty-five head of cattle that had been stolen."[94] After gathering the cattle, Stockton and his men were able to move away some distance before the lower country cowboys discovered the theft and gave chase. They followed Stockton and his men to the outskirts of Durango, but the outlaws had a head start and reached town before they could be overtaken. The lower Animas men were few in number and not prepared to enter Durango. They returned to New Mexico and spread the news.[95] Stockton and his men made a quick profit on the stolen herd. The *Republican* noted, "They butchered and sold them. They claimed that these cattle belonged to them, and that they were engaged in the cattle business. The fact is neither Stockton nor any of his gang own a hoof of cattle in that country."[96] The *Los Angeles Daily Herald* asserted, "citizens dare not write an impartial statement of affairs to the papers for fear of death. A Denver newspaper man who was suspected of writing an account for the Denver papers, was a few days ago stopped on the street at the point of a revolver by Ike Stockton. Six Marshals are on duty but are unable to cope with the outlaws."[97]

One of the men who trailed Stockton and Lacy's stolen cattle into Colorado was Big Dan Howland. After Bob Dwyer fired him, Big Dan remained in Lacy's employment and was rounding up horses in preparation for the spring roundup.[98] The men who chased the cattle thieves reported that they ran into "A Mexican, a spy from the Stockton crowd" about six miles from Durango. They shot and killed him.[99] Although he was never charged for this crime, the shooter was Big Dan Howland.[100] Several days later the *Durango Record* carried a clueless article that said "A Mexican sheep-herder was found dead three miles below town yesterday." The shepherd worked for Dona S. Hersey of Hermosa and the newspaper speculated that he was killed to get possession of his outfit.[101] It's doubtful that the sheepherder was a "spy." More than likely the doomed flock master was an innocent victim whose main concerns were coyotes, staying dry and keeping out of the way of the warring parties. Howland was turning into I.W. Lacy's loose cannon.

In the aftermath of Stockton's most recent rustling raid, the Rio Arriba County Grand Jury took on an added urgency, but the New Mexico cattlemen could not stand by and wait for that process to be completed. They believed that more cattle would be stolen. This, and the threats against the family of Wash Cox and others, spurred the men to take action. In all likelihood the seasoned Texas trail driver took the lead in a developing plan to get Stockton. Word was soon spread along the lower Animas and San Juan Rivers, and men began to gather, probably at the Cox place. They were tired of performing picket duty on the Colorado line. They wanted support from territorial officials, but were not convinced that it would be forthcoming. They gathered supplies and ammunition and prepared to deal with Stockton on his own turf. They hedged their bets and that's why a handful began the three day journey to Tierra Amarilla to plead their case before Max Frost and present testimony before the grand jury. Wash Cox, Mose Blancett, W.B. Haines, Tom Nance and others traveled to Tierra Amarilla. At least one of the travelers knew about Stockton's most recent raid and the killing of the sheepherder.[102] It's possible that one or more of them were part of the group which had trailed the cattle thieves toward Durango. But as the New Mexicans prepared to deal with Stockton on two fronts, events in Durango took an ugly turn.

"Colorado. - Incidents of a Trip to the Mining Town of Durango," from Frank Leslie's Illustrated Newspaper, *May 28, 1881, artist J.J. Reilly. (Author's collection.)*

Chapter Twelve

Baptism of Blood

> *Retribution shall prove that the just liveth still,*
> *And its horrors and dangers our hearts can abide,*
> *That safety and honor may tread in our path;*
> *The vengeance of Heaven shall speed at our side,*
> *As we follow unwearied our mission of wrath.*[1]

The instability and conflict which had come to define Durango exploded on the 10th and 11th of April, 1881. The chaos was kicked off by a Stockton-Eskridge hanger-on named Henry Read Moorman. Before his arrival in the Animas valley Moorman worked as a constable in Buena Vista, Colorado and later was a stage driver for Barlow and Sanderson. He quickly made his presence known in Durango and was reported to have been involved in several "gun plays," but without serious consequences.[2] Only a week before, Dison Eskridge and Moorman made a man remove his shoes while he "danced" on one of Durango's snow and ice covered boardwalks. Their bullets plowed into the boards just inches from the dancer's feet. The terrorized tenderfoot endured this treatment for almost an hour. Eskridge and Moorman followed that up by taking their victim into the Haverty and Eskridge Saloon, where they set him up with a shot of whiskey, told him to put his shoes on and advised him to attend to his business.[3] On another occasion Dison rode his horse into one of Durango's saloons and began shooting the ceiling. Bob Dwyer, who one contemporary described as having "plenty of nerve and … the coolest man I ever saw," responded to the disturbance. With calm indifference he told the mounted, pistol wielding intruder, "Dice, I'll take those guns." Eskridge was just trying to liven up the town and meekly handed over his weapons.[4] Henry Moorman, on the other hand, was looking for more than fun.

The *Durango Record* declared that recently "[Moorman] had announced his desire and intention to do some 'killing.' " The police force had been keeping an eye on him with growing apprehension.[5] The stoutly built, florid-faced ex-stage driver was about thirty-five years old and had ridden into Durango in late March. According to the *Denver Republican* he had participated in the most recent Stockton rustling raid.[6] On the evening of the 9th Dison Eskridge and Moorman attended the show at the Coliseum. They took box seats and were accompanied by Alice Harrison and "Big Emma." Eskridge and Moorman drank heavily during the show and afterwards went down to Hargo's Eclipse Saloon for even more libations.[7] As Saturday turned to Sunday (April 10th) events went downhill.

An *Extra* edition of the *Durango Record* said, "Just at the commencement of the dance which takes place at the dance house, just after the nigger show is over, a disturbance occurred on the sidewalk which was created by a Henry R. Moorman." Local officers stopped the disturbance and thought they had the situation under control. Moorman was patient, found his opportunity and when he saw it, entered the Coliseum.[8] He was accompanied by Henry Watts, Jack Wilson and Dison Eskridge. As he walked through the doors he drew his pistol and yelled out, "Damn my soul!"[9] He then proceeded to bring his exhortation to fruition. According to the *Record*, Moorman "immediately began blazing away." One bullet struck Perry Steffey in the arm. He was slightly injured. The same bullet then struck James Knox Polk Prindle, lodging in his hip. Falling to the ground, he had time enough to shout "You've shot the wrong man pard!" He was bleeding profusely, and like Thomas Greatorex, he was placed on one the tables in the Coliseum. Within twenty minutes, Prindle was dead.[10] One of the dance hall girls retrieved a bed sheet from her room and covered the body.[11] The victim was described as an "old miner," who had lived for a time in Georgetown and Central City before moving to Durango from the Gunnison country, where he had been doing some prospecting.[12] He was considered to be a quiet, peaceable man and had interests in three valuable claims near Buffalo Basin, Colorado.[13] He also had claims on Leavenworth Mountain near Georgetown. He had, up until March 1st, been working at a mill in the Florida valley, but had quit that and was making preparations for a spring prospecting expedition into the Needle Mountains. His body remained in the Coliseum until Monday morning, when Coroner Wright held an inquest on scene. After that, undertaker E.F. Nelson moved Prindle's remains "to a tent on Railroad street, near Charlie King's butcher shop, where it was properly laid out." King, who the year before had been butchering Gus Hefferman's stolen cattle in Rico, was now operating a large meat market in Durango. Services for Prindle were held at the recently completed St. Mark's Episcopal Church with Parson C. Montgomery Hoge officiating. He was interred in the Animas City Cemetery until his relatives could be contacted.[14] While Polk Prindle's cares expired with his last breath, Moorman's were on the upswing.

After the shooting, Jim Marshall immediately offered a $100 reward for Moorman's capture.[15] Marshall was particularly upset and concerned that his establishment had developed a reputation as host to several fatal and non-fatal confrontations. Shortly after the shooting, Justice of the Peace J.C. Craig was roused and quickly produced a complaint for the arrest of Moorman for murder, and then a second complaint charging three men as "accessories to the murder of one Polk Prindle." Those three men were Dison Eskridge, Jack Wilson and a third man whose name may have been Charles or John Harphan. Justice Craig's obviously hurried writing makes it difficult to clearly decipher the man's first or last name.

Even though Watts was clearly part of the group, he was not named as an accessory (his name does not resemble the undecipherable name). Craig handed the warrants over to Deputy Sheriff Bob Dwyer.[16] It was probably before the complaints were issued that constable T.R. (Tom) Payton, accompanied by Jim Garrett and Tom Lynch, found Moorman and Henry Watts hiding in a woodpile on Railroad Street near the Williams's lumberyard. Moorman had a revolver in each hand and told them to stay back. Payton took aim with his shotgun and demanded Moorman's surrender. Moorman called out, "Is that you, Tom? Well, I will surrender to you if you promise to protect me." Payton would offer no guarantees, but his shotgun was persuasive and Moorman and Watts soon gave up.[17] The ease of tracking and quick apprehension was enabled by a one inch snowfall that evening.[18] In the San Juan Mountain mining burgs, Moorman had a less than stellar reputation. The *Lake City Mining Register* was surprised to learn that he was still alive. A few weeks before, they had carried a report of his death. As for his recent arrest, the *Register* said, "Six policemen, under the command of Policeman Dwyer, caught all the parties, who are now in jail."[19] It is inconceivable that Jim Garrett helped apprehend Dison Eskridge and if others were incarcerated with Moorman, they were soon released. Moorman was not so fortunate. In Durango feelings were running hot.

As the sun rose, the town was filled with anticipation. Mrs. Romney's newspaper noted, "All day long knots of men were in the streets and on the corners discussing the terrible crime which had been perpetrated and every one accepted it as a foregone conclusion that Moorman would be lynched." At the same time, the Farmington vigilantes, heavily armed and prepared for action, were headed up the Animas. The *Durango Record* later estimated the number of men as ranging from twenty-five to fifty.[20] Members of this group included Alf Graves, Al Dustin and Ed Thomas.[21] Graves's brother-in-law, John Cox, and Burr Milleson also rode on the expedition.[22] According to Pete Knickerbocker other New Mexicans who rode to Durango that night included himself, Lew Coe, George Thompson (the nephew and namesake of Lacy's partner), Will, Charles and Harv McCoy, George Lockhart, the Claytons, the Eldridges, Pete Scott and Big Dan Howland. Much of the time the men rode in the dark. They arrived on the outskirts of Durango in the late hours on Sunday night. At least one or possibly more of the riders, most likely those who were least well known in Durango, were sent into town to reconnoiter.[23]

Their timing could not have been worse. According to the *Record*, about an hour before midnight two shots rang out and at that signal three hundred Durango citizens converged around Moorman's lockup. In a scenario played out many times on the western frontier, the vigilantes "overpowered the guards," who could now say they had performed their duty.[24] Moorman, the unwilling participant in this dance, put up a struggle, but was soon overwhelmed. The leader of the mob was probably fifty-seven-year-old Cap Stanley, who had only recently dealt death to Jack Roberts.[25] One witness said Moorman begged to be allowed to stand trial. He continued making so much noise that the men gagged him and then marched him to the pine tree in front of the Post Office on G Street. The vigilantes circled the tree and all of the lights facing the tree were extinguished. The noose was placed over Moorman's head, he was raised up and the rope was secured to the tree.[26] It's not known if the lower Animas reconnaissance party witnessed the lynching or only its aftermath, but they did view Moorman's body dangling in the moonlight. After hanging Moorman, Durango's vigilantes stayed on scene for about fifteen minutes. Then, according to the *Record*, "the Superintendent of the picnicers announced that any person who should cut down the body before daylight would do so under penalty of death."[27] With the warning issued the men moved on and went their separate ways. Soon afterwards, a large number of gawkers proceeded to the post office and viewed the body. As the crowd grew, the situation remained volatile and sporadic gunshots pierced the chill night air.[28] With gunfire echoing off the mesa behind them, the Farmington vigilantes grew tense and apprehensive, wondering if Stockton and Eskridge had discovered their spies.

The lower Animas scouting party had stepped into a hornet's nest. They headed out of town to deliver the surprising news. With everyone's nerves on edge, the approach to the rendezvous site was ripe with danger. Cool heads prevailed and the spies safely joined their very relieved companions. Overflowing with curiosity, the men gathered round to hear the report. The lynching of Moorman was described, but more importantly the scouts warned that large numbers of people, many of them well-armed, were still on the streets, a circumstance that was likely to continue for some time. After discussing the situation, they realized that now was not the time to take on Stockton and his men. The disappointed and weary group rode upriver toward Animas City, where several of them had friends. They made camp on Junction Creek and settled in for a sleep-deprived night. At the time, Deputy U.S. Marshal Heffernan lived on Junction Creek. The men did not care. They knew their presence would soon be relayed to Stockton, if not by Heffernan, then by others. Dawn came early. The element of surprise they had counted on was gone. They had lost their opportunity to get Ike Stockton.[29]

Morning in Durango was subdued. The citizenry followed the directions given by the vigilantes and Moorman's body still decorated the post office pine tree. The *Record* described the scene: "No one was disposed to cut it down, so it remained until morning swaying to and fro in the breeze, as a warning to the many other thieves and murderers that infest the town of Durango."[30] Like the doomed Tex Anderson, it was discovered that Moorman was carrying a letter from his sweetheart. The note was dated March 24th and had been sent from Stephensport, Kentucky. Kate was her name and she had not seen Moorman for almost four years. It was evidently a poorly kept secret that she considered herself to be engaged to the former stage driver. In the letter she tells Moorman that, "I have so many to advise me not to marry you; that you was such a wild fellow, and I knew nothing about you, being so far away from me, that you would not do to trust." Evidently, Kate had some perceptive friends who were not afraid to tell her the truth.[31]

As the sun began to climb above the mountains, the New Mexicans met with thirty-year-old Luke Hunter, the sheriff of La Plata County. He was accompanied by local residents D.W. Wood and Barney Watson.[32] Hunter had been elected sheriff in the fall of 1880. He was from Posey County, Indiana and had moved to Parrott City in May 1876, where he was a mechanic on steam engines. The next year he took up mining interests in the Needles with his partner, William Valliant.[33] The men later owned the Valliant and Hunter Saloon in Animas City, which was in operation when Port Stockton was the town marshal.[34] Hunter's saloon partner had known the Stockton boys for many years. In 1866 Valliant had moved from Tennessee to Erath County, Texas where he worked as a deputy sheriff.[35] The lower Animas men told Sheriff Hunter they were looking for stolen cattle and he assured them that he would guarantee their safety and they could enter Durango to look for their cattle and for hides. They were not confident in Hunter's guarantee of safe passage through Durango. In fact, most of them believed the sheriff was a Stockton-Eskridge sympathizer.[36] Hunter had never offered the New Mexicans any assistance in dealing with Ike Stockton or his associates. According to one account, he was aware of the sale of stolen beef in Durango, but had declined to make it his concern.[37] Self-preservation was definitely one reason for Hunter's lack of interest. After the meeting, some of the men felt that Hunter was setting them up for an ambush, somewhere along the main road leading into Durango.[38] Ike Stockton himself said, "We were told they were coming, and one of the Marshals came to me and said: 'For God's sake go out of town, and have no fighting here among the women and children.' "[39]

About 10:00 AM, the New Mexicans struck camp and headed down a lesser used route that trailed along the eastern edge of what is now downtown Durango.[40] They traveled along the low bench that is now traversed by East Second, Third and Fourth Avenues. Their destination was the gulch which housed Charlie King's slaughter pens. King owned the Parlor Meat Market on the corner of Railroad and G Streets in Durango. Not surprisingly, they had received reports that thirty of the stolen cattle could be found in King's pens.[41] The butcher was benefiting from the same illegal cattle trade which had supplied his business in Rico, yet he somehow managed to adroitly duck any blame for Ike Stockton's cattle stealing activities. He clearly took advantage of the situation by obtaining cattle at less than wholesale value. By Monday morning there were few people who did not know that the Farmington cowboys were in the area looking for their cattle. King was no fool and preferred that the animals not be found in his pens. As the men rode down the trail, they saw what they believed were their stolen cattle, grazing on the hillside. They began to inspect brands.[42] It was about noon when the horsemen were spotted by Stockton's sentinels as the rode along the mesa east of downtown. The alarm was spread and Stockton's supporters left their comforts on lower F Street and ran toward the sagebrush covered slope at the edge of town. A few isolated pops broke the sleepy noon day quiet and as more men entered the fray, the tempo of shots quickened. The *Durango Record* said, "The Eskridge, Garrett, Stockton crowd made a break in that direction and commenced firing. The fire was returned and from fifty to one hundred shots were exchanged, by the two parties."[43] The smoke and smell of exploded gunpowder wafted through downtown Durango. Ike Stockton later said, "I can't say who did the first firing. They were shooting at me and I returned the compliment." He added, "There were probably 200 shots fired."[44] On the hillside bullets were whizzing through the air, thudding into the ground and shredding the oak brush. John Cox was doing his best to ride out of the line of fire, but he was leading a pack mare that refused to be rushed. He turned to Burr Milleson, who was behind the mare and with his remnant Texas twang said, "poke up that hoss," which Milleson did and they finally reached some cover. One of the other men was riding a horse that was known to suddenly back up without cause. As the air filled with lead, the horse had even more inclination to do that and soon the horse and rider piled up on the hillside. At the sight of it the Stockton men whooped, but the horse and rider soon rose and rode for the safety of some boulders.[45] The next day the *Record* reported, "One horse was seen to fall on the other side." Ike's recollection as to who fired first was faulty. Editor Romney declared, "it is nevertheless true that the firing was commenced on this side, and had this not been the case we do not believe that the Farmington men would have fired upon the town, as they did not return the fire for some time."[46] The New Mexicans were presented with a choice to turn tail or fight and they chose the latter. They grabbed their rifles and their bullets whined into Durango striking buildings, pounding into the ground, scattering the residents. Harg Eskridge and Jack Wilson were conspicuous, brazenly standing in the open as bullets tore up the ground at their feet.[47] Despite the danger, some were unwilling to miss the show. Two innocent victims were struck, Conrad Pulvermiller was hit in the calf and Henry Wilson in the hand. One shot struck the West End Hotel on Second Street, smashing into the wall just over the head of Mr. Rouse, one of the owners. Another struck the Brunswick Billiard Parlor sign on I Street. Several buildings on First Street were also hit.[48] Despite the mayhem, the actual combatants were entirely safe and the Farmington men soon extricated themselves and rode south. The Battle of Durango was over, but Durango's battle over the fate of Ike Stockton had just begun.

Burr Milleson, left with Jim Cox. The photo is not dated. Milleson was born in 1860 and Cox in 1864. Photo by J.A. Boston, Durango, CO. (Courtesy Aztec Museum Association Historic Photo Collection, No. 83.63.01.)

One witness to the shootout was William (Billy) Devere. At the time Devere was preparing for the April 15th grand opening of his recently constructed two story high Clipper Theatre on First Street.[49] Devere also had literary aspirations and sixteen years after the incident he published a book of poetry. The gun battle between the Stockton forces and the New Mexico cowboys is immortalized in the book, which is titled, *Jim Marshall's New Pianner and Other Western Stories*. On the cover Devere calls himself the "Tramp Poet of the West." One of the poems is titled, " 'The Parson's Box.' A Tale of the San Juan." The first line reads, "Knowed Parson Hogue, well I should say." The poem goes on to chronicle some of the other characters Devere knew in Durango. It includes this brief passage:

> Big "Tex," "Ike Stockton," who stood off "Coe,"
> When he brought the gang from New Mexico,
> To take "Hargue Eskridge" and "Dyson's" lives,
> But the boys went out with their "forty-fives"

And winchesters, and they called them down
On the mesa outside of Durango town.⁵⁰

    The Farmington men who had faced the forty-fives and Winchesters believed that had they taken the main road half of them would have been killed. The planned ambush and the subsequent attack by Stockton's men confirmed their suspicion that Sheriff Hunter was on friendly terms with Stockton and his allies and that Durango was not safe for them.⁵¹ The next day Caroline Romney of the *Durango Record* was quick to attack, saying, "The Farmington people have made a grave mistake in attacking this town, firing in among residences containing women and children, and endangering the lives of people who have no part in their quarrels." Romney warned, "There are a thousand armed men in Durango, ready to repel any forcible invasion of this place." Mrs. Romney noted, "Had they had a warrant issued by the governor of this state to the sheriff of this county, in answer to a requisition from the governor of New Mexico, as the law provides, it would then have been the duty of the sheriff, in the language of the statute, to 'convey such fugitive to any place within the state which the executive in his warrant shall direct.' "⁵² That's how the law should work, but as time would tell, the words of the law and the actions of those selected to enforce it were two different things.

    Romney's complaint that the Farmington cowboys were attempting to act outside of the law was a bit ironic, considering the *Record's* opinion about the lynching of Henry Moorman, which was published in the same issue. In regard to Durango's vigilantes the *Record* said, "They have proclaimed to the world that good order, peace, quietude and safety to person and property must and shall prevail in Durango; they have thrown down the gauntlet to lawlessness and disorder." At the time, Durango's incorporation and first municipal election were close at hand and Romney wrote, "Judge Lynch holds sway and will protect the town until the town officers are duly elected." As for the troubled infancy of the town, she commented, "All new western towns have to pass through a baptism of blood and mis-rule."⁵³ Like a good Baptist, Durango was going through a total immersion and since it was April, the Animas was beginning to run muddy. The turmoil was not over. As the Farmington men rode down the Animas toward their homes, they were disappointed that they had been unable to get Stockton or Eskridge and believed their trip had been a total failure. They were wrong. The battle had a sobering effect on the residents of Durango, who now began to see that their support of Stockton was dangerous for residents and bad for the town's reputation, and that made it bad for business. As the D&RG rail lines drew closer the town was filled with optimism about its limitless future. However, the infestation of rowdies and desperadoes was throwing a monkey wrench into those expectations. The raging gun battle marked the beginning point of a steady erosion of Stockton's support in Durango.

Members of the McCoy family – Standing are Xuella and brother Harvey, seated left to right are George William, father Levi Allen and James. Brothers Harv, G.W. and James participated in the Battle of Durango. (Author's collection, from Ella Ann Spargo.)

Many Durangoans felt it was time to rid the town of not only the Stockton gang, but other saloon crowd ne'er do wells. The men who had lynched Moorman were calling themselves the "Committee of Safety."[54] The leaders of the Committee were Mr. Fisher, the president of one of Durango's lumber companies, the smelter's master mason Cap Stanley, and James Luttrell, land agent for the Denver and Rio Grande Railroad.[55] The Fisher in question was probably George L. Fisher, a former employee of the D&RG Railroad and after that the superintendent of the San Juan Lumber Company.[56] In a belated report to Governor Wallace, Max Frost described the sentiment which was slowly beginning to gather steam: "The best citizens of Durango are getting tired of the dominion of these men and that there will soon be a clash."[57] Within hours of the shootout with the Farmington cowboys, at 4:00 PM, a meeting was held at the Congregational Church Hall in Durango's Post Office block. Charles M. Hilliker served as the chairman. According to the *Durango Record* they voted on a proposal to have Marshal Dwyer "give notice to every disturber of the peace, and every disreputable character" to leave town immediately. The names were to be provided by the town marshal. That motion was voted down. They finally adopted a motion for a committee "to wait on the parties and give them notice to leave by Tuesday noon." The committee was composed of James Luttrell, C.M. Williams and I.E. Grout. The

Durango Record reported that among those who were to be told to leave the town were Jack Wilson, Dison Eskridge, James Garrett and Isaac Stockton. Some of them were present at the meeting. It's not known if others were being invited to leave town. After the meeting the three committee members in the company of Marshal Dwyer and Deputy U.S. Marshal Heffernan found the Eskridge brothers and perhaps others, and delivered the ultimatum. The Eskridge boys did not take the news well and drew their guns on Marshal Dwyer. According to the *Record*, "The General [Heffernan] walked up to the muzzle of the loaded guns and compelled the boys to listen to reason, and to go home and keep quiet."58 Not long after this meeting, Mr. Fisher of the Committee of Safety was "waited upon by some of this crowd, and told he had to leave, to which he answered, he would not and that he would see them all hanged yet."59 Up until this time, few in Durango dared to speak out against Ike Stockton or the Eskridge brothers. The tide was beginning to turn, but many of Durango's best citizens stubbornly refused to admit that they were harboring outlaws.

In fact, the friends of Ike Stockton and the Eskridge boys wasted no time calling for a second meeting to discuss what they called the "Farmington matter." This one was well attended by their supporters, many of whom were well known as leading citizens in La Plata County. Stockton's meeting took place in front of Myers and West's Livery Stable on F Street at 7:30 that evening. C.W. Long was elected chairman.60 A large crowd (one witness estimated the number at three hundred) gathered in the early lamp light.61 After some speechmaking, a committee was appointed, composed of Captain G.S. Flagler, attorney and Animas City justice of the peace; James Hunter, possibly Sheriff Luke Hunter's twenty-five-year-old brother; William DeVere, owner of the Clipper Theater; and Eugene Engley, former editor of the *Animas City Southwest*, who was by then working as an attorney in Durango. In 1892 he would be elected attorney general of the state of Colorado. Other committee members included Charles Shaw, a twenty-four-year-old freighter and son of John Shaw, the owner of the Shaw Hotel; and twenty-eight-year-old Ohioan Lucien Nunn, who was the co-owner of Durango's Pacific Grotto Restaurant. He also dabbled in real estate. Nunn had attended the Harvard School of Law and later moved to Telluride, where he innovated in the practical usage of alternating current power systems. Others on the pro-Stockton committee were J.M. Kelsey and E. Calkins. The main purpose of the meeting was to denounce the resolution passed by the Safety Committee. According to the *Durango Record*, Stockton's committee passed a resolution which said in part,

> Be it Resolved, That whereas at a meeting of what was or is called a meeting of the law abiding citizens, we the undersigned claim to be just as good law abiding citizens as any of the parties who attended the meeting this afternoon. Therefore *Resolved*: That

we the law-abiding citizens of La Plata county, believing that Jack Wilson, Dison Eskridge, Jas. Garrett and Isaac Stockton are good citizens and as yet have violated no law in the County of La Plata or State of Colorado, pledge ourselves to protect them against the assaults of any committee or set of persons not acting in accordance with law and order.[62]

The crowd applauded the resolutions and some prominent attorneys spoke on how the current turbulence could best be settled. There was some concern that the two groups might clash and the Animas City militia was called out by Sheriff Hunter. Militia members camped out in Durango that night. Jim Marshall announced the closure of the Coliseum for the next two weeks out of fear that bad blood between the Durango groups would lead to another murder in his establishment.[63]

The next day members of the two appointed committees held a conference. The men discussed what would be the best and most proper way to end the "Farmington troubles" as far as they concerned Durango. Both groups pledged their support to Sheriff Hunter. Later that evening about fifty friends of Ike Stockton, the Eskridge brothers and James Garrett met in the back room of a local saloon and, according to the *Record*, they "swore to stand by each other to the death." The *Record* editorialized that, "while wishing well to the Stockton and Eskridge party, our people as a rule, think it would be wise for them to close up their business matters and remove to some place more remote from their enemies." Concern over the blockade in business affairs between La Plata and Rio Arriba counties and the negative impact on the reputation of the community was rising to the forefront.[64] It appears that the prominent Durango and Animas City cattlemen did not take a leading part with either group. Most had no use for Ike Stockton, but they chose not to openly antagonize Ike or his followers.

Stockton's loss of support was coupled with the pressure being brought to bear by authorities in New Mexico. On April 12th Wash Cox, William Haines, Tom Nance, Mose Blancett and others were gathered in Tierra Amarilla to testify before the grand jury.[65] Some belated pioneer narratives place Blancett, Cox and Nance at the Battle of Durango on April 11th. Nance for one could ride like the wind, but even he couldn't cover that much ground in one day. It is unknown how they traveled, other than it was not by train; passenger service on the D&RG still reached only as far as Chama.[66] Nance was the star witness and he related the story of the killing of Aaron Barker and his narrow escape. The actual grand jury testimony evidently no longer exists, but the outcome was just about everything territorial officials could have hoped for. On April 12th, Max Frost sent an urgent dispatch to the governor: "I have the honor to inform you that indictments for murder, assault with intent to kill and horse stealing have this day been found by the grand jury against Isaac Stockton, Harge Eskridge, James W. Garrett, Charlie Allison, Wilson Hunter, Thomas Radigan and 3 others."[67] In his haste to get word to Wallace, Frost had garbled some of the information. Wilson Hunter was really Wilson Hughes (alias Texas Jack) and there were only two others indicted. Those two were Bill Hunter (alias Tex) and Lark Reynolds.[68] Gus Hefferman and a man identified only as Painter, who both may have participated in the raid, were not indicted. Max Frost was aware of the allegations against the two men and wrote, "2 of Stocktons [sic] men, in his gang during the recent raids and killing of Barker, Painter and Heffernan [sic], have left him and left the country on Monday last."[69] Hefferman left Durango, but he would turn up again. Painter, who was probably Erath County cattle thief, Bill Painter, disappeared.

The Barlow and Sanderson stagecoaches were usually full going both to and from Durango. "Colorado.- Incidents of a Trip to the Mining Town of Durango," Frank Leslie's Illustrated Newspaper, *May 28, 1881, artist J.J. Reilly. (Author's collection.)*

The San Juan men gave Frost the latest update on the situation. They were unaware of the pitched battle that had taken place in Durango. Wash Cox told Frost about the most recent Stockton rustling operation, which had occurred less than a week before. Frost's subsequent dispatch to Wallace reported that Stockton's group had recently stolen four hundred head belonging to Wash Cox and to Thompson and Lacy. The estimated number was too high by a substantial amount, although Stockton and his associates were no doubt continually picking at the edges of the large herds owned by Cox and I.W. Lacy. Cox and the others told Frost that their men traveled in numbers and heavily armed. The situation was bringing business and agricultural activities to a halt, with most men performing guard and patrol duties. The Rio Arriba County sheriff appointed a deputy to serve the western portion of the county (no election was required for deputy appointments). The new deputy was identified by Frost as Moses Blanchard. Blanchard was Mose Blancett. Immediately after the grand jury proceedings Judge Prince produced arrest warrants for the wanted men and Blancett had them in hand and was ready to serve them, should Ike and his men return to New Mexico. Blancett was highly respected, fearless and well suited for the position.[70]

Blancett observed his 48th birthday on April 11th, either traveling to or already in Tierra Amarilla.[71] Frost described the stockman as "a man of splendid reputation and of means."[72] In the mid-1870s, Marcellus (Cell) Blancett, the son of Moses, passed through northwest New Mexico, while serving in the U.S. Army.[73] He took note of the broad valleys and later described the San Juan country to his family. Prior to moving to New Mexico the Blancett family lived in Fremont County, Colorado. In October 1875, the Blancett men took part in the bloody battle for the Pocahontas mine in the Hardscrabble mining district near Rosita. The battle ended with the killing of a hired gun named Major Graham and the discovery that the town had been swindled by a notorious bank robber, forger, and conman named Walter C. Sheridan. Sheridan fled the town with all of the bank's deposits. Many of the miners were thrown out of work and Rosita began to fold up.[74] The Pocahontas Mine dispute would for many years remain an ugly memory for the Blancett family.[75] On October 6, 1877 one of the Blancett men was shot in the mouth at Texas Creek in Fremont County by a ne'er do well named Jerry Liner. Blancett confronted Liner, who was trying to steal a horse.[76] Not long after this incident the Blancett family moved to the San Juan country. The Blancetts who came to New Mexico included brothers Moses, Enos and John.[77] The Blancetts knew about the reputation of Ike's notorious brother. Two weeks after Port Stockton was killed, the Blancett family attended the Bloomfield wedding of Harvey McCoy and Angie Hart, who was Cap Hart's daughter. At the same ceremony En Blancett married Jennie McCoy.[78] Before the 1880s were over both Enos and John were shot and killed in separate incidents.[79] Mose first came to the San Juan country with his wife Lucinda Adams "Monie" Blancett, their son Cell, and the widowed matriarch of the clan, Elizabeth (Mrs. Josiah) Blancett.[80]

After accepting his appointment, Deputy Blancett and his companions were anxious to return home. The San Juan men were accompanied on their return by Max Frost. After reaching Bloomfield in mid-April, Frost eagerly dove into his investigation of the troubles in western Rio Arriba County. Many of the local residents were anxious to tell Frost their take on the situation. The adjutant general stayed at the residence of William Haines. He was meticulous about duplicating letters before he mailed originals to the governor. In Bloomfield he carefully transcribed them on Haines and Hughes letterhead. Several lower Animas

Mose Blancett's cattle brand, from the Northwest New Mexican *(Bloomfield, NM), Feb. 8, 1887. (From the collection of Robert L. Maddox, Jr.)*

expatriates were still living in Durango and elsewhere in southwest Colorado. Frost reported, "There are several refugees from here up at Durango, principally Mr. Locke - who, I am informed by every man I have spoken to, at least 50 - can return and live here with perfect safety and unmolested. The only man against whom I find a strong sentiment is Seth Wellfoot."[81] The Englishman was unable to control his feelings or his tongue. The consistently outspoken La Plata valley rancher George Lockhart speculated that Welfoot was spreading falsehoods and said "he is too contemptible to notice."[82] Frost did not confine his investigation to Ike Stockton, but tried to sort out the details of turbulent events going back to the lynching of Tex Anderson. The adjutant general, no doubt, interviewed some men who assisted with the lynching. Those who were not there probably knew the details of the lynching and the identification of the vigilantes, but all of them deemed it in their best interests to plead ignorance. Although it was one of the most memorable events to occur in the newly settled area, Frost could only report that "no one seems to remember, how it occurred." Frost learned that Mrs. Hubbard, who had supposedly been run out of the country, was still there. He noted that the locals described Oscar Puett as "a quarrelsome young fellow, hand in hand with Eskridge and Garrett." The Eskridge/Garrett herd, which Dow Eskridge said numbered five hundred, was said to actually number only two hundred. Frost said that, "the most prominent citizens will help him to round up and take out." Frost also learned that Emily Stockton was totally recovered from her wounds. He advised the governor that, "J.H. Razor, an old man and family, left because he was afraid of Ike Stockton killing him." Both his sons, Cal and James, were implicated in the killing of Port Stockton. Frost was advised that several other families left because they feared the Coes, or the Stocktons, or because of the general turmoil.[83] The adjutant general laid much of the blame for the turmoil on the Coe family. He told the governor that "Lou and George Coe have been assuming the lead of affairs and their braggadocio and threaths [sic], aided by one or more reckless cowboys, (Thomas Nance, for one) have made these men Locke, Wellfoot, Sterrit [i.e. Starriett], Pierce, Vaughn and Phelps leave."[84] (Parentheses are in Frost's letter.) Just as Ike Stockton was losing support in Durango, the Coe men were losing support in northwest New Mexico. Frost learned that one of the Coes, whom he did not name, had moved out. Significantly, Frost found that the Coe men who remained were now "regarded as black sheep and have nothing to say." He also noted that some of the prominent local men were implicated in the death of Port Stockton, "but public opinion upholds them."[85]

Frost found that C.H. McHenry had returned to his home in New Mexico. The letters he received from Frank Coe and A.F. Miller induced his return. Despite the vitriolic letter he sent to Governor Wallace, even McHenry had to admit that he was not being molested.[86] William Locke was also being encouraged to return, and even though the Coes themselves may have had nothing to do with his expulsion, his forced exodus was a critical factor in the diminishment of their influence along the lower Animas.

While Max Frost investigated the troubles in northwest New Mexico, the Denver press concentrated on events on their side of the border. The *Denver Republican* wondered if Durango would save herself and rid the town of outlaws. The Denver daily kept up a steady stream of reports on Durango and Ike Stockton during this period from their correspondent who is identified only as "Agate." Agate's sources were either as ill-informed as he was or he was unable to weed out the falsehoods from the facts. He provided some fanciful accounts of activities in Durango. On April 15th the *Republican* carried a long-winded, dime novel type dispatch from their man on the scene. Agate began by identifying the Eskridge brothers as Dixon and Harry. He declared that the Stockton brothers took a prominent part in the Lincoln County War and attributes to them four or five murders during "their" stay there. There is, of course, no evidence to support that claim. The article said that Porter Stockton was killed while on "one of his raids upon the cattle men." Porter's death then brought about Ike's return "from his retirement in Texas." The *Republican* reported that Ike then opened a dance hall in Durango. In describing the shooting of Aaron Barker, the *Republican* uses the words "cattle man" to describe Barker and his partner, whom they repeatedly call "Nanc." In the terminology of the time, there was a huge distinction between Nance and Barker who were "cow boys" or "herders," and Lacy and Cox, who were cattlemen. The *Republican* also carried portions of a letter purportedly written by a person described by Agate as "a man of wide experience, cool and deliberate judgment, and unbiased mind." The letter writer noted, "Durango is now to all intents and purposes in the hands of the worst set of thieves and murderers that I ever saw in all my travels. There is a regular old-fashioned Lincoln County, New Mexico, war on hand right here now." He declared that one marshal found Durango "too hot." So "he stole a pile and lit out one night for Tombstone, Arizona." The correspondent said, "I came awful near getting it a short time ago from the 'gang,' and right in the back. Have been packing a Winchester and shooter ever since, and yet don't know what minute they will down me. They may kill me, but can't run me out of the country as they have others."[87] Unfortunately, whether newspaper stories were exaggerated or not, they were a hindrance to the business interests of the area.

To the *Republican's* credit, several days later they carried a letter by A.W. Hudson, which replied to the letter above and commented on Agate's reports. Hudson identified Agate as Judge W.B. Sloan of Ohio and said, "the trouble with him is that he don't understand the country, and gets excited too easily. I don't think you would feel very much in danger were you here, but Sloan thinks the town is hell. The fact is, it's the average frontier town, rather more orderly than the average, except the fight between the Farmington factions. So tone your man down, and don't give us a black eye without cause."[88] The *Durango Record* announced the receipt of a private letter from Rico, which asked, "Why don't you run the correspondent of the Denver *Republican* out of Durango? He ought to be hanged." [89]

In the meantime, Max Frost was busy organizing the San Juan Guards as the new militia were being called.[90] Governor Wallace was a strong supporter and the driving force behind the organization of the militia. Three years before he had personally organized the Lincoln County Riflemen.[91] Even the *Dolores News* noted Frost's presence in western Rio Arriba County. They said he would be traveling from Bloomfield to Farmington to help organize the militia.[92] Frost, Haines and Blancett issued a public notice:

> Citizens of Rio Arriba Co.
> Territory New Mexico
> Governor Lew Wallace having directed the organization of a Militia Company under Sec. 11, Militia Law 1880 – for the protection of life and property of the Citizens on the San Juan, Animas and La Plata Rivers – and as a Posse Comitatus for the

Deputy Sheriffs of the County, you will be present at 4 oclock P.M. Monday the 18th Inst. at the school house on the Animas River known as the Cole school house, for the purpose of aiding and joining in the formation of said Company.
And herein fail not under penalty of Law.
By the Governor of the Territory of New Mexico:
[signed] Max Frost
Adjutant General
[signed] M. Blancett
Deputy Sheriff
[signed] Wm. B. Haines
Captain San Juan Guards[93]

Over seventy men gathered at the school house. In addition to Haines as captain, Hiram W. Cox was selected as first lieutenant and Alfred F. Stump as second lieutenant. The Guards served only as requested by the governor or by the county sheriff and his deputies. Their jurisdiction was limited to the boundaries of Rio Arriba County. In addition to Mose Blancett, thirty-four-year-old William Shane was appointed as a deputy sheriff. Like his La Plata valley neighbors, George Lockhart and Edward Thomas, Shane had witnessed firsthand, and probably been a victim to, the Stockton-Eskridge rustling epidemic. Enlisted men in the militia included First Sergeant Charles W. Rash, Sergeant Levy A. Hughes, Sergeant Isaac N. Covert, Sergeant Juan A. Manzanares, Sergeant George Lockhart, Corporal William B. Horn, Corporal Juan N. Jaquez, Corporal M.M. Blancett (Mose Blancett's son Marcellus Blancett), Corporal R.W. Williams and seventy-five privates. In organizing the militia Frost was careful to put in writing their limited geographical jurisdiction.[94]

The militia were given their orders and responsibilities. Lieutenant Wash Cox was assigned ten men with rations for ten days with orders to patrol the approaches from Colorado in and near the Animas River valley. Lieutenant Stump was assigned to patrol the La Plata valley. Manuel Gonzales of the so-called "Cañon Largo Gang" had also been indicted during the Tierra Amarilla court session. At Deputy Shane's request, Sergeant Manzanares and twenty-two men were issued five days rations and started in pursuit of "bands of thieves under one Manuel Gonzales," in Cañon Largo. Shane carried with him the arrest warrant for Gonzales.[95] Unbeknownst to Shane, Gonzales was aware of the indictment and had already posted bond with the court. The indictment was obtained because of the testimony of David Lobato and Guadalupe Arellano at the recent grand jury proceedings in Tierra Amarilla. Gonzales who lived near Coyote (northeast of Cuba, New Mexico) was a cattleman, and was not in hiding. According to Gonzales, on the morning of April 20th twenty-four men surrounded his bed and demanded his surrender. He identified the men as the sheriff and posse, which were in fact Deputy William Shane, Sergeant Manzanares and the twenty-two San Juan Guardsmen. He asked to see the warrant and saw that it was for the charges for which he had already posted bond. He heard some of the men saying that he "would never reach the San Juan river alive." Gonzales was steady under pressure. In a letter he claimed that he resisted the arrest and "had the satisfaction to make five of the men drop their guns." He removed their bullets and returned their weapons and forced the men to leave his home. Deputy Shane and the San Juan Guards were thoroughly cowed. The warrant remained unserved.[96] It was after this incident that he went to the *Alcalde* of Coyote and asked that warrants be issued for the arrest of the entire party. He told the *Alcalde* that the men were after him because of personal animosity and they intended to kill him. According to the *New Mexican*, Gonzales swore out an affidavit to that effect. *Alcalde* Sandoval obliged Gonzales and issued warrants for the arrest of Deputy Shane and the San Juan Guardsmen who had invaded his home.[97]

For the time being, Max Frost was blissfully unaware of developments at Coyote and concerned himself with the principal players. In the *Santa Fe New Mexican* he speculated that Ike Stockton and his gang might head for Blue Mountain in Utah or even to Texas. The *New Mexican* noted that Frost, "feared they may make one more raid and endeavor to kill the Coe Brothers, Thomas Nance and some others who were engaged in the killing of Port Stockton."[98]

The territorial government was doing its best to overcome the law enforcement vacuum in western Rio Arriba County and in that effort, somehow, Wallace's admonition that Justices of the Peace had to be elected and not appointed fell by the wayside. According to Max Frost the Rio Arriba County Commission would appoint justices of the peace and constables, effective as of May 1st. In addition to being appointed captain of the San Juan Guards, William Haines was designated as a justice of the peace in Precinct 19 with P.F. Salmon as constable. W.G. Markley was designated as the justice of the peace for Precinct 20, with the recently returned Boyd Vaughan as constable.[99]

Stockton and his men were well informed about events in Rio Arriba County via the newspapers and from the few travelers who managed to slip across the border. They stayed close to Durango. During this period the same *Ouray Times* correspondent who had witnessed Eskridge in action while on a hack trip from Animas City, decided to put a face on both Ike Stockton and Hargo Eskridge. The reporter was a personal acquaintance of both men. He described Stockton as being "peaceable and quiet; never talking of his troubles unless closely questioned, and then he is very guarded in what he says." The newsman acknowledged that his quiet disposition changes when he is aroused. He noted that Stockton did not appear to be desperate, but his eyes told a different story. The correspondent said, "You would not notice anything wild about him, only his restless eyes which seem to be continually glancing here and there."[100]

At the same time the newsman described the man he names as Eskridge. He fails to give the man's first name, but there is no doubt he is describing Hargo and not Dison. Both brothers were in Durango, but after Dison's row at the Hamblet home, it was Hargo who stepped forward as the most active, outspoken, and feared Eskridge. He described Hargo as "a tall, raw-boned young man, dark complexioned, with a fine black moustache, heavy jaw-bone and large, prominent chin."[101] (A description of Dison Eskridge described him as having a light complexion, standing five feet ten inches tall and weighing about 155 pounds.)[102] The newsman said that Hargo seldom laughs and seldom speaks aloud. His walk was slow with one hand always in his coat pocket. He was prepared to meet the enemy at any moment; his head was on a swivel, as he constantly surveyed his surroundings. He was described as a crack shot, desperate and cold-blooded. Hargo was well known for blackguarding anyone who spoke out in favor of the Coes. In Durango one day he made one such "fellow dance, shooting between his legs, and cursing him to everything he could lay his tongue to." The reporter gave a sarcastic twist in summing up the situation in Durango: "How Eskridge can be classed as one of 'Durango's peaceable citizens' I can't imagine. Yet he is said to be 'a very nice boy,' and 'should be protected by the citizens of Durango.' "[103]

During the last two weeks of April, a lot of pressure was brought to bear on Stockton and Eskridge. Adding to that was an April 20th meeting of La Plata County cattlemen. John Reid, who had a large presence in the La Plata valley, was selected as chairman of the informal group. A committee was appointed "to confer with the Animas valley cattle men, who have had trouble with each other, and arrange matters with them so that the round-up parties will not be interfered with." The *Durango Record* carried an account of the meeting, but they did not include any specific information concerning cattle rustling. The *Record* said that the organization of a more formal stock growers association was hindered because no one wanted to take the lead in the matter. The memory of Aaron Barker and the reputation of Ike Stockton may account for this reluctance. However, the coming together of the cattlemen to solve their problems did not bode well for Stockton and his cohorts.[104]

Then there was the matter of Wallace's requisitions. There was much speculation in the press, in barrooms and elsewhere that the requisitions would soon be received by Governor Pitkin. Ike and the others did not wait for official word in the matter. On April 29th the *Record* declared,

> The Stockton, Eskridge, Garrett party, together with their aiders and abettors, have left Durango for good. They sold out,

a few days since, and one by one,

> *They folded their tents*
> *Like the Arabs,*
> *And silently stole away.*[105]

The Rio Arriba County indictments were having their desired effect and Stockton and his men were worried that their safe haven in Durango was about to vanish. The *Record* said, "the citizens of Durango would not protect them against any legal demand for their surrender." Romney's newspaper offered this opinion, "We believe that they have also left the state; as the requisition would take them anywhere in the state. They will never return here under any circumstances, as a return would mean certain arrest."[106] The *Record's* assessment was overly optimistic, to say the least. At about the same time the Eskridge brothers received other bad news. In late April Max Frost told the *New Mexican* that a jury from Conejos County had indicted the two brothers for stealing livestock.[107]

Stockton did leave, temporarily, and his exit from Durango was facilitated by a financial arrangement. The *New Mexican* declared, "And now when the law and public sentiment becomes too strong, they buy the Stockton gang off."[108] The *Trinidad News* concurred, saying that, "While Durango has hired these fellows to leave town, Gov. Wallace has offered a handsome reward for their capture." The *News* went on to suggest that, "A good way for Durango to get even would be to turn out and earn the reward. At all events Durango is to be congratulated on being rid of these lively fellow citizens, who have succeeded in knocking a big hole in the boom."[109] Ike and his men made an arrangement to pay for about one hundred head of cattle. At the time cattle were selling for between $15 and $20 each. In return $700 in cash was raised and presented to Stockton.[110] Part of this money was probably payment for Ike and Hargo's Tent Saloon and Club Room. As late as April 30th the *Durango Record* carried an advertisement for the establishment, a portion which said, "Stockton & Eskridge, Proprietors." The same issue carried an advertisement for the Eclipse Saloon.[111] Hargo was apparently compensated in some fashion for his share of the Eclipse. In a later report the *Record* said, "The citizens finally, to get rid of the Eskridge crowd, seven or eight of whom remained in the town, one or two engaged in business, bought their property and induced them to go."[112] At the same time the *Durango Record* held out the olive branch to the citizens of Farmington, saying, "Durango and Farmington can now shake hands over the bloody chasm. The good citizens of the two towns, have nothing against each other. Indeed, their interests are identical. Durango is well rid of the men whom the Farmington people feared." The newspaper advised that while Farmington had its own ruffians, the town's "better elements" were gaining the upper hand. Seeking to re-establish business with the New Mexicans, the newspaper noted, "The people of that section, need have no fears in regard to visiting Durango; as not one of their enemies, is now left here." The *Record* declared that the lawless situation which existed could never occur again because Durango was now incorporated, with an election of municipal officers to be held soon, which would undoubtedly elect a law and order group who would favor swift punishment of lawbreakers.[113] Once again the *Record's* assessment of the situation was overly optimistic and it also didn't take into consideration the dangers of traveling the sparsely settled roads into and out of Durango. It was about this time that unidentified members of the Stockton crowd ran across a man named Roberts north of Durango. The traveler was said to be one of the men who had pursued Eskridge and Garrett after the Hamblet house shootings. An anonymous source wrote the *New Mexican* and said that Roberts was pulled from his horse and severely pistol whipped.[114] The *Chicago Tribune* reported that Roberts was killed by "the Stockton, Eskridge party," and that one of the Farmington men had been killed during the Battle of Durango. They based their story on a telegram sent by someone living up the Animas near Cascade Creek. Shortly thereafter the *Durango Record* pointed out that both accounts were wrong.[115]

All of the talk about law and order and what would happen upon the delivery of a requisition were soon to be tested. On April 29th, Governor Wallace signed the much anticipated requisition and sent it to Governor Pitkin. The requisition noted "that the said offenders had fled from justice, and taken refuge in Durango, La Plata County Colorado." Thirty-year-old Arkansas native, Tony Neis, the chief deputy marshal of New Mexico, was appointed the agent from New Mexico to receive the wanted men. (Only a month before Neis had escorted Billy the Kid to Mesilla for trial. Along the way he held off a mob intent on taking the Kid.)[116] The *Dolores News* suspected that the delivery of the requisition was imminent and Hartman and Jones were frantic. They predicted that if Stockton and his men were arrested and turned over to authorities in Rio Arriba County, they would never stand trial, but would be lynched. They grasped at straws, refusing to recognize that the courts or the governor of New Mexico had any authority to pursue charges for crimes committed within the territory. The editors asked, "Should they be taken to New Mexico, where would the case be tried?" The young newspapermen preposterously proposed that if the men were arrested, they should "be protected by a regular company of Colorado militia," even though their trial would be in New Mexico. They noted that Stockton and his men have expressed a willingness to be tried on the charges against them.[117] The Rico newspapermen also wrote that they had received several "intimidating letters" from the Farmington crowd. One of the letters said, "our Captain has fixed a good many ropes and we guess he will fix a good many more, so look out."[118]

Stockton and his allies at the *Dolores News* were surprised when they realized that it was not the Coes who were leading the militia in Rio Arriba County. The *News* attempted to influence events along the lower Animas and foment feuds between the Coes and the leaders of the San Juan Guards. They alleged that the formation of the Guards was causing discord in Rio Arriba County. Hartman and Jones declared, "The harmony in that section was broken by the organization of the militia company, known as the San Juan Guards, to which association several of the leaders (including the self-styled 'Captain') of the old mob were denied admittance." The *News* said, "Even now they [the Coe mob] are secretly and in private threatening the lives of various parties for the action they have taken in this fight, saying that they shall settle with them after the trouble is over."[119] The newspapermen were missing the point. When Wash Cox and Mose Blancett teamed up to take an open and active role in the hostilities, the power of the Coes was gone, forever. The Cox and Blancett families included a sizable number of young fearless men, who would not back down from a fight. Not only that, but Wash Cox employed a large number of cowboys to ride the range protecting the COX brand. Cox's reputation throughout the San Juan country was impeccable. The Coes had seen enough and they had no taste for challenging the Cox and Blancett families. The Coe men also viewed the change as their way out of the hostilities. Hartman and Jones were evidently unfamiliar with the Blancetts, but they could not explain away the prominent role of Wash Cox and wrote of him, "We know of one man in the outfit who is universally acknowledged to be a white man and that is H.W. Cox, the owner of the largest band of cattle in the lower country." The *News* then characterized the majority of Cox's associates as "grossly ignorant and malicious men."[120]

There was good reason for Cox's stellar reputation. He was a cowman with ethics. If a calf strayed out of its normal range and did not bear one of the brands associated with one of his roundups, there was an overwhelming temptation to lay claim to it by branding it. Cox had seen rampant mavericking and worse in Texas, and had worked as one of the first brand inspectors in Erath County. He would have none of it. He had certainly seen men killed and lynched for the same. Even his sons told him he needed to adjust his sense of right and wrong in order to keep even with the other outfits. Cox would not bend, and his instructions to his boys and punchers were clear: "Don't you boys bother their cattle, that will never do." If one of his cowboys brought in a yearling without a brand, Cox was not averse to branding it, but he advised his punchers to be positive beyond all doubt that it was no longer a suckling calf.[121] Hartman and Jones, on the other hand, allowed their hatred of the Coes and their friendship with Stockton and the Eskridge boys get in the way of their ethics.

They were relentless in their drive to generate sympathy for Ike and his allies. The wounding of Emily Jane Stockton when her husband was shot and killed presented Hartman and Jones the perfect opportunity to blast the lower Animas vigilantes. The newspapermen took full advantage of the situation. Under the headline, "Think Of It!" the *News* carried the following article,

> The wife of Port Stockton, who was murderously assaulted at the time Port was killed, and who is known as a good kind hearted exemplary lady, is now a cripple for life, suffering the tortures of hell. One shot fired at her passed through the right hand and on through the left arm, paralyzing that limb, and rendering both limbs useless. Another shot entered the lower part of the left breast, ranging downward into the left side, where it is now lodged. This unfortunate woman has left to her support, three helpless children. Mrs. Stockton is destitute of any means of support, except the aid she will receive at the hands of Ike Stockton the surviving brother. It is reliably stated that the men who killed Port Stockton strictly forbade any of the neighboring women to go to the aid of Mrs. Stockton.[122]

Emily Jane moved to La Plata County soon after the shooting. The article fails to note that her brother John Cowan was living in La Plata County and her mother and sister were living along the Animas as well. The Morrison and O'Neal families were also part of the extended Stockton support network.[123] Emily probably did have lifelong effects from her wounds, but a second marriage and the birth of two more children, indicate that she was not the helpless cripple Hartman and Jones depicted.[124]

While the Rico newspapermen stewed, the New Mexicans and Dow Eskridge came to a tentative agreement which allowed Eskridge to round up his cattle. Formal papers were drawn up and signed by Eskridge and unknown parties from western Rio Arriba County. It is likely that Wash Cox was working behind the scenes, trying to wring out a peaceful solution with Dow Eskridge. The agreement stipulated that Eskridge could round up his cattle and those belonging to "his brothers and the Garrett boys."[125] If successful the agreement would have forced a wedge between Stockton and the Eskridge family. Unfortunately, the simmering bad blood between the parties initially derailed the venture. According to a letter written by William Haines, "The brothers of Eskridge and Garrett came down to round up their cattle." The lower Animas cattlemen were unable to assist them because of their own time commitments to their livestock and to the San Juan Guards. Mose Blancett sent word or met with Dow

Eskridge and advised him that the feelings of the community were still at "fever heat." He told Dow that he "could not answer for their lives." According to Haines, Deputy Blancett advised the Colorado men that there should be "no gathering of cattle at present time in order to prevent bloodshed." Haines assured Governor Wallace that, "The cattle are perfected [sic] safe and will receive no harm."[126]

On the other side, the *Dolores News* reported that the lower Animas men "made a demand on Dow for the delivery to them of Ike Stockton before they would allow him to gather his cattle, which of course was an impossibility." The *News* believed that so many of the Eskridge cattle had been stolen and killed that "they would not make a respectable showing." Dow Eskridge continued a dialog with the New Mexicans in order to revive the agreement.[127] At the same time Governor Wallace prepared a reward notice as a means of turning up the pressure on Ike Stockton and his gang. The governor had other concerns as well. In the last week of April, Billy the Kid made a daring escape from the Lincoln County jail, killing deputies Robert Olinger and J.W. Bell in the process. The territory's outlaw troubles stretched from north to south.[128]

By the first week of May the *New Mexican* carried two reward notices from the governor. One was for $500 for "William Bonny, alias The Kid" and directly below that was another reward notice: a total of $2250 for Isaac Stockton and his gang. Like the Kid, Ike had a price of $500 on his head. The reward offered for Hargo Eskridge, Jim Garrett and the other members of the gang was $250 each. Even one-legged Thomas Radigan had a $250 price on his head.[129] The following week the same reward notice appeared in the *Denver Republican*. Soon other Colorado papers, like the *Aspen Weekly Times*, printed it.[130] It's possible that Levy Hughes, who was in Santa Fe in early May, paid a visit to the governor and facilitated the initial publication of the notice. Hughes may also have been the source of an article in the May 6th issue of the *New Mexican* which said that Stockton was rustling cattle from the lower Animas, butchering them and openly selling the meat in Durango. From the proceeds, he was supplying his men with "rifles, revolvers and horses." The article repeated the allegation that Stockton and his men had recently stolen four hundred cattle from the lower Animas. The *New Mexican's* informant reported that Stockton was supported by Durango's saloon crowd, gamblers and others of a similar nature.[131]

Stockton's rustling activities attracted the attention of every cattleman in the area. I.W. Lacy had hoped to get to the bottom of the Stockton problem or perhaps even rid the country of Ike Stockton through his employment of Big Dan Howland. As it turns out, hiring Howland was the biggest mistake of Lacy's life.

Chapter Thirteen

Death of a Cattle King

> *We live upon the mesas high,*
> *And in the piñons on the plain;*
> *They'll never catch us, though they try ---*
> *They hunt the rustler all in vain.*[1]

Cattle were disappearing from I.W. Lacy's herd at an alarming rate, compelling the stockman to personally oversee his San Juan operations. He was furious with the inept performance of Big Dan, his cattle detective. Not only was Ike Stockton selling stolen beef to Durango's butchers, according to at least one account Stockton's crowd was bold enough to run their own slaughterhouse at Lightner Creek west of Durango.[2] At the time, Lacy and his partner, George Thompson, had a new market for their La Plata valley cattle. The day after Aaron Barker was killed, bids were taken for the Fort Lewis beef contract. It was a sure thing, as Irvin Lacy was the one and only bidder.[3] Normally, that would have been a positive development. For Lacy, however, his San Juan operations proved to be nothing but trouble.

On April 12, 1881, he vented his concerns to personnel at Fort Lewis. Below is the summary of Lacy's statement from the fort's files,

> [Lacy] States that it has become absolutely necessary, to enable him to fill the beef contract properly at this time at this post that he be allowed to keep at least twelve (12) men at this [illegible]. The cattle are being stolen by the hundred, the lives of his men and himself threatened because they interfere. The parties live in Durango and are making raid after raid and as his herders and butchers have to go in bands for their own protection it becomes necessary to have at least a dozen men to go and receive his cattle from his employees on the lower La Plata.[4]

Perhaps Lacy did not use Stockton's name, or perhaps Ike's reputation made the transcriber understandably hesitant about naming names. In any case, the reference to rustlers coming out of Durango clearly implicates Stockton and his associates. By exclusion, Lacy's accusations exonerate the "Farmington mob" as they were called in the *Dolores News*. There were others in Durango who might rustle cattle. Some of them had little or nothing to do with Stockton. It did not matter. Ike had made himself the most notorious member of the crowd and if he was arrested, killed or run out of town, others would depart like rats fleeing a sinking ship, and the boldness of those who remained would be diminished.

Thompson and Lacy's herd filled the La Plata valley, and despite the volatile situation, Lacy was planning on increasing and diversifying his investments in the San Juan country. On May 2nd, the *Durango Record* announced, "Mr. I.W. Lacy will, within ten days, establish in this city, a wholesale beef business, on a scale second to none in the state. Mr. Lacy is one of the cattle kings of the west, and will [kill?] the choicest specimens of beeves from his herds in the La Plata and Montezuma valleys for this market."[5] The establishment of a large slaughterhouse would put financial pressure on Durango's butchers and assured that a bright spotlight would shine on anyone who herded, corralled or accepted cattle bearing the brands used by Lacy.

Up to this time, Lacy and his partner George Thompson had generally been absentee owners. Thompson lived in Trinidad, where he was no longer the sheriff, but was serving in a less precarious position as a Las Animas County Commissioner. Lacy was still living south of the border at his ranch on the Vermejo.[6] Two of Lacy's children attended school in Trinidad.[7] That spring George Thompson was close to consummating the sale of a large portion of his Colorado land holdings. The land deal encompassed parts of Bent, Las Animas and Huerfano counties and was worth close to $1,000,000. If completed, it was said to be the second largest land sale in Colorado history up to that time.[8] In early May, he sold the Las Animas Land Grant, also known as the Vigil and St. Vrain Grant, to William Craig for $150,000.[9] While Thompson was making six-figure land deals, Lacy, who may not have been in that league, was nonetheless acknowledged as a "cattle king" in Colorado and New Mexico. In the spring of 1881 the *New Mexican* said that Lacy's San Juan herd numbered close to ten thousand head.[10] Present day Cortez was the center point of the massive LC herd. From there, the cattle ranged sixty miles southeast toward Farmington and sixty miles northwest toward Utah's Blue Mountain. Given Port Stockton's habit of stealing Thompson and Lacy cattle, it is not shocking that Ike continued the tradition. The LC cattle grazed over a far-flung, rugged and unpopulated region of mesas, mountains and river valleys, making them easy pickings. Once the animals were butchered, their skins could be buried, burned or otherwise destroyed. In cold weather the quartered beeves might find their way to Silverton, Telluride, Ouray or elsewhere. As far as re-branding was concerned, Thompson and Lacy used several simple brands, all of which lent themselves to the creative use of a running iron. However, Stockton and his allies were not interested in building up a cattle herd and all of the work that entailed. They wanted a quick payoff, so the stolen cattle were quickly skinned and butchered.

Lacy's plans for his stock detective, whatever they were, fizzled. If he had hoped to get the goods on Stockton and his crew through Big Dan, he was out of luck. Along with the planned opening of his own slaughterhouse, Lacy put even more pressure on Ike and his accomplices. In early May he stopped by the offices of the *Durango Record* and placed this advertisement.

$100 REWARD!

For information that will lead to the proof of any unauthorized person using or driving cattle branded as follows:

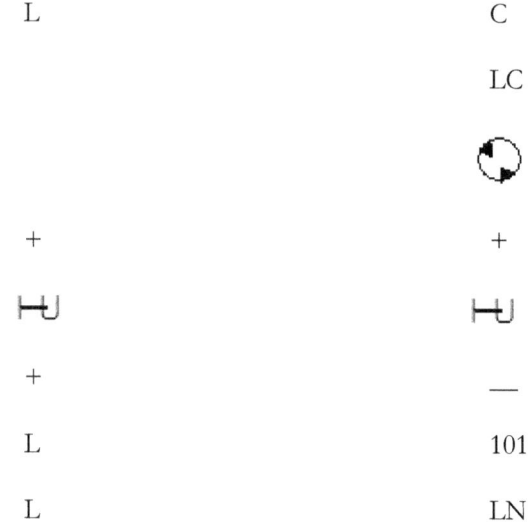

L	C
	LC
+	+
⊢⊔	⊢⊔
+	—
L	101
L	LN

G.W. Thompson and C.H. Goodman are the only persons authorized to use or sell cattle bearing above brand
        Signed   I.W. Lacy

Lacy was beginning to tighten the noose around the necks of Stockton and his fellow cattle rustlers, and Ike knew it. The notice makes it clear that Henry Goodman was a top hand in Thompson and Lacy's outfit. The G.W. Thompson in the advertisement was the young nephew and namesake of the Trinidad cattleman. The large number of varied brands illustrates the enormous scope of the LC cattle empire. The ad ran throughout the first three weeks of May.[11] While Lacy's advertisement pointed the accusatory finger at Ike Stockton, in some ways it was cautious. Unlike the $2000 reward offered by Wash Cox and other lower Animas cattlemen, Lacy's ad did not mention Stockton by name. The fact that Mrs. Lacy was a cousin to both Ike and to Ike's wife may have contributed to the discretion apparent in the reward notice. Since Ike denied that he was stealing any cattle, he could hardly object publicly to the reward notice, although privately he seethed. Lacy's notice had an added benefit, since it might serve to identify others besides Stockton's crowd who were stealing his cattle. The obvious drawback to Lacy's plan was that for $100 few were likely to volunteer to get on the wrong side of Ike Stockton.

The threat to cattle posed by Ike Stockton was not Lacy's only concern. Out in Lacy's western range another threat was beginning to grow. A combined band of Indians were making their presence known in the canyon country along the southern portions of the Utah and Colorado border. At the same time, the pressure being brought to bear on Stockton was mounting daily. Why he would take an active interest in the growing Indian problems is difficult to explain. Yet, he would. Stockton and a handful of his associates would soon feel the wrath of the deadly Ute/Paiute band. They were loath to give up their traditional way of life and roamed the border country with impunity. The San Juan Paiutes had no Indian agency and no reservation.[12] They were joined in their forays by an unmanageable faction of the Weeminuche Utes.[13] A handful of intractable Indians from other tribes joined them. In a May 23, 1881 letter to Colonel Crofton, Deputy U.S. Marshal Heffernan summed up his view on the matter in an underlined sentence, saying, "When west of the Rio Mancos all Southern Utes become Pi utes."[14]

As Lacy and other cattlemen moved more and more cattle into the area the renegades became more aggressive. Their way of life was under intense, relentless pressure as more and more "Americans" entered the area. They fought back desperately and the futility of their situation drove them to employ some horrific methods to stop the unending wave that would inevitably overwhelm them. Cattle were an easy target. In 1893, Rico newspaperman Charles Jones writing under the pseudonym Jones Adams for the *Overland Monthly* magazine provided a colorful narrative about the conditions found on the range that spring. He recalled, "Poor tottering brutes bawled everywhere in pain upon the prairie, hair clotted with blood from gaping crevices upon their hips, or with flesh exposed in strips where rawhide had been torn in ribbons from their sides. Sometimes an animal was found knee-deep in the luxuriant bunch-grass of the foot-hills, making pitiful efforts to graze upon the abounding richness, yet starving because of the severing of its tongue by an Indian hunting knife."[15] According to the account of a man named Griffith, who visited Oliver D. "Lot" Loutsenhizer's cattle camp that May, "seventy-three head of dead three year olds were found near the mouth of the Uncompahgre during one day's ride on the round-up. The brains and the tongues were the only portion utilized and the Uncompahgre Utes beyond doubt are the guilty parties."[16]

Trouble between the whites and the Indians began to reach the boiling point in late April, when large numbers of Indians began heading for the Uncompahgre country of western Colorado. Ike Stockton's friend and neighbor, Deputy U.S. Marshal Heffernan, said, "Ignatio and his squaws came to my house on Junction Creek near Animas City and remained during the night." Ignacio had several complaints against the white men. He advised Heffernan that there was to be a large gathering of

Ignacio, revered Chief of the Weeminuche Utes. He was born in 1828 and helped lead his people through the transition brought on by the overwhelming tide of white settlement. Photo by J.A. Boston. (Courtesy La Plata County Historical Society, from Annette Pauline Cobb Collection, No. 92.22.267.)

Indians at the Big Bend of the Dolores to discuss the coming of the railroad. (The Big Bend, which is now inundated by McPhee Reservoir, is about two miles below the town of Dolores.) Heffernan reported that Ignacio said "when he was in Washington they told him the railroad would not come through the Ute land, now it is here - all white men were liars and they were going to stop it." Heffernan asked if he, Peter Keegan of the D&RG railroad, Dolores area cattleman Pat O'Donnell, and W.A. Bennett could go to the "pow wow," as he called it. Ignacio told Heffernan that the Indians didn't like the white men anymore and that he could go, but not the others. The Ute chief departed the next morning. Heffernan stayed home.[17] If Ike Stockton was at home in Animas City, he soon learned of the big pow wow and the potential for Indian difficulties. Stockton's involvement would change the dynamics of the ongoing turmoil in the San Juan country.

According to Al Puett, the Indians traveling to the Big Bend were becoming increasingly hostile. During the last week of April, they had several conflicts with local residents. He said that Mariano, one of the Ute's head men, stopped by the home of George May and the two men traded antagonistic barbs. Mariano drew his revolver, but no bloodshed ensued. There was simmering bad blood between the Utes and the three May brothers, George, William and Richard. The Indians also accosted cattleman D.D. Williams. He felt the danger was so great he moved out of his home.[18]

The convergence of a large number of Indians along the Dolores River increased the chances for a major conflict with the sizable number of cattlemen and their cowboys, who were in the area for the spring roundup. The stockmen's remudas were a tremendous attraction to the Indians. Among the horse herds was one owned by Joshua H. Alderson and John Thurman. They were not cattlemen, but horse traders. According to Alderson, he and Thurman brought 150 head of horses and eight mules into the country in November 1880. Alderson left the animals in Thurman's care and returned to his home in Eureka, Nevada. Shortly afterwards he moved to San Francisco. Thurman's headquarters was a cabin, which he and Mr. Willis (probably Dave Willis) built. It was located about seven miles southwest of what is now the town of Dove Creek, Colorado at what was then known as Pine Springs and which is now known as Burnt Cabin Springs.[19] The location put Thurman on the far edge of civilization and in the middle of the most troublesome Indians. Astute and experienced frontiersmen had been living in precarious circumstances in the midst of large Indian populations for decades, and the wise and wary ones knew there were tradeoffs they had to make to keep the peace and keep their hair. Thurman was neither wise nor wary. If he had been, he never would have placed a large remuda of fine horseflesh along the Utah/Colorado line. Soon after his arrival he had his first run-in with the Indians. Presenting a courageous front was important, but Thurman stepped over the line from courage to vindictiveness. He caught a Ute of Narraguinnep's band stealing one of his horses. He retrieved the horse and then proceeded to tempt fate by giving the Indian a thorough whipping.[20]

By late April, Thurman was feeling safety in numbers. The spring roundup was in full swing and cowboys combed through the area, gathering cattle. He was at the cabin when he received two visitors, Richard (Dick) May and Byron Smith. (Byron, a sometime resident of Rico, is sometimes misidentified as Frank Smith.)[21] Dick May was there to purchase horses and was carrying about $400 in cash. Smith accompanied him as a hired hand. The Indians still had their eyes on the horse herd as well. On Sunday May 1st a sizable group of well-armed Indians rode up to the cabin. Trouble ensued and the Indians attacked the men with deadly intent. Thurman ran south, away from the cabin. Smith also made a run for it.

Dick May sought cover in the cabin, which proved to be a deadly trap.[22] After killing the white men, the Indians looted the ranch, taking guns, ammunition, an estimated $1000 in cash and a large supply of flour, coffee, bacon and other provisions, estimated to weigh almost two thousand pounds.[23] Despite the fact that numerous cowboys were working on the roundup in the area, the Paiutes and Utes boldly torched the cabin, sending up a smoke plume that was visible for miles. They rounded up all of Thurman and Alderson's horses and with whoops and hollers they trailed the herd north, leaving a dust cloud in their wake.[24]

Frederic Remington's "Branding A Horse," from Theodore Roosevelt's "The Round-up," The Century Illustrated Monthly Magazine, *Vol. 35, No. 6, April 1888. (Author's collection.)*

Later that day one of the O'Donnell brothers, either Pat or Mike, and several other cowboys saw the smoke plume curling ever higher in the sky. They rode that direction. Despite their hopes otherwise, with each step they became certain that the smoke was coming from Thurman's cabin. Wary, apprehensive, with the smell of smoke filling their nostrils, the cowboys rode into the clearing and saw the burned out remains of Thurman's horse camp. The men saw evidence of a struggle, including a dead pony which had been shot. The eerie scene and the growing darkness spooked them and they made only a cursory search. They found no bodies.

The men gathered up their livestock (a small herd of horses) and spurred toward the Big Bend.²⁵

The trail worn cowboys arrived at Henry Goodman's and Charles A. Frink's roundup camp at 10:00 AM the next day. Upon hearing the news, the cowboys at the Big Bend camp stopped the roundup and began to gather supplies. At 2:00 PM a group of seventeen well-armed men rode out for Thurman's. Besides Al Puett and the May brothers, some of the other men who joined the expedition were Henry Goodman, Charlie Frink, M.W. Reid, George Phelps, Mike O'Donnell and Benjamin (Benny) Quick.²⁶ Others rode for Rico, Fort Lewis and Durango to spread the news. The much feared, much anticipated and inevitable Indian outbreak had come to pass. The Big Bend cowboys spent much of the night on the trail. Tuesday at 9:00 AM the weary and wary men rode up to the still smoldering remains of Thurman's cabin. They were not long in discovering the fate of their friends. Richard May's burnt body was found lying against the charred south wall of the cabin. Al Puett reported, "his two brothers, George and William May, could only identify the body by a small piece of clothing, that lay under the body, a silver ring, and lastly but surely, by two old copper cents, that some time ago, William May gave him." At that point Billy May swore an oath to avenge the death of his brother. Thurman's body was found three quarters of a mile south of the cabin. Puett noted that, "He was shot in several places, one ball entering just above the left nipple and passing directly through the body, which must have caused instant death. His head was horribly mutilated, being almost cleft in twain with an axe or hatchet." The cowboys buried him where he fell. Despite their best efforts, the men could not find the body of Byron Smith. Dick May's body was loaded on a pack animal and taken back to the Dolores.²⁷ Fittingly, he was buried at the Big Bend, near the residence of his brothers, George and William.²⁸ The three May brothers had always been exceptionally close and the surviving brother's despair was overwhelming. They were children of the frontier, all of them born in Missouri between the years of 1835 and 1839. In 1870, the three men were stock raisers residing in the same residence in Huerfano County, Colorado.²⁹ When the San Juan country opened up to settlement, they sought greener pastures.

By May 3ʳᵈ accounts of the attack and deaths of Thurman, May and Smith reached Fort Lewis.³⁰ Lieutenant Colonel Robert Erskine Anderson Crofton received the news with an equanimity bordering on disinterest. Crofton was a native of Ireland and about forty-six years old. He was one of twelve Papal Zouaves who left the army of Pope Pius IX at the start of the Civil War. During the war he fought at Corinth, Shiloh and Stone River. He was wounded at Chickamauga and won honors at Missionary Ridge. After the war he served at several posts in the American west. During his service at Fort Lewis the press normally referred to him as

Colonel Crofton.³¹ By all appearances, Crofton was unconcerned about the situation. Perhaps he was just being cautious. Whatever the case, he would eventually be forced to act.

Crofton's inbox was full on May 2nd. One piece of correspondence was from local rancher D.D. Williams. The cattleman had lived in Colorado for twenty years, most of that time among the Utes and he maintained open communication with those who were peaceably disposed. His closest neighbor was the recently deceased, Richard May. Williams advised Crofton that there was a large influx of Indians in the area. He warned the colonel that from all appearances the Utes were preparing for war. Williams reported seeing a band of "about one hundred fifty bucks with their squaws, families [and] goats" headed to join up with the Uncompahgre Utes. Within the last twenty-four hours he had seen other large bands, including a band of Paiutes with 150 lodges, crossing the Big Bend and heading to the Uncompahgre, all of them traveling with "goats and sheep and many horses." He declared that many of the Indians were well-armed with Winchesters and plenty of ammunition. Williams said that even before the large gathering, the Indians had been making "threats of an alarming character against me and the men hired by me." He also complained that they had wantonly shot down thirty-five of his cattle in acts of "vandalism and deviltry" and seldom did they use the meat. He did his utmost to prod Crofton to act, telling him that every day he and his neighbors found dead cattle and sometimes cattle were not killed but "wounded and left to suffer in a horrible condition."³² Williams was desperate and clung to the forlorn hope that his pleading prose would jolt Crofton out of his paralytic stupor.

It was also in early May that Billy May rode to the Fort to ask for help. He was met with apparent indifference. A letter written to the *Durango Record* said, "Mrs. Cavendish" (probably La Plata valley rancher Henry Caviness's wife Nancy) reported that May was told there was nothing they could do for him. They refused to send out troops to look for Smith, who was missing, and he was told "the troops were there to protect the Indians."³³

On May 5th a Durango resident wrote up a narrative of the incident and gave it to a traveler heading to Amargo, which was at the end of the advancing telegraph line. The dispatch was wired to Governor Pitkin on May 9th. It was the first notice of the attack received outside of the San Juan country. The governor telegraphed General Pope, commander of the Department of Missouri, at Fort Leavenworth for more information. Pope wired back the same day and said he was unaware of the attack.³⁴ The *Denver Republican* said that Pope doubted the reliability of the accounts that were coming in about the killings since "the commandant of that post [Fort Lewis] has not sent a particle of official information on the matter, an omission which, the General thinks, throw a doubt on the credibility of the private reports."³⁵ General Pope or his staff members were misinformed or uninformed about telegraph facilities in the region. The *Republican* reported that his dispatch noted, "if these depredations were committed it was strange that no report of such was made to his headquarters, as the fort was but a day's journey from the telegraph station."[36]

"Ignatio, [sic] chief of the Southern Utes, escorting the women, children and stock in the Amimas [sic] valley to a place of safety," Frank Leslie's Illustrated Newspaper, *June 18, 1881, artist J.J. Reilly. (Author's collection.)*

Crofton's superiors soon began to realize that there was something to the accounts coming out of southwest Colorado. Crofton had committed an egregious error in failing to notify his superiors. His inaction placed him in a difficult situation as military dispatches sizzled through the telegraph wires to Amargo. On May 11th he received a telegram from the Department of Missouri asking about the attack. Two days later he received a communication from his superiors in New Mexico asking about the information they were receiving involving murders and robberies committed by the Utes near Rico and on the Dolores. This message concluded with a comment and clear orders: "Nothing received from you on the subject. Ascertain about it and inform this office at once."[37]

The *Republican* said that Governor Pitkin was trying to learn if the killings were done by Southern Utes or renegades and if Ignacio was at the

Ute Agency. Then the newspaper veered into wild speculation and proclaimed, "A reporter of *The Republican* conversed with a number of gentlemen acquainted with the situation in the South, in regard to the matter, last evening, and found them almost universal in the belief that the triple murder had been committed by the Stockton band of outlaws." The *Republican* speculated that Stockton and his gang then made off with Alderson's horses. The newspaper imagined that the action was done "in one bold effort to fly the country." They reasoned the impetus for the attack was the $2250 reward offered by Governor Wallace. The account was pure nonsense, but the sensationalistic rag was in business to sell papers, whether their articles were truthful or not.[38]

About a day before this article appeared, Tony Neis disembarked in Denver after a long train ride from Española.[39] He was there at the request of Governor Wallace and his purpose was to hand-deliver the requisition for the arrest of Ike Stockton and others to Governor Pitkin.[40] During his brief stay Neis was cornered in the rotunda of Denver's Windsor Hotel by a reporter for the *Republican,* who asked him about his business in town. Neis replied, "No; I can't tell you my mission here. You newspaper fellows are always giving things away. I am on a hard case, and it would destroy what hope I have of clearing it up successfully if I were to tell you what it was." Neis was described as "a bronzed and handsome specimen of the frontiersman" as well as "one of the most unrelenting and fearless officers that ever started in pursuit of a border criminal." Neis was interviewed about his recent trip from Santa Fe to Mesilla with his prisoner, Billy the Kid. Neis described holding off a large group of men at the end of the railroad tracks at Rincon. They were intent on releasing the Kid. Neis pointed a shotgun at the Kid and told them "if they wanted him they would have to take him dead after killing me." The Kid believed him and told his friends, "Boys, for God's sake, don't make any break, or this fellow will kill me." (The *Republican* was notoriously unreliable, so the account may not be accurate.) Neis delivered the Kid to Mesilla, where in early April he stood trial for the murder of Sheriff William Brady. He was found guilty without the testimony of witness Ike Stockton and was sentenced to hang, but escaped shortly thereafter. About New Mexico's desperadoes, Neis said the state of affairs was, "Very bad. In fact, I don't think that it was ever worse." He predicted that the pursuit of criminals would soon improve. The construction of railroads, which contributed much to the crime of the era, also brought the telegraph. This device would soon prove be an effective crime fighting tool. Neis captured the essence of the desperado era and perfectly described how Port Stockton and his brethren operated, saying, "When a man killed another in the Territory without provocation, he jumped a horse, left the country, and within a few days the crime would fade from the public mind. Again, if there was the slightest cause for the killing, the man put on a bold front and stood his ground. To be sure the bluff always won, and he was unmolested."[41] Neis's interview was published on May 14th. He had left town on the evening of May 10th. On May 11th the *Republican* printed a short notice which said that Pitkin had issued arrest warrants for the Durango outlaws. Another article in the same issue breathlessly declared that Stockton and his men "are said to have their rendezvous in a blind cañon near Farmington." The May 11th newspaper did not identify Neis by name, but said, "A member of the Rocky Mountain Detective Association departed last night with the papers. He will be joined at Durango by an armed posse."[42] The *Republican* was both out of touch with reality and woefully misinformed. Stockton had no reason to hide in a blind canyon, especially in New Mexico. He was still living openly in southwest Colorado and the chances of getting up a posse of men in Durango to arrest him were non-existent.

While Neis was headed south, I.W. Lacy was learning more about the killings of Thurman, Smith and May. The life of the cattle king was rustic. He was staying at his dugout next to Fort Lewis and had been there for about a month. After burying John Thurman, Henry Goodman traveled over to the La Plata valley to meet with Lacy.[43] What to do about Ike Stockton and how to stop the Indian depredations were on the top of their discussion list. After the murder of Thurman and May, local cattlemen hoped that troops would be sent out to punish the recalcitrant Indians and the problem would be solved. As time passed, the locals became increasingly concerned about the lack of action at Fort Lewis. Some cattlemen began to make plans to take matters into their own hands.

Lacy was besieged with problems: Stockton's rustling, Indian depredations, and his personal loose cannon, Big Dan Howland. As a detective, Howland was like a bull in china shop. He'd been fired by Bob Dwyer, killed a more than likely innocent and noncombatant sheepherder, and he was known as being a member of the Farmington forces at the Battle of Durango on April 11th. Despite his poor performance he was almost certainly one of the sources who reported that Sheriff Luke Hunter turned a blind eye to Stockton's stock rustling.[44] Thompson and Lacy relied on J.F. Bond, the Durango saddler, to handle business affairs for them in Durango. Bond received a $10 check as payment for Howland's work as Durango constable. He forwarded the check on to Fort Lewis. While he was preparing for the La Plata valley roundup, Howland asked Rube Baldock, one of his co-workers, to pick up his mail. Baldock picked up the $10 check for Howland and gave it to Lacy.[45] Howland later asked for his $10 and Lacy refused to give it to him, saying that Howland owed him money.[46] This was probably only the tip of the iceberg in terms of bad blood between the two men. The ten dollar dispute provided the thin rationale for Howland's subsequent actions.

Howland brooded over his treatment by Lacy. On May 10th the La Plata valley roundup commenced. Big Dan would not let matters rest and

Tony Neis, standing, and Robert Olinger. In late March 1881, the two men escorted Billy the Kid from Santa Fe to stand trial in Mesilla. A month later Olinger was shot and killed by the Kid. That May Neis delivered Governor Wallace's requisition for Ike Stockton's arrest to Governor Pitkin in Denver. (Courtesy L. Tom Perry Special Collections, Harold B. Lee Library, Brigham Young University, Provo, Utah, MSS P645, B1, F1.)

the trouble between the two men continued. Finally, the Texas trail driver had enough and fired his disgruntled employee.[47] According to the *Durango Record*, at about 3:30 PM on Thursday, May 12th, Lacy, Tom Nance and a butcher were together at what the *Record* referred to as "Lacy's slaughterhouse near the Fort."[48] There is some question whether Nance was there at the time.[49] Big Dan's motives were most likely more sinister than trying to obtain his ten dollar payment. He badgered Lacy and according to the *Dolores News*, Lacy said, "Dan, I settled bills for you in Durango amounting to a good deal more than that; but if you insist that it is due you, I will get the money for you." To which Big Dan replied, "You had better do it; you will either give it to me, or I will give you something worse." Lacy started out the door, perhaps headed to the post to get some cash, although he may have gone to retrieve a Winchester that was leaning outside the building. Big Dan stood up and as Lacy disappeared around the door casing he drew his weapon, peeked out the doorway and fired a round, before ducking back inside. He peeked out again and then went outside and fired three more rounds.[50] James Davis, a cattleman, and an unidentified man were near the scene and they hurried over to see what had happened. Howland kept the two men at gunpoint and ordered them to take a look at how Lacy was shot and claimed he fired in self-defense.[51] The Winchester was found cocked and lying next to Lacy. Some accounts say it was found underneath Lacy's body. According to the *Dolores News*, it held no cartridges, and no one witnessed how the rifle came to be in that position. Of course, Howland knew, and Lacy might have, but neither was in any position (or condition) to explain. The *News* reported that Lacy was shot in the back, in the side near the back and twice in the chest.[52] After the fireworks, Howland mounted a horse and was last seen riding on the road in the rear of the Fort, headed toward Parrott City. The *Record* (probably incorrectly) said that Nance rode Lacy's horse to the Fort to get a doctor. The doctor hurriedly rode to the scene, but the cattleman was already dead.[53]

Lieutenant Colonel Crofton sent twenty soldiers out in pursuit of Howland, who was poorly mounted and had only a twenty minute lead.[54] Howland was riding a horse which the *Dolores News* said had been stolen from Lark Reynolds. The *News* speculated that the stolen horse was then purchased by I.W. Lacy.[55] It is no surprise that Reynolds's horse turned up in Lacy's remuda; Reynolds was one of the men implicated in the murder of Aaron Barker, a raid in which several of Lacy's horses were stolen.

Another allegation of horse theft was made against another Lacy herder. Two days before Lacy was killed, George West complained to Colonel Crofton that one of his horses which was "in dispute by the Indians is now in possession of Thos' Nance, foreman for I.W. Lacy." West's claim to the horse may have been about as firm as Lark Reynolds's claim to his horse. He wisely chose not to confront Nance directly in the matter. A summary of the situation noted that West had decided to pursue the matter through civil authorities.[56]

When Lacy was murdered, Henry Goodman was still on the La Plata. He too set out after Big Dan.[57] The soldiers gave up the search at dusk and returned to the Fort. It was a half-hearted effort, considering the lengths civilian groups often went to when pursuing horse thieves and other outlaws. While the soldiers were gone, Colonel Crofton held an inquest into Lacy's death. Shortly afterwards, the body was transported to Durango by wagon, arriving on Thursday night.[58] An enraged and motivated Goodman spent a week trying to track down Howland, without success.[59] After the chase, a weary and disappointed Goodman returned to the Montezuma Valley. As he had been doing before Lacy arrived on the La Plata, Goodman took charge of his mentor's San Juan cattle operations.[60]

At the time Lacy was killed, William Haines was camped across the state/territorial line directly down the La Plata valley with the San Juan Guards. Haines reported the killing to Governor Wallace, saying, "From all evidence the killing of Lacey was perfectly in self defense one of my company now in camp being present at time. Lacey seizing his gun, and firing first. The man that did the killing is in no way connected with this community, and being one of Lacey's hired men." Haines does not identify the San Juan Guardsman who was present during the shooting. He was either clueless or unwilling to admit to the governor that Howland had been an active member of the Farmington crowd for almost two months. His letter to Wallace tacitly indicates that he knew Howland on sight: "I am not at all informed where the man is. I have not seen him, nor have any of my Company."[61]

The day of the shooting, Ignacio and his wives traveled on the road between Mancos and Durango. This would have placed them on portions of the same road which Big Dan used for his escape. The big pow wow was over and Ignacio went to Animas City, where he met again with Deputy Marshal Heffernan. According to Heffernan, Ignacio told him that the Thurman cabin murders were committed by "Piutes of the lower San Juan together with the renegade Navajos and Indians from the Moqui [Hopi] villages." Heffernan reported, "Ignatio said he was sorry it was done, but the Indians did not like the May brothers." Ignacio's initial account did not mention that any Utes were involved. Heffernan told Ignacio that one of the O'Donnell brothers believed the murders were committed by Utes from Mariano's and Narraguinnep's bands. Ignacio advised him to "ask Mariano he knew it all."[62] According to Al Puett, after the killings, Mariano's band was seen herding some of Thurman's horses across the Dolores.[63] That evening Durango and Animas City were abuzz with the shocking news of Lacy's death and the passage of Ignacio through town.

That was not the only news. Tony Neis departed Denver on the evening of May 10th. He probably arrived in Durango on the day Lacy was killed. Neis hand-delivered the arrest warrants for Ike Stockton and others indicted for the murder of Aaron Barker to Luke Hunter or to others with the La Plata County Sheriff's office.[64] He received a cold reception. It's likely that the man who had successfully delivered Billy the Kid for trial at Mesilla left Durango with his tail between his legs.

Neis may have traveled into Durango with Trinidad resident Major T.K. Gash. Passenger service on the D&RG was inaugurated into Amargo on April 25th.[65] From there, travelers took a stagecoach or found other means of transportation to Durango. Major Gash was passing through the area, on his way to Rico, when he learned about the murder of his friend, I.W. Lacy. Gash was on the payroll of Thompson and Lacy and his trip to Rico was possibly part of the effort they were making against Ike Stockton. Whatever his plans, he changed them. Lacy's body was prepared in Durango and on Saturday morning, May 14th, the trail driver's remains were loaded onto a spring wagon. With Major Gash in charge, the 107 mile journey to Amargo began.[66]

Lacy was killed on Thursday. It was not until Saturday that a messenger reached the communications hub of the San Juan country, the telegraph station in Amargo. The operator tapped out this message,

> Fort Lewis, Colo., May 12, 1881.
> Geo. W. Thompson:
> Lacey has been killed, this date. Come as soon as you can. Killed by Dan Howland.
> R.J. Balldoc[67]

Baldock's message was stunning news. Unaware that Major Gash had taken charge of the situation, Thompson immediately sent a telegram to their man in Durango, J.F. Bond. It said, "Send Lacey's body in best condition possible to Trinidad at once. Spare neither pains nor expense."[68] He then sent word to Sarah Lacy at the LC headquarters on the Vermejo. Telegrams were soon sent out notifying other family members about the tragedy. J.C. and Delila Brumley of Cleburne, the widow's father and mother, and one of her brothers began the journey to Trinidad.[69] Lacy was well known in Colorado, New Mexico, and in parts of Texas and was soon eulogized in the press. "Mr. Lacey was a quiet man," reported the *Trinidad News*, "and of a nature to avoid personal difficulties." They were unaware that behind Lacy's quiet demeanor was a steely-eyed determination, strong will, and the already proven capacity to use a pistol in settling personal conflicts. The *News* estimated his personal worth at one hundred thousand dollars and noted that he was survived by his wife, three daughters and two young boys.[70] The *Dolores News* offered a succinct characterization, saying

"[Lacy] was possessed of all those qualities of frontier manliness for which cow-men of the old-time days are so noted."[71] The *Durango Record* said, "at an early age [he] removed to Texas where he made his home in the saddle, and mastered all the minutiae of the cattle business, and afterwards engaged in it on his own account. Later he went to New Mexico, where he amassed an immense fortune, and became a veritable cattle king."[72]

Ike Stockton was in Animas City on the day Lacy was killed. It was early the next day, Friday, May 13th, that he asked the *Durango Record* to publish a reward notice. On May 14th, the *Record* featured a half page printing of the notice, which said,

> $2,000 REWARD!
> The undersigned will pay a reward of
> TWO THOUSAND DOLLARS
> for the capture and delivery,
> DEAD OR ALIVE!!!
> of one Dan Howland, to the sheriff of La Plata County, Colorado, or to any sheriff of Colorado.
>
> Dan Howland murdered Col I. W. Lacy near Fort Lewis, La Plata County Colorado.
>
> Howland is about 28 years of age, light complexon [sic], light hair, light moustache and gotee [sic] weighs about 200 pounds, is generally known as "Big Dan."
>
> Mrs. I. W. Lacy,
> May 13th.   By ISAAC STOCKTON, her Agent.[73]

Ike Stockton's intense interest in the fate of Dan Howland was, to say the least, peculiar. Like William Haines, Ike knew Lacy's one-time cattle detective on sight. Since Irvin Lacy already had an advertising account with the *Record*, it's probable that Ike did not even have to pay for its printing. The notice was widely circulated and Ike's role in posting the ad caused much speculation. A few days later the *New Mexican* commented, "The circulars were distributed, and a good many reached Santa Fe. They created a good deal of comment, it being thought strange that Stockton, the enemy of Mr. Lacy, should be acting as agent of the widow of the deceased in an effort to punish the murderers, and it was generally suspected that there was something crooked about the reward business."[74]

There was something crooked about the reward business. Ike Stockton could not have had the approval of Lacy's widow to publish the notice or to offer a $2000 reward in her name. When Ike went to the offices of the *Record* to ask that the notice be published, Mrs. Lacy did not even know her husband was dead. That news was telegraphed to Trinidad the following day and then it had to be relayed to the Vermejo valley ranch.

Adjacent to the *Durango Record's* notice was a small blurb which said, "An order was sent by Isaac Stockton, to Fort Lewis, on Thursday, for the body of I.W. Lacy. It arrived here the same evening, was embalmed by undertaker Nelson, and this morning, was expressed to his late home near Cimarron."[75] The reporters of the *Durango Record* were strangely apathetic and accepted Ike's words and the motives behind those words at face value. If Lacy had been a cow herder, his body would have already been buried near Fort Lewis. As a prominent citizen there was no doubt he would be transported across the Continental Divide and buried near his family, whether Ike was involved or not. He almost certainly expounded on what he claimed was his close friendship and business relationship with Mr. Lacy to the reporters at the *Record*. To their credit, they did not publish those lies. Hartman and Jones were not interested in printing the truth when it came to Ike Stockton and the *Dolores News* would soon carry a fictitious account of his relationship to I.W. Lacy. Soon after visiting the offices of the *Record*, Ike left for Amargo.

Major Gash and the body of I.W. Lacy arrived in Amargo late on Sunday night.[76] Along the way they crossed paths with Hargo Eskridge who was rapidly riding in the other direction. Hargo's haste was occasioned by the death of former Rico resident Jim "Kid" White. According to the *Dolores News*, which provided the Eskridge side of the story, White ran pack trips into Rico during the summer of 1880 and then spent the winter there, where he made himself very unpopular. He also became acquainted with Hargo. The *News* reported that on Sunday morning, Hargo passed through Amargo on a return trip from Alamosa. After disembarking from the train, he secured a four-seated wagon for himself and others to complete the trip to Durango. "Kid" White asked Eskridge for a ride and the two men and others left Amargo. About two miles out of town, a horse and rider appeared behind them and soon they were overtaken by the outlaw Jimmy Catron. He said he needed to speak to Hargo. Catron told Eskridge that he had just learned that White intended to kill him. White was offered $900 to do the job and hoped to secure the $250 reward offered by territorial officials as well. Hargo turned and spoke to White, who went for his gun, but was beaten to the draw and disarmed. Eskridge then pulled White from the wagon. Up to this point the Hartman and Jones version is plausible. However, Hargo's next move defies belief. According to the *News*, Eskridge told White to defend himself and then returned his pistol. Eskridge shot White in the stomach, took Catron's horse and left for Durango. White was taken back to Amargo.[77] There was no relief for the gut-shot man. He lingered for three days, groaning out tirades laced with profanities and steadfastly refusing to provide any details about the shooting. Kid White died on May 18th; shortly before his death, he divulged that his real name was Cherry.[78] His deathbed revelation was too little and too late and his true identity remains a mystery.

The *New Mexican* presented a version of the shooting that was not so favorable to Eskridge. Unlike the *Dolores News*, which said the killing occurred on the morning of the 15th, they said the killing occurred on Saturday evening, the 14th. The Santa Fe daily declared that not only was Eskridge in Amargo, he was accompanied by Jim Garrett and Ike Stockton. Both Garrett and Eskridge had family in Conejos County and had good reason to ride the D&RG rails over Cumbres Pass. The *New Mexican* said the men spent several days in Amargo. Ike could not have been there for several days. He was in Animas City on Thursday, the day Lacy was killed. If he left Durango on Friday morning, that would have put him in Amargo sometime on Saturday. Reportedly Kid White kept company with Hargo and Garrett during the week. The newspaper announced, "On Saturday last they were drinking and riding about the place in a hack, when the difficulty resulted in Eskridge drawing a revolver and shooting Kid in the back." If portions of the *New Mexican* article are true, it means that after Tony Neis delivered arrest warrants in Durango, he then passed through Amargo on his way to Santa Fe. This would place him in Amargo on one of the days that Garrett and Eskridge were partying, possibly on the 15th, when even Ike was there. If that did happen, Neis apparently made no attempt to arrest the men. It's conceivable that Neis was the source of the *New Mexican's* article. The *New Mexican* said that White had also killed a few men and offered this opinion: "If the 'gang' would have a few more such difficulties among themselves it would be a good thing for the country."[79] That sentiment was at one time echoed by Lew Wallace, who declared, he was "not of the opinion that the killing of outlaws by outlaws is of importance."[80]

Stockton had at least one reason for visiting the railroad camp. It was about this time that the Stockton Gang gained a new member. Ike's latest recruit was a tough Texan who called himself M.C. Cook and it's possible that Stockton was meeting Cook at the Amargo station. Cook was actually former Erath County resident Marion H. "Bud" Galbreath. His stepmom was a sister to the sisters who were the mothers of the Stockton boys and their wives.[81] Galbreath was wanted for attempted rape and for the murder of a Bosque County officer.[82] Some accounts say that Galbreath had at one time joined up with notorious Texas outlaw John Wesley Hardin.[83] Galbreath was listed in the 1878 edition of the Texas Rangers' Black Book.[84] His outstanding arrest warrant in Texas prevented him from testifying in a December 1877 civil suit brought in Erath County. The court ruled in favor of the claim of John Dupuy and he was awarded property near Belknap and Broadway streets in Stephenville which had been bequeathed to Galbreath and his younger brother, Madison.[85] (Throughout his time in the San Juan country Galbreath used Cook as his alias name and we shall use it as well.) The exact nature of Cook's crimes in Texas was not common knowledge in the San Juan country, but soon persistent rumors that Cook was not a man to be trifled with began to make the rounds. Stockton and Cook were an inseparable and fearsome combination from this point forward.

On Sunday, while Stockton was in Amargo, George Thompson took the southbound train out of Trinidad, bound for Las Vegas. I.W. Lacy had been dead less than a week. Around ten in the morning on Monday, May 16th, the attention of George Thompson and fellow cattleman Wilson South was drawn to the occupants of two wagons being driven into Las Vegas. South and another companion, Lou Horn, noticed that one of the group appeared to be a man dressed as a woman. After Lacy's murder, George Thompson could not get Ike Stockton out of his mind and subsequently believed the suspicious wagon travelers might be Stockton associates. The wagons were being driven by a boy who was about ten years old and by a woman. While others in the suspicious group were busy purchasing supplies, South and Thompson began to question the boy and the woman. They also questioned at least one of the men with the group. They completed their inquiry and shortly thereafter the suspect group hurried out of town. Thompson and South could not shake their suspicions, so they followed the group out of town. They rode past the four horse wagon driven by the woman and stopped the lead wagon which had a mile lead and re-interviewed the boy. He boldly refused to allow them to search his wagon, and since they had no lawful authority, they did not press the issue. As they rode back toward the woman's wagon, they saw it now only had three horses and off in the distance was a mounted horse, loping off across the prairie. They stopped and spoke to the woman and she told them they were from the Wind River Mountains and were headed to Kansas. The *Trinidad News* later reported, "Thompson told her she was giving him wind (no joke intended), for the man interviewed in town said they were from Arizona and were on their way to the Black Hills." (Parentheses are in the original article.) Thompson and South returned to Vegas and looked up Marshal Louis Kreeger. The marshal gathered up Frank Loving and James Masterson (brother to Bat Masterson). They mounted up, well-armed with Winchester rifles and tracked the group toward the now forgotten little burg of Chicoso in Colfax County. The woman and boy had done everything they could to make their trail difficult to follow. At one point the wagon tracks backtracked for several miles and then headed east toward the A.T. and S.F. Railroad right of way. Upon reaching the tracks, the wagons followed the rails for some time. The three man posse was persistent and finally caught up with their quarry. Only the boy and woman were present and Marshal Kreeger's search turned up nothing of significance. With no reason to detain them, the disappointed posse returned to Las Vegas.[86] The incident was odd, but uneventful. However, it demonstrates that on the heels of Lacy's murder, George Thompson unambiguously viewed Ike and his allies as enemies.

Thompson's actions fly in the face of Stockton's public relations blitz in Durango, in which he tried to fabricate evidence that he was an ally and business associate to Irvin Lacy.

In the meantime, the press continued to speculate about Lacy's murder. According to the *Trinidad Times*, Lacy had written to George Thompson about the firing of Big Dan and the *Times* believed that Big Dan had written to Thompson "complaining that money matters had not been satisfactorily arranged between them."[87] It seems that Howland was trying to squeeze an exorbitant amount of money out of Thompson and Lacy. The firing of a mere cowhand would not necessitate any special communication between Lacy and Thompson. The true urgency of the matter arose because of Howland's demands for money and because Howland did not follow through with his duties as Lacy's stock detective.

Exactly a week after Lacy's murder, Tom Nance wrote a letter to the *Durango Record*. The *Record* had been taken to task by their fellow journalists for not publishing Nance's account of the murder of Aaron Barker and his harrowing escape. This time they published his letter, which read,

> Farmington, N.M.,
> May 18, 1881.
> Editor, *Durango Record*
>
> I would like to have you correct the statement which came in your columns, this week about the killing of I. W. Lacey at the Post. I wish to state that I left there before the shooting took place and went to my work on the round-up on La Plata. Dan Howland never was in the employ of Lacey, at any time. I did not know that there was any bitter feeling between them, until the day before, when Lacey told me that he would kill him if he didn't mind, because he had not done what he brought him here for.
>
> Thomas Nance.[88]

Nance can't keep his stories straight. His assertion that Howland never worked for Lacy is at odds with the next sentence of the letter. His other assertion that he was working on the La Plata roundup when Lacy was killed may be true. Howland would have been less anxious to force a deadly dispute with Lacy, especially while Nance was around. Nance was not afraid of gunplay and might have stopped Howland in his tracks. It's also unlikely that Big Dan's horse could have outraced Nance and Ol' Turp.

It is clear from Nance's letter that Lacy was thoroughly riled with Howland because of his poor performance as a cattle detective. The exact nature of "what he brought him here for" will in all likelihood remain forever a mystery. Certainly, Lacy wanted evidence against Stockton, but he may well have hired Howland to effect a final solution to the Stockton problem. Despite his total failure to obtain the results Lacy desired, Howland added insult to injury by trying to force more money out of him. Nance's statement that Howland never worked for Lacy is also at odds with the 1880 Las Animas County census which shows Nance and "Ben Howlan" living in the same household and employed as "cattle herders." Looking at the relationship between Howland, Nance, and Lacy as well as the all too common inaccuracies of local census enumerators, it is certain that Ben Howlan and Dan Howland were one in the same. The *Record* added a postscript to Nance's letter, saying, "[It seems that Howland was not in the employ of Lacey, in connection with his cattle business; but Mr. Lacey told us himself, that he employed Howland to come out here, as a detective. – Ed. Record.]" (Brackets are in the original article.)[89]

At 1:30 in the afternoon on Tuesday, May 17th, the train carrying the body of I.W. Lacy pulled into the D&RG's El Moro station, just north of Trinidad. Mrs. Lacy was in Trinidad with her three daughters, Ecce Homo, Ruth Norma and Lucy Fair, as well as her two sons, Irvin W. and Clay. They had taken up temporary residence at St. Joseph's Academy and the funeral was arranged to take place in Trinidad at 2:00 PM on Wednesday.[90] Mid-May in Trinidad can be glorious, but I.W. Lacy's funeral service was accompanied by the final blast of winter. "A cold east wind carrying rain, snow and sleet prevailed throughout the day," reported the *Trinidad News*. In spite of the weather, a large crowd gathered to pay homage to the slain cattleman and to offer condolences to the family.[91] He was laid to rest in the northern portion of the Catholic Cemetery just north of town. Mrs. Lacy would later purchase a monument which featured an approximately sixteen foot tall spire. Less than two years later, her father was interred next to the remains of her husband.

Lacy's killing coupled with the pervasive San Juan country turmoil sent the *Dolores News* into overdrive. As the month of May drew to a close, Hartman and Jones claimed to "have been busily at work trying to ferret out the true inwardness of the dastardly murder and gathered all the facts which it is possible for those outside of the Farmington mob of murderers to know."[92] Gathering all of the facts consisted solely of embellishing what Ike Stockton told them. Ike, Hargo, M.C. Cook and Lark Reynolds rode into Rico on about May 22nd.[93] The *Dolores News* was a weekly publication and Stockton's version of events was published on May 28th. Their account was a clever mixture of truths, half-truths and outright lies. Despite its intent to do just the opposite, many of the assertions in the article are so wildly at odds with the facts that they serve to implicate Ike Stockton as being complicit in the murder of I.W. Lacy. The confusion sowed by Hartman and Jones lives on in latter day accounts of Lacy's murder.

The *News* alleged that "Dan no doubt treasured resentment against Lacy and after association with the lower Animas mob, who all wanted Lacy killed, he evidently was on the lookout for an opportunity to murder him." They *News* outrageously asserted that Stockton and Lacy were on the best of terms and that the Farmington crowd developed a plan to force them apart. They reported that members of the Farmington faction had written several letters to Lacy, telling him that Ike was stealing his horses and killing his cattle. They also said Mrs. Lacy had received letters from the Farmington crowd which warned that Ike was threatening Lacy's life. The *News* carried a purported quote from a letter Mrs. Lacy wrote to her husband, which said, "You may be safe, but I cannot believe you are; I think there will be trouble from some source and I wish you and Ike would both come home." Sarah Lacy's true opinion of her cousin Ike would soon become abundantly clear and she certainly never wrote those words. Ike and his wife and children had no home in Colfax County and they were clearly not welcome at Lacy's home. The Stocktons had lived in Animas City for almost two years and they had not lived in Colfax County for over four years. According to the *News*, Stockton and Lacy "had been intimate friends for the past 15 years and Stockton has had charge of his cattle and business for a long time."[94] The suggestion that Ike was in charge of Lacy's cattle business was preposterous. If that was the case he would have been shown in Lacy's notice as one of those authorized to use or sell cattle bearing the LC or other related brands. In the weeks prior to his murder, Lacy let it be known by his words and deeds that he believed Ike was stealing his cattle. Ike had been on the run from Colfax County authorities since Port's jailbreak in September 1876 and after that he faced the threat of arrest anytime he entered Lacy's home range. In fact, it was Lacy's long-time friend and ally, Sheriff Peter Burleson, who trailed the Stockton boys when they did venture into Colfax County. Ike had lived for over two of the past four and a half years in Lincoln County, running a saloon in a locale where Lacy had no cattle herds. Ike's mission to avenge the death of his brother, had made him a pernicious irritant in Lacy's life. The insinuation that Lacy regarded Ike as anything more than a blight on the San Juan country is distinctly absurd; that Ike would take the opportunity to raise his standing in Lacy's absence, however, isn't.

With Lacy gone, his wife needed someone to step up and take charge of the day to day operations. Henry Goodman did that. If Goodman needed help with the spring roundup, which was just beginning, he wouldn't get it from Ike Stockton. Ike went to Rico and for the next month, while his whereabouts were generally known, he was out of contact with the rest of the world. The *News* said the two men were "just like brothers" and that Lacy lived with Stockton and his family when he was in Animas City. Yet it was Durango saddler J.F. Bond, and not Stockton, who received George Thompson's telegram asking him to send Lacy's body to

Trinidad. After Lacy's death, Ike did not act like Lacy's brother. He was not the one who telegraphed George Thompson about the murder and, most telling, he did not gather his men and go out in search of Big Dan. If Ike was so close to Lacy, he certainly would have accompanied Lacy's body to Trinidad, where he could have consoled his grieving cousin. The *Dolores News* alleged that the lower Animas crowd threatened Lacy because of his close relationship with Stockton and tried to force him to put up a reward for the capture of Stockton and his men or else he would be killed. The *News* reported that Lacy said, "I guess I will have to die then, for I will never put up my money to have one of my best friends murdered." The *News* said that the day before Lacy was killed he learned that F.M. Hamblet warned that there was a rope waiting for him if he refused to put up reward money for Ike. At the time, Lacy was already doing just that by posting a reward for information that would prove who was stealing his cattle. The *News* also said that Tom Nance threatened Lacy's life "if Lacy did not walk a chalk line," the inference being that Lacy had to oppose his good friend, Ike Stockton. The assertion that Nance threatened Lacy is without merit. If Nance had a problem with Lacy, he would not have continued to work for him. Nance was one of Thompson and Lacy's top hands and all of Lacy's known La Plata valley herders had always been and continued to be allied with the Farmington crowd. The participation of at least one and possibly two of Thompson and Lacy's employees (Nance and Joe Caldwell) in the killing of Porter Stockton, which was followed by Ike Stockton's murder of herder Aaron Barker and attempted murder of Tom Nance, provides clear and damning evidence that Lacy and Stockton were deadly enemies. Despite all the evidence to the contrary, the *News* said, "I.W. Lacy, to-day, lies in his grave, the victim of a cowardly assassin, because he was too true to a friend to betray him."[95] Certainly during the early portion of the 1870s Porter and Ike Stockton at times worked for I.W. Lacy, but Porter Stockton's threats and bald-faced theft of Lacy's cattle brought an abrupt end to that relationship. In the months immediately prior to Lacy's death, there are no newspaper articles or other sources which report that Lacy and Ike Stockton were on friendly terms. In contrast, there are many that say just the opposite.

Ike's article in the *Dolores News* makes clear that he saw some obvious benefits to being Lacy's friend and business associate, even if only posthumously. Lacy's one hundred dollar reward for information which could prove the identity of those who were stealing his cattle was published only one week before his murder. Given Howland's short-lived employment with the Durango police force, and Durango's roiling rumor mill, Ike doubtless knew he was Lacy's detective. Lacy's reward notice and the planned opening of his own slaughterhouse put intense pressure on Ike and perhaps motivated him to make a deal with Big Dan. If Ike hired or induced Howland to murder Lacy, the presumptuous reward notice for the capture of Howland, dead or alive, had two purposes. It served as evidence that Ike was a close friend and agent for Lacy, and it assured that the only witness who could implicate Ike in Lacy's murder would disappear. With a large reward notice on his head, Big Dan would leave for parts unknown and, if he was cornered, he would likely take his chances in a gunfight, since lynching was certain if he was captured.

Hartman and Jones had one thing right; Big Dan was a despicable character. However, the two newsmen resorted to further outrageous allegations to impugn his character. They said that Big Dan was known to carry a photo of four hanged outlaws, one of whom was Dave Rudabaugh. He would pull out the photo and proudly proclaim that Rudabaugh was his cousin.[96] There is no doubt that Rudabaugh was a first-rate desperado who deserved to be hung. He was an associate of the Dodge City Gang in Las Vegas, New Mexico and later joined forces with Billy the Kid. He then made the mistake of murdering a jailer in Las Vegas.[97] For this crime, he was sentenced to hang. The execution was set for May 25, 1881, but that was delayed when the case was appealed.[98] In early December 1881, Rudabaugh, J.J. Webb and five others escaped from the Las Vegas jail.[99] On January 16, 1886, the *Albuquerque Evening Democrat* reported that Rudabaugh had been killed by an angry mob in Parral, Mexico after he killed two men in a drunken cantina rampage.[100] The aroused Mexicans then decapitated him with a meat cleaver, placed his head on a pike, and paraded through town.[101]

Less than a week after the *Record* published the reward notice for Howland, a copy reached Sarah Lacy. Shortly after reading it, she fired off a notice of her own. It said,

> Trinidad, Colo., May 20, 1881.
> To the editor of the *Durango Record*.
> Dear Sir - The enclosed poster, purporting to be a reward offered by me, through the agency of Isaac Stockton, for the capture of one Dan Howland, has just been exhibited to me. I will say that the same was published and circulated without my authority or knowledge. I will further say that Isaac Stockton is not now my agent, never has been, and never will be. You will confer a favor by publishing the poster in connection with my disclaimer of it, in your paper, and by requesting other papers to copy. By doing so you will oblige
> Mrs. I.W. Lacy

Those are not the words of a dear cousin or someone whose husband had a close, personal and friendly relationship with Ike Stockton. Sarah Lacy's repudiation of Ike and his reward notice make it clear that Ike had an overabundance of interest and sinister motives when it came to the fate of Dan Howland. The *Santa Fe New Mexican* published Mrs. Lacy's letter with a postscript: "What Stockton's idea was in publishing the reward circular it is hard to say. It may have been done in order to work evil to Howland. His action showed a good deal of cool impudence on his part, and it is just as well to let the boys know that the reward 'don't go.' "[102]

Catholic Cemetery, Trinidad, CO. (Author's collection.)

It would be most satisfying to place the smoking gun in Stockton's hands. Unfortunately, the evidence linking him to Lacy's murder, while substantial, is entirely circumstantial. If Stockton was involved, the reward notice served its purpose. Dan Howland was never captured and he never told his tale. There will always be the chance that Howland fired in self-defense, or that he murdered Lacy in a fit of rage over a diminutive amount of money, but that does not explain Stockton's curious actions in the aftermath of Lacy's death. It is clear that Stockton generated turmoil in the San Juan country and fate brought Lacy and Howland together in the La Plata River valley. Lacy led a remarkable life, moving out of Kentucky to the Texas frontier at a young age and then faced extraordinary and innumerable dangers while trailing herds out of Texas. Had he lived to a ripe age, and had he been inclined to reminisce about his life, there is no doubt he would now be remembered in the same vein as some of his contemporaries, like Charles Goodnight and John Chisum. Lacy was known for hiring herders with rough edges and that contributed to his undoing. In the end, for whatever reason, an ill-tempered, short-fused, part-time policeman, part-time herder and full-time loose cannon did him in. Lacy had seen just the beginning of the Indian trouble on the Utah/Colorado border. Within days of his death those events would reach the point of no return and would engulf many of the cowboys and other residents of the area.

Frederick Remington's "Roped!" from Theodore Roosevelt's "The Round-up," The Century Illustrated Monthly Magazine, *Vol. 35, No. 6, April 1888. (Modified, author's collection.)*

Chapter Fourteen

Cowboys and Indians

Twenty of us ridin' bronks, headed for the war;
Twenty top-hand saddlemen, up in bustin' lore;
Off the ranges fast they come, hosses black and gray,
Hosses roan and calico, hosses brown and bay;
Saddle, bridle, cinch and ride ---- buck, you big hoss, buck![1]

The Colorado cowboys were intent on rounding up their cattle in southeastern Utah. They were being harassed by the same wayward band of Indians who had killed Thurman, May and Smith. Unbelievably, Ike, Hargo and M.C. Cook were about to be caught up in these troubles. They would soon be headed toward a deadly rendezvous in a remote canyon near Moab, Utah.

The cocksure killers of Thurman, Smith and May were surprised they had not been pursued by anyone. After the killings they left the Dove Creek area and headed west with their stolen loot and purloined horse herd. The Indians were in no hurry to leave the area and on May 15th the assessor for San Juan County, Utah visited their camp in Utah's Abajo Mountains just west of Monticello. The small scenic range is also known as the Sierra Abajo and the locals refer to it singularly as Blue Mountain. The assessor later reported the Indians were holding stock belonging to John Thurman. As was common practice, the county offices no doubt held a brand book where local stockmen registered the brands and earmarks of their cattle, sheep and horses. He said that the camp held about one hundred people, including women and children. About thirty-five of that number were men. He also said that in addition to the Paiutes, there were several Navajos and some Utes from Narraguinnep's band.[2]

Back in Colorado, Billy May was obsessed with avenging the death of his brother. In a letter to the *Durango Record*, a traveler calling himself Arcade Ambo advised that, "On our way out we passed William May, brother of one of the murdered men. He was very quiet and determined. Poor fellow! we all felt for him."[3] May was incensed with the lack of concern and lack of action at Fort Lewis. Ike Stockton continued to hear accounts coming out of the Utah border area, and they piqued his interest.

While Billy May smoldered, life at Fort Lewis seemed carefree. On Wednesday, May 18th, officers of the Fort hosted a ballroom dance with single ladies and others driven in by coach from Durango. Hosts included Captain and Mrs. Benjamin H. Rogers, Captain Pratt, Lieutenant W.S.

Davies, and Mrs. Byrne, wife of the surgeon. Guests from Durango included the widowed newspaper editor, Caroline Romney, Mrs. Pennington, Mrs. James Heffernan, Lilly Heffernan, Laura Will and several others.[4] As the partiers returned to Durango, the cowboys near the Utah/Colorado border began to face increasing difficulties from the fractious band of Indians.

On May 16th Green Robinson, chief herder for "Spud" Hudson, and twelve other men had left for Blue Mountain to look for stock. On May 20th another twelve men from the Dolores joined up with this group. With the large number of men, a branding camp was kept busy and many of the cowboys spread out in small groups to scour the countryside for their horses and cattle. On May 22nd a group of six men were herding some horses into camp when they were fired on by two Indians from about two hundred yards away. According to horse trader J.H. Alderson, who was one of the six men, they returned fire and chased the Indians toward the woods. Alderson noted "the Indians left and we captured the two horses they had been riding." Green Robinson added that the horses were still saddled. The story seems only half told, since it's unlikely that live Indians would willingly abandon their saddled horses. In any case, the Indians kept up their attacks. D.D. Williams said that three Indians encountered one of the Willis brothers and chased him back to camp. Green Robinson said that after this, a group of men went out to gather cattle; "the Indians were watching us and bound to kill the party we came back to get a larger party." The cowboys also reported seeing Indian signal fires. The stockmen were game and well-armed, but the deadly intent of the Indians was clear. Having seen enough, they retreated from Blue Mountain and returned to the Big Bend of the Dolores. Williams estimated the value of the stock left on Blue Mountain at $150,000, with the same amount of stock in the vicinity of Coyote and the La Sal Mountains. The cowmen were desperate to be rid of the Indians. Several of them wrote letters to Colonel Crofton, hoping the army would take action. If not, they intended to take matters into their own hands.[5] The roundup in southeastern Utah would be put on hold while the cowboys prepared to battle marauding Indians.

After coming off the roundup Green Robinson rode into Durango and took time out to visit the offices of the *Durango Record*. Robinson declared that out of Spud Hudson's one hundred horse remuda, eighty were missing. The *Record* said, "It is the intention of the stockmen to return sufficiently reinforced to recover their range, ranches and stock, which the Indians now hold by force." They newspaper continued, "These thieving and murdering fiends are what are known as the Pah-Utes. They should be exterminated on short notice, and we hope the stockmen will not let up until it is done."[6]

On May 21st the *Dolores News* commented, "It seems strange that nothing has as yet been done in regard to the massacre of May, Thurman and Smith."⁷ Unbeknownst to May and others, the day before the *Dolores News* article and almost three weeks after the murders, Crofton received a dispatch from the Military District of New Mexico which ordered him to immediately send out the mounted company of his command and one infantry company. The order specified that the troops should be sent "fully armed and equipped to the scene of the late reported depredations by the Pi Ute Indians, near the Dolores, to thoroughly scout the vicinity, and cover the exposed settlements" and to send a full report.⁸ Colonel Crofton ordered C Company mounted infantry and E Company, Thirteenth Infantry to take the field. The mounted troops were under the command of Captain Benjamin Rogers.⁹ Deputy U.S. Marshal James Heffernan volunteered his services as a guide for the troops. During the 1870s Heffernan had lived in Goose Creek, Corrine and Salt Lake City, Utah. He may have traveled through the region on one of his prospecting sojourns.¹⁰ In late May, Colonel Edward Hatch ordered four companies of the Ninth Cavalry under Captain Henry Carroll to proceed to Santa Fe and then to Fort Lewis for field service in the Ute country. Carroll's command was composed of Buffalo Soldiers from the southern part of the territory. Colonel Crofton was advised that "Captain Henry Carroll with four companies of the Ninth Cavalry, thoroughly fitted and with transportation, pack train and one Hotchkiss Gun" were on their way to Fort Lewis. Carroll and his men were "ordered to La Plata to be used in event of Indian troubles and will be used for no other purpose."¹¹

If he was not aware of it, Crofton soon found out that the same "Pah-Ute" band had been the cause of trouble for the last few years. They were implicated in the murders of two prospectors, Ernest Mitchell and another whose name may have been Merrick. The two had made the mistake of prospecting in the Navajo country of northeastern Arizona. The Navajos said the "Pi-Utes" and White River Utes were responsible.¹² Henry Goodman was one of a party of ten well-armed men from the lower Mancos who went out to bury the bodies. According to the *La Plata Miner*, a Navajo guided the group to the location. The bodies were found about two miles apart, each had been shot. The remains of both men were partially eaten by coyotes and rats.¹³ Mitchell's father, Henry L. Mitchell, added his two cents to the information piling up on Crofton's desk, saying, "These Pah Utes are renegades and known to be such by all the Navajos in that region." He advised Crofton that they killed his son in 1879. He said they were led by Poca (Poco) Narraguinnep. Mitchell advised Crofton that the Navajo accounts were reliable, "so much so that the Navajo chiefs have voluntarily offered to go and catch these renegades if permitted, and if necessary, fight them."¹⁴

Meanwhile, down on the lower Animas, Indian-related news was traveling through the country like wildfire. The Ute problems and the rumored solution was the cause of the discontent. Even before the Meeker

Massacre, the Utes were the pariahs of Colorado. As more settlers entered Colorado, there was intense political pressure to force the Utes out. The slogan which permeated the Colorado press was "The Utes Must Go."[15] The pressure in the press ramped up after the Meeker Massacre and remained at a steady boil into the 1880s. Now the Ute Commission was proposing to create a Ute reservation in western Rio Arriba County. Settlers who had uprooted themselves, moved to the area, started farms, brought in cattle herds and started businesses were in a state of disbelief. New Mexico newspapers railed against the proposal.[16] William Haines penned a frantic letter to Adjutant General Frost. Part of the problem was that even though some had lived on their claims since 1876, they had not been able to perfect their titles to the land because the surveyor general had not completed surveys in the western portion of Rio Arriba County. Despite that, the residents considered their property to be on the open market and valuable. Haines was of the opinion that the government would surely have to compensate residents for their land. In the same letter, Haines referred to the brewing Indian turmoil on the Utah/Colorado border. He advised Frost, the former army officer, that local residents were unhappy with the perceived "cowardice of the Regulars." Colonel Crofton and his soldiers were rapidly becoming the butt of much derision by the local civilian population. Haines also alerted Frost about local rumors, saying, "I hear it openly talked, that the intention is to bring on an Indian war as soon as possible." Haines correctly advised Frost, "Inside one month from now you will see the war going full blast."[17]

Max Frost, who now had business interests in western Rio Arriba County, acted even before he received Haines's letter.[18] At Governor Wallace's request he worked up a fact sheet packed with information to fight the reservation proposal. He laid out the development of the area, pointing out that there were five hundred primarily Hispanic residents along the upper San Juan and between one thousand and twelve hundred residents on the lower San Juan and Animas River valleys, as well as twenty thousand head of cattle, fifty thousand sheep and several established communities. Eventually the ill-conceived idea was dropped from consideration.[19]

While Haines dealt with the proposed Ute reservation, he continued to receive and pass on reports about the activities of Stockton, Eskridge and their allies. In the aftermath of the Battle of Durango, concerned citizens hammered out a transaction to purchase Ike and Hargo's Tent Saloon and Hargo's Eclipse Saloon. In exchange, the two men were supposed to stay out of Durango.[20] That transaction was completed in late April, and Ike and Hargo gladly took the money, but they had no intention of keeping their end of the bargain. They reappeared in Durango and contemptuously defied anyone to do anything about it. Haines soon advised Frost that Stockton and his men were once again appearing publicly in Durango and, in fact, had voted in Durango's first election and elected "their ticket."[21] The election was held during the second week of May. John "Doc" Taylor, Jr., a druggist, was elected mayor and the town trustees were O.F. Boyle, James Reed, John Foley, and M.B. Marshall, the owner of the Coliseum.[22] Haines advised Governor Wallace that Stockton and his men, "laugh at the rewards offered by your excellency and posted in Durango. They could easily be arrested, but no steps are taken."[23] He also reported that it was a great hardship on the men, keeping the militia in the field, and "Their crops are suffering for water, & attention, & the stock men have not been able to round up, & have to leave their cattle unbranded."[24]

Haines spent several days camped on the La Plata, with what he called "the American portion of my company" as opposed to the "Mexican" portion, which was composed of primarily Hispanic men who lived in the San Juan River valley in and above Bloomfield. After their aborted attempt to arrest Manuel Gonzales near Coyote, the Hispanic Guardsmen moved north to Cañon Largo to look for one of Aaron Barker's murderers, Bill "Tex" Hunter. After the Battle of Durango, "Tex" decided it was time to leave. Unaware that the San Juan Guardsmen were in the vicinity, he had been seen riding up Cañon Largo. Meanwhile, over in the La Plata valley, the western contingent of the San Juan Guards discovered a camp of thirteen armed men. Haines and his militia gave chase, but "they escaped across line to their stronghold in Colorado."[25] Haines does not identify the interlopers, but they certainly included Ike Stockton, Hargo Eskridge and M.C. Cook. At the time, Ike and his two lieutenants were making their way from Durango to Rico. Cook was a new arrival in the San Juan country and Ike hoped to show him the lay of the land, but the guided tour was cut short by the warm greetings received from Haines's militia. In a letter from his La Plata valley camp, Haines asked Wallace if Colorado Governor Frederick Pitkin intended to act and expressed his fears that if the situation continued "we cannot prevent the depopulation of this portion of New Mexico."[26] Up in Rico, Hartman and Jones received a copy of the *New Mexican* which carried portions of Haines's letter, and the newsmen responded with typical invective, "Wm. B. Haines, Captain of the San Juan Guards, whom we believe to be a malicious liar, residing at the seat of the Farmington, New Mexico trouble, favors Gov. Wallace, of New Mexico, with another mess of trash." Adding to their diatribe the Rico newspapermen added, "Gov. Wallace is a victim to the misrepresentation of a handful of rogues and desperadoes that infest the western portion of Rio Arriba county."[27]

Wallace was walking a tightrope with Governor Pitkin. He wanted action taken, but since he could not tell a fellow governor what to do, he did his best to be respectful while insisting that something be done. He informed Pitkin: "It is precisely as if there was open war between them and neighboring citizens of Colorado. Possibly you may not be aware that the militia are on duty under summons from the sheriff of that county as a posse, and that they are being maintained while so engaged at the expense of the Territory. Yet such is the case." He advised the governor that the militia and sheriff's deputies were under strict instructions to observe the sovereignty of the State of Colorado and forbidden to cross the line in pursuit of the outlaws. Wallace noted, "Upon the appearance of pursuers they make haste to get behind the division line in your state where they are safe." Governor Wallace assured Pitkin that Colorado authorities would have the full cooperation of territorial and county officials. Utilizing his best lawyerly idiom, Wallace wrote, "I have, therefore, to respectfully request that you will take speedy measures, which will suggest themselves, to secure energetic effort to capture the banditti or drive them from the border." He also carefully asked Pitkin about the possibility of obtaining permission for Captain Haines, the militia, and Rio Arriba County deputies to cross the line and go in pursuit of Stockton and his men. Pitkin never gave permission for cross border operations.[28]

After the issuance of warrants and the publication of wanted fliers, Stockton hysteria spread throughout New Mexico and Colorado. The *South Pueblo Banner* reported, incorrectly, that four men were killed during a Stockton raid near Farmington.[29] Sightings of members of the Stockton Gang became fairly commonplace. Down in Las Cruces the *Rio Grande Republican* carried an account that said, "A party consisting of five Americans, two negroes and one Mexican, six of them well armed and mounted" were said to be traveling east through the *Jornada Del Muerto* at Upton's Siding. One of the men drove a wagon carrying a wounded man. With dubious reasoning the article speculated, "From the appearance and actions of the party it was thought to have been a part of Stockton's gang from the San Juan country."[30]

Back in northwest New Mexico one of Captain Haines's San Juan militia, Corporal Juan Jaquez, rode into Coyote and was promptly arrested on the warrant issued by *Alcalde* Sandoval at the request of Manuel Gonzales. The *New Mexican* reported that the judge assessed Jaquez with a fine of $700, although the fine may have only been $100. The corporal did not pay the fine. He was then taken to the jail in Tierra Amarilla.[31] Captain Haines soon received a letter from Corporal Jaquez. Haines hastily penned a letter to Governor Wallace with a heading which noted that he was still "In camp on La Plata," followed by a description of the arrest of Jaquez. Haines dispatched Private J.C. Trujillo to travel as quickly as possible to the long, low slung, one story adobe office and hacienda on the north side of Santa Fe's plaza, the seat of territorial government known as the Palace of the Governor's.[32]

One can only wonder at Wallace's reaction to the news. It had to be priceless. He was the man who once said, "Every calculation based on experience elsewhere fails in New Mexico."³³ The governor wrote a letter to *Alcalde* Sandoval. It's likely that he utilized the courier services of Private Trujillo to deliver the correspondence to Coyote. According to the *New Mexican,* the governor informed Sandoval that "he was pursuing an iniquitous course and that unless he changed it he would be more than likely to get into serious trouble." According to Sandoval, he never received the letter, but within days both Sandoval and Gonzales turned up in Santa Fe in Max Frost's office. The newspaper claimed that both men were "very anxious to put themselves on the right track as regards the troubles in their county." The two men, who had run roughshod over Jaquez, now asked for the protection of officers of the law because they feared violence from the people residing in Rio Arriba County. The paper noted that Gonzales was "under indictments and bonds, and his case will have to take its course." Corporal Jaquez was ordered to be released from the Tierra Amarilla lockup.³⁴

While Haines was camped on the La Plata, he detailed at least one man to guard the Haines and Hughes Store. That was wise, since his store was a possible target of Stockton and his men. At dusk on May 24th, Haines reported "the boys were badly woke up" when three men rode close by the store and fired several rounds in the direction of En Blancett and Private Dan Sullivan who were standing outside the door. Young Blancett was not a member of the San Juan Guards and evidence suggests that prior to this incident he sustained some life altering misfortune requiring the use of at least one crutch, and perhaps two, to move about. Blancett was armed, but only had one round in his revolver. He fired off his round and Private Sullivan grabbed his rifle and took two shots at the retreating men. (Sullivan became the first Sheriff of San Juan County, when it was created in 1887.) The attackers were perhaps supporters of Manuel Gonzales of the so-called "Cañon Largo Gang." Haines was of the opinion that they were not Stockton's men.³⁵

Haines was right because it was about two days before the incident that Ike Stockton, Hargo Eskridge, M.C. Cook and Lark Reynolds rode into Rico. At this juncture, Ike was unaware that Mrs. Lacy had written the letter repudiating him and his actions in the aftermath of her husband's murder. During their time there, they heard additional accounts about the depredations of the intractable band of Ute Indians along the Utah border. The wanted outlaws remained in town for two days and then traveled to Expectation Mountain to work on the Lookout Mine, which was owned by Eskridge, Stockton and young Bert Wilkinson. The mine assay was promising and it was believed it might contain a profitable concentration of silver. Despite the rewards being offered for Stockton and Eskridge, the *Dolores News* openly published news of their arrival and offered this slanted assessment: "They do not appear to be reckless, desperate characters, but behaved themselves like gentlemen, as those who are acquainted with them know them to be. We wish them all sorts of good luck in their mining interests."[36]

Before he made the climb up Expectation Mountain, Ike had a little excitement. On the afternoon of Monday, May 23rd, Marshal Jim Cart received word that a man had fallen in the Dolores River, which was swollen with snow melt. The victim was seen bounding down the rapids with his head submerged. His horse was still standing in the stream. Cart and Stockton mounted up and proceeded immediately to the scene, where they found another man named Vroman pulling the body of forty-two-year-old rancher J.B. Horton from the river. Horton was from the Potato Valley in Piute County, Utah. It was later learned that he had been drinking heavily when he left town for his camp. Stockton was not without redeeming qualities. Offering assistance during an emergency was typical of men raised on the frontier and that type of act was one reason Ike had numerous supporters in southwest Colorado, including Marshal Cart.[37]

Cart, like other law enforcement officers in the nearby towns, picked his battles. He was a firm ally of Stockton and his associates. He knew he could possibly obtain a reward from New Mexico authorities for arresting Stockton. It was not a task he desired to undertake. He was not without courage and while not all crimes in Rico were penalized, he kept the lid from blowing completely off. He was a native of Arkansas and had spent time near Fort Concho in Texas before arriving in Colorado. He had been a drinker in Texas, but gave that up, which was unusual in Colorado's mining camps. His sobriety contributed to his success as an officer of the law. He was a large man and his control of the town was based on a combination of fear and respect. In the earliest days of Rico, he was also often backed up by his deputy marshal, Jim Sullivan, a man whom Charles Jones described as having "a natural killer instinct." One of Cart's closest friends was Barney Watson who would soon be the sheriff of La Plata County. Watson and Jim Sullivan were destined to play a key role in the saga of Ike Stockton. When young Charles Jones first arrived in the San Juan country, Cart was the marshal of Silverton and notwithstanding their age difference, they began a lifelong friendship. At that time Cart was thirty-three and Jones was seventeen. Cart was also close friends with Hargo Eskridge, enlisting him on a temporary basis to work as a deputy marshal. The arrangement is evidence that Hargo was viewed as a man who could take care of himself. The relationship kept Hargo's wild side in check. Cart, like many at that time, was uneducated. He said he had attended school for three weeks and according to Jones he often said, "and I'm sorry I went that long."[38]

The Rico trip was the last time that Stockton or Eskridge would be heard from for a long time and they made the most of it. They found time to write a letter to the governor of New Mexico, with a similar letter going to Governor Pitkin. They alleged that the New Mexico requisitions "were obtained by misrepresentation and perjury of men who have sworn to kill us." The letter was printed in its entirety in the *Dolores News*. It proclaimed, "We have never committed a crime against the laws of the United States, of Colorado or of New Mexico." The two men offered to turn themselves into New Mexico authorities, so long as it was not in Rio Arriba County. They advised the governor that they were in Rico tending to their mining interests and said that any communications sent to Rico would reach them. The letter ends with a cordial closing, "Yours, very respectfully, J.H. Eskridge, I.T. Stockton."[39] Years later, Charles Jones acknowledged that he had actually written the letters.[40] The letter does not appear in the correspondence to Governor Wallace for the period in question, but that does not necessarily mean it was not sent and received. A week after the *Dolores News* printed the letter, the *New Mexican* said that a visitor from Colorado claimed "Ike Stockton is anxious to 'play quits,' and would give up if he could make favorable terms with the authorities." The newspaper said some people did not place much confidence that Stockton would keep his word in the matter.[41] It seems that Stockton was actually trying to extricate himself from the situation he now faced. However, there is no record that Ike made a firm proposition or that New Mexico authorities followed up on any feelers. Even though Stockton and Hargo Eskridge had a safe refuge in southwest Colorado, they faced steady unending pressure because of the New Mexico warrants and rewards.

In the meantime, Indian trouble simmered on the Utah/Colorado border. On May 28th, the much aggrieved and aggravated Billy May turned up in Rico. He was loaded for bear.[42] He proceeded to recruit men for a Civilian Punitive Expedition against the Indians. In the view of May and others, if Colonel Crofton was not going to take action, then the people would have to do it. At the same time cattleman Louis Paquin was recruiting volunteers in the Mancos valley and one of the Willis brothers was doing the same in Parrott City.[43] May used the story of the gruesome death of his brother to spur the Rico men to action. May reported that during the months prior to the killing many Indians had stopped by Thurman's ranch and partook of his hospitality. He also said that after the attack the Indians mutilated the horses they did not take. According to May, they gouged the eyes out of some, hamstrung others, and further mutilated horses by cutting their ears off. He topped that off with accounts of the cowboys being chased off the Blue Mountain roundup. A large motivated contingent of Ricoites responded to the call. Ike Stockton, Hargo Eskridge and M.C. Cook were part of that group.[44]

Hargo may have played the leading role in convincing Stockton and Cook to join the Civilian Punitive Expedition. Eskridge knew May. When he had lived in the *Dolores News* office/residence with Hartman, Jones and Wilkinson, their next door neighbor was Billy May.[45] Other factors also played into the decision. Perhaps Stockton and Cook were motivated by the horrific Kiowa or Comanche atrocities which were commonplace during their early years in the Cross Timbers of Texas, just as their Indian counterparts were driven by stories they had heard or acts they had witnessed committed by white men. Ike felt that the benefits of his participation outweighed any risks. The effort would take them far away from the New Mexico border and it would be viewed as a commendable action. As the month of May drew to a close, cowboys, miners, prospectors, freighters and others gathered at the Big Bend. Rico men represented the largest contingent. The *Dolores News* noted, "The party from Rico number 31 and they are all stayers." In the same vein, Hartman and Jones continued, "It is said by those who are personally acquainted with nearly all the men who are in the outfit that it is the best lot of men who ever started out for a purpose of this kind, having been on the frontier for many years and have had brushes with Indians before."[46]

Before the civilians were fully organized, the ponderously slow U.S. Army swung into action. In late May, Captain Rogers finally moved out from Fort Lewis. On May 26th he sent a dispatch to the Fort from his camp seventeen miles from the Dolores at Chicken Creek. Crofton had already sent orders that E Company, Thirteenth Infantry and five wagons return to Fort Lewis. The O'Donnell brothers, Louis Paquin and other cowboys were also camped at Chicken Creek. Rogers was advised about the recruitment effort that was going on in Rico and elsewhere. The captain was under the impression that the cowboys intended to gather their stock and only if necessary fight the Indians. He proposed to travel to the vicinity of the roundup along Blue Mountain to offer his protection. In a dispatch to Crofton he said, "I think there will be trouble out there within 8 days."[47] Marshal Heffernan, with a bit of intrigue, wrote Crofton a letter, which began, "This note is private." He advised the colonel that the cattlemen were determined to fight the Indians. He said in three days one hundred armed civilians would start their pursuit.[48] Some of the soldiers were not so anxious for battle. Shortly after arriving in camp at the Big Bend, two of them deserted, taking their rifles and pistols. On May 29th, Captain Rogers delayed the start of his scheduled foray into Utah. Instead of searching for Paiutes and Utes, his men spent the day looking for the two deserters. It seems they had no luck. He did report that the D.D. Williams Ranch had been burned by Indians. He advised Colonel Crofton that his intent was to leave for Blue Mountain on May 30th for a ten day scout.[49]

Captain Rogers and his soldiers would not be part of the hostilities, but the Indian war Captain Haines had predicted was about to begin. Consequently, the nerve-wracked residents of western Rio Arriba County would see a lengthy cessation in the activities of the Stockton Gang. But where Ike went, action followed close behind. Ike Stockton, Hargo Eskridge and M.C. Cook were joining a larger struggle which began when Christopher Columbus first set foot in the Americas. The wanted outlaws would participate in a chase and battle that was one of the last of its kind, and they would have the attention of America from coast to coast.

Perhaps like one of the "stayers" from Rico appeared as the Coloradoans prepared to pursue Utes. Frederic Remington's "Old-style Texan Cowman," from Theodore Roosevelt's "Ranch Life in the Far West," The Century Illustrated Monthly Magazine, *Vol. 35, No. 4, February 1888. (Author's Collection.)*

Chapter Fifteen

Battle in the La Sals

A winding, wooded canyon road
That mortals seldom tread
Leads up this lonely mountain
To this desert of the dead.[1]

While Ike and others gathered at the Big Bend, a wave of Indian hysteria rolled across southwest Colorado. Reports verged on the fantastic. Families from the Mancos valley and points to the west were streaming into Animas City and Durango to take refuge.[2] A stunned James I. (Jimmie) Hall, the Mancos school teacher, sent his account of events to the *Durango Record*. He reported that numerous signal fires were visible on the mesas and hills around the little village and one was even found within twenty yards of the school house. No one knew how it started.[3] The *Record* said, "They report four hundred braves encamped in their neighborhood, without their women, children, or old men, which they considered a sufficient indication of hostile intentions."[4] Those who remained behind gathered in numbers as a deterrent. The *Record* advised that they "have built a stockade around the school house, near [George] Bauer's Store, and are making all possible preparations for protecting themselves in case of attack."[5]

Over at the Big Bend, Stockton, Eskridge and Cook were preparing to move out with the rest of the civilians. The men believed the Indians would be routed in any fight and some believed they would run rather than fight. They may have been encouraged by a letter written by Governor Pitkin, which was printed in the *Durango Record* on May 23rd. It had originally been written in response to an inquiry by J.E. Clark, who was identified as the "Acting" deputy sheriff of Gunnison, Colorado. The letter described the limitations and authority as Pitkin saw them for apprehending Indian outlaws. Pitkin said, "The decision of the United States Court was that the State courts had no jurisdiction over criminals who commit crimes on the reservation." On the other hand he said, "If the crime was committed off the reservation, you can follow the criminals on to the reservation if necessary to make the arrests." But then he added a caveat, saying, "You had better advise with the District Attorney, who knows all the facts."[6] The cowboys on the Dolores were not concerned with legalities, but if the renegades sought sanctuary on Indian lands, Pitkin's words had given them a loophole they could ride a horse through.

The Four Corners region from an edited portion of a map of Colorado, Utah, New Mexico and Arizona. Rand McNally Standard Atlas of the World, *1888. (Map page is from the author's collection.)*

Billy May had gone to great effort to recruit men, yet he was not chosen to lead the expedition. The men selected William H. "Bill" Dawson, a thirty-eight-year-old native of Missouri as their captain. Billy May may have acquiesced to this decision, but his judgment was clouded by the loss of his brother, and he determined to go his own way if he believed circumstances called for it. May's lust for revenge, combined with his fragile emotional state did not bode well for the cohesive military style action which was essential for the expedition's success.[7] On June 2nd

Dawson and his men crossed the Utah line and headed toward Blue Mountain, which loomed on the western horizon.[8]

Captain Rogers had already left the Big Bend and set up camp about a mile north of O'Donnell's cow camp cabin on Blue Mountain. They found the cabin intact, but the insides ransacked. Spud Hudson's cabin had suffered a similar fate. Stockton and his associates arrived at Captain Rogers's camp on the evening of June 3rd. They were part of a group of fifty-four men and they traveled with three wagons. That same night Louis Paquin and three others began a scout toward the crest of Blue Mountain. Marshal Heffernan reported that Paquin was riding a white horse and characterized it as a "bold and gamy enterprise." The soldiers had standing orders that if they encountered Indians to fire if fired upon. The *Durango Record* carried an account based on information received from Heffernan, who proclaimed, "All of the men were perfectly crazy to get a whack at the redskins." Heffernan said that on June 4th the troops did approach an Indian camp, but the Paiutes "fled from the village, and built barricades." After the scouting expedition by Paquin and other similarly aggressive actions by the cattlemen, Captain Rogers finally realized that the civilians were not there to gather cattle and they intended to seek out the Indians and force a fight. According to Heffernan's account, "On Sunday, June 5th, the military being out of rations, moved back to the Big Bend of the Dolores." Ike Stockton and the rest of the civilians were on their own.[9]

The day after the soldiers departed the Indians made their presence known by stealing several horses. According to Heffernan a group of cowboys "pursued them and kept on their trail until they had made a circuit of the south and west sides of Blue Mountain, to Indian Creek."[10] Spud Hudson was leading this group and their circuitous and tortuous path took them through the mesmerizing canyon and rimrock country common in southeast Utah and out of the looming battle.[11]

At some point Dawson sent Green Robinson and one of the O'Donnell brothers to kill and butcher a beef. While cutting out a steer, Marshal Heffernan said that they were attacked by eight Indians. They took off without looking back, arriving at the Big Bend thirty-six hours later. Heffernan reported that Billy May and five other men went out to find Robinson and O'Donnell.[12] They did not locate the two cowboys and soon rejoined Dawson's command.

Once Captain Rogers left Blue Mountain, reports from the civilian forces became sparse and narratives gathered from witnesses many years later are confusing and at times contradictory. Even accounts made at the time are muddled. On June 18th, the *Dolores News* reported that the cattlemen had killed two Indians near the Big Bend.[13] This was no doubt a belated version of the earlier J.H. Alderson and Green Robinson reports which said two saddled Indian horses had been seized, although both men failed to mention that two Indians had been killed in the process.[14] The

Indians were also out for blood and eighteen miles east of Monticello they encountered a lone prospector. He was unaware and uninvolved in the trouble, but the Indians killed him anyway.[15]

In most of New Mexico and Colorado, newspapers were not yet aware that Ike Stockton and Hargo Eskridge were out pursuing Indians. There was a sudden break in activity by Stockton and his men in northwest New Mexico and many were erroneously attributing the cool down to the border patrols of the San Juan Guards. The *Rio Grande Republican* of Las Cruces said that the militia were "keeping desperadoes out of their section of Rio Arriba county."[16] Even Dison didn't know that Ike and Hargo were out chasing Indians. On June 7th he showed up in Rico looking for his brother.[17]

Ike, Hargo and M.C. Cook were still traveling with Captain Dawson, while Spud Hudson's cowboys crept north along the west side of Blue Mountain. Dawson's men believed the Indians would head to the La Sal Mountains, just east of Moab. They left Blue Mountain behind and headed directly toward the La Sals, confident that they would find their quarry. Along the way, the euphoria of the early days of the expedition began to fade. In a later account, Colonel Henry Page, the Southern Ute Indian Agent, said that, "dissensions arose among them" and "the ranks of the men were weakened from day to day."[18] There is no doubt that the ardor found at the Big Bend was long gone. While some headed back to their homes in Colorado, Stockton, Eskridge and Cook stayed. The next day Dawson's remnant band continued their trek toward the La Sals. The long expected battle was imminent and that night Dawson sent a man down toward the Grand River (now known as the Colorado), to the tiny community of Moab to get help. Captain Dawson's fatigued men and horses were in desperate shape, yet they pushed on.[19]

At this point, nothing had been heard from the Civilian Punitive Expedition since the reported killing of two Indians in early June. Some general information showed up in the press. On June 16th, the *Cimarron News and Press* announced that, "most of the Ike Stockton gang have gone where they will do the most good and joined May's company."[20] (Since May's intensive recruitment efforts had sparked the expedition, he was still viewed as the defacto leader.) Three days later the *Santa Fe New Mexican* editorialized that, "Stockton and his men are reported as hunting for Utes, an employment in which they are better engaged than is usual for them."[21] In the middle of June a hint of accurate new information and misinformation finally reached the Dolores valley. The *Dolores News* announced that Mr. Frink had just come into Rico and carried news that two of Captain Dawson's men had recently arrived at the Big Bend to get provisions. They said that the civilians had pursued the Indians toward the Grand River where they overtook them. They believed a large-scale battle had already taken place. According to the newly arrived men, the expedition force numbered about one hundred and the number of Indian warriors was about the same.[22] Based on that news, Dison Eskridge and another man named J.F. Hume made plans to ride toward the Big Bend.[23] George West's herder, the mulatto Kid Thomas, also headed to the Big Bend.[24]

By this time the Coloradoans had reached the La Sals. Many years later, Jordan Bean recalled that before the battle began the men determined that those who survived would rendezvous at their camp on Mill Creek. They also acknowledged the fearful necessity to retain at least one round in their weapon for themselves.[25] Dawson's initial force had dwindled to about thirty-eight, including Stockton, Eskridge and Cook. At about 8:30 on Thursday morning, June 16th, Ike Stockton and the others happened upon about one hundred Indians in their encampment near the forks of Mill Creek. (Many accounts say the battle began on June 15th.) A *Dolores News* account of this encounter put the number of warriors at sixty-five with "35 being old men and squaws." (The exact opposite of what the San Juan County Assessor reported on May 15th.) The Indians were breaking camp when they spotted the Colorado men, who were three-quarters of a mile away. The Indians left much of their camp trappings on the ground, and pulled out. It was the moment Dawson and his men had been waiting for and they prepared for battle.[26] At the same time a party of twelve men were on their way from Moab. Two of those men were L.F. Flood and William Shea. In a letter written just five days later, Flood and Shea said that the Colorado men came within sight of the Indian camp and "They [the Indians] were packing up to leave and the boys were anxious for a fight and made an attack."[27]

However, a later account in the *Durango Herald* said that before the battle began, "May ordered a halt and displayed a white flag, indicating that he wished to have a parley. This friendly advance was met with a volley of about forty shots, and the whites had no other recourse left but to fire back, which their captain ordered them to do."[28] Whatever happened, the two forces began a battle that would last most of the day. The *Dolores News* later described the action, saying, "The squaws with the papooses were driving what stock they could, while the bucks retreated more slowly, fighting and giving way." Early in the battle the Coloradoans were able to capture about 140 horses which had broken away. Holding the horse herd may have further reduced Dawson's fighting force.[29] The battle began about three miles from the ranch of Alfred Wilson, one of the first settlers of Moab. The combatants battled their way north through the La Sals, crossing Wilson's summer stock range, which included Bald Mesa. A narrative of the fight provided by Wilson described the action as "a fierce and bloody struggle, the Indians backing toward the ranch and fighting desperately all the time." Wilson's two sons, Alfred and Isadore, were at the ranch cabin and about noon the battle overtook them. They joined forces with the Coloradoans.[30]

Near Mason Spring the men stopped and gathered round.[31] The spring is about 8300 feet in elevation and the view is panoramic. Red rock spires and a round bluff jut above the valley floor and beyond in the distance are the sheer red rock bluffs along the west side of the Colorado River. The most intense fighting was still ahead and the men were already worn out from the day's action. The Indians fled down the Pinhook valley or, as it is sometimes called, Pinhook Draw. The drainage eventually feeds into the Castle valley. The head of the Pinhook valley is about three-quarters of a mile east of Mason Spring. The men left the spring and trailed the Indians eastward, across a steep hillside. Stopping at the heights, they were in an area that featured Douglas fir and other species common to the higher slopes of the mountains. They peered down into the three mile long and normally waterless Pinhook valley.[32] Behind them were the lofty peaks of the La Sals and the verdure of the high mountains. The view to the northwest, down the valley, is unobstructed. The bottom of the valley is about one-third to one-half mile wide with steep slopes on both sides. The valley bottom is covered with thickets of scrub (Gambel's) oak, with the occasional piñon and juniper jutting above it. The slope is moderate and easily traversed on foot. The bottom of the valley is virtually devoid of boulders, but it is so wide that it is transected by three ravines which run parallel with each other for almost two miles before they finally converge. There are a few boulders against the southwestern side of the valley, but none in sufficient quantity to provide cover for a large group of men. About a mile and a half below their vantage point on the northeastern side of the valley is a rocky promontory which juts out from the hillside. Below that is a talus slope of rolled boulders, many of them suitable for hiding one or several men. From the heights, the Coloradoans caught glimpses of the flocks of goats and sheep as the women and children herded them down the valley. Floating above the oak was a hazy trail of dust created by the moving flocks. Dawson and his men could not be sure if the men were also with the flocks. The problem confronting the Coloradoans was that once they entered the oak thickets, their view would become very limited. Some of the men did not like the lay of the land and there was a vociferous debate about their next course of action.

The outcome of the battle was determined at this juncture. According to Frank Silvey, Captain Dawson advocated a direct pursuit into the draw. Billy May wanted to travel along the edge of the mesa, colorfully named the Porcupine Rim, on the southwestern side of the valley. May hoped to find a cut in the vertical sandstone bluff into the valley and intercept the Indians.[33] It seems strange that the Wilson boys, who were intimately familiar with the local terrain, did not argue forcefully against the futility of that action. It is apparent that not all of the battle's participants made it to the parley and perhaps the Wilsons and others straggled in later. Including the Wilson boys, the white men were forty strong, but only a meager nineteen men would continue on with Captain Dawson. This group included Ike Stockton, Hargo Eskridge and the Wilsons. They headed into the Pinhook valley. That left twenty-one men.[34] Some of that number may have been guarding captured horses. Billy May took the rest and began the ride down the Porcupine Rim in a fruitless search for a drop-off, where they could cut off the Indians.

View of the Castle Valley and the canyon of the Colorado from near Mason Spring in the La Sal Mountains. Close to this location Ike Stockton, Hargo Eskridge and other members of the Colorado forces gathered to prepare for their battle with Indians in the Pinhook Valley. (Author's collection.)

Dawson's tiny force was also on a foolhardy mission. While the white men argued, the Indians had decided to make a stand. The Paiutes and Utes had the disadvantage of traveling with women, children and animals, but that was balanced out by their knowledge of the terrain.[35] According to Bean, "Dawson picked Dick Curtis, Harg Eskridge, Ike Stockton, Harg [Hardin or Hard] Tartar, Billy Parks and myself to overtake the Indians."[36]

Ike, Hargo and the other men moved downstream toward the dust being raised by the goats and sheep. The Indian warriors were ready for the battle they hoped would allow their wives and children to escape. The white men stayed well away from the boulder strewn slope, which was the obvious site for an ambush. The path taken by Dawson's men played right into the Indian's hands. The bulk of the Indian forces gathered on the southwestern side of the valley, opposite the bouldered slope, about a mile and a half down the valley, using scrub oak for concealment. The dearth of boulders on that side meant only a few of their number had bulletproof barriers. The waiting Indians were patience personified.[37] The men dismounted and advanced on foot.[38] The decision to travel on foot was hastened by the thousands of sharp edged cobbles, which stick two to five inches above the ground about a foot apart and cover every portion of the valley floor. Despite Dawson's desire to maintain two separate forces, most of his men were now in close proximity. According to Frank Silvey, the wary Coloradoans advanced slowly, eventually entering an opening in the oak thicket. The Indians had been waiting for just this moment. As about a dozen of them neared the center of the opening, the Indians opened fire; four of the Coloradoans fell in the initial volley. The others were in total disarray and dashed for the nearest ravine.[39] At about three to five feet deep, with gently sloping sides, the valley's ravines did not provide a safe haven. The tilt of the valley floor is too steep to provide for the development of cutbanks and vertical walls common to the arroyos of the American southwest. Hargo Eskridge and James Hall, by sheer luck, plunged into one of the rare sections with a modest cave-like cut in the bank. There they would make their stand.[40] Hall and Eskridge shared some similarities. While Hall had been born in Alabama, he spent most of his childhood in the east, in Pennsylvania. When he was sixteen he headed west to Texas, where he joined in the last great buffalo hunt and later became a cowboy. In 1878 he moved to Colorado and joined the search for mineral riches. That quest had taken him to Rico. Now he was burrowed into a sandy arroyo, surrounded by Indians who had just killed several of his friends.[41]

Not all of Hall's allies were on foot. Jordan Bean was riding with Hard Tartar when Tartar's horse was shot out from under him. They soon found an old Ute mare and roped it. Tartar continued the battle, riding bareback using a rope halter.[42] Those who sought shelter in the ravine were pinned down and unable to escape. The Indian's ambush was well planned, but a few men escaped the initial volley. Those who were not trapped included Captain Dawson, Ike Stockton, Charles Bullock, Dick Curtis, Billy Parks and Tim Jenkins.[43] They were still mounted and rode in as close as possible. After dismounting, Stockton and his companions began to pour fire into the area where they believed many of the Indians were hidden.[44] Their position provided them with an ample view of the hillside, but their view down the valley floor was limited. The Paiutes and Utes still held the advantage.

In the ravine, the cornered men held on. They faced attacks from mounted horsemen, while other Indians advanced on foot and fired on their position. According to one account, as many as sixteen mounted Indians armed with Winchesters harried the trapped men.[45] In addition to

Frederic Remington's "An Episode in the Opening Up of a Cattle Country," from Theodore Roosevelt's "Ranch Life in the Far West," The Century Illustrated Monthly Magazine, *Vol. 35, No. 4, February, 1888. (Author's collection.)*

the four already killed, six of those trapped in the ravine would be killed before the day was through. Hargo Eskridge and Jimmie Hall were surrounded and had serious gunshot wounds, but they had an ample supply of ammunition, which they used judiciously. The Indians kept up their attack, but to advance on Eskridge and Hall proved to be a deadly task. The two men waited for a final attack or for rescue. Dawson knew the two trapped men were alive and called for a volunteer to go in and encourage them to come out. Several men volunteered and Pat McKenney an Irish prospector was chosen. (Some accounts identify Tim Jenkins as the man who went to aid Eskridge and Hall.) He removed his chaps and stripped down to his underwear. He crawled part way and upon reaching the edge of the open area, made a mad dash for the arroyo. The Indians opened fire, but McKenney was fleet of foot and dove over the embankment. He found Eskridge and Hall huddled in the sand beneath the undercut ravine. With their wounds, there was no way they could make a sprint to safety. The men decided their only hope was to wait until dark. As the sun dropped below the red sandstone bluffs along the Colorado, the three men ventured out from their sandy redoubt, made their way up the valley, and rejoined Dawson's ragged band.[46] Jordan Bean was not so fortunate. He had been struck in the head by a bullet, rendering him unable to leave the battlefield as darkness fell. He spent a long, lonely night separated from his companions.[47]

Billy May and his group were still missing in action, but help was on the way.[48] According to L.F. Flood and William Shea, they and several other men from Moab arrived on the scene at dusk. They wrote, "Our party got up after the battle was over, and night coming on we could not do anything until next day."[49] With the night time arrival of McKenney, Eskridge and Hall, the Coloradoans realized that nine of their comrades were missing. That number included Jordan Bean, but not the two Wilson brothers.[50]

The next morning Dawson was anxious to search for possible survivors. With extra men now available, he left a protective guard with Eskridge and Hall, while the others rode out toward the scene of the battle.[51] Jordan Bean was found alive. He recovered from his wounds and lived a very long life. Many of his comrades suffered fatal wounds in the battle and fifty-nine years later, knowing that fate would soon exact its final toll, the old cowboy recalled the fight and paid tribute to the faithfulness of his fallen friends: "I lost my horse a big dapple grey but knowing that bunch of boys as I did I know they will take care of him until I get there."[52]

Surprisingly, the Indians had not fled during the night. They believed they held the upper hand, not realizing that the men from Moab had reinforced Dawson's group. Flood and Shea recalled that second morning, saying, "[We] went out of camp with ten Colorado boys, making twenty men of our company. Coming on to the battle ground we were going to bury Mr. Willis, who got killed the day before, when the Indians under cover of heavy cedar on the mountain side, poured in a heavy fire on us."[53] Like the day before, the white men found themselves in an untenable position. They returned fire and retreated. During the battle, a white-haired Indian woman, worn out from the events of the previous days and separated from the other Indians, was shot and killed.[54] Some reports said she was killed while herding sheep.[55] The white men rode for the cover of an aspen grove on the hillside of Bald Mesa.[56] The Indians were intent on total annihilation and kept up their attack. According to Flood the Indians fought "with as much desperation and courage as any Indians ever known to our most experienced frontiersmen, but with all the Indian cunning our boys poured in such a galling, fire that they had to retreat, with a loss of 5 or 6 warriors."[57] The Colorado cattlemen and their Moab allies were stunned by the ferocity of the Indians. Dawson sent D.G. Taylor and Tom Pepper on a desperate 140 mile journey to the populated areas of southwest Colorado, hoping one of them would get through. Taylor was bound for Rico and Pepper for the Mancos valley.[58] Dawson certainly realized that reinforcements from southwest Colorado would never arrive in time to save them, but Taylor and Pepper could at least bear witness in case all of Dawson's men were killed. As the day wore on, the Indian casualties mounted and they realized that the white men were not the same demoralized group they had faced the day before. At about 5:00 PM the renegade band moved out.[59]

It is unclear what happened to Billy May and his group after they rode down the Porcupine Rim. According to one account he did rejoin Dawson's group after the first day of battle.[60] That is incorrect, since the couriers sent out by Dawson, on the second day, had not seen him and did not know where he was, but they did know details from the second day of battle. Perhaps May's band rejoined with Dawson on the evening of the second day or sometime thereafter. The *Durango Record* later reported that, "It is supposed that the May party, who were cut off by the Indians, went to join the McCarthy party, as they have not been heard from."[61] (The McCarthy party was no doubt the McCarty family who lived near La Sal.)[62] One account said May and his men had ridden for miles along the ridge of the Porcupine Rim.[63] The cowboys viewed a panorama that beggars description; in places the sheer vertical drop from the top of the bluff was greater than four hundred feet and the floor of the Castle valley was an incredible two thousand feet below the rim. As the Wilson brothers could have told him, there was no pathway into the valley. Billy May had missed his opportunity to strike back at the Indians.[64]

After two days of carnage, the white men were of the same mind as the Indians. They rode out of the La Sals. The Moab rescue party still feared an Indian attack, so they rode home through the night. That evening Moab's residents sought shelter in the old "Mormon Fort." The Indians were headed in the other direction and that day they were seen about fifteen miles northwest of Moab in the Onion valley, still herding a sizable number of horses.[65] Moab's residents remained forted up for several days.[66]

According to the *Dolores News*, "The dead bodies were found on the fourth day, (Sunday) and were so decomposed that it was almost impossible to bury them at all, but were buried about where they fell."[67] (Parentheses are in the original article.) The father of the two dead Wilson brothers reported that the bodies of his sons "were found in a pile with those of six other white men, who had evidently fallen while struggling shoulder to shoulder." The body of Dave Willis was found about 150 yards away.[68] John B. "Tarheel Jack" Galloway was found with one of his hands neatly bound with a white handkerchief. The men never found the body of T.C. Taylor and he was presumed dead. Willis was buried where he was found. Alfred and Isadore Wilson were interred with "Tarheel Jack," Hiram Melvin and Tom Click. Three other Colorado men, Hard and Wiley Tartar and James A. Heaton were buried separately, but nearby.[69] Jordan Bean said the men were buried "chaps and all."[70] The results of the battle were horrific for both sides. The total Indian casualties are not known. In a letter written to the *Deseret News* on July 6, 1881, Alfred Wilson and two other men said, "It is believed that there were 25 or 30 Indians killed, but cannot say definitely."[71] The *Dolores News* said that about eighteen Indians were killed.[72] In September 1881, William Boot drove a herd of beef cattle into Ouray from Utah. He had passed through portions of the battlefield and reported it still held evidence of a desperate fight. On the same excursion, he learned that the Utes were admitting that sixteen of their number had been killed during the fight.[73] Mancos Jim, who ended up with Dave Willis's Sharps rifle, said twenty-two of his Indian comrades were killed.[74]

On the same day that the nine men were buried (Sunday, June 19th), Dawson's messengers, D.G. Taylor and Tom Pepper, reached the Big Bend. Durango butcher Charles A. King happened to be there and rapidly rode to Durango, arriving late on the 21st or early on the 22nd.[75] Taylor rode into Rico on the evening of June 21st. Both towns were thrown into an uproar. In Rico, Taylor said that as many as seven of Dawson's men may have been killed and that Eskridge, Hall and Bean were wounded. The *Dolores News* announced that, "Mr. Wm. May, who has the death of a brother to avenge seems to have become displeased, and left the main party. It is not known by the courier where he is with his squad."[76] Despite the distance and what looked like a hopeless situation, a rescue expedition was organized. Many of those who volunteered were residents of Rico. Men began to gather their horses and supplies. Dison Eskridge, Kid Thomas and others were already at the Big Bend, ready to go.

In the meantime news of the battle was telegraphed across the nation from Amargo. The generally erroneous stories were riveting, colorful, exaggerated and filled with the prejudice of the time. The exploits of the wanted outlaw, Hargo Eskridge, received prominence. The *Sacramento Daily Record-Union* carried a Denver dispatch which reported that, "J.H. Eskridge, the Wilson Brothers and all the settlers in Grand Valley are supposed to have been killed. Eighteen or twenty of the original party of cattlemen have been missing for several days, and are supposed to be killed. Among them is Ike Stockton."[77] The *Denver Republican* declared that Eskridge was killed as the result of six bullets.[78] The *Saguache Chronicle* declared "A.G. Eskredge" was alive, but his foot had been shot off.[79] According to the *Durango Record*, "J.H. Eskridge was cut off from the party and 30 Indians charged on him. He laid down in a clump of bushes and picked them off with his rifle until it was too hot, when he opened on them with two revolvers, killing twelve Indians. The boys then came to his rescue, and found that he had received only one wound in the ankle and his clothes were riddled with bullets."[80] The *Chicago Times* carried extensive coverage of the skirmish gathered from reports coming out of Durango and Rico. The *Salt Lake Herald* carried news of the battle in their territory from the Chicago dispatch and noted that, "Ike Stockton was not killed as reported."[81] The *Dolores News* said that, "Eskridge, whom it is supposed the Indians believed to be captain, (as he had a large, gaudy Chihuahua hat,) had the hat riddled with bullets so that it cannot be worn, and his hair was nearly all cut off with scalp wounds and grazing bullets." At the *News*, Hartman and Jones worried that Eskridge's ankle wound was so serious it would require amputation, if he survived long enough to reach a doctor.[82] The *Ouray Times* carried a letter about the battle from F.W. Raymond, who reported, "Our boys fought them hand to hand, killing the red devils with their revolvers, Eskridge alone killing four and receiving twenty bullet holes through his clothing."[83]

The *Dolores News* under the headlines, "WAR! WITH THE INDIANS" and "Rico Sends Forth Another Bold Little Army," hysterically proclaimed that the Indians had received reinforcements and now numbered several hundred warriors.[84] Some later estimates put the number of Indian warriors as thirty or less.[85] Charles Jones joined the Pinhook Rescue Expedition. He reported that the initial group numbered forty-six men.[86] By the time they reached Piute Springs that number was reduced to twenty-six men because of weakening mounts. Among the twenty-six were Charles Jones, Dison Eskridge, Kid Thomas, D.G. Taylor and Gus (Heffron) Hefferman. Worden (Ward) Grigsby, who served on the Rico town council, was unanimously selected as captain of the expedition. They made the approximately 140 mile trip to the Coyote Ranch (near present day La Sal, Utah) in two and half days, arriving there at 11:00 at night. Along the way two more men dropped out because their horses could not keep up the pace. At Coyote they met two of Dawson's party, horse trader J.H. Alderson and Bob Brown. They confirmed the stunning news and gave the full details of the tragedy. Most of the men realized that the so-called war was over and the next day some of the rescue party set out for Rico. Nineteen continued on to the battle site, guided by local rancher George McCarty. Charles Adam Jones and Dison Eskridge were part of this group and they still hoped to find Indians to fight.[87] In 1893, Jones recalled the rescue mission in an article for the *Overland Monthly* magazine. Under the penname Jones Adams, he recalled the ride into the La Sals: "Upon the high mesa to the left were many poles of abandoned teepees sharply outlined against the western sky, and as the trail led under a bluff, the bloody hat of Jimmie Heaton was picked up." Before reaching the main battlefield, nightfall came. They made camp, tying their horses in a grove of aspens.[88] The next day they searched for more clues to what had happened and descended into Pinhook Draw. The battlefield was littered with debris from both the Indians and the Colorado men. They found Jimmy Heaton's notebook, a letter to one of the Tartars, as well as arrows and some jingle-bobs used to ornament Indian bridles. The men also found the body of the dead Indian woman. She was left where she was found.[89] Further on they found Jack Galloway's old Spencer carbine with an exploded shell in the breech, rendering the weapon useless. They left it on the side of the arroyo.[90]

Somewhere along the trail they came across Jimmy Heaton's black stallion. The horse had been shot, but it was only a flesh wound. One of the men appropriated it to replace his worn out mount. Upon their return to Rico the horse was returned to Heaton's grieving father. Before leaving the area, the men spread out and conducted an intensive search for the body of T.C. Taylor, but never found his remains. The search party theorized that he had been wounded in the battle and managed to crawl to a concealed crevice or other hiding place. (Indeed, thirty-three years after the battle, Taylor's body was finally found. On May 22, 1914, Moab's *Grand Valley Times* reported that Robert G. Bryant had located Taylor's remains under a rock on a hillside near the battlefield. An old saddle was laying nearby.) After failing to find Taylor's body, the searchers moved away from the scene of the fight and followed the trail of the Indians for several miles. Along the way they found two sites with bloody rags strewn about, where the Indians had stopped to dress wounds. Finally, the Coloradoans were ready to return to Rico. At the edge of the La Sals they stopped at a ranch where an elderly couple, Mr. and Mrs. Tom Goshorn, lived. As Jones recalled, "They had a few milk cows and never was milk so appreciated." Afterwards the group called themselves the "Buttermilk Rangers," an appellation they retained throughout their time in the San Juan country.[91]

About noon on the same day that D.G. Taylor arrived in Rico (June 21st), Captain Carroll and the Buffalo Soldiers left Fort Lewis on an extended patrol, taking with them a supply train of sixteen wagons.[92] The chances that Carroll would ever catch up to the Indians while operating a wagon train were less than slim. Some of Carroll's soldiers were unwilling to take that chance. The day before Carroll left, he charged three privates with desertion and theft. Some were unwilling to desert, but had no stomach for fighting Utes. Two days after leaving Fort Lewis, Carroll reported that two men had "accidentally" shot themselves.[93] The rest of the troops were ready for action. In newspapers Carroll is often identified as "a noted Indian fighter."[94] He had been busily engaged fighting Apaches in southern New Mexico for several years. In September 1876, Ninth Cavalry troops under his command killed fourteen Chiricahua Apaches near the Florida Mountains south of Deming.[95] In the spring of 1880, Carroll and seven of his soldiers had been wounded while battling Mescalero Apaches in the San Andres Mountains north of Las Cruces.[96]

On their return trip Dawson's bedraggled men and members of the Rico Rescue Expedition crossed paths with Captain Carroll and his troops.[97] Carroll asked for help tracking the Indians. Dick Curtis and Gus Hefferman of Rico volunteered.[98] Hefferman was apparently not concerned that he was implicated in the murder of three members of the Ninth Cavalry back in Cimarron. The men were accompanied by artist J.J. Reilly of *Frank Leslie's Illustrated Newspaper*.[99] Carroll and his troops did not return to Fort Lewis until noon on July 10th and soon went out on another scout.¹⁰⁰ Their search was fruitless as the deadly and cantankerous band of Indians had evaporated.

When Dawson and his men met with Captain Carroll they sought treatment for Hargo Eskridge and James Hall from Fort Lewis post doctor Bernard Byrne. The doctor was an acquaintance and friend of Tom Nance and knew that Eskridge had attempted to murder Nance. Byrne was not disposed to provide any more help than necessary for Eskridge. The *Dolores News* said "The army surgeon Byrnes [sic], who charged Eskridge and Hall $12 for telling them they were 'shot in bad places,' should also be shot in a bad place. Had he rendered aid at that time, they would have been out of danger ere this time."¹⁰¹

Upon their return to civilization some of the men grudgingly expressed a new appreciation for their Indian foes. Bob Brown, who was in on portions of the battle, said that he had heard all his life that in a fight one white man was worth a dozen Indians. After the battle, he said, "it should be turned right around. We fought them all day and never saw anything to shoot at, except now and then a puff of smoke, or a quick glimpse of an Indian head up among the rocks." It was a costly lesson.¹⁰²

The dusty, grimy men who rode into Rico and Durango were greeted as heroes, but for Ike Stockton the consequences of his participation in the Civilian Punitive Expedition were devastating. His chief ally, Hargo Eskridge, was out of action. In Durango he found that many of his associates had left and many of those who remained were looking out for themselves. As a consequence, he lost some of his zeal for continuing his battle with the Farmington crowd.

(Author's collection.)

Chapter Sixteen

The Albuquerque Capture

> *Then swift upon my steed I lept;*
> *My streaming eyes the desert swept;*
> *I saw the accursed where he crept*
> *Against the blood-red sun.*[1]

Stockton found that much had happened during his absence. In New Mexico, Governor Wallace was gone. When James A. Garfield was elected president in 1880, Wallace followed the custom of the time and submitted his resignation, with a note saying that he would accept reappointment. He was probably offered reappointment, but he had changed his mind. At the height of the Stockton turmoil in April, Wallace was anxious to turn over the reins of power to his successor. He noted, "In six years more I shall be sixty. I have spent enough time in this place."[2] On May 31st his wish was granted. The June 1, 1881 issue of the *New Mexican* announced that Lew Wallace had left town the day before for his home in Indiana. The new governor was General Lionel A. Sheldon.[3]

Governor Wallace had done much to improve conditions in New Mexico, but his successor still faced many of the same problems. Like Wallace, Sheldon was an attorney and former Union general. Among other duties during the War Between the States he served under Colonel James A. Garfield and then for General Grant at Vicksburg. As an Ohio delegate to the 1880 Republican convention he played a key role in securing the presidential nomination for his old commanding officer. After Garfield became president, Sheldon and his wife spent several weeks as guests at the White House. In early May 1881, Garfield appointed him as governor of New Mexico. The new governor and his wife arrived in Santa Fe on the evening of June 3rd.[4]

Just two days before his arrival, Ike Stockton and the Colorado cowboys crossed into Utah to begin their epic Indian chase. Six days before that, a group of highwaymen began a crime spree along the border of New Mexico and Colorado. The torrent of lawlessness was led by Charlie Allison and other former associates of the Stockton-Eskridge crowd. Many residents in New Mexico and Colorado did not know that Allison had been blackballed from Ike's gang. Allison was a loud-mouthed, dangerous ne'er-do-well and Ike wisely shed him like a blood-gorged tick. At that point, Stockton should have stomped on him, but Allison was allowed to roam free and his road agent rampage would have catastrophic consequences for Ike and his closest allies. Allison had never been one for honest toil and he saw opportunity in the stage line operating between Amargo and Durango. Until the rail lines closed the gap, travelers, businessmen and others had few options but to ride the stage. In early May, Pueblo's *Colorado Chieftain* reported that the general superintendent for J.L. Sanderson and Company's stage lines, Harley Sanderson, had recently purchased "one hundred head of first class stage horses" in St. Louis. The horses were to be shipped by rail to Chama. The company planned on increasing end of the track service to Durango to three stages a day.[5]

As artist J.J. Reilly depicted his stagecoach trip to Durango. "Colorado.- Incidents of a Trip to the Mining Town of Durango," Frank Leslie's Illustrated Newspaper, *May 28, 1881. (Author's collection.)*

The packed coaches presented the perfect target for Charlie Allison and his road agents. Allison's entourage included Henry Watts, Lewis Perkins and Thomas Seely. Watts was twenty-three years old and had been raised in Tennessee. He had worked as cowboy in south Texas and in Colorado since he was fifteen or sixteen years old. Descriptions of the time note that he had a very dark complexion and black curly hair.[6] In fact, he may have been black or at least partly so. Watts and the recently lynched Henry Moorman had been captured in the Durango lumberyard after the murder of Polk Prindle.[7] Lew Perkins may have been from North Carolina and later moved to Nebraska. He was twenty years old. In recent years he had spent a fair amount of time in Albuquerque and was well known there.[8] Later press accounts often referred to him as the "Cross-eyed Kid"[9]. Seely, because of his small size, was known as "Little Tommy."[10]

Allison and his gang of coach robbers lived openly in a big tent in a small grove of trees below Amargo.[11] Those traveling to and from Durango often had no choice but to carry large sums of money or other valuables. They developed ingenious methods to hide their loot, but not all hiding places were foolproof. The stagecoach strong box was such an obvious target that many travelers disdained its use. Train passengers boarded the usually full stage in Amargo and traveled north to Pagosa Springs and then west to Durango. It was a scenic trip, but not much improved since the Cox and Graves families traveled over it a few years earlier. The road was isolated and sparsely populated.

Steam rises above the hot springs at Pagosa. "Colorado.- Incidents of a Trip to the Mining Town of Durango," Frank Leslie's Illustrated Newspaper, *May 28, 1881, artist J.J. Reilly. (Modified, author's collection.)*

At twilight on May 26, 1881 as the westbound coach traversed a rocky canyon about three miles west of Pagosa Springs, four unmasked armed men forced the driver to stop. The passengers were ordered out and their personal valuables were taken. The robbers took between $500 and $600 in cash, plus gold watches and other valuable jewelry. In addition, Peter Keegan, the D&RG Railroad contractor, was robbed of a company draft worth $3300. Passenger T.K. Gash was unable to travel to Durango without the occurrence of some noteworthy event. The major had only recently returned to the area from performing escort service for the body of I.W. Lacy. The bandits took one of the lead horses and replaced it with a small worn out dun "broncho" pony. After the highwaymen's work was done they shared a drink of whiskey with their victims and spoke openly of their plan to rob the eastbound coach and steal the stage horses, which were some of the new stock recently imported from St. Louis. Afterwards the Durango bound coach met the Amargo bound coach and shared their story; the eastbound travelers made camp for the night and avoided the highwaymen.[12]

Charles Allison, Colorado State Penitentiary, 1881. (Courtesy Royal Gorge Regional Museum and History Center, Cañon City, CO, No. 84.000.167.)

Allison and his men gave up waiting and rode into Pagosa Springs, arriving about 10:00 P.M. They entered James Voorhees's store, which also served as the express and stage office. They forced him to open his safe and retrieved $467 in cash and a watch and chain worth $450. The bold band then walked out of the store and rode away. Harley Sanderson and one of his employees, John Foshay, the Barlow and Sanderson Division Superintendent, witnessed the robbery. Cattleman E.A. Taylor and an unidentified constable were also present, but were not robbed. Once again, the highwaymen wore no masks and some of the witnesses recognized Charlie Allison from his days as a Conejos County deputy sheriff. The

Denver Republican reported that the rest of the thieves were "members of one of the bands of cattle thieves who have been operating in the neighborhood of Farmington for some months past." According to the *Republican*, the day before the stage robbery Allison and his confederates robbed a store in Amargo "of guns, pistols, ammunition and everything of value in sight."[13]

Henry Watts, Colorado State Penitentiary, 1881. (Courtesy Royal Gorge Regional Museum and History Center, Cañon City, CO, No. 84.000.168.)

Shortly afterwards, the bandits stole three horses at Monero, about six miles east of Amargo. According to the *Durango Daily Record*, "they have stolen three very valuable horses, two of them belonging to A.C. Hunt, Jr., and one to Gov. Hunt, the latter being his elegant trotter Moro, for which he paid over $1,000."[14] The horses were being sent to Durango at the time. Stealing cash and watches was one thing, but stealing horses, especially valuable horses from a former governor, was another. Upon hearing of the theft, A.C. (Bert) Hunt, Jr. of Durango applied for a deputy sheriff's badge and gathered a posse. If Allison's gang met untimely ends, the Colorado badge could provide the cover of law for the posse members. On June 1st, Hunt and his group rode out of Durango intent on recovering the stolen horses and meting out justice. In the meantime, Allison learned that the horses belonged to former Governor Hunt and his son. Hoping to avoid the scrape of hemp around their necks, the men left the horses in Amargo (or possibly in the Monero stable) and liberally spread the word where they could be found. After recovering the animals, Hunt's posse gave up the chase. Upon returning to Durango, Hunt celebrated by hiring a Tabor and

Wasson coach, which happened to be named "Gov. Hunt," and filled it with his friends. They proceeded to the photographer's tent on Railroad Street to capture the moment, and then rode up to Animas City for hardened refreshments. Stage line owner Perly Wasson drove the inebriated group back to Durango.[15]

Lewis Perkins, aka "The Cross-eyed Kid," Colorado State Penitentiary, 1881. (Courtesy Royal Gorge Regional Museum and History Center, Cañon City, CO, No. 84.000.170.)

Even before the Hunt posse was headed their way, Allison was headed for Chama. On the last day of May or first day of June, Allison and four other men laid siege to the town, flourishing their six-shooters and cowing local law enforcement. In broad daylight they robbed the wholesale liquor house of C.L. Petherbridge and the house of Wilmot. E. Broad.[16] The *New Mexican* reported that Allison and his crew "held up" the town and said, "They are said to have used the point of their six-shooters to good advantage, and with the aid of those little persuaders to have accumulated in a short time quite a pretty pile of wealth." The band made off with a substantial amount of ammunition, as well.[17] The *Cimarron News and Press* wondered, "Would it not be well for the Governor of Colorado to actively assist the New Mexico authorities in this matter?"[18] The crime wave was not over. On June 2nd, Allison and his gang tempted fate and risked a run in with Hunt's posse. They rode to the familiar canyon west of Pagosa Springs and again held up the Barlow and Sanderson Stage. They took seventeen dollars from an unidentified young man, but then returned two dollars. Mr. Schrock, formerly of Morrison, Colorado, traveled on to

Rico where he reported that he had $400 stolen in the robbery. The victims of this outrage said that there were seven robbers.[19] The highwaymen broke open several trunks, but took nothing except some women's hose. At the time, Allison was still nursing the leg wound he had accidentally self-inflicted when he shot carpenter Andy Guinan. The victims recalled that one of the robbers, upon examining the hose said, "[they] would be good for his sore leg; as they would be large and warm." One of the robbers addressed another as "Pete." The *Durango Record* concluded: "This will be their last robbery, however, as the wires are laid for their apprehension, and they will either be taken or driven from the state, at once."[20]

"Colorado.- Incidents of a Trip to the Mining Town of Durango," Frank Leslie's Illustrated Newspaper, May 28, 1881, artist J.J. Reilly. (Author's collection.)

The continued antics of the Allison Gang played into the hands of New Mexico authorities. Finally, Colorado officials were beginning to realize that the presence of Stockton and his associates, whether Stockton claimed them or not, was harmful to the state and its residents. On the morning of June 4th, Governor Pitkin received a telegram with a desperate plea for help from Conejos County Sheriff Joe Smith. It read, "Antonito, Colo. – To Governor Pitkin, Denver. - The county is powerless against armed desperadoes. C. Allison, late deputy sheriff is the leader. Life and property are in danger; stages, stores ranches are being robbed of money, and stock, threatened with attack on Antonito and Conejos. Assistance is wanted. Have good men but no arms." At the time Conejos County extended over the Continental Divide into the area around Pagosa Springs. Pitkin issued a proclamation offering $1000 for the capture of Allison and $200 for the capture of the other robbers. He also ordered the shipment of arms to the county.²¹ New Mexico authorities were offering $250 for Allison's capture for his part in the murder of Aaron Barker. There was also reward money waiting in Eureka, Nevada for the capture of the same man, the man Nevadans knew as Charles Ennis.

In Silverton, the Amargo troubles were seen as a business opportunity. As news of Allison's crimes reached the mining town, the *La Plata Miner* reported other Amargo outrages. One man was robbed of $37 while he was standing on the D&RG's depot platform. When he later met the robbers in town, they laughed at him. The *Miner* strongly recommended that travelers avoid Amargo all together, by leaving the rail line at Alamosa and traveling via Del Norte and then over the pass to Silverton. Upon reaching the mining town, travelers could continue on to Durango in a Tabor and Wasson Concord coach, pulled by a four horse team. Portions of the mountainous route were precarious, so the stage line restricted their operation to daylight hours. The glare of sunlight also discouraged would be highwaymen.²²

As word of Allison's plundering spree spread, newspapers in New Mexico misinterpreted events along the Colorado/New Mexico border. While Ike Stockton was in Utah chasing Indians, his reputation as an outlaw was growing by leaps and bounds. News accounts insisted on binding Allison tightly to Stockton, erroneously inferring that the highwayman was a respected and accepted member of Stockton's gang. Commenting on the Rio Arriba turbulence, the *Rio Grande Republican* in Las Cruces hopefully speculated that, "Governor Pitkin seems to have now come to a clearer understanding of the case, brought about by attacks of some of the Ike Stockton gang on Colorado towns, Colorado stage coaches and Colorado citizens."²³ The *New Mexican* carried similar accounts, saying that, "Stockton's gang is divided into two parties one of which is with him at Rico while the other is headed by Charlie Allison who has been doing the robbing in Rio Arriba recently." As for the trouble around Durango, the Santa Fe daily made Ike sound like General Grant at the Battle of Spotsylvania, reporting: "Ike Stockton says that he intends to fight it out all summer."²⁴ Commenting on the situation in Conejos County, the *Alamosa Independent* said, "There is little doubt that the devil has broke loose in the lower country, and our State authorities should lose no time in taking decisive measures." The *Independent* called on Pitkin "to organize a sufficient force of militia and send them into the field with instructions to hunt high and low and stay there until every desperado is lodged in jail, or still better spread out as a banquet on some side hill for the turkey buzzards."²⁵

South of the border, the saga of Manuel Gonzales and the "Cañon Largo Gang" was not over. It became the subject of a war of words in the *New Mexican*. As it turns out Max Frost had been misled when he concluded that Manuel Gonzales was the leader of that gang of desperadoes. Gonzales described his chief accusers, David Lobato and

Guadalupe Arellano, as "two of my bitterest enemies in that portion of Rio Arriba County." Gonzales asserted that the situation arose when he made a deal to sell forty-six head of cattle to Arellano and John W. Baker. He contended that Arellano had tried to swindle him out of the proceeds from the sale. Gonzales had the misfortune at the same time to run into the man he believed to be a constable from Bernalillo, who may have been a constable as well as an outlaw. Gonzales assisted him in obtaining an endorsement from a local justice of the peace on a writ of replevin from Bernalillo County, which resulted in the seizure of a horse from David Lobato. The *New Mexican* said that Gonzales was a man of means and Gonzales himself said he looked forward to seeing the matter settled in court where he would prove that his accusers had tried to take his cattle first by force and then "by false pretenses under a color of justice."[26]

Back in the Animas valley, Dow Eskridge was continuing to round up his cattle on a limited basis. In early June, the *Durango Record* noted, "the round-up party is now working on this side of the New Mexico line, having abandoned for the present any idea of obtaining their stock from below." Dow's negotiations with the New Mexico cattlemen would continue, but for the time being no Colorado cattlemen would be allowed to drive their stock out of the northwest portion of New Mexico until Ike Stockton was arrested. At the same time the *Dolores News* declared that the "Farmington mob" was "harboring Dan Howland in their midst to 'a dead moral certainty' although it is reported that he was in the vicinity of Trinidad." The *Trinidad News* confidently asserted, "Dan Howland is no nearer Trinidad than the day he murdered I.W. Lacy, sensational rumors to the contrary, notwithstanding. His address is Farmington, where it will probably be for some time to come." The *News* was at least partly right; not even Howland would have been stupid enough to travel to Trinidad, where George Thompson and others would have greeted him with a rope. However, the chances are slim that he found refuge along the lower Animas. Hartman and Jones appreciated the Trinidad newspaper's take on the situation and added, "People are beginning to realize that Farmington is headquarters for a set of thieves and murderers who have compelled all decent citizens to leave."[27]

Howland's fellow cowpuncher Tom Nance did leave the San Juan country, although he would later return. Two days before the decisive Indian battle in the La Sals, the June 14th issue of the *New Mexican* reported that, "Tom Nance reached the city yesterday from Bloomfield, Rio Arriba county. He is the chap who rid the country of Port Stockton, for which service he has since enjoyed the pleasure of having the Ike Stockton gang going for him." The newspaper said that he was "seeking a more congenial neighborhood." He likely made the trip with Levy Hughes, although the paper reported that Hughes arrived in town the day before Nance's arrival.[28] Nance only stayed in town for one night. The next day he left for

Trinidad where the newspaper noted he had relatives.[29] Nance obviously intended to meet with his uncle, George Thompson.

While Nance and Hughes were in Santa Fe, another visitor familiar with the San Juan country informed the *New Mexican* that Ike Stockton and Charlie Allison were not friends, but bitter enemies. The same informant declared "that the reports about the bad breaks made by the desperadoes up there are exaggerated and that the Colorado authorities are not to blame."[30] There was no need to exaggerate the "bad breaks" made by Charlie Allison or Ike Stockton. And Colorado authorities were indeed very much to blame for the continuing strife, since they had consistently refused to take any steps whatsoever to arrest Ike or others involved in the murder of Aaron Barker.

For Charlie Allison, that changed after he began robbing stagecoaches in southern Colorado. After creating bedlam around Amargo and Pagosa Springs, Allison's little band suddenly became quiet. Then on Sunday, June 12th, one of the suspected robbers, Thomas Seely, appeared in Alamosa and was quickly arrested.[31] Conejos County Deputy Sheriff Frank Hyatt, who had been in Santa Fe after horse thieves, hastened back to Alamosa to interview Seely. Hyatt learned that Allison and his men were traveling by horseback to Albuquerque. It was a slow journey and their route probably followed down the Rio Chama and Rio Grande valleys. Hyatt hoped to beat them, by taking the train to Española.[32] He gathered up three men he knew he could trust: saloon keeper, Miles Blain; Cy Afton, a painter; and forty-three-year-old cattleman, H.C. (Hank) Dorris.[33]

After disembarking in Española, the men traveled on to Santa Fe where they received the go ahead from Governor Sheldon to arrest Allison, even though they had no requisition. The men boarded the recently completed spur line to Lamy, where the tracks joined the main line to Albuquerque. Upon their arrival, they ascertained that Allison had not yet reached Albuquerque. Hyatt began to wonder if "Little Tommy" had sent them on a wild goose chase. Allison's group was still on the road. Very early the next morning Hyatt boarded the train and headed up the Rio Grande valley to Bernalillo to look around and see if he could find out anything about the Allison Gang.[34] In Bernalillo he stopped near the train station to eat breakfast.[35] After a few minutes he heard the shuffle of spurs as someone entered the eating house. As he glanced toward the noise, who should he see but Charlie Allison and two other men. He knew Allison on sight. The two other men were Lew Perkins and Henry Watts. Allison walked around the room and took a seat opposite Hyatt and then pulled his pistol and put it in his lap. Hyatt's heart jumped a little as he thought he had been recognized. He coolly continued talking with the owner.[36] After a short while he paid for breakfast, turned his back on Allison and sauntered out the door. He walked over to the train station which provided a safe and inconspicuous location to keep watch on the little restaurant. The outlaws soon exited the eating establishment, mounted up, and rode toward Albuquerque. Hyatt telegraphed his men in Albuquerque and advised them that Allison was headed their way.[37]

The deputy was desperate for a horse. Hyatt recalled that an "old Mexican" rode up in his wagon, pulled by two horses. The wagon driver agreed to provide the horses and ride along with Hyatt for one hundred dollars. They rode out of Bernalillo and soon came in sight of the marauding band. They slowed up, and for a long while kept the easy pace set by their quarry.[38] Hyatt's telegraph zipped to Albuquerque at the speed of light, however, the messenger's delivery of the paper telegram traveled at the slower pace common in New Mexico. As the bandits drew closer and closer to town, Hyatt became uneasy. Sensing that his chance of surprising and capturing the gang was diminishing with each stride, he crossed the river and spurred his horse into Albuquerque. Upon meeting his men he learned that they had just received the telegram and were preparing to head toward Bernalillo.[39] Hyatt quickly recruited the assistance of several locals including Jeff Grant of the Grant Brother's Stable and Justice of the Peace Daniel J. Sullivan. Most of the posse holed up in Grant's livery barn to await Allison's arrival.[40]

Hyatt kept a lookout upriver with field glasses. Allison and his companions were finally spotted riding slowly toward Albuquerque. As they neared the outskirts of town, they stopped by some trees, dismounted and disappeared from view. Hyatt feared that the stagecoach robbers might elude him and Jeff Grant was selected to go out and look for them. Grant rode up on Allison's group unexpectedly, but smoothly engaged them in conversation. In short order, the affable liveryman convinced the three highwaymen to accompany him back to his stable. Back at the livery Hyatt and his posse watched as Grant blithely led the Allison Gang into Albuquerque. The posse members hid from view and waited. Tension rose as they heard Grant's entourage approach. Soon Allison and the other men rode into the barn and Hyatt and the others emerged from the shadows with their guns drawn. The crestfallen desperadoes quickly gave up their weapons. The siege of Charlie Allison and his fellow highwaymen was over. An exultant Hyatt walked up to Allison and said, "Well, Charlie, I took breakfast with you this morning." To which Allison replied, "Yes, God damn you, and I was dead on to you all the time. I had a notion to take you prisoner then, and was a fool for not doing it, but I watched you pretty close and didn't think you knew me or were on this lay."[41] The men were placed in irons and taken to the room over the livery office and placed in the custody of Richard Helen.[42]

That same day (June 17th), the *Albuquerque Daily Journal* carried news of the arrest. The paper reported that immediately afterwards, "Grant's stables were thronged this afternoon with excited men who were discusing [sic] the capture." There was some talk of lynching the men, but as Albuquerque had not been the site of their crime spree, that talk soon died away. The paper included news of Hyatt's telegram from Bernalillo warning of the men's approach. Despite that, they passed on the Justice Sullivan version of events, saying, "The capture was made without any assistance whatever from the Colorado officials."[43]

The fun was just beginning. Allison was worth a lot of money, in three jurisdictions, although at the time New Mexico and Colorado officials had no idea he was wanted in Nevada. While still in the barn, Justice of the Peace Sullivan immediately claimed the reward money. No account exists of Hyatt's reaction to this treachery, but that he was furious would qualify as a diluted understatement. A flurry of telegrams followed. Several came into Governor Sheldon's office asking about the reward money.[44] Hyatt sent a telegram to Governor Pitkin, who in turn telegraphed Governor Sheldon saying he heard there was some difficulty with the reward money and asking if requisitions were needed. Sheldon telegraphed back to send the requisitions, but he would send the prisoners in any case.[45]

Hyatt also fired off a telegram to Mayor D.P. Broadwell in Alamosa: "We have got Allison and his gang in irons. I followed them eighteen miles alone." News of the arrests created pandemonium in Alamosa.[46] Conejos County authorities were surprised by the arrests. It wasn't until the next day that Justice of the Peace J.H. McHolland issued a John Doe criminal complaint calling for the arrest of the stagecoach robbers.[47] Back in Santa Fe, Governor Sheldon telegraphed Sheriff Perfecto Armijo of Bernalillo County and asked that he aid Hyatt in holding the prisoners. Hyatt had agreed to give up any claim to the New Mexico reward, but Sullivan continued to hold the prisoners until he was assured he would receive the reward money. If Lew Wallace enlightened Sheldon about the problems he might encounter in New Mexico is unknown, but Sheldon was finding out in any case. Sheldon was thoroughly disgusted with Justice Sullivan. According to the *New Mexican* he said, "that in all his experience he had never encountered an official who had as much presumption, or who would attempt to interfere with the course of the law or the execution of justice for the sake of $200, but that Sullivan would not let the prisoners go until the Governor became responsible for the reward." Upon learning this, the governor sent Adjutant General Frost to Albuquerque with writs for the arrest of the outlaws and with instructions that they were to be taken from Bernalillo County to Santa Fe County.[48] In Albuquerque, Frost found that Hyatt himself had just been placed under arrest. It's not known what role Justice of the Peace Sullivan played in this matter, but given the level of his greed, it seems that he was the power behind the arrest. Hyatt was charged with reneging on his hundred dollar deal with the Bernalillo horse owner. Now the deputy felt the Colorado reward money slipping from his grasp. He quickly posted bond and was released.[49]

While their captors argued over the reward money, the three stage robbers were growing in notoriety. One of them was interviewed, probably Allison, and asked if he was afraid of being mobbed in Colorado. He boasted that he would take his chances with a mob if they gave him his pistols.[50] That wouldn't be possible because shortly after they were jailed their money, rifles, revolvers and everything but their horses had been stolen. In light of their recent stage robberies and the robbery of Voorhees's Store, they had to be carrying a considerable amount of money and other loot. Sheriff Armijo was said to be looking into the matter.[51] Despite his incarceration, Allison presented a cheerful facade and denied the charges he faced, babbling to reporters that he had tried mining for a while and supported himself from $1700 he had made by selling some claims in Arizona. Watts and Perkins were despondent and feared lynching would be their fate.[52]

Allison and his men were transported to Santa Fe on June 20th guarded by Hyatt and his posse, as well as Justice Sullivan and John Phelan, who had been deputized by Sheriff Armijo for the trip. Max Frost accompanied the group on what had to be a rather strained journey. The *Albuquerque Daily Journal* reported that Perkins would be held for extradition to Colorado and Watts and Allison would be tried in Santa Fe for the murder of Aaron Barker. That account was in error, since Allison was the only one of the threesome indicted in the Barker case.[53] That same day, Governor Sheldon issued a letter certifying that Daniel J. Sullivan of Albuquerque would receive the $250 reward for the arrest of Charles Allison for his role in the murder of Aaron Barker. The letter was co-signed by Territorial Auditor, Trinidad Alarid.[54]

On June 23rd, Sheldon received the requisitions from Colorado. At the time Hyatt and his men were running out of funds, but that problem was solved when, along with the requisitions, a motivated Pitkin sent word to Hyatt to draw on him for any funds needed to defray expenses. New Mexico authorities decided not to hold Allison. After receiving a written order from Governor Sheldon, Santa Fe County Sheriff Romulo Martinez turned all three prisoners over to Frank Hyatt. The deputy and his prisoners quickly departed Santa Fe by stagecoach for Española, where they boarded the train to Alamosa. There was some fear that the men might be lynched when they arrived in Conejos County.[55] There was also concern that Allison's friends might attempt to free the outlaws. Jimmy Catron was one of those friends. Catron and Allison had probably first met when Allison worked as deputy sheriff in the San Luis Valley. The *New Mexican* reported that before departing Santa Fe, Hyatt wired ahead and provided misleading information that they would travel to Denver first and not arrive in Alamosa until Saturday evening. Allison's friends were not fooled and continued their vigil in Antonito. According to the *New Mexican*, when the train carrying the Allison Gang arrived, his would be rescuers "in a seemingly indifferent way looked through the train for him; the prisoners were locked up in the baggage car, however, and were not discovered."[56] On Friday, June 24th, the men were placed in the Alamosa jail. Shortly afterwards a crowd began to gather and it was feared the stage robbers would be lynched. Mayor Broadwell sent a messenger to Hyatt's residence and he quickly returned to the jail. Hyatt, Broadwell and several other citizens, including Alva Adams (a future governor of Colorado), managed to get the prisoners to the train yard, where they boarded a tiny train consisting of only the caboose and an engine. As a crowd converged, the engine and caboose chugged out of the station. The prisoners would spend the next few weeks in Denver for their own safety.[57]

Ike Stockton did not know it, but the arrest of Allison, Watts and Perkins would entrap him in a cataclysmic progression of events. The arrest of the Allison Gang would also have lifelong consequences for the Eskridge family. Allison was captured just a day after the big killing in Utah's Pinhook valley. After the long Indian chase Stockton and Eskridge made their way back to southwest Colorado. Hargo and Ike split up. While Eskridge headed for Rico, Ike and M.C. Cook rode on toward Animas City.

Chapter Seventeen

The Calm Before the Storm

> *When she hove in sight far up the track,*
> *She was workin' steam, with her brake shoes slack,*
> *She hollered once at the whistle post,*
> *Then she flitted by like a frightened ghost.*[1]

A weary, worn out Stockton and his shadow, M.C. Cook, rode into Animas City on Friday, July 1st.[2] Ellen and their two children, Delilah and toddler Guy had not seen him for over a month. It is likely that Cook lived with the Stocktons. Later that summer, Cook began work as one of Animas City's town marshals.[3] One of Stockton's admirers and associates, Bert Wilkinson, was now living in Animas City, close to the Stockton place, and often visited Stockton at his home.[4] Shortly after his return, Ike stopped by the offices of Durango's new newspaper, the *Herald*, and told his story of the Indian fight. J.H. Alderson visited the *Herald* that same week. The *Herald* summed up their stories, saying, "The white company, after a fatiguing march of thirty-three days, during which they endured hardships unspeakable, much of the time without food; and in which they had fought, considering the numbers engaged, one of the bloodiest battles on record."[5] That same week it was reported that Ike regaled "a crowd of eager listeners yesterday, while he was relating his hair-breadth escape from the 'immanent [sic] deadly, breach,' etc."[6] Despite the efforts of the lower Animas men and New Mexico territorial officials, Ike was safe in southwest Colorado. No one bothered him and he maintained a close relationship with most of the law enforcement officials in the area. While Ike settled in, lower Animas residents were trying to repair their relations with southwest Colorado. But the partial travel and trade embargo at the territorial/state line continued to hinder development on both sides of the border.

A few days after Ike's return, Henry Goodman came into Durango on a business trip. While Stockton had been out chasing Indians, Goodman had different worries. The *Record* noted, "Mr. Henry Goodman, who is at present – in the absence of an administrator – the agent for I.W. Lacy, deceased, was in town last week." The newspaper noted that Goodman, since he brought Lacy's cattle into southwest Colorado, had "managed the business of Mr. Lacy with credit to himself and profit to his employer."[7] So much for the claims of the *Dolores News* that Stockton had some benevolent interest in Lacy's business affairs or that he had ever been in charge of Lacy's cattle operations. Goodman was assisting Mrs. Lacy as she worked to settle her late husband's estate.[8]

THE CALM BEFORE THE STORM 299

Just before Ike's return, the *San Juan Herald* in Silverton did their part to mend the border enmity. The newspaper did not name names, but they took a direct shot at Hartman and Jones and the *Dolores News*. The *Herald* noted that men who had recently been to western Rio Arriba County "have no hesitancy in saying that a gross injustice has been done that section by certain individuals and newspapers." Their correspondent said the residents there, who had been "represented as a band of outlaws and cut-throats," were not. A Silverton merchant said that, "he never met a more peaceable or hospitable sort of people anywhere east or west." The merchant described W.B. Haines as "a perfect gentleman and a straightforward business man," and he said, "Mr. Cox & Sons, who are heavy cattle men, rank among the best dealers of the lower Animas."[9] The article was a step in the right direction, but so long as Ike Stockton lived openly in Animas City, the situation would show little improvement. Not long afterwards, Haines himself wrote the *Herald*. He thanked them for their kind comments and said the New Mexico men were after no man's blood, but wanted only respect for the law. He lauded the efforts of Deputy Sheriff Blancett in helping to bring an end to the "reign of terror." However, he noted that few residents "dared cross the line of Colorado into the town of Durango, knowing full well that death would be our fate."[10] It was most likely through the efforts of Mose Blancett and Wash Cox that Dow Eskridge was allowed to enter New Mexico and round up his stock. The *Durango Record* reported that Dow had recovered all but one of his horses. The cattle count was still uncertain until the completion of the roundup.[11] The public relations efforts of Haines and others kept the pressure on Ike Stockton. And the recovery of Eskridge's stock did the same, as Dow almost certainly influenced his younger brothers to avoid hostilities with the lower Animas cowboys.

Stockton was beginning to feel the strain of his precarious position. There was no more Stockton Gang. There would be no more raids into New Mexico. The Territorial militia had made it a dangerous proposition to rustle cattle in New Mexico. This put the pinch on Ike for money. He began to consider his options. He could negotiate his surrender. He could pack up and leave town, but like his older brother, it was not in his nature to run from trouble. Some of Durango's citizens were biding their time, ready to pounce if and when Ike became vulnerable. New Mexicans continued to demand his arrest. Desperate times call for desperate measures and Ike was rapidly reaching that point. Even those who had not taken sides in the feud wished he would just go away.

In late June, William Locke and William Hendrickson traveled to Santa Fe to meet with Governor Sheldon personally. They gave him an update on the situation in the San Juan country. The *New Mexican* said the two men "report matters quiet in the San Juan and Animas River settlements."[12] They were two of the most thoughtful men in the area and throughout all of the troubles they worked to find solutions to the conflict. Because they refused to take sides, some residents along the lower Animas viewed them as being sympathetic to Ike Stockton. As the summer dragged on residents on both sides of the border realized that so long as Ike Stockton was around, the situation would never be resolved. It is apparent that Locke, Hendrickson and others from the San Juan country advised Sheldon that Ike Stockton was once again living openly in Animas City and Durango, while arrest warrants from New Mexico remained unserved. A couple of weeks after their visit, Max Frost traveled to Denver. The trip was reported in the *New Mexican*, but the article offered few details, saying only, "Business of importance called him to that city."[13] The New Mexicans had finally realized that announcing every action in the newspapers was not to their advantage. It seems likely that Frost visited Pitkin to ask that the warrants be served. Pitkin had options other than relying on Sheriff Luke Hunter. Under the General Laws of Colorado he had the authority to appoint anyone "the said executive may think fit" to execute such warrants within Colorado.[14] Pitkin was inclined to rely on the goodwill and best judgment of Sheriff Hunter. As time would tell, reliance on Sheriff Hunter's goodwill and judgment was a risky proposition.

In early July, Hargo Eskridge was able to read about himself in the *Denver Republican*. On June 22nd the *Republican* carried more than three columns worth on the first page, based on an interview with a man they identified as one of the "Durango outlaws." The *Republican* said that on June 21st a well-known Durango merchant cornered one of their reporters on Larimer Street. The merchant said he could introduce him to one of Stockton's gang, who would provide the newsman with the first full account of the Farmington trouble from the Stockton perspective. The merchant requested that he not be named and that the newsman simply state the facts as told. The reporter could not believe his good luck and eagerly agreed to the conditions. He was taken to a less than first rate hotel in the north part of town. The merchant asked for the room number of James Smith. Mr. Smith was in, so the two men proceeded down the hallway. While walking, the merchant revealed that Smith was notorious Stockton lieutenant, Hargo Eskridge. Upon entering the room the newspaperman noticed "two formidable looking double-action Colts," which were lying on a table. When the man called Hargo learned the newsman was from the *Republican,* he "eyed the scribe suspiciously," and said, "A *Republican* reporter," then with anger rising in his voice he continued, "that's the paper that gave Stockton and the boys such a rough deal a little while ago."[15] The newspaperman wondered what might happen next, but he had no need to worry. The man was not Hargo. On the day of the interview, Eskridge was still in Utah, unable to ride a horse while nursing the bullet wound in his leg. The impersonator laid it on thick and the newsman swallowed all of it. Within a few days copies of the interview reached Rico and Durango and were the subject of much mirth. The *Durango Democrat* commented on the article and revealed that the Durango merchant's last name was Williams. They did not reveal the name of the Eskridge impersonator, but said, "The 'guy' is evidently well acquainted with this part of the country and the details of the quarrel and persons engaged in it." They concluded that the *Republican's* "reporter is too fresh for Durangoites."[16]

The *Dolores News* was not as diplomatic to a reporter from the *Conejos County Times* who had the nerve to comment that southern Colorado was an unhealthy locale for the "Stockton gang" and Allison's band of robbers. Hartman and Jones were not fond of the term "Stockton gang" and addressed their response to the editor of the *Times* as "You poor, idiotic, stupid fool."[17]

The real Hargo had to be astounded to learn that Charlie Allison was achieving status as Colorado's most noted desperado. Up in Denver, Allison was the talk of the town. His arrival in Denver had been thoroughly publicized and that day a large crowd gathered at the depot. As the engine huffed toward the station, anticipation grew. The engine hissed and groaned and steam and smoke filled the air. The car carrying the desperadoes was soon identified and the crowd swarmed. There was a slight delay and as the car door opened, the spectators eagerly crowded forward, chains and ankle irons clanked as the three stage robbers stepped out of the car. Living up to their image, they wore hats described as large light colored sombreros. Over a dozen weapon-laden lawmen surrounded the prisoners for the short walk to the omnibus which would carry them to jail. Frank Hyatt and H.C. Dorris stepped off the train, very much surprised at the frenzy created by the Allison Gang.[18] On July 9th, Hargo and others learned from the *Dolores News* that hundreds of curious people had applied to the county jail to see Allison. It was said that he was lighthearted and jovial during his confinement.[19]

While Allison inspected his Denver jail cell, Dison Eskridge was returning from Utah to Colorado. The Pinhook Rescue Expedition found no Indians to fight. Dison reached Rico on July 13th. That same week Ike Stockton and M.C. Cook traveled up from Animas City. Hargo spent the first two weeks of July hoping that his foot would heal up. It would not. On the day Dison arrived, two surgeons, J.P. Landon and A.J. McDonald, operated on Hargo's foot. They laid it open and removed several pieces of decayed bone, cleansed the wound, sewed him up, and hoped for the best. Stockton and Cook returned to Animas City that same week. About a week later a three-year-old bay roan filly, "well broke to saddle and gentle," was raffled off to help pay for the operation, with twenty-five tickets sold at $3 a piece.[20]

Upon his return to Animas City, Ike learned that one of his acquaintances had been shot and killed by Pat Garrett in Fort Sumner. Billy the Kid was dead and now Ike Stockton took his place as the most wanted man in New Mexico. About the same time, constable Jim Sullivan came to Rico after a trip to New Mexico and Arizona. The Stockton sympathizer was warmly welcomed in Rico.[21] Not long afterwards, Sullivan found employment on the police force in Durango. As fate would have it, Sullivan's appointment was just in time for the most well-known shooting in the early history of Durango. At the same time, Sullivan's friend, Hargo Eskridge, was hobbling around on crutches.[22] In Durango, news of Billy the Kid's death was soon overshadowed.

From left to right, Hargo Eskridge, Tom Radigan and James Hall, ca. July 1881, probably in Rico, CO. Hall and Eskridge were recovering from wounds inflicted by Indians at the mid-June battle in the Pinhook valley in Utah's La Sal Mountains. Tom Radigan was shot in the leg on March 1, 1881 when he rode with Ike Stockton, Hargo Eskridge and others on the raid to kill Tom Nance. Nance escaped, but his companion Aaron Barker was killed. Tom Radigan's leg was amputated by the post surgeon at Fort Lewis. (Photo courtesy of Southwest Collection, Special Collections Library, Texas Tech University, Lubbock, TX, Clifford B. Jones Collection, No. 422 E5.)

In late July, the Denver and Rio Grande Railroad was finally on the outskirts of town and plans were being made for an elaborate party to celebrate the arrival of the first train.[23] Shortly before the tracks reached Durango, Mrs. I.W. Lacy and George Thompson took the train as far as Arboles, then headed for the La Plata valley and points west to check her late husband's cattle holdings.[24] While passing through Durango, Mrs. Lacy stayed at the Grand Central Hotel, not at the home of her cousins, Ike and Amanda Ellen Stockton.[25] Not long afterwards, George Thompson purchased Mrs. Lacy's interest in the "HU" and "Double Cross" brands in

La Plata County for $20,000.[26] Even so, Mrs. Lacy held on to a substantial portion of her late husband's cattle herd.

That summer the forces involved in the final Stockton conflagration began to drift into Durango. The new terminus at Arboles didn't provide the same excitement as Amargo and by the middle of July, outlaw Jimmy Catron showed up in Durango, where he proceeded to become a public nuisance. Shortly afterwards Bob Dwyer arrested him for carrying a concealed weapon. He was fined $25.[27]

Over in Alamosa the citizens who had tried in vain to lynch Charlie Allison and his gang were fed up with persistent lawlessness and took their wrath out on an unusual target. On July 21st the vigilantes lynched local Justice of the Peace George C. O'Connor. The *Denver Tribune* declared that, "All had become disgusted with the gang of thieves who were headed by O'Connor, and, of course, as all criminals had to be tried before him, the trial were farces, and they in all cases were acquitted." The vigilance committee would brook no misunderstandings and the *Tribune* reported that after O'Connor's hoisting, "The rest of the gang were notified to leave town inside of forty-eight hours."[28] Allison, when told about O'Connor's fate, was elated, and claimed he held no love for the judge.[29] The former stage robber was an adept liar, so it is difficult to tell if this was one of his lies or if he truly harbored some grudge against O'Connor. Meanwhile, back in Allison's old stomping grounds, a big change was taking place.

On July 27th the iron rails were finally laid inside the town limits of Durango. The telegraph lines followed a few days later. The town proudly sent out this telegraph, "Durango, Colo., July 30. – This is the first telegraphic dispatch from Durango to the outside world. To all our fellow-countrymen: Durango sends cordial greetings and hearty all hails. The first passenger train will arrive here on the first of August and the authorities and citizens of Durango will celebrate this event by a grand Jubilee on August 5th. The business men here are preparing and will soon publish a pamphlet exposition of Durango and the San Juan."[30] On July 28th, the *Durango Herald* noted, "The iron horse arrived in Durango about five o'clock yesterday afternoon. A large crowd gathered soon after at the corner of G and Railroad streets to witness the driving of the silver spike." Ike Stockton's ardent supporter, Eugene Engley, made "a few well chosen remarks." Then the spike, which had been formed out of ore mined on Junction Creek, was "driven home by the well directed and vigorous blows of Mayor Taylor." Durango was no longer a backwater town.[31] The advance of civilization was not good news for Ike Stockton. The arrival of the railroad added more urgency to the desire of progressive citizens to put an end to news stories about Durango's desperadoes which impeded progress and discouraged businesses and families from relocating to the area.

Up in Denver plans were being finalized for an excursion train which would travel from the capital city to Durango, carrying dignitaries to the August 5th celebration. Aboard the train were mayors, councilmen and other residents from Denver, Leadville, Colorado Springs, Pueblo, and elsewhere.[32] When the big day arrived the dignitaries were stuck a mile and a half outside of Amargo. Heavy rains had damaged the tracks, making them impassable. The excursionists were expected to make it in the following morning, having to spend all night on the train or bedded down in the brush beside the tracks. Governor Pitkin, U.S. Marshal P.P. Wilcox, A.C. Hunt, former Lieutenant Governor Lafayette Head and some of the Denver press were already in town. They came in on the first train to arrive in Durango after the construction train. The conductor of the special train was A.R. Hill and the engineer was John Fuller.[33] Despite the missing dignitaries, most of the celebration went on as planned. Ike Stockton and his family were, no doubt, among the throng who enjoyed the day's festivities. A parade through Durango concluded at the horse track, where Governor Pitkin delivered a speech to the full grandstand. That afternoon an estimated three thousand spectators enjoyed the races, which included not only horse races, but also mule and burro races.[34] Ike Stockton entered his bay mare, Nellie, in the first race of the day, a two hundred yard sprint for horses fourteen hands or under. Nellie was also entered in the third race, a quarter horse event at four hundred yards. Only the results for horses that came in first or second were reported and Nellie did not place.[35] In the evening what one newspaper called an "eat hop" was held at the smelter works. The banquet was served on the blast furnace floor and the dance was held in the sampling room, with about 250 couples in attendance. The next day, Durango's baseball team beat Silverton's ten to three.[36]

The days of celebration passed with relative peace. The pacification was assisted by the arrest of Jimmy Catron, which took place about four in the morning on August 2nd. According to an eyewitness, Catron "had been drinking some." As was usually the case he was unable to control himself when drunk. Deputy Marshal Newt Moreland had befriended Catron. While Moreland was eating at an establishment on lower F Street, Catron passed by and he invited the outlaw to sit down and have something to eat. Catron sat down and not long afterwards he told Moreland, "Newt, look me in the eye." He repeated that and then said, "Fix yourself, Do you hear what I say? Get yourself ready Newt." As Catron went for his pistol, Moreland put him in a clinch. After the struggle, Moreland could not find Catron's pistol, which the outlaw had managed to place in one of his boots. As if nothing had happened, Catron told Moreland, "Let's go and get a cigar." Moreland was not in a forgiving mood and the hidden pistol was finally discovered. Officer Dwyer showed up about the same time and after another scuffle, Catron was finally subdued and placed under arrest. The trouble was not over. R.F. Blackmer, a friend of Catron's who was off some distance down the street, fired a round at Dwyer and said anybody who arrested Catron could not live. Dwyer returned fire and Blackmer took to his heels, disappearing into the darkness. Moreland captured him early the next morning hidden amongst the shavings under a workbench in a shed behind the depot. The two men were probably taken before Justice Flagler later that day. It appears that both men spent the duration of the celebration in the lockup.³⁷

Governor Pitkin and the other excursionists passed through the breathtaking Toltec Gorge on their journey to Durango. "Colorado.- Incidents of a Trip to the Mining Town of Durango," Frank Leslie's Illustrated Newspaper, *May 28, 1881, artist J.J. Reilly. (Modified, author's collection.)*

While he was in town Pitkin met with local law enforcement officials, which would have included Sheriff Luke Hunter and Deputy U.S. Marshal Heffernan. They discussed the Stockton situation and the still unserved arrest warrants. After his trip to Durango, Governor Pitkin wrote Governor Sheldon a letter in which he said the difficulty in arresting Stockton was that officers believed that Stockton could not be taken alive, and if he was killed in the process, the officers would not receive the reward offered by New Mexico. Pitkin added, "It was also believed that one or two men would be killed by Stockton in any [attempt?] to arrest him." The Colorado governor said that, "The sheriff of [this?] county and [others] to whom I applied, refused to engage in the [attempt] of making his arrest for the reasons stated."[38] Stockton used the D&RG celebration to his advantage. He made it a point to look up a reporter from the *Denver Republican*. He found his man at Durango's Inter-Ocean Hotel.[39]

The *Republican's* reporter, C.O. Ziegenfuss, said he was approached "by a pleasant faced, mild-mannered gentleman, who said he had a grievance."[40] Stockton laid on the charm. According to the newsman, Ike told him, "You have come down here into my home; you will mingle with the best people here; all I ask is that you inquire fully into my character and into my conduct since here, and publish what you find without prejudice." Judging from the article, the reporter was unaware that many, if not most of those with grievances against Stockton, were not inclined to air their complaints to be read later in newspapers across the state and elsewhere. According to Stockton, his brother was killed because he wasn't afraid to speak his mind. Ike added Aaron Barker's name to the list of men who were present when his brother was shot. Ike seems to be the only one who says Barker was there and it is apparent that he added Barker's name to the list so he could justify Barker's killing. Ike even claimed that it was Barker and Alf Graves who fired the fatal shots into Porter's breast and neck. According to Ike, five other men fired, but missed. When asked about his enemies in Farmington, Ike claimed to have met some of the Farmington people that very day, saying he had dinner with the sheriff's brother, the sheriff's wife, and other prominent Farmington residents. If Ike was not telling a tall one, he probably meant he met with Deputy Sheriff Mose Blancett's brother, which would be either John or En Blancett and the "sheriff's" wife, Monie Blancett. Ike told Ziegenfuss that they were working on a compromise, but added, "I can never compromise with the men who shot my brother. I mean that those men shall be tried by the courts, and I will not rest until they are tried and punished." The newsman made it clear, though, that avenging his brother's death was Stockton's purpose in life and speculated that Ike may kill those who killed his brother or be killed himself. Ike repeated his assessment of the now famous stage robber Charles Allison, saying, "Allison was with us only one trip – the first. The whole party was so disgusted with him that all declared they would never go out again if he went along." Stockton said when Allison healed up after shooting himself (while trying to shoot Andy Guinan), "he started on his own hook, and got himself where he belongs." Ike offered to surrender under the same ridiculous conditions outlined in the *Dolores News*. He professed his innocence and said he had never stolen any cattle, nor had he killed any white men. The newsman noted that Ike lived in a pleasant home in Animas City with his "fair-faced and pleasant young wife" and his two young children. The *Republican* was not known for its accuracy and the newspaperman was completely captivated. He proclaimed: "In Durango public sympathy is entirely with Stockton." Ziegenfuss reported that Durango's citizens regarded Stockton as an enterprising, peaceful and quiet man, who was being persecuted. He said the wanted outlaw moved openly in and around Durango and Rico where he was confident that he would never be arrested. The article concluded: "The writer found Stockton anything but a ruffian, and was impressed with the truthfulness of his story."[41] Ziegenfuss did not travel south to see what the men on the lower Animas might have to say.

While Ike impressed the reporter, his financial situation was deteriorating. The day after the big D&RG celebration, Ike ran Nellie in a match race against a horse put up by John T. Trimble. Trimble's horse was actually owned by Robert Caviness and was named Brown Kate. The men wagered $200 a side. Even an August thunderstorm did not stop the contest and the horses made the mud fly. Stockton's mare got off well and never relinquished the lead. It was Nellie's third dash in two days. Stockton's racing mare had become his chief source of income.[42]

The relative peace along the Animas could not last forever and on August 6th the *Dolores News* made this observation: "We have not heard of Frank Coe, who made some faithful promises to the boys. We will give him thirty days more."[43] The next day the *New Mexican* took a shot at Governor Pitkin. They complained that no action had been taken in regard to requisitions from Governor Wallace, even though Ike and others in his gang lived openly in southwest Colorado. They noted that New Mexico's governors had in every case complied without delay to requisitions from Governor Pitkin. The *Dolores News* responded to the *New Mexican* with their customary claims of innocence for Ike Stockton and his allies. The *News* also said that they believed that Stockton had called upon Governor Pitkin while he was in Durango because they heard that was his intent. Stockton certainly had the nerve to do that, but if they did meet, accounts of the encounter were never made or are well hidden. The *Pueblo Chieftain* blasted the *New Mexican* article, saying they did not believe "that any requisition by Governor Wallace had been neglected at the state department." The *Chieftain* also commented, "Whenever the matter is properly presented to the notice of Governor Pitkin, we presume he will take some action upon it, but in the meanwhile, it would be well enough for [New] Mexico to help herself a little, and not get down on her knees to Colorado every time a brawling cowboy steps inside her limits."[44] The *Chieftain* was woefully uninformed about events in Denver or had selective amnesia, or else they would have acknowledged or been aware that New Mexican authorities had hand-delivered a requisition to Pitkin on about May 9th. The subsequent trip to Durango by Tony Neis with arrest warrants signed by Pitkin was reported in the *Denver Republican* at the time.[45] To New Mexicans it was apparent that Colorado authorities had ample opportunity to arrest Ike and his indicted allies, yet no action had been taken.

Robert Dwyer, one of the first settlers in La Plata County. He served in several law enforcement positions during the rough and rowdy early days. (Courtesy La Plata County Historical Society.)

It was clear that Sheriff Luke Hunter had no intention of trying to arrest Ike Stockton, Hargo Eskridge or their associates. As the month of August passed, Stockton was quiet, except for racing Nellie. But Durango's lower F Street continued to be the center of mayhem. On August 18th, two members of the Durango police force were involved in a fatal shooting. At about 5:00 PM, officer Newt Moreland attempted to arrest a French Canadian named Jean Baptiste Laboeuf, who was drunk and disorderly. Laboeuf was about thirty years old and had been working construction jobs out of the D&RG camps prior to his arrival in Durango. He was an impressive physical specimen. Moreland was having difficulty effecting the arrest and Bob Dwyer ran up to assist. During the struggle, which occurred behind the Cabinet Saloon, Moreland struck Laboeuf with his pistol causing it to discharge. The bullet struck the drunk in the back of the neck and exited his right ear. Still unspent, it plowed into Dwyer's face, to the left of his nose and remained lodged in his head. Blood was flowing profusely from the wound. He was placed in a hack and driven rapidly to Dr. H.A. Clay's office on 1st Street. Several men assisted him upstairs to Clay's office. After examining and cleaning the wound, Clay elected to not remove the projectile. Dwyer was later placed in the daily care of Mrs. Heffernan. Some residents placed the blame entirely on Moreland, but Dwyer absolved his assistant, calling the shooting an accident. The *Record* speculated that "a good hickory billy is the proper weapon in such cases."[46] Dwyer survived, and within two weeks he was out on the streets, though still in a weakened condition.[47] Laboeuf was not so fortunate. He lingered for a month and then died.[48] Dwyer's extended recovery time worked in his favor, as the lingering Stockton tumult was rolling inexorably toward its final bloody conclusion.

The inappropriately timed and blood-drenched nativity of the Stockton trouble had burst forth on Christmas Eve 1880 when Dison Eskridge shot and killed George Brown at F.M. Hamblet's house near Farmington. At the same party Os Puett was also shot dead. That same evening Puett's cousin, Bert Wilkinson, killed "Comanche Bill" Swinford in a Durango saloon. Those three killings began a chain of violent events which were not over. Up to now, the most notable links in that chain were the brutal deaths of Porter Stockton and Aaron Barker. As August 1881 drew to a close, Ike Stockton, Dison and Hargo Eskridge, Jimmy Catron, Bert Wilkinson, Kid Thomas and others, whose lives had intersected in the past would converge one last time. No one could have imagined the startling, twisted sequence of events which were about to shatter the San Juan country. The tragic trigger which kicked off those events and which would inevitably lure Ike Stockton to his final cataclysm was a seemingly unrelated occurrence: the return of Charlie Allison, Henry Watts and Lew Perkins to Conejos County.

Chapter Eighteen

Blood in Silverton

> *The morn burst red, a gory wound,*
> *O'er iron hills and savage ground;*
> *And there was never another sound*
> *Save beat of horses' hoofs.*[1]

The man with his finger on that trigger was Kid Thomas, a normally harmless, light-skinned black cow herder, who had only recently returned from the mission to rescue Ike Stockton, Hargo Eskridge and the other men involved in the Pinhook valley battle.[2] Thomas told George West, his boss, that his brother was jailed in Denver.[3] He said his wayward sibling would soon be in Conejos County to stand trial for stage robbery. He asked West for some time off, so he could attend the trial.[4] The only stage robbers fitting that description were Charles Allison, Henry Watts and Lew Perkins. If one of those robbers was a brother to Kid Thomas, it had to be Henry Watts. A photo of Watts reveals a man with a dark complexion and black wavy hair.[5] Unlike Kid Thomas, descriptions of Watts never convey that he was a black man. Thomas left his cattle herding duties behind and rode out of the La Plata valley, headed for Alamosa. He needed help, so one of his first stops was Durango's lower F Street, where he had no trouble recruiting Jimmy Catron. The normally drunken desperado did not need much encouragement. Thomas also induced Bert Wilkinson to join the cause.[6] Based on those he gathered around him, it is clear that Kid Thomas intended to break his brother out of the Conejos County jail.

It's not known if Kid Thomas was literate. If not, he had friends who were and they kept him informed about the activities of the Allison gang. On August 12th, the *Rocky Mountain News* reported that Allison and his two accomplices, all of them still sporting their trail worn, light-colored sombreros, exited a carriage and were led into Denver's Union Depot. They were escorted by two Arapahoe County deputy sheriffs, Charles Linton and Barney Cutler. To the accompaniment of clanking ankle chains, they entered the gentlemen's waiting room. Heads swiveled in response to the distinctive noise. The men sat on the north side of the room and soon a large crowd gathered around to gawk and listen to the outlaws, who were enveloped in the aromatic smoky haze of their cigars. Allison, Perkins and Watts were glad to be out of the lockup and were cheerful and talkative. The loquacious Allison held the crowd in the palm of his hand. When asked by a reporter if he expected trouble on the southbound trip, Allison blustered, "Trouble? No; there ain't a going to be any trouble – not when Joe Smith is along, and he'll be there, you bet!" Smith was the Conejos County sheriff, Allison's former boss. When the questioner persisted, Allison added a comment which typified why he had become the subject of derision among the Stockton Gang. He boasted, "The devil! Give me a couple of six-shooters and I'll lick all of Alamosa and Conejos county put together!" Watts and Perkins had a good laugh at this comment. The southbound trip was cancelled after it was learned that there was track washout down the line, but reports of the aborted trip were wired around the state, alerting Kid Thomas to the intentions of Conejos County officials.[7]

Two days later, on Sunday morning, August 14, 1881, the three men left Denver on the D&RG rail line under the guard of Sheriff Smith and Deputy Hyatt of Conejos County, and Deputy Linton of Arapahoe County. The train did not reach Pueblo until Monday morning. While in Pueblo, word was received that a lynch mob was waiting for them in Alamosa. It was deemed unsafe for the men to continue and after some discussion the prisoners were placed in a hack and transported to the Pueblo jail under the escort of Pueblo County Sheriff H.R. Price and several deputies. For those who might harm Allison and his band as well as those who intended to rescue them, news of their every move was conveniently published in Denver's newspapers and wired around the state. It was also reported that the men would be held in Pueblo, until the next Conejos County Court term in November.[8] This was a ploy to throw off any lynch mobs. Not all of the state's newspapers carried that misinformation. On Saturday, August 20th, the *Durango Record* asserted, "Allison and his gang, it seems, will not be taken south after all, until the first of the month."[9] The *Record's* account was also incorrect as Conejos County officials planned to escort the Allison gang to Alamosa before the end of the month.

While Allison was still in Pueblo, Kid Thomas and his companions left Durango and rode up the Animas valley, but they soon veered wildly away from their planned journey to Alamosa. On Sunday afternoon, August 21st, the men passed by the Pinkerton ranch, south of Baker's bridge. Just above Pinkerton's, Jimmy Catron and Bert Wilkinson held up M.J. Miller at his saloon, taking a watch, $15 and two pistols. On August 23rd warrants were issued for their arrest and deputy sheriffs Newt Moreland and Frank Trimble started out to the find the men.[10] According to the *La Plata Miner*, after the robbery Catron turned up in Durango, where the lure of alcohol was more than he could resist. Officers soon found the desperado, arrested him and took him to jail. His incarceration was brief. The *Miner* reported that his companions "took the top off the jail and he made his escape."[11] When Kid Thomas and Bert Wilkinson resumed their journey to Alamosa, Catron was not with them. Whatever his reasons, Catron would soon be thankful that he had parted ways with Wilkinson and Thomas. Once again the men left Durango and headed up the Animas toward Silverton. At this juncture, Kid Thomas had recruited Dison Esridge to the cause. All three men were connected by the friendships developed during their prior misadventures. All of the men were implicated in the La Plata valley rustling ring, and Dison owed a debt of gratitude to Kid Thomas, who had eagerly volunteered his services to help rescue Hargo Eskridge and others after the Pinhook valley battle. Kid Thomas needed reckless men in order to break his brother out of jail and he had them. Bert Wilkinson and Dison Eskridge were two men who would use their pistols if necessary. They had proven as much on that fateful Christmas Eve the year before.

On Wednesday, August 24th, Silverton stable owner Charles W. Hodges was also on his way to Silverton. Just below the Rico House, Thomas and the other men passed him. Hodges had been in Durango and was aware that the men had been involved in the robbery of Miller's Saloon. Soon after arriving in Silverton, Hodges saw the men and notified local law enforcement authorities that they were wanted in La Plata County. San Juan County Sheriff George Thorniley and Silverton Marshal David Clayton (Clate) Ogsbury wanted more than a hearsay account before they took action. That evening they checked the Durango mail and found no warrants. They hoped the outlaws would move on and decided to wait and see what tomorrow might bring.[12]

In the meantime, La Plata County Sheriff Luke Hunter was on his way up the Animas with warrants in hand. Around midnight, he rode into Silverton. He placed his horse in the care of the Herr, Hodges and Herr's stable and in the company of Charles Hodges went to find Marshal Ogsbury. He inquired about Ogsbury in the Senate Billiard Hall and was told that he could be found asleep in his room at the rear of Goode's Saloon at the southeast corner of 13th and Greene Streets. Upon arriving at Goode's, Hunter told Mr. Goode that he was looking for Wilkinson and the other men because of their involvement in a robbery and the jail break of Jimmy Catron. Goode took Hunter and Hodges to Ogsbury's sleeping room. Hunter soon learned that Wilkinson and the others were at the Diamond Saloon (commonly referred to as the lower dance hall), which was on the southeast corner of 11th and Greene Streets. A one-time Rico resident, Dick Simms, overheard some of the conversation and immediately left for the Diamond Saloon, where he asked Wilkinson and the others about the jail break of Catron. Simms regularly put his nose where it did not belong, and was known in the mining camps as "Broke-Nose" Simms. When Simms was asked how he knew about the jail break, he said he had just heard it from Luke Hunter. Back at Goode's Saloon, Ogsbury finished dressing, put on his gun belt, and prepared to make the arrests.[13] He was a bit apprehensive and advised Sheriff Hunter that they needed more men.

Hunter blandly assured him that they were fine. Ogsbury was probably aware that Hunter knew Eskridge and Wilkinson and accepted his word that the men could be arrested without incident, so he deferred to Hunter's judgment and good will. The two officers and Hodges strode out into the darkness and headed for the Diamond Saloon.[14] The Diamond was going full blast.

As the Diamond's crowd reveled, Bert Wilkinson and his companions prepared for Hunter's arrival. Marshal Ogsbury was taking the lead. He was wary, but might have been more so had he known that because of Hunter's loud mouth and Dick Simms's treachery, the wanted men had been alerted. Upon approaching the dance house and saloon Ogsbury saw a figure in the shadows leaning against the northwest corner of the building. As Ogsbury leaned into the shadow to get a better view, he saw Wilkinson. Bert pointed his pistol and fired, striking the marshal in the left side near the heart. The marshal fell forward on his face and Hodges leaned down to check on his condition. Ogsbury groaned. Hodges rolled the wounded marshal on to his back, but with sporadic gunshots still piercing the air, he soon sought shelter across the street. After only about a dozen shots, the deadly portion of the mayhem was over. The Diamond Saloon had a full house and some of the bullets passed through the walls. Most of the patrons sought safety on the floor. Charles Edwards was shot in the side and the bar keeper had two bullet marks in his clothing. Wilkinson, Eskridge and Thomas fled the scene on foot, leaving their horses and their rifles at Carlisle's Livery. Hodges went back over to Ogsbury, who was still alive but mortally wounded. He tried to get help in the dance hall, but found that pandemonium prevailed. Shortly afterwards, Hiram Herr and another man came along and they carried Ogsbury two blocks to Goode's Saloon. If the marshal was not dead, he soon would be.[15]

At the time Silverton had a new telephone line that went over to Lake City. A phone call was placed and soon the word was spread via telegraph to Alamosa, Durango and elsewhere. The town fire bell rang out and men gathered in the cool evening air. Several posses spread out looking for the men.[16] Reports about the role of Kid Thomas are varied. Some say he remained in town, others say he left. According to one account, Wilkinson and Eskridge induced him to return to town to see what was going on and more importantly to return with horses. Silverton residents quickly identified Eskridge, Wilkinson and Thomas as the perpetrators and made no distinction about who fired the fatal shots. Witnesses reported that Thomas was in the thick of the action, firing as many as four shots during the fracas. As bedlam reigned, rumors sprang up that Thomas was wanted in Texas with a $1200 reward for his capture.[17] If Thomas had indeed fled town and then returned, it was a catastrophic blunder. Within a half hour of the shooting he showed up at the back door of the Grand Central Hotel and demanded admittance, while at the same time inexplicably offering to give up his gun. In short order he was captured and placed in the Silverton jail.[18]

Hiram Herr and others rode out of town and headed up Mineral Creek. In the pitch black they cut the trail of the outlaws about three miles upstream. By lantern light the posse could discern in the black mountain fastness where Eskridge and Wilkinson unwittingly passed through a marshy area near the stream. The fugitives left gashes in the mud, where they had sunk past their knees in the gunk. Dison's boots were lost when the mire sucked them off his feet. It was a normal summer at over nine thousand feet and the temperature sank as the night wore on. Soaked with water and mud, trailed by a posse bristling with pistols, shotguns and rifles, Eskridge and Wilkinson spent a miserable night running for their lives. Despite being afoot, the two men could not be found. They were gone, but not forgotten.[19]

Silverton's enraged residents were in a state of shock and one thing at least was certain: there would be hell to pay. Ogsbury's parents lived in Albany, New York and he was well known and well liked in the mining town, where he had lived since 1875.[20] Like many others in the San Juans, the town marshal was an active prospector, always hoping to become the next "Midas of the Rockies."[21] He had been appointed as marshal early in the spring and was dedicated to his job, so much so, that he had joined the Rocky Mountain Detective Association.[22] The marshal's pay was $1500 a year. Regular constables were paid $1000 per year.[23] At 9:00 AM the next day a coroner's jury was assembled, consisting of S.W. Mathews, B.A. Taft, A. Loring, E.M. Johnson, Major W.W. Ross and T.E. Bowman. Their finding was that Bert Wilkinson fired the fatal shot.[24]

The day after the shooting, the talk in town was about lynching and the consensus was that Wilkinson and Eskridge were headed to Rico. Indeed, the men were headed over Ophir Pass toward the mining town of Ophir and then to the Fish Lakes, which were about fifteen miles from Rico. (Nowadays the Fish Lakes area is known as Trout Lake. The name was changed in about 1882.)[25] Their partner in crime Kid Thomas, or the Black Kid as he was being called in the press, found no escape from the Silverton jail. He was well aware what fate awaited him and his wait was not long. According to the *Denver Republican*, about 9:00 o'clock that night, Kid Thomas was taken from his cell and hung in the wood house which adjoined the jail. A dispatch from Silverton said, "It can simply be stated that one of the gang of desperadoes has tasted the availability of hemp, and Marshal Ogsbury's death is partly avenged."[26]

That same evening (August 25th), on the other side of the Continental Divide, Charles Allison, Lew Perkins and Henry Watts were placed in the Conejos County jail.[27] The men had narrowly avoided their own lynch mob thanks to the guile of Sheriff Joe Smith who made a show of loading the prisoners in the mail car, but it was a ruse. At La Veta a mob stormed the mail car, but the prisoners were not inside.[28] While vigilantes searched for them, the outlaws were transported from Pueblo by wagon via Poncha Springs and Saguache. At the same time it was reported in Antonito that Catron and three others held up two saloons in Animas City and now all four desperadoes were in jail. This was no doubt a slightly confused version of the earlier robbery north of Durango. The *Denver Republican* carried a dispatch from Antonito which said that Conejos County residents feared that a rescue attempt was being organized from the area near Chama. Conejos County's aroused citizens let it be known they "expect a visit from the gang but are prepared for them."[29] Jimmy Catron did not show up in Conejos County, Wilkinson and Eskridge were preoccupied, and Kid Thomas was dead. Allison and his gang did not escape nor were they lynched. In October 1881, the men were tried and convicted for robbery. They would spend the next several years in the penitentiary in Cañon City.[30]

A trial, verdict and jail term for Eskridge and Wilkinson were not part of the plan for Silverton's angered citizens. They were out for blood. Up in Rico, Wilkinson and Eskridge had many friends who would help them, including newspapermen Charles Jones and Frank Hartman. There was also a rumor that Harry Bennett, a proprietor of a Silverton dance hall, was trying to help the two wanted men. Silverton's residents were aware that the fugitives might head for Rico. Sheriff Thorniley and his men had headed that direction at about 3:00 in the morning. At 7:00 AM, Jack Pendleton and J.W. Brady were at the Fish Lakes, on the trail to Rico, when they saw three men on the upper end of the lake, two of them on horseback and one on foot. They rode out for Silverton to advise authorities.[31] They may not have been on the trail for long, when they ran into Thorniley's posse. A short time later the Sheriff and his men rode into Neumeyer's lodge on the lake. That summer Mrs. A.W. Neumeyer was operating "The Summit House," a wayside inn and eatery with stable facilities for travelers and tourists at the lake.[32] It was a twenty mile ride from Silverton to the Fish Lakes, so Thorniley and his posse took a respite from their labors. Little did they know that while still on the Fish Lakes trail, they had passed right by Dison Eskridge and Bert Wilkinson.[33]

While Jones's *Dolores News* was kind in its characterization of Wilkinson, the rest of the San Juan country press was not so circumspect. The *Silver World* of Lake City said Wilkinson was "known to be a murderer, thief and habitue of dance houses."[34] Newspapers marveled at how such a hardened outlaw had emerged from such a respected and distinguished family.[35] In Silverton, local citizens used the shooting to clean up the seedier side of town. Both dance houses were shut down. It was said that the girls would move to Animas Forks, but the *Lake City Mining Register* predicted that they would find no lodging there either.[36] The sudden temperance mattered little; no mining town could exist without a dance house and Silverton's own noble experiment was predictably short.

The citizens of Silverton intended to catch Wilkinson and Eskridge. San Juan County, Colorado offered a $1500 reward for their capture. The town of Silverton offered a $1000 reward. Citizens of the town added $1000 of their own money to the kitty and Governor Pitkin added another $1000, for a grand total of $4500.[37] Notices described Wilkinson as being about twenty-two years old (he was only nineteen), not quite six foot tall and weighing 160 pounds with a freckled face and bony appearance. He was reported to be wearing a "suit of light clothes." Dison Eskridge was described as being in his early twenties, about five feet ten inches tall and 155 pounds.[38] Over five hundred post cards were printed up featuring the reward and descriptions of the men. The cards were sent to sheriff and marshal offices in Colorado, New Mexico, Arizona, Utah and Texas.[39] Down in Durango, as the reward total grew, it drew attention from a surprising source. Ike Stockton began to take notice. A plan to betray his young admiring gang members, and make some money in the process, began to form in Stockton's mind. He approached his friend, Sheriff Luke Hunter, and asked to be commissioned as a deputy. Hunter obliged.[40]

Hillside Cemetery, Silverton, CO. (Author's collection.)

The substantial reward attracted wide attention. Captain Charles A. Hawley of the Rocky Mountain Detective Association came from Denver to see if he could help capture the fugitives. Greed may not have been his sole motivation, as he had been personally acquainted with Ogsbury.[41] The *Rocky Mountain News* declared that, "The detective association was very anxious to effect a capture as Ogsbury had been such a popular and valued member of the force." Hawley evidently felt he was so well known and highly regarded as a detective that he furtively traveled in disguise from Denver to Durango. Other "detectives" and bounty hunters descended on the San Juan country, all of them anxious for the reward money. The *News* was unaware of the growing reward and reported that Wilkinson was worth only $2000 dead or alive.[42]

The close call with Thorniley's posse made it clear that Rico would not be a safe haven. There was one other obvious destination for the two men and that was the Castle Rock stage station above Durango. (The Castle Rock Station was located about a mile south of the entrance to the present day ski area.)[43] The station was strategically located near the fork of the Rico and Silverton roads. Bert Wilkinson had good reason to go to there; his sister Flora Pyle and her husband Orville operated the station. The Pyles found sanctuary north of Durango after being run out of Farmington shortly after the murder of Os Puett at the Hamblet's Christmas Eve party, the same shootout where Dison Eskridge killed George Brown. Seth Welfoot, the one-armed Englishman who had helped bury Os Puett, lived with the Pyles. For this act and others, he too was forced out of Farmington. The teenaged cousins, Os Puett and Bert Wilkinson, had allied themselves with Dison Eskridge and that alliance brought death to Os Puett and eight months later was contributing to an ever slimmer chance of survival for Bert Wilkinson. As Eskridge and Wilkinson struggled through timber falls and across the high mountain meadows of the San Juans, they did not have the time or inclination to reflect on their relationship. With every turn of the trail they knew they might encounter Thorniley's posse and with that in mind they had no intention of separating. They bored on, seeking sanctuary at Castle Rock. Ike Stockton was also aware that the two men would eventually end up at the Pyle home, so on Saturday, August 27th, he traveled to Castle Rock and arranged to spend the night. He told Flora that, "he had heard that a party would arrive from Silverton and that he had come to warn the boys" if they were there.[44]

That same day Silverton held what was probably the town's largest funeral up to that time. Ogsbury was laid out, without a casket, in the San Juan County Courthouse. Those who wished to gaze upon the slain marshal passed through the building. After the viewing, his body was placed in a casket for burial. The funeral service was conducted by Reverend Harlan P. Roberts of the First Congregational Church. It was an open casket service so mourners could take one last look at Ogsbury. Almost five hundred people overflowed the pews and spilled into the lobby. After the service a funeral procession consisting of eighteen mounted horsemen and fifteen double teams followed by a large crowd of pedestrians traveled up Reese Street to 13th Street. From there, they proceeded up Greene Street to the cemetery. Business houses were closed and flags flew at half-mast. At the grave the mourners sang "Nearer, My

God, To Thee." After the benediction was given, Clate Ogsbury was laid to rest. Clate's final resting place would not remain on the mountainside above Silverton. Two days later he was disinterred at the telegraphed request of his family and shipped to Dunnsville, New York on the Hudson. Reverend Roberts escorted the slain marshal's corpse.[45]

The desperate flight of Eskridge and Wilkinson continued. Stockton spent Saturday night at the Pyle place and remained there on Sunday. At midnight on Sunday night, August 28th, Flora Pyle awoke to light knocking on the door. Upon answering, she found Bert and Dison, looking much the worse for wear. Bert's first words were, "Flora, we are awful hungry, but have you got anything that will fit Dison's feet; he is barefooted." Flora gave them a meal, which they ate outdoors. They never entered her home. Their mud-caked clothes contributed to that situation. There was a house across from the Pyle home used by travelers, and it was then occupied by Stockton. Flora told the two men and they were overjoyed that their ally was there to help them. They wanted to see him immediately and someone was sent for Stockton, who went out to meet the fugitives.[46]

When Stockton arrived, he was trembling and his teeth were chattering. According to Flora he commented, "It is very cold this evening." Perhaps the enormity of the betrayal he was contemplating contributed to his nervous appearance, but Ike was not prepared to take on both Eskridge and Wilkinson, so he set about preparing a trap. Bert was anxious to know who was getting the blame for the shooting. His reaction to finding out that he had been identified as the murderer is not known. After considering that another Silverton posse might show up, and not wishing to further entangle the Pyles, Eskridge and Wilkinson decided to make their stay short. Flora arranged to provide them with horses and sufficient provisions for several days. Before leaving, Dison asked Flora to tell Hargo that he was going to see their brother Dow in Conejos and from there he and Bert intended to go out on the plains. Stockton suggested that the two men might have a better chance if they separated. They were not receptive to the idea, but they did say that when they reached a place where they could live and work, they intended to mend their ways and live honorable lives. Stockton made arrangements for a rendezvous and the fugitives rode off.[47]

After they left, Flora invited Stockton and Welfoot to have breakfast. Eight months before, Welfoot had denounced the men who killed Porter Stockton and shot Mrs. Stockton. His outspoken criticism of Port's killers was one reason he was now living with the Pyles. He was not so quick to condemn Bert Wilkinson for killing a respected peace officer like Ogsbury. His reliance on the goodwill of his current hostess clearly dampened his outspoken manner. As they ate breakfast, Stockton and Welfoot conversed about their situation. Flora Pyle was busy with her domestic duties and later recalled their conversation. Ike spoke about living in dread of the law and said that many of his friends had advised him to leave the country and change his name. He joked with Welfoot, saying he should go down to Farmington with him. Of all the men who had been forced out of the lower Animas, Seth Welfoot was the most unpopular. By this time almost all of the New Mexico expatriates had returned to their homes. (Some had found success in Colorado and there they would remain.) Welfoot's condemnation of his neighbors had managed to engender long-lasting ill will and so he was still reviled by many residents in and around Farmington. Those residents were just glad to be rid of Porter Stockton. Ike Stockton and Welfoot would have received heated greetings in Farmington. Unfortunately, Flora found the rest of their conversation to be "about matters of small consequence."[48] As for Stockton, that day he set in motion a course of action which he hoped would enable him to leave the country and start anew.

On Monday, August 29th, Wilkinson and Eskridge spent the night at the rendezvous site. Ike Stockton returned to Animas City where he enlisted the aid of his friend, M.C. Cook, who was working as the deputy town marshal in Animas City. The city fathers were either fearless or clueless, since M.C. Cook followed in Port Stockton's brutish footsteps as the second town marshal who was wanted for murder in Texas.[49] La Plata County's new law enforcement officers wasted no time. They rode up the Animas and on to the Castle Rock Station. They stopped at the Pyle place and Ike asked Orville Pyle for the $10 that Bert owed him, a loan which Orville had agreed to pay. Considering what Ike was planning to do, finances were obviously foremost in his mind. According to Flora, her husband had been holding the $10 for a while, but had recently used it and was unable to pay Stockton. To avoid arousing suspicion, Ike did not press the matter and told the Pyles he was in no hurry for payment.[50] Stockton and Cook soon left for the rendezvous site. Different accounts place the hideout as close as seven and as far as twenty miles north of town. The refuge was also said to be in the Needle Mountains. One version places it on a mesa west of the Animas, but other accounts place it on a mesa east of the Animas.[51] Eskridge and Wilkinson were probably high up on Missionary Ridge, hidden from view, but with easy access to a long distance view which would reveal any riders approaching their redoubt.

On Tuesday morning the four men met up as planned. Eskridge and Wilkinson did not suspect Stockton's true motives. If Ike ever thought about capturing Dison for the reward money, he quickly discarded that idea. In Dison's case, Stockton either remained true to his friend Hargo, or the fear of reprisal from Hargo influenced his decision. Stockton left Cook with Wilkinson on the pretext that he and Dison were going to cross over the divide to get horses.[52] Ike's longtime ally, George Morrison, was to provide the fresh mounts.[53] At 3:00 PM Stockton returned without Dison.

Stockton told Wilkinson that Dison's brother Hargo had joined them. He enticed Wilkinson, reporting that the Eskridge boys were holding Morrison's fresh mounts five miles away. Bert rose and walked over to cinch his saddle, leaving his pistol on a blanket. Stockton placed himself between Wilkinson and the blanket and told Bert to throw up his hands. Bert put his hands up with a laugh, thinking Ike was joking. But after seeing the look on Stockton's face, he asked, "Ike, do you mean it?" To which Stockton replied, "Yes, I do mean it – money is what makes men in this country." Bert responded, "You've got the drop on me, Ike, but I'd rather you'd kill me." Stockton told Wilkinson that he would not be turned over to the authorities unless he had something to defend himself.[54] Ike justified his actions, at one point telling Wilkinson, "You know you are a murderer and there is no chance for Eskridge while you are with him."[55]

Ike and M.C. Cook headed down the ridge with their prisoner. Before traveling onto Animas City and Durango, they stopped at Frank Williams's ranch and Wilkinson was left there under guard.[56] The next day the *Durango Record* announced, "Ike Stockton rode into town last evening, claiming that he had captured Burt Wilkinson in the mountains, some fifteen to twenty miles north of here." Everyone wanted to see Bert Wilkinson, but Ike refused to tell anyone where he was, except for his attorney, James L. Russell.[57] Stockton met with Sheriff Hunter, who advised him to send a man to Silverton to let Sheriff Thorniley know that at least one of their men was in custody. Frank Williams was dispatched to Silverton.[58] Naturally, everyone was surprised and many were suspicious when it was learned that somehow Dison Eskridge had escaped capture. Stockton told reporters that Eskridge and Wilkinson had been together, but now Eskridge was gone, he knew not where.[59]

On Wednesday night Wilkinson was brought into Animas City and placed in Keith's City Hotel on the east side of the Animas about one hundred yards from the Animas bridge. Wilkinson was kept under heavy guard and the fear that vigilantes would soon arrive was heavy in the air. The prisoner was wearing shoes with holes in the bottoms and no socks, and still wore his cartridge belt. He smoked a meerschaum pipe. The *Durango Record* said that he had a long talk with his uncle, "Mr. Puitt[sic]." At the time, Austin Puett was working as a milkman and lived up the Animas valley. A few years before, his wife worked as the first teacher in the first school house in Animas City. The one room log cabin was the first school on the western slope of the San Juans. Bert's other uncle, Al Puett, was probably still running cattle on the Utah/Colorado border. While being held in Animas City, Wilkinson absolved Eskridge of any responsibility for the shooting of Marshal Ogsbury. Ike introduced a newsman from the *Durango Southwest* to Wilkinson. The teenaged murderer was lying on one of the six beds in the hotel's lodging room, perusing a newspaper. The young outlaw told the newsman that they had come close to being captured after the trouble in Silverton. He said that while he and Eskridge were headed toward the Fish Lakes, they saw the sheriff and his posse, but they managed to avoid being discovered. As for their run for freedom Wilkinson said, "I don't know where I did go. I wandered around in the mountains, and got lost. I hardly know myself where I have been." While part of that assessment was for the protection of his sister, Flora, some of it was certainly accurate. Speaking of his predicament, he remarked, "All I have to say myself is that I would like to have a square trial." About the lynching of Kid Thomas he noted, "It was a murder when they hung him, and a foul murder too." Commenting further he observed, "I would like to go to trial, but if I do not, I guess I can stand it. The country is old enough now to be governed by law and order." When asked to explain his actions he replied, "I don't believe it would do any good, to tell the truth. I do not think that the people are prepared to hear it. They are for strangling." He asked the reporter to tell W.G. Brien, a Durango attorney, to come over and see him immediately. The newsman concluded that "from the drift of his remarks it would seem that he considered himself responsible entirely for the killing of Ogsbury."[60]

Silverton's *La Plata Miner* made no secret of what fate awaited Wilkinson. An article describing his capture had this to say; "Our people will rejoice at the positive assurance which they now have that this murderer and thief will soon receive his just dues. He will be hung."[61] Stockton had hoped to hold the prisoner in Animas City until the reward money was deposited in the Bank of Durango. He wanted the San Juan County sheriff to come to Animas City and pick up Wilkinson. Stockton played cat and mouse with potential vigilantes by periodically moving Wilkinson out to the woods for safekeeping. He was protected by a heavy guard consisting of Mayor E.E. Fox, Marshal M.C. Cook, John Hull (or Hall), Mark Shannon, George Enslow, Howard Culver and J.B. Doe. Additional guards hid in the brush and hills, ready to spread the alarm, should a vigilante party show up. For Stockton, the cost of protecting Wilkinson was proving to be a potentially expensive proposition.[62]

Bert's mother and stepfather, Ellen and Simeon Hendrickson, lived up the Animas valley near the Cascade Lakes. On the evening of August 31st, Flora Pyle joined them as they visited Wilkinson in the hotel room which served as his cell. Facing the strong possibility that her son would be lynched, the strain on Mrs. Hendrickson was tremendous. Outlaws in Bert's circumstances seldom had a reunion of this kind. Young Bert had a long conversation with his family and they remained in Animas City overnight.[63] Bert deserved his reputation as a killer, but newspaper accounts of the heart-wrenching encounter between the prisoner and his mother heightened the perception that Ike Stockton's role in the affair was something less than honorable, even among outlaws.

Frank Williams returned from Silverton the next morning and told Ike that Silverton authorities would not pay the reward until Wilkinson was delivered to Silverton. Ike was very apprehensive about making the fifty mile journey up the Animas. He feared that Wilkinson, and thus his reward money, would be taken from him before he reached the mining town. He sent word back to San Juan County and Silverton authorities that they would have to come and get Wilkinson.[64] Silverton's *San Juan Herald* reported that Ike "was somewhat squeamish about invading the precincts of San Juan county, as he had reason to believe that the people of our section made rather summary work of those who had associated with outlaws and murderers." Ike was playing a losing hand. Having to guard Wilkinson around the clock was placing him in an untenable position, and above all else, he needed the reward money. Ike soon caved and made arrangements to deliver Bert Wilkinson to Silverton.[65]

On Saturday, September 3rd, Wilkinson was taken out of Animas City under the guard of Stockton, Animas City's Mayor Fox, John Hull and M.C. Cook. Stockton's small group was met between Silverton and Animas City at Carson's Ranch by Sheriff Thorniley and one deputy. Sheriff Luke Hunter, the appropriate person to represent La Plata County during the proceedings, was nowhere to be seen. Upon meeting Stockton's group, Thorniley sent his deputy back to Silverton to secure a large escort party. A posse of twelve armed men left Silverton at about 1:00 PM and met the group near the Ten Mile House in the Animas River canyon. As the river bubbled and gurgled its way south, D&RG grading crews worked in the narrow canyon bottom to extend the rails. They had advanced to within eight miles of Silverton. Perhaps some of the crewmen looked up from their picks, shovels and sledges and watched as the solemn convoy rode past. Despite the increased guard, Stockton was still concerned that Wilkinson might be lynched and the tension remained high as the men rode upriver. It was about 6:00 PM when Wilkinson finally returned to the town that was the location of his most heinous crime. The town was a tinderbox. Just one match and it would explode. If any of Silverton's residents had thoughts of lynching Wilkinson right then and there, they were dissuaded after watching the resolute and well-armed escort party. The reputations of Ike Stockton and M.C. Cook, and the respect accorded Sheriff Thorniley, worked in their favor and Wilkinson was successfully delivered to the Silverton jail. A heavy guard was placed in and around the jail. Visitors were restricted to "officers in charge, and members of the press." Meanwhile Ike Stockton and his men proceeded to the side door of the bank and, according to the *San Juan Herald*, received reward monies totaling $2500, which represented only the money put up by the Town of Silverton and San Juan County and not the $1000 from Governor Pitkin nor the $1000 pledged by the citizens of the area.[66] The *Herald* was misinformed about the amount of money Stockton received. Stockton received only $850.00 from

San Juan County and $571.43 from the Town of Silverton, for a total of $1421.43.67 Stockton feared that he too might become the victim of vigilante justice and did not want to give up his pistol while in town. Authorities told him to keep his weapon and Thorniley assured him that he would not be bothered. The Animas City men checked into the Walker House and prepared to spend the night. Stockton did not go out to celebrate his new found fortune. He stayed close to the hotel and went to bed early.68 Flora and Orville Pyle had followed Stockton's party up the Animas and they rode into Silverton that same evening. Flora was intent on trying to secure a trial for her beleaguered brother.69 The mood in Silverton remained agitated until three or four in the morning, when Clate Ogsbury's friends, and others who simply hoped to see a lynching, finally accepted that Bert Wilkinson would live to see another dawn. As might be expected, there were several suspicious characters skulking about and it was feared they were there to break Wilkinson out of jail. The *San Juan Herald* reported that they were shadowed all night.70 As for Wilkinson's survival, the *Dolores News* reported that only the presence of Flora Pyle saved his life.71

That Sunday in Silverton was a day made for lynching. Residents woke to a gloomy morning, with an intermittent drizzle drenching the town. Ike Stockton and his men donned their slickers and rode down the Animas at 7:30 that morning. Flora and Orville left about 9:00 AM, leaving Wilkinson to his own devices.72 Flora had been told that Bert would be hung, whether she was in town or not. Sheriff Thorniley promised that Bert's body would be sent to her.73

During the day, Captain Hawley was allowed into the jail to interview the doomed man. He engaged Wilkinson in conversation, trying to divine the location of Dison Eskridge. It was a fruitless exercise. While in the Silverton lockup, Wilkinson tried a different strategy and now said that Dison Eskridge was equally implicated in the murder of Ogsbury, as both men fired at the same time and he could not be sure who fired the fatal shot. He said his intent that night was to kill Sheriff Luke Hunter. Wilkinson made clear his absolute disgust with Ike Stockton, his one-time friend, who had betrayed him for the reward money. According to the *San Juan Herald*, "Wilkinson said if he could only see Stockton hung he would die singing – and begged that Ike might be brought in the jail so that he could shoot him, and then he would let them put the noose around his [own] neck when he could die shouting." About noon a photographer entered the jail, and while Wilkinson smoked a cigar and chatted with Hawley, a photo of the living, breathing Wilkinson was taken for posterity.74 Wilkinson was familiar with the gruesome post-mortem photos often taken of desperadoes and asked that no photos be taken after he was hung. It was noted that, "He showed during the day the grandest bravery ever shown by any man in the face of death."75 The *Durango Herald* echoed that opinion, saying, "The nerve he manifested was simply wonderful."

They reported that Wilkinson blamed the shooting on whiskey and when questioned about his religion he said, "he knew nothing about religion."[76] As darkness fell, James Everingham, a reporter for the *San Juan Herald*, stayed close to the jail. Mayor Francis M. Snowden encountered the reporter, asked him what he was doing and then told him to leave. Everingham resisted, but Snowden told others that he made the reporter "git up and git."[77]

The Pyle family in 1895. Standing are Harry, Frank, Carroll and Louisa. Seated in front are mother Flora Wilkinson Pyle, Cleaver, father Orville D. and Dorothy. Flora followed Ike Stockton and the other men holding her brother Bert Wilkinson into Silverton, but did not succeed in her efforts to save him from vigilantes. (Courtesy Frank and Sandra Pyle.)

In contrast to the previous night, Silverton's Sunday night was unusually quiet. Wilkinson knew his time was near when most of the guardsmen in and around the jail melted away into the night and only the jailer and two other men remained. The streets were almost empty when at about 9:30 a party of masked men made their way down the street to the lockup. As was invariably the case, later newspaper accounts described the guards as being "overpowered." Unlike many frontier lynchings, there would be no public spectacle in the moonlight. Wilkinson was kept in his cell. A noose was placed over his neck and according to some he stepped onto a chair of his own accord and assisted the vigilantes with the hanging. When asked if he had anything to say, he replied, "Nothing, gentlemen, *adios!*" The chair was removed and he dropped, showing little struggle. He was composed until the very end. The tightly orchestrated execution proceeded to the next step as Wilkinson's body was soon discovered hanging in the cell and the very unsurprised coroner was notified. It was now two down and one to go. The *San Juan Herald* reported Wilkinson's death and added, "Silverton does nothing by halves. Her people started out for justice and spared neither expense or vigilance and the result is that Wilkinson has met his just deserts. Now for Eskridge."[78] According to one account, the prostitute who had been at the center of the killing of "Comanche Bill" was in Silverton and she asked to see the body. While in the cell she tried to remove a diamond ring from one of Wilkinson's blood-gorged fingers. She had to resort to using her teeth to retrieve the prize. She may have initially planned on keeping the ring, but then she had second thoughts and shortly afterwards she gave the ring to Flora Pyle.[79]

The next day, after the coroner's inquest, Wilkinson's body was placed in a coffin and delivered to his relatives by Sheriff Thorniley. Bert would have turned twenty years old on October 23rd. After his death, newspapers reminded readers that Ogsbury was not his first killing. That was most likely the killing of "Comanche Bill" in December 1880. Evidently he murdered someone else. According to the *San Juan Herald*, Wilkinson sent at least three men to their graves.[80] The identity of Bert's third victim remains a mystery. For a nineteen-year-old youth, it was an alarming total.

The Puett and Pyle families buried Bert near the Castle Rock Station.[81] By that time his former ally, Ike Stockton, was at home in Animas City. If he intended to leave southwest Colorado, he found the blood money he received in Silverton was too small to start a new life, especially after he split it with M.C. Cook. Payments made to those who had helped guard Wilkinson may have further reduced his take. Ike remained in Animas City and held out hope that he would receive the $1000 reward offered by Governor Pitkin and the $1000 offered by the citizens of Silverton, although the reward money pledged by the citizens presumably dried up after Bert swung. Not long after his return to Animas City, rumors swirled that La Plata County Sheriff Luke Hunter would soon resign. The *San Juan Herald* reported that Stockton was in line to take his place.[82] The *Rocky Mountain News* declared that the capture of Wilkinson "will result in making Stockton one of the most popular men in his section."[83] For some reason, the Colorado press failed to grasp the truth of the matter. Support for Ike Stockton in southwest Colorado had been steadily declining since the Battle of Durango. His participation in the Pinhook fight provided a temporary boost, but his support was as soft as the sand in the bottom of the Pinhook valley. If anyone but Stockton had arrested Ogsbury's killer, they would have been feted in Silverton and Durango as a courageous hero. Local citizens were thankful that Wilkinson had been arrested, but along the Animas acclaim for Ike was not forthcoming. Loyalty was a trait highly valued across the frontier, and while the frontier was rapidly disappearing, loyalty was still held in high regard. Stockton had committed a grievous error when he delivered nineteen-year-old Bert Wilkinson to the citizens of Silverton for money. Ike's betrayal would be one of the last notable acts of a desperate man.

Bert Wilkinson ca. 1880. Lynched inside the Silverton jail on September 4, 1881, just fifty days short of his twentieth birthday. (Courtesy of Frank and Sandra Pyle.)

Chapter Nineteen

Durango's Judas

> *The long trail ends today,---*
> *The long trail ends today,*
> *The punchers go to play*
> *And all you weary cattle*
> *May sleep in peace for sure,---*
> *May sleep in peace for sure,---*
> *Sleep, sleep for sure.*[1]

The first indication of trouble for Ike Stockton began even before Wilkinson was lynched. After the shock of Ogsbury's murder began to wear off, the conduct of La Plata County Sheriff Luke Hunter became the subject of much conversation in Silverton. The *San Juan Herald* reported the consensus in Silverton: "To say the least, the actions of Sheriff Hunter in the affair are somewhat suspicious."[2]

Hunter's friendship with Ike Stockton, Dison Eskridge and Bert Wilkinson put his actions under close scrutiny. The La Plata County sheriff was taken to task for advertising the purpose of his arrival in Silverton as he greeted acquaintances at the Senate Billiard Hall, Johnny Goode's Saloon and elsewhere. Silverton's residents wondered why he had not quietly gone about his business. His relationship to "Broke-Nose" Simms, who had given the warning to Wilkinson and his friends, was the focal point of much conjecture. The *San Juan Herald* said that while Hunter arrived on horseback, he left by coach. The *Herald* said it was Simms who rode Hunter's horse out of Silverton. The newspaper speculated that Hunter purposely announced his arrival in the belief "that the gang, hearing of his presence, would at once skip." That misguided plan resulted in the ambush which followed. As for the dozen or so shots fired after Ogsbury was hit, none of them came from Hunter's firearm. It seems that all of the shots were fired by the fugitives as they covered their escape. Not only did Hunter fail to defend the fallen marshal, he did not join the posses pursuing the outlaws. The *Herald* laid it out, saying Ogsbury's murder "is indirectly traceable to criminal carelessness and foolhardiness on the part of the sheriff of La Plata County." The Silverton paper also noted that anyone "implicated in the affair, either directly or indirectly, will be liable to smell of powder or taste of hemp." Luke Hunter was persona non grata in Silverton and San Juan County.[3]

While Hunter was feeling the wrath of Silverton, Ike Stockton began to feel the wrath of his former friends. On September 17th the

Durango Record published correspondence they had received from Rico, which said, "Durango's Judas, (Ike Stockton) who numbered many friends at one time, is probably sensible enough not to come to Rico soon, without any warning from us."[4] (Parentheses are in the original article.) Charles Jones and Frank Hartman had used the printing press of the *Dolores News* like a running iron, but some brands cannot be altered and Ike Stockton's true character proved to be as difficult to obscure as the C-O-X burned into the flanks of Wash Cox's cattle. In the end, Ike's inherent nature showed through, crisp and clear, when he hand-delivered Bert Wilkinson to his lynchers.

Now that one of their closest friends had been strung up by men who were their friends and acquaintances in Silverton, Hartman and Jones reassessed their editorial stance when it came to Ike Stockton. They noted "Since the shooting of Comanche Bill last winter, in the early days of Durango, [Wilkinson] has been a sort of outlaw, although many thought that killing perhaps justifiable." The newspapermen continued, "Wilkinson had a right to expect assistance from Stockton, as he was a man of his own stripe." They noted that the man who arrested Wilkinson had a "blacker heart" than the man he captured. After backing up Stockton in all of his actions, the newsmen now claimed that they "have taken pains to inquire into the life of Stockton for many years past. His record is not what it should be." After defending Stockton and his allies for months and asserting that they were upstanding citizens, the Rico newspaper made a stunning admission: "Stockton and Wilkinson were two of a band of outlaws." The *News* went on saying, "the idea of the treachery of Stockton in delivering up his comrade to be hung for a monied consideration solely, is an action which has caused the loss of all the friends he had." They characterized Wilkinson as "a misguided boy, encouraged in his misdeeds by Stockton and his companions."[5] Hartman and Jones had at last corrected their assessment of Ike Stockton, but they could not undo the damage they had already done. The two young men wielded tremendous influence through the opinions they recklessly expressed in the *Dolores News*. Readers of their dispatches in Denver and even Durango and elsewhere were left with a slanted impression of the unrest, which made it difficult to determine what was true and what was not. The motives of some of the good citizens like Wash Cox, Alf Graves, Mose Blancett and others were ignored, minimized and ridiculed by the Rico newspaper. Conflict may have been reduced and tragedies avoided had the newspapermen checked into or revealed what they already knew about Stockton's past at an earlier date. Their blind faith in and support of Stockton and his associates damaged business affairs in southwest Colorado and northwest New Mexico, and indirectly contributed to the calamitous sequence of murders, stage robberies and other mayhem that flowed out of the lawless situation on both sides of the border. Had they seen the light sooner, their friend Bert Wilkinson might have been saved from the perilous path which ultimately led to his lynching.

Down in Animas City, Isaac Stockton was not pleased with his latest press clippings. During their stay at the Walker House in Silverton, Stockton and M.C. Cook had been interviewed by a reporter from the *San Juan Herald*. After reading the subsequent article, Stockton wrote the *Southwest* and blasted the *Herald's* account of the capture of Wilkinson and related events. Copies of Stockton's letter are not available, but the *Herald* responded and suggested that it was Ike's own excitement during the interview which accounted for any discrepancies. The *Herald* did not apologize, but said they had no desire to commit any injustice upon Stockton, calling his criticism the result of "overweening sensitiveness on his part."[6]

Ike's concern about the *Herald's* article was a waste of time and effort. The rumor that Luke Hunter was out as the sheriff of La Plata County was true. The speculation that Ike Stockton would take his place was not. The new sheriff was Barney Watson. He was appointed to the position by the La Plata County Commission to fill out the remainder of the term, which ran until December 31, 1881.[7] His deputy was Stockton-Eskridge ally Jim Sullivan. Sullivan had also been a friend to young Bert Wilkinson. When Bert shot and killed "Comanche Bill" Swinford, it was Jim Sullivan who took no interest in arresting Wilkinson.[8] Sullivan had no use for traitors. Stockton's hold on La Plata County's law enforcement authorities was over.

Watson assumed his new responsibilities in mid-September. Not long afterward he had a visit with Rio Arriba County Deputy Sheriff Mose Blancett and let him know that he was ready to assist New Mexico authorities in any way he could, but he also told the deputy that Hunter had given him no documents authorizing the arrest of Ike Stockton.[9] Luke Hunter had made sure that Stockton's arrest warrant was long gone.[10] Watson asked that Governor Sheldon be contacted about the situation. He said that as soon as he had the requisition in his hands he could guarantee the delivery of Ike Stockton. Watson was no fool and he had one more request. He asked that all notice of his communication and of the requisition be kept out of the newspapers. Blancett informed William Haines and Haines penned a letter to Governor Sheldon. According to Haines's letter, Watson requested direct delivery of the requisition from Governor Sheldon's office to his office, a procedure which bypassed Colorado's Governor Pitkin. Governor Sheldon could not do this, however another requisition was drafted for delivery to Pitkin. Near the end of his letter to Sheldon, Haines noted, "This seems to be bringing the end very near."[11] In a letter written a few days later, Haines advised Max Frost that Ike Stockton now had as many enemies in Durango as he had in Rio Arriba County and noted "His [Stockton's] days are numbered."[12]

Ike Stockton's former friends knew many of his secrets. They were aware that M.C. Cook was actually Marion H. "Bud" Galbreath. Stockton's former allies realized that Galbreath was one loose end they needed to tie up. While Watson attempted to secure a requisition and warrant for Ike Stockton's arrest, he was fortuitously advised that Cook/Galbreath was wanted by Texas authorities for murdering a deputy sheriff in Bosque County in 1874. Watson contacted officials in Meridian, Texas to confirm these reports. Not long afterwards Bosque County officials advised him that a deputy was headed to Colorado carrying a requisition for Bud Galbreath.[13] The noose was beginning to tighten.

While the authorities were plotting his arrest or a more expeditious end to the situation, Ike's gang was in the final stages of disintegration. The process had begun in the second week of April in the aftermath of the Battle of Durango and with the Rio Arriba County Grand Jury indictments. After the lynching of Wilkinson and the resignation of Luke Hunter, the last of Stockton's associates began to leave town. The *Denver Republican* reported that in the middle of September, Hargo Eskridge left Durango and headed to Rico when several men ambushed him and he was hit by two bullets.[14] If that is the case, the wounds were not life threatening. No other contemporary accounts of this assault seem to exist. Hargo did not stay long in Rico.

On September 21st he rode into the town then called Gunnison City. He had dispensed with his crutches, but was using a cane and his arm was in a sling. He was seen in the Gunnison House by a porter named Fred Scherrer, who recognized him. Knowing that there was a reward in New Mexico for Hargo's capture, Scherrer informed two local policemen, J.H. Roberts and officer Myers. The next day the three men set out to find Eskridge and finally located him at the train depot sitting in an eastbound car that was about to leave the station.[15] The *Lake City Silver World* reported, "He was heavily armed – with a pair of Colt's revolvers and a Winchester rifle, but held up his hands at the first command."[16] The officers of Gunnison City had done what Durango authorities refused to do. On September 22nd, Captain Charles Hawley, who was in Gunnison, sent a telegram to Durango which read, "*To the Mayor of Durango*: Do you want H. Eskridge? We have him in jail here." The mayor wired back that he was not wanted in Durango, but was still wanted in New Mexico.[17] Hawley, of the Rocky Mountain Detective Association, had only recently left Silverton after the manhunt for Dison Eskridge and Bert Wilkinson. The captain was somehow unaware that it was the territory of New Mexico which had issued an arrest warrant and reward for the capture of Hargo Eskridge for the murder of Tom Nance's cowboy partner, Aaron Barker.

Despite all of his troubles, Eskridge led a charmed life, as Gunnison authorities proceeded to muck up what would be the best chance to bring the wanted murderer to justice. Hargo was immediately taken before Judge J.P. Harlow and charged with carrying concealed weapons. He was fined $25 and costs, which he promptly paid. The *Gunnison News-Democrat* reported, "Another warrant charging him with murder was sworn out and he is now held until the officers can hear from Governor Wallace." At the time Wallace had not been governor of New Mexico for over three months, not to mention the fact that Hargo had committed no murders in Gunnison County. Gunnison's hold on Hargo Eskridge was based on Scherrer's hearsay testimony and imprecise knowledge about murders committed outside the state of Colorado. Hargo was carrying a lot of cash and he immediately hired Colonel Baker as his counsel. As word of Eskridge's arrest spread, a crowd began to gather. Hargo had friends in Gunnison and they tried to convince authorities that there were no outstanding charges against the outlaw. Scherrer claimed that Eskridge was wanted for the murder of the man he identified as "Kit" White in Amargo in June. Eskridge's supporters told the Gunnison newspaper reporter that White's murder was a case of self-defense and Eskridge had been acquitted on the charges. In fact, Hargo never faced charges for the murder of Kid White. He fled Amargo on the day of that killing, went to Durango and on to Rico, and from there he went to Utah on the Indian chase. Since then he had been nursing his injured foot. Scherrer also claimed that Eskridge had killed a man "down on the borders of Mexico." This is probably a confused account of the murder of Aaron Barker. Gunnison authorities had every right to hold Eskridge for Barker's murder, but it seems that they were unaware that months earlier Governor Pitkin had responded to New Mexico's requisition by issuing a warrant for Eskridge's arrest. As for the killing of Kid White, the *News-Democrat* reported: "White testified before his death that Eskridge acted in self defense, so, if this is the only charge against him, it is very doubtful if he can be held."[18] Actually, White did not absolve Eskridge. The *New Mexican* reported that while lying on his deathbed, White refused to say what happened.[19] Not that it mattered, since there was no warrant or requisition calling for the arrest of Hargo Eskridge for the murder of Kid White.

A telegram to Governor Pitkin would have revealed that Colorado authorities had the right and in fact the duty to arrest and hold Hargo for Aaron Barker's murder, but no telegram was sent. Scherrer and others were in line to receive portions of the $250 New Mexico reward offered for Hargo. However, they were intent on bungling their opportunity. Judge Harlow's role is difficult to fathom. Perhaps he was angling to receive some of the reward money, or he had been lied to, or he mistakenly thought that Kid White was murdered in Colorado. Whatever the case, he had no firm information which allowed him to detain Hargo. The news of Hargo's arrest was wired out of Gunnison and warmly received in Santa Fe. The *New Mexican* reported the arrest and added that Stockton's lieutenant, "Harris" Eskridge, was wanted for murder, cattle rustling and robbery of the U.S. Mail. (The Rio Arriba County indictment was actually for murder, attempted murder and horse theft.) The newspaper advised its readers that Hargo would be extradited to New Mexico and placed in the Santa Fe jail, since the jail in Tierra Amarilla was deemed to be "insecure."[20] On September 23rd Governor Sheldon sent a second requisition for Eskridge to Governor Pitkin.[21] Before that process was completed, Eskridge's attorney had succeeded in securing his release.[22] Hargo wasted no time leaving the Gunnison valley. He eluded authorities and never paid for his crimes. As for others in Stockton's crowd, an article in the *New Mexican* noted that Dison Eskridge had fled Colorado and that Jim Garrett had gone to Texas.[23] Not long afterwards the *Dolores News* carried news about what it correctly described as a false rumor that Dison had been arrested on the Chiquita Colorado, 185 miles southwest of Durango and was being brought to Silverton under guard.[24] Like his brother, Dison never paid for his crimes.

Newspapers in the region were quick to blame any crime on members of the Stockton Gang, and any and all desperadoes who moved out of Durango during this period were inevitably labeled as members. On the evening of September 23rd, four heavily armed men robbed the Browne and Manzanares Store at Lamy Junction, south of Santa Fe. They pilfered the store, took all of the cash on hand, saddles and two horses belonging to Placido Sandoval. They also took every pistol and gun they saw, which "disarmed the pursuit."[25] A week later the *New Mexican* reported: "It is said that the men who committed the robbery at Lamy recently were a remnant of Ike Stockton's gang." They headed to the Rio Grande valley and later accounts placed them south of Albuquerque in Los Lunas.[26]

Stockton was content to remain in southwest Colorado. On the morning of Monday, September 26th, he said goodbye to his wife and children and headed down to Durango with M.C. Cook. The two men traveled the two miles by wagon, arriving in Durango about 11:30 that morning. Stockton's mode of transportation make it clear that he was unaware that he was in imminent danger. Sheriff Watson and Deputy Jim Sullivan had been expecting their arrival and had maintained a steady watch.[27] Watson's timing was predicated by at least two factors. First, the deputy carrying the requisition and arrest warrant for M.C. Cook had recently arrived from Texas, and second, the longer he waited, the more likely the chances that Ike would learn of Watson's intentions. The arrival of a deputy from Bosque County was just one of many events which might tip off Ike and blow Watson's plans apart. Watson still had not received an arrest warrant for Stockton, but he decided it was now or never. It seems likely that Stockton was a creature of habit, who normally came into Durango every Monday a little before noon. Whatever the case, Watson and Sullivan were ready. As Stockton's wagon wheels churned up Durango's dirt, the trap was sprung. The lawmen stayed out of sight as

Stockton and Cook parked the wagon at the corner of First and H Streets. Stockton climbed down and walked away, while Cook remained in the wagon. Watson and Sullivan knew that now was their chance. With Stockton out of sight, they walked up, one on each side of the wagon, and took aim at Cook's head with their six-shooters. They coolly told Cook to put his hands up, which he quickly did.[28] While Sullivan kept a steady aim, Watson pounced into the wagon and put Cook in cuffs. Now they had Stockton outnumbered. They left their stunned prisoner in the charge of former Stockton supporter Jack Wilson and several other armed men.[29]

Sullivan and Watson split up, each headed around the same block. Sullivan turned the corner toward the Pacific Club rooms. As both men rounded the far corners of the block, they saw Stockton in the company of Major William S. Peabody standing opposite a new building which adjoined the Brunswick Billiard Parlor. Their surprise was complete as both lawmen were able to closely approach Stockton. The outlaw was still talking with Peabody when he felt a hand on his shoulder. It was Jim Sullivan's and he advised Stockton that he was under arrest. Just as everyone had predicted, Stockton would not go down without a fight. He wrenched away from Sullivan, ducked into a nearby doorway, and began to draw his pistol. Sullivan and Watson were ready and before Stockton could bring his gun into firing position, they pulled their triggers.[30] Close against the building, the roar was deafening. Their excitement was high and their aim not true, but fortunately for both men one bullet struck Stockton in the right thigh, shattering the bone.[31] Stockton squeezed off a round which exploded harmlessly into the board sidewalk, sending splinters flying into the befouled air.[32] With only one leg to stand on, Stockton teetered and then collapsed, crashing against the door. Watson rushed in, took Ike's pistol, and placed him in custody.[33] As the sound of gunshots echoed through downtown Durango, M.C. Cook was wondering what had happened. Men bolted toward the noise. As the crowd grew, news of the shooting rippled through those streaming to the scene. According to one account which may or may not be reliable, Stockton "squealed like a pig" and "in many ways behaved in a manner unbecoming the desperado of the story books." Unless one has lived through it, it is hard to imagine the pain brought on by a bullet smashing into the femur and the prodigious blood loss associated with such a wound. Somehow Stockton remained conscious. As the spectators pressed forward, visions of Bert Wilkinson and Kid Thomas must have flashed through Ike's head and he begged not to be hung.[34]

Someone staunched the flow of blood and Stockton was placed in a wagon for transport across the Animas to the new offices of the New York and San Juan Mining and Smelting Company. Along the way he "complained bitterly on account of the pain he was suffering and stimulants were administered to him freely, to keep him from fainting from the loss of blood." By now, a surprised and bewildered Cook had probably met the satisfied deputy from Bosque County, who insisted on calling him Galbreath. The wheels were turning inside his head, but it was reported that a stoic Cook "rode quietly through the town to the smelter." Both men were placed under a heavy guard.[35] Watson's location for holding the men was shrewdly selected, as no one could approach the smelter unseen. Sometime during the day or possibly very early the next day Watson telegraphed Governor Pitkin's office asking for delivery of the warrant for Stockton's arrest based on the New Mexico requisition. Within about a twenty-four hour period Pitkin also signed the new arrest warrant for Hargo Eskridge and issued a warrant for the arrest of Charles Allison based on a requisition from Nevada. Sheriff Matt Kyle, who had been guarding Charles (Ennis) Allison during his daring train escape, was the Nevada agent assigned to pick up Allison, if Conejos County gave him up.[36]

The New York and San Juan Smelter where surgeons amputated Ike Stockton's leg in an attempt to save his life. (Courtesy La Plata County Historical Society, No. 92.21.215.)

While some of Ike's associates knew that M.C. Cook was wanted for murder in Texas, to others the news came as a complete surprise. The *Dolores News* reported that Cook's troubles began when he and a partner went to a Swedish settlement in Bosque County and threw a widow into a well and then "ravished her three daughters." The account in the *News* said that shortly after his arrest for rape, he managed to shoot and kill the sheriff guarding him and made his escape.[37] The *Durango Record* said that the killed sheriff was from Grayson County, Texas.[38] The actual victim was Bosque County Deputy Sheriff Jabez Pierson.[39] Reportedly, a Pinkerton detective had spent twelve months trying to track down Cook.[40] He had been on the run for seven years and for the prior five months had been virtually attached at the hip to Ike Stockton.

The two men would soon be separated. Stockton was in dire need of medical care and soon after his arrival at the smelter, several doctors were summoned to the scene. Close to the same time his twenty-three-year-old wife, Ellen, his six-year-old daughter, Delilah, and his almost two-year-old son Guy arrived at the smelter. They almost certainly traveled to the scene with M.C. Cook's young and very pregnant wife and their baby. Mrs. Cook was allowed to visit her husband.[41] Parson Hoge also made his way to the smelter. After examining Stockton, the doctors agreed that amputation was his only hope for survival.[42] Stockton feared that at any moment a mob would overpower the guards and he would be summarily lynched. Despite the severity of his injury, he was still conscious and would not allow the doctors to operate until Dr. Davis from Animas City was present. Finding Davis proved to be difficult and as the minutes stretched into hours Stockton's condition worsened. Davis finally arrived at the smelter after darkness had fallen.[43] All the while, Stockton's wife and children held vigil nearby. Finally, Dr. H.A. Clay, Dr. Smith and Dr. Davis performed the impossibly difficult operation, amputating Ike's leg at mid-thigh. The bone was splintered for a length of about three inches and broken up into about twenty pieces. Doctors Tracy, Griffith and Bellinger were also in attendance.[44] Parson Hoge had remained all day and he was joined by Dr. Folsom, a dentist, who moonlighted as an undertaker. The operation was completed at 11:30 that night. Stockton was described as being in "very feeble condition" and his prognosis was extremely guarded.[45] After the surgery, Ellen and her two children maintained their sad watch, praying and weeping. About Ike's family the *Record* said, "his wife is recognized by all as being a lady, and the little children, a credit to any family." Describing the scene the *Record* reported, "The oldest child is a lovely little girl, about four or five years of age, and her cries of grief were heart-rending. The second child, it seems, is a boy instead of a girl [the *Record* had earlier identified Guy as a girl] and not two years old, so of course, was unconscious of what was passing." At 2:45 that morning, with his wife and children at his side, Ike Stockton, cattle rustler, Indian fighter and wanted murderer breathed his last.[46]

Later that morning, Ellen took Ike's remains back to their home in Animas City.[47] A collection was taken up and Stockton's friends donated $100, which was used to purchase a casket. A silver engraved plate was attached which read, "Isaac T. Stockton, aged 29 years." The plate was the work of J.R. Shoemaker. On the afternoon of Wednesday, September 28th, a large group of family, friends, and the curious attended the funeral which was presided over by Durango's pioneering frontier clergyman, Parson C.M. Hoge. For the interment, the attendees walked and rode up the steep hillside on the east side of the Animas River, across the valley from Animas City. At the time only a few graves dotted the narrow hillside bench which is home to the Animas City Cemetery. The mourners looked out on spectacular views of the La Plata Mountains and northward up the Animas River valley. Rising above them was a scrub oak covered hillside. Many of the leaves had turned red, some had a brownish hue, while others remained green in defiance of the cooler weather and shorter days. At 2:00 PM, Stockton was laid to rest.[48] The *New Mexican* reported "His funeral was largely attended and his burial was the occasion of appropriate and impressive ceremonies."[49]

Ike Stockton's forlorn and misdated tombstone in the Animas City Cemetery. (Author's collection.)

As Ike Stockton was lowered into the ground, residents of the San Juan country heaved a sigh of relief. The nightmare was over. Farmers, merchants, miners and others had uprooted their families and moved into the mountains and valleys to pursue a better, more prosperous life. Their pursuit of the dream was relentless and those who got in the way were swept aside. Many who impeded progress, like the Stockton brothers and Bert Wilkinson, were condemned to the grave. Some were more fortunate; Hargo and Dison Eskridge made it out with their lives. The pioneering residents of northwest New Mexico and southwest Colorado looked to heal the raw and ragged wound which had been clawed along the border. As time moved on, the story of the Stocktons dimmed and blurred, like the faded, hair-covered brand on a mossy horned Cross Timbers longhorn. In some cases their history was as difficult to find as a rustler's stolen hides, buried deep in the bowels of archives and libraries throughout the west. In other instances portions of their tale were easy to find, like the stolen hides which Porter Stockton brazenly peddled to his neighbors. Remnants of their story are still out there, well hidden, but awaiting excavation by others.

Chapter Twenty

Reflection

> *For a man is a man, but he's partly a beast ---*
> *He kin brag till he makes you deaf,*
> *But the one, lone brute, from the West to the East,*
> *That he kaint quite break, is himse'f.*[1]

Considering that there were no telegraph lines into northwest New Mexico, news of Ike Stockton's death traveled down the Animas valley in lightning time. During the morning hours of September 29th, just two days after Ike's death, Wash Cox, Mose Blancett and E.A. Clayton rode into Durango. Clayton was a neighbor to the Lockhart and Thomas families in the La Plata valley. The three men met with Sheriff Watson and offered him their congratulations on a job well done. There is no word of any money being given to Watson, but since Cox and others privately raised a $2000 reward for Stockton, it's possible that some sort of payment was made to both Watson and Sullivan. Watson was riding the crest and he and the New Mexicans went over to the offices of the *Durango Herald* for a brief interview. The newspaper noted, "They inform us that hereafter Durango will be considered the market and trading point for the large and rich scope of agricultural country around Farmington. Both Durango and Farmington will undoubtedly reap much benefit from the amicable relations that now exist between the communities."[2] Despite the glowing business prospects, some decided it was in their best interests to leave town. One of those was butcher Charlie King, who had held stolen cattle in his Durango pens.[3] King was not a desperado, but like some, he clearly benefitted from southwest Colorado's illicit cattle trade. Less than a week after Ike's death the *Dolores News* reported that King was moving to Pueblo where he would open a "wholesale and retail meat market."[4]

With Ike's passing the *Durango Herald* unleashed their honest opinion of the situation, saying, "Sheriff Watson deserves much credit for the courage and coolness he manifested in effecting the arrest of these men. They were both known to be desperate characters, with rewards on their heads, and are about the last of a gang of hard citizens who have caused a world of trouble in Southwestern Colorado and Northern New Mexico. Pity for the innocent wives and children is universal, but there are but few to mourn over the fate of the men."[5] The *Record* heaped more praise on Watson, saying, "We now have a sheriff, who has some back-bone, and it will no longer be a reproach to Durango and La Plata county, that men with prices on their heads, are allowed to roam the country, without fear of arrest."⁶ From Durango, word of Ike's death spread across America. The *Iola (Kansas) Register* carried an article which attributed crimes to Ike, some which he had never committed, saying, "Ike Stockton, one of the leaders of the notorious Stockton-Eskridge gang of desperadoes, who was wanted in New Mexico for murder, rape, arson and other crimes, was fatally shot while resisting arrest."⁷ The *Milan (Tennessee) Exchange,* the *Lancaster (Pennsylvania) Daily Intelligencer* and other faraway newspapers carried similar accounts.⁸ The *Dodge City Times* carried a report from the *Las Vegas Optic* which incorrectly advised that, "Tom Stockton, a peaceable citizen of Colfax county, this territory, is the only remaining brother." The *Optic* concluded, "Several of the boys have bit the dust during the last six months and nothing is left but to declare all further depredations off."⁹ Durango's *Record* offered a final thought about Ike's killing: "His death undoubtedly seems very hard to the stricken ones, but when one remembers how much worse it might have been, it is doubtless a mercy. There will now always be a shadow of doubt as to the guilt of the father and husband and the disgrace attendant upon what might have been, will be spared his survivors."¹⁰ Commenting on Ike's death the *New Mexican* said, "The days of ruffianism in New Mexico are fast drawing to a close, and the fact is a good thing for the Territory."¹¹

Stockton's end was the death knell of widespread turmoil in the San Juan country. There would be other troubles, but none so severe as those associated with Ike Stockton. In Santa Fe, on the day of his death, a second requisition for the arrest of "Isaac Stockton and others" was written up for delivery to Governor Pitkin.¹² Where Ike Stockton had gone, there was no extradition. Three days after Stockton's death, the *New Mexican* noted that, "The Stockton and Eskridge gang, which at one time numbered one hundred ten men in and around Durango, has recently dispersed."¹³ The Stockton-Eskridge gang certainly never numbered one hundred and ten men, but Stockton's death ensured that most of the residual bad men left the San Juan country. As they were leaving, the railroad was importing civilization on a massive scale.

Afterword

Loose Ends and Later Lives

When my old soul hunts range and rest
Beyond the last divide,
Just plant me in some stretch of West
That's sunny, lone and wide.
Let cattle rub my tombstone down
And coyotes mourn their kin,
Let hawses paw and tramp the moun',---
But don't you fence it in![1]

The Allison Gang – Charlie Allison, Lew Perkins and Henry Watts stood trial and were sentenced to thirty-seven years in the Colorado State Penitentiary in Cañon City. All of the stage robbers served only a small portion of their sentence before they were released. Lew Perkins was the first one to leave prison. In the 1890s he was reportedly living in Trinidad, Colorado, where he operated a large saloon and gambling hall. Watts and Allison both served about ten years. Charlie Allison was said to have moved to Butte, Montana where he worked as a bartender. According to one account, Watts joined a band of train robbers and was killed in Arizona in about 1895.[2]

Blancett, Moses (Mose) – After the death of Ike Stockton, Mose Blancett's life was filled with a series of tragic and violent deaths. On August 4, 1882, Blancett's son-in-law C.W. Rash was shot and killed by Blancett's other son-in-law, William McCoy. The men and their families were staying at the new town of La Plata, about five miles above Parrott City, and working at prospecting and mining. Rash had been drinking whiskey and then began to fire a Winchester, recklessly, endangering the lives of his own children and others. The drunken Rash would not listen to reason and kept firing, giving McCoy little choice in the matter.[3]

On October 24, 1882 Moses Blancett's brother, John Blancett, accompanied a man named Smith to Cañon Largo to retrieve a wagon that was being held by Justice of the Peace Guadalupe Archuleta. The wagon was the subject of a replevin lawsuit. Upon their arrival in Cañon Largo they found that Archuleta was not disposed to release the wagon. Some reports say that Smith's party opened fire. Another account says that Smith was taking the wagon away when Justice Archuleta opened fire. However it began, John Blancett was shot in the neck, the ball entering at his Adam's apple, severing his spine and exiting between his shoulders. Dr. Clay, who had tried to save Ike Stockton a year earlier, was summoned, but Blancett died two days later.⁴ William Haines reported to Governor Sheldon that, "G. Archuleta gave himself up to me, and was placed in the hands of Mose Blancett, deputy sheriff. The Mexican population was certain that Archuleta would be lynched and gathered at Bloomfield to the number of about 150 men." In response, Haines called out the militia to maintain order. He advised Sheldon that, "I now have about fifty men under arms, and think that by moderation and good judgment law will be allowed to take its course."⁵ Though Haines was saying all the right things to the governor, his bias against the Hispanic population was evident in a September 1881 letter to Adjutant General Max Frost: "It is a decided fact here that no more prisoners will go to Tierra Amarilla, to be tried by Mexican penetentes [sic] (don't know if spelt right) and get off. We must have a new county and this must be county seat."⁶ As events spiraled out of control, the *Santa Fe New Mexican* carried the following dispatch, which was received at the territory's military headquarters in Santa Fe:

> Matters are very serious at Bloomfield. The wounded man is dead, and his friends say the Mexican must die. Blancett, brother of the man killed, and leader of the party, is sheriff. Haines, justice of the peace and captain of militia, is powerless. The best citizens are for law and order and a fair trial. The sheriff says the man shall never be taken to Tierra Amarilla alive. There are 150 Mexicans present, armed and ready to attack Blancett and party if the prisoner is killed. The women and children have all left the place.

Governor Sheldon dispatched Max Frost to the scene.⁷ Before he could arrive, the men holding Archuleta convened an impromptu court and he was sentenced to hang. Al Dustin later recalled that Archuleta was placed in En Blancett's buckboard and driven to a nearby butcher frame, probably at the Haines and Hughes Store. He was noosed to the windlass normally used to hoist cattle and the buckboard was driven away. Some of Archuleta's friends witnessed the lynching.⁸ That did not prevent a celebration. Mr. Kutz told the *Durango Herald* that, "as soon as the deed had been done, the participators in it threw their hats into the air and cheered loudly."⁹ One of those assisting the Blancetts that day was Tom Nance.¹⁰

An *Albuquerque Review* headline said, "The Bloomfield Murderer Swings and the People Disperse Satisfied."¹¹ A military dispatch noted, "The prisoner was hanged at Bloomfield to-day. I am informed that the Mexicans were convinced that he was guilty. The people have now dispersed and no further trouble is anticipated." The *New Mexican* said the lynching party was led by Deputy Sheriff Mose Blancett and noted that Blancett had "heretofore borne a good character" and "was virtually sheriff of that portion of the county."¹² Miraculously, despite the administration of summary justice, a bloodbath did not result.

It seems that after Archuleta's death, the Blancett misfortunes multiplied. In November 1885, Cell Blancett's five-year-old son got hold of a pistol and accidentally shot and killed his three-year-old brother.[13] Two years later, tragedy struck again.

In December 1887, Mose's brother Enos was involved in a two-day-long dispute with Hank Parrish in Eureka, Utah. Six years earlier, Blancett had been using crutches and he was still using them in Utah. Despite his permanent physical impairment, Blancett was not one to back down from a battle.[14] In 1875, Parrish had been an associate of the notorious Major Graham in Rosita, Colorado, where the Blancett family was then living.[15] Graham was one of the leading hired gunman during the deadly Pocahontas Mine dispute.[16] The Blancetts joined those who had opposed Graham and his associates.[17] Blancett and Parrish met in McDonald's Saloon. After Blancett recognized Parrish, he told his former San Juan country neighbor Tom Nance to kill Parrish, but Nance refused to get involved.[18] Blancett should have taken that as a hint. The next day Blancett and Parrish again showed up at McDonald's Saloon. Blancett challenged Parrish to a shootout at Pat Shea's Corral and Parrish accepted. Blancett left the saloon and went home to retrieve his firearms. Parrish secured a double-barreled shotgun. Blancett then headed out for Shea's Corral using two crutches, carrying a shotgun, and packing a pistol. Parrish proceeded to the Haws's house which was near the path that Blancett would take to the corral. He stayed hidden near the house. When Blancett hobbled into view, Parrish fired a blast, breaking one of Blancett's crutches. Blancett fell and said, "You have not got me yet." Parrish let loose the second barrel and the pellets struck Blancett in the chest. He died shortly thereafter.[19]

In July 1890 calamity struck again. Mose and Lucinda's son, Cell, and the horse he was riding on were killed by lightning. At the time he was gathering cattle with Jim Cox, Al Dustin and others in the San Juan River valley. Cell was a deputy sheriff for the recently created San Juan County.[20] Mose Blancett's life ended prematurely at dawn on Monday morning, February 19, 1894. He was sixty years old.[21] He was fatally injured trying to regain control of a runaway team.[22]

<u>Browne and Manzanares Store Robbers</u> – Whether the Lamy robbers were part of Stockton's crowd is open to question. They are not mentioned in any of Ike Stockton's activities in the San Juan country and seem only to turn up in the press for their activities in central New Mexico. They certainly may have been part of the rough crowd that left Durango after the lynching of Bert Wilkinson. These supposed remnants of the Stockton Gang left Lamy and were seen in the Rio Grande valley south of Albuquerque. On Wednesday, October 5, 1881 they showed up in Socorro and two of them were arrested. The men identified themselves as Frenchy Elmoreau and Bush Clark. (The *Durango Herald* identifies Bush as "Butch"

Clark.) Both of Elmoreau's names were evidently descriptive aliases. The French translation of *moreau* is "dark black." Elmoreau was probably white, but was described as having dark hair. One of the horses they rode belonged to Browne and Manzanares and the other was stolen north of Albuquerque. Some of their associates escaped, including Bush Clark's brother. On the night of October 6th//7th Socorro vigilantes removed the two men from captivity. They were taken to Palisade Alley and lynched from a cottonwood tree located behind the livery stable. Placards were placed on their backs which read, "This is the way Socorro treats horse-thieves and foot-pads." The men's bodies were cut down early the next morning and placed in the livery stable. The coroner's jury assembled there at 9:00 AM and inevitably found "that they came to their deaths by strangulation caused by a rope tied around their necks by unknown parties." A dispatch from Socorro offered another speculative alternative to lynching, saying that both men had the unbelievably bad luck to try and jump an adobe fence and they had both become entangled in ropes which had been tied with hangman's nooses. Before that happened, they did confess to the Browne and Manzanares robbery. A dispatch from Socorro said they died game and that, "They all belonged to the late Ike Stockton's gang of Colorado."[23]

Catron, James – After the lynching of Bert Wilkinson and Kid Thomas, Jimmy Catron left Durango and that fall was living near Antonito. At that time the *Dolores News* noted, "The gang of outlaws who hoped to release Charlie Allison and his pals from the Alamosa jail, reside promiscuously in the San Luis valley, south of Conejos." Hargo and Dison Eskridge may have also holed up nearby at Dow Eskridge's ranch. In its November 19, 1881 issue, the *Dolores News* carried a cryptic report which mentioned no names saying that San Luis Valley residents raided a camp of horse thieves, who were known for stealing livestock in the San Juan and Animas River valleys. Four of the thieves were captured and two others escaped. Two of the captured men were wounded and one of them died from his wounds.[24] Perhaps Catron was part of this group.

There are several different versions of Catron's eventual fate. One account from 1899 claims that Catron joined with Denver and Rio Grande Railroad forces in their war against the Bat Masterson led forces of the Atchison, Topeka and Santa Fe. The article misdates this 1879 trouble as occurring in 1886. The same narrative claims that Catron then moved to Dodge City, Kansas where he "pre-empted eighty acres near the city" and held off numerous attempts to take it from him, including one led by "Mysterious Dave" Mather. The imaginative story notes that in 1893 he headed for the Indian Territory and participated in the Cherokee Strip land run. In 1898 "he was stricken with paralysis."[25] In 1926 Charles Valiton, a San Juan country old timer, but not always an accurate source of information, said that Catron got out of the country and moved back to Missouri, where he had grown up.[26]

Another press story describes a much different fate for Jimmy Catron. On May 11 or May 12, 1882, Catron and a companion went looking for trouble in the little village adjacent to Fort Garland. The *Durango Herald* reported, "the noted desperado, well known in this city, filled up with poor whiskey and undertook to run things to suit himself at Fort Garland."[27] "The two roughs marched through the town with guns in hand," said the *Pueblo News*, "threatening to shoot the first g[od] d[amn] s[on of a] b[itch] that shoved his head out a doorway." This went on for several hours. Tiring of that, the two men went over to the Fort and commenced shooting. Three soldiers were sent out to meet the men and were met with "a shower of bullets."[28] A lieutenant from the camp told Catron to leave. Catron threatened the lieutenant, who then ordered the soldiers to shoot. "Catron was fatally shot," the *Herald* said, "through the bowels and his companion, Wash Triplet, was instantly killed by a bullet that passed through his brain. At last accounts Catron was in a dying condition."[29] The *Pueblo News* declared, "Catron was shot and killed at 8 o'clock on the night of the 11th inst."[30] The *Herald* concluded, "No one will regret the death of Catron. He ought to have been hung in Durango a year ago. One by one the roses fall; one by one the bad men die with their boots on."[31]

<u>Coe, Frank</u> – After their difficulties in northwest New Mexico, Frank Coe and his family moved to Lincoln County, where he began farming.[32] He kept out of trouble, most of the time. In October 1898, Coe shot and killed Irvin Lesnett who was trying to elope with his fifteen-year-old daughter. A year and a half later Coe was acquitted. It seems the young man fired the first shot in the fray.[33] Frank died on September 16, 1931 and is buried in the George Coe Cemetery in Glencoe, Lincoln County.[34]

<u>Coe, George,</u> - The Coe cousin and his wife moved to Lincoln County where they lived out the rest of their days.[35] In November 1931 the one-time terror of the San Juan country traveled to Chicago. There he regaled a wide-eyed reporter with accounts of his battles alongside Billy the Kid and told of the Battle of Blazer's Mill, where he lost his trigger finger.[36] George died on November 12, 1941 in Roswell and is buried in the George Coe Cemetery.[37]

<u>Coe, Lew</u> – The elder Coe stayed in the Farmington area. Some of the alliances and the feuds along the lower Animas shifted after the death of Ike Stockton. On April 11, 1883, Lew Coe had a falling out with Henry Hanson. Only two years before, the Coes, in alliance with Hanson, had run Justice Halford out of the San Juan country. The nature of this later dispute is unknown, but Coe was charged with "Threatening in a Menacing Manner" after he accosted Hanson with a pistol. Robert Smith and Frank Coe's wife, Helena Anne, were summoned as witnesses. Frank Coe and

Frank Pierce served as sureties in the matter. Pierce was one of the men who had been forced out of Farmington by the Coes and their allies in early 1881. Disposition in this case is unknown, but any punishment was certainly minor. For most folks along the lower Animas, Lew Coe grew to become a respected citizen.[38] In 1887, San Juan County was created out of the western portion of Rio Arriba County. Even though some folks continued to harbor ill will toward Coe, he was elected in 1888 to serve on the new County Commission. Coe's old enemy, Frank Hartman, praised the election in the *Santa Lulu Independent* newspaper.[39]

Cook, M.C. aka M.H. Galbreath aka Bud Galbreath – On the day Ike Stockton died, prisoner Bud Galbreath left Durango via the D&RG rails guarded by Deputy Jim Sullivan and the Texas officer who had delivered the requisition.[40] Galbreath's wife Florence was also traveling to Texas by rail. She went to Sherman and initiated habeas corpus proceedings. At the same time, she contacted her brother to help plan her husband's escape. The *Durango Record* reported that Sullivan delivered Galbreath to authorities in Denison, Texas on the first day of October. Shortly after his arrival, Grayson County Special Deputy Sheriff J.W. Jenkins served the writ of habeas corpus on the marshal and jailer in Denison. Jenkins guarded Galbreath on the ten mile trip to Sherman, where the writ was to be heard. On October 3, 1881, Jenkins and Galbreath were in Sherman waiting for the hearing to start. With time to kill, Jenkins took Galbreath to a nearby hotel where Mrs. Galbreath and her brother were staying. Galbreath managed to walk away, made his way through the rear door, where he mounted a waiting horse and escaped custody. Once again, Marion "Bud" Galbreath was a free man. Sullivan received no reward from Texas.[41]

Marion and Florence hid out in Texas and in December 1881 Florence gave birth to their daughter Vinta. They were living in Kansas when Edgar was born in July 1887.[42] The couple had an older child, who lived with them in Animas City in 1881. It appears that the eldest child did not reach adulthood.[43] The family came to Oklahoma in September 1891 for the Land Run which opened Pottawatomie County to settlement. At the time Galbreath was calling himself Marion Lee. He soon opened the Hotel Lee in Tecumseh.[44] Life was good. In 1897 the *Tecumseh Republican* described Mr. Lee as "one of our best and foremost citizens."[45] That same year the wheels of Texas justice creaked into action. Someone notified authorities that the man who murdered Deputy Jabez Pierson was living in Oklahoma. Governor Charles Culberson soon signed a requisition for Galbreath's arrest and forwarded it to Governor Cassius Barnes of Oklahoma. On November 20, 1897, an officer from Bosque County, Texas arrested Mr. Lee for murdering Deputy Pierson back in 1874.[46] The arrest was greeted with shock and disbelief by the residents of Pottawatomie County.

Galbreath's twenty-three year run from authorities was over. Newspapers reported that a cousin had turned Galbreath in for a paltry reward of fifty dollars. The identity of the cousin is unknown, but it is clear that Galbreath was taking a poor risk residing a mere 250 miles from his childhood home in Stephenville. Mr. Lee denied that he had ever gone by the name Galbreath and asserted that he had no knowledge of the murder in question. He secured an attorney and sought his release through a writ of habeas corpus.[47] Many folks in Tecumseh believed that Mr. Lee was the victim of misidentification and the *Tecumseh Republican* reported that his friends and family hoped for a "speedy vindication."[48] As for the habeas corpus writ, Texas authorities convincingly proved they had the right man, and in the middle of December the *Oklahoman* of Oklahoma City reported that Marion H. "Bud" Galbreath and the sheriff of Bosque County passed through the city on their way to Meridian, Texas.[49] Galbreath made an initial appearance in the Bosque County District Court on January 18, 1898. Interest in the case was high and the presiding judge ordered the sheriff to summon a pool of seventy potential jurors.[50]

Before the trial, Galbreath told his version of events. He reported that he had been working on a ranch west of Bosque County and that he and several of his fellow cowboys came into Meridian. Galbreath's companions were soon intoxicated and there was some sort of incident with a Swedish woman. Galbreath claimed the woman alleged that the cowboys had made an indecent proposal. He said the cowboys denied that and blamed the woman's inability to speak English for the confusion. According to Galbreath he was never intoxicated and he was never at the woman's house.[51] In fact, Bosque County records show that authorities were certain that Galbreath was there, and the incident was much more than an indecent proposal. Galbreath was indicted in June 1874 for "an assault with intent to commit a rape." In Galbreath's case the victim was apparently able to fight off her attacker.[52] Even in his 1898 alibi story, Galbreath acknowledged that the incident resulted in arrest warrants for himself and several of his companions, although he does not specify the charges. The cowboys, except Galbreath, headed for the cattle range, and he was soon arrested. Galbreath recalled that a mob of enraged Swedes quickly gathered and threatened to lynch him. The extreme reaction of the Swedes, indicates that they believed more than an attempted rape had occurred. Galbreath reports that authorities had his wrists and ankles shackled at a blacksmith's shop, loaded him in a covered wagon and then chained him to the wagon's rear standard with rivets. The plan was to take him to a nearby county and away from the enraged Swedes. The situation was so dire that Galbreath recalled that a contingent of ten Rangers guarded him out of town, but after twenty miles broke away leaving him in the care of Deputy Pierson. Shortly thereafter one of Galbreath's fellow cowboys appeared and demanded Galbreath's release. Deputy Pierson refused and in the ensuing fight the unidentified cowboy struck Deputy Pierson with a wagon brake rod, took his pistol and shot him with fatal effect. Galbreath and his friend managed to remove the wagon standard and then unharnessed a horse and left the scene. A few miles away they found a blacksmith, who freed Galbreath from his shackles. Galbreath reported that he and his friend then fled to Colorado. Galbreath adds additional embellishment to his incredibly self-serving story, reporting that he and his unnamed ally entered the cattle industry, accumulating $35,000 in the process. Galbreath's account then veers toward the truth, noting that he was arrested in Colorado for the charges he faced in Texas. He says his friend escaped apprehension. He conveniently failed to mention the location of his lucrative Colorado cattle business, making it impossible for newspapers or others to verify the veracity of his claims. He also failed to mention his October 1881 escape from authorities in Sherman, Texas. In fact, he claimed that he was never extradited from Colorado, but was released due to technical problems with the requisition. After that brush with the law, Galbreath said he left Colorado and moved to Iowa. He sought to protect his wife, who had lived with him in Animas City, and facilitated his escape, and reported that he married her in Iowa. He also noted that the man who actually killed Deputy Pierson died only one month after he left Colorado. Galbreath, relentlessly sought to lay the blame elsewhere, and claimed that as his pardner lay on his deathbed, he confessed to his wife that he had murdered Deputy Pierson. Despite facing a long prison term or worse, Galbreath nobly refused to call the widowed woman as a witness "because the community in which she lives knows nothing of the tragic life her husband lived."[53] Galbreath's protection of the widow points circumstantially to Amanda Ellen Stockton, who was widowed hours after Galbreath's arrest. Since Amanda Ellen's aunt was Galbreath's stepmother, he may have kept up with news of Amanda Ellen's life after the death of Ike Stockton.[54] It's clear that Galbreath was a consummate liar. It can't be said with any degree of certainty that his companion was Ike Stockton. Perhaps the companion never existed at all, or was someone else entirely. However, given the exceptionally close relationship between Ike and Bud Galbreath, the similarity between Galbreath's account of events and the actual story of Ike Stockton, it appears that Ike may well have had some involvement in the murder of Deputy Jabez Pierson.

On the other hand, one version making the rounds in 1897, which held Galbreath solely culpable for the murder, reported that after Galbreath's 1874 arrest, he was placed in the back of the wagon when he complained that he was ill. He had some freedom of movement and was not so ridiculously shackled and riveted as he alleged. Unfortunately, the wagon bed was partially covered with straw and that concealed the iron wagon brake rod, which Galbreath soon found. He used it to strike Deputy

Pierson's head, inflicting a fatal wound.[55] Seventeen years earlier, in September 1881, the *Durango Southwest* carried an account of Galbreath's escape, which reinforces the contention that the escape was facilitated when he feigned illness. The *Southwest* noted that "Cook [Galbreath] claimed to be sick, and could not ride horseback. He was handcuffed and placed in wagon driven by a Deputy Sheriff, the Sheriff and Cook's pard [who had been arrested at the same time] riding ahead on horseback." The *Southwest's* account is confused about Galbreath's victim, when it notes that Galbreath seized the deputy's pistol and in the fight which followed the sheriff, not the deputy, was killed.[56] In Colorado, Galbreath had no closer pard than Ike Stockton. In spite of Galbreath's dissimulation, both his twenty-three years on the lam, and the statute of limitations worked in his favor. On February 22nd the jury determined the fate of Bud Galbreath. The confusing verdict was reported this way: "We the jury find the defendant guilty of manslaughter and as the offense was committed more than three years prior to the finding of this indictment we find him not guilty of that offense." Galbreath was "discharged from all further liability upon the charge."[57] A death caused by a wagon brake rod, and not by pistol, certainly left the door open for a manslaughter conviction. The killer of Deputy Jabez Pierson returned to Oklahoma and retained the name Lee.

In 1900 he was still operating a hotel in Tecumseh.[58] While Lee had escaped punishment in Texas, his sterling reputation in Tecumseh was now tarnished. Perhaps that is one explanation for the family's move to Sulphur, Oklahoma during the first decade of the new century. The Lee's operated the Summit Hotel in Sulphur.[59] Marion and Florence Lee remained in Sulphur and were still alive in 1930.[60]

Cox, Hiram Washington and Graves, Alf – Wash Cox was old enough to be the father of the Stockton boys, yet he and his wife Nancy outlived the Stocktons by almost twenty years. In his later years he was known to many as "Uncle Washington" or "Uncle Wash."

Opposite page: In the foreground is sixty-nine-year-old Texas trail driver Hiram Washington "Wash" Cox. This photo is described as "The Last Roundup," ca. 1894. None of the cowboys are identified, but they probably include Wash Cox's sons George, John, Jim and Ike as well as Alf Graves and his sons Bruce and John. The photo was probably taken as the boys and men gathered for the first day of the roundup near the Cox home at Cedar Hill. In the background, the chuck wagon is loaded and ready to go. (Courtesy Aztec Museum Association Historic Photo Collection.)

The $100,000 offer Cox once refused for all of his branded stock, even if it was made during the last year of his life, would have been worth over $2,400,000 in 2007, accounting for inflation. One account said he died a pauper, but that may have overstated the financial hardships which befell him.[61] In 1888, former Cox foe Frank Hartman said, "Every active man in the territory knows Wash Cox, and no man in New Mexico has or deserves more friends."[62] On August 10, 1890 his youngest son, eighteen-year-old William A. (Willie) Cox, was killed. Willie and other cowboys were cooling off in the Animas after rounding up cattle all day. He rode his horse into the river and was thrown from the saddle, striking his head.[63] The Panic of 1893, drought conditions and barb wire brought an end to the open range in the San Juan country. As Ike Cox put it, "fellows we called nesters" became troublesome. Soon all of the big cattle outfits were gone. The last general roundup of Cox cattle took place in the mid-1890s.[64]

As the open range days drew to a close, so did the life of Wash Cox. He paid a horrific price for the sixty years he spent out on the range.[65] In the late 1890s, he was afflicted with cancer of the face.[66] At the time, he and Nancy moved into the nearby home of Alf and Nancy Belle Graves.[67] Uncle Wash died at the age of seventy-three on December 16, 1898. Mrs. Cox died at the Graves's home on January 28, 1900. In recalling Wash and Nancy Cox, the *Durango Democrat* noted they "gave liberally to those who passed their door in need."[68]

Alf Graves died on March 2, 1909. Graves had gone out early to do the spring cleaning on his ditches. As the morning wore on he was overcome by a terrific headache. Finally, he could no longer work, so he went home to rest. He died of apoplexy (what is now called a stroke) that afternoon.[69] Nancy Belle died on May 4, 1932 from pneumonia.[70] All of them are buried in the Cedar Hill, New Mexico Cemetery. Wash Cox's son, Ike Cox, and his grandson John Graves were two of the principal men involved in the deadly Cox-Truby range war feud, which engulfed the Animas River valley from 1911 to 1913.[71] In the 1950s and into the sixties San Juan County transitioned from a primarily agricultural economy to one centered around the San Juan Basin's energy resources. Wash Cox's "Texas house" did not survive the transition. It was torn down to accommodate highway construction north of Aztec.[72]

Dawson, William H. – After the battle in the Pinhook valley, Bill Dawson returned to Rico. He was nominated for sheriff of Dolores County in the fall of 1881 and was subsequently elected to the position.[73] In early June 1882, Rico's city marshal, George Smith, was shot and killed by Tom Wall and "Trinidad Charley" Cummings. Both men had recently been kicked out of Durango. Dawson was with Marshal Smith at the time. He was not shot, but had powder burns on his face.[74] A few days later, Wall and Cummings were taken into custody by Barney Watson and two of his La Plata County deputies, Lambert and Bacon. They caught up with the fugitives in New Mexico at Bowen's Ferry on the San Juan River. Wall gave up immediately, but Watson had to enlist the aid of a dozen or more Navajo men to flush "Trinidad" out of the brush along the river. The men were lynched in Johnny Gault's stable behind the Rico jail.[75]

Eskridge, Dison – After being sent on his way by Ike Stockton, Dison disappeared altogether. Perhaps he changed his name and lived up to the vow he had made at Flora Pyle's Castle Rock home to mend his ways and live an honorable life. Or perhaps not. According to the often unreliable Charles Valiton, Dison was shot and killed by the night marshal of Yuma, Arizona.[76] Durango's dentist and undertaker, Dr. W.H.C. Folsom, reported that Dison was killed in a saloon in Alaska. Of course, Folsom also says he met Billy the Kid when he came up to the San Juan country to visit Port Stockton, which was certainly not accurate.[77]

Dison and Hargo's older brother, Lorenzo Dow Eskridge, continued to live in the San Luis Valley for most of his life. In 1902 he served as an appointee of the governor as a commissioner on Colorado's State Board of [Livestock] Inspection, which oversaw the state's brand inspectors.[78] Dow passed away in a Denver hotel on October 30, 1916.[79]

Eskridge, Hargo – After his arrest in Gunnison City, Hargo Eskridge remained in Colorado. He lived in Conejos County and in late May or early June 1882 the *Alamosa Independent* reported that Eskridge went on a tear in Antonito, firing off his six-shooter and generally raising hell. While in a hotel dining room he confronted John Bennett and asked him, "What are you looking at me for, you son of a bitch." Bennett did not reply and walked out. Eskridge followed Bennett and despite the efforts of a man named Bittner, who tried to smooth things over, Eskridge pulled his revolver and shot Bennett behind the left ear, killing him. The *Dolores News* noted that when Eskridge was sober he killed with little provocation and if inebriated he was known to kill just "for the fun of it." Immediately after the shooting Eskridge left Antonito and went to Conejos, to say goodbye to Dow and other members of his family. That same day he returned to Antonito, where no one tried to arrest him. He then took the train to La Jara, where he jumped off. It was assumed he went to New Mexico. At that time he disappeared from Colorado for good.[80]

Dr. Folsom reported that Hargo moved to San Diego where he prospered in real estate.[81] Charles Valiton related an entirely different story. He says Hargo moved to Pittsburgh and became a druggist and upstanding citizen.[82] Folsom is correct when he places Hargo in San Diego and Valiton's assertion that Hargo lived in Pennsylvania is also accurate. Hargo married a Delaware girl named Ella in 1886.[83] He became a respected citizen in Centre County, Pennsylvania. In late April, 1896, the Bloomsburg, Pennsylvania *Columbian* reported that J.H. Eskridge passed through town while on his way to the Democratic state convention in Allentown and noted, "He is one of the prominent Democrats of that county."[84] Hargo and Ella had two children, Robert Lee born in 1891 in Pennsylvania and a daughter Marion (Mary) E., born in 1899 also in Pennsylvania. In 1900 Hargo was living with his family in Phillipsburg and working as a salesman.[85] He also served on the town council for three years, beginning in 1900.[86] During the aught decade the Eskridge family left Pennsylvania and in 1910 they lived in southern California. Hargo was a Pasadena insurance salesman.[87] By 1915 the family had moved to San Diego where Hargo and his business partner, J.L. Haines operated the Coronado Realty Company. They made loans, offered rental properties and sold real estate and insurance from their office on the corner of Orange and B Avenues on Coronado Island.[88] Charles Jones said he once consulted a San Diego acquaintance concerning the reward offered for the killers of Clate Ogsbury.[89] Ella and Hargo did not finish out their lives on the west coast. By 1920 they had returned to Phillipsburg with their twenty-year-old daughter. Hargo continued to work as an insurance agent.[90] In June 1923 Eskridge spoke at Clearfield, Pennsylvania's Jordan Hotel to the local Rotary Club. The *Clearfield Progress* reported, "The speaker graphically described a battle in which he participated, in which 31 Indians were [killed] and eight wounded by his party of ten white men." The article referred to Hargo as the "Deacon" and reported that one of his comrades in the battle was James Hall who now lived in Kylertown (about seventeen miles from Clearfield). Hargo, it was reported, still bore the visible scars from five bullet wounds. The article failed to mention Hargo's history as a desperado.[91] Eskridge was a member of the Ancient Arabic Order of the Nobles of the Mystic Shrine (the Shriners) and a respected member of the Jaffa Shrine in Altoona. The man who killed John Bennett, Kid White and probably several Indians in the Pinhook valley lived a long life and died with his boots off on August 15, 1928.[92]

Hargo's son Robert Lee did not return to live in Pennsylvania. He became a highly regarded artist, well known for his Hawaiian-themed paintings. He also befriended artist Georgia O'Keefe, when she traveled to Hawaii in the late 1930s.[93] He wrote and illustrated *Manga Reva: The Forgotten Island*, *Umi: The Hawaiian Boy Who Became a King*, and *South Sea Playmates*.

Frost, Max – The adjutant general was a whirlwind of activity and an effective self-promoter. His name is liberally sprinkled throughout territorial newspapers from the time he first arrived in Santa Fe. A New York City newspaper in reporting his death said the local Indian and "native Mexicans" thought of him as having supernatural power because he was "the man who made the wires talk."[94] His early work for the Signal Corps gave him a devoted and long-lasting group of supporters. After leaving active duty, Frost remained a member of the Army National Guard until 1886, with the rank of colonel.[95] He also served as register of the New Mexico Land Office. He was indicted for numerous improprieties while serving in that position and in 1887 he was convicted of receiving illegal fees and sentenced to serve a year in prison. He appealed that verdict and was granted a new trial in 1888.[96] The guilty verdict was reversed. After the mysterious loss of some records from the Office of the United States District Court Clerk, all of the charges he faced were dismissed.[97] In addition, he served as Secretary of the New Mexico Bureau of Immigration. He was a Thirty-third Degree Freemason and prior to his death he had begun work to establish the Scottish Rite Cathedral in Santa Fe. Shortly before his death he joined in the effort to establish a public library in Santa Fe. He was a member of the Odd Fellows, treasurer of the New Mexico Historical Society, and a member of the Archaeological Society. He was also a member of the New Mexico Bar Association and became the editor of the *Santa Fe New Mexican*.[98] For the last ten years of his life he was stricken with locomotor ataxia. This horrific affliction eventually paralyzed Frost, took his eyesight and then took his life on October 13, 1909.[99]

Garrett, James W. (Jim) – Garrett had been one of those indicted for the murder of Aaron Barker, but he was less inclined to seek trouble than were Ike Stockton and the Eskridge brothers. After memories began to fade, he moved to the family's home area near La Jara. For the rest of his life he split his time between La Jara and Creede, Colorado. He worked in the mines around Creede and was a member of the Creede Miners Union. In 1886 he married Sarah Chapman and they had three children: Harriet, Mancil and Jean. In January 1904, while living in Creede, he suffered a minor injury to his hand and developed blood poisoning. He was thought to be recovering, but then developed pneumonia and on the 28th of January, at the age of forty-seven, he succumbed to his ailments. His aged parents survived him. His body was taken to La Jara for burial.[100]

Haines, William Bullock – Captain Haines did not make a go of it in the San Juan country. It seems likely that his Hispanic customer base dried up after the lynching of Guadalupe Archuleta in 1882. The Haines family eventually moved to the state of Washington. By 1893, Haines had formed the Haines Oyster Company. In 1907, the company worked out of Puget Sound with two boats, the Alta and Zebeitka.[101]

Hartman, Frank – Hartman sold out his interest in the *Dolores News* to Charles Jones on September 2, 1882 and left Rico.[102] He stayed with the newspaper business mostly in southwest Colorado for the rest of his life. After leaving Rico he was editor of Durango's *Daily Idea*. He also worked at the *Great Southwest*, a Durango paper owned by John Reid.[103] In 1888 Hartman was publisher of a short-lived New Mexico newspaper the *Santa Lulu Independent*. Santa Lulu was a new townsite being promoted on the west side of the Animas River, about one-half mile south of the Aztec Ruins. Hartman was the promoter and backed by funds provided by Wash Cox. It was an odd combination, since Cox had at one time offered a substantial reward for the "capture" of Hartman's friend, Ike Stockton.

Describing Wash Cox in the Santa Lulu newspaper, Hartman said, "No man is more capable of distinguishing between the right and the wrong than is Mr. Cox."¹⁰⁴ While living in Durango, Hartman was involved in at least two fights involving gunfire. In 1903 he engaged in a long, bombastic, journalistic war of words with Dave Day, the editor of the *Durango Democrat*. On May 18, 1903 Hartman and Day met on the street and engaged in a gunfight during which about twelve shots were fired. Hartman was struck in the leg and ran into a nearby saloon for cover. The *Alamosa Journal* said, "The grievances between editors should not be aired in their own papers, nor should Day be so poor a marksman."¹⁰⁵ In August 1906, Hartman was witnessed on a Durango street whipping a boy for an unspecified offense when Bob Ogden interfered. Hartman drew a weapon from his pocket and fired twice at Ogden. Bill Starr, who was nearby, popped Hartman in the jaw with his fist, laid him out, and disarmed him. The *Durango Democrat* commented, "Judging from Frank's record as a shootist we are of the opinion that he could not hit a barn at two feet range."¹⁰⁶ Hartman's punishments for such activities were slight, if any. In 1911 he was editor of both the *La Plata Miner* and the *Alamosa Empire*.¹⁰⁷ In 1914, he and Charles Valiton co-founded the *Moffatt Times*. In 1926 he moved to Farmington and started the *Farmington Republican*, which he owned and operated for eight years. He died in the Durango hospital on October 15, 1934 and was buried in Durango.¹⁰⁸

Howland, Big Dan – On June 25, 1881, the *Durango Record* reported that Howland was seen by some cowboys at Cross Canyon in the company of a Mr. Plumto. The pair split up and Howland headed into Utah.¹⁰⁹ The *Durango Southwest* under the headline "The Rustlers" reported that Dan Howland and two companions, known only as Doc Baker and Big Dave, shot and killed four men of Chinese heritage near Clifton, Arizona in August 1883. Howland was struck by a bullet in the side, but recovered. The *Southwest's* article does not confirm that this Dan Howland was Big Dan Howland, but they did note that the Arizona criminals had "a dread of Colorado."¹¹⁰ The identification of Big Dan Howland as being a member of the Clifton rustlers may be in error, or perhaps not. On Saturday evening, December 8, 1883, several outlaws attempted to rob the Castañeda store in Bisbee, Arizona. The robbery went awry and several innocent victims were shot and killed.¹¹¹ It was later determined that the robbers were members of the "Gang of Rustlers" who were "well known in Clifton." One of the gang was identified as Big Dan, but this man was known as Big Dan Dowd. One of the men who did not participate in the Bisbee fiasco, but who normally traveled with the Bisbee murderers was identified as the previously mentioned Doc Baker.¹¹² In May 1881, when Big Dan Howland shot and killed I.W. Lacy, he was described as being about twenty-eight years old, with a light complexion, light hair and a light mustache and goatee.¹¹³ Less than three years later a description of Big Dan

Dowd said he was about thirty years old, with a light complexion and blonde mustache.[114] Dowd and his associates were captured not long after the murders. The coincidences continue to mount as testimony at his trial in Tombstone indicated that Dowd had been in the area for only about two or three years.[115] Dowd and the others involved were tried and convicted of capital murder. On March 28, 1884, Big Dan and four of his associates from the Bisbee murders were hung in Tombstone. A crowd estimated at one thousand witnessed the mass execution.[116] At the time, Frank Hartman was editor of the *Durango Southwest*. His newspaper does not appear to mention the Tombstone hangings. Charles Jones was still running the *Dolores News*. About the multiple hanging he said only this, "The five Bisbee murderers were hung at Tombstone last Saturday."[117] The timing of the article in the *Durango Southwest* associating Big Dan Howland with the Clifton rustlers is conspicuous. It was published on the 15th of March, a month after the conviction of Big Dan Dowd and two weeks before his execution. The incomplete newspaper collections from southern Arizona do not note the Dowd/Howland connection.

Hunter, Sheriff Luke – Hunter was in his late twenties and a widower when he first arrived in the San Juan country. Evidently he never remarried. After abdicating his position as sheriff, he worked at least part time as a machinist, mostly for San Juan country mining companies. Like many others in the region, he did some prospecting and had some mining claims.[118] In the early 1900s he worked for the Old Hundred and Silver Lake Mines in the Silverton area. He spent the cold months in San Diego.[119] In 1910 he was living up the Animas River from Silverton in Howardsville. Sometime after 1910 he may have permanently relocated to San Diego. Census records show him living there in 1920 and still living there in 1930, when he was seventy-nine years old.[120]

Jones, Charles Adam – The co-owner of the *Dolores News* stayed in Rico for several more years, eventually becoming the sole owner and publisher of the Rico newspaper. In January 1884 he married Virginia (Jennie) Bartlett.[121] Their son Clifford was born in Rico. The little mining town faced tough times in the mid-1880s and Jones sold his newspaper. In 1887 he moved to Kansas City, Missouri where he worked for his father at the National Water Works Company. Mrs. Jones gave birth to their son Hoyle in Kansas City. Jones later worked twelve years as purchasing agent for Kirk Armour at the Armour Packing Company. In the first decade of the 1900s he took over management of the Spur Ranch in the southern portion of the Texas Panhandle for brothers S.A. and E.P. Swenson. At times over 25,000 head of cattle ranged across over 430,000 acres which comprised the ranch. Sixty cowboys and several hundred horses were required for the operation which used a spur-shaped branding iron as well as the SMS brand for its Herefords.[122] In 1909, Jones helped establish the town of Spur, Texas out of ranch lands subdivided for that purpose.[123] E.P.

Swenson later organized the Freeport Sulphur Company and Jones helped establish the town of Freeport, Texas and assumed management of their Freeport, Texas operations. In the early 1900s Jones traveled the world in connection with the Swenson's far-flung business interests. He eventually moved to the corporate offices in New York City.[124] His son Clifford became President of what was then called Texas Tech College in Lubbock. Charles Jones died on November 25, 1934 in Spur, Texas.[125]

Lacy, Sarah – Irvin Lacy's widow did not sell all of her San Juan country cattle herd to George Thompson. She retained a sizable number of cattle and set her family up in the cattle business. Jim, John and William Brumley and Milt McConnell managed the family's San Juan cattle operations.[126] A few years after the Brumley's move to Colorado, Henry Goodman married John Brumley's daughter, Mary Louise.[127] In 1885 Mrs. Lacy estimated that her San Juan herd numbered twelve thousand. Her son-in-law, P.J.S. Montgomery, played a major role in Mrs. Lacy's cattle business. Lacy's widow retained her Vermejo residence, but in 1885 she was building a home in Trinidad.[128] During portions of 1885 Mrs. Lacy lived on the Dolores, just below the Big Bend with the Brumleys. At the time the *Dolores News* reported that she was known as the "cattle queen of the south west."[129] At least two of Mrs. Lacy's children moved to Tulare County, California. Irvin Lacy, Jr. married Mabel Horne (or Horner) there in 1895.[130] Ruth Lacy Montgomery, who had married her husband, P.J.S. Montgomery, in 1884 in Trinidad Colorado, also lived there. Mr. Montgomery was foreman of the San Joaquin Valley's Paige ranch and farm properties.[131]

Lockhart, George – The La Plata valley farmer and possible assailant of Port Stockton was a noted trouble maker. After the Stockton troubles Lockhart, Tom Nance and Sherman Helton accosted a newly arrived preacher named Hugh Griffin in Bloomfield and tried to make him drink with them. Griffin refused and they fired shots all around his feet. The preacher still refused. Helton respected the preacher's courage and called off his friends. In about 1885 a traveling showman presented a stereopticon show featuring biblical characters at the Farmington school house. Lockhart, Nance and others put an end to the show by shooting up the screen. As the gunfire erupted the showman leapt out the window. Several accounts say that Lockhart was killed in Gallup, New Mexico.[132]

That is not exactly correct. In 1887 Lockhart was working as a deputy sheriff in Apache County, Arizona in the northeastern part of the territory. The *St. Johns Herald* described the man who had hoorawed preacher Griffin as "a large stockowner, and one of the most highly esteemed and respected citizens of Apache county."[133] In early February, Tom King reported that his horse had been stolen. It was believed that a Navajo named Hosteen Chee was the culprit as he had been seen riding the mare at Bennett's Store near Houck's Tank on the Atlantic Pacific rail line.

(Houck's Tank is now Houck, Arizona, which is about thirty-three miles southwest of Gallup.)[134] On February 7th Lockhart, King and Ed Palmer left Navajo Springs and entered the Navajo Reservation to recover the horse and arrest the horse thief. [135] Lockhart would have been wise to tell the victim to take the matter up with the Indian agent, but that was not in his nature. According to the *St. Johns Herald,* "They found Hostine [sic] Chee at his tepee and served the warrant on him." Events deteriorated from there. Chee's son was sent to retrieve the horse, but he returned in the company of several Navajos. A fiery argument ensued and Lockhart was shot and killed. One account indicates that Lockhart was struck from behind by a Navajo woman wielding a hatchet. Given the circumstances, Lockhart would have been wary, although he certainly would not have expected that. Palmer and King made a run for it, but after a chase of over two miles, they too were killed. Chee was also killed and another Indian was believed to be seriously, if not mortally, wounded.[136] Several of the Indians raided Bennett's store, gathered a supply of provisions and took to the hills.[137]

Later reports dispute the initial accounts of that day and lay the blame for the outcome of this incident on the overbearing attitude of Lockhart and his two man posse. U.S. Army Captain John Brown Kerr reported, "Hosteen Chee, a very respectable Indian, finding a horse astray took the trouble to drive it over to Mr. Bennett's ranch to have it identified." Bennett recognized that the horse belonged to E.L. Palmer, who Kerr described as "a worthless white man – said to be a deserter from the United States Army." The horse was left at Bennett's, but when Palmer examined the horse he found a "small abrasion," and for this he swore out a warrant for horse theft against Chee. According to Captain Kerr, the King involved was named J.V. King. Kerr reported that Palmer and King took two horses from Mr. Bennett without permission and Bennett's horses were killed in the shootout with the Indians. The *St. Johns Herald* vehemently disputed Captain Kerr's version of events and described the incident as "a conflict between thieving, murderous Indians and respectable white persons." The *Herald* decried the vilification of whites by the army and Indian agents.[138] Some accounts report that Lockhart and his companions had been scalped. At the request of his widow, Mary Ann, Burr Milleson, Frank Allen and John Cox traveled to Arizona. They rounded up and sold his cattle, and trailed his herd of horses to the La Plata valley.[139] Whatever the whole truth of the story, it is clear that all of the men died needlessly. The victims failed to recognize, until it was too late, that their actions were leading to their own demise.

Morrison, George W. – After the turmoil of 1881, Morrison continued to live near Bayfield. In 1896, the Lewis Publishing Company published a history of central Texas which included a biography of George's father, William Morrison. The book noted that his son George W.

Morrison died when he was eighteen years old. Of course, that was not true. It's unclear if this misinformation was included because the Morrison family had disowned George or if they did it to protect him from Texas authorities.[140] As he had demonstrated during his youth in Stephenville, his fuse remained short. On Tuesday, April 18, 1899, Morrison encountered Sam Logan in Henry Arnold's Store in Bayfield. Logan's father-in-law was former Erath Country resident M.V.B. Salyer. Mrs. Salyer was I.W. Lacy's sister. As was consistently the case with George Morrison, there had been a simmering dispute between the families over ownership of cattle and some other unspecified disagreement. At 6:30 that evening Logan rode into Bayfield carrying a slaughtered beef in his wagon. He was armed with a pistol and Winchester rifle. He entered Arnold's Store. Morrison saw this and he entered the store and used his cane to strike Logan over the head. Morrison still retained much of the strength of his youth and the force of the blow drove Logan to the floor. Logan rolled under the counter and ran out the door headed for his wagon. Morrison was on his tail and pulled his Colt pistol and fired a round which struck Logan. The injured man continued to run, drew his weapon and returned fire. Morrison's bullet took effect and Logan fell to the ground, mortally wounded. The *Durango Democrat* reported, "Morrison mounted his horse drew his Winchester from his scabbard and rode over to where the body of Logan lay apparently to ascertain if he was dead. He then coolly rode towards home." At the time, Morrison lived about two miles west of Bayfield. His eighteen-year-old son Dudley and Ben Pargin assisted Morrison as he left his home and rode over the little divide to the Florida valley and disappeared. Pargin and Dudley returned home with Morrison's horse. That evening Undersheriff Bill Thompson and Deputy Billie Bay led a posse which surrounded the Morrison home. The *Durango Democrat* noted that, "As the old man is known to be a dead shot and has a record the posse contented itself with preserving a rigid blockade." At daybreak they rode up to the house and found that George Morrison was gone, but they did arrest Dudley and Ben Pargin. The next day a coroner's jury found that Morrison shot Logan "through the heart done with felonious intent." That same day, Morrison's wife, Marinda, came into Durango and met with her husband's attorney, Charles Johnson. Of the onetime staunch ally of Porter and Ike Stockton the *Democrat* said, "George Morrison is well known here. He is rather over middle age and has the reputation of being a dead shot and having a bad temper especially when in his cups. He has already gone through several duels and has been shot through the body again and again. He is a physical wreck and with his age will not be able to endure great exposure. He has the reputation of being a good friend and a dangerous foe."[141]

At noon on Thursday, April 20th, Charles Johnson rode out of Durango to Bayfield, where he met with Morrison near his home. They left Bayfield for Durango and along the way they were surrounded by an angry mob intent on lynching Morrison. Attorney Johnson had himself escaped a lynch mob in Amargo, when he was working as a Rio Arriba County deputy sheriff. He faced down the crowd and he and Morrison proceeded without further interruption. They rode through the dark and at 1:15 AM they entered Durango's Horseshoe Saloon where Morrison turned himself into Sheriff Joseph P. Airy.[142] There was a quid pro quo involved, as the sheriff released Dudley Morrison later that day.[143] Morrison was held without bond until July, when long time La Plata County attorney and now Judge James L. Russell placed the bond at fifteen thousand dollars.[144]

Morrison went to trial in April 1900 for murder. Through the able representation of Charles Johnson, he was found guilty of the lesser charge of voluntary manslaughter and was sent to the Colorado Penitentiary.[145] Efforts were made on Morrison's behalf to secure his early release because of his poor physical condition and advanced age. In July 1902 he walked out of the penitentiary a free man. On Independence Day the *Democrat* noted that now Morrison could spend his "declining years" amongst his family and friends. The newspaper said, "we feel assured that the rest of his days will be devoted to less of anger and more of peace and patience."[146] The *Democrat's* assessment was wrong.

After his release, Morrison and his family moved close to the Utah line, to Dove Creek, Colorado. Despite the claims of Morrison's frailty, he was still able to ride a horse five years after his release from prison. At that time the *Democrat* estimated his age as between seventy and seventy-five. Two census records place his year of birth as being about 1847, making him about sixty years old in 1907. Whatever his age was, he continued to make enemies. On Friday, June 14, 1907, Morrison and Bill Hinton had an argument over, of all things, cattle. The disagreement had been on a low boil for several years. Perhaps age had slowed Morrison down. Hinton drew his weapon, fired, and struck Morrison in the arm and just below the shoulder. The bullet wounds were survivable, but when Morrison was thrown from his horse, he sustained serious injuries. His condition worsened and on June 18th, he was brought into Durango by train accompanied by his children, Minnie, Maud and Dudley. He was admitted to the Oschner Hospital. Peritonitis had developed and early the next morning irascible George W. Morrison died from his wounds.[147] His body was placed in the care of the Hood Undertaking Company and his remains were shipped to Dolores for burial.[148] In March 1908, Bill Hinton stood trial in Rico for the killing. He was acquitted.[149]

<u>Nance, Tom</u> – Nance was a hell raiser with few peers. His antics ranged from mischief to mayhem. On June 2, 1882 he was arrested by Durango's Marshal Foley for being drunk and disorderly after he berated the marshal and then recklessly discharged his pistol. At the time Nance was still working for George Thompson.[150] Although by this time it is not totally clear for which George Thompson he was working. Young George

W. Thompson, the namesake of his uncle, arrived in the San Juan country prior to I.W. Lacy's murder. His brother William moved to southwest Colorado soon after Lacy's demise. Their father, Doctor Alfred Thompson, also moved to southwest Colorado shortly after Lacy's death. Doctor was his given name and not a title. The Thompson boys, who were considerably younger than Tom Nance, were soon handling the bulk of the elder George Thompson's San Juan country cattle business.[151] Tom Nance had faced death in dealing with Porter and Ike Stockton and, like the Thompson boys, he too was a nephew of the elder George W. Thompson. That the upstart and latecomer Thompson brothers were now in charge of affairs could not help but rub Nance the wrong way. With his future uncertain and his options limited, Nance sold the few cattle he owned to William Thompson and Joe Caldwell and left the area, but that deal only added to the bad blood between Nance and young William Thompson.[152]

On November 1886 he returned, determined to collect $290 which he claimed was owed to him by Thompson and Caldwell. Reports indicate he filed a court claim in the matter, but before the court date, he became impatient. For several days he made a habit of frequenting the local saloons. Once liquored up, he would issue threats against his Thompson cousins and then he would make a showy display of his impressive, razor sharp bowie knife. On the evening of Monday, November 22, 1886, Nance met with William Thompson at the Henderson Brothers Saloon in Durango. The two moved to a back room of Henderson's and engaged in a quiet conversation. Bystanders were aware of the dispute between the men, but believed they were working out their differences. According to the *La Plata Miner* one witness said "Thompson was particularly quiet and seemed anxious to avoid trouble." Their talk deteriorated and soon both men rose. An angry Nance baited Thompson, daring him to use his pistol. Thompson carefully kept his hands away from his gun and raised them palms open. Nance pressed in close to Thompson, drew his bowie knife and began slashing away with deadly intent. Thompson drew his pistol and fired off two wild rounds. One of them put out the lights. He clubbed Nance with his pistol. Nance was undeterred. When it was over Thompson was left with his intestines hanging out of his belly, a serious stab wound in his side, two lesser wounds in his back, and his cheek and jaw had a gaping wound, which exposed his facial bones. Nance was almost none the worse for wear. He had a slight scalp wound. Town Marshal McDevitt and officers Webb and Wynne took the men to the Inter Ocean Hotel and then Strater's drug store was opened and they were moved there. Dr. Winters and Dr. Bellinger soon arrived to care for the wounded. Nance was taken to the town jail, where he proclaimed that he acted only in self-defense. Thompson was clinging to life. Chloroform was administered and with much difficulty, Dr. Winters was finally able to place Thompson's intestines back through the hole in his abdomen. All of the wounds were then sewed up, cleaned and dressed. He was still alive, barely.[153] (Thompson survived and in the early 1900s was the sheriff of La Plata County. A little before noon on January 9, 1906, while serving as sheriff, Thompson was shot and killed by Durango police officer Jesse Stansel in front of Durango's El Moro Saloon.)[154] As of January 1887, Tom Nance was still housed in the Durango jail, awaiting trial.[155] But perhaps Nance's claim of self-defense worked out because in the fall of 1887 he arrived in Eureka, Utah in the company of Mose Blancett's crutch-bound brother, En. After En was shot to death in December, Nance remained in Eureka and in March 1888 he shot Silva La Boa in the arm. He was quickly arrested and brought into Provo for an appearance before the Utah County Grand Jury.[156] Nance was indicted and brought to trial. In October he was found guilty of assault with intent to murder. He was sentenced to serve forty-two months in the Utah Territorial Penitentiary.[157]

After serving his time, he moved to northern Arizona and probably worked for the Aztec Land and Cattle Company (commonly known as the Hasknife outfit). On September 18, 1892 he got into a quarrel with Hashknife cowboy J.B. (Ben) Mitchell in a Holbrook bar. Nance had been unemployed for several months. As the fight progressed, Mitchell knocked Nance to the ground and it was thought the matter was over. Then Nance approached Mitchell from behind with a chair raised over his head. Once again Mitchell put Nance on the ground and commenced kicking him in the head. Despite the vicious assault, Nance was not thought to be seriously hurt and was taken outside. About fifteen minutes later, around midnight, someone went out to check on Nance and found that he was dead. Mitchell left the country immediately. A coroner's jury ruled that Mitchell had killed Nance by hitting and kicking him to death.[158]

Radigan, Tommy – After the Stockton gang disbanded, the one-legged Radigan was a popular man in Rico. According to Governor Pitkin, by the fall of 1881, he may have been the only indicted member of the Stockton Gang who was known to still be in Colorado. Residents of the mountain town submitted a petition to Governor Pitkin concerning his status as a wanted man in New Mexico and asked his assistance in obtaining a pardon for Radigan. In October 1881, Pitkin sent the petition to Governor Sheldon and told the New Mexico governor that Radigan was not a member of the Stockton-Eskridge gang, but merely accepted employment from them. Pitkin asserted that, "he [Radigan] had no knowledge of their [Stockton and Eskridge] relations to the other citizens of Rio Arriba county."[159] Considering the continual bombastic stories about those relations printed in the *Dolores News,* that assertion is beyond preposterous. In any case, Sheldon wisely refused to consider the request. The June 1885 state of Colorado census shows that he was living in San Miguel County, Colorado, probably in Telluride. Despite being one-legged, Radigan's occupation was listed as "Cow-Boy."[160]

Stockton, Samuel – In 1892, thirty-seven-year-old Sam Stockton took a fifteen-year-old bride and in 1900 he and his wife, Bertha, were living in Eastland County.[161] He was the likely source of the Eastland County salt saga story of Ike Stockton, which was published by Mrs. Langston in 1904.[162]

The Stockton Widows – Mrs. Porter (Emily Jane) Stockton and Mrs. Ike (Amanda Ellen) Stockton. The Stockton women were accustomed to high drama and that did not end with the violent deaths of their husbands. After Port Stockton was killed, Emily Jane had at least two suitors. One was George N. Woods. Mr. Woods had evidently been part of Ike's crowd in Durango. The Missouri native was about thirty-four years old and had lived most of his life in the gold rush mining town of Grass Valley in Nevada County, California. He had some unspecified trouble there in about 1875 and then drifted through Oregon, Washington, Idaho and Wyoming before entering Colorado in 1880.[163] When it came to women, Woods's recollections are questionable and may be clouded with what he wished might have been. While he was slightly off plumb, his infatuations were real, and they would have deadly consequences. In a letter, he claimed to "have lived in the house with her [Emily Jane] for two or three months." Through the first few months of 1882, he said he gave "$135 worth of provisions and clothing to her and the orphan children." Emily spurned Woods and began seeing Joel Estes Jr., a small time stockman. Estes ran his cattle with the help of his longtime employee, M.G. Buchanan. His cattle ranged up and down the Animas and Florida valleys and he spent much of his time in and around Durango. Woods knew Estes and claimed that at one time they had been good friends.[164] Fate has a way of picking strange bedfellows. As it turns out, Estes was the widower who employed Port Stockton's widow victim, Lucy Cooper, after Stockton jumped her Flora Vista land claim. It seems likely that Estes would have married the widow Cooper, had she not found caring for his six children along with her three children much more than she wanted to handle.[165] The ironies do not end there. On April 18, 1881 Estes was part of a large group of men sworn in by Max Frost to be members of the San Juan Guards assigned to protect western Rio Arriba County from the raids of Ike Stockton.[166] It's unclear when their relationship began, but on March 12, 1882, Emily married Joel Estes. Woods unwisely attended the wedding dance which was held two days later in Farmington. "That was where Estes first gave me the cold shoulder," he reported, "and he tried to raise a row with me then and has threatened me ever since that time."[167]

Well before Port's widow married Joel Estes, Woods had turned his attention to Ike's widow. Shortly after the death of her husband, Ellen wrote a letter to Governor Pitkin inquiring if Sheriff Barney Watson and Deputy Jim Sullivan had any authority to arrest her husband. Although he had no standing in the matter, George Woods wrote Pitkin a similar letter.

Pitkin gave Woods a one page reply. Ike's widow received a five page letter. In his letter to Ellen, Pitkin recounted receiving the requisitions from Governor Wallace and that he in turn had issued warrants for the arrest of Ike Stockton and others. Pitkin asserted that as far as he knew the warrants were delivered to the sheriff in Durango by Tony Neis and he received confirmation of this from Governor Wallace. Of course, the warrants were then conveniently lost by Barney Watson's predecessor, Luke Hunter. Pitkin advised Ike's widow that, "I have never heard from him [Neis], nor from the Sheriff of any county in relation to this matter."[168] Giving the governor the benefit of the doubt, it appears that he had a memory lapse. The *Denver Republican* reported that on the day Stockton died, Pitkin's office received a telegram from Watson asking for copies of Ike's arrest warrant.[169] After receiving Pitkin's reply, Ellen apparently dropped the matter. George Woods continued to pursue her.

Those efforts ended abruptly when the fickle thirty-four-year-old saw fifteen-year-old Lizzie Cowan. Thoroughly infatuated, Woods set his sights on the nubile teenager. According to Joel Estes, "Woods was making love to John Cowan's daughter." That was probably only in the Victorian sense of the saying. The fact that Lizzie was also the niece of both Stockton widows was unimportant to the love crazed Woods.[170] Needless to say, Mr. Cowan was not impressed with his daughter's thirty-four-year-old suitor.[171] At the time, Cowan's sister (the former Mrs. Porter Stockton and now Mrs. Joel Estes) was living in Animas City.[172] Cowan hoped to hide Lizzie and sent her to live with the Estes family, but Woods found her and continued his pursuit. According to Estes, "Wood [sic] had been paying some attention to her, but we discouraged her attention to Wood [sic], and when he saw that the girl's attention had been attracted from him, he very naturally felt a little piqued at all of us." Woods's hostility extended to Estes's hired hand M.G. Buchanan.[173] A desperate Cowan then sent Lizzie to Durango to live with her widowed aunt, Mrs. Ike Stockton. Woods quickly found Lizzie and continued to make a nuisance of himself. As for John Cowan, he claimed that his daughter wanted nothing to do with Woods. That may have been his fervent hope, but it appears that Lizzie offered Woods some encouragement, even if slight. In desperation, Cowan finally packed his daughter off to the Catholic girl's school in Trinidad.[174] Woods had managed to gain the deep-seated enmity of each Stockton widow and both Joel Estes and M.G. Buchanan made no secret of their animus toward Woods. The infatuated man later claimed that both Estes and Buchanan had threatened to kill him, saying, "These two men have been hunting me down for some time." Witnesses to the threats included "Henry Woods, Mrs. Tucker and Guy Sutton."[175] Mrs. Tucker was Angeline Tucker, who Woods identified as his aunt. While George Woods had grown up in California, Mrs. William Lafayette Tucker, whose maiden name was Wood (not Woods), had grown up in Erath County, Texas.[176]

On May 25, 1882 the trouble came to a head in Kincaid's Pacific Slope Saloon in Durango. About 9:00 AM, Woods entered the saloon and was greeted by Buchanan who said he wanted to have a talk with him. Woods replied that they had no business to talk about. Buchanan disagreed and accused Woods of threatening his life. Both men walked to the door and Woods left the saloon. Shortly afterwards, Buchanan left, but returned just before 11:00 AM. He ordered a drink and commented that he needed to go out and look after some cattle over on the Florida.[177] Before that happened, Woods re-entered the saloon, sat down with four men, and commenced a game of cribbage. Buchanan caught sight of Woods and imprudently commented that he had met a man who would not speak to him. Woods jumped up and said, "God damn you, I will speak to you!" He drew his .45 caliber long barrel pistol and fired a shot in the direction of Buchanan. It struck a drinking glass held by Buchanan's drinking companion. Woods fired again, striking Buchanan, who fell on his back, exclaiming "I'm killed." Woods paused, and then to make sure Buchanan's words were accurate, he shot the prone man a few more times. At the sound of gunfire, Policeman Charley O'Connor sprinted toward the Pacific Slope and encountered Woods just outside the saloon. Woods immediately admitted, "I have killed a man and want to give myself up."[178] Later reports said that as Woods advanced on Buchanan and fired his final two or three shots, he repeated himself, saying, "[God] damn you, I'll talk to you." Woods determined that his only hope was to claim self-defense. He alleged that Buchanan had threatened to draw on him near Wickline's Saloon earlier that day and while in the Pacific Slope Buchanan had threatened him with a large knife. Woods also asserted that before he pulled his pistol, Buchanan had reached for his own sidearm. Other witnesses said Buchanan was unarmed. Woods proclaimed, "I did it, to save my life, Estes and Buchanan have both threatened to shoot me. Twenty persons knew this."[179]

Buchanan was taking it easy that morning because he needed a saddle. According to Joel Estes, he brought the saddle into town and was looking for Buchanan, but could not find him. Emily Jane received word that Buchanan had been killed and she delivered the news to her husband. Estes believed that his employee was not armed and told a reporter, "Buchanan came up with a bunch of cows yesterday. Left his pistol at Animas City, and came in town to-day."[180] The *Dolores News* claimed that the animosity between Woods and Buchanan was inevitably headed for fatal results because Lizzie was in love with Woods and "Buchanan was indignantly and wildly jealous."[181]

Woods had chosen a most inopportune time to gun down Buchanan, since the La Plata County District Court was holding one of its few sessions of the year. The next day, the grand jury swiftly indicted him for murder. His trial was placed on the court's docket for the following week.¹⁸² Sheriff Watson was determined to foil those who desired immediate justice. Woods was guarded night and day. Initially, he was held in the district clerk's office. A locomotive light was mounted at the top of the back stairs to light up the surroundings.¹⁸³ Less than a week after the murder, Woods was brought to trial where he was represented by attorneys James L. Russell and Colonel H.B. Wilson. The District Attorney, Frank C. Goudy, was assisted by James Hoffmire. The defense asked for a change of venue, which was denied by Judge William M. Burris. A continuance was also denied.¹⁸⁴ Even without a lynching, frontier justice was swift. On the evening of May 31ˢᵗ the jury found Woods "guilty of deliberate and premeditated murder."¹⁸⁵ Before the week was out Judge Burris pronounced sentence, death by hanging. The defendant was given less than a month to live. Burris set the date of execution as June 23, 1882. The *Durango Herald* reported that the doomed man walked out of the courtroom with a smile on his face.¹⁸⁶

While awaiting his hanging, Woods vented his wrath at Ellen Stockton in a letter to his Aunt Ange. In it he alleged that Ellen broke up his relationship with Lizzie with "obscene lies, saying that I lived with a bad woman." Woods said Ike Stockton's widow "will do anything to flirt with N.C. Caldwell [also known as Coldwell] and to keep up appearance." He said, "Ellen is smart. No matter what she does, she will meet a person with one of those cute smiles and cunning words to hide all her evil doings from the world, outside of the man she is criminating with." He begs his Aunt Ange "to keep poor Lizzie from her, for she will be the ruin of her." He spews venom thickly, saying, "she has beat me out of my money, my work and my life, and beat me out of the one that I loved, for she could not see me marry her, knowing how me and her were before I saw the loved one." In the same rambling letter he assesses the character of the former Mrs. Porter Stockton: "Jane Estes is a virtuous woman," adding "she is a good woman, and I can forgive her for what she said against me."¹⁸⁷

Woods did not have long to stew in the mess he had made for himself. Sometime after sentencing, he was moved to a room next to the sheriff's office and kept chained to the wall. His feet and hands were shackled. Some of the precautions may have been to prevent Woods from foiling the executioner, since his cribbage set was clearly missing several pegs. A few days before his scheduled execution, he sat for a photo in his cell. Conspicuously displayed on his chest was a photo of his last obsession, Lizzie Cowan. In his hand he held a cigar. When interviewed by a *Durango Herald* newsman, Woods reported that he ate well and slept soundly. He expressed no regret over killing Buchanan, but did regret that he was unable to kill Joel Estes. Local resident James O. Harris had known Woods's father, William D. Woods, since 1849. Harris served as the messenger between George and his family in California. After the death sentence was delivered, Harris wired the family home in Grass Valley and requested a thousand dollars to pay for an appeal. George Woods later advised his father to not waste money on the effort. Many speculated that Woods was insane, a claim he vehemently denied to the *Herald's* reporter. As the newsman departed the makeshift dungeon, Woods was devouring a box of strawberries.[188]

The day before the scheduled hanging Woods had weakened and was beginning to look emaciated and worn out. The *Herald* reported that "his limbs twitch nervously." He had lost some of his cheer, but the condemned man proclaimed that he felt "first rate" and said, "I will meet death like a man." In the days prior to his execution he perused several catalogs from Dr. Folsom's undertaking establishment and selected an imitation rosewood casket with nickel plated handles. (It was also reported that he had selected a metallic casket.) He ordered a silver plate for the lid to be engraved with his name and other pertinent information. To complete the arrangements, he hired a hearse and selected pall bearers for the occasion. Woods planned on being shipped out of Durango by rail to California to be buried next to his twin brother, who had died at the age of nineteen. To add to the ghoulish scene, he kept the coffin in his cell during the night preceding his execution.[189]

A state-of-the-art gallows was constructed in a grassy field, a very short walking distance from downtown. At the time the location was described as being "on the ground opposite the new county building, and under the brow of the mesa." "The plan adopted contemplates the sudden elevation of the poor wretch skywards," reported the *Durango Herald*, "by means of a heavy weight attached to a pulley, instead of the old trap door device."[190] The new mechanism added new symbolism to the term, "jerked to Jesus." The execution took place about 11:00 AM on the prescribed day with a large crowd in attendance, mostly men, but there were a few women and children. Sheriff Barney Watson's arrangements went off without a hitch.[191]

Just two days after the hanging, Ellen Stockton married N.C. Coldwell in La Plata County.[192] Coldwell, an attorney, was a native of Arkansas. Both his parents were from Tennessee.[193] He opened a law practice in Durango. The Coldwell family lived in La Plata County until the latter half of the 1880s when they moved to the San Joaquin Valley in California.[194]

Opposite page: Durango's residents and others gather on a glorious, but somber summer day for the hanging of George N. Woods, June 23, 1882. (Courtesy La Plata County Historical Society.)

By that time they had produced two children. Colbert was born in Durango on April 11, 1883.[195] His sister, Julia was born in Durango in 1885. Their brother Cedric was born in California in 1890. In 1900 the family lived in the center of the valley in Fresno. The 1900 census included Ike's son Guy, but not his daughter, Delilah.[196] N.C. Coldwell died on May 30, 1913. The widow of Ike Stockton and N.C. Coldwell died in San Francisco on January 7, 1924. She did live long enough to see Colbert's success in business. In 1903, Colbert started his career in real estate sales.

During the early 1900s he was a founding member of the firm Coldwell, Cornwall and Banker, which became Coldwell Banker Real Estate.[197] Accounts indicate that the real estate tycoon was unaware of Ike's true story or had selective amnesia when it came to his mother's first husband. His father told acquaintances that Ike had been "killed by unidentified outlaws."[198] California was a long way from Colorado, so very few knew the truth of the matter.

A less than modest headstone in the Animas Cemetery bearing the initials GNW which is reported to mark the grave of fickle and foolhardy George N. Woods. (Author's collection.)

As for Porter Stockton's widow, Emily Jane, after marrying Joel Estes, she took on the care of their large blended family. In 1885, the couple and seven children were living in La Plata County.[199] In the mid-1880s, Emily Jane gave birth to two boys, Cleve and Lev.[200] Even before she was shot and injured by vigilantes in Flora Vista, Mrs. Stockton/Estes was described as being in poor health. Her frailties are unknown, but her bullet induced injuries probably worsened her lingering health troubles. On Saturday April 22, 1893 the *Durango Herald* reported, "Yesterday morning occurred the death of Mrs. Joel Estes of Animas City. Funeral services this morning at 10 o'clock."[201]

Sullivan, Jim – One year after the shooting of Ike Stockton, the former Durango law enforcement officer was arrested for cattle rustling north of Pagosa Springs. When captured, Sullivan, Alf Dunham and two other men were herding about two hundred head of cattle. The men were jailed in Conejos County.[202] Sullivan may have been acquitted because in 1883 or early 1884 he was reportedly killed near Chama. Then in February 1885 friends reported seeing him at the New Orleans Exposition. They said that he had quit his wild and wooly ways, but was a physical wreck. The *News* of Rico assured its readers that he had been killed near Chama as they had "seen a number of papers that were taken from the body."[203]

Watson, Sheriff Barney – In November 1881, Watson was elected to a two-year term as county sheriff.[204] About a week later (six weeks after the death of Ike Stockton) he traveled to Farmington with George W. Clarke.[205] There is no word on his business in Rio Arriba County, but there is no doubt that he was greeted as a hero along the lower Animas. Watson was not without his detractors. In April 1882 the *Durango Record* reported that he was using his position to bully private individuals and was guilty of indecent activities. They accused him of living openly with a girl named Julie who worked for Madam Cora Leslie in less than honorable pursuits. When Julie removed to Silverton, Watson trekked up the valley and succeeded in inducing her return.[206] In January 1884 he was arrested by Deputy U.S. Marshal Robert Dwyer for stopping an omnibus in the fall of 1883 and releasing two U.S. Army deserters.[207] Watson evidently overcame those charges. At that time he was represented by attorneys N.C. Coldwell and James Hoffmire. It's not known how Ike's widow felt about her second husband representing one of the men who had killed her first husband.[208] In May 1884 Watson was re-arrested on the same charge by sheriff and acting Deputy U.S. Marshal Sam Pedgrift in Durango.[209] According to the *Aspen Times* a few days later, after a preliminary examination, Watson was discharged.[210] There was bad blood between Sheriff Pedgrift and Barney Watson. Shortly after the November 1883 elections, allegations of voter fraud against Pedgrift were made by the defeated sheriff's candidate, Henry Goodman. When Watson served the necessary papers on Pedgrift, he refused to acknowledge that they had been served.[211]

Welfoot, Seth – The stubborn one-armed Englishman remained in Colorado up until early 1882. In January that year, he was working on some mining property on what was then commonly known as Nigger Baby Hill near Rico. In February he left Rico and traveled to Durango and then went on to Santa Fe. By arrangement he met several other residents of the lower

Animas, who were there to serve as witnesses for each other's land claims. C.H. McHenry was part of the group. The men were in a celebratory mood when they left Santa Fe on February 28th. McHenry later reported that on the return trip Welfoot began to feel poorly and developed a fever. As they passed through Chama, the men still believed it was not a serious condition. Welfoot made it back to Bloomfield, where he stayed a few days to recover. On March 11th he was placed in the care of the widow Eliza Vaughan and other neighbors who lived near his Farmington land. His condition worsened and he told his friends that his cousin in the east should have his possessions. After being pushed off his property for a year and finally proving up on his claim, he died before he could live on his land.[212]

<u>West, George E.</u> – West remained in the cattle business. In 1883 he was running a herd on Utah's Blue Mountain.[213] He was a member of the Colorado Stock Grower's Association until at least 1899.[214] He was highly respected in southwest Colorado and in the early 1900s he served as a state senator from La Plata County.[215]

Appendix

Muster Roll of the San Juan Guards – April 1881

Captain William B. Haines	1st Lt. H.W. Cox	2nd Lt. Alfred F. Stump
Sgt. Charles W. Rash	Sgt. Levy A. Hughes	Sgt. Isaac N. Covert
Sgt. Juan A Manzanares	Sgt. George Lockhart	Cpl. William B. Horn
Cpl. Marcellus M. Blancett	Cpl. R.W. Williams	Cpl. Juan N. Jaquez

<u>and the privates were</u> -

	E.W. Mead	Frank Creighton
Thomas Fulcher	Edward P. Stone	J.W. Snyder
Dan Sullivan	J.T. Quiringo?	Charles Virden
Fred W. Townsend	H. Lushbaugh?	Thomas K. Raley
Peter M. Salmon	Jasper N. Coe	O.H. Hansen
José Trujillo	M. Cordoba	James A. Cox
José Manzanares	E..cion Bender?	Gabriel Chavez
J. Isidro? Cales?	Gu ??	Antonio Munoz
E.? Archuleta	Guadalupe Archuleta	David Lobato
Julian Sanchez	Manuel Sanchez	F.M. Hamblet
John T. Hamblet	H. Benning	Thomas Cream?
E.A. Clayton	John Brown	Louis Fontaine
Charles McCoy	Harvey McCoy	George W. Cox
G.W. McCoy	D.F. Sharp	Joel Estes
John Blancett	J. Scott	A.U. (Alf) Graves
Fred Tully	L.Green Barlow	J.H. [Joseph] Foster
Charles B. Sharp	H. James Kiffin	D.C. Cole
John Truan, Jr.	S.E. Peck?	Peter Knickerbocker
D. Coryell	Burr Milleson	John Cox
John Milleson	Joseph Harris	J.H. (Jake) Bohannon
Samuel Howe	H.M. Sharp	James Tully
James Helton	J.H. Ferguson	Lee Hamblet
P.K. Williams	L.A. McCoy	

Those on the San Juan Guards muster roll were duly sworn into service. Militia operations were governed "in conformity with the Rules and Regulations and Articles of War governing the United States Army." There may be some errors on the names in the list. The names are taken from the signatures of the San Juan Guardsmen on the muster roll. In some cases their signatures were very difficult to read. According to the article, "The Rio Arriba Troubles," *Santa Fe Daily New Mexican*, April 27, 1881, there were seventy-five privates. There are slightly less than that on the April 18th muster roll. Those holding rank above private are from the April 27th *New Mexican*. All of the names of the privates are from the Muster Roll, San Juan Guards, April 18, 1881. The Special Orders for Organization of San Juan Guards, April 15 and April 16, 1881, Campaign, TANM, NMSRCA and the *United States Census 1880*, Rio Arriba County, New Mexico, FLC-CSWS were used to help decipher some of the names on the muster roll.

Notes

The author endeavored to make the endnotes more thorough and complete than is common to most books. Hopefully this will make it easier for writers, historians, genealogists and others to follow up on their own research.

All illustrations are credited on the same page as the image, except the frontispiece (see credit on page iv) and those shown on the cover. The cover illustrations are:

Top front cover – "Colorado.- Incidents of a Trip to the Mining Town of Durango," image titled "Mount Blanca" *Frank Leslie's Illustrated Newspaper*, May 28, 1881, artist J.J. Reilly. (Modified, author's collection.)

Bottom front cover – "Cattle-raising on our Great Plains.- Cowboys checking a stampede of thunder-frightened cattle, near Kerrville, Texas," *Frank Leslie's Illustrated Newspaper*, May 28, 1881, artist L.W. MacDonald. (Modified, author's collection.)

Back Cover – "Colorado.–View of Durango, The Magic City of the Southwest," *Frank Leslie's Illustrated Newspaper*, 1881, artist J.J. Reilly. (Modified, newspaper print is from the author's collection.)

Top Spine - "An Arizona Type," from "The Round-up," by Theodore Roosevelt, *The Century Illustrated Monthly Magazine*, Vol. 35, No. 6, April 1888, artist Frederic Remington. (Modified, author's collection.)

INTRODUCTION

¹ *New Mexico v. Porter Stockton,* case no. 417, August 30, 1879, Colfax County District Court Records, New Mexico State Records Center and Archives (hereafter abbreviated as NMSRCA).

² Ibid.; "State and Vicinity," *Fairplay (CO) Flume,* June 19, 1879, p. 3, from the *Otero Optic;* "The Withers Murder At Otero," *Denver Daily Tribune,* June 22, 1879, p. 6, from the *Trinidad News.*

CHAPTER ONE – THE TEXANS

¹ Charles B. Clark, Jr., "The Outlaw," *Songs of the Cattle Trail and Cow Camp,* comp. by John A. Lomax (New York: The MacMillan Company, 1920), p. 140.

² "Robbery," *La Plata Miner* (Silverton, CO) December 18, 1880, from the *Animas City (CO) Southwest.*

³ Ibid.

⁴ "Capture of the Stolen Horses," *Animas City (CO) Southwest,* December 18, 1880; "Another Tragedy," *Durango (CO) Weekly Record,* January 10, 1881.

⁵ Isaac Hiram Cox, "Tales," transcribed by Joeen Johnson Sutton, 1920s, courtesy of Les Sutton, p. 3.

⁶ John B. Arrington and Eleanor D. MacDonald, *The San Juan Basin - My Kingdom Was A County* (Denver: Green Mountain Press, 1970), pp. 136-138. Arrington's account is very confused in many of the details and he does not identify the thief by name, but it is a virtual certainty, based on information in the January 10, 1881 issue of the *Durango Record* and in the December 18, 1880 issue of the *Animas City Southwest,* that the victim was Den Gannon.

⁷ "Another Tragedy," *Durango (CO) Weekly Record,* January 10, 1881.

⁸ W.P. Hendrickson to Colonel Crofton, March 9, 1881, Fort Lewis Military Post Federal Records Inventory (hereafter abbreviated FLMP), Coll. M 118, box 1, series 4, folder 37, Fort Lewis College, Center of Southwest Studies (hereafter abbreviated FLC-CSWS).

⁹ *U.S. Census 1850,* Upshur County, TX, r. 916, p. 183b, Albuquerque/Bernalillo County Library System - Special Collections Library (hereafter abbreviated ABCLS), from the records of the U.S. Bureau of the Census, National Archives and Records Administration (NARA); Betty Ann Burton- Cruber, comp., *The Marriage Records of Itawamba County, Mississippi, 1837-1866, with Heads of Families, 1840 Federal Census* (Memphis: The Milestone Press, 1973), p. 78, ABCLS; *U.S. Census 1860,* Hopkins County, TX, r. 1297, p. 128b, ABCLS; *U.S. Census 1880,* La Plata County, CO, r. 91 p. 572c and Rio Arriba County, NM, r. 803, p. 225c, ABCLS. The 1850 Upshur County census shows the "Stocton" family; husband Samuel - thirty-six, wife S. - twenty-three, daughter M.A. - six, daughter S.M. - four, daughter E.G - three, son G.H. - two, son Wm. - less than one year. The parents were born in Tennessee, with all the children born in Mississippi, except William who was born in Texas. The 1860 Hopkins County census shows the following family; No husband is shown, mother Jane Stockton – age thirty-six and born in Mississippi, daughter Mary - sixteen, Sarah - fourteen, Emily - thirteen, no son

with the initials G.H. is listed, Porter - ten, Isaac - nine, daughter Matisha - seven, Samuel - five and Amanda - two. All of the children are shown as being born in Texas. As with virtually all census record comparisons, there are inconsistencies, but there are numerous similarities as well. The 1880 United States census for La Plata County, Colorado shows William P. Stockton - twenty-nine, born in Texas with both his parents shown as being born in Mississippi. The 1880 census for Rio Arriba County, New Mexico shows Isaac Stockton - twenty-nine, born in Texas, with both his parents being born in Tennessee.

[10] From a personal viewing of Ike Stockton's tombstone on October 3, 2009.

[11] *U.S. Census 1860*, Hopkins County, TX, r. 1297, p. 128b, ABCLS.

[12] Ibid.

[13] "Another Tragedy," *Durango (CO) Weekly Record*, January 10, 1881.

[14] C.O. Ziegenfuss, "Ike Stockton," *Dolores News* (Rico, CO), August 20, 1881, p. 1, from the *Denver Republican*. Colorado's Historic Newspaper Collection. This Rico, Colorado newspaper is just one of many of Colorado's historic newspapers which can be can be accessed from http://www.coloradohistoricnewspapers.org. This online collection began when the Collaborative Digitization Program joined with the Colorado Historical Society and the Colorado State Library, and began a project to digitize Colorado newspapers published before 1923 as well as those which were already copyright cleared. The article cited is from the August 12, 1881 *Denver Republican* interview with Ike Stockton.

[15] Lewis Publishing Company, comp., *A Memorial and Biographical History of Johnson and Hill Counties, Texas*, (Chicago: Lewis Publishing Company, 1892), http://archive.org/details/memorialbiograph01chic (accessed August 12, 2013).

[16] "A Historical Character," *Wichita (KS) Daily Eagle*, May 4, 1890, p. 4. Jesse Chisholm opened a trading post on the North Canadian in 1866.

[17] C.O. Ziegenfuss, "Ike Stockton," *Denver Republican*, August 12, 1881.

[18] Mrs. George Langston, *History of Eastland County Texas* (Dallas, TX: A.D. Aldridge & Co., 1904), pp. 75, 194 http://www.archive.org/details/cu31924028801310 (accessed November 22, 2009). The Internet Archive at archive.org contains many digitized publications from books, periodicals, government reports, U.S. Census records and more.

[19] *U.S. Census 1870*, Eastland County, TX, r. 1583, pp. 300a-301a; *U.S. Census 1860*, Eastland County, TX, r. 1293, pp. 1a-2b. Available from The Internet Archive from the collections of the Genealogy Center of the Allen County (Indiana) Public Library (IA-ACPL). "Weatherford Sun," *Fort Worth Daily Gazette*, October 6, 1884, p. 4, from the *Weatherford (TX) Sun*. From the Library of Congress, Chronicling America: Historic American Newspapers. Sponsored jointly by the National Endowment for the Humanities and the Library of Congress as part of the National Digital Newspaper Program (NDNP). These historical newspapers can be accessed at http://chroniclingamerica.loc.gov/. This obituary for Mrs. Oliver (Susan) Loving notes that "deadly forays of the Indians forced" him to move his family from Loving's Valley in Palo Pinto County to Weatherford. While this occurred one year before the outbreak of the Civil War, that situation only grew worse when the men on the Texas frontier left their families behind to fight Yankees.

[20] Lewis Publishing Company, comp., *History of Texas*, Central Texas ed. (Chicago: The Lewis Publishing Company, 1896), p. 289. http://archive.org/details/historyoftexassu00lewi (accessed March 1, 2013).

[21] *U.S. Census 1860*, Erath County, TX, r. 1293, pp. 114a-144b, IA-ACPL; *U.S. Census 1870,* Erath County, TX, r. 1583, pp. 454a-476b, IA-ACPL.

[22] J. Frank Dobie, *The Longhorns* (New York: Grosset and Dunlap, 1941), p. 114.

[23] W.H. Fooshee, "Early Days in Stephenville," *Stephenville (TX) Tribune*, July 27, 1923. Microfilm of the *Stephenville Tribune* are available at the Dick Smith Library at Tarleton State University in Stephenville (hereafter abbreviated TSU-DSL).

[24] W.H. Fooshee, "Early Days in Stephenville," *Stephenville (TX) Tribune*, July 6, 1923.

[25] "About Texas," *Bolivar (TN) Bulletin,* January 5, 1872, p. 1. Besides Erath and Palo Pinto, the other prime grazing counties listed were Johnson, Throckmorton, Jack, Young, Callahan, Coleman, Brown, Tarrant, Comanche, Hill and Stephens.

[26] *U.S. Census 1860*, Palo Pinto County, TX, r. 1302, pp. 332a, 334a, 336a and 342b, IA-ACPL.

[27] *Santa Lulu Independent* (Aztec, NM), November 2, 1888, San Juan College, Farmington, NM.

[28] Mrs. Frances Terry Ingmire, comp., *Marriage Records of Hopkins County, Texas, 1846-1880* (St. Louis, MO: 1979), p. 2. The Cox-Allard marriage record is dated February 11, 1849. It notes Nancy's birth date as being August 14, 1836. H.W. Cox's headstone in the Cedar Hill, NM Cemetery says he was born on January 26, 1825. Nancy's headstone says she was born in 1836 and an engraving on the side of H.W.'s headstone, closest to Nancy's headstone says, "Nancy Wife of H.W. Cox Born Aug. 14, 1836 Died Jan. 28, 1900." See also Stanley M. Cox, comp., *Joseph Cox, Ancestors and Descendants* (Kansas City, MO: 1955), p. 103. This Cox family genealogy notes that Nancy Cox was the daughter of Aaron Hardin Allard and Polly Weaver and was born in northern Missouri. The family moved to Hopkins County, Texas in the early 1840s.

[29] Mary Atwood, curator, "Portrait of Nancy Cox," *Aztec (NM) Museum Association Newsletter,* July 1, 1987; Cox, "Tales," the title page of "Tales" notes that Nancy arrived in Texas in the early 1840s. At that time Texas was its own republic.

[30] Lewis Publishing Company, comp., *History of Texas,* Central Texas ed. p. 353.

[31] *U.S. Census 1860*, Erath County, TX, r.1293, p. 122b, ABCLS; *U.S. Census 1870,* Erath County, TX, r. 1583, p. 460b, IA-ACPL.

[32] Cox, "Tales," p. 123. Isaac boldly claimed that his father was considered to be the best shot and best hunter in Texas.

[33] Floyd B Streeter, *Ben Thompson, Man With A Gun* (New York: Frederick Fell, Inc., 1957), p. 26. Streeter's account based in part on an article from the *Southern Intelligencer* (Austin, TX), October 13, 1858.

[34] J.W. Wilbarger, *Indian Depredations in Texas* (Austin: Hutchings Printing House, 1890) pp. 507 and 508, http://archive.org/details/indiandepredatio00wilb (accessed August 24, 2013). Wilbarger does not say the women were raped, but the chances they were not is less than slim. *U.S. Census 1860*, Palo Pinto County, TX, r. 1302, p. 343b, IA-ACPL; *U.S. Census 1860*, Erath County, TX, r. 1293, p. 114b, IA-ACPL; U.S. *Census 1870,* Erath County, TX, r. 1583, p. 454b, IA-ACPL. The census sheet dated July 4, 1860 shows the Lemley family living in Palo Pinto County in precinct no. 4. The Lemley family in the 1860 census included four

sisters; Lucinda - twenty, Hulda - fifteen, Lida - thirteen and Nancy - twelve. The 1860 Erath County census shows Lucinda Lemley's soon to be husband, twenty-eight-year-old William Wood, living with the family of William Roberts. That family includes eleven-year-old Lydia Roberts and twelve-year-old Robert H. Wood. It appears that after Lucinda's death, Mr. Wood married Lydia Roberts. In 1870 William Wood was still living in Erath County and had a twenty-one-year-old wife named Lydia. A member of their household was twenty-one-year-old Robert Hunter Wood.

[35] James Cox, *Historical and Biographical Record of the Cattle Industry and the Cattlemen of Texas and Adjacent Territory* (St. Louis: Woodward and Tiernan Printing Company, 1895), p. 306; *U.S. Census 1860*, Palo Pinto County, TX r. 1302, pp. 332a and 334a, IA-ACPL; *U.S. Census 1860*, Buchanan County, TX, r. 1302, p. 348b, IA-ACPL.

[36] J. Marvin Hunter, comp. and ed., *The Trail Drivers of Texas* (Nashville: Cokesbury Press, 1925), p. 903, http://archive.org/details/traildriversofte00hunt (accessed June 8, 2013). This book is a compilation of firsthand accounts written by the cowboys and cattlemen of the era.

[37] J. Evetts Haley, *Charles Goodnight - Cowman and Plainsman*, new ed. (Norman and London: University of Oklahoma Press, 1949, first copyright 1936 by J. Evetts Haley), pp. 20-21.

[38] *U.S. Census 1860*, Erath County, TX, r. 1293, p. 122b, ABCLS; *U.S. Census 1870*, Erath County, TX, r. 1583, p. 460b, ABCLS.

[39] Hunter, comp. and ed., *The Trail Drivers of Texas*, pp. 20, 414-415 and 646.

[40] Joseph Carroll McConnell, "Incident No. 371," *The West Texas Frontier*, vol. 2 (Palo Pinto, TX: Texas Legal Bank and Book Company, 1939), p. 111, http://www.forttours.com/pdf%20files/Mcconnell%20MERGED.pdf (accessed December 1, 2009)

[41] Lewis Publishing Company, comp., *History of Texas*, Central Texas ed., pp. 353-354, 784-785; *U.S. Census 1860*, Erath County, TX, r. 1293, pp. 121a and 122b, IA-ACPL, for Ed Cox, J.B. Allard, and H.W. Cox, respectively. Ed Cox and J.B. Allard are on the same census page.

[42] McConnell, "Incident No. 512," *The West Texas Frontier*, p. 333; *U.S. Census 1860*, Erath County, TX, r. 1293, p. 117a, IA-ACPL.

[43] *U.S. Census 1860*, Erath County, TX, r. 1293, p. 120a, IA-ACPL.

[44] Lewis Publishing Company, comp., *History of Texas*, Central Texas ed., pp. 354 and 785.

[45] Hunter, *The Trail Drivers of Texas*, pp. 864-865 and 903-904.

[46] Maurice W. Frink, Turrentine Jackson and Agnes Wright Spring, *When Grass Was King* (Boulder: University of Colorado Press, 1956), p. 356.

[47] Hunter, *The Trail Drivers of Texas*, pp. 908-913.

[48] *Smoky Hill and Republican Union* (Junction City, KS), July 9, 1864.

[49] "How the Cattle Rustlers Were Driven Out At Last," *St. Paul (MN) Globe*, July 3, 1904, p. 61. This article is about stock thieves "Flat Nose" George Curry and Tom O'Day who utilized running irons and other methods to steal cattle in the latter 1800s and early 1900s.

[50] Record of Marks and Brands, Erath County, Texas (Under law of 1874), p. 36, no. 9, TSU-DSL.

[51] Delphine Dawson Wilson, *John Barkley Dawson – Pioneer, Cattleman, Rancher* (n.p.: Delphine Dawson Wilson, 1997), p. 57.

[52] George B. Anderson, comp., *History of New Mexico - Its Resources and People*, vol. 2 (Los Angeles, Chicago, New York: Pacific States Publishing Co., 1907), p. 703.

[53] "Glimpses Into the Past," *Las Vegas (NM) Weekly Optic and Stock Grower*, May 11, 1901, p. 2, from the *Springer (NM) Sentinel*.

[54] "The Late I.W. Lacey," *Trinidad (CO) Daily News*, May 22, 1881.

[55] Erath County Commissioners Court Minutes, vol. A, 1867-1879, pp. 46 and 47, TSU-DSL.

[56] *U.S. Census 1870*, Erath County, TX, r. 1583, pp. 460b, 469a, 469b, IA-ACPL. Fifty-four-year-old Bosque Creek farmer Sterling Cruse also valued his personal estate at $13,000.

[57] City of Waco, *Fugitives From Justice - The Notebook of Texas Ranger Sergeant James B. Gillett*, with a foreword by Michael D. Morrison (Austin: State House Press, 1997), pp. 20 and 21.

[58] *Texas v. John Middleton*, p. 313, case no. 313, vol. B, 1871-1874, Erath County District Court Minutes, TSU-DSL.

[59] *Texas v. John Middleton*, p. 186, case no. 235, State Docket Book A, Palo Pinto County District Clerk Records.

[60] Wilson, *John Barkley Dawson*, pp. 9-10.

[61] "Damning Evidence," *Dolores News*, May 28, 1881, p. 1; Christopher A. Meek, *The Meek/Meeks Family of Tennessee and Arkansas*, revised draft, May 16, 2009, p. 34-35, http://meekgenealogy.com/Articles/The%20Meek%20Family%20TN_AR.pdf (accessed October 20, 2009). I.W. Lacy's father-in-law was J.C. Brumley. They lived in Johnson County, Texas in 1880. His wife was named Delila and she was born about 1821 in Tennessee. See *U.S. Census 1880*, Johnson County, TX, r. 1313, p. 216d, IA-ACPL; "Death of I.W. Lacy," *Cimarron (NM) News and Press*, May 19, 1881, portions as reported by the *Trinidad Times*.

[62] "The Late I.W. Lacey," *Trinidad Daily News*, May 22, 1881. This account notes that Lacy was born in Hazel Grove in Wood County, Kentucky. There is no Hazel Grove nor is there a Wood County in Kentucky. However there is a Hazel Green in present day Wolfe County and the right fork of Lacey Creek flows nearby. *U.S. Census 1860*, Erath County, TX r. 1293, pp. 123b and 141a, IA-ACPL; S.C. Lacy, "Dictation of the widow of I.W. Lacy," Western Americana Collection, The Bancroft Collection, Bancroft Library, University of California, Berkeley, CA, from microfilm archived at the Center for Southwest Research, University of New Mexico, Albuquerque, NM. Mrs. Lacy reports her father's name was Jefferson and that she was born in Arkansas in 1847.

[63] *U.S. Census 1870*, Erath County, TX, r. 1583, p. 458b, IA-ACPL.

[64] Record of Marks and Brands, Erath County, Texas (Under law of 1874), p. 12, no. 219, TSU-DSL.

[65] *Texas v. I.W. Lacy*, box 1, case nos. 40 and 42, Erath County District Clerk Records. The witness statement for the sticky case no. 40 is from these records. Case no. 43, which is the other charge of retailing liquors, is not found in these records. Records for all three cases can also be found on pp. 78, 97, 105, 107, 108, 139, 154 and 163, vol. A, 1860-1870, Erath County District Court Minutes; and on pp. 43, 84 and 176, vol. B, 1871-1874, Erath County District Court Minutes, TSU-DSL. Final judgment for case no. 40 is noted on page 84, vol. B. Also see case no. 130 on page 176, vol. B, which finalizes the forfeiture of the sureties.

[66] *U.S. Census 1870*, Johnson County, TX, r. 1593, p. 580b, IA-ACPL.

⁶⁷ *Texas v. I.W. Lacy*, box 1, case no. 132, Erath County District Clerk Records; *U.S. Census 1870*, Erath County, TX, r. 1583, pp. 455b and 457a, IA-ACPL; *U.S. Census 1880*, Erath County, TX, r. 1302, p. 23a, IA-ACPL; *U.S. Census 1850*, Drew County, AR, r. 21, p. 76b, IA-ACPL. The Drew County census identifies Rena as Serena Berry. By 1880 Rena was widowed and living with her father and mother in Stephenville.

⁶⁸ *Texas v. I.W. Lacy*, p. 14, case no. 132, vol. B, 1871-1874, Erath County District Court Minutes, TSU-DSL.

⁶⁹ W.H. Fooshee, "Early Days in Stephenville," *Stephenville (TX) Tribune*, October 19, 1923.

⁷⁰ *Texas v. Porter Stockton*, box 1, case no. 142, Erath County District Clerk Records; *U.S. Census 1900*, Taylor County, TX, r. 1672, p. 21b, IA-ACPL.

⁷¹ *Texas v. Porter Stockton*, box 1, case no. 142, Erath County District Clerk Records.

⁷² Erath County Genealogical Society, *Erath County, Texas Marriage Records 1869-1891*, vol. 1 (Stephenville, TX: Erath County Genealogical Society, 1980), book A, p. 2, ABCLS. As for onetime slave Taylor Avant, he eventually moved to Abilene, where he lived with his wife and their children while working as a cook. See *U.S. Census 1900*, Taylor County, TX, r. 1672, p. 21b, IA-ACPL. Stockton was never one to de-escalate an unpleasant situation and if later behavior is any indication, it appears that Avant was also a quarrelsome man. On December 20, 1883, the *Fort Worth (TX) Daily Gazette* reported that correspondence from Eastland County advised that "A few nights ago two negroes got into a dispute over a dusky maiden" in Cisco, Texas. The row ended when Avant shot and wounded Sandy Williams.

⁷³ Like all genealogy research, the ancestry track of the Stockton brothers and their wives is at times elusive. Their marriage records can be found in the Erath County Marriage Records, Vol. A, 1869-1877, TSU-DSL, pp. 29 and 95. Porter Stockton and Emily Jane's marriage record is dated November 8, 1870. Anyone authorized to perform marriage rites was "hereby authorized to celebrate the rites of matrimony" for the couple. Other records for the Stockton brothers, their wives and families can be found in the *U.S. Census 1880*, La Plata County, CO, r. 91, p. 572c, ABCLS; *U.S. Census 1880*, Rio Arriba County, NM, r. 803, p. 225c, Collection I 002, FLC-CSWS. (The collection number is not noted in subsequent notes.) The remarriage of Ike's widow is shown in the La Plata County, CO, Marriages, 1876-1889, La Plata County Government Records, Coll. M 028, series 3.2, FLC-CSWS. Port and Ike's father, Samuel Stockton, married Jane Hickey on August 16, 1843 in Itawamba County, Mississippi. (See Burton-Cruber, comp., *The Marriage Records of Itawamba County*, p. 78.) Other useful records include: *U.S. Census 1850*, Titus County, TX, r. 915, p. 122a, ABCLS; *U.S. Census 1860*, Erath County, TX, r. 1293, p. 124b, ABCLS. The 1850 census for Titus County, Texas shows that William Cowan, age thirty-eight, was married to Sally Cowan, age thirty-three. They had the following children; James - sixteen, Polly - fourteen, John - twelve, Delila - ten, West - eight, Isaac - four and Elizabeth - two. The 1860 census for Erath County shows the following family; Isaac Robinson, age fifty-three, a stock farmer, who is married to Sarah, age forty-four. Living with Isaac and Sarah were; James - twenty-five, Polly - twenty-four, John - twenty-two, Delila apparently married and moved away, Wml? - fourteen (probably West Cowan with an error on his name

and age), Elizabeth - twelve, Emily J. - ten (evidently born right after the 1850 census), and Amanda Robinson - two. Living next door to the Robinson/Cowans was West W. Hickey - thirty-seven, Mary M. Hickey - twenty-seven, Sarah Bibb - sixty, James G. Moving? - four and Martha E. - two. Christopher A. Meek, *The Meek/Meeks Family of Tennessee and Arkansas,* revised draft, May 16, 2009, p. 34-35. Many published accounts about Port Stockton say that his wife's father was a minister. That does not appear to be the case. In the 1850 census, William Cowan said he was a farmer and in the 1860 census and Isaac Robinson said he was a stock farmer.

[74] *Texas v. Porter Stockton,* box 1, case no. 142, Erath County District Clerk Records.

[75] Ibid. Also see prior footnote which provides details of the Stockton family genealogy. See also, *U.S. Census 1870,* Erath County, TX r. 1583, pp. 455b and 466a, IA-ACPL. The portion of the Erath County census for Bosque Creek shows the following families living in close proximity; William C. Bibb and family, John R. O'Neal and family and Mrs. Sarah Bibb, who was residing with twelve-year-old John Riley Bibb. They lived next door to George and Marinda Morrison. The West Hickey family also lived on Bosque Creek. See also the *U.S. Census 1850,* Titus County, TX, r. 915, p. 123b, ABCLS. In 1850 John Bibb and his wife, the former Sarah Meek Hickey (age fifty-one) lived in Titus County with their eighteen-year-old son William and other children.

[76] *Texas v. Porter Stockton,* box 1, case no. 155, Erath County District Clerk Records.

[77] *Texas v. Porter Stockton,* box 1, case no. 179, Erath County District Clerk Records.

[78] Andy Adams, *The Log of a Cowboy: A Narrative of the Old Trail Days* (Boston and New York: Houghton Mifflin Company, 1903), p. 100.

[79] "State News," *Brenham (TX) Weekly Banner,* June 4, 1880, p. 2.

[80] City of Waco, *Fugitives From Justice,* p. 21.

[81] *Texas v. George W. Morrison,* box 1, case no. 178, Erath County District Clerk Records; *U.S. Census 1870,* Erath County, TX, r. 1583, pp. 455b, 457b and 458a, IA-ACPL; Erath County Marriage Records, Vol. A, 1869-1877, TSU-DSL, p. 33.

[82] *Texas v. Geo. Morrison,* box 2, case no. 331, Erath County District Clerk Records; *U.S. Census 1870,* Erath County, TX, r. 1583, p. 476b, IA-ACPL.

[83] City of Waco, *Fugitives From Justice,* p. 22.

[84] Lewis Publishing Company, comp., *History of Texas,* Central Texas ed., pp. 800-801.

[85] *Texas v. William Painter,* box 1, case no. 215 – the Parr case, case no. 217 – the "Hyat" case, case no. 220 – the Waller case and case no. 228 – the Blankenship case, Erath County District Clerk Records; Record of Marks and Brands, Erath County, Texas (Under law of 1874), p. 10, nos. 11 and 57, TSU-DSL; *U.S. Census 1860,* Erath County, TX r. 1293, p. 117a, IA-ACPL; *U.S. Census 1870,* Erath County, TX, r. 1583, p. 457a IA-ACPL.

[86] *U.S. Census 1860,* Erath County, TX. r. 1293, p. 118a, IA-ACPL; Randy Farrar, e-mail message to author, August 3, 2010. Farrar's research notes that James Galbreath's first wife is not known, his second wife was Elvira Garrison. She was the mother of Marion Galbreath. His third wife was Elizabeth Ann Hickey. Farrar noted that more research was needed to firm up this data.

[87] Christopher A. Meek, *The Meek/Meeks Family of Tennessee and Arkansas*, revised draft, May 16, 2009, p. 34-35. The exceptionally close relationship between Ike Stockton and Marion Galbreath, while not definitive proof, certainly lends credence to the notion that Elizabeth Ann was an aunt to the Stockton boys and to the women who became their wives.

[88] *Texas v. Samuel Stockton,* box 1, case no. 227, Erath County District Clerk Records; *Texas v. Samuel Stockton,* p. 399, case no. 227, vol. B, 1871-1874, Erath County District Court Minutes, TSU-DSL.

[89] *Texas v. Porter Stockton,* p. 133, case no. 179, vol. C, 1874-1884, Erath County District Court Minutes, TSU-DSL.

[90] W.H. Fooshee, "Early Days in Stephenville," *Stephenville (TX) Tribune,* June 15, 1923.

[91] W.H. Fooshee, "Early Days in Stephenville," *Stephenville (TX) Tribune,* June 29, 1923.

[92] *Texas v. I.W. Lacy,* p. 60, case no. 212, vol. B, 1871-1874, Erath County District Court Minutes, TSU-DSL.

[93] *Texas v. I.W. Lacy,* p. 107, case no. 212, vol. B, 1871-1874, Erath County District Court Minutes, TSU-DSL; *U.S. Census 1870,* Erath County, TX, r. 1583, p. 457b, IA-ACPL. Mrs. Salyer's name was P.J. Lacy Salyer and, like I.W. Lacy, she was born in Kentucky.

[94] W.H. Fooshee, "Early Days in Stephenville," *Stephenville (TX) Tribune,* June 29, 1923.

[95] L.F. Roberts, "L.F. Roberts Came Here From Virginia in 1859," *Stephenville (TX) Empire Tribune,* 66th Anniversary Edition, January 1936; *U.S. Census 1870,* Erath County, TX, r. 1583, p. 466a, IA-ACPL.

[96] F. Stanley, *Ike Stockton* (Denver: World Press, Inc., 1959), p. 82.

[97] Maxine Benson, "Port Stockton," *Colorado Magazine,* vol. 43, no. 1 (Winter, 1966): p. 23.

[98] *U.S. Census 1880,* La Plata County, CO, r. 91, p. 572c, ABCLS.

CHAPTER TWO – CHAOS IN COLFAX COUNTY

[1] "The Texas Cowboy and the Mexican Greaser," *Songs of the Cattle Trail and Cow Camp,* comp. by John A. Lomax (New York: The MacMillan Company, 1920), p. 11.

[2] "Sale of the 'Maxwell Grant,' " *Colorado Weekly Chieftain* (Pueblo), July 28, 1870, p. 2.

[3] "Latest News," *Colorado Weekly Chieftain,* March 2, 1871, p. 2.

[4] Victor Westphall, *Thomas Benton Catron and His Era* (Tucson: The University of Arizona Press, 1973), pp. 101-102.

[5] *Santa Fe Daily New Mexican,* April 16, 1873, from the *Cimarron (NM) News.*

[6] *U.S. Census 1870,* Colfax County, NM, r. 893, p. 142a, IA-ACPL; *U.S. Census 1880,* Colfax County, NM, r. 0802, p. 217d, IA-ACPL. Mathias B. Stockton is shown living in Colfax County in 1880 with his wife and four children, including a son born in New Mexico in 1873.

[7] Delphine Dawson Wilson, *John Barkley Dawson – Pioneer, Cattleman, Rancher* (n.p.: Delphine Dawson Wilson, 1997), p. 25.

[8] *U.S. Census 1860,* Buchanan County, TX, r. 1302, p. 349a, IA-ACPL.

⁹ George B. Anderson, comp., *History of New Mexico - Its Resources and People,* vol. 2 (Los Angeles, Chicago, New York: Pacific States Publishing Co., 1907), p. 707.

¹⁰ "New Mexico," *Colorado Weekly Chieftain* (Pueblo), June 20, 1872, p. 1. This article identifies Wilburn as being a partner with Stockton. *U.S. Census 1870,* Colfax County, NM, r. 893, p. 142a, IA-ACPL. In this census Stockton and Frank Wilburn are shown as the only two residents living in their household. "New Mexico," *Colorado Weekly Chieftain,* June 20, 1872, p. 1. This article notes that the Canadian River was commonly known as the Red River. It should not be confused with the Red River which flows westward into the Rio Grande above Taos. Upon leaving the Sangre de Cristos, the Canadian (Red) River flows eastward across the plains and into the Texas Panhandle and onto Oklahoma. Eventually it empties into the Arkansas River.

¹¹ F. Stanley, *The Grant That Maxwell Bought* (Denver: World Press, 1952), pp. 204.

¹² "New Mexico," *Colorado Daily Chieftain* (Pueblo), March 15, 1873, p. 2.

¹³ T.M. Pearce, ed., *New Mexico Place Names - A Geographical Dictionary* (Albuquerque: University of New Mexico Press, 1965), p. 36.

¹⁴ *Santa Fe Daily New Mexican,* July 27, 1872, from the *Cimarron News.* For more information on Finis Ernest, see Harry E. Kelsey, Jr., "Finis P. Ernest," *The Colorado Magazine,* vol. 31, no.4 (October, 1954): pp. 290-296. Fine Ernest served under General Sterling Price and moved to Palo Pinto County, Texas in 1867. He married seventeen-year-old Sarah Elizabeth Stockton in New Mexico in 1869. After her death Ernest married John Hittson's daughter. Kelsey does not mention the Van Valser/Cunningham incident. *U.S. Census 1860,* Buchanan County, TX, r. 1302, p. 349, IA-ACPL. Tom Stockton's parents and siblings are enumerated on this page.

¹⁵ *U.S. Census 1870,* Colfax County, NM, r. 893, p. 139b and 140a, IA-ACPL. Van Valser is identified as Leonard Vanbelzer.

¹⁶ *New Mexico v. Thomas Stockton et al,* case nos. 194 and 195, September 1872, Colfax County District Court Records, NMSRCA.

¹⁷ Colfax County District Court Records, Civil and Criminal Record Book no. 2, 1871-1874, pp. 171, 262, 273-274, NMSRCA.

¹⁸ *Colorado Transcript* (Golden), August 7, 1872, p. 2; Stanley, *The Grant That Maxwell Bought,* pp. 67-68. Stanley credits the killing of Morris to Chunk Colbert. Old newspaper accounts often did not use full names, resulting in the confusion between the activities of "Chuck" Arrington and "Chunk" Colbert. They were different people. Chunk was killed in January 1874. Milton Arrington was still alive and five months later on June 12, 1874 on page 3 of the *Las Animas Leader* (West Las Animas, CO) it was reported that Milton J. "Chuck" Irington [sic] was arrested on suspicion of stealing a horse belonging to Tom Stockton.

¹⁹ *New Mexico v. Charles Morris, Fred J. Ames and Charles Farrand,* case no. 153, April 1872 and March 1873, Colfax County District Court Records, NMSRCA.

²⁰ *Santa Fe Daily New Mexican,* November 15, 1871.

²¹ "The Pistol at Cimarron," *Rocky Mountain News* (Denver), July 24, 1872, p. 4.

²² *Colorado Daily Chieftain,* August 2, 1872, p. 2, from the *Cimarron (NM) News and Press.*

²³ Colfax County District Court Records, Civil and Criminal Record Book no. 2, 1871-1874, case no. 460, pp. 228-229 and 243, NMSRCA, records for *New Mexico v. Milton J. Arrington.* The victim is not named in these records, but Charles Morris

is the most likely candidate. The actual case file no. 460 in the Colfax County District Court Records, box 2, case nos. 3-700, 1869-1883 does not match this case. Case no. 460 in those records is *New Mexico v. Robert Stepp and Albert Morgan* for permitting gaming.

[24] "About Texas," *Bolivar (TN) Bulletin*, January 5, 1872, p. 1.

[25] "Cattle Thieving," *Rocky Mountain News* (Denver, CO), April 29, 1873, p. 4.

[26] Charles L. Kenner, "The Great New Mexico Cattle Raid – 1872," *New Mexico Historical Review* vol. 37, no. 4 (October 1962): p. 256. http://archive.org/details/newmexicohistori37univrich (accessed June 5, 2013).

[27] Letter from James Patterson, "The Loma Parda Tragedy," *Santa Fe Daily New Mexican*, September 27, 1872; *Santa Fe Daily New Mexican*, August 2, 1872, p. 1. This article noted, "James Patterson, Esq., who has been engaged for some time in hunting up Texas cattle throughout our Territory, left yesterday for the Pecos." Apparently, he had the ear of the *New Mexican's* editors. A week later, on April 9th, the newspaper carried an editorial favorable to Hittson's cattle gathering operation.

[28] Hulda's father was Wash Cox's brother Solomon B. Cox. Lady E. Dalton, December 11, 2012, email to author; Elizabeth Berry Buffa, comp., "Cox Family Outline," Pacific Palisades, CA, 1977, p. 16, http://archive.org/stream/coxfamilyoutline00buff#page/n17/mode/2up (accessed February 25, 2013); *U.S. Census 1850*, Harrison County, MO, r. 400, p. 435a, IA-ACPL. Hulda was fourteen at the time of her marriage to Mart Childers. *U.S. Census 1860*, Lampasas County, TX, r. 1299, p. 173a, IA-ACPL. The family name is shown as Childers and in 1860 Hulda and Mart had a three-year-old child named Lemuel.

[29] Joseph G. McCoy, *Historic Sketches of the Cattle Trade of the West and Southwest* (Arthur H. Clark Company, 1966; Bison Book ed. Lincoln and London: University of Nebraska Press, 1985), p. 132.

[30] *Bolivar (TN) Bulletin*, August 31, 1871, p. 1.

[31] "Cattle Thieving," *Rocky Mountain News*, April 29, 1872, p. 4; *Santa Fe Daily New Mexican*, August 10, 1872; Letter from James Patterson, "The Loma Parda Tragedy," *Santa Fe Daily New Mexican*, September 27, 1872; "Brutal Murder," *Colorado Daily Chieftain*, September 22, 1872, p. 1.

[32] "The Escape of M. Childers," *Santa Fe Daily New Mexican*, January 6, 1873.

[33] "The Late John Hittson, Cattle King," *Dodge City (KS) Times*, January 29, 1881, p. 2. Hittson was thrown from a carriage and killed. Mart Childers later moved to Grant County in southwest New Mexico. On October 1, 1897 the *Silver City (NM) Enterprise* under the headline "The Killing of Mart Childers" reported that Childers was killed by a sheriff's posse who was after him for the murder of Ed Moss. Members of the posse included the brother and uncle of Ed Moss. "Local and Personal," *Western Liberal* (Lordsburg, NM), January 29, 1915, p. 4. Tom Stockton also moved to southwest New Mexico, where he ran cattle in the Gila River country.

[34] Charles L. Kenner, "The Great New Mexico Cattle Raid – 1872," *New Mexico Historical Review* vol. 37, no. 4 (October 1962): p. 258-259.

[35] S.A. Bull to J. Evetts Haley, February 27, 1927, J. Evetts Haley Collection, Nita Stewart Haley Memorial Library and J. Evetts Haley History Center, Midland, TX (hereafter abbreviated JEHC-HMLHC), p. 2.

[36] "Obituary," *Raton (NM) Daily Range*, April 8, 1910.

37 Hazel Noble, "Hazel Noble Remembers," *Aztec (NM) Museum Association Newsletter,* June 1, 1983. When Cox made the final move to Colfax County is not certain. "Obituary," *Raton (NM) Daily Range,* April 8, 1910. This is Marion Littrell's obituary. It notes that he first drove cattle into Colfax County in the fall of 1872 and that Cox settled there at that time.

38 "He Was Feared," *Las Vegas (NM) Weekly Optic and Stock Grower,* July 13, 1901, p. 2, from the *Springer (NM) Sentinel.*

39 Howard Bryan, *Robbers, Rogues and Ruffians* (Santa Fe: Clear Light Publishers, 1991), pp. 25-26.

40 Barbara Marriott, *Outlaw Tales of New Mexico* (Guilford, CT: TwoDot/Globe Pequot Press, 2007), p. 5.

41 "He Was Feared," *Las Vegas (NM) Weekly Optic and Stock Grower,* July 13, 1901, p. 2, from the *Springer (NM) Sentinel.*

42 Ruth W. Armstrong, *The Chases of Cimarron* (Albuquerque: New Mexico Stockman, 1981), pp. 21 and 26.

43 "He Was Feared," *Las Vegas (NM) Weekly Optic and Stock Grower,* July 13, 1901, p. 2, from the *Springer (NM) Sentinel.*

44 S.C. Lacy, "Dictation of the widow of I.W. Lacy," Western Americana Collection, The Bancroft Collection, Bancroft Library, University of California, Berkeley, CA, from microfilm archived at the Center for Southwest Research, University of New Mexico, Albuquerque, NM.

45 Brand Record Book B, 1870-1890, Colfax County. The pages are not numbered. Colfax County Clerk Records, NMSRCA.

46 Chuck Parsons, *Clay Allison – Portrait of a Shootist* (Seagraves, TX: Pioneer Book Publishers, 1983), p. 11.

47 Dick Dalrymple, "Henry Goodman: Moab's Forgotten Icon," *Canyon Legacy,* Journal of the Dan O'Laurie Canyon Country Museum, vol. 45 (Summer 2002): p. 4.

48 Norman Cleaveland and George Fitzpatrick, *The Morleys-Young Upsarts on the Southwest Frontier* (Albuquerque: Calvin Horn Publisher, Inc., 1971), p. 121.

49 *U.S. Census 1860,* Erath County, TX, r. 1293, p. 130a, ABCLS.

50 J.N. Doyle, "David Crockett," *Weekly Kansas Chief* (Troy), March 4, 1880, p. 1.

51 "Interesting Career of Indian Scout, Pioneer Cattleman, Comes to Close," *Moab (UT) Times-Independent,* May 31, 1934; "$100 REWARD," *Durango Weekly Record,* May 7, 14 and 21, 1881. In this reward notice Henry Goodman and G.W. Thompson (the cattleman's namesake and nephew) are shown as the only ones authorized to sell LC cattle. It misidentifies Henry C. Goodman as C.H. Goodman. "Killed By The Indians," *Edgefield (SC) Advertiser,* June 19, 1873, p. 3.

52 "Obituary," *Raton (NM) Daily Range,* April 8, 1910.

53 Delbert Littrell Hughes and Lenore Harris Hughes, *Give Me Room!* (El Paso: The Hughes Publishing Co., 1971), p. 23.

54 Isaac Hiram Cox, "Tales," transcribed by Joeen Johnson Sutton, 1920s, p. 56, courtesy of Les Sutton.

55 "Obituary," *Raton (NM) Daily Range,* April 8, 1910.

56 *U.S. Census 1860,* Buchanan County, TX, r. 1302, p. 348b, IA-ACPL. "Zenes" Curtis lived in Buchanan County with his father Joel W. and mother Henrietta Curtis. Living next door to them was Henrietta's brother, John B. Dawson.

57 Hughes, *Give Me Room!* p. 61.

[58] "Obituary," *Raton Daily Range*, April 8, 1910. When Alf Graves married Wash Cox's daughter, Nancy Isabelle Cox, the Colfax County Clerk recorded that the wedding took place at the home of the bride's father on the Red River.

[59] "State Items," *La Plata Miner* (Silverton, CO), June 5, 1880. Lacy lived on the Vermejo.

[60] Margaret Ward, *Cousins by the Dozens* (n.p.: 1966), p. 5, University of New Mexico, University Libraries, Center for Southwest Research, Call no. F391 C8 W37x.

[61] Erath County Marriage Records, Vol. A, 1869-1877, TSU-DSL, p. 95, Ike and Amanda Ellen Robinson's county marriage record is dated June 11, 1873. They were probably married a few days after that.

[62] *Texas v. Isaac Stockton*, pp. 352, 353 and 359, case nos. 299 and 300, vol. B, 1871-1874, Erath County District Court Minutes, TSU-DSL.

[63] "New Mexico Items," *Las Animas Leader*, October 4, 1873, p. 3, from the *Cimarron News; U.S. Census 1880*, Colfax County, NM, reel 0802, p. 224a, IA-ACPL.

[64] Glenn D. Bradley, *Winning the Southwest – A Story of Conquest* (Chicago: A.C. McClurg and Co., 1912), pp. 73-77, 86-87, 97-98, http://archive.org/details/winningsouthwes02bradgoog (accessed September 8, 2013).

[65] "Trinidad," *Colorado Daily Chieftain*, December 30, 1873, p. 1.

[66] "Trinidad," *Colorado Daily Chieftain*, December 30, 1873, p. 1; "Territorial Items," *Daily Colorado Miner* (Georgetown), January 8, 1874, p. 3, from the *Trinidad (CO) Enterprise*. The *Chieftain* identifies the participants as Chunk, Doss and George Waller and says the event took place at the San Francisco Ranch. The *Enterprise* says the participants were John Chunk, Race Dorse and Walton Waller. It also mentions "Dutch Bill" and Mr. Folis. See also the *Colorado Weekly Chieftain*, January 13, 1870, p. 3 which carries an article about Sam Doss and horse races at Trinidad. The *Colorado Weekly Chieftain*, March 18, 1875, p. 3, notes that George W. Thompson and Sam Doss wish to sell five hundred cattle.

[67] "Territorial Items," *Daily Colorado Miner*, January 8, 1874, p. 3, from the *Trinidad Enterprise*.

[68] "Trinidad," *Colorado Daily Chieftain*, December 30, 1873, p. 1.

[69] "Territorial Items," *Daily Colorado Miner*, January 8, 1874, p. 3, from the *Trinidad Enterprise*.

[70] North Dakota Cowboy Hall of Fame, "Ranching – James William 'Bill' Follis," n.d. http://www.ndcowboy.com/Hall_of_Fame/Ranching/follis_james.asp (accessed January 3, 2011).

[71] *U.S. Census 1870*, Eastland County, TX, r. 1583, p. 300a, IA-ACPL.

[72] *New Mexico v. Noah Camblin and others*, case no. 277, March, 1874, April 2, 1877, Colfax County District Court Records, NMSRCA; Requisition from New Mexico to Colorado, for Porter Stockton and others, March 16, 1875, roll 1, microcopy 364, Coll. I 023, Interior Department, Territorial Papers, New Mexico, 1851-1914, RG 48, NARA, FLC-CSWS. Stockton and others shot the wrong man in their haste to get Chunk Colbert.

[73] George B. Anderson., comp., *History of New Mexico - Its Resources and People*, vol. 1 (Los Angeles, Chicago and New York: Pacific States Publishing Co., 1907), pp. 106-107.

[74] "Shooting of Chunk," *Trinidad (CO) Enterprise*, January 9, 1874, p. 3.

[75] Anderson., comp., *History of New Mexico - Its Resources and People*, vol. 1, p. 107.

76 Adams Peabody, "Kansas," *State Journal* (Jefferson City, MO), June 26, 1874, p. 4. The 1870 U.S. census for Trinidad shows a largely Hispanic population with most of the parents of families being born in New Mexico.

77 "Death of Patrick McBride," *Colorado Weekly Chieftain,* July 26, 1877, p. 2, from the *Denver Democrat.*

78 Requisition from New Mexico to Colorado, for Porter Stockton and others, March 16, 1875, roll 1, microcopy 364, Coll. I 023, Interior Department, Territorial Papers, New Mexico, 1851-1914, RG 48, NARA, FLC-CSWS; "The [illegible] Judge Mezick," *Trinidad Enterprise,* April 16, 1874, p. 2 and in the same issue on page 3 see a dispatch from the *Cimarron News* headlined "Outrage." Also see "Assault? On Judge Mezick," *Trinidad Enterprise,* April 29, 1874, p. 2. The *Enterprise* identifies "Tex" as both Bakewell and Blackwell and Camblin as Nick and as Noah. Las Animas County Commissioner's Record Book no. 2, January 1, 1872 to December 1874, pp. 251-253. On page 257 from January 10, 1874, S.D. Hays is identified as a deputy sheriff. John Selles is identified as a deputy sheriff on page 284 which is dated February 5, 1874 and as a constable on page 238, which is dated December 2, 1873. Those records identify him as John Sellers, but numerous newspaper and other accounts use the name Selles. Charleton and Selles are shown in the Las Animas County records as being paid for their part in the pursuit of Chunk Colbert, but neither man was indicted for the murder which occurred as a result of that pursuit.

79 "Trinidad," *Colorado Weekly Chieftain,* January 1, 1874, p. 3. Later that evening the men arrived at the Red River Station, so late in the night that everyone was asleep.

80 Howard L. Conard, *"Uncle Dick" Wootton,* Classics of the Old West ed. (Chicago: W.E. Dibble and Co., 1890; reprint, n.p.: Time-Life Books, Inc., 1980), pp. 437–438.

81 "Trinidad," *Colorado Weekly Chieftain,* January 1, 1874, p. 3. The article does not identify the Clifton House by name, but it was the only inn and eating establishment at the Red River.

82 *New Mexico v. Noah Camblin and others,* case no. 277, March, 1874, April 2, 1877, Colfax County District Court Records, NMSRCA.

83 "Trinidad," *Colorado Weekly Chieftain,* January 1, 1874, p. 3.

84 *New Mexico v. Noah Camblin and others,* case no. 277, March, 1874, April 2, 1877, Colfax County District Court Records, NMSRCA.

85 "Trinidad," *Colorado Weekly Chieftain,* January 1, 1874, p. 3.

86 *New Mexico v. Noah Camblin and others,* case no. 277, March, 1874, April 2, 1877, Colfax County District Court Records, NMSRCA. The indictment dates the murder as occurring on December 28, 1873. Given the distances traveled by Porter Stockton and then by the posse, it seems more likely that the shooting took place in the early morning darkness on December 29th. Requisition from New Mexico to Colorado, for Porter Stockton and others, March 16, 1875, roll 1, microcopy 364, Coll. I 023, Interior Department, Territorial Papers, New Mexico, 1851-1914, RG 48, NARA, FLC-CSWS.

87 Las Animas County Commissioner's Record Book no. 2, January 1, 1872 to December 1874, pp. 251-253. A notation on p. 253 clearly identifies Hays as S.D. Hays and notes that he was paid $16.80 for his part in the pursuit of Chunk Colbert.

[88] *New Mexico v. Noah Camblin and others,* case no. 277, March, 1874, April 2, 1877, Colfax County District Court Records, NMSRCA.

[89] "Assault on Judge Mezick," *Trinidad Enterprise,* April 29, 1874, p. 2.

[90] *New Mexico v. Patrick McBride,* case no. 132, April 7, 1871, Colfax County District Court Records, NMSRCA. Witnesses in the case included Samuel Cameron, Joseph Kinney, W.D. Dawson and M. Bloomfield.

[91] Morris F. Taylor, *Trinidad, Colorado Territory* (Pueblo: Trinidad State Junior College, 1966), pp. 145-146; See also "Fatal Duel," *Colorado Daily Chieftain,* June 9, 1876, p. 4. On June 8, 1876, Jessup was shot and killed by O. Davis at River Bend, Colorado. Davis was the son of a wealthy stockman. River Bend was located out on the plains about sixty miles east of Denver on the Kansas Pacific (KP) Railway line.

[92] "Sentence Commuted," *Leadville (CO) Daily and Evening Chronicle,* October 14, 1890, p. 4. This article notes that Bakewell's sentence was commuted to twenty years and that with good behavior he was scheduled to be released on December 7, 1891, which would be a little over eleven years after he was sentenced.

[93] *Santa Fe Daily New Mexican,* December 31, 1873; "New Mexico," *Colorado Daily Chieftain,* December 31, 1873, p. 1. This dispatch says Carney was murdered on his ranch on the Vermejo about noon on Saturday.

[94] "Territorial Items," *Daily Colorado Miner,* January 3, 1874, p. 3.

[95] "A Murderer Lynched in Colorado," *New York Sun,* December 31, 1873, p. 1.

[96] "New Mexico," *Colorado Daily Chieftain,* December 31, 1873, p. 1.

[97] "Here's Interesting, Authentic History of a N.M. Pioneer's Life," *Raton Daily Range,* March 27, 1930, from the *Trinidad Chronicle-News; U.S. Census 1870,* Colfax County, NM r. 893, p. 143a, IA-ACPL.

[98] *Santa Fe Daily New Mexican,* December 31, 1873.

[99] "Here's Interesting, Authentic History of a N.M. Pioneer's Life," *Raton Daily Range,* March 27, 1930, from the *Trinidad Chronicle-News.*

[100] "Hung to a Telegraph Pole," *Denver (CO) Daily Times,* December 30, 1873, p. 4.

[101] *Santa Fe Daily New Mexican,* January 7, 1874, from the *Cimarron News.*

[102] "Hung to a Telegraph Pole," *Denver Daily Times,* December 30, 1873, p. 4.

[103] *Dallas (TX) Daily Herald,* February 17, 1874, p. 1.

[104] "Territorial Items," *Daily Colorado Miner,* January 15, 1874, p. 3, from the *Cimarron News.*

[105] "Shooting of Chunk," *Trinidad Enterprise,* January 9, 1874, p. 3.

[106] "A Desperado Shot," *Colorado Daily Chieftain,* January 18, 1874, p. 4.

[107] George E. Crocker, "Memories of Cimarron, New Mexico, 1871-1872," n.d., p. 37, http://archive.org/details/memoriesofcimarr00croc (accessed May 12, 2012).

[108] "West and South," *Jasper (IN) Weekly Courier,* February 4, 1876, p. 6.

[109] Parsons, *Clay Allison,* p. 24.

[110] J. Marvin Hunter, comp. and ed., *The Trail Drivers of Texas* (Nashville: Cokesbury Press, 1925), pp. 22-23, 122-123, 405 and 924, http://archive.org/details/ traildriversofte00hunt (accessed June 9, 2013).

[111] "The Maxwell Land Grant," *Denver Mirror,* March 29, 1874, p. 1.

[112] *Cimarron (NM) News,* February 7, 1874.

[113] Cleaveland, *The Morleys,* p. 112.

[114] George Coe to J. Evetts Haley, August 12, 1927, pp. 7-8, and Frank Coe to J. Evetts Haley, August 14, 1927, p. 4, JEHC-HMLHC. George Coe arrived in Colfax County in August 1874 with a herd of cattle for Lew Coe. Frank Coe and Ab Saunders soon left Colfax County and moved to Lincoln County.

[115] George Coe to J. Evetts Haley, August 18, 1927, p. 8, JEHC-HMLHC. In this letter George Coe says Lew Coe purchased the Sugarite property from "Gaddus" and Fount Miller for about eleven hundred dollars.

[116] *U.S. Census 1880,* Hemphill County, TX r. 1310, p. 101a, IA-ACPL. In 1880 the still single Clay Allison was living in the northeast corner of the Texas Panhandle next to his sister and brother-in-law L.G. Coleman. Coleman's wife is listed with the name SAM and they had a five-year-old son enumerated only by the initials R.L who was born in New Mexico. The *Las Vegas (NM) Daily Optic* of March 11, 1880 reported a false rumor that Clay Allison had killed his brother-in-law, Coleman.

[117] "Stock Association," and "County Fair," *Cimarron (NM) News,* September 5, 1874, New Mexico Highlands University, Thomas C. Donnelly Library, Las Vegas, NM.

[118] *New Mexico v. James Kelly,* case no. 284, August, 1875 and case no. 285 (also numbered as no. 477), September 3, 1875, Colfax County District Court Records, NMSRCA.

[119] S.A. Bull to J. Evetts Haley, February 27, 1927, JEHC-HMLHC, p. 2. Bull says that the Cox herd also went through Winfield and Wichita, Kansas via the Shawnee Trail, a detour of some two hundred miles compared to the more direct south to north route from Stephenville to Dodge City. Bull dates the drive as 1874. *U.S. Census 1870,* Erath County, TX r. 1583, p. 470a, IA-ACPL.

[120] Hughes, *Give Me Room!* pp. 24-28 and 61.

[121] *Cimarron News,* August 29 and September 26, 1874.

[122] C.O. Ziegenfuss, "Ike Stockton," *Denver Republican,* August 12, 1881.

[123] "Story of Lee of Tecumseh," *Wichita (KS) Daily Eagle,* March 6, 1898; *Texas v. M.H. Gilbreath [sic],* p. 12, case no. 101, State Docket, District Court, Bosque County District Clerk Records. This case from the June 1874 term of court is for "An assault with intent to commit a rape." See also "Ike Stockton Killed," *Dolores News,* October 1, 1881, p. 1, from the *Durango Southwest.*

[124] Clifford R. Caldwell and Ron DeLord, *Texas Lawmen, 1835-1899: The Good and the Bad* (Charleston, SC: The History Press, 2011), pp. pp. 28-29.

[125] "Story of Lee of Tecumseh," *Wichita (KS) Daily Eagle,* March 6, 1898, this is Lee's version of events; "After Twenty Years," *Guthrie (OK) Daily Leader,* November 23, 1897.

[126] Cox, "Tales," p. 85.

[127] "The Raid," *Las Animas Leader,* July 17, 1874, p. 1, from the *Cimarron (NM) News,* July 11, 1874.

[128] Ibid. *U.S. Census 1880,* Colfax County, NM, r. 893, pp. 141a and 143a, IA-ACPL. A.J. (Tony) Meloche was a horse and cattle raiser.

[129] "The Raid," *Las Animas Leader,* July 17, 1874, p. 1, from the *Cimarron (NM) News,* July 11, 1874.

[130] "Eye Witness," "Disturbance At Cimarron," *Colorado Weekly Chieftain,* January 28, 1875, p. 1.

[131] Crocker, "Memories of Cimarron, New Mexico, 1871-1872," p. 14.

[132] "The Cimarron Tragedy," *Las Animas Leader,* February 5, 1875, p. 4, from the *Cimarron News and Press.*

[133] "Eye Witness," "Disturbance At Cimarron," *Colorado Weekly Chieftain,* January 28, 1875, p. 1.

[134] "The Cimarron Tragedy," *Las Animas Leader,* February 5, 1875, p. 4, from the *Cimarron News and Press.*

[135] "Bayfield Tragedy," *Durango (CO) Democrat,* April 20, 1899, p. 4.

[136] "Condensations Territorial," *Santa Fe Daily New Mexican,* February 9, 1875.

[137] *New Mexico v. James Spiller,* case no. 345, August 1875, February, 1876 and March 1877, Colfax County District Court Records, NMSRCA.

[138] *New Mexico v. John Alexander,* case no. 348, August and September, 1875, Colfax County District Court Records, NMSRCA.

[139] *Texas v. Porter Stockton,* box 1, case no. 142, Erath County District Clerk Records.

[140] *Texas v. Porter Stockton,* box 1, case nos. 142, 155 and 179, Erath County District Clerk Records.

[141] *Texas v. Porter Stockton,* box 1, case no. 155, Erath County District Clerk Records.

[142] *Texas v. Porter Stockton,* box 1, case no. 142, Erath County District Clerk Records. See also, *Texas v. Porter Stockton,* p. 116, case no. 142 and p. 121, case no. 155, vol. C, 1874-1884, Erath County District Court Minutes, TSU-DSL; *U.S. Census 1870,* Erath County, TX r. 1583, pp. 456b and 466a, IA-ACPL.

[143] *Texas v. Porter Stockton,* box 1, case no. 179, Erath County District Clerk Records. The summons for William Bibb and Eugene Wood was in the file for case no. 142, however, an original notation on the bottom of the summons says, "assault with intent to kill." That indicates that it should have been filed with case no. 179. See also, *Texas v. Porter Stockton,* p. 133, case no. 179, vol. C, 1874-1884, Erath County District Court Minutes, TSU-DSL; *U.S. Census 1870,* Erath County, TX, r. 1583, p. 455b, IA-ACPL.

[144] Requisition from New Mexico to Colorado, for Porter Stockton and others, March 16, 1875, roll 1, microcopy 364, Coll. I 023, Interior Department, Territorial Papers, New Mexico, 1851-1914, RG 48, NARA, FLC-CSWS.

[145] "The Early History Southwestern Colorado," *Durango (CO) Wage Earner,* March 14, 1907, p. 2; "Local News, *Durango Wage Earner,* May 22, 1902, p. 3, death notice for John Turner.

[146] "Second Day Session of New Mexico M.E. Conference," *Albuquerque (NM) Citizen,* October 24, 1907, p. 3.

[147] "New Mexico's Land Ring," *New York Sun,* November 29, 1885, p. 6.

[148] "The Case of Rev. O.P. McMains," *Pueblo Weekly Chieftain,"* May 25, 1876, p. 3. The *Chieftain* also offers another motive for the murder of Tolby involving politically powerful Reverend Joe Brooks.

[149] "New Mexico's Land Ring," *New York Sun,* November 29, 1885, p. 6.

[150] "Lively Times At Cimarron," *Colorado Weekly Chieftain,* November 4, 1875, p. 3.

[151] *New Mexico v. James Kelly,* case no. 477, September 3, 1874, Colfax County District Court Records, NMSRCA.

[152] "Lively Times At Cimarron," *Colorado Weekly Chieftain,* November 4, 1875, p. 3.

153 O.S. Clark, "Clay Allison of the Washita," *Some Western Gun Fighters*, comp. by Ed Bartholomew (Toyahvale, TX: Frontier Book Company, 1954), p. 17.

154 Colfax County Records, Proceedings of Board of County Commissioners, 1876-1884. p. 31, NMSRCA.

155 Outsize Record Books, Colfax County Records, County Sheriff, 1869-1884, Coll. 1973-025, subseries 7.1, box 4, p. 214, NMSRCA.

156 Colfax County Records, Proceedings of Board of County Commissioners, 1876-1884. p. 37, NMSRCA.

157 *New Mexico v. Porter Stockton*, case no. 416, August 30, 1879, Colfax County District Court Records, NMSRCA. The original case number was 65.

158 "Another Tragedy," *Durango (CO) Weekly Record*, January 10, 1881.

159 Local History Project, comp., "Index Marriage Records, Colfax County, NM," Arthur Johnson Memorial Library, Raton, NM, p. 2. Copy available at ABCLS. This is an index for records filed from November 30, 1869 to April 14, 1905. The record for the marriage of Antonio Arcibia and Rita Herera (not the common Herrera spelling) is dated August 26, 1874.

160 National Park Service, Civil War Soldiers and Sailors System, http://www.nps.gov/civilwar/soldiers-and-sailors-database.htm (accessed November 30, 2012).

161 *New Mexico v. Porter Stockton*, case no. 416, August 30, 1879, Colfax County District Court Records, NMSRCA.

162 "New Mexico," *Colorado Weekly Chieftain*, March 30, 1876, p. 2.

163 Outsize Record Books, Colfax County Records, County Sheriff, 1869-1884, Coll. 1973-025, subseries 7.1, box 4, pp. 80-84, NMSRCA.

164 Frank Hall, *History of the State of Colorado*, vol. 4 (Chicago: Rocky Mountain Historical Company, 1895), pp. 383-384. http://archive.org/stream/historyofstateof04hall#page/n9/mode/2up (accessed February 13, 2013).

165 Jose Emilio Fernandez, *The Biography of Casimiro Barela*, translated and annotated by Anthony Gabriel Melendez (Albuquerque: University of New Mexico Press, 2003), pp. 35 and 36. Barela's biography mistakenly identifies the arrestee as Ike Stockton.

166 F. Stanley, *Desperadoes of New Mexico* (Denver: World Press, Inc., 1953), p. 178.

167 F. Stanley, *Ike Stockton* (Denver: World Press, Inc., 1959), p. 84.

168 Stanley, *Desperadoes of New Mexico*, p. 178.

169 Las Animas County Commissioner's Record Book no. 3, January 14, 1875 to May 21, 1880, pp. 169, 176 and 187.

170 Requisitions for Extraditions to New Mexico, Governor Samuel Axtell Papers, Records of the Territorial Governors, 1846-1912, Territorial Archives of New Mexico (hereafter abbreviated TANM), NMSCRA. Stockton's arrest and subsequent requisition were reported in the *Colorado Daily Chieftain*, September 3, 1876, p. 4.

171 *Albuquerque (NM) Review*, August 26, 1876.

172 "The Taos Court," *Santa Fe Daily New Mexican*, September 13, 1876.

173 "The Case of Rev. O.P. McMains," *Colorado Weekly Chieftain*, May 25, 1876, p. 3. Also see the *Colorado Weekly Chieftain*, May 10, 1877, p. 1, under the headline "New Mexico Justice," the newspaper alleged that the annexation of Colfax County to Taos County for judicial purposes was just part of the Santa Fe Ring's plans to control the Maxwell Land Grant and other land grants and to ensure the

indictment of Reverend McMains. The paper was virulently anti-Mormon and alleged that Governor Axtell was attempting to turn the territory into a Mormon enclave. The Ring was blamed for much of the turmoil in Colfax County and Lincoln County. Governor Axtell's support of the Ring was a major factor in the loss of his position as governor.

[174] "The Taos Court," *Santa Fe Daily New Mexican*, September 13, 1876.

[175] "New Mexico's Land Ring," *New York Sun*, November 29, 1885, p. 6. Reverend McMains reported that he was tried before a jury of "Americans and Greasers. The latter were naturally bent upon a conviction." "Lively Times At Cimarron," *Colorado Weekly Chieftain*, November 4, 1875, p. 3. The *Chieftain* says William Lowe hired Cruz Vega to watch his corn crop. The lonely duty was clearly a set up to assure Vega could be easily captured. The *Chieftain* confuses events and says Lowe was implicated in the murder of Tolby. The subsequent arrest of McMains and Lowe clearly indicate their alliance and involvement in the lynching of Vega.

[176] *Santa Fe Daily New Mexican*, Sept. 18, 1876; *New Mexico v. Isaac Stockton*, case no. 420, August 30, 1879, assault in a menacing manner and case no. 421, August 30, 1879, rescuing a prisoner, Colfax County District Court Records, NMSRCA.

[177] "Another Tragedy," *Durango Weekly Record*, January 10, 1881.

[178] Crocker, "Memories of Cimarron, New Mexico, 1871-1872," p. 39.

[179] "Cimarron Affairs," *Santa Fe Daily New Mexican*, October 4, 1876, p. 1.

[180] October 3, 1876 letter to the editor signed by "Justice," "Letter From Cimarron," *Santa Fe Weekly New Mexican*, October 17, 1876, p. 1.

[181] Anderson, *History of New Mexico*, vol. 2, p. 685; "Justice," "Letter from Cimarron," *Santa Fe Weekly New Mexican*, October 17, 1876, p. 1. The letter from "Justice" refers to Holbrook as being a deputy.

[182] "Justice," "Letter From Cimarron," *Santa Fe Weekly New Mexican*, October 17, 1876, p. 1.

[183] Anderson, *History of New Mexico*, vol. 2, p. 685.

[184] "Cimarron Affairs," *Santa Fe Daily New Mexican*, October 4, 1876, p. 1; "Justice," "Letter From Cimarron," *Santa Fe Weekly New Mexican*, October 17, 1876, p. 1.

[185] William A. Keleher, *The Maxwell Land Grant* (Santa Fe: Rydal Press, 1942; 2nd ed. New York: Argosy-Antiquarian, 1964; reprint, with an introduction by John R. Van Ness, Albuquerque: University of New Mexico Press, 1984), p. 70. An excerpt from the *Las Vegas (NM) Gazette*, October 7, 1876.

[186] *Santa Fe Daily New Mexican*, November 1, 1876.

[187] *U.S. Census 1880*, Ouray County, CO, r. 92, p. 176d, ABCLS.

[188] Bill O'Neal, *Encyclopedia of Western Gunfighters* (Norman: University of Oklahoma Press, 1979), pp. 301-302. The author could find no contemporary accounts of the murder of Juan Gonzales in Colfax County. Territorial records and newspaper stories could not be located for this murder. They may exist and were just not found. Newspapers for the local area in that date range are sparse. Also at the time, killings sometimes went unpunished and at times unpublished. There were numerous residents with that name in New Mexico at the time.

[189] Tom Hilton, *Nevermore, Cimarron, Nevermore* (Fort Worth: Western Heritage Press, 1970), p. 25, copy from the University of New Mexico, Zimmerman Library.

[190] Frank Coe to J. Evetts Haley, August 14, 1927, p. 7, JEHC-HMLHC.

¹⁹¹ Frank Coe to Haley, August 17, 1927, p. 19, JEHC-HMLHC.

¹⁹² Ibid., p. 23.

¹⁹³ "Lincoln Refugees," *Santa Fe Weekly New Mexican*, April 26, 1880. In this confused account the *New Mexican* notes the arrival of George "Cole" and his brothers in Rio Arriba County. Brothers Lew, Frank and Jasper (Jap) Coe were cousins to George Coe.

¹⁹⁴ Frank Coe to Haley, August 14, 1927, p. 4, JEHC-HMLHC; Frank Coe to J. Evetts Haley, August 17, 1927, p. 26, JEHC-HMLHC.

¹⁹⁵ Frank Coe to Haley, August 17, 1927, pp. 1 and 11- 12, JEHC-HMLHC.

¹⁹⁶ "Gleanings," *Rocky Mountain News* (Denver), July 11, 1870, p. 4, from the *Pueblo (CO) Chieftain*.

¹⁹⁷ Frank Coe to Haley, August 17, 1927, p. 19, JEHC-HMLHC.

¹⁹⁸ Frank Coe to J. Evetts Haley, August 17, 1927, pp. 1 and 19, JEHC-HMLHC.

¹⁹⁹ Ibid., pp. 26 and 27

²⁰⁰ Ibid., p. 27.

²⁰¹ Ibid., pp. 19- 21.

²⁰² John Becker to B. Stevens, November 16, 1876, *Albuquerque Review*, November 18, 1876.

²⁰³ "One More," *Albuquerque Review*, November 25, 1876.

²⁰⁴ "Killed By A Sheriff's Posse," *Santa Fe Daily New Mexican*, November 23, 1876.

²⁰⁵ O'Neal, *Encyclopedia of Western Gunfighters*, pp. 301-302.

²⁰⁶ *U.S. Census 1860*, Hopkins County, TX, r. 1297, p. 187b, IA-ACPL.

²⁰⁷ "Supposed Stage Robber Killed," *La Plata Miner* (Silverton, CO), February 19, 1881. This article is from a special dispatch to the *Denver Daily Republican* from Alamosa. "The Stage Robbers Captured," and "Those Mail Robbers," *Durango (CO) Weekly Record*, February 19, 1881; "After the Stage Robbers," *Colorado Springs Daily Gazette*, February 8, 1881, from the *Denver Republican*.

CHAPTER THREE – THE SAN JUAN COUNTRY

¹ James Barton Adams, "A Cowboy Toast," *Songs of the Cattle Trail and Cow Camp*, comp. by John A. Lomax (New York: The MacMillan Company, 1920), p. 176.

² *Santa Fe Daily New Mexican*, March 19, 1873.

³ *Colorado Weekly Chieftain* (Pueblo), September 25, 1873, p. 1, from the *Rocky Mountain News*.

⁴ *Daily Colorado Miner* (Georgetown), September 23, 1873, p. 2.

⁵ Charles Jones, "The Memoirs of Charles Adam Jones," n.d., p. 68, Clifford B. Jones Papers, 1814-1973 and undated, Accession Nos. 96-0122-B and 98-0001-B, Southwest Collection/Special Collections Library, Texas Tech University, Lubbock.

⁶ Rev. George M. Darley D.D., *Pioneering in the San Juan* (Chicago, New York and Toronto: Fleming H. Revell Company, 1899), p. 14, http://archive.org/details/pioneeringinsanj00darl (accessed June 9, 2013).

⁷ *Santa Fe Daily New Mexican*, January 23, 1874.

⁸ *Annual Report of the Commissioner of Indian Affairs to the Secretary of the Interior* (Washington, DC, 1875), p. 327, http://archive.org/details/usindianaffairs75usdorich (accessed June 7, 2013).

⁹ Veronica E. Velarde Tiller, *The Jicarilla Apache Tribe - A History*, rev. ed., Bison Book ed. (Lincoln: University of Nebraska Press, 1992), pp. 80-81.

¹⁰ *Annual Report of the Commissioner of Indian Affairs to the Secretary of the Interior* (Washington, DC, 1876), p. 103, http://archive.org/details/usindianaffairs76usdorich (accessed June 7, 2013).

¹¹ Olive Frazier Cornelius, "Pioneer History and Reminiscences of the San Juan Basin," *Aztec (NM) Independent Review*, March 10, 1933.

¹² Sandra Gwilliam, July 10, 2011, email to author about Alf Graves's father. See also Lewis Publishing Company, comp., *History of Texas*, Central Texas ed. (Chicago: The Lewis Publishing Company, 1896), p. 463. http://archive.org/details/historyoftexassu00lewi (accessed March 1, 2013). The parents of Alf and Leana Graves were William and Caroline (Cowder) Graves.

¹³ "A.V. Granes [sic] Is Believed To Be First Settler in San Juan," *Farmington (NM) Daily Times*, August 15, 1956. According to the account, the neighbor shot at the Indians and killed one of them.

¹⁴ *U.S. Census 1870*, Erath County, TX, r. 1583, p. 459a, IA-ACPL.

¹⁵ *San Juan Democrat* (Aztec, NM), March 5, 1909. Older newspapers from Aztec are archived on microfilm at the Aztec Museum and Pioneer Village. Marriage Record Book no. 1, Colfax County Clerk's Office, Raton, New Mexico. Cox lived on the Vermejo River and evidently it was also sometimes referred to as the Red River as was the Canadian River.

¹⁶ *U.S. Census 1880*, Rio Arriba County, NM, r. 803, p. 225c, FLC-CSWS. According to Alf Graves's headstone in the Cedar Hill, NM cemetery, he was born on January 1, 1853. The obituary in the *San Juan Democrat* (Aztec, NM), March 5, 1909, says he was born in 1851. According to Nancy Belle Cox Graves's obituary in the *Aztec (NM) Independent Review*, May 13, 1932, she was born on April 7, 1860.

¹⁷ "Historial Nubs of Early Day Farmington," *Farmington (NM) Times Hustler*, April 5, 1940. Frank Wood recalled learning that Alf Graves worked as a Texas Ranger with fellow Ranger K. Meek who was a brother of Frank's mother.

¹⁸ Hazel Noble, "Hazel Noble Remembers," *Aztec (NM) Museum Association Newsletter*, June 1, 1983.; *U.S. Census 1880*, Rio Arriba County, NM, r. 803, p. 225c, FLC-CSWS. Sources for H.W. Cox's time in the San Juan country include; Olive Frazier Cornelius, "Pioneer History and Reminiscences of the San Juan Basin." This is a collection of articles published weekly in the *Aztec Independent Review* beginning on February 24, 1933 and ending on August 11, 1933. Copies of the newspaper are available at the Aztec (NM) Museum. Another source on Cox is Edith Rhodes, "The H.W. Cox House," *Bulletins Pioneer Association San Juan County*, New Mexico, 1953 to 1976 (1963): pp. 10-11, Farmington (NM) Public Library. This bound volume covers the early history of San Juan County, New Mexico. It contains one volume for each year, except for 1970, when evidently no bulletin was issued. Two bulletins were issued in 1957, one in March and one in July. Each bulletin is written by several authors. Not all of the authors are identified.

¹⁹ "Over the Range," *Colorado Weekly Chieftain*, July 13, 1876, p. 1.

²⁰ Ibid.

²¹ C.S. Peterson, comp., *Representative New Mexicans* (Denver: C.S. Peterson, 1912), p. 33, http://archive.org/details/representativene01denv (accessed August 10, 2013).

²² "Over the Range," *Colorado Weekly Chieftain*, July 13, 1876, p. 1.

[23] Frank Hall, *History of the State of Colorado*, vol. 4 (Chicago: Rocky Mountain Historical Company, 1895) p. 169, http://archive.org/stream/historyofstateof04hall#page/n9/mode/2up (accessed February 13, 2013). Animas City was located in the area near the 32nd Street bridge in Durango.

[24] Cornelius, "Pioneer History," *Aztec Independent Review*, March 10, 1933.

[25] C.V. Koogler and Virginia Koogler Whitney, *Aztec: Old Aztec From Anasazi to Statehood* (Fort Worth: American Reference Publishing Co., 1972), pp. 13-14.

[26] Colfax County Records, Proceedings of Board of County Commissioners, 1876-1884. pp. 55 and 57. Cox attended a meeting on October 15, 1877. On January 7, 1878, he was not a commissioner. The trail over Cumbres Pass was rapidly becoming popular with travelers and those trailing cattle. It was their most likely route, since other trails required major detours to the south, to avoid the Sangre De Cristo Mountains or to get south of the Rio Grande Gorge.

[27] *Colorado Transcript* (Golden), July 18, 1877, p. 2, from the *Cimarron News and Press*, July 5, 1877.

[28] Cornelius, "Pioneer History," *Aztec Independent Review*, March 10, 1933.

[29] J. Marvin Hunter, comp. and ed., *The Trail Drivers of Texas* (Nashville: Cokesbury Press, 1925), pp. 261-262, http://archive.org/details/ traildriversofte00hunt (accessed June 9, 2013).

[30] Cornelius, "Pioneer History," *Aztec Independent Review*, March 10, 1933; *U.S. Census 1880*, Rio Arriba County, NM, r. 803, p. 224b, FLC-CSWC.

[31] "A.U. Graves Is Believed To Be First Settler in San Juan," *Farmington Daily Times*, August 15, 1956.

[32] Cornelius, "Pioneer History," *Aztec Independent Review*, March 10, 1933, May 19, 1933 and June 16, 1933.

[33] Colfax County Records, Proceedings of Board of County Commissioners, 1876-1884. pp. 55 and 57.

[34] William Hendrickson to America McHenry, 1892, "Wm. Hendrickson and Brother," *Farmington (NM) Times Hustler*, August 8, 1941, p. 1 and p. 6.

[35] "John Moss," The History Committee of the Fort Lewis Mesa Reunion, *Pioneers of Southwest La Plata County Colorado* (Bountiful, UT: Family History Publishers, 1994), p. 336

[36] "Parrot [sic] City," *Colorado Daily Chieftain* (Pueblo), December 19, 1875, p. 4; "Rest Came Soon," *The Morning Call* (San Francisco, CA), November 6, 1894, p. 12. Tiburcio Parrott was a native of Mexico and the son of banker John Parrott. He inherited a considerable fortune, but lost much of it on a variety of mining speculations. He died in California on November 5, 1894 at the age of fifty-four.

[37] William Hendrickson to America McHenry, 1892, "Wm. Hendrickson and Brother," *Farmington (NM) Times Hustler*, August 8, 1941, p. 1 and p. 6.

[38] Ibid.

[39] Hol. Gordon, "Animas City," *Colorado Weekly Chieftain*, February 1, 1877, p. 3.

CHAPTER FOUR – IKE, THE KID AND THE COES

[1] Arthur Chapman, "The Border Riders," *Out Where the West Begins and Other Western Verses* (Boston and New York: Houghton Mifflin Company, 1917), p. 73.

[2] "The Taos Court," *Santa Fe Daily New Mexican*, September 13, 1876. Ike was on the run after breaking Porter out of the Cimarron jail.

[3] Frederick W. Nolan, *The Life and Death of John Henry Tunstall* (Albuquerque: The University of New Mexico Press, 1965), pp. 9, 155, 180, 184 and 448.

[4] Emerson Hough, *The Story of the Outlaw: A Study of the Western Desperado*, (New York: Grosset and Dunlap, 1907), p. 204. https://archive.org/stream/storyofoutlawstu00houguoft#page/n5/mode/2up (accessed June 25, 2013).

[5] *U.S. Census 1850*, Upshur County, TX, r. 916, p. 183b, ABCLS; *U.S. Census 1860*, Hopkins County, TX, r. 1297, p. 128b, ABCLS. Father Samuel Stockton is shown in the 1850 census, but does not appear in the 1860 census or thereafter.

[6] George W Coe, *Frontier Fighter - The Autobiography of George W. Coe who fought and rode with Billy the Kid* (Boston and New York: Houghton and Mifflin Co., 1934; 2nd ed. Albuquerque: University of New Mexico Press, 1951; The Lakeside Classics ed., ed. by Doyce B. Nunis, Jr. with historical introduction by Doyce B. Nunis, Jr. Chicago: The Lakeside Press, R.R. Donnelly and Sons Co., 1984), pp. 154-155. A map of the town of Lincoln.

[7] Frederick Nolan, *The Lincoln County War - A Documentary History* (Norman and London: University of Oklahoma Press, 1992), p. 565.

[8] "The Final Farewell," *Las Vegas (NM) Daily Optic*, September 29, 1881.

[9] "Former Pal Lauds 'Billy the Kid,' " *Douglas County Record Journal* (Castle Rock, CO), November 13, 1931, p. 7.

[10] Pat F. Garrett, *The Authentic Life of Billy the Kid*, Western Frontier Library ed. (1882; reprint, with an introduction by J.C. Dykes, Norman: University of Oklahoma Press, 1954), p. 62.

[11] Hough, *The Story of the Outlaw*, pp. 199-200, 204.

[12] "Ring-Ridden New Mexico," *New York Sun*, July 14, 1878, p. 6.

[13] Maurice G. Fulton, *History of the Lincoln County War - A Classic Account of Billy the Kid* (Tucson: The University of Arizona Press, 1968), pp. 115-116.

[14] Frederick Nolan, *The West of Billy the Kid* (Norman: University of Oklahoma Press, 1998) p. 108.

[15] Nolan, *The Lincoln County War*, p. 203.

[16] *Santa Fe Weekly New Mexican*, May 25, 1878.

[17] Fulton, *History of the Lincoln County War*, p. 141.

[18] Hough, *The Story of the Outlaw*, pp. 207, 212, 213.

[19] Charles A. Siringo, *History of "Billy the Kid"* (Santa Fe: 1920), pp. 51-52, http://archive.org/details/historyofbillyki00siririch (accessed June 25, 2013).

[20] Fulton, *History of the Lincoln County War*, pp. 159.

[21] Garrett, *The Authentic Life of Billy the Kid*, p. 62.

[22] "Particulars of the Lincoln County Shooting Affrays," *Santa Fe Weekly New Mexican*, April 13, 1878, from the *Mesilla Valley Independent* (Mesilla, NM), April 9, 1878.

[23] Ibid.

[24] Hough, *The Story of the Outlaw*, pp. 287-288.

[25] "Particulars of the Lincoln County Shooting Affrays," *Santa Fe Weekly New Mexican*, April 13, 1878, from the *Mesilla Valley Independent*, April 9, 1878.

[26] "Former Pal Lauds 'Billy the Kid,' " *Douglas County Record Journal* (Castle Rock, CO), November 13, 1931, p. 7.

[27] "Particulars of the Lincoln County Shooting Affrays," *Santa Fe Weekly New Mexican*, April 13, 1878, from the *Mesilla Valley Independent*, April 9, 1878. The *New Mexican* obtained this report via a military telegraph.

[28] Cara Mae Coe Marable Smith, *The Coe's Go West: From Billy the Kid Land to Movie and Other Entertainment Lands* (El Paso: C.M. Smith, 1988), p. 42.

[29] Hough, *The Story of the Outlaw,* pp. 215-219.

[30] Walter Noble Burns, *The Saga of Billy the Kid* (New York and Garden City, NY: Doubleday, Page and Company, 1926), pp. 116 and 138-139.

[31] Nolan, *The West of Billy the Kid*, pp. 172-173.

[32] *New Mexico v. Frank McNab et al,* case no. 264, April 23, 1878, Lincoln County District Court Records, Criminal Cases, NMSRCA.

[33] George Coe to J. Evetts Haley, August 12, 1927, p. 4, JEHC-HMLHC.

[34] George Coe to J. Evetts Haley, August 18, 1927, p. 6, JEHC-HMLHC.

[35] George Coe to J. Evetts Haley, March 20, 1927, p. 26, JEHC-HMLHC.

[36] Marilu Waybourn and Vernetta Mickey, *Meet Me At The Fair* (Farmington, NM: San Juan County Fair Association, 1984), p. 1. Lew Coe's farm was close to the present day intersection of San Juan Boulevard and Main Street.

[37] "Mary Brothers Recalls Era of Just Rio Arriba," *Farmington (NM) Daily Times,* August 15, 1956. Pueblo's *Colorado Weekly Chieftain,* June 7, 1877, p. 1 published an April 25th letter from Hol Gordon which noted that Milton Virden's home had been burned down about a month before and the Navajos had "torn down and fired" several other houses at the same time.

[38] The author could find no evidence of Porter Stockton's presence in Lincoln County.

[39] George Curry, *George Curry 1861-1947 An Autobiography*, ed. H.B. Hening (Albuquerque: University of New Mexico Press, 1958), pp. 36-37.

[40] Hough, *The Story of the Outlaw,* p. 222-224.

[41] "Telegraphic," *Weekly Arizona Miner* (Prescott), February 28, 1879, p. 2.

[42] Frazier Hunt, *The Tragic Days of Billy the Kid,* (New York: Hastings House, 1956), p. 156.

[43] "General Lew Wallace's Picturesque Outlaw Hero," *St. Louis (MO) Republic,* July 6, 1902, s. 1, p. 11.

[44] John P. Wilson, *Merchants, Guns, and Money – The Story of Lincoln County and Its Wars* (Santa Fe: Museum of New Mexico Press, 1987), p. 118.

CHAPTER FIVE – TROUBLE IN OTERO

[1] Burke Jenkins, "The Cowboy to his Friend in Need," *Songs of the Cattle Trail and Cow Camp,* comp. by John A. Lomax (New York: The MacMillan Company, 1920), p. 91.

[2] *Texas v. I.W. Lacy,* p. 107, case no. 212, vol. B, 1871-1874, Erath County District Court Minutes, TSU-DSL. Burleson apparently lived in Erath County in the early 1870s and served as one of I.W. Lacy's sureties in the case noted above.

[3] Victor Westphall, *Thomas Benton Catron and His Era* (Tucson: The University of Arizona Press, 1973), p. 159.

[4] Arie Poldervaart, "Black-Robed Justice in New Mexico, 1846-1912," *New Mexico Historical Review,* vol. 22, no. 4, (October 1947): p. 368-369, http://archive.org/details/newmexicohistori22univrich (accessed September 1, 2013).

[5] Mrs. Mary E. Burleson, "Pioneer Story," transcribed by Edith L. Crawford in Carrizozo, NM, U.S. Works Progress Administration, Federa Writer's Project (Folklore Project, Life Hisories, 1936-1939), Manuscript Division, Library of

Congress, http://www.loc.gov/resource/wpalh1.19040404/seq-1#seq-1 (accessed September 18, 2013).

[6] *Colorado Weekly Chieftain* (Pueblo), May 23, 1878, p. 1.

[7] "Solonic Saunterings," *Colorado Weekly Chieftain*, February 20, 1879, p. 1.

[8] "A Moving Town," *Las Vegas (NM) Daily Optic*, May 30, 1880.

[9] "Solonic Saunterings," *Colorado Weekly Chieftain*, Feb. 20, 1879, p. 1.

[10] "New Mexico Mining," *Santa Fe Weekly New Mexican*, June 21, 1879, from the *St. Louis Globe-Democrat*.

[11] "Solonic Saunterings," *Colorado Weekly Chieftain*, Feb. 20, 1879, p. 1.

[12] "On to Mexico," *Colorado Weekly Chieftain*, Feb. 13, 1879 p. 1.

[13] "Solonic Saunterings," *Colorado Weekly Chieftain*, Feb. 20, 1879, p. 1.

[14] *Santa Fe Weekly New Mexican*, June 21, 1879, from the *St. Louis Globe-Democrat*.

[15] Miguel Antonio Otero, *My Life on the Frontier 1864-1882* (New York: Press of the Pioneers, 1935; reprint, with an introduction by Cynthia Secor-Welsh, Albuquerque: University of New Mexico Press, 1987), p. 134.

[16] *Las Vegas (NM) Daily Optic*, November 19, 1879. The *Optic* does not mention the location of the *Daily News*, but it was probably the Trinidad newspaper.

[17] "The Withers Murder At Otero," *Denver (CO) Daily Tribune*, June 22, 1879, p. 6, from the *Trinidad News*.

[18] Hervey E. Chesley, *Adventuring with the Old-Timers: Trails Travelled - Tales Told* (Midland, TX: Nita Stewart Haley Memorial Library, 1979), p. 94.

[19] Justice of the Peace Inquisition upon the body of Edward Withers, deceased, n.d., part of the record of *New Mexico v. Porter Stockton*, case no. 417, August 30, 1879, Colfax County District Court Records, NMSRCA.

[20] "Indian News," *Emporia (KS) News*, July 17, 1874, p. 2.

[21] "Washington News and Gossip," *Washington (DC) Evening Star*, July 27, 1874, p. 1.

[22] "State Items," *Leavenworth (KS) Weekly Times*, January 21, 1875, p. 1.

[23] Edgar Rye, *The Quirt and The Spur – Vanishing Shadows of the Western Frontier* (Chicago: W.B. Conkey Company, 1909), pp. 74 and 103. http://archive.org/details/quirtandspurvan00ryegoog (accessed June 28, 2013).

[24] *Texas v. Hannah Eizenstein and Edward a Mexican*, p. 67, case no. 17, Book A, 1875-1884, Minutes District Court, Shackelford County District Clerk Records.

[25] *Texas v. Molly McCabe, Jim Oglesby, Hurricane Bill, Long Kate, Helen, Etta, Liz, Minnie*, p. 47, case no. 16, Book A, 1875-1884, Minutes District Court, Shackelford County District Clerk Records.

[26] *Texas v. Frank Smith, Griffin Long Kate, Mollie McCabe, Minnie*, p. 3, case no. 7, Book A, 1875-1884, Minutes District Court, Shackelford County District Clerk Records.

[27] Gary L. Roberts, *Doc Holliday - The Life and Legend* (Hoboken: John Wiley and Sons, Inc., 2006), p. 432, footnote no. 72.

[28] *Texas v. Mike Lynch and Dock Holladay [sic]*, p. 49, case no. 34, Book A, 1875-1884, Minutes District Court, Shackelford County District Clerk Records. See also, *Texas v. Mike Lynch and Dock Holladay [sic]*, p. 16, case no. 34, vol. A, 1875-1884, Shackelford County District Court Minutes, TSU-DSL. Lynch and Holliday were charged with playing cards in a house which sold spirituous liquors.

[29] Frances Mayhugh Holden, *Lambshead Before Interwoven: A Texas Chronicle, 1848-1878* (College Station: Texas A&M University Press, 1982), pp. 151-153.

³⁰ City of Waco, *Fugitives From Justice - The Notebook of Texas Ranger Sergeant James B. Gillett* (Austin: State House Press, 1997), p. 167.

³¹ Ed Bartholomew, *Wyatt Earp 1848-1880 The Untold Story* (Toyahvale, TX: Frontier Book Company, 1963), p. 294.

³² *New Mexico v. John McClelland*, case no. 399, March 31, 1879, Colfax County District Court Records, NMSRCA.

³³ *New Mexico v. Frank Randal*, case no. 400, March 31, 1879, Colfax County District Court Records, NMSRCA.

³⁴ *U.S. Census 1870*, Colfax County, NM, r. 893, p. 142a, IA-ACPL.

³⁵ *New Mexico v. Noah Camblin and others*, case no. 277, March, 1874, April 2, 1877, Colfax County District Court Records, NMSRCA.

³⁶ Colin Rickards, *Mysterious Dave Mather* (Santa Fe: Press of the Territorian, 1968), pp. 7 and 11.

³⁷ Randy Russell, *Billy the Kid – The Story The Trial* (Lincoln, NM: The Crystal Press, 1994), p 4. The notation "Sr" for Mr. Ellis is parenthesized in the original document. Stockton is not identified by his first name, however Ike is identified by several sources as being a witness to at least portions of the incident. See also pp. 2, 16, 46, 48. Several different case numbers are used in relation to the murder charges.

³⁸ The progress of the twice yearly northern circuit of the district court through San Miguel, Colfax, Taos and Rio Arriba counties is normally described in varying detail in the issues of the *Santa Fe New Mexican*.

³⁹ "Court in Colfax County," *Santa Fe Weekly New Mexican*, April 12, 1879.

⁴⁰ "Fatal Shooting Affray," *Santa Fe Weekly New Mexican*, April 5, 1879, from the *Cimarron News and Press*.

⁴¹ "Court in Colfax County," *Santa Fe Weekly New Mexican*, April 12, 1879.

⁴² *New Mexico v. John Hill*, case no. 390, *New Mexico v. Henry Gorden [Sic]*, case no. 389 and *New Mexico v. Robert Leigh*, case no. 388, March 28, 1879, Colfax County District Court Records, NMSRCA.

⁴³ *New Mexico v. George Hill*, case no. 395, carrying a deadly weapon, case no. 403, assault with intent to murder, March 28 and March 31, 1879. Colfax County District Court Records, NMSRCA.

⁴⁴ Colfax County District Court Records, Civil and Criminal Record Book no. 3, 1874-1879, p. 279, NMSRCA. The attempted murder charge was originally case no. 52.

⁴⁵ "In the Long Ago," *Las Vegas (NM) Weekly Optic and Stock Grower*, May 18, 1901, p. 3, from the *Springer (NM) Sentinel*.

⁴⁶ *New Mexico v. George Morrison*, case no. 391, April 1, 1879, Colfax County District Court Records, NMSRCA. All of the cases are in one file, making it somewhat difficult to decipher. S. Morgan Friedman, "The Inflation Calculator," *Ceci n'est pas une* homepage, n.d., http://www.westegg.com/inflation/infl.cgi (accessed December 8, 2010).

⁴⁷ *Santa Fe Weekly New Mexican*, May 17, 1879, from the *Cimarron News and Press*.

⁴⁸ "New Mexico," *Trinidad (CO) Enterprise*, April 19, 1879, p. 4.

⁴⁹ *New Mexico v. Isaiah Rinehart, Joseph Holbrook and John B. McCullough*, case no. 363, March 1, 1878, Colfax County District Court Records, NMSRCA; Erath County Genealogical Society, *Erath County, Texas Marriage Records 1869-1891*, vol. 1

(Stephenville, TX: Erath County Genealogical Society, 1980), book A, p. 2, ABCLS. Wilson L. South married Louisa Langston in Erath County in 1869.

[50] "The Court in Taos County," *Santa Fe Weekly New Mexican*, April 19, 1879.

[51] *Colorado Weekly Chieftain*, June 19, 1879, p. 1. Virtually the entire first page and much of the rest of this issue is filled with articles about Colorado's railroad war. The June 12th issue of the *Weekly Chieftain* is also replete with stories on the battling railroads.

[52] Bartholomew, *Wyatt Earp 1848-1880*, p. 296.

[53] *New Mexico v. Robinson and Henry*, case no. 370, March 26, 1879, *New Mexico v. Robinson and Henry*, case no. 422, September 1, 1879, Colfax County District Court Records, NMSRCA.

[54] "Doc Holliday, Gun Fighter and Some Stirring History," *Bisbee Daily Review*, July 31, 1910, p. 2, from the *New York Herald* from an interview with Bat Masterson; *Colorado Miner* (Georgetown), August 2, 1879, p. 1. About three years after his run-in with Doc Holliday, the *Miner* contained a mail notice for "Budd" Ryan.

[55] "Holliday's Trail of Blood," *Omaha Daily Bee*, January 2, 1888, p. 3, from the *Denver (CO) Republican*.

[56] *New Mexico v. Porter Stockton*, case no. 417, August 30, 1879, Colfax County District Court Records, NMSRCA; "State and Vicinity," *Fairplay (CO) Flume*, June 19, 1879, p. 3, from the *Otero Optic*; Also see "The Withers Murder At Otero," *Denver Daily Tribune*, June 22, 1879, p. 6, from the *Trinidad News*. One of the witnesses, Bill Wootton, was one of the small fry desperadoes infesting Otero. In the late 1870s, his half-brother, R.L. Wootton, Jr. was the Sheriff of Las Animas County. See also, "The Pistol at Trinidad," *Colorado Weekly Chieftain*, December 12, 1878 p. 2, from the *Trinidad (CO) Daily News*. The *Daily News* reported that Wootton shot and killed Kendrick Washburn at the Olympic Theatre in Trinidad. He later surrendered to officer Kriegbaum of the Trinidad police force and was escorted into custody by his half-brother and Marshal Selles of Trinidad. The *Colorado Weekly Chieftain* of December 19, 1878, p. 3, reported that Wootton was discharged a few days later after no one testified against him at a preliminary hearing. Wootton continued to court trouble. According to the article titled, "Court Proceedings of San Miguel County," *Santa Fe Weekly New Mexican*, March 22, 1879, shortly after killing Washburn, young Bill headed to San Miguel County, New Mexico. There he got in another fight and ended up with a broken arm. In March he faced charges for this affray. He entered a plea of guilty to aggravated assault and was sentenced to time served plus $150 and costs. Still looking for excitement, he turned up in Otero.

[57] "State and Vicinity," *Fairplay (CO) Flume*, June 19, 1879, p. 3, from the *Otero Optic*.

[58] "The Withers Murder At Otero," *Denver Daily Tribune*, June 22, 1879, p. 6, from the *Trinidad News*.

[59] "State and Vicinity," *Fairplay (CO) Flume*, June 19, 1879, p. 3, from the *Otero Optic*.

[60] "The Withers Murder At Otero," *Denver Daily Tribune*, June 22, 1879, p. 6, from the *Trinidad News*.

[61] Chesley, *Adventuring with the Old-Timers*, p. 94. Stockton is identified as Porter Shagdon.

⁶² "Otero Sparks," *Trinidad Daily News*, June 13, 1879.

⁶³ *Santa Fe Weekly New Mexican*, June 21, 1879

⁶⁴ Justice of the Peace Inquisition upon the body of Edward Withers, deceased, June 11, 1879, part of the record of *New Mexico v. Porter Stockton*, case no. 417, August 30, 1879, Colfax County District Court Records, NMSRCA.

⁶⁵ Request for payment of expenses incurred during the pursuit of Port Stockton submitted by Sheriff Burleson probably during the summer of 1879, n.d., part of the record of *New Mexico v. Porter Stockton*, case no. 417, August 30, 1879, Colfax County District Court Records, NMSRCA.

⁶⁶ Bartholomew, *Wyatt Earp 1848-1880*, p. 295.

⁶⁷ *Santa Fe Daily New Mexican* of August 5, 1880.

⁶⁸ *New Mexico v. Porter Stockton*, case no. 417, August 30, 1879, Colfax County District Court Records, NMSRCA.

⁶⁹ Howard Bryan, *Wildest of the Wild West* (Santa Fe: Clear Light Publishers, 1988), p. 105.

⁷⁰ "Doc Holliday, Gun Fighter and Some Stirring History," *Bisbee Daily Review*, July 31, 1910, p. 2, from the *New York Herald* from an interview with Bat Masterson.

⁷¹ *New Mexico v. Porter Stockton*, case no. 417, murder, August 30, 1879 and case no. 416, murder, August 30, 1879; also see *New Mexico v. Isaac Stockton*, case no. 420, assault in a menacing manner, August 30, 1879, and case no. 421, rescuing a prisoner, August 30, 1879, all four cases are from the Colfax County District Court Records, NMSRCA. A list of grand jurors can be found in Colfax County District Court Records, Civil and Criminal Record Book no. 3, 1874-1879, p. 295, NMSRCA; *U.S. Census 1870*, Colfax County, NM, r. 893, p. 141b, IA-ACPL; *Trinidad Enterprise*, June 20, 1879. Witness John J. Selles worked for Sheriff Wootton as his only deputy in Las Animas County, Colorado.

⁷² *New Mexico v. Porter Stockton*, case no. 417, August 30, 1879, Colfax County District Court Records (1879, 1880, 1881), NMSRCA.

⁷³ Emerson Hough, *The Story of the Outlaw: A Study of the Western Desperado* (New York: Grosset and Dunlap, 1907), pp. 212-213, https://archive.org/stream/storyofoutlawstu00houguoft#page/n5/mode/2up (accessed June 25, 2013).

⁷⁴ Russell, *Billy the Kid*, p. 32. The Kid went to trial in April 1881.

⁷⁵ George Coe to J. Evetts Haley, August 12, 1927, p. 6, JEHC-HMLHC. Coe says the Stocktons arrived in late 1879. C.O. Ziegenfuss, "Ike Stockton," *Denver Republican*, August 12, 1881. In this article Ike says he arrived on the Animas in 1879.

⁷⁶ *U.S. Census 1880*, Rio Arriba County, NM, r. 0803, p. 225c, FLC-CSWS. The census enumerator spells Ellen Stockton's name as "Alan." The area where the Coes and Stocktons resided was called the Animas Arriba by the U.S. Census enumerator, which means the upper Animas. That is somewhat of a misnomer. The Animas River from Aztec to the Colorado line could be considered the upper Animas, when looking at the river from only a New Mexico perspective. But in terms of the river's entire length, the upper Animas is that area around Silverton and up to the high ranges of the San Juan Mountains which encompass the Continental Divide, with one side being the Animas River drainage and the other side being the headwaters of the Rio Grande.

⁷⁷ Book of Brands and Earmarks, San Juan County Clerk's Office, Aztec, NM.

NOTES 401

[78] "State Notes," *Colorado Weekly Chieftain*, October 23, 1879, p. 4.

[79] *Colorado Weekly Chieftain*, November 27, 1879, p. 5.

[80] "Shooting Affray in Otero," *Cimarron (NM) News and Press*, November 27, 1879.

[81] Delbert Littrell Hughes and Lenore Harris Hughes, *Give Me Room!* (El Paso: The Hughes Publishing Co., 1971), p. 82.

[82] "Shooting Affray in Otero," *Cimarron (NM) News and Press*, November 27, 1879.

[83] *Santa Fe Weekly New Mexican*, November 29, 1879.

[84] Hughes, *Give Me Room!* p. 59.

[85] *Las Vegas (NM) Daily Optic*, November 28, 1879, from the *Trinidad Enterprise*.

[86] *Cimarron (NM) News and Press*, November 20, 1879; "Cow-Punchers," *Cimarron News and Press*, November 27, 1879.

[87] *Las Vegas (NM) Daily Optic*, January 17, 1881.

[88] "A New Town," *Cimarron (NM) News and Press*, June 24, 1880.

[89] "K.E.Y." "Letter from Baughl's Siding," *Las Vegas (NM) Daily Optic*, March 29, 1880.

[90] R.E. Lay, "Letter from Baughls," *Las Vegas (NM) Daily Optic*, April 19, 1880.

[91] "A New Town," *Cimarron (NM) News and Press*, June 24, 1880.

[92] "K.E.Y." "Letter From Baughl's Siding," *Las Vegas (NM) Daily Optic*, March 29, 1880.

[93] Ibid.

[94] *Las Vegas (NM) Daily Optic*, March 3, 1880.

[95] R.E. Lay, "Letter from Baughls," *Las Vegas (NM) Daily Optic*, April 19, 1880.

[96] "Bullets," *Santa Fe Daily New Mexican*, January 14, 1881.

[97] "Horse Thieves Captured," *Las Vegas (NM) Daily Optic*, April 14, 1880; Mandate upon requisition from State of Texas for Ike Stowe (alias) and West Brown (alias), April 26, 1880, roll 1, microcopy 364, Coll. I 023, Interior Department, Territorial Papers, New Mexico, 1851-1914, RG 48, NARA, FLC-CSWS.

[98] *U.S. Census 1860*, Hopkins County, TX, r. 1297, p. 128b, ABCLS.

[99] *Brenham (TX) Weekly Banner*, May 25, 1877, p. 1; "Another Stage Robbery," *Frontier Echo* (Jacksboro, TX), August 11, 1876. The *Echo* is available for viewing at Abilene Christian University, Brown Library. The *Echo* reported that the Fort Worth to Weatherford stage was robbed on August 3rd.

[100] City of Waco, *Fugitives From Justice*, p. 131.

[101] *Fort Griffin (TX) Echo*, April 10, 1880. Abilene Christian University, Brown Library.

[102] "Horse Thieves Captured," *Las Vegas (NM) Daily Optic*, April 14, 1880.

[103] Ibid. The *Optic* noted that "J. Greathouse" aided in the capture of the horse thieves. The Greathouse/Kuch Ranch was well known as a rendezvous for the region's horse thieves and the *Optic* apparently misunderstood Greathouse's role in the affair.

[104] J. Steck, "Reminiscenses," *Lincoln County Leader* (White Oaks, NM), December 7, 1889, p. 1.

[105] "Horse Thieves Captured," *Las Vegas (NM) Daily Optic*, April 14, 1880. *Oche de Mil Egre* may have been the wildly anglicized version of *Ojo de Milagro* or Miracle Spring. It's unclear if this was the location of another Greathouse ranch property.

[106] "Home At Last," *Las Vegas (NM) Daily Optic*, June 10, 1880, from the *Henrietta (TX) Shield*.

[107] "Jail Delivery," *Emporia (KS) News*, October 15, 1880, p. 4, from the *Arkansas City Traveler*.

[108] "A Moving Town," *Las Vegas (NM) Daily Optic*, May 30, 1880.

CHAPTER SIX – THE ESKRIDGE BOYS

[1] Charles Badger Clark, Jr., "The Old Cowman," *Songs of the Cattle Trail and Cow Camp*, comp. by John A. Lomax (New York: The MacMillan Company, 1920), p. 165.

[2] "The Territories," *Colorado Miner* (Georgetown), August 23, 1879, p. 1, from the *Cimarron (NM) News and Press*.

[3] Ibid.

[4] "The Maxwell Land Grant," *Colorado Weekly Chieftain* (Pueblo), June 12, 1879, p. 3, from the *Tribune* (probably the *Denver Tribune*).

[5] "Settlers Fight," *Iola (KS) Register*, August 31, 1888, p. 2.

[6] "In Splendid Condition," *Santa Fe Weekly New Mexican*, April 12, 1880.

[7] "A New Enterprise in El Moro," *Colorado Weekly Chieftain* (Pueblo), November 8, 1877, p. 3.

[8] J. Evetts Haley, *The XIT Ranch of Texas*, Western Frontier Library ed.(Norman: University of Oklahoma Press, 1953), p. 43; "Murder Most Foul!" *Dolores News* (Rico, CO), May 21, 1881, p. 2.

[9] Elmo Scott Watson, "Fifty Famous Frontiersman," *Douglas County Record Journal* (Castle Rock, CO), December 1, 1933, p. 3.

[10] "City and Vicinity," *Colorado Daily Chieftain* (Pueblo), May 10, 1876, p. 4.

[11] Laura V. Hamner, *Short Grass and Longhorns* (Norman, University of Oklahoma Press, 1945), p. 195.

[12] William S. Speer and Hon. John Henry Brown, ed., *The Encyclopedia of the New West* (Marshall, TX: The United States Biographical Publishing Company, 1881; 2nd ed. Easley, SC: Southern Historical Press, The Rev. S. Emmett Lucas, Jr., 1978), p. 58.

[13] "The Maxwell Land [illegible]" *Trinidad (CO) Enterprise*, December 13, 1877, p. 2; "The Great Legal Fight," *Colorado Daily Chieftain*, May 1, 1872, p. 2; "Fat Contributor," "The Maxwell Land Grant," *Denver (CO) Republican*, March 29, 1881. Mrs. Bent-Thompson believed her Bent children were the rightful heirs to a one-fourth portion of the Maxwell Land Grant.

[14] "Official Directory," *Trinidad (CO) Enterprise*, September 12, 1873, p. 1; "The Trinidad Murder," *Colorado Weekly Chieftain*, February 15, 1872, p. 2.

[15] "In Splendid Condition," *Santa Fe Weekly New Mexican*, April 12, 1880.

[16] *Colorado Weekly Chieftain*, October 9, 1879, p. 1, from the *Santa Fe New Mexican*.

[17] "$100 REWARD," *Durango (CO) Weekly Record*, May 7, 14 and 21, 1881. In this reward notice Henry Goodman and G.W. Thompson (the cattleman's namesake and nephew) are shown as the only ones authorized to sell LC cattle. It misidentifies Henry C. Goodman as C.H. Goodman.

[18] "Death of John H. Reid," *Silverton (CO) Standard*, March 8, 1890, p. 2. Reid's death was brought on by typhoid fever.

[19] Report No. 1, Adjutant General Max Frost to Governor Wallace, April 2, 1881, Campaign, TANM, NMSRCA. From TANM roll 87.

[20] George B. Anderson., comp., *History of New Mexico - Its Resources and People*, vol. 2 (Los Angeles, Chicago and New York: Pacific States Publishing Co., 1907), p. 863.

[21] *U.S. Census 1860*, Sussex County, DE r. 99, page number is illegible, IA-ACPL; *U.S. Census 1870*, Sussex County, DE r. 122, p. 474a, IA-ACPL; *U.S. Census 1880*, Sussex County DE, r. 117, p. 411b, IA-ACPL; Chapman Publishing Company, comp., *Portrait and Biographical Record of the State of Colorado* (Chicago: Chapman Publishing Company, 1899), p. 193, http://archive.org/stream/portraitbiograph00chaprich#page/193/mode/1up (accessed March 3, 2013).

[22] National Park Service, Civil War Soldiers and Sailors System, http://www.nps.gov/civilwar/soldiers-and-sailors-database.htm (accessed November 30, 2012).

[23] *U.S. Census 1870*, Labette County, KS, r. 436, p. 102a, IA-ACPL.

[24] *U.S. Census 1880*, Conejos County, CO, r. 89, p. 181a, IA-ACPL; *U.S. Census 1860*, Schuyler County, MO, r. 646, p. 759, IA-ACPL; *U.S. Census, 1870*, Sussex County, DE, r. 122, p. 474a, IA-ACPL; *U.S. Census 1880*, Sussex County DE, r. 117, p. 411b, IA-ACPL.

[25] Chapman Publishing Company, comp., *Portrait and Biographical Record of the State of Colorado*, p. 193.

[26] Ann Lee Fulcher Clarkson, "Rio Grande County, Interview 367-18," *The First We Can Remember*, ed. Lee Schweninger (Lincoln and London: University of Nebraska Press, 2011), pp. 38-39. Clarkson was interviewed by Laura White on December 18, 1933. The work was funded by the Civil Works Administration, an agency created as part of President Franklin Roosevelt's New Deal.

[27] "James W. Garrett Crosses the Dark River," *Creede (CO) Candle*, January 30, 1904, p. 1; *U.S. Census 1900*, Mineral County, CO, r. 127, p. 159b, IA-ACPL. The *Creede Candle* article says that Garrett was forty-eight when he died and that would mean he was born in 1856. However, the 1900 census for Mineral County, Colorado says he was born in January 1857.

[28] Report No. 1, Frost to Wallace, April 2, 1881, Campaign, TANM, NMSRCA.

[29] "The Ute Outbreak," *Colorado Weekly Chieftain*, October 9, 1879, p. 1.

[30] Fred H. Werner., *Meeker – The Story of the Meeker Massacre and the Thornburgh Battle – September 29 ,1879* (Greeley, CO: Werner Publications, 1985), p. 55

[31] Marshall D. Moody., "The Meeker Massacre," *The Colorado Magazine*, vol. 30, no. 2 (April 1953): p. 100.

[32] "Warlike Utes!" *Colorado Weekly Chieftain*, October 9, 1879 p. 3.

[33] Werner, *The Story of the Meeker Massacre*, pp. 61 and 78 and 114; *U.S. Census, 1870*, Weld County, CO r. 95, p. 513b, IA-ACPL. Provides the approximate age of Josie Meeker.

[34] "Arrival of the Captives" and "The Rescued Captives," *Colorado Weekly Chieftain*, October 30, 1879, p. 2.

[35] "The Meeker Outrage," *Colorado Weekly Chieftain*, January 15, 1880, p. 1, as reported by the *Kansas City Times*.

[36] "The Indian War," *Colorado Weekly Chieftain*, October 16, 1879, p. 3. This information came from two dispatches from Silverton, one from attorney A.W. Hudson.

37 "The Indian War - The Day's Doings," *Colorado Weekly Chieftain*, October 16, 1879, p. 3.
38 *Colorado Weekly Chieftain*, October 9, 1879, p. 2.
39 "Outbreak of the Utes," *Colorado Weekly Chieftain*, October 9, 1879, p. 5.
40 "Soldiers in the San Juan," *Dolores News*, November 8, 1879, p. 1.
41 Raymond M. Beckner., *Old Forts of Southern Colorado* (Cañon City, CO: self-published, 1975), p. 52.
42 Report No. 1, Frost to Wallace, April 2, 1881, Campaign, TANM, NMSRCA.
43 Ibid.
44 *U.S. Census 1880*, Rio Arriba County, NM, r. 803, p. 230b, FLC-CSWS; See also "Twilight Land!" October 9, 1880, *La Plata Miner* (Silverton, CO). This article lists the many of the farms located on the Animas River in New Mexico as well as other information about the lower country. Eskridge and Garrett and a few others are not listed, probably because they had no lands under cultivation. Much of the information was provided by lower Animas resident Seth Welfoot.
45 "Farmington Items," *La Plata Miner*, March 20, 1880. This article describes the size of Farmington.
46 *U.S. Census 1880*, Rio Arriba County, NM, r. 803, p. 225d, FLC-CSWS; *U.S. Census 1860*, Schuyler County, MO, r. 646, pp. 759 and 760, IA-ACPL. Thomas Fulcher's father Silas and his family lived in Schuyler County, Missouri very near to the Garrett family in 1860.
47 Clarkson, "Rio Grande County, Interview 367-18," *The First We Can Remember*, ed. Lee Schweninger, pp. 36-39; *U.S. Census 1880*, Conejos County, CO, r. 89, pp. 186c and 193a, IA-ACPL.
48 *U.S. Census 1870*, Schuyler County, MO, r. 804, pp. 389b and 390b, IA-ACPL.
49 J.N. Coe, "A Reign of Terror," *Colorado Springs Daily Gazette*, March 27, 1881.
50 "In Splendid Condition," *Santa Fe Weekly New Mexican*, April 12, 1880.
51 *Cimarron (NM) News and Press*, July 15, 1880.
52 *New Mexico v. Richard L. Wooten, Jr.[sic]*, case no. 446, also referred to as case no. 95, September 4, 1880, Colfax County District Court Records, NMSRCA. The full name of "Uncle Dick," who was Wootton's father, was Richens Lacy Wootton.
53 "Twilight Land!" *La Plata Miner*, October 9, 1880.
54 "A Local Protest," *La Plata Miner*, April 3, 1880, from the *Santa Fe New Mexican*.
55 Charles F. Coan, Ph.D., *A History of New Mexico*, vol. 1 (Chicago and New York: The American Historical Society, Inc., 1925), p. 542.
56 Report No. 2, Frost to Wallace, April 2, 1881, Campaign, TANM, NMSRCA. This letter identifies the precincts as No. 19 and No. 20. *Dolores News*, April 3, 1880, p. 2; "Refutation of a Slander," *Dolores News*, April 23, 1881, p. 1.
57 Anderson, *History of New Mexico*, Vol. 2, p. 868. Less than a year after Locke's arrival in Denver, in late February 1861, Colorado became a territory.
58 Mary Atwood, ed., "The Vaughan Family," *Aztec (NM) Museum Association Newsletter*, August 1, 1991.
59 Anderson, *History of New Mexico*, vol. 2, pp. 865-868.
60 "Refutation of a Slander," *Dolores News*, April 23, 1881, p. 1.
61 Report No. 2, Frost to Wallace, April 2, 1881, Campaign, TANM, NMSRCA.
62 George W Coe, *Frontier Fighter - The Autobiography of George W. Coe who fought and rode with Billy the Kid* (Boston and New York: Houghton and Mifflin Co., 1934;

2nd ed. Albuquerque: University of New Mexico Press, 1951; The Lakeside Classics ed., ed. by Doyce B. Nunis, Jr. with historical introduction by Doyce B. Nunis, Jr. Chicago: The Lakeside Press, R.R. Donnelly and Sons Co., 1984), pp. 251-252.

[63] Robert W. Duke, "Political History of San Juan County, New Mexico 1876-1926" (master's thesis, University of New Mexico, June 1947), p. 175. This information is from Appendix 3 which is titled "Early San Juan County From Journal of Wm. Locke." A copy of Duke's thesis is available at the San Juan County Archaeological Research Center and Library at the Salmon Ruins near Bloomfield, NM.

[64] *U.S. Census 1880*, Rio Arriba County, NM, r. 803, p. 223d, FLC-CSWS.

[65] Frank Coe to J. Evetts Haley, August 17, 1927, pp. 21-22, JEHC-HMLHC.

[66] Philip J. Rasch, "Feuding at Farmington," *New Mexico Historical Review*, vol. 40, no. 3 (July 1965): p. 217.

[67] O.H. Hanson, "Mob Law on the Lower Animas a Hoax," *La Plata Miner*, July 17, 1880; Mary Atwood, ed., "San Juan County's First Postmasters," *Aztec (NM) Museum Association Newsletter*, August 1, 1984.

[68] *U.S. Census 1870*, Colfax County, NM, r. 893, p. 132b, IA-ACPL. The census shows Halford as Henry H. Holford, a resident of Elizabeth City. National Park Service, Civil War Soldiers and Sailors System, http://www.nps.gov/civilwar/soldiers-and-sailors-database.htm (accessed November 30, 2012). The NPS database shows Halford as Hannibal H. Holford.

[69] George Coe to J. Evetts Haley, August 12, 1927, pp. 7-8, JEHC-HMLHC.

[70] "Take a Reasonable View," *Dolores News*, April 30, 1881 p. 2.

[71] Ibid.

[72] Rasch, "Feuding at Farmington," p. 216.

[73] J.N. Coe, "A Reign of Terror," *Colorado Springs Daily Gazette*, March 27, 1881.

[74] Coe, *Frontier Fighter*, pp. 255-256.

[75] L.W. Coe, "New Light on the Hanging!" *Dolores News*, April 17, 1880, p. 1.

[76] McHenry to Wallace, March 22, 1881, Campaign, TANM, NMSRCA. McHenry lists the members of what he calls "the mob." Given that more than a dozen men were involved in Anderson's lynching, it seems likely that a similar number were involved in his capture. McHenry's list was written a year after Anderson was hung and the number of men in McHenry's so-called mob had grown quite large.

[77] "A Little Hell in New Mexico," *Dolores News*, March 13, 1880, p. 1.

[78] O. Henry Hanson, "Mob Law on the Lower Animas a Hoax," *La Plata Miner* (Silverton, CO), July 17, 1880; C.H. McHenry to Governor Wallace, March 22, 1881, transcribed by Albert W. Puett on March 30, 1881, Campaign, TANM, NMSRCA.

[79] "A Little Hell in New Mexico," *Dolores News*, March 13, 1880, p. 1.

[80] C.H. McHenry to Governor Wallace, March 22, 1881, transcribed by Albert W. Puett on March 30, 1881, Campaign, TANM, NMSRCA. The letter was transcribed onto Executive Office letterhead.

[81] "A Little Hell in New Mexico," *Dolores News*, March 13, 1880, p. 1, portions are as reported in the *Animas City (CO) Southwest*. The *Dolores News* and the McHenry letter both say Anderson and the officers were headed for Taos. The lynching occurred very close to the same time as the boundary change, which took the area out of Taos County and placed it in Rio Arriba County on February 10, 1880.

Tierra Amarilla was the county seat of Rio Arriba County, but Anderson's escorts were probably well aware that Tex would never make it to Taos or Tierra Amarilla.

[82] Agnes Miller Furman, *Tohta - An Early Day History of the Settlement of Farmington And San Juan County, New Mexico 1875-1900* (Wichita Falls, TX: Nortex Press, 1977), pp. 81-82; *U.S. Census 1880*, Rio Arriba County, NM, r. 803, p. 225c, FLC-CSWS. The census taker shows Adams and Crouch as living in the same household. However, that is contradicted by correspondence from Adjutant General Frost to Governor Wallace, April 16, 1881, LSRAGT, TANM, NMSRCA. According to Frost, Adams and Crouch lived on neighboring ranches.

[83] McHenry to Wallace, March 22, 1881, Campaign, TANM, NMSRCA.

[84] *U.S. Census 1880*, Rio Arriba County, NM, r. 803, 225c, FLC-CSWS. The census taker recorded Jane as "Jaen" Adams.

[85] "Flora Vista, N.M." *Dolores News*, March 27, 1880, p. 1.

[86] L.W. Coe, "New Light On the Hanging!" *Dolores News*, April 17, 1880, p. 1; *New Mexico Territorial Census, 1885*, Rio Arriba County, NM, M846, r. 3, La Plata District p. 3, ABCLS. Peter Fox was still living on the La Plata in 1885.

[87] *U.S. Census 1880*, Chaffee County, CO, r. 89, p. 39a, FLC-CSWS.

[88] L.W. Coe, "New Light on the Hanging!" *Dolores News*, April 17, 1880, p. 1.

[89] *U.S. Census 1880*, Chaffee County, CO, r. 89, p. 39a, FLC-CSWS.

[90] O.L. Baskin and Co., comp., *History of the Arkansas Valley, Colorado* (Chicago: O.L. Baskin and Co., 1881), pp. 494 and 528.

[91] L.W. Coe, "New Light on the Hanging!" *Dolores News*, April 17, 1880, p. 1.

[92] "At Last," *Dolores News*, July 24, 1880, p. 1, from the *Denver (CO) Tribune*.

[93] "The First Pack Train of the Season," *La Plata Miner*, May 15, 1880.

[94] "Rico," *La Plata Miner*, April 24, 1880, from the *Animas City Southwest*.

[95] "Rico," *La Plata Miner*, April 24, 1880, from the *Animas City Southwest*; "Colorado's Census," *Lake City (CO) Silver World*, October 1, 1881.

[96] *Dolores News*, October 25, 1879, p. 4 and June 26, 1880, p. 4.

[97] Rev. George M. Darley D.D., *Pioneering in the San Juan* (Chicago, New York and Toronto: Fleming H. Revell Company, 1899), pp. 60-62. http://archive.org/details/pioneeringinsanj00darl (accessed June 9, 2013).

[98] "State Notes," *Colorado Weekly Chieftain*, October 30, 1879, p. 2, from the *Dolores News*.

[99] *Dolores News*, October 25, 1879, p. 4.

[100] "Local Summary," *Dolores News*, May 29, 1880, p. 3. In the 1880s the *Durango Record* and *Dolores News* always spelled the parson's name as Hoge. Some later accounts mistakenly use the name Hogue.

[101] "Parsons Hoge and Griffin," *Durango Wage Earner*, March 14, 1907, p. 4.

[102] Charles Jones, "The Memoirs of Charles Adam Jones," n.d., pp. 170-171, Clifford B. Jones Papers, 1814-1973 and undated, Accession Nos. 96-0122-B and 98-0001-B, Southwest Collection/Special Collections Library, Texas Tech University, Lubbock. Charles Jones's son, Clifford, was a President of Texas Technological College (now Texas Tech University) in the late 1930s and early 1940s.

[103] Darley, *Pioneering in the San Juan*, pp. 141-142.

[104] Jones, "The Memoirs of Charles Adam Jones," p. 171.

[105] "Parsons Hoge and Griffin," *Durango (CO) Wage Earner*, March 14, 1907, p. 4.

[106] John R. Curry, "To The People," *Dolores News*, May 1, 1880, p. 1.

[107] *Farmington (NM) Times Hustler*, October 19, 1934.

[108] "It Was in 1876 That A.F. Miller Saw Adobe-Town Farmington," *Farmington Daily Times*, August 15, 1956.

[109] Jones, "The Memoirs of Charles Adam Jones," p. 96.

[110] Ibid., pp. 1- 3, 9, 14, 19, 34-36 and 44.

[111] Ibid., pp. 44-45, 65-72, 140.

[112] Ibid., pp. 73, 75, 77, 89.

[113] *U.S. Census 1880*, Ouray County, CO, r. 92, p. 176c, ABCLS.

[114] Jones, "The Memoirs of Charles Adam Jones," p. 148.

[115] *Dolores News*, March 19, 1881, p. 3 and "A Terrorized Community," *Dolores News*, May 14, 1881, p. 1. In the March blurb the *News* falsely accuses the "Coe Mob" of having killed William H. Sockrider. The article from May 14th rails against the influence of the "Coe Mob." In his memoirs, Jones references the Simmons Gang and Frank Simmons of Farmington. It is clear that Charles Jones substituted the name Simmons for the name Coe. At the end of the memoirs (p. 380), Charles Jones says, "In some places in this sketch I have purposely substituted fictitious names for the real ones when unpleasant references have been necessary. This in order to not visit any possible unhappiness to connections or descendants who are in no way responsible for the conduct described." George Coe outlived Jones by seven years and it seems Jones substituted the name Simmons with the knowledge that his old nemesis was still alive and kicking. Unfortunately, some subsequent stories about the Stockton Gang relied on Jones's account and other accounts used those accounts, causing the accursed, but falsely named Simmons Gang to live on and on as a self-perpetuating error.

[116] "It Was in 1876 That A.F. Miller Saw Adobe-Town Farmington," *Farmington (NM) Daily Times*, August 15, 1956; Marilu Waybourn and Vernetta Mickey, *Meet Me At The Fair* (Farmington, NM: San Juan County Fair Association, 1984), p. 1.

[117] "Durango's Newspaper Fight," *Alamosa (CO) Journal*, May 21, 1903, p. 2 and "Target Practice," *Durango (CO) Democrat*, August 31, 1906. These newspapers indicate that Frank Hartman fired pistols in anger on at least two occasions.

[118] William Hendrickson to America McHenry, 1892, "Wm. Hendrickson and Brother," *Farmington Farmington (NM) Times Hustler*, Farmington, NM, August 8, 1941, p. 1 and p. 6.

[119] "Wilkinson's Capture," *Dolores News*, September 10, 1881, p. 2, from the *La Plata Miner* and the *Durango Record*.

[120] "Animas City Notes," *Colorado Weekly Chieftain*, April 5, 1877, p. 4; La Plata County, CO, Marriages, 1876-1889, La Plata County, CO, Government Records, Coll. M 028, series 3.2, FLC-CSWS. The La Plata County records say the Wilkinson and Hendrickson wedding occurred on June 19, 1877. The April 5, 1877 issue of the *Chieftain* carries the March 16, 1877 date. La Plata County records show Mrs. Wilkinson's name as Ellen Louisa Wilkinson. Interview with Frank and Sandra Pyle, December 14, 2009. According to the Pyles, the family called Simeon Hendrickson "Simon."

[121] *U.S. Census 1880*, La Plata County, CO, r. 91, p. 577b, ABCLS; *U.S. Census 1880*, Ouray County, CO, r. 92, p. 176c, ABCLS; "Wilkinson's End," *Lake City (CO) Mining Register*, September 9, 1881. This article inferred that Wilkinson was born on October 23, 1861. Bert Wilkinson's name is often spelled Burt in contemporary newspapers. However, in most instances the *Dolores News* uses the

"e" spelling and since one of the owner/editors of the paper, Frank Hartman, was related to Bert, that is the spelling used here. Bert's name is sometimes given as A.W. Wilkinson. One of his maternal uncles was named Albert W. Puett, however it is unclear if his name was also Albert. See the *Dolores News*, February 5, 1881, p. 1.

122 Interview with Frank and Sandra Pyle, December 14, 2009. According to the Pyles, Bert was not alone in his dislike of Simeon Hendrickson, Bert's sister Flora Pyle felt the same way.

123 William Hendrickson to America McHenry, 1892, "Wm. Hendrickson and Brother," *Farmington (NM) Times Hustler*, August 8, 1941, p. 1 and p. 6.

124 *U.S. Census 1880*, Ouray County, CO, r. 92, p. 176c, ABCLS. Bert Wilkinson, Hargo Eskridge, Charles Jones and Frank Hartman are shown living in the same household.

125 *Annual Report of the Secretary of War*, vol. 1 (Washington, DC, 1879), p. 227. http://archive.org/details/annualreportswa68deptgoog (accessed June 9, 2013).

126 Dr. Robert W. Delaney., *Blue Coats, Red Skins and Black Gowns - 100 Years of Fort Lewis* (Durango CO: Durango Herald, 1977), pp. 7-8.

127 "The Selections of Lands on the La Plata Completed," *Dolores News*, September 25, 1880, p. 1, from the *Denver Tribune*.

128 "That Military Post," *Dolores News*, August 21, 1880, p. 4, from the *Animas City Southwest*.

129 "The Selections of Lands," *Dolores News*, Sept. 25, 1880, p. 1, from the *Denver Tribune*.

130 Senator George E. West, "The Oldest Range Man," *Pioneers of the San Juan Country*, vol. 2, comp. and ed. Sarah Platt Decker Chapter D.A.R. (Durango, CO: Sarah Platt Decker Chapter D.A.R., 1946), p. 117.

131 Delaney, *Blue Coats, Red Skins and Black Gowns*, p. 8.

132 *Dolores News*, November 26, 1881, p. 1. Beef cattle were selling for $4.55 to $5.25 per cwt.

133 West, "The Oldest Range Man," p. 117-118.

134 F. Stanley, *Ike Stockton* (Denver: World Press, Inc., 1959), p. 118.

135 "Blood in the San Juan," *Denver Republican*, August 29, 1881, from the *La Plata Miner*. In August 1881, Kid Thomas, Dison Eskridge and Bert Wilkinson were all involved in the murder of Marshal Clate Ogsbury. "Return of Rico's Reinforcements," *Dolores News*, July 9, 1881, p. 2. In June 1881, Kid Thomas joined forces with Dison Eskridge and others on an expedition to rescue Hargo Eskridge, Ike Stockton and others who were besieged by Indians in Utah.

136 Zuni, "Lower Animas Valley," *Dolores News*, October 9, 1880, p. 1. Zuni mentions the army beef supply controversy and complains about the men who lynched Tex Anderson. Zuni may have been Frank Hartman or his sister, Lillie.

137 George Lockhart, "Farmington," *Dolores News*, April 23, 1881, p. 2.

138 Lily Klasner, *My Girlhood Among Outlaws* ed. by Eve Ball (Tucson: The University of Arizona Press, 1972), p. 156; Isaac Hiram Cox, "Tales," transcribed by Joeen Johnson Sutton, 1920s, p. 5. Ike Cox noted that West "had a good many partners" during his time in the cattle business and he "was always the one that put [in] the money and the one that made it," if there was any to be made. Cox would have his own troubles later in life, when he participated in a deadly range war in the early twentieth century.

CHAPTER SEVEN – MARSHAL STOCKTON

[1] Charles Badger Clark, Jr., "A Ranger," *Songs of the Cattle Trail and Cow Camp*, comp. by John A. Lomax (New York: The MacMillan Company, 1920), pp. 134-135.

[2] "Bullets," *Santa Fe Daily New Mexican*, January 14, 1881. The article mentions the "Glorietta" shooting, which may have actually taken place at Baughl's Siding.

[3] *New Mexico v. Isaac Stockton*, case no. 420, August 30, 1879, assault in a menacing manner and case no. 421, August 30, 1879, rescuing a prisoner, Reimbursement request, March 26, 1880 from Colfax County Sheriff, Colfax County District Court Records, NMSRCA.

[4] *U.S. Census 1880*, La Plata County, CO, r. 91, p. 572c, ABCLS.

[5] "Lincoln Refugees," *Santa Fe Weekly New Mexican*, April 26, 1880.

[6] "Bullets," *Santa Fe Daily New Mexican*, January 14, 1881. Also see George Lockhart's letter, "Farmington," *Dolores News* (Rico), April 23, 1881, p. 2. The letter says that Port was forced to leave Animas City and then moved to the Farmington area.

[7] "Take a Reasonable View," *Dolores News* (Rico, CO), April 30, 1881, p. 2.

[8] J.H. Eskridge, "The Other Side," *Dolores News*, Jan. 15 1881, p. 1. Hargo's letter which was dated January 6th was first printed in the *Southwest*, which moved from Animas City to Durango about that time.

[9] From the Brown family plot headstone.

[10] O. Henry Hanson, "Mob Law on the Lower Animas a Hoax," *La Plata Miner* (Silverton, CO), July 17, 1880; C.H. McHenry to Governor Wallace, March 22, 1881, transcribed by Albert W. Puett on March 30, 1881, Campaign, TANM, NMSRCA. This letter specifies the debt as being $40. *U.S. Census 1880*, Rio Arriba County, NM, r. 803, p. 230b, FLC-CSWS.

[11] O.H. Hanson, "Mob Law on the Lower Animas a Hoax," *La Plata Miner*, July 17, 1880.

[12] McHenry to Wallace, March 22, 1881, Campaign, TANM, NMSRCA. McHenry names the members of what he calls "the mob." Topping the list is Lew Coe, followed by Frank and Jasper Coe.

[13] *Dolores News*, May 8, 1880, p. 3, from the *Animas City (CO) Southwest*.

[14] Adjutant General Max Frost to Governor Wallace, April 16, 1881, LSRAGT, TANM, NMSRCA. From TANM roll 78.

[15] "Local and Personal," *Dolores News*, May 15, 1880, p. 3.

[16] *U.S. Census 1880*, Ouray County, CO, r. 92, p. 176c, ABCLS.

[17] Charles Jones, "The Memoirs of Charles Adam Jones," n.d., p. 96, Clifford B. Jones Papers, 1814-1973 and undated, Accession Nos. 96-0122-B and 98-0001-B, Southwest Collection/Special Collections Library, Texas Tech University, Lubbock.

[18] *U.S. Census 1880*, Ouray County, CO, r. 92, p. 176d, ABCLS.

[19] *U.S. Census 1880*, Conejos County, CO, r. 89, p. 195d, IA-ACPL.

[20] H.C. Schroeder, December 31, 1929, La Plata County, pp. 12-13, Civil Works Administration (CWA) Pioneer Interviews, Special Collections, Steven H. Hart Library and Research Center (SHHLRC), History Colorado Center (HCC), from an article in the *Durango (CO) Herald Democrat*, December 31, 1929. On May 15,

1880, the *Dolores News* reported, "Charlie King, the well-known cattleman from Los Pinos" had opened a first class meat market across the street from the offices of the *News*.

[21] *Santa Fe Daily New Mexican*, November 1, 1876.

[22] Dick Dalrymple, "Henry Goodman: Moab's Forgotten Icon," *Canyon Legacy*, Journal of the Dan O'Laurie Canyon Country Museum, vol. 45 (Summer 2002): p. 10, footnote no. 25.

[23] "Business Houses," *Dolores News*, July 24, 1880, p. 3.

[24] Ramon F. Adams, *The Cowman Says It Salty* (Tucson: The University of Arizona Press, 1971), p. 82.

[25] *Dolores News*, June 12, 1880, p. 3.

[26] "Burt Wilkinson Captured by Marion Cook and Ike Stockton," *Dolores News*, September 3, 1881, p. 1. An excerpt from the *Durango Record* which reported that Bert's uncle, "Mr. Puitt" came to see him in the Animas City lockup. *U.S. Census 1880,* Ouray County, CO, r. 92, p. 182a, IA-ACPL; *U.S. Census 1870*, Knox County, IN, r. 331, p. 155a, IA-ACPL. The 1870 census shows that thirty-five-year-old Austin W. Puett was married to Maria L. Puett and had four children, including a nine-year-old son named Oscar B. and a four-year-old son named Albert. Ten years later the census for Ouray County, Colorado showed the following family members living in the same household; eighteen-year-old O.B. Puett, fifteen-year-old A.M. Puett, Jr., forty-four-year-old A.M. Puett and forty-seven-year-old Albt. W. Puett. The penmanship of the census enumerators was at times undecipherable. In the elder Austin's case the 1870 middle initial clearly resembles a "W," but his 1880 middle initial is clearly an "M." *U.S. Census 1880*, Conejos County, CO, r. 89, p. 195d, IA-ACPL.

[27] *Dolores News,* May 15, 1880, p. 3.

[28] Jones, "The Memoirs of Charles Adam Jones," pp. 178-180. Jones identifies Wilkinson's companion as Al Puett, but then says Al was killed at a country dance near Farmington. Os Puett was the one killed at a dance.

[29] Frank Coe, "Frank Coe Answers," *Dolores News*, July 3, 1880, p. 1.

[30] McHenry to Wallace, March 22, 1881, Campaign, TANM, NMSRCA.

[31] Frank Coe, "Frank Coe Answers," *Dolores News*, July 3, 1880, p. 1.

[32] *La Plata Miner,* July 31, 1880; "On the Wing," *La Plata Miner,* June 19, 1880, from the *Del Norte Prospector*.

[33] *U.S. Census 1880,* La Plata County, CO, r. 91, p. 572c, ABCLS; *U.S. Census 1880*, Rio Arriba County, NM, r. 803, p. 225c, FLC-CSWS; *U.S. Census 1860,* Erath County, TX, r. 1293, p. 124b, ABCLS.

[34] *U.S. Census 1880*, La Plata County, CO, r. 91, p. 572c, ABCLS; "Cattle Men," *Durango Herald,* May 13, 1882.

[35] *U.S. Census 1860*, Palo Pinto County, TX, r. 1302, pp. 331b and 332a, IA-ACPL. These two pages show Billy Wilson, his parents and his siblings.

[36] That Animas City's "One Armed" Billy Wilson is also Goodnight's and Loving's "One Armed" Billy Wilson is based in part on the following census records: *U.S. Census 1880*, La Plata County, CO, r. 91, p. 572c, ABCLS; *U.S. Census 1860*, Palo Pinto County, TX, r. 1302, p. 331b and 332a, IA-ACPL.

[37] "Cattle Men," *Durango (CO) Herald,* May 13, 1882. The *Herald* noted that the spring roundup would commence at Thompson's lower camp on the La Plata and

the other would extend into Utah. Another roundup covered the Animas, Florida and Los Pinos valleys. It was noted that W.J. Wilson owned cattle in both areas.

[38] J. Marvin Hunter, comp. and ed., *The Trail Drivers of Texas* (Nashville: Cokesbury Press, 1925), pp. 903-913, http://archive.org/details/traildriversofte00hunt (accessed June 8, 2013). This section of Hunter's classic book contains the riveting firsthand accounts of the fate of Oliver Loving as recalled by Charles Goodnight and Bill Wilson.

[39] "In Memoriam," *Fort Worth (TX) Daily Gazette*, October 6, 1884, p. 4, from the *Weatherford (TX) Times*.

[40] "The Trinidad Murder," *Colorado Weekly Chieftain* (Pueblo, CO), February 15, 1872, p. 2, from the *Trinidad (CO) Enterprise*.

[41] J. Evetts Haley, *Charles Goodnight - Cowman and Plainsman*, new ed. (Norman and London: University of Oklahoma Press, 1949), p. 205-206.

[42] Register of Male Citizens of La Plata County, La Plata County, p. 155, CWA Pioneer Interviews, Special Collections, SHHLRC, HCC. A notation on the register says it was made in 1877 or 1878. It notes that thirty-four-year-old W.J. Wilson was living in Animas City and in the remarks section next to Wilson's name it says "cripple." In J. Marvin Hunter's, the *Trail Drivers of Texas*, page 908, Wilson is identified as William J. Wilson. The census records indicated above, the *Durango Herald* article from May 13, 1882, the description of Wilson as a "cripple," the fact that "One Armed" Billy Wilson's brother, George, spent a short time in the San Juan country in 1877 make it certain that Palo Pinto's Billy Wilson was also Animas City's Billy Wilson.

[43] "Wilson Heard From," *Colorado Weekly Chieftain* (Pueblo), June 28, 1877, p. 3; "Gone Up – George Wilson Dies With His Boots On," *Colorado Weekly Chieftain*, November 1, 1877, p. 1; "The Case of George Wilson," *Colorado Weekly Chieftain*, May 17, 1877, p. 3; "The Victims Of Their Own Folly," *Weekly Arizona Miner*, October 19, 1877, p. 2.

[44] *U.S. Census 1880*, La Plata County, CO, r. 91, p. 572c, ABCLS.

[45] *U.S. Census 1880*, La Plata County, CO, r. 91, pp. 568a-579b, ABCLS.

[46] "Bullets," *Santa Fe Daily New Mexican*, January 14, 1881.

[47] Police Magistrate Court Records, January 1879 – December 1883 and Business Licenses 1879 - 1896, Animas City, CO, Government Records, Coll. M 120, FLC-CSWS and their website at http://swcenter.fortlewis.edu/inventory/AnimasCity.htm#licenses (accessed August 14, 2008).

[48] Andy Chitwood, "Animas City, As I Remember," *Pioneers of the San Juan Country*, vol. 2, comp. and ed. Sarah Platt Decker Chapter D.A.R. (Durango, CO: Sarah Platt Decker Chapter D.A.R., 1946), p. 101 and associated map.

[49] Board of Trustees Ordinance Book, December 24, 1878 - March 13, 1888, Police Magistrate Court Records, January 1879 – December 1883 and Business Licenses 1879 - 1896, Animas City, CO, Government Records, Coll. M 120, FLC-CSWS and their website at http://swcenter.fortlewis.edu/inventory/AnimasCity.htm#licenses (accessed August 14, 2008); Jones, "The Memoirs of Charles Adam Jones," p. 163. Jones describes the arrival of the daily stage in Rico.

[50] Board of Trustees Ordinance Book, December 24, 1878 - March 13, 1888, Animas City, CO, Government Records, Coll. M 120, FLC-CSWS.

[51] *U.S. Census 1880*, Rio Arriba County, NM, r. 803, p. 224b, FLC-CSWS.

[52] "Personalities," *Dolores News*, September 4, 1880, p. 3.

53 Hol Gordon, "Lower Animas and San Juan," *Colorado Weekly Chieftain* (Pueblo), April 18, 1878, p. 1.

54 Mary Atwood, ed., "San Juan County's First Postmasters," *Aztec (NM) Museum Association Newsletter*, August 1, 1984.

55 Board of Trustees Ordinance Book, December 24, 1878 – March 13, 1888, Animas City, CO, Government Records, Coll. M 120, FLC-CSWS.

56 Olive Frazier Cornelius, "Pioneer History and Reminiscences of the San Juan Basin," *Aztec Independent Review*, March 31, 1933; "Shooting in Animas City," *Dolores News*, July 10, 1880, p. 2.

57 *Santa Fe Daily New Mexican*, April 9, 1881. The *New Mexican* mistakenly says the man shot was named Caphart and the shooting occurred in Farmington. The story of the shooting of the nonexistent Mr. Caphart has found its way into latter day accounts.

58 Cornelius, "Pioneer History," *Aztec Independent Review*, March 31, 1933.

59 "Personalities," *Dolores News*, September 4, 1880, p. 3.

60 "Shooting At Animas City," *Dolores News*, Sept. 18, 1880, p. 2; "A Dastardly Act," *La Plata Miner*, Sept. 25, 1880, from the *Animas City Southwest*.

61 "Shooting At Animas City," *Dolores News*, Sept. 18, 1880, p. 2.

62 *U.S. Census 1880*, Ouray County, CO, r. 92, p. 179c, ABCLS.

63 Raymond M. Beckner, *Guns Along the Silvery San Juan* (Cañon City, CO: self-published, 1975), pages not numbered.

64 "A Dastardly Act," *La Plata Miner*, Sept. 25, 1880, from the *Animas City Southwest*.

65 Ibid.

66 "Shooting At Animas City," *Dolores News*, Sept. 18, 1880, p. 2. The *News* says that J.W. Allen, the Black barber, was shaving Stockton "and in some way became engaged in difficulty."

67 Ibid.

68 "A Dastardly Act," *La Plata Miner*, Sept. 25, 1880, from the *Animas City Southwest*.

69 Helen M. Searcy, "Mr. Nagelin Responds," *Pioneers of the San Juan Country*, vol. 1, comp. and ed. Sarah Platt Decker Chapter D.A.R. (Durango, CO: Sarah Platt Decker Chapter D.A.R., 1942), p. 162. Advertisements for his blacksmith shop use the spelling Naegelin.

70 *U.S. Census 1880*, La Plata County, CO, r. 91, p. 575b, ABCLS.

71 Charles Naegelin interviewed by A.L. Soens, January 17, 1934, La Plata County, p. 52, CWA Pioneer Interviews, Special Collections, SHHLRC, HCC.

72 *U.S. Census 1860*, Erath County, TX, r. 1293, pp. 126a and 126b, IA-ACPL.

73 *U.S. Census 1880*, La Plata County, CO, r. 91, p. 575b, ABCLS.

74 *Texas v. George W. Morrison*, box 1, case no. 178, Erath County District Clerk Records.

75 Isaac Hiram Cox, "Tales," transcribed by Joeen Johnson Sutton, 1920s, pp. 99-101, courtesy of Les Sutton. There was a substantial amount of hostility between the Cox family and George Morrison. Ike Cox reported that Morrison owed his father $5000 and "never paid a penny." The Cox family also said that Morrison had welshed on a deal involving two hundred head of Cox cattle. Morrison continually had trouble with other cattle owners as well. Those problems would eventually cost Morrison his life.

[76] "Bayfield the Town," *Pioneers of the San Juan Country,* vol. 4, comp and ed. Sarah Platt Decker Chapter N.S.D.A.R. (Durango, CO: Sarah Platt Decker Chapter N.S.D.A.R., 1961), p. 66.

[77] "Public Surveys," *Colorado Springs Gazette,* April 24, 1875, p. 4. Ranchers, farmers and other settlers needed these surveys so they could perfect their land title. "Squatters' Sovereignty," *Dolores News,* November 15, 1879, p. 4. Squatter's rights were a common consideration throughout the newly settled regions of the west.

[78] "Mary Brothers Recalls Era of Just Rio Arriba," *Farmington Daily Times,* August 15, 1956.

[79] "Public Surveys," *Colorado Springs Gazette,* April 24, 1875, p. 4. New Mexico, Colorado and all of the mountainous states and territories faced similar problems as settlers moved into the river valleys coming out of the Rocky Mountains. Convincing their respective Surveyor General to survey their river valley was a top priority.

[80] Victor Westphall, *The Public Domain in New Mexico - 1854-1891* (Albuquerque: University of New Mexico Press, 1965), pp. 1 and 164-165.

[81] Barry Cooper, "Coopers Were Early Pioneers Here," *Aztec (NM) Museum Association Newsletter,* September 1, 1988.

[82] Ibid.

[83] Cornelius, "Pioneer History," *Aztec Independent Review,* March 24, 1933. Cornelius reported "it was weeks before he [Leslie] could return to Lake City." Cooper, "Coopers Were Early Pioneers Here." This article reports that Leslie returned to Colorado after recuperating for two weeks. According to an article first reported in the *Rosita (CO) Index,* which appeared under the headline "State News," *Fairplay (CO) Flume* of May 1, 1879, p. 2, there was a John Leslie who reportedly owned some "very valuable mining property in San Juan." George Lockhart, "Farmington," *Dolores News,* April 23, 1881, p. 2. Lockhart's letter says that after clubbing the "negro" in Animas City with his pistol, Stockton moved to the lower Animas and did the same thing to a "white man."

[84] "Bullets," *Santa Fe Daily New Mexican,* January 14, 1881.

[85] Cooper, "Coopers Were Early Pioneers Here." Barry Cooper reports that Mrs. Cooper eventually moved to Durango. She married a third time and died on May 7, 1932 in Pueblo, Colorado. Her great-grandson Barry Cooper was Superintendent of the Aztec Ruins National Monument in the 1980s. Interview with Frank and Sandra Pyle, December 14, 2009. According to the Pyles, the descendants of Joel Estes Sr. lamented that he traded his Estes Park property for a span of oxen.

[86] Mary Alverda Estes Taylor interviewed by Anna Florence Robison, March 9, 1934, Montezuma County, pp. 98-99, 104 and 107, CWA Pioneer Interviews, Special Collections, SHHLRC, HCC. Mrs. Taylor also says that the Estes Park property was traded for a team of oxen.

[87] Cooper, "Coopers Were Early Pioneers Here."

[88] Cornelius, "Pioneer History," *Aztec Independent Review,* June 16, 1933. In those days, the loss of the breadwinner made life especially difficult for the surviving family. After Port's callous treatment of Mrs. Cooper, the community's heart went out to the widow and they did their best to help her. It was during the winter of 1881 that Mrs. Cooper worked as the Aztec school teacher. The little school house

was reportedly located near the Animas River, probably close to the current location of the old Aztec bridge. The article said the school house was on property that later became the Current family pear orchard.

CHAPTER EIGHT – HERE I AM, COME ON BOYS

[1] Larry Chittenden, "The Cowboys' Christmas Ball," *Songs of the Cattle Trail and Cow Camp*, comp. by John A. Lomax (New York: The MacMillan Company, 1920), p. 114.

[2] "The First Spike," *Rocky Mountain News* (Denver, CO), July 29, 1871, p. 1.

[3] "City and Vicinity," *Colorado Daily Chieftain* (Pueblo, CO), February 22, 1876, p. 4.

[4] "Railroad Notes," *Colorado Weekly Chieftain* (Pueblo, CO), July 4, 1878, p. 3.

[5] E.B.C., "On the Road," *Dolores News* (Rico, CO), February 19, 1881, p. 1.

[6] "On the Wing," *La Plata Miner* (Silverton, CO), June 19, 1880.

[7] "The Denver and Rio Grande," *Colorado Weekly Chieftain* as reported by the *Chicago Tribune*, November 15, 1877, p. 2..

[8] "A Mile a Day," *La Plata Miner*, March 13, 1880.

[9] "Durango," *Dolores News*, August 14, 1880, p. 1, from the *Animas City (CO) Southwest*.

[10] "Durango Doings," *Dolores News*, September 18, 1880, p. 2.

[11] "Denver and Rio Grande R'y Extension!" *Dolores News*, August 7, 1880, p. 1.

[12] "Ollapodrida, *Colorado Miner* (Georgetown), December 18, 1880, p. 1. This information was probably obtained from the *Animas City Southwest*.

[13] Report No. 2, Adjutant General Max Frost to Governor Wallace, April 2, 1881, and Report No. 3, Frost to Wallace, April 3, 1881, includes an extract of an April 2nd letter from C.R. Fife to T.D. Burns, Campaign, TANM, NMSRCA.

[14] "Our Mines," *Dolores News*, July 24, 1880, p. 2.

[15] "Personalities," *Dolores News*, Sept 4, 1880, p. 3.

[16] Olive Frazier Cornelius, "Pioneer History and Reminiscences of the San Juan Basin," *Aztec (NM) Independent Review*, May 12, 1933.

[17] *U.S. Census 1880*, Rio Arriba County, NM, r. 803, pp. 224b and 225c, FLC-CSWS. The census provides some haphazard idea of the relative locations of the residents on the Animas River in 1880, including Bohannon and Jake E. Bull. *U.S. Census 1870*, Erath County, TX, r. 1583, p. 470a, IA-ACPL. This census shows Jacob E. Bull, living with his family and brother, one-time Cox herder, Solon Bull.

[18] L.W.C., "Farmington Notes," *Cimarron (NM) News and Press*, September 9, 1880, Western New Mexico University, Miller Library.

[19] George Coe to J. Evetts Haley, August 18, 1927, p. 7, JEHC-HMLHC.

[20] L.W.C, "Farmington Notes," *Cimarron (NM) News and Press*, September 9, 1880.

[21] Isaac Hiram Cox, "Tales," transcribed by Joeen Johnson Sutton, 1920s, p. 78, courtesy of Les Sutton.

[22] "Personalities," *Dolores News*, Sept 4, 1880, p. 3 and *Dolores News*, October 2, 1880, p. 3; *U.S. Census 1880*, Ouray County, CO, r. 92, p. 176c, IA-ACPL.

[23] Chas. L. Valiton, "Forty-five Years in Colorado," *Silverton (CO) Standard*, June 5, 1926.

[24] George Lockhart, "Farmington," *Dolores News*, April 23, 1881, p. 2.

25 "Will Exterminate Cattle 'Rustlers,' " *Coconino Sun* (Flagstaff, AZ), August 9, 1912, p. 6.

26 Ramon F. Adams, *The Cowman Says It Salty* (Tucson: The University of Arizona Press, 1971), p. 84.

27 *U.S. Census 1880*, Rio Arriba County, NM, r. 803, p. 226a, FLC-CSWS.

28 *Santa Fe Daily New Mexican*, February 18, 1881. This article mentions Mr. L. Hughes of Ilfeld and Company. *U.S. Census 1880*, Santa Fe County, NM, r. 804, p. 71c, IA-ACPL.

29 "Bullets," *Santa Fe Daily New Mexican*, January 14, 1881.

30 W.P. Hendrickson to Colonel Crofton, March 9, 1881, FLMP, Coll. M 118, box 1, series 4, folder 37, FLC-CSWS.

31 *Durango (CO) Weekly Record*, January 10, 1881.

32 J.N. Coe, "A Reign of Terror," *Colorado Springs Daily Gazette*, March 27, 1881.

33 Letter from Military District of New Mexico to Fort Lewis (correspondents names not given and titles unclear), September 2, 1880, FLMP, Coll. M 118, B 1, S 4, F 29, FLC-CSWS; First Lieutenant Cavenaugh to Fort Lewis, September 30, 1880, FLMP, Coll. M 118, B 1, S 4, F 30, FLC-CSWS; First Lieutenant Cavenaugh to Fort Lewis, October 28, 1881, FLMP, Coll. M 118, B 1, S 4, F 32, FLC-CSWS; First Lieutenant Cavenaugh to W.B. Haines, October 27, 1880, FLMP, Coll. M 118, B 1, Se 4, F 32, FLC-CSWS.

34 The Nance and Thompson relationship is from a copy of the Thompson family tree the author received from George W. Thompson.

35 *U.S. Census 1860*, Fannin County, TX, r. 1293, pp. 211a and 211b, IA-ACPL.

36 William S. Speer and Hon. John Henry Brown, ed., *The Encyclopedia of the New West* (Marshall, TX: The United States Biographical Publishing Company, 1881; 2nd ed. Easley, SC: Southern Historical Press, The Rev. S. Emmett Lucas, Jr., 1978), p. 58.

37 From an undated copy of the obituary for Martha Jane Thompson given to the author by George W. Thompson. Martha Jane was the wife of Doctor A. Thompson, who was the brother of George W. Thompson, the Trinidad cattleman.

38 The Enloe ancestors are shown in George Thompson's biography in William S. Speer and Hon. John Henry Brown's, *The Encyclopedia of the New West*, p. 58. As for Lincoln's paternity, websites espousing and debunking this theory are legion. Thompson descendants contacted by the author were aware that there was a family connection to Lincoln.

39 *Memphis (TN) Daily Appeal*, July 11, 1868, p. 2.

40 James M. Smallwood, Barry A. Crouch and Larry Peacock, *Murder and Mayhem – The War of Reconstruction in Texas* (College Station: Texas A&M University Press, 2003), pp. 65-69.

41 "A Good Man Gone," *Raton (NM) Comet*, June 8, 1883. The *Comet* provides a southerner's view of Bowman's alliance with Robert Lee.

42 *U.S. Census 1870*, Harrison County, MO, r. 778, p. 180b, IA-ACPL.

43 *U.S. Census 1880*, Las Animas County, CO, r. 92, p. 120c, IA-ACPL; *U.S. Census 1860*, Fannin County, TX, r. 1293, p. 212, IA-ACPL; Rube Baldock's father may have been the James Baldock who was killed by the forces of Bob Lee. In 1870 Rube and his sister and mother were living in Albany, Missouri without a

husband or father. Mrs. Baldock was working as a servant at her brother's hotel. See *U.S. Census 1870*, Gentry County, MO, r. 776, p. 544a, IA-ACPL.

44 "Death of I.W. Lacy," *Cimarron (NM) News and Press*, May 19, 1881, from the *Trinidad Times*.

45 "Stabbing Affray at Durango," *La Plata Miner*, November 27, 1886, from the *Durango Herald; The San Juan* (Silverton, CO), November 25, 1886.

46 Bernard James Byrne, M.D., *A Frontier Army Surgeon - Life In Colorado In The Eighties*, 2nd rev. and enlarged ed. (New York: Exposition Press, 1962), pp. 34-35.

47 Zuni, "Lower Animas Valley," *Dolores News*, October 9, 1880, p. 1; Lillie Hartman, "Between the Navajoes and the Southern Utes," *Dolores News*, November 15, 1879, p. 1.

48 J.H. Eskridge, "The Other Side," *Dolores News*, January 15, 1881, p. 1, from a letter to the *Animas City Southwest*.

49 *U.S. Census 1880*, Rio Arriba County, NM, r. 803, p. 230b, FLC-CSWS.

50 C.H. McHenry to Governor Wallace, March 22, 1881, transcribed by Albert W. Puett on March 30, 1881, Campaign, TANM, NMSRCA.

51 National Park Service, Civil War Soldiers and Sailors System, http://www.nps.gov/civilwar/soldiers-and-sailors-database.htm (accessed November 30, 2012).

52 McHenry to Wallace, March 22, 1881, Campaign, TANM, NMSRCA.

53 Report No. 2, Frost to Wallace, April 2, 1881, Campaign, TANM, NMSRCA.

54 "Refutation of a Slander," *Dolores News*, April 23, 1881, p. 1, from the *Durango Record;* George B Anderson, comp., *History of New Mexico - Its Resources and People*, vol. 2 (Los Angeles, Chicago and New York: Pacific States Publishing Co., 1907), p. 876. Anderson's history notes that Boyd Vaughan's sister was Nettie Locke. Charles H. Leckenby, *The Tread of Pioneers* (Steamboat Spring, CO: The Pilot Press, 1945), pp. 84-92. Leckenby describes the capture of David Lant and Harry Tracy.

55 "Durango and Animas City," *Dolores News*, November 27, 1880, p. 4.

56 *Durango (CO) Herald*, November 17, 1881, Durango Public Library.

57 Mary C. Ayres, "The Founding of Durango, Colorado," *The Colorado Magazine*, vol. 7, no. 3 (May 1930): pp. 89-90.

58 "Durango," *La Plata Miner*, October 23, 1880, from the *Animas City Southwest;* "Durango Doings," *La Plata Miner*, November 27, 1880.

59 "Durango Doings," *La Plata Miner*, November 27, 1880.

60 William Devere, "Tramp Poet of the West," *Jim Marshall's New Pianner - And Other Western Stories* (New York, Chicago and London: M. Witmark and Sons, 1908), p. 37.

61 "Durango," *Denver (CO) Republican*, August 6, 1881.

62 "Durango Doings," *La Plata Miner*, November 27, 1880.

63 Ibid. C.O. Ziegenfuss, "Ike Stockton," *Denver Republican*, August 12, 1881. The *Republican* reported Ike's trip to Texas.

64 "Animas City Items," *La Plata Miner*, December 11, 1880, from the *Animas City Southwest*.

65 Sarah Ann Menefee (Mrs. William A.) interviewed by A.L. Soens, March 23, 1934, La Plata County, pp. 99-100, CWA Pioneer Interviews, Special Collections, SHHLRC, HCC.

66 "Dolores Horses at Chicago," *Dolores News*, September 5, 1885, p. 2 The *News* reported that in late August Charles Johnson raced Jim Douglas and Red Girl in

Chicago, probably at the Washington Park Club. At that time Johnson had moved from the Pine River and lived at the Big Bend of the Dolores River. Hattie Johnson Porter (Charles Johnson's daughter) interviewed by Anna Florence Robison, March 26, 1934, Montezuma County, pp. 173, 176, CWA Pioneer Interviews, Special Collections, SHHLRC, HCC.

[67] "Robbery," *La Plata Miner*, December 18, 1880, from the *Animas City Southwest*.

[68] Elbert (Al) Nunn interviewed by Anna Florence Robison, March 28, 1934, Montezuma County, pp. 198-199 and 206, CWA Pioneer Interviews, Special Collections, SHHLRC, HCC.

[69] On December 5, 1874 the *Santa Fe New Mexican* reported that Charles Johnson was scheduled to race Blue Bird in Santa Fe against Maria Grey, a horse owned by O. Willburn. The stakes were one thousand dollars a side.

[70] "Robbery," *La Plata Miner*, December 18, 1880, from the *Animas City Southwest*. Additional information on Charles "Race Horse" Johnson and this incident can also be found under the headline, "Durango," in the *Denver Republican*, March 29, 1881. The writer of the article also mentions meeting Charles Johnson at the Pine River Stage Station.

[71] Cornelius, "Pioneer History," *Aztec Independent Review*, March 24, 1933; "Capture of the Stolen Horses," *Animas City Southwest*, December 18, 1880, FLC-CSWS. This report identifies the posse members. Cox, "Tales," p. 2. Cox said Johnson's runner met them at the river crossing three miles above Bondad.

[72] "Capture of the Stolen Horses," *Animas City Southwest*, December 18, 1880. Dave [Mur]ray's name was illegible, but it is likely that he was David Murray, who was a thirty-three-year-old stockman who is shown as living on the Florida River. No other names in the La Plata County Census seem to come close. See the *U.S. Census 1880*, La Plata County, CO, r. 91, p. 574c, ABCLS.

[73] Cox, "Tales," pp. 2-3. Cox says the "fine mair" fell. Al Nunn says Blue Bird "was crippled" during the pursuit and later died. See Elbert (Al) Nunn interviewed by Anna Florence Robison, March 28, 1934, Montezuma County, p. 200, CWA Pioneer Interviews, Special Collections, SHHLRC, HCC.

[74] "Capture of the Stolen Horses," *Animas City Southwest*, December 18, 1880.

[75] Elbert (Al) Nunn interviewed by Anna Florence Robison, March 28, 1934, Montezuma County, pp. 199-200, CWA Pioneer Interviews, Special Collections, SHHLRC, HCC.

[76] "Capture of the Stolen Horses," *Animas City Southwest*, December 18, 1880.

[77] "Another Tragedy," *Durango Weekly Record*, January 10, 1881.

[78] "Durango," *Denver Republican*, March 29, 1881.

[79] Elbert (Al) Nunn interviewed by Anna Florence Robison, March 28, 1934, Montezuma County, p. 200, CWA Pioneer Interviews, Special Collections, SHHLRC, HCC.

[80] "Another Tragedy," *Durango Weekly Record*, January 10, 1881.

[81] Cox, "Tales," p. 3. According to Ike Cox, the horse thief who died was shot at least once by Johnson, saving George Cox's life. Cox only mentions Johnson the race horse owner, not Johnson's son, in his collection of "Tales."

[82] Cornelius, "Pioneer History," *Aztec Independent Review*, March 24, 1933. Cornelius reports that Thomas B. (Cap) Hart was part of the posse. That seems unlikely, given that only five months before Stockton had shot Cap Hart in the mouth.

83 Cox, "Tales," p. 3. Cox reported that the dead man wore only one diamond ring.

84 "An Unprovoked Murder," *La Plata Miner*, January 8, 1881, from the *Durango Daily Record*.

85 Robert W. Duke, "Political History of San Juan County, New Mexico 1876-1926" (master's thesis, University of New Mexico, June 1947), p. 169, this portion from "Extracts From Letter by W.P. Hendrickson;" *U.S. Census 1880*, Rio Arriba County, NM, r. 803, p. 222a, FLC-CSWS.

86 "An Unprovoked Murder," *La Plata Miner*, January 8, 1881, from the *Durango Daily Record*.

87 *U.S. Census 1880,* Ouray County, CO, r. 92, p. 182a, IA-ACPL.

88 *U.S. Census, 1880*, Rio Arriba County, NM, r. 803, p. 230b, FLC-CSWS.

89 W.P. Hendrickson to Colonel Crofton, March 9, 1881, FLMP, Coll. M 118, box 1, series 4, folder 37, FLC-CSWS.

90 "Published in a Tent," *Durango (CO) Weekly Record*, January 10, 1881.

91 J.H. Eskridge, "The Other Side," *Dolores News*, January 15, 1881, p. 1, from a letter to the *Animas City Southwest*.

92 "An Unprovoked Murder," *La Plata Miner*, January 8, 1881, from the *Durango Daily Record*. The misinformation that Oscar's last name was Pruett and not Puett was sprinkled throughout the *Record's* account. It is a misspelling that has found its way into several latter day articles and books.

93 Ibid.

94 J.H. Eskridge, "That Shooting at Hamlet's," *Durango Weekly Record*, January 10, 1881.

95 Miss C.L. Garrett and response by the *Record*, "More About the Killings at Hamlet's," *Durango Weekly Record*, January 22, 1881; *U.S. Census 1880*, Conejos County, CO, r. 89, p. 186c, IA-ACPL; *Alamosa (CO) Journal*, April 17, 1884, p. 2. This is an advertisement for I.W. Hill, the successor firm to Field and Hill. Advertisement for Ed Schiffer and Co., *Durango Weekly Record*, April 30, 1881.

96 J.N. Coe, "A Reign of Terror," *Colorado Springs Daily Gazette*, March 27, 1881.

97 J.H. Eskridge, "The Other Side," *Dolores News*, January 15, 1881, p. 1, from a letter to the *Animas City Southwest*.

98 James Garrett, "A Communication," *Dolores News*, January 29, 1881, p. 2. A description of the San Juan country's pioneer dances and the issuing of numbers was provided by Sherman Howe in "Sherman Howe Student of Ancient Ones," *Farmington Daily Times,* August 15, 1956. Howe noted that some of the cowboys "could dance very well but others could only stomp around like old cows." He likened the sound of the cowboy's high heeled boots on the floor as being similar to the roar of a band of horses running across a plank bridge. He noted that watching some of the cowboys in their clumsy attempts to keep up with the changes of the caller was as much as much fun as being on the dance floor. *U.S. Census 1880*, Rio Arriba County, NM, r. 803, p. 225d, FLC-CSWS, source for the age of Lee Hamblet.

99 J.H. Eskridge, "The Other Side," *Dolores News*, January 15, 1881, p. 1, from a letter to the *Animas City Southwest*.

100 James Garrett, "A Communication," *Dolores News*, January 29, 1881, p. 2.

101 J.H. Eskridge, "The Other Side," *Dolores News*, January 15, 1881, p. 1, from a letter to the *Animas City Southwest*.

NOTES 419

[102] James Garrett, "A Communication," *Dolores News*, January 29, 1881, p. 2.

[103] "Refutation of a Slander," *Dolores News*, April 23, 1881, p. 1, from the *Durango Record*.

[104] J.N. Coe, "A Reign of Terror," *Colorado Springs Daily Gazette*, March 27, 1881.

[105] *Durango Weekly Record*, February 26, 1881; Arrest records for early Durango show the arrest of Pete Haverty for fighting and carrying a concealed weapon in November 1881. See Durango, Colorado, Police Ledgers Index, List of Arrests, 1881-1885: by name, Durango, CO, City Government Records, Coll. M 027, series 6.6, 2003 and 2004. FLC-CSWS, from their website at http://swcenter.fortlewis.edu/inventory/DgoArrests18811885.htm#1881-1885 (accessed May 12, 2009).

[106] J. H. Eskridge, "The Other Side," *Dolores News*, January 15, 1881, p. 1, from a letter to the *Animas City Southwest*.

[107] "Refutation of a Slander," *Dolores News*, April 23, 1881, p. 1, from the *Durango Record*.

[108] J.H. Eskridge, "The Other Side," *Dolores News*, January 15, 1881, p. 1, from a letter to the *Animas City Southwest*.

[109] Raymond M. Beckner, *Guns Along the Silvery San Juan* (Cañon City, CO: self-published, 1975), pages not numbered; Barbara Marriott, *Outlaw Tales of New Mexico* (Guilford, CT: TwoDot/Globe Pequot Press, 2007), p. 36.

[110] J.H. Eskridge, "The Other Side," *Dolores News*, January 15, 1881, p. 1, from a letter to the *Animas City Southwest;* James Garrett, "A Communication," *Dolores News*, January 29 1881 p. 2; Miss C.L. Garrett, "More About the Killings at Hamlet's," *Durango Weekly Record*, January 22, 1881; "An Unproved Murder," *La Plata Miner*, January 8, 1881, from the *Durango Daily Record;* "A Rico Boy Shot," *Dolores News,* January 8, 1881, p. 3, from the *Animas City Southwest;* McHenry to Wallace, March 22, 1881, Campaign, TANM, NMSRCA; George Lockhart, "Farmington," *Dolores News*, April 23, 1881, p. 2.

[111] Duke, "Political History of San Juan County," p. 169, this portion from "Extracts From Letter by W.P. Hendrickson;" *U.S. Census 1880*, Rio Arriba County, NM, r. 803, p. 230b, FLC-CSWS. Provides the approximate age of John "Doc" Brown.

[112] Anderson, *History of New Mexico,* vol. 2, p. 867.

[113] Duke, "Political History of San Juan County," p. 169, this portion from "Extracts From Letter by W.P. Hendrickson."

[114] Duke, "Political History of San Juan County," pp. 169-170, this portion from "Extracts From Letter by W.P. Hendrickson." For the Pyle, Puett and Wilkinson relationship see the "Wilkinson's Capture," *Dolores News*, September 10, 1881, p. 2, from the *La Plata Miner* and the *Durango Record*. See also the *U.S. Census 1880*, Rio Arriba County, NM, r. 803, p. 230b, FLC-CSWS; *U.S. Census 1870,* Henry County, IA, r. 395, p. 175b, IA-ACPL, see the Mahlon Wilkinson family in Center Township; Frost to Wallace, April 16, 1881, LSRAGT, TANM, NMSRCA. This letter identifies Oscar Puett as Al Puett's nephew. Anderson., comp., *History of New Mexico*, vol. 2, p. 866. Anderson credits the arrival of William Locke with the erection of Farmington's first school house. J.H. Eskridge, "The Shooting at Hamlet's," *Durango Weekly Record*, January 10, 1881. Hargo says Austin Puett and his wife were living in Pagosa Springs. The *Farmington (NM) Republican*, October 30, 1929, reported the death of Flora W. Pyle in California and noted that the Pyle

family lived on the San Juan River on the peninsula in 1878. This article was reprinted in the *Farmington Daily Times* on October 30, 2011.

[115] Lillian Hartman Johnson, "In Memory of Orville D. Pyle," n.d., Courtesy of Frank and Sandra Pyle.

[116] Harry V. Pyle (son of O.D. Pyle) interviewed by Anna Florence Robison, March 16, 1934, Montezuma County, p. 135, CWA Pioneer Interviews, Special Collections, SHHLRC, HCC.

[117] *U.S. Census 1880*, Rio Arriba County, NM, r. 803, p. 230b, FLC-CSWS.

[118] Duke, "Political History of San Juan County," pp. 169-170, this portion from "Extracts From Letter by W.P. Hendrickson;" "Death of Seth Welfoot," *Dolores News*, March 18, 1882, p. 3; *U.S. Census 1880*, Rio Arriba County, NM, r. 803, p. 224a, FLC-CSWS.

[119] "Charles Holliday McHenry 1838-1913," *Bulletins Pioneer Association San Juan County, New Mexico*, 1953 to 1976 (1953): p. 15, Farmington (NM) Public Library.

[120] Duke, "Political History of San Juan County," pp. 169-170, this portion from "Extracts From Letter by W.P. Hendrickson;" *U.S. Census 1880*, Rio Arriba County, NM, r. 803, p. 222a, FLC-CSWS.

[121] "Fatal Shooting at Durango," *Dolores News*, January. 1, 1881, p. 2.

[122] "Wilkinson's Capture," *Dolores News*, September 10, 1881, p. 2, from the *La Plata Miner* and the *Durango Record*.

[123] *Durango Weekly Record*, January 10, 1881.

[124] *Dolores News*, February. 5, 1881, p. 1. This article mentions Jerry Bartol's involvement. The Rector of Saint Mark's Church, "Saint Mark's Church's 'Parson' Hogue," *Pioneers of the San Juan Country*, vol. 4, comp. and ed. Sarah Platt Decker Chapter of the N.S.D.A.R. (Durango, CO: Sarah Platt Decker Chapter N.S.D.A.R., 1961), p. 97. This article identifies the Christmas Eve Durango shooting victim as Samuel Swinford.

[125] Interview with Frank Pyle, November 18, 2009.

[126] "Fatal Shooting at Durango," *Dolores News*, January 1, 1881, p. 2.

[127] Ibid. "More Shooting at Durango," *Dolores News*, March 26, 1881, p. 1, from the *Durango Record*. At the time of the shooting the *News* reported that Marshal Sullivan was several blocks away. Even though Durango was not incorporated until the spring of 1881, newspaper articles and pioneer accounts often refer to various citizens as being the "marshal" of Durango during this period. The marshals were probably commissioned as deputy sheriffs although it is possible that they may have received some pay through subscriptions offered by the saloon and gambling hall owners, who needed someone to keep order.

[128] "Shot In a Dance Hall," *Durango Weekly Record*, January 10, 1881.

[129] *Durango Weekly Record*, January 10, 1881.

CHAPTER NINE – VIGILANTES AND RUFFIANS

[1] Margaret Ashmun, "The Vigilantes," *Songs of the Cattle Trail and Cow Camp*, comp. by John A. Lomax (New York: The MacMillan Company, 1920), p. 150.

[2] "Refutation of a Slander," *Dolores News* (Rico, CO), April 23, 1881, p. 1, from the *Durango (CO) Record*.

[3] C.O. Ziegenfuss, "Ike Stockton," *Denver (CO) Republican*, August 12, 1881.

[4] "Bullets," *Santa Fe Daily New Mexican*, January 14, 1881.

[5] Adjutant General Max Frost to Governor Wallace, April 16, 1881, LSRAGT, TANM, NMSRCA; "Historial Nubs of Early Day Farmington," *Farmington (NM) Times Hustler*, April 5, 1940, San Juan College Library Microfilm Archives. Frank Wood recalls learning that Alf Graves worked as a Texas Ranger with fellow Ranger K. Meek who was a brother of Frank's mother.

[6] Report No. 5, Frost to Wallace, April 5, 1881 and Frost to Wallace, April 16, 1881, LSRAGT, TANM, NMSRCA.

[7] Undated, unsigned scribbled notation probably associated with the wording found in the letter from Frost to Wallace, April 16, 1881, LSRAGT, TANM, NMSRCA. The scribbled notation was apparently initially attached to the letter from C.H. McHenry to Governor Wallace, March 22, 1881, transcribed by Albert W. Puett on March 30, 1881, Campaign, TANM, NMSRCA.

[8] Walter A. and James Clayton, "Letter from Jamestown, California," *Bulletins Pioneer Association San Juan County, New Mexico*, 1953 to 1976 (1954): p. 8, Farmington (NM) Public Library.

[9] *U.S. Census 1880*, Rio Arriba County, NM, r. 803, p. 224a, FLC-CSWS.

[10] *U.S. Census 1880*, Ouray County, CO, r. 92 p. 162c, IA-ACPL.

[11] *U.S. Census 1880*, Rio Arriba County, NM, r. 803, p. 224a, FLC-CSWS.

[12] McHenry to Wallace, March 22, 1881, Campaign, TANM, NMSRCA.

[13] Joe E. Boettcher, "Who Killed Porter Stockton?" n.d., p. 11, Aztec (NM) Museum. Joe Boettcher, of Aztec, was a student and teacher of New Mexico history. He says he heard the story from Harry McWilliams about 90 years after Port Stockton was killed. That would be about 1971. A young Harry McWilliams participated in the last Cox roundup. In his twilight years, he was well known for the richness of the details he recalled from the old days.

[14] C.O. Ziegenfuss, "Ike Stockton," *Denver Republican*, August 12, 1881.

[15] Ed Thomas, Jr. "George and Mary Ann (Molly) Thomas Lockhart," The History Committee of the Fort Lewis Mesa Reunion, *Pioneers of Southwest La Plata County Colorado* (Bountiful, UT: Family History Publishers, 1994), p. 296.

[16] Frank Hartman, "Tragedy of the Toll Road," *Alamosa (CO) Empire*, April 16 and April 23, 1919. Hartman was traveling with Lockhart when events spiraled out of control south of Conejos.

[17] *U.S. Census 1880*, Rio Arriba County, NM, r. 803, pp. 223c and 223d, FLC-CSWS.

[18] Boettcher, "Who Killed Porter Stockton?" p. 11.

[19] George B. Anderson., comp., *History of New Mexico - Its Resources and People*, vol. 2 (Los Angeles, Chicago and New York: Pacific States Publishing Co., 1907), p. 870.

[20] Patti Chavez, "A Short History, 1876-2003," Research by Sergeant Dewayne Faverino, San Juan County Sheriff's Office [New Mexico], n.d., http://www.sjcso.com/OfInterest/AgencyHistory/history.pdf (accessed March 2, 2009).

[21] Robert W. Duke, *San Juan County, New Mexico: The Early Years* (Farmington, NM: San Juan County Historical Society, 1999), p. 17.

[22] "A Dead Horse Thief," *Dolores News*, September 29, 1883, p. 2. In September 1883 Joe Caldwell was part of a group of thirteen cowboys from the La Plata valley area who formed a punitive posse whose members included George W. Thompson (the elder George W's nephew), Will (Bill) Thompson, Pete Winkle and Matt Caviness. The men were after four horse thieves who had made their living in and

around La Plata County for close to three years. They had recently swindled a Rico livery owner and followed that up by stealing over a dozen horses in the La Plata valley. The posse caught up with the thieves in Cañon Blanco (New Mexico) and killed one man. The *News* noted that the *Durango Herald* later reported that a few days afterwards the three other thieves sought safety and turned themselves into Rio Arriba County Deputy Sheriff Willets.

[23] George Coe to J. Evetts Haley, August 12, 1927, pp. 6-7, JEHC-HMLHC.

[24] "The Rio Arriba Troubles," *Santa Fe Daily New Mexican*, April 27, 1881.

[25] "Bullets," *Santa Fe Daily New Mexican*, January 14, 1881.

[26] George Coe to J. Evetts Haley, August 12, 1927, p. 6, JEHC-HMLHC.

[27] Boettcher, "Who Killed Porter Stockton?" pp. 8 and 11-13. According to McWilliams, while Tom Nance was shooting Porter Stockton, Alf Graves fumbled around for the pistol buried in his mackinaw. That may be, but Graves certainly brought a rifle to the shootout as well. "Bullets," *Santa Fe Daily New Mexican*, January 14, 1881. This account says Stockton's wife grabbed a Winchester.

[28] Frost to Wallace, April 16, 1881, LSRAGT, TANM, NMSRCA.

[29] "Another Tragedy," *Durango Weekly Record*, January 10, 1881.

[30] Ibid.

[31] "Bullets," *Santa Fe Daily New Mexican*, January 14, 1881.

[32] *Las Vegas (NM) Daily Optic*, January 17, 1881.

[33] "Durango [Deviltries?]," *Las Vegas (NM) Daily Optic*, March 29, 1881.

[34] McHenry to Wallace, March 22, 1881, Campaign, TANM, NMSRCA.

[35] C.O. Ziegenfuss, "Ike Stockton," *Denver Republican*, August 12, 1881.

[36] *Dolores News*, Jan. 22, 1881, p. 3. The *News* does not credit the *Durango Record*, but they also carried the eighteen assailant version of the story.

[37] "A Call On Stockton," *Sedalia (MO) Weekly Bazoo*, February 1, 1881.

[38] C.O. Ziegenfuss, "Ike Stockton," *Denver Republican*, August 12, 1881.

[39] "Think of It!" *Dolores News*, April 30, 1881, p. 2.

[40] "Bullets," *Santa Fe Daily New Mexican*, January 14, 1881.

[41] Duke, *San Juan County, New Mexico: The Early Years*, p. 18.

[42] *Durango (CO) Weekly Record*, February 5, 1881.

[43] Frost to Wallace, April 16, 1881, LSRAGT, TANM, NMSRCA.

[44] Robert W. Duke, "Political History of San Juan County, New Mexico 1876-1926" (master's thesis, University of New Mexico, June 1947), p. 169-170, this portion from "Extracts From Letter by W.P. Hendrickson."

[45] Arrington, John B. and Eleanor D. MacDonald, *The San Juan Basin - My Kingdom Was A County* (Denver: Green Mountain Press, 1970), p. 140. Boettcher, "Who Killed Porter Stockton?" pp. 2, 3 and 7. During Boettcher's lifetime the land where Porter Stockton was killed and buried was commonly known as the Brett place because it had been owned by George Brett and his wife, Estella. Brett farmed the land on the south side of the Animas River beginning in the very late 1800s and it remained in the family into the 1920s. County clerk records indicate that the Brett's land began about one quarter mile upriver from the Flora Vista bridge and extended for another mile upriver. Boettcher reported that up until the 1970s Stockton's grave was marked by a single post, but the post was later removed and several mobile homes were moved into the area. Such is progress.

[46] C.O. Ziegenfuss, "Ike Stockton," *Denver Republican*, August 12, 1881.

[47] J.N. Coe, "A Reign of Terror," *Colorado Springs Daily Gazette*, March 27, 1881.

⁴⁸ "The Mob's Madness," *Dolores News*, Feb. 5, 1881, p. 1.

⁴⁹ *Dolores News*, January 29, 1881, p. 3 and "The Mob's Madness," *Dolores News*, Feb. 5, 1881, p. 1.

⁵⁰ D.H. Fisher and others to Colonel Crofton, Jan. 28, 1881, FLMP, Coll. M 118, box 1, series 4, folder 36, FLC-CSWS. This letter says the incident occurred on Monday, January 25th. The problem is that January 24, 1881 was a Monday. The letter writer was probably right on the day of the week and wrong on the day of the month. Others who signed the letter include; L.W. Coe, W.P. Hendrickson and F.M. Pierce.

⁵¹ *Santa Fe Daily New Mexican*, February 18, 1881.

⁵² *Durango Weekly Record*, February 12, 1881.

⁵³ "The Indian Troubles at Farmington," *Durango Weekly Record*, February 19, 1881.

⁵⁴ "More About the Indian Troubles," *Durango Weekly Record*, February 5, 1881.

⁵⁵ Anderson, *History of New Mexico*, vol. 2, p. 866.

⁵⁶ "Fuller Particulars as to the Indian Troubles," *Durango Weekly Record*, February 5, 1881.

⁵⁷ *Santa Fe Daily New Mexican*, February 18, 1881.

⁵⁸ Robert W Duke, "Political History of San Juan County, New Mexico 1876-1926" (master's thesis, University of New Mexico, June 1947), p. 171, this portion from "Extracts From Letter by W.P. Hendrickson;" *U.S. Census 1880*, Rio Arriba County, NM, r. 803, p. 222a, FLC-CSWS.

⁵⁹ Second Lieutenant W.P. Davies, "Report of Scout in San Juan Valley," December 7, 1880, FLMP, Coll. M 118, B 1, S 4, F 34, FLC-CSWS.

⁶⁰ Duke, "Political History of San Juan County," p. 171, this portion from "Extracts From Letter by W.P. Hendrickson."

⁶¹ Anderson, *History of New Mexico*, vol. 2, p. 866.

⁶² D.H. Fisher and others to Colonel Crofton, Jan. 28, 1881, FLMP, Coll. M 118, B 1, S 4, F 36, FLC-CSWS.

⁶³ "Warlike Navajoes," *Santa Fe Daily New Mexican*, February 13, 1881.

⁶⁴ "Fuller Particulars as to the Indian Troubles," *Durango Weekly Record*, February 5, 1881.

⁶⁵ Ibid.

⁶⁶ Frost to Wallace, April 8, 1881, and Frost to Wallace, April 16, 1881, LSRAGT, TANM, NMSRCA. The quote is from the April 8th letter. According to a letter from an unidentified Durango resident, which was published in the Feb. 26, 1881 issue of the *Santa Fe Daily New Mexican* under the headline "Mob Law," it was Meyers who took the lariat and a third man named Banks was also involved in the shooting. This is somewhat at odds with the Feb. 18, 1881 account in the *New Mexican*.

⁶⁷ Police Magistrate Court Records Jan. 1879 to Dec. 1883, Animas City, CO Government Files, Coll. M 120, FLC-CSWS.

⁶⁸ *U.S. Census 1880*, Ouray County, CO, r. 92, p. 178a, IA-ACPL.

⁶⁹ *Dolores News*, July 17, 1880, p. 3 and July 24, 1880, p. 3.

⁷⁰ Carl F. Mathews, "Rico, Colorado – Once a Roaring Camp," *The Colorado Magazine* vol. 28, no. 1 (January 1951): p. 41.

⁷¹ Police Magistrate Court Records Jan. 1879 to Dec. 1883, Animas City, CO Government Files, Coll. M 120, FLC-CSWS; *Dolores News*, October 9, 1880, p. 3.

[72] "Durango and Animas City," *Dolores News*, November 27, 1880, p. 4, from the *Animas City Southwest*.

[73] "Durango," *Dolores News*, February 5, 1881, p. 2.

[74] "Clubbed with Pistols," *Durango Weekly Record*, February 5, 1881.

[75] Charles Jones, "The Memoirs of Charles Adam Jones," n.d., pp. 125-128, Clifford B. Jones Papers, 1814-1973 and undated, Accession Nos. 96-0122-B and 98-0001-B, Southwest Collection/Special Collections Library, Texas Tech University, Lubbock. For information about the Davis's business see the following; Advertisement for T.A. and E.L. Davis store, *Dolores News*, January 29, 1881, p. 2; "Closing Out Sale!" *Dolores News*, April 2, 1881, p. 3. and "Transfers," *Dolores News*, April 23, 1881, p 2; "Charles Jones Stabbed," *La Plata Miner* (Silverton, CO) February 26, 1881. This article, which was based on a letter from Frank Hartman, places the bar fight as occurring on February 18, 1881.

[76] Clifford R. Caldwell, *Dead Right: The Lincoln County War* (Kerrville, TX: 2008), pp. 146-147.

[77] "Durango's Desperadoes," *Aspen (CO) Weekly Times*, May 21, 1881, p. 4; "La Plata County," *Colorado Weekly Chieftain* (Pueblo), March 7, 1878, p. 1.

[78] Dr. Robert W. Delaney, *Blue Coats, Red Skins and Black Gowns - 100 Years of Fort Lewis* (Durango, CO: Durango Herald, 1977), p. 8.

[79] "Durango's Desperadoes," *Aspen (CO) Weekly Times*, May 21, 1881, p. 4. The author of the article is described as the Durango correspondent for the *Ouray Times*. Unfortunately, he only identifies Eskridge by his last name, never divulging his first name. Was he describing Hargo or Dison? Most likely it was Hargo. As events progressed Hargo developed the reputation as the tougher and more feared of the two Eskridge brothers.

[80] "Durango," *Dolores News*, February 5, 1881, p. 2.

[81] Stanley W. Zamonski, "Rougher Than Hell," *1957 Brand Book of the Denver Westerners*, vol. 13, ed. Numa L. James (Boulder: Westerners, Inc., Johnson Publishing Company, 1958), p. 318; "Personalities," *Dolores News*, September 4, 1880, p. 3.

[82] *Dolores News*, February, 5, 1881, p. 2.

[83] "Durango's Desperadoes," *Aspen Weekly Times*, May 21, 1881, p. 4, from the *Ouray Times*.

[84] Ibid.

[85] "Durango's Desperadoes," *Lake City (CO) Mining Register*, May 13, 1881, from the *Ouray Times;* "Durango," *Dolores News*, February 5, 1881, p. 2. Myers and West operated a line of hacks and sleighs between Animas City and Durango.

[86] "Durango's Desperadoes," *Lake City (CO) Mining Register*, May 13, 1881, from the *Ouray Times*.

[87] "Warlike Navajoes," *Santa Fe Daily New Mexican*, February 13, 1881.

[88] "Durango's Desperadoes," *Lake City (CO) Mining Register*, May 13, 1881, from the *Ouray Times*.

[89] *La Plata Miner*, February 19, 1881, from the *Durango Southwest*, formerly the *Animas City (CO) Southwest*. For more information on the genesis and route of Boren's proposed toll road see the *Colorado Weekly Chieftain*, Pueblo, March 16, 1876, p. 2, from the *Santa Fe New Mexican*.

[90] "Troubles at Farmington," *Santa Fe Daily New Mexican*, February 23, 1881.

[91] "Mob Law," *Santa Fe Daily New Mexican*, February 26, 1881.

⁹² Anderson, *History of New Mexico*, vol. 2, pp. 864, 872 and 876; "Mob Law Still Rules," *Dolores News*, March 12, 1881, p. 1. The *News* carried the same letter as the *New Mexican* with Pierce's correct name.

⁹³ "Fassbinder's Addition to Durango," and "Hotel Arrivals," *Durango Weekly Record*, February 12, 1881.

⁹⁴ "Mob Law," *Santa Fe Daily New Mexican*, February 26, 1881.

⁹⁵ *Albuquerque Daily Citizen*, July 6, 1901, p. 2, from the *Springer (NM) Sentinel*.

CHAPTER TEN – MURDER ON THE LA PLATA

¹ "The Cowboy," *Songs of the Cattle Trail and Cow Camp*, comp. by John A. Lomax (New York: The MacMillan Company, 1920), p. 127.

² C.O. Ziegenfuss, "Ike Stockton," *Denver Republican*, August 12, 1881.

³ *New Mexico v. Isaac Stockton*, case no. 420, August 30, 1879, assault in a menacing manner and case no. 421, August 30, 1879, rescuing a prisoner, Colfax County District Court Records, NMSRCA.

⁴ Adjutant General Max Frost to Governor Wallace, April 8, 1881, LSRAGT, TANM, NMSRCA.

⁵ J.N. Coe, "A Reign of Terror," *Colorado Springs Daily Gazette*, March 27, 1881.

⁶ "Durango's Desperadoes," *Aspen (CO) Weekly Times*, May 21, 1881, p. 4, from the *Ouray (CO) Times*.

⁷ C.O. Ziegenfuss, "Ike Stockton," *Denver (CO) Republican*, August 12, 1881.

⁸ "Durango's Desperadoes," *Aspen Weekly Times*, May 21, 1881, p. 4, from the *Ouray Times;* C.O. Ziegenfuss, "Ike Stockton," *Denver Republican*, August 12, 1881.

⁹ "Another Man Killed at Farmington," *La Plata Miner* (Silverton, CO), March 12, 1881, from the *Durango (CO) Southwest*. The *Southwest* says Ike and eight men left on Sunday afternoon. "Death by the Bullet," *Durango (CO) Weekly Record*, March 5, 1881. This article reported that the men left Durango at the first of the week.

¹⁰ C.O. Ziegenfuss, "Ike Stockton," *Denver Republican*, August 12, 1881.

¹¹ "Local Items," *Durango Weekly Record*, January 17, 1881.

¹² "Death by the Bullet," *Durango Weekly Record*, March 5, 1881.

¹³ Frost to Wallace, April 12, 1881, LSRAGT, TANM, NMSRCA and Reward Notice for Isaac Stockton and others, n.d., GLWP, TANM, NMSRCA; *U.S. Census 1880*, Ouray County, CO, r. 92, 181c, ABCLS. This census page lists Tom Radigan.

¹⁴ "Durango's Doom," *Denver Republican*, April 15, 1881.

¹⁵ Frost to Wallace, April 12, 1881, LSRAGT, TANM, NMSRCA and Reward Notice for Isaac Stockton and others, n.d., GLWP, TANM, NMSRCA; "Trouble in Conejos County," *Saguache (CO) Chronicle*, June 10, 1881, p. 5.

¹⁶ Frost to Wallace, April 18, 1881, GLWP, TANM, NMSRCA.

¹⁷ "Death by the Bullet," *Durango Weekly Record*, March 5, 1881.

¹⁸ Robert W Duke, "Political History of San Juan County, New Mexico 1876-1926" (master's thesis, University of New Mexico, June 1947), pp. 36-37, see footnote nos. 61 and 62. Edward Thomas and George Lockhart's remarried widow, Mary Dicus, identify Aaron Barker as a range rider for "Billy Watson's" Two Circle outfit. Thomas was the brother of Mary Dicus. The author has never come across "Billy Watson" in other sources and it seems certain that the cattleman referred to was actually "One-armed" Billy Wilson. Edward Thomas appears in the 1880 United States census for western Rio Arriba County. At the

time the nineteen-year-old native of Wales lived with his parents (his father was also named Edward) and siblings in the area described on the census form as the Rio San Juan Abajo. See *U.S. Census 1880*, Rio Arriba County, NM, r. 803, p. 223c, FLC-CSWS.

[19] J.N. Coe, "A Reign of Terror," *Colorado Springs Daily Gazette*, March 27, 1881.

[20] Ibid.

[21] Duke, "Political History of San Juan County," p. 37. Duke's thesis contains Al Dustin's version of the incident. Isaac Hiram Cox, "Tales," transcribed by Joeen Johnson Sutton, 1920s, p. 49, courtesy of Les Sutton. Ike Cox said they shot Nance through the "coat sholder." W.P. Hendrickson to Colonel Crofton, March 9, 1881, FLMP, Coll. M 118, B 1, S 4, F 37, FLC-CSWS. Hendrickson mentions that one bullet passed through Nance's clothing. Bernice Gardner Bowra, "Cemeteries of San Juan County," *New Mexico Genealogist*, vol. 1, no. 1 (October 1962): p. 9-10. Bowra reported that Aaron Barker was buried near the site of Farmington's first cemetery at the corner of Butler and Apache Streets. The old cemetery later became the Farmington High and then the Tibbetts School football field. The body was reportedly reburied in Greenlawn Cemetery. If that is the case, Aaron Barker was still not at his final resting place. His remains are now buried in a small cemetery near San Juan College in Farmington. That cemetery holds the mortal remains of George Brown, who was killed by Dison Eskridge. Buried alongside George are his parents John and Hattie and his brother and sister-in-law, Lee and Julia Brown.

[22] "Neighborhood Notes," *Dolores News* (Rico, CO), August 20, 1881, p. 1, from the *Durango Record*.

[23] Olive Frazier Cornelius, "Pioneer History and Reminiscences of the San Juan Basin," *Aztec (NM) Independent Review*, March 24, 1933.

[24] "Death by the Bullet," *Durango Weekly Record*, March 5, 1881.

[25] J.N. Coe, "A Reign of Terror," *Colorado Springs Daily Gazette*, March 27, 1881; See also, Frost to Wallace, April 16, 1881, LSRAGT, TANM, NMSRCA. Frost says they robbed Barker and stole four horses.

[26] "Death by the Bullet," *Durango Weekly Record*, March 5, 1881; "Another Man Killed at Farmington," *La Plata Miner*, March 12, 1881, from the *Durango Southwest*; J.N. Coe, "A Reign of Terror," *Colorado Springs Daily Gazette*, March 27, 1881. Jap Coe says they "lost no time in putting before the public, through the *Durango Record*, their story."

[27] "Another Man Killed at Farmington," *La Plata Miner*, March 12, 1881, from the *Durango Southwest*; "Wilkinson's Capture," *Dolores News*, September 10, 1881, p. 2; "Grand Ball at the New Post," *Durango Weekly Record*, February 19, 1881. The *Record* carries an article which identifies Dr. Cochran as the Post Surgeon and Dr. Byrne as the Assistant Surgeon.

[28] Cornelius, "Pioneer History," *Aztec Independent Review*, March 24, 1933.

[29] "Death by the Bullet," *Durango Weekly Record*, March 5, 1881; "Retaliation," *Dolores News*, March 12, 1881, p. 1, from the *Durango Record*.

[30] "Another Man Killed at Farmington," *La Plata Miner*, March 12, 1881, from the *Durango Southwest*.

[31] "Farmington Matters," *Durango Weekly Record*, March 19, 1881.

[32] "Farmington," *Trinidad (CO) Daily News*, April 5, 1881, from the *Durango Southwest*.

33 "Farmington Matters," *Denver Republican,* March 30, 1881, from the *Trinidad News.*

34 *Dolores News,* March 12, 1881, p. 1.

35 "Durango [Deviltries]," *Las Vegas (NM) Daily Optic,* March 29, 1881, p. 1.

36 *Santa Fe Daily New Mexican,* March 12, 1881. The *New Mexican* and other newspapers offer different locations for the killing of Aaron Barker. The Santa Fe daily places the location near Port's house in Flora Vista, the *Southwest's* description (six miles from Port's cabin) matches the location of the Garrett/Eskridge house near Lew Coe's place, which was about two miles east of what is now downtown Farmington. Those areas were well populated and the subsequent horse chase of six or seven miles would have passed by several farm houses, where Nance could have given the alarm, even if only by the sound of his gunfire. The Barker Arroyo drains the area west of the La Plata toward the Colorado line. George Morrison's winter camp was probably in this vicinity. Pete Knickerbocker, "Uncle Sam Not Present," *San Juan County Index* (Aztec, NM), July 1, 1904, pp. 2-3. *BLM Surface Management Status Map,* Farmington, New Mexico, U.S. Dept. of the Interior, Bureau of Land Management, 1991.

37 *Santa Fe Daily New Mexican,* March 12, 1881.

38 *Dolores News,* March 12, 1881, p. 2, from the *Durango Southwest.*

39 "Thos. A Greatorex Shot," *Dolores News,* March 12, 1881, p. 2, from the *Durango Record;* "Tom Greatorex Is Dead," *Dolores News,* March 26, 1881, p. 2; *U.S. Census 1880,* San Juan County, CO, r. 92, p. 368b, IA-ACPL.

40 "Durango in Mourning," *Durango Weekly Record,* March 19, 1881; "Thos. A Greatorex Shot," *Dolores News,* March 12, 1881, p. 2, from the *Durango Record.*

41 "Thos. A Greatorex Shot," *Dolores News,* March 12, 1881, p. 2, from the *Durango Record.*

42 Advertisement for the Palace of Pleasure, *Durango Weekly Record,* January 22, 1881.

43 "Business Houses," *Dolores News,* July 24, 1880, p. 3

44 *U.S. Census 1880,* Ouray County, CO, r. 92, p. 176c, IA-ACPL.

45 "A Sad Day in Durango," *Durango Weekly Record,* March 12, 1881; "A Sad Day in Durango," *La Plata Miner,* March 12, 1881. The *Miner* identifies Haskell as "Fat Alice."

46 "A Sad Day in Durango," *La Plata Miner,* March 12, 1881.

47 "Thos. A Greatorex Shot," *Dolores News,* March 12, 1881, p. 2, from the *Durango Record; U.S. Census 1880,* Ouray County, CO, r. 92, p. 176d, ABCLS. The census notes Hefferman was a stock dealer residing with three butchers and one teamster. "Grand Ball at the New Post," *Durango Weekly Record,* February 19, 1881. This article identifies Dr. Byrne as the Assistant Surgeon.

48 "A Sad Day in Durango," *La Plata Miner,* March 12, 1881, from the *Durango Record.*

49 "$500 REWARD," *Dolores News,* March 19, 1881, p. 4.

50 *Dolores News,* March 19, 1881, p. 3; "Tom Greatorex Is Dead," *Dolores News,* March 26, 1881, p. 2.

51 "Lynched," *Durango Weekly Record,* March 26, 1881.

52 "Served Him Right," *Arizona Weekly Citizen* (Tucson, AZ), April 3, 1881, p. 3; *U.S. Census 1880,* La Plata County, CO, r. 91, p. 570c, IA-ACPL.

53 "Fell By the Wayside!" *Dolores News,* March 26, 1881, p. 3.

⁵⁴ "Dead Pioneer," *Durango (CO) Democrat,* January 30, 1900, p. 3.

⁵⁵ Mary Atwood, curator, "Cedar Hill," *Aztec (NM) Museum Association Newsletter,* September 1, 1983.

⁵⁶ Edith Rhodes, "The H.W. Cox House," *Bulletins Pioneer Association San Juan County, New Mexico,* 1953 to 1976 (1963): p. 10.

⁵⁷ Cornelius, *"Pioneer History," Aztec Independent Review,* April 21, 1933.

⁵⁸ "Fell By the Wayside!" *Dolores News,* March 26, 1881, p. 3.

⁵⁹ Cox, "Tales," p. 4.

⁶⁰ "Fell By the Wayside!" *Dolores News,* March 26, 1881, p. 3.

⁶¹ "Lynched!" *Durango Weekly Record,* March 26, 1881. The *Record* says the lynching occurred on Tuesday, March 22, 1881 or possibly very early on the morning of the 23rd. In their article, "Fell by the Wayside!" the *Dolores News,* March 26, 1881, p. 3 puts the lynching date as Wednesday, March 16, 1881.

⁶² Cox, "Tales," p. 4; *U.S. Census 1880,* Rio Arriba County, NM, r. 803, p. 224b, FLC-CSWS. Canadian-born James Barrie, his wife Teanie and infant daughter Birthy are shown as being the neighbors of John Cox.

⁶³ "Fell By the Wayside!" *Dolores News,* March 26, 1881, p. 3.

⁶⁴ "Passed In His Checks," *La Plata Miner,* March 26, 1881.

⁶⁵ "Refutation of a Slander," *Dolores News,* April 23, 1881, p. 1, from the *Durango Record.*

⁶⁶ William Locke and John Fulcher to Colonel Crofton, March 10, 1881, FLMP, Coll. M 118, B 1, S 4, F 38, FLC-CSWS.

⁶⁷ Frost to Wallace, April 16, 1881, LSRAGT, TANM, NMSRA; "Orange Phelps," *Bulletins Pioneer Association San Juan County, New Mexico,* 1953 to 1976 (1955): p. 6, Farmington (NM) Public Library. An article on the family of Orange Phelps.

⁶⁸ Colfax County Records, Proceedings of Board of County Commissioners, 1876-1884. p. 31.

⁶⁹ Frost to Wallace, April 18, 1881, portions of the letter were based on a statement from an unnamed Durango resident, GLWP, TANM, NMSRCA.

⁷⁰ *U.S. Census 1880,* Rio Arriba County, NM, r. 803, p. 224a, FLC-CSWS.

⁷¹ Harry Jackson, "Harry Jackson and Mrs. Jackson," dictated to Ella Jackson Birkhimer, *Pioneers of the San Juan Country,* vol. 1, comp. and ed. Sarah Platt Decker Chapter D.A.R. (Durango, CO: Sarah Platt Decker Chapter D.A.R., 1942), pp. 108-109.

⁷² Frost to Wallace, April 18, 1881, portions of the letter were based on a statement from an unnamed Durango resident, GLWP, TANM, NMSRCA.

⁷³ "Mob Law Still Rules," *Dolores News,* March 12, 1881, p. 1; George B Anderson, comp., *History of New Mexico - Its Resources and People,* vol. 2 (Los Angeles, Chicago and New York: Pacific States Publishing Co., 1907), p. 876.

⁷⁴ "Latest Eastern News," *Los Angeles Daily Herald,* July 12, 1878, p. 2.

⁷⁵ Bonnie Baker, "The Origins of the Posse Comitatus Act," *Air and Space Power Journal* (November 1, 1999), from the website of the Air and Space Power Journal, the Professional Journal of the United States Air Force at http://www.airpower.maxwell.af.mil/airchronicles/cc/baker1.html (accessed December 18, 2008).

⁷⁶ John R. Brinkerhoff, "The Posse Comitatus Act and Homeland Security," *Journal of Homeland Security* (February 2002), from the website of the federally

funded Homeland Security Institute at http://www.homelandsecurity.org/journal/Articles/brinkerhoffpossecomitatus.htm (accessed February 2, 2009).

[77] Governor Pitkin to Colonel Crofton, April 13, 1881, FLMP, Coll. M 118, B 1, S 4, F 39, FLC-CSWS. This letter includes a transcription of Heffernan's March 14, 1881 letter to Governor Pitkin. See also *U.S. Census 1880*, La Plata County, CO, r. 91, p. 578d, IA-ACPL.

[78] Lucien B. Crooker, Henry S. Nourse, John. G. Brown and Milton L. Haney, *The Story of the Fifty-fifth Regiment Illinois Volunteer Infantry in the Civil War 1861-1865* (Clinton, MA: W.J. Coulter, 1887), pp. 33, 185, 361-364, 466 and 502, http://archive.org/stream/ofthefiftyfifth00illirich#page/n0/mode/2up (accessed Feb. 4, 2013). General Heffernan died in St. Louis in 1885.

[79] "Obituary: Death of Sister M. Rita," *Intermountain Catholic* (Salt Lake, City, UT), July 30, 1910, p. 8.

[80] "Charles Holliday McHenry 1838-1913," *Bulletins Pioneer Association San Juan County, New Mexico*, 1953 to 1976 (1953): p. 15, Farmington (NM) Public Library.

[81] Governor Pitkin to Colonel Crofton, April 13, 1881, FLMP, Coll. M 118, B 1, S 4, F 39, FLC-CSWS. This letter includes a transcription of Heffernan's letter to the governor.

[82] "Some Farmington Letters," *Durango Weekly Record*, March 26, 1881; "Prospects of Peace," *Colorado Springs Daily Gazette*, April 2, 1881, from the *Durango Record*.

[83] "Blood Upon the Streets," *Durango Weekly Record*, March 19, 1881; *U.S. Census 1880*, Gunnison County, CO, r. 90, p. 149b, IA-ACPL.

[84] "Local," *Durango Weekly Record*, April 9, 1881.

[85] C.O. Ziegenfuss, "Ike Stockton," *Denver Republican*, August 12, 1881.

[86] *Denver Republican*, September 28, 1881.

[87] *Sacramento Daily Union*, May 1, 1879. From the California Digital Newspaper Collection. The CDNC is a project of the Center for Bibliographical Studies and Research (CBSR) at the University of California, Riverside. The CDNC is supported in part by the U.S. Institute of Museum and Library Services under the provisions of the Library Services and Technology Act, administered in California by the State Librarian. Web portal at http://cdnc.ucr.edu/cdnc.

[88] "News Items," *Arizona Weekly Citizen*, September 11, 1881, p. 3.

[89] "A Leap for Liberty," *Ogden (UT) Standard Examiner*, June 25, 1879, p 2, from the *Reno Gazette*. Utah Digital Newspapers operated by the University of Utah's J. Willard Marriott Library. *Standard Examiner* courtesy of the Weber County Library.

[90] "Trouble in Conejos County," *Saguache (CO) Chronicle*, June 10, 1881, p. 5.

[91] *Durango Weekly Record*, February 5, 1881; "Lodged in Limbo," *Denver Republican*, June 27, 1881.

[92] *Durango Weekly Record*, February 5, 1881.

[93] "Lodged in Limbo," *Denver Republican*, June 27, 1881.

[94] *Durango Herald*, July 28, 1881.

[95] "A Clever Capture," *Denver Republican*, June 24, 1881.

[96] "The Conejos Stage Robber," *Bismarck (ND) Tribune*, July 15, 1881, p. 7, from the *Denver Tribune*.

[97] "Lodged in Limbo," *Denver Republican*, June 27, 1881.

[98] C.O. Ziegenfuss, "Ike Stockton," *Denver Republican*, August 12, 1881.

[99] J.N. Coe, "A Reign of Terror," *Colorado Springs Daily Gazette*, March 27, 1881.

100 Report No. 2, Frost to Wallace, April 2, 1881, Campaign, TANM, NMSRCA.

101 "Durango [Deviltries]," *Las Vegas (NM) Daily Optic*, March 29, 1881, p. 1.

102 C.H. McHenry to Governor Wallace, March 22, 1881, transcribed by Albert W. Puett on March 30, 1881, Campaign, TANM, NMSRCA.

103 In mid-April, when Adjutant General Max Frost called for volunteers for a militia to patrol western Rio Arriba county, he had no trouble finding volunteers. About seventy men signed up, even though it was a hardship for them and their families. See Muster Rolls of the San Juan Guards, Campaign, TANM, NMSRCA.

CHAPTER ELEVEN – THE ADJUTANT GENERAL

1 Glenn Norton and L.F. Post, "The Gila Monster Route," *Songs of the Cattle Trail and Cow Camp*, comp. by John A. Lomax (New York: The MacMillan Company, 1920), p. 170.

2 Lew Wallace, *Lew Wallace: An Autobiography*, vol. 2 (New York and London: Harper and Brothers Publishers, 1906), p. 912. http://archive.org/stream/lewwallacevolii002480mbp#page/n3/mode/2up (accessed January 30, 2012).

3 Harwood P. Hinton, Jr., "John Simpson Chisum, 1877-84," *New Mexico Historical Review*, vol. 31, no. 4 (October 1956): p. 328, http://archive.org/details/newmexicohistori31univrich (accessed August 24, 2013).

4 Irving McKee, *"Ben-Hur" Wallace* (Berkeley and Los Angeles: University of California Press, 1947), p. 46.

5 Wallace, *Lew Wallace: An Autobiography*, vol. 2, pp. 750-753, 807, 847-848, 852, 900-901 and 912.

6 Ibid., p. 919.

7 Ibid., pp. 921 and 936.

8 Larry D. Ball, *The United States Marshals of New Mexico and Arizona Territories 1846-1912* (Albuquerque: University of New Mexico Press, 1978), pp. 102-103.

9 Governor Wallace to Justice L. Bradford Prince, March 25, 1881, GLWP, TANM, NMSRCA. From TANM roll 99.

10 Governor Wallace to General D.C. Dodge, March 27, 1881, GLWP, TANM, NMSRCA.

11 "Nature Exacts Final Tribute," *Santa Fe New Mexican*, October 14, 1909.

12 "Personal," *Colorado Springs Gazette*, December 11, 1875, p. 4.

13 "Nature Exacts Final Tribute," *Santa Fe New Mexican*, October 14, 1909.

14 "Rio Arriba," *Santa Fe Daily New Mexican*, March 30, 1881.

15 "News and Notes," *Iola (KS) Register*, April 8, 1881.

16 Max Frost's Journal of the Events and Investigation of the troubles in Rio Arriba County, March 30, 1881 to April 1, 1881 and Report No. 1, Adjutant General Max Frost to Governor Wallace, April 2, 1881, Campaign, TANM, NMSRCA; "The Early History Southwestern Colorado," *Durango (CO) Wage Earner*, March 14, 1907, p. 2. This article identifies Head as a former Colorado lieutenant governor. "A Clever Capture," *Denver (CO) Republican*, June 24, 1881. The article notes San Antonio is now called "Antonita." *U.S. Census 1880*, Conejos County, CO, r. 89, p. 181a, IA-ACPL; David F. Myrick, *New Mexico's Railroads - A Historical Survey*. Revised ed. (Albuquerque: University of New Mexico Press, 1990), p. 110. Myrick says the D&RG rail line to Española was opened on December 31, 1880.

[17] W.J. Buffington, "Our Legislators," *Daily Colorado Miner* (Georgetown), February 4, 1874, p. 1, from the *Denver Daily World*.

[18] "Chama," *Denver Republican*, March 23, 1881.

[19] Frank Hall, *History of the State of Colorado*, vol. 4 (Chicago: Rocky Mountain Historical Company, 1895), p. 92, http://archive.org/stream/historyofstateof04hall#page/n9/mode/2up (accessed February 13, 2013).

[20] "The Early History Southwestern Colorado," *Durango Wage Earner*, March 14, 1907, p. 2.

[21] "Further From Santa Fe," *Edgefield (SC) Advertiser*, April 21, 1847, p. 2, from the *St. Louis Reveille*.

[22] "The Early History Southwestern Colorado," *Durango Wage Earner*, March 14, 1907, p. 2.

[23] Ball, *The United States Marshals of New Mexico and Arizona Territories*, p. 25.

[24] "Over the Range," *Colorado Daily Chieftain* (Pueblo), July 6, 1876, p. 2.

[25] "The Early History Southwestern Colorado," *Durango Wage Earner*, March 14, 1907, p. 2.

[26] "Official Directory," *Colorado Springs Gazette*, November 11, 1876, p. 1.

[27] Report No. 1, Frost to Governor Wallace, April 2, 1881, Campaign, TANM, NMSRCA.

[28] Ibid.

[29] Max Frost's Journal of the Events and Investigation of the troubles in Rio Arriba County, March 30, 1881 to April 1, 1881, Campaign, TANM, NMSRCA.

[30] Ibid.

[31] "Chama," *Denver Republican*, March 23, 1881.

[32] *Santa Fe Daily New Mexican*, March 9, 1881.

[33] *Santa Fe Daily New Mexican*, April 7, 1881, FLC-CSWS; The microfilmed copy of this newspaper displays three dates, April 6, 7 and 8, 1881. Apparently the typesetters forgot to change out the dates on all of the pages.

[34] "Chama," *Denver Republican*, March 23, 1881. It is unknown if Dr. Cole was the owner of Cole's Restaurant.

[35] "Chama," *Leadville (CO) Daily Herald*, January 7, 1881, p. 4.

[36] "C?ock," "Chama Currency," *Las Vegas (NM) Daily Optic*, March 26, 1881.

[37] *Santa Fe Daily New Mexican*, March 9, 1881.

[38] T.M. Pearce, ed., *New Mexico Place Names - A Geographical Dictionary* (Albuquerque: University of New Mexico Press, 1965), pp. 7 and 94.

[39] "Territorialities," *Santa Fe Daily New Mexican*, April 7, 1881. This could be the April 6th issue, based on the date of the adjacent page.

[40] "Chama," *Leadville Daily Herald*, January 7, 1881 p. 4.

[41] Report No. 3, Frost to Wallace, April 3, 1881, includes an extract of April 2nd letter from C.R. Fife to T.D. Burns, Campaign, TANM, NMSRCA. Frost refers to the site of the shooting as "Almagre about 20 miles west of Chama," at the Graves's Railroad camp.

[42] "Durango," *La Plata Miner* (Silverton, CO), April 16, 1881; "Two Men Shot While in Bed Near La Count's Camp in El Magre Canon," *Durango (CO) Weekly Record*, April 9, 1881.

[43] "Territorialities," *Santa Fe Daily New Mexican*, April 7, 1881. This could be the April 6th issue, based on the date of the adjacent page.

[44] Ibid.

45 Report No. 3, Frost to Wallace, April 3, 1881, includes an extract of April 2nd letter from C.R. Fife to T.D. Burns, Campaign, TANM, NMSRCA; *U.S. Census 1870*, Lafayette County, MO, r. 786, p. 240a, IA-ACPL.

46 *U.S. Census 1880*, Conejos County, CO, r. 89, pp. 181a and 182c, IA-ACPL.

47 "First Forced On Him," *Kansas City (MO) Journal*, September 17, 1899, p. 9, from the *Chicago Inter Ocean*.

48 *U.S. Census 1880*, Conejos County, CO, r. 89, p. 180b, IA-ACPL.

49 "Territorialities," *Santa Fe Daily New Mexican*, April 7, 1881. This could be the April 6th issue, based on the date of the adjacent page.

50 "Murder on the Rio Grande," *Dolores News* (Rico, CO), September 11, 1880, p. 1, from the *Denver News*.

51 Report No. 3, Frost to Wallace, April 3, 1881, includes an extract of April 2nd letter from C.R. Fife to T.D. Burns, Campaign, TANM, NMSRCA.

52 "Territorialities," *Santa Fe Daily New Mexican*, April 7, 1881. This issue has pages dated April 6th and 7th. The fast advance of the D&RG rails caused some confusion in describing the shooting location. The *New Mexican* reported that it took place "at Almagre, a town about two miles west of Chama."

53 Report No. 3, Frost to Wallace, April 3, 1881, includes an extract of April 2nd letter from C.R. Fife to T.D. Burns and Max Frost's Journal of the Events and Investigation of the troubles in Rio Arriba County, April 1, 1881, Campaign, TANM, NMSRCA. Fife's confusing letter is the only source linking Jimmy Catron to Deputy Johnson's predicament and whatever Catron's role, it is clear he held Johnson's fate in his hands.

54 Max Frost's Journal of the Events and Investigation of the troubles in Rio Arriba County, April 1, 1881, Campaign, TANM, NMSRCA.

55 Report No. 4, Frost to Wallace, April 4, 1881, LSRAGT, TANM, NMSRCA. Concerning Frost's mistaken identification of H.W. Cox; there were only two J. Coxes in the 1880 Rio Arriba County census for the San Juan area. Both were sons of H.W. Cox. John Shriver Cox was twenty-two years old and James Allard Cox was sixteen years old at the time of the census. Data from the *U.S. Census 1880*, Rio Arriba County, NM, r. 803, pp. 224b and 225c, FLC-CSWS; *Dolores News*, April 3, 1880, p. 2. Cox was a member of the territorial legislature.

56 Report No. 6, Frost to Wallace, April 5, 1881, LSRAGT, TANM, NMSRCA.

57 Report No. 2, Frost to Wallace, April 2, 1881, Campaign, TANM, NMSRCA.

58 Reign of Terror, *Rocky Mountain News* (Denver, CO), March 31, 1881.

59 "The People of Rio Arriba in a State of Terror," *Los Angeles Daily Herald*, April 2, 1881; "Murderous Desperadoes," *New York Tribune* (New York, NY), April 2, 1881.

60 "Murderous Desperadoes," *New York Tribune*, April 2, 1881, p. 1.

61 "Murderers' Carnival," *National Republican* (Washington, DC), April 2, 1881, p. 1.

62 "Local Intelligence," *Dolores News*, March 26, 1881, p. 3.

63 L. Bradford Prince, Chief Justice, "The Rio Arriba Court," *Santa Fe Daily New Mexican*, April 3, 1881.

64 Adjutant General Max Frost to Wm. B. Haines, April 6, 1881, LSRAGT, TANM, NMSRCA.

65 Frost to W.B. Haines, A.F. Miller and J.H. Cox, April 7, 1881, LSRAGT, TANM, NMSRCA.

[66] Report No. 4, Frost to Wallace, April 4, 1881 and Frost to Wallace, April 8, 1881, LSRAGT, TANM, NMSRCA.

[67] "Rio Arriba," *Santa Fe Daily New Mexican*, April 12, 1881.

[68] "By Telegraph," *Santa Fe Daily New Mexican*, December 30, 1880, p. 1.

[69] Report No. 4, Frost to Wallace, April 4, 1881 and Frost to Wallace, April 8, 1881, LSRAGT, TANM, NMSRCA. Frost mistakenly identifies Moses Blancett as Blanchard. Blancett plays a key role in future events and Frost misnames him in several future dispatches as well. Guadalupe Arellano's last name was spelled phonetically as "Ariano" in Frost's dispatch.

[70] *Santa Fe Daily New Mexican*, April 9, 1881.

[71] Letter from Adjutant General, U.S. Army to Commanding Officer of Fort Lewis, received April [23?], 1881, FLMP, Coll. M 118, box 2, series 4, folder 1, FLC-CSWS.

[72] W. M. Rambo, H. Delush, S. Bowen, K.S. Kelser, E. Proles, H. Sanftenberg, "Another Indian Murder," *Durango Weekly Record*, April 9, 1881. The Rambo letter dates the murder as April 2nd. Frost to Wallace, April 12, 1881, LSRAGT, TANM, NMSRCA. Haines advised Frost that an American freighter had been slain by Navajos at the "Lower San Juan Crossing." He mistakenly reported the date of the murder as "five days ago," and mistakenly reported that the freighter's team had been stolen.

[73] W. M. Rambo, H. Delush, S. Bowen, K.S. Kelser, E. Proles, H. Sanftenberg, "Another Indian Murder," and W.M. Rambo, From Bowen's Ferry, New Mexico, *Durango Weekly Record*, April 9, 1881. Rambo identifies the rifle as an "1853 model." He does not name the manufacturer, but in Costiano's presence he took down the serial number, which he said was 48-987. Enfield also produced a Model 1853 rifle.

[74] "The Utes," *Denver Republican*, March 29, 1881.

[75] Frost to Wallace, April 8, 1881, LSRAGT, TANM, NMSRCA.

[76] "News from Rio Arriba," *Santa Fe Daily New Mexican*, April 8, 1881.

[77] Two letters from Frost to Wallace both dated April 8, 1881, LSRAGT, TANM, NMSRCA.

[78] Western Union Telegram Frost to Wallace, April 8, 1881, LSRAGT, TANM, NMSRCA.

[79] Frost to Wallace, April 6, 1881 and April 8, 1881, LSRAGT, TANM, NMSRCA.

[80] Report No. 1, Frost to Wallace, April 2, 1881, Campaign, TANM, NMSRCA.

[81] Report No. 5, Frost to Wallace, April 5, 1881, LSRAGT, TANM, NMSRCA.

[82] "Damning Evidence!" *Dolores News*, May 28, 1881, p. 1.

[83] *U.S. Census 1880*, Las Animas County, CO, r. 92, p. 120c, IA-ACPL; "Death of I.W. Lacy," *Cimarron (NM) News and Press*, May 17, 1881, from the *Trinidad Times*.

[84] "Cold Blooded Murder," *Durango Record*, May 14, 1881; "Damning Evidence!" *Dolores News*, May 28, 1881, p. 1. Lacy paid tabs for Howland during this period.

[85] "Cold Blooded Murder," *Durango Record*, May 14, 1881. The *Record* says Howland was hired by Lacy "to find out the status of affairs existing between the Farmington and the Stockton, Eskridge parties." That seems like an odd way of phrasing his mission, since everybody in the country knew how matters stood between the two groups. "Death of I.W. Lacy," *Cimarron (NM) News and Press*, May 17, 1881, from the *Trinidad Times*. According to this article Howland worked as a Trinidad policeman "for some time."

86 "Cold Blooded Murder," *Durango Record*, May 14, 1881. Constables and deputies who were known to be sympathetic toward Stockton and his associates included Jim Sullivan, Sheriff Luke Hunter, Jack Wilson and Deputy U.S. Marshal James Heffernan.

87 "Saddles and Harness," advertisement *Trinidad (CO) Enterprise*, April 29, 1874, p. 1.

88 Robert W Duke, "Political History of San Juan County, New Mexico 1876-1926" (master's thesis, University of New Mexico, June 1947), p. 35.

89 Governor Wallace to Adjutant General Max Frost, April 11, 1881, GLWP, TANM, NMSRCA. From TANM roll 99.

90 Wallace to Frost, April 7, 1881, GLWP, TANM, NMSRCA.

91 Wallace to Frost, April 11, 1881, GLWP, TANM, NMSRCA.

92 "What the Interior Department Directs," *Santa Fe Daily New Mexican*, April 8, 1881.

93 "Another Man Killed at Farmington," *La Plata Miner*, March 12, 1881, from the *Durango Southwest*.

94 "Durango's Doom," *Denver Republican*, April 15, 1881.

95 Frost to Wallace, April 12, 1881, GLWP, TANM, NMSRCA.

96 "Durango's Doom," *Denver Republican*, April 15, 1881.

97 "Marauding Bands in New Mexico," *Los Angeles Daily Herald*, April 16, 1881, p. 1, from the *Denver Republican*.

98 "The Death of Lacy," *Denver Republican*, May 21, 1881, from the *Trinidad Times*.

99 Frost to Wallace, April 12, 1881, GLWP, TANM, NMSRCA.

100 "Damning Evidence!" *Dolores News*, May 28, 1881, p. 1.

101 *Dolores News*, April 23, 1881, p. 1, from the *Durango Record*.

102 Frost to Wallace, April 12, 1881, LSRAGT, TANM, NMSRCA.

CHAPTER TWELVE – BAPTISM OF BLOOD

1 Margaret Ashmun, "The Vigilantes," *Songs of the Cattle Trail and Cow Camp*, comp. by John A. Lomax (New York: The MacMillan Company, 1920), p. 151.

2 "Murder Most Foul!" *Durango (CO) Weekly Record*, April 16, 1881.

3 Charles L. Valiton, "Forty-five Years in Colorado," *Silverton (CO) Standard*, March 13, 1926.

4 George Doughty interviewed by A.L. Soens, January 24, 1934, La Plata County, p. 31, CWA Pioneer Interviews, Special Collections, SHHLRC, HCC.

5 "Murder Most Foul!" *Durango Weekly Record*, April 16, 1881.

6 "Disrupted Durango," *Denver (CO) Republican*, April 20, 1881.

7 Valiton, "Forty-five Years in Colorado," *Silverton Standard*, March 13, 1926.

8 "Durango," *La Plata Miner* (Silverton, CO), April 16, 1881, from the *Durango Record Extra*.

9 "Twice Dead," *Lake City (CO) Mining Register*, April 22, 1881.

10 "Durango," *La Plata Miner*, April 16, 1881, from the *Durango Record Extra*.

11 Valiton, "Forty-five Years in Colorado," *Silverton Standard*, March 20, 1926.

12 "Durango," *La Plata Miner*, April 16, 1881, from the *Durango Record Extra*.

13 "Disrupted Durango," *Denver Republican*, April 20, 1881.

14 "Murder Most Foul!" *Durango Weekly Record*, April 16, 1881.

15 Ibid.

[16] Justice of the Peace J.C. Craig, Docket Ledger, March 4, 1881 - December 29, 1881, La Plata County, CO, Government Records, Coll. M 028, RG 17, FLC-CSWS.

[17] "Murder Most Foul!" *Durango Weekly Record*, April 16, 1881.

[18] Valiton, "Forty-five Years in Colorado," *Silverton Standard*, March 13, 1926.

[19] "Twice Dead," *Lake City Mining Register*, April 22, 1881.

[20] "Murder Most Foul!" and "Another Great Excitement!" *Durango Weekly Record*, April 16, 1881.

[21] John B. Arrington and Eleanor D. MacDonald, *The San Juan Basin - My Kingdom Was A County* (Denver: Green Mountain Press, 1970), p. 146.

[22] Olive Frazier Cornelius, "Pioneer History and Reminiscences of the San Juan Basin," *Aztec (NM) Independent Review*, April 7, 1933.

[23] Pete Knickerbocker, "Uncle Sam Not Present," *San Juan County Index* (Aztec, NM), July 1, 1904, pp. 2-3. Knickerbocker said that Mose Blancett, Tom Nance and Wash Cox rode on the Durango expedition. This is incorrect because the Farmington vigilantes stayed in the area until Monday afternoon, and on Tuesday, April 12th, Tom Nance was in Tierra Amarilla to testify before the grand jury investigating the death of Aaron Barker. Mose Blancett and Wash Cox were also in Tierra Amarilla that day. Knickerbocker also notes that five men, including Nance and Big Dan, were sent into town to check things out. That also does not seem likely, as the presence of Nance and Howland would have certainly added to an already lively evening. The George Thompson named was the nephew of cattleman George W. Thompson. The issue of the *Index* is available at the Aztec (NM) Museum. The *Durango Weekly Record* of May 14, 1881 (see the article "Cold Blooded Murder") reported that Dan Howland was at the battle. Another reference to the presence of at least one of the Coe men comes from William Devere, "Tramp Poet of the West," *Jim Marshall's New Pianner - And Other Western Stories* (New York, Chicago and London: M. Witmark and Sons, 1908), p. 37.

[24] "Murder Most Foul!" *Durango Weekly Record*, April 16, 1881.

[25] Valiton, "Forty-five Years in Colorado," *Silverton Standard*, March 20, 1926.

[26] "Disrupted Durango," *Denver Republican*, April 20, 1881.

[27] "Durango," *La Plata Miner*, April 16, 1881, from the *Durango Record Extra*.

[28] "Disrupted Durango," *Denver Republican*, April 20, 1881.

[29] Adjutant General Max Frost to Governor Wallace, April 18, 1881 portions of the letter were based on a statement from an unnamed Durango resident, GLWP, TANM, NMSRCA; Heffernan to Crofton, May 23, 1881, FLMP, Coll. M 118, B 2, S 4, F 2, FLC-CSWS. Heffernan noted that he lived on Junction Creek near Animas City.

[30] "Durango," *La Plata Miner*, April 16, 1881, from the *Durango Record Extra*.

[31] "Twice Dead," *Lake City Mining Register*, April 22, 1881.

[32] "Disrupted Durango," *Denver Republican*, April 20, 1881. This article says Hunter was in the company of Captain D.W. Wood and Barney Patterson.

[33] "Luke Hunter," *Durango Weekly Record*, April 9, 1881; *U.S. Census 1880*, La Plata County, CO, r. 91, p. 571a, ABCLS.

[34] Business Licenses issued 1879-1896, Animas City, CO, Government Records, Coll. M 120, FLC-CSWS.

[35] William Valliant interviewed by A.L. Soens, n.d., La Plata County, p. 20, CWA Pioneer Interviews, Special Collections, SHHLRC, HCC.

NOTES

[36] Frost to Wallace, April 18, 1881, portions of the letter were based on a statement from an unnamed Durango resident, GLWP, TANM, NMSRCA.

[37] "The Rio Arriba Troubles," *Santa Fe Daily New Mexican*, April 27, 1881.

[38] Frost to Wallace, April 18, 1881, GLWP, TANM, NMSRCA.

[39] C.O. Ziegenfuss, "Ike Stockton," *Denver Republican*, August 12, 1881.

[40] "Durango," *La Plata Miner*, April 16, 1881, from the *Durango Record Extra*.

[41] "Murder Most Foul!" and "To Those Contemplating Coming to Durango," *Durango Weekly Record*, April 16, 1881; Advertisement for C.A. King's Parlor Meat Market, *Durango Weekly Record*, April 30, 1881.

[42] Frost to Wallace, April 18, 1881, portions of the letter were based on a statement from an unnamed Durango resident, GLWP, TANM, NMSRCA.

[43] "Another Great Excitement," *Durango Weekly Record*, April 16, 1881.

[44] C.O. Ziegenfuss, "Ike Stockton," *Denver Republican*, August 12, 1881.

[45] Cornelius, "Pioneer History," *Aztec Independent Review*, April 7, 1933.

[46] "Another Great Excitement" and "To Those Contemplating," *Durango Weekly Record*, April 16, 1881.

[47] Valiton, "Forty-five Years in Colorado," *Silverton Standard*, December 19, 1925. Valiton's series of articles would appear in the *Standard* sporadically through June 1926.

[48] "Another Great Excitement," *Durango Weekly Record*, April 16, 1881.

[49] "The Clipper," *Durango Weekly Record*, March 26, 1881.

[50] William Devere, *Jim Marshall's New Pianner*, p. 37.

[51] Two Letters from Frost to Wallace both dated April 18, 1881, GLWP, TANM, NMSRCA. Portions of one of the letters was based on a statement from an unnamed Durango resident.

[52] "Durango Attacked By Farmington," *Dolores News* (Rico, CO), April 16, 1881, p. 2, from the *Durango Record*.

[53] "Murder Most Foul!" and "To Those Contemplating," *Durango Weekly Record*, April 16, 1881.

[54] "Murder Most Foul!" *Durango Weekly Record*, April 16, 1881.

[55] Frost to Wallace, April 18, 1881, portions of the letter were based on a statement from an unnamed Durango resident, GLWP, TANM, NMSRCA.

[56] Frank Hall, *History of the State of Colorado*, vol. 4 (Chicago: Rocky Mountain Historical Company, 1895) p. 447, http://archive.org/stream/historyofstateof04hall#page/n9/mode/2up (accessed February 13, 2013). Hall's brief biography of Fisher notes that he "took part in many stirring incidents connected with the founding and progress of that city." Two other possible Fishers appear in an advertisement for Fisher and Fisher in the *Durango Daily Record*, May 23, 1881. These Fishers were brothers and building contractors D.M. and J. G. Fisher, who operated out of an office in the Williams's Lumber Company.

[57] Frost to Wallace, April 18, 1881, portions of the letter were based on a statement from an unnamed Durango resident, GLWP, TANM, NMSRCA.

[58] "Still Farther Excitement," *Durango Weekly Record*, April 16, 1881.

[59] Frost to Wallace, April 18, 1881, portions of the letter were based on a statement from an unnamed Durango resident, GLWP, TANM, NMSRCA.

[60] "Still Farther Excitement," *Durango Weekly Record*, April 16, 1881.

[61] "They Seem to Have Friends," *Dolores News*, April 30, 1881, p. 1, from the *Ouray Times;* "Disrupted Durango," *Denver Republican*, April 20, 1881.

NOTES   437

⁶² "Still Farther Excitement," *Durango Weekly Record*, April 16, 1881. Biographical information in this paragraph can be found in the *U.S. Census 1880*, La Plata County, CO, r. 91, p. 571a, IA-ACPL. These records show Luke Hunter and Charles Shaw's family in La Plata County. *U.S. Census 1870*, Posey County, IN, r. 352, p. 293, IA-ACPL. These records show the family of Luke and James Hunter living in Harmony Township in Posey County. Justice of the Peace G. S. Flagler Docket Ledger, June 11, 1878 – November 9, 1881, La Plata County, CO, Government Records, M 028, RG 17, FLC-CSWS. These records identify Flagler as a justice of the peace. "Griffin S. Flagler," *Durango Weekly Record*, May 7, 1881. This article promoted Flagler's candidacy for mayor of Durango. It says he was born in New York City in 1829 and served in the Civil War. He was promoted to captain at the Battle of Fair Oaks (Seven Pines) and wounded at Malvern Hill. He moved to the area near the present day ghost town of Howardsville in 1874. He reportedly hauled in the first load of lumber for the first house in Animas City and was elected mayor of that town in 1879. Advertisement for attorneys, Broyles and Engley, *Durango Weekly Record*, January 10, 1881; "Eugene Engley Has Fought His Last Fight," *Alamosa (CO) Journal*, April 22, 1910, p. 1; "The Life of L.L. Nunn as recorded by the Western Colorado Power Company Collection," M 002, FLC-CSWS. From their website http://swcenter.fortlewis.edu/inventory/Nunn.htm (accessed September 6, 2009).

⁶³ *Dolores News*, April 30, 1881, p. 1, from the *Ouray (CO) Times*.

⁶⁴ "Still Farther Excitement," *Durango Weekly Record*, April 16, 1881.

⁶⁵ Frost to Wallace, April 12, 1881, LSRAGT, TANM, NMSRCA.

⁶⁶ "Amargo," *La Plata Miner*, April 30, 1881. Train service to Amargo began on April 25, 1881.

⁶⁷ Frost to Wallace, April 12, 1881, LSRAGT, TANM, NMSRCA.

⁶⁸ Reward Notice for Isaac Stockton and others, n.d., GLWP, TANM, NMSRCA.

⁶⁹ Frost to Wallace, April 18, 1881, GLWP, TANM, NMSRCA.

⁷⁰ Two letters from Frost to Wallace, both dated April 12, 1881, LSRAGT, TANM, NMSRA.

⁷¹ Mary Atwood, curator, "The Blancett Hotel," *Aztec (NM) Museum Association Newsletter*, September 1, 1984; *U.S. Census 1880*, Rio Arriba County, NM, r. 803, p. 226a, FLC-CSWS.

⁷² Frost to Wallace, April 12, 1881, LSRAGT, TANM, NMSRCA.

⁷³ Tweeti Walser Blancett and Kathy Summers Price, *Step Back Inn To Aztec's Roots* (Aztec, NM: Step Back Inn, 1994), p. 5.

⁷⁴ "The Rosita Row," *Colorado Daily Chieftain* (Pueblo, CO), October 13, 1875, p. 4; "Rosita's Ex-Banker," *Colorado Daily Chieftain*, April 12, 1876, p. 4.

⁷⁵ "Homicide at Tintic," *Deseret News* (Salt Lake City, UT), December 28, 1887.

⁷⁶ "The Pistol," *Colorado Weekly Chieftain* (Pueblo, CO), October 11, 1877, p. 3.

⁷⁷ Cornelius, "Pioneer History," *Aztec Independent Review*, March 17, 1933.

⁷⁸ "A Double Wedding," *Durango Weekly Record*, February 5, 1881.

⁷⁹ "Homicide at Tintic," *Deseret News* (Salt Lake City, UT), December 28, 1887; "Deputy Sheriff Killed," *Dolores News*, October 28, 1882, p. 2, from the *Durango Herald*.

80 *U.S. Census 1860*, Nemaha County, KS, r. 351, pp. 452 and 453, IA-ACPL; *U.S. Census 1880*, Rio Arriba County, NM, r. 803, pp. 224a and 226a, FLC-CSWS. The 1880 census shows brothers Enos and John evidently living with their mother, who is identified only by her last name. According to Ella Ann Spargo, Monie was pronounced "Ma Knee." From an interview with Ella Ann Spargo on April 21, 2009.

81 Frost to Wallace, April 18, 1881, portions of the letter were based on a statement from an unnamed Durango resident, GLWP, TANM, NMSRCA. Haines's letterhead read, "Office of Haines & Hughes - Wholesale and Retail Dealers in General Merchandise - Wool, Hides and Pelts."

82 George Lockhart, "Farmington," *Dolores News*, April 23, 1881, p. 2.

83 Frost to Wallace, April 16, 1881, LSRAGT, TANM, NMSRA; *U.S. Census 1880*, Rio Arriba County, NM, r. 803, p. 224a, FLC-CSWS. The Raser family is shown as living at the "Mouth of the Animas."

84 Frost to Wallace, April 18, 1881, portions of the letter were based on a statement from an unnamed Durango resident, GLWP, TANM, NMSRCA.

85 Frost to Wallace, April 16, 1881, LSRAGT, TANM, NMSRA.

86 Frost to Wallace, April 18, 1881, portions of the letter were based on a statement from an unnamed Durango resident, GLWP, TANM, NMSRCA.

87 "Agate" (Judge W.B. Sloan) and other unidentified correspondent, "Durango's Doom," *Denver Republican*, April 15, 1881.

88 A.W. Hudson, "Life and Property as Safe," *Denver Republican*, April 27, 1881.

89 *Durango Daily Record*, May 4, 1881.

90 "The Rio Arriba Troubles," *Santa Fe Daily New Mexican*, April 27, 1881.

91 William A. Keleher, *Violence in Lincoln County: 1869-1881* (Albuquerque: University of New Mexico Press, 1957), p. 213.

92 *Dolores News*, April 23, 1881, p. 2.

93 Undated notice from Adjutant General Frost, Dep. Sheriff Mose Blancett and Captain of the San Juan Guards, W.B. Haines, LSRAGT, TANM, NMSRA. The school house was apparently named for the family of thirty-five-year-old Dave Cole. Mr. Cole and his wife and three children lived on the Animas near George and Jap Coe.

94 "The Rio Arriba Troubles," *Santa Fe Daily New Mexican*, April 27, 1881; *U.S. Census 1880*, Rio Arriba County, NM, r. 803, p. 223d, FLC-CSWS.

95 "Historial Nubs," *Farmington (NM) Times Hustler*, May 17, 1940. As reported in a letter by William B. Haines and published by the *Santa Fe Daily New Mexican*, April 27, 1881.

96 Manuel Gonzales, letter to the editor, *Santa Fe Daily New Mexican*, June 3, 1881.

97 "The Rio Arriba Trouble," *Santa Fe Daily New Mexican*, June 1, 1881. According to the *New Mexican*, Gonzales asked *Alcalde* Sandoval for the warrants before the San Juan Guards arrived at his home, but based on the timing of the subsequent arrest of one of the Guardsmen, it seems likely that the warrants were issued after his confrontation with the San Juan Guards. For another account see William B. Haines to Governor Wallace, May 21, 1881, Campaign, TANM, NMSRCA.

98 Max Frost, "The Rio Arriba Troubles," *Santa Fe Daily New Mexican*, April 27, 1881.

99 Ibid.

[100] "Durango's Desperadoes," *Lake City (CO) Mining Register*, May 13, 1881.
[101] Ibid.
[102] "Blood in the San Juan," *Rocky Mountain Sun* (Aspen, CO), September 3, 1881, p. 3.
[103] "Durango's Desperadoes," *Lake City Mining Register*, May 13, 1881.
[104] "Meeting of the Cattle Men," *Durango Weekly Record*, April 23, 1881.
[105] "Durango At Peace," *Durango (CO) Daily Record*, April 29, 1881.
[106] Ibid.
[107] Max Frost, "The Rio Arriba Troubles," *Santa Fe Daily New Mexican*, April 27, 1881.
[108] "Historial Nubs," *Farmington Times Hustler*, May 24, 1940, from the *Santa Fe Daily New Mexican* of May 10, 1881.
[109] "The Durango War," *Trinidad Daily News*, May 7, 1881.
[110] *Cimarron (NM) News and Press*, May 12, 1881, Western New Mexico University, Miller Library Microfilm Archives; "Rio Arriba," *Santa Fe Daily New Mexican*, May 14, 1881. Lists the price of cattle.
[111] Advertisements for the Tent Saloon and the Eclipse Saloon, *Durango Weekly Record*, April 30, 1881.
[112] "Southwest Colorado," *Durango Weekly Record*, August 6, 1881.
[113] "Durango at Peace," *Durango Daily Record*, April 29, 1881.
[114] "Rio Arriba Items," *Santa Fe Daily New Mexican*, May 24, 1881.
[115] "More Unreliable Correspondents," *Durango Weekly Record*, May 28, 1881.
[116] Requisition from New Mexico to Colorado, for Isaac Stockton and others, April 29, 1881, roll 1, microcopy 364, Coll. I 023, Interior Department, Territorial Papers, New Mexico, 1851-1914, RG 48, NARA, FLC-CSWS; "New Mexico Murderers," *Denver Republican*, May 14, 1881; *U.S. Census 1880*, Santa Fe County, NM, r. 804, p. 46d, IA-ACPL. In 1880 Neis resided in Santa Fe and was working as a railroad contractor, probably as a detective.
[117] "Take A Reasonable View," *Dolores News*, April 30, 1881, p. 2.
[118] "A Terrorized Community," *Dolores News*, May 14, 1881 p. 1.
[119] Ibid.
[120] Ibid.
[121] Isaac Hiram Cox, "Tales," transcribed by Joeen Johnson Sutton, 1920s, p. 122, courtesy of Les Sutton.
[122] "Think of It!" *Dolores News*, April 30, 1881, p. 2.
[123] *U.S. Census 1880*, Rio Arriba County, NM, r. 803, p. 225c, FLC-CSWS. This census sheet shows Ike and his family, his mother-in-law, sister-in-law and brother-in-law (John Cowan) all living on the Animas River in New Mexico. John Cowan and Ike and his family would later move to La Plata County, Colorado. The Morrison and O'Neal families lived on the Pine River near present day Bayfield, Colorado.
[124] Wilma Crisp Bankston, *Where Eagles Winter - History and Legend of the Disappointment Country* (Cortez, CO: Mesa Verde Press, 1987), pp. 43 and 108
[125] "Damning Evidence!" *Dolores News*, May 28, 1881, p. 1.
[126] Haines to Wallace, May 21, 1881, Campaign, TANM, NMSRCA.
[127] "Damning Evidence!" *Dolores News*, May 28, 1881, p. 1.
[128] "The Particulars of the Kid's Escape," *Santa Fe Daily New Mexican*, May 3, 1881.

129 "Billy the Kid," *Santa Fe Daily New Mexican*, May 4, 1881.
130 *Denver Republican*, May 11, 1881; *Aspen (CO) Weekly Times*, May 21, 1881, p. 4.
131 *Santa Fe Daily New Mexican*, May 5, 1881; "The Difficulty at Durango," *Santa Fe Daily New Mexican*, May 6, 1881.

CHAPTER THIRTEEN – DEATH OF A CATTLE KING

1 Arthur Chapman, "The Range Pirates," *Out Where the West Begins and Other Western Verses* (Boston and New York: Houghton Mifflin Company, 1917), p. 75.
2 Robert W. Duke, "Political History of San Juan County, New Mexico 1876-1926" (master's thesis, University of New Mexico, June 1947), p. 36, footnote no. 60.
3 Military District of New Mexico to A.C.S. at Fort Lewis (correspondents names not stated), May 19, 1881, FLMP, Coll. M 118, box 2, series 4, folder 2, FLC-CSWS.
4 I.W. Lacy to Fort Lewis (evidently transcribed from a verbal communication), April 12, 1881, FLMP, Coll. M 118, box 1, series 4, folder 39, FLC-CSWS.
5 "Another Wholesale [Enterprise?]," *Durango (CO) Daily Record*, May 2, 1881.
6 *U.S. Census 1880*, Las Animas County, CO, r. 92, p. 96a, IA-ACPL.
7 "Murder Most Foul!" *Dolores News* (Rico, CO), May 21, 1881, p. 2.
8 "Fat Contributor," and "The Maxwell Land Grant," *Denver (CO) Republican*, March 29, 1881.
9 "City Splinters," *Trinidad (CO) Daily News*, May 12, 1881. The *News* reported that Thompson sold the Las Animas Grant for $150,000. *Durango Daily Record*, May 11, 1881. The *Record* reported that he purchased the Las Animas Grant for $100,000. Since Thompson resided in Trinidad, the report of the *News* is probably the correct one.
10 *Santa Fe Daily New Mexican*, May 18, 1881.
11 "$100 REWARD," *Durango (CO) Weekly Record*, May 7, 14 and 21, 1881. There were some minor variations from week to week on the brands depicted. The representation shown is as it appeared in the May 21st issue.
12 Ute Indian Agent Henry Page to Colonel Crofton, May 26, 1881, FLMP, Coll. M 118, B 2, S 4, F 2, FLC-CSWS.
13 *Dolores News*, January 17, 1885, p. 2. The *News* identifies Poco Narraguinnep as a chief of the Southern Utes, also known as the Weeminuche Utes. H.L. Mitchell to Colonel Crofton, June 21, 1881, FLMP, Coll. M 118, B 2, S 4, F 4, FLC-CSWS. Mitchell identified Poco Narraguinnep as the leader of the renegade band.
14 Deputy U.S. Marshal James J. Heffernan to Colonel Crofton, May 23, 1881, FLMP, Coll. M 118, B 2, S 4, F 2, FLC-CSWS.
15 Jones Adams [Charles Adam Jones], "In The Stronghold of the Piutes," *Overland Monthly*, vol. 22, issue 132 (December 1893): p. 584, http://archive.org/stream/overlandmonthly221893sanf#page/583/mode/1up (accessed February 28, 2013).
16 "Uncompahgre Utes Making Mischief," *Durango Weekly Record*, June 4, 1881.
17 Heffernan to Crofton, May 23, 1881, FLMP, Coll. M 118, B 2, S 4, F 2, FLC-CSWS.
18 Albert W. Puett, "The Late Indian Atrocities," *Durango Weekly Record*, May 21, 1881.

NOTES 441

[19] J.H. Alderson to Colonel Crofton, May 26, 1881, FLMP, Coll. M 118, B 2, S 4, F 3, FLC-CSWS; Albert W. Puett, letter to the editor, *Durango Daily Record*, May 12, 1881. Puett identifies the cabin location as Pine Springs.

[20] "The Southern Utes," *Durango Daily Record*, June 1, 1881.

[21] "Raiding a Ranch," *Denver Republican*, May 10, 1881; "Interesting Indian Intelligence," *Dolores News*, May 14, 1881, p. 2.

[22] Albert W. Puett, a letter to the editor, *Durango Daily Record*, May 12, 1881.

[23] "Interesting Indian Intelligence," *Dolores News*, May 14, 1881, p. 2.

[24] J.H. Alderson to Colonel Crofton, May 26, 1881, FLMP, Coll. M 118, B 2, S 4, F 3, FLC-CSWS; "Raiding a Ranch," *Denver Republican*, May 10, 1881.

[25] D.D. Williams to Colonel Crofton, May 2, 1881, FLMP, Coll. M 118, B 2, S 4, F 1, FLC-CSWS; Albert W. Puett, letter to the editor, *Durango Daily Record*, May 12, 1881.

[26] Mrs. W.C. Ormiston, "Settlement of the Mancos Valley," *Mancos (CO) Times-Tribune*, August 16, 1907, p. 1; *U.S. Census 1880*, La Plata County, CO, r. 91, p. 568, IA-ACPL. In 1880, Benny Quick resided with Henry Goodman on the Rio Mancos.

[27] Albert W. Puett, a letter to the editor, *Durango Daily Record*, May 12, 1881; Adams, "In The Stronghold of the Piutes," p. 584. In this December 1893 article, Jones Adams (Charles Adam Jones) reported the unsubstantiated rumor that Smith had turned up alive and well, living in Santa Fe.

[28] "More About the Indian Outrages," *Durango Weekly Record*, May 14, 1881. This report noted that Thurman had six bullet wounds and an axe or hatchet splitting open his head. The crows had been picking at his brains through the gash.

[29] *U.S. Census 1870*, Huerfano County, CO, r. 95, p. 323b, IA-ACPL.

[30] Mrs. W.C. Ormiston, "Settlement of the Mancos Valley," *Mancos (CO) Times-Tribune*, August 16, 1907, p. 1.

[31] "Was a Brave Soldier," *Aspen Tribune*, July 24, 1898, p. 3.

[32] Williams to Crofton, May 2, 1881, FLMP, Coll. M 118, B 2, S 4, F 1, FLC-CSWS.

[33] Arcade Ambo, "More About the Indians," *Durango Weekly Record*, May 21, 1881; *U.S. Census 1880*, La Plata County, CO, r. 91, p. 570c, IA-ACPL.

[34] "Raiding a Ranch," *Denver Republican*, May 10, 1881.

[35] "Troops Moving," *Denver Republican*, May 12, 1881.

[36] "Raiding A Ranch," *Denver Republican*, May 10, 1881.

[37] Telegram from Department of the Army, Missouri to Commanding Officer of Fort Lewis on the La Plata, May 9, 1881 and what is probably a transcribed telegram from District of New Mexico to Commanding Officer at Fort Lewis, May 11, 1881, FLMP, Coll. M 118, B 2, S 4, F 2, FLC-CSWS.

[38] "Raiding a Ranch," *Denver Republican*, May 10, 1881.

[39] "After Outlaws," *Denver Republican*, May 11, 1881; "New Mexico Murderers," *Denver Republican*, May 14, 1881.

[40] Requisition from New Mexico to Colorado, for Isaac Stockton and others, April 29, 1881, roll 1, microcopy 364, Coll. I 023, Interior Department, Territorial Papers, New Mexico, 1851-1914, RG 48, NARA, FLC-CSWS.

[41] "New Mexico Murderers," *Denver Republican*, May 14, 1881.

[42] "After Outlaws," *Denver Republican*, May 11, 1881.

[43] "Murder Most Foul!" *Dolores News*, May 21, 1881, p. 2.

44 "The Rio Arriba Troubles," *Santa Fe Daily New Mexican*, April 27, 1881.

45 "The Death of Lacy," *Denver Republican*, May 21, 1881, from the *Trinidad Times;* "Murder Most Foul!" *Dolores News,* May 21, 1881, p. 2. The *News* says J.F. Bond sent the $10 to Howland via Lacy.

46 "Murder Most Foul!" *Dolores News*, May 21, 1881, p. 2.

47 "Death of I.W. Lacy," *Cimarron (NM) News and Press,* May 17, 1881, from the *Trinidad Times.*

48 "Cold Blooded Murder," *Durango Weekly Record*, May 14, 1881.

49 Thomas Nance, "A Correction," *Durango Daily Record*, May 20, 1881.

50 "Damning Evidence!" *Dolores News*, May 28, 1881, p. 1.

51 "The Death of Lacy," *Denver Republican*, May 21, 1881, from the *Trinidad Times.*

52 "Damning Evidence!" *Dolores News*, May 28, 1881, p. 1; "The Death of Lacy," *Denver Republican* May 21, 1881, from the *Trinidad Times.*

53 "Cold Blooded Murder," *Durango Weekly Record*, May 14, 1881.

54 Ibid.

55 "Damning Evidence," *Dolores News*, May 28, 1881, p. 1.

56 George West to Colonel Crofton, May 10, 1881, FLMP, Coll. M 118, B 2, S 4, F 2, FLC-CSWS.

57 "Murder Most Foul!" *Dolores News*, May 21, 1881 p. 2.

58 "The Death of Lacy," *Denver Republican* May 21, 1881, from the *Trinidad Times.*

59 Dick Dalrymple, "Henry Goodman: Moab's Forgotten Icon," *Canyon Legacy,* Journal of the Dan O'Laurie Canyon Country Museum, vol. 45 (Summer 2002): pp. 5-6.

60 "Local," *Durango Weekly Record,* July 9, 1881.

61 William B. Haines to Governor Wallace, May 21, 1881, GLWP, TANM, NMSRCA.

62 Heffernan to Crofton, May 23, 1881, FLMP, Coll. M 118, B 2, S 4, F 2, FLC-CSWS.

63 Albert W. Puett, "The Late Indian Atrocities," *Durango Weekly Record*, May 21, 1881.

64 "After Outlaws," *Denver Republican,* May 11, 1881; Governor Pitkin to Mrs. A.E. Stockton, November 8, 1881, Governor Frederick W. Pitkin, correspondence outgoing, Colorado State Archives.

65 "Amargo," *La Plata Miner* (Silverton, CO) April 30, 1881.

66 "Murder Most Foul!" *Dolores News,* May 21, 1881, p. 2; "The Death of Lacy," *Denver Republican*, May 21, 1881; "The Dead Cattle King," *Trinidad (CO) Daily News,* May 18, 1881. This article notes that Gash was a Thompson and Lacy employee. Some newspaper accounts outside of Trinidad identify Major Gash as Colonel Gash.

67 "Murder." *Trinidad Daily News,* May 15, 1881.

68 Ibid.

69 "Death of I.W. Lacy," *Cimarron (NM) News and Press*, May 19, 1881, portions as reported by the *Trinidad Times; Trinidad Daily News,* May 17 and May 19, 1881.

70 "Murder." *Trinidad Daily News,* May 15, 1881.

71 "Murder Most Foul!" *Dolores News,* May 21, 1881, p. 2.

72 "Cold Blooded Murder," *Durango Weekly Record,* May 14, 1881.

73 *Durango Weekly Record,* May 14, 1881; "An Unauthorized Action," *Santa Fe Daily New Mexican,* May 27, 1881, portions as reported by the *Durango Record.*

[74] "An Unauthorized Action," *Santa Fe Daily New Mexican*, May 27, 1881, portions as reported by the *Durango Record*.

[75] *Durango Weekly Record*, May 14, 1881.

[76] "The Death of Lacy," *Denver Republican*, May 21, 1881, from the *Trinidad Times*.

[77] "Got His Dose," *Dolores News* (Rico, CO), May 21, 1881, p. 2.

[78] "A Kid Gone," *Santa Fe Daily New Mexican*, May 19, 1881; "Got His Dose," *Dolores News*, May 21, 1881, p. 2.

[79] "A Kid Gone," *Santa Fe Daily New Mexican*, May 19, 1881.

[80] Irving McKee, *"Ben-Hur" Wallace* (Berkeley and Los Angeles: University of California Press, 1947), p. 160.

[81] *U.S. Census 1860*, Erath County, TX. r. 1293, p. 118a, IA-ACPL; Randy Farrar, e-mail message to author, August 3, 2010. Farrar's research notes that James Galbreath's first wife is not known, his second wife was Elvira Garrison. She was the mother of Marion Galbreath. His third wife was Elizabeth Ann Hickey. Farrar noted that more research was needed to firm up this data.

[82] "Ike Stockton Killed," *Dolores News*, October 1, 1881, p. 1; *Texas v. M.H. Gilbreath [sic]*, p. 12, case no. 101, State Docket, District Court, Bosque County District Clerk Records. This case from the June 1874 term of court is for "An assault with intent to commit a rape."

[83] Clifford R. Caldwell and Ron DeLord, *Texas Lawmen, 1835-1899: The Good and the Bad* (Charleston, SC: The History Press, 2011), pp. 28-29.

[84] City of Waco, *Fugitives From Justice - The Notebook of Texas Ranger Sergeant James B. Gillett*, with a foreword by Michael D. Morrison (Austin: State House Press, 1997), pp. 6 and 173.

[85] *John A. Dupuy v. Marion Galbreath et al*, p. 333, case no. 441 and *John A. Dupuy v. Marion Galbreath et al*, p. 354 and 355, case no. 441, vol. C, 1874-1884, Erath County District Court Minutes, TSU-DSL

[86] "Mysterious Outfit," *Trinidad Daily News*, May 17, 1881. The quote is from the *News*. The incident is also briefly referred to in "Town and Country," *Santa Fe Daily New Mexican*, May 20, 1881.

[87] "Death of I.W. Lacy," *Cimarron (NM) News and Press*, May 19, 1881, from the *Trinidad Times*.

[88] Thomas Nance, "A Correction," *Durango Daily Record*, May 20, 1881.

[89] Thomas Nance, "A Correction," *Durango Daily Record*, May 20, 1881; *U.S. Census 1880*, Las Animas County, CO, r. 92, p. 120c, IA-ACPL.

[90] "The Dead Cattle King," *Trinidad Daily News*, May 18, 1881; S.C. Lacy, "Dictation of the widow of I.W. Lacy," Western Americana Collection, The Bancroft Collection, Bancroft Library, University of California, Berkeley, CA, from microfilm archived at the Center for Southwest Research, University of New Mexico, Albuquerque, NM. Mrs. Lacy names her children in a dictation which was taken at her home on the Vermejo on September 4, 1885 by J.T. Grayson. Two of her daughters were married at that time.

[91] "Funeral of Mr. Lacy," *Trinidad Daily News*, May 19, 1881.

[92] "Damning Evidence!" *Dolores News*, May 28, 1881, p. 1.

[93] "Local Intelligence," *Dolores News*, May 28, 1881, p. 3; "Drowned in the Dolores," *Dolores News*, May 28, 1881, p. 2.

[94] "Damning Evidence!" *Dolores News*, May 28, 1881, p. 1.

[95] Ibid.

⁹⁶ Ibid.
⁹⁷ "Escape of Desperado Convicts," *Los Angeles Daily Herald*, December 4, 1881, p. 2.
⁹⁸ *Dodge City (KS) Times*, April 28, 1881, p. 5.
⁹⁹ "Escape of Desperado Convicts," *Los Angeles Daily Herald*, December 4, 1881, p. 2.
¹⁰⁰ Howard Bryan, *Wildest of the Wild West* (Santa Fe: Clear Light Publishers, 1988), p. 193.
¹⁰¹ "A New Mexican Episode," *Washington (DC) Evening Star*, December 26, 1896, p. 15.
¹⁰² "An Unauthorized Action," *Santa Fe Daily New Mexican*, May 27, 1881, portions as reported by the *Durango Record*.

CHAPTER FOURTEEN – COWBOYS AND INDIANS

¹ Arthur Chapman, "The War-Horse Buyers," *Out Where the West Begins and Other Western Verses* (Boston and New York: Houghton Mifflin Company, 1917), p. 59.
² D.D. Williams to Colonel Crofton, May 26, 1881, FLMP, Coll. M 118, box 2, series 4, folder 3, FLC-CSWS.
³ "Arcade Ambo" and "More About the Indians," *Durango (CO) Weekly Record*, May 21, 1881.
⁴ "Fort Lewis Invaded!" *Durango (CO) Daily Record*, May 19, 1881.
⁵ Green Robinson to Colonel Crofton, May 26, 1881, J.H. Alderson to Colonel Crofton, May 26, 1881, D.D. Williams to Colonel Crofton, May 26, 1881, FLMP, Coll. M 118, B 2, S 4, F 3, FLC-CSWS.
⁶ "Red Murderers in the Blue Mountains," *Durango Weekly Record*, May 28, 1881. The *Record* identified their roundup informant as G.W. Robinson.
⁷ *Dolores News*, May 21, 1881, p. 2.
⁸ Military District of New Mexico to C.O. (Colonel Crofton), May 13, 1881, FLMP, Coll. M 118, B 2, S 4, F 2, FLC-CSWS.
⁹ "The Renegade Utes on the Warpath!" *La Plata Miner* (Silverton, CO), June 25, 1881.
¹⁰ "Obituary: Death of Sister M. Rita," *Intermountain Catholic* (Salt Lake, City, UT), July 30, 1910, p. 8. Sister Rita was the daughter of Animas City resident James J. Heffernan.
¹¹ Military District of New Mexico to Colonel Crofton, May 26, 1881, FLMP, Coll. M 118, B 2, S 4, F 3, FLC-CSWS.
¹² "Murder by the Indians at the Field of New Discovery," *Dolores News* (Rico, CO) March 13, 1880, p. 1.
¹³ "Pah-Utes on the War Path," *La Plata Miner*, March 13, 1880; "Interesting Career of Indian Scout, Pioneer Cattleman, Comes to Close," *Moab (UT) Times-Independent*, May 31, 1934.
¹⁴ H.L. Mitchell to Colonel Crofton, June 21, 1881, FLMP, Coll. M 118, B 2, S 4, F 4, FLC-CSWS.
¹⁵ "The Indian Ring," *Colorado Weekly Chieftain* (Pueblo, CO), December 25, 1879, p. 2; "Carbonates, Nuggets, Squibs and General News," *Dolores News*, Jan. 31, 1880, p. 1.
¹⁶ "Rio Arriba," *Santa Fe Daily New Mexican*, May 14, 1881.

[17] William Haines to Adjutant General Max Frost, May 26, 1881, LRRAGT, TANM, NMSRCA. From TANM roll 73.

[18] Ibid. Apparently Frost was involved in the development of a new irrigation ditch in western Rio Arriba County.

[19] "Rio Arriba," *Santa Fe Daily New Mexican*, May 14, 1881.

[20] "Historial Nubs," *Farmington (NM) Times Hustler*, May 24, 1940, from the *Santa Fe Daily New Mexican* of May 10, 1881.

[21] Haines to Frost, May 26, 1881, LRRAGT, TANM, NMSRCA.

[22] "Municipal Election!" *Durango Weekly Record*, May 14, 1881; Jno. Taylor Jr., Druggist advertisement, *Durango Weekly Record*, May 21, 1881.

[23] "Rio Arriba," *Santa Fe Daily New Mexican*, May 29, 1881.

[24] William B. Haines to Governor Wallace, May 21, 1881, Campaign, TANM, NMSRCA.

[25] Haines to Wallace, May 21, 1881, Campaign, TANM, NMSRCA. See also, "Rio Arriba," *Santa Fe Daily New Mexican*, May 29, 1881, which carries portions of the same dispatch from Haines.

[26] Haines to Wallace, May 21, 1881, Campaign, TANM, NMSRCA.

[27] *Dolores News*, June 11, 1881, p. 1.

[28] "Rio Arriba," *Santa Fe Daily New Mexican*, May 29, 1881. A copy of a May 28, 1881 letter from Wallace to Pitkin.

[29] *Durango Daily Record*, May 6, 1881. A refutation of the *South Pueblo Banner* article.

[30] *Rio Grande Republican* (Las Cruces, NM), May 28, 1881.

[31] "The Rio Arriba Trouble," *Santa Fe Daily New Mexican*, June 1, 1881; Justo Sandoval, letter to the editor, *Santa Fe Daily New Mexican*, June 3, 1881.

[32] Haines to Wallace, May 21, 1881, Campaign, TANM, NMSRCA.

[33] Lew Wallace, *Lew Wallace: An Autobiography*, vol. 2 (New York and London: Harper and Brothers Publishers, 1906), p. 925, http://archive.org/stream/lewwallacevolii002480mbp#page/n3/mode/2up (accessed January 30, 2012).

[34] "The Rio Arriba Trouble," *Santa Fe Daily New Mexican*, June 1, 1881. In the June 3, 1881 *Daily New Mexican* Sandoval in a letter to the editor asserts that up to that time he had never seen the letter from Governor Wallace. While in Santa Fe, he says Max Frost showed it to him.

[35] Haines to Frost, May 26, 1881, LRRAGT, TANM, NMSRCA. En was Enos Blancett and according to his great niece Ella Ann Spargo he was always referred to as En, which rhymes with bean. Interview with Ella Ann Spargo on July 5, 2008; Workers of the Writers' Program of the Work Projects Administration, *New Mexico – A Guide to the Colorful State –American Guide Series* (New York: Coronado Cuarto Centennial Commission, Hastings House, 1940), p. 365. The WPA article reports that Blancett used crutches when he lived near Bloomfield. A list of potential San Juan Guard members can be found in a letter from Adjutant General Frost, Dep. Sheriff Blancett and Wm B. Haines (Captain San Juan Guards), April 15 and 16, 1881, Campaign, TANM, NMSRCA. The list includes Dan Sullivan who became sheriff of the newly created San Juan County, New Mexico in 1887.

[36] "Local Intelligence," *Dolores News*, May 28, 1881, p. 3; "Drowned in the Dolores," *Dolores News*, May 28, 1881, p. 2. This article indicates Ike was in Rico by at least May 23rd.

37 "Drowned in the Dolores," *Dolores News*, May 28, 1881, p. 2.
38 Charles Jones, "The Memoirs of Charles Adam Jones," n.d., pp. 90, 148, 149 and 158, Clifford B. Jones Papers, 1814-1973 and undated, Accession Nos. 96-0122-B and 98-0001-B, Southwest Collection/Special Collections Library, Texas Tech University, Lubbock.
39 *Dolores News*, May 28, 1881, p. 1.
40 Jones, "The Memoirs of Charles Adam Jones," p. 97.
41 *Santa Fe Daily New Mexican*, June, 4, 1881.
42 "Ugly Utes," *Durango (CO) Herald*, July 7, 1881.
43 "War with the Pah-Utes," *Denver (CO) Republican*, June 25, 1881.
44 "Ugly Utes," *Durango Herald*, July 7, 1881.
45 *U.S. Census 1880*, Ouray County, CO, r. 92, p. 176c, ABCLS.
46 "Indian Intelligence," *Dolores News*, June 4, 1881, p. 2. Also see Jonathon C. Horn, principal investigator, *Landscape Level History of the Canyons of the Ancients National Monument Montezuma and Dolores Counties, Colorado* (Dolores, CO: Bureau of Land Management, 2004), p. 17, http://www.blm.gov/heritage/adventures/research/StatePages/PDFs/Colorado/Studies/Ancients%20Report.pdf. (accessed March 15, 2009). Horn lists the civilian contingent. Those who survived were Billy May, Jordan Bean, Tom Pepper, Jess Seeley, Hi Barber, M.C. Cook, Hargo Eskridge, Ike Stockton, D.G. Taylor, Tim Jenkins, Billy Parks, Charlie Reynolds, James Hall, Bill Dawson, (first name not known) Purdy, Ed Summers, Bill Robins and Tex La Fone.
47 Captain Rogers to Colonel Crofton, May 26, 1881 and Patrick O'Donnell and others to Fort Lewis, May 26, 1881, FLMP, Coll. M 118, B 2, S 4, F 3, FLC-CSWS.
48 Marshal Heffernan to Colonel Crofton, Friday, May 27, 1881 (5:00 AM), FLMP, Coll. M 118, B 2, S 4, F 3, FLC-CSWS.
49 Captain Rogers to Colonel Crofton, May 29, 1881 FLMP, Coll. M 118, B 2, S 4, F 3, FLC-CSWS.

CHAPTER FIFTEEN – BATTLE IN THE LA SALS

1 MacMahon, "Jack Dempsey's Grave," *Songs of the Cattle Trail and Cow Camp*, comp. by John A. Lomax (New York: The MacMillan Company, 1920), p. 52.
2 *Dolores News* (Rico, CO), June 4, 1881, p. 1, from the *Durango Record*.
3 James I. Hall, *La Plata Miner* (Silverton, CO), June 11, 1881, as reported in a letter to the *Durango (CO) Record*. The June 4, 1881 issue of the *Record* identified Hall as the Mancos school teacher.
4 *Dolores News*, June 4, 1881, p. 1, from the *Durango Record*.
5 "A 'Quien Sabe' Case," *Dolores News*, June 11, 1881, p. 2, from the *Durango Record*.
6 Frederic W. Pitkin, letter to J.E. Clark, "The Indian Atrocities," *Durango Daily Record*, May 23, 1881.
7 "Last Version of the Grand Valley Battle," *Dolores News*, July 2, 1881, p. 2. This article identifies Dawson as Captain. "War! With the Indians!" *Dolores News*, June 25, 1881, p. 1. This article notes that as the battle developed May became displeased and left the main group taking "his squad." *Colorado State Census, 1885*, Dolores County, r. 3, p. 16, ABCLS.
8 "Indian Intelligence," *Dolores News*, June 4, 1881, p. 2.

[9] "The Renegade Utes On The Warpath!" *La Plata Miner*, June 25, 1881, from the *Durango Record*.

[10] Ibid.

[11] Frank Silvey, "Rambling Thoughts Of A Rimrocker," *San Juan Record* (Monticello, UT), October 10, 1935.

[12] "The Renegade Utes On The Warpath!" *La Plata Miner*, June 25, 1881, from the *Durango Record*.

[13] "Interesting Indian News," *Dolores News*, June 18, 1881, p. 1.

[14] Green Robinson to Colonel Crofton, About May 26, 1881 and J.H. Alderson to Colonel Crofton, May 26, 1881, FLMP, Coll. M 118, B 2, S 4, F 3, FLC-CSWS.

[15] Hugh O'Neil, "Crude Tombstone Marks Early Utah Prospector's Grave," *San Juan Record*, March 10, 1938.

[16] "Santa Fe Squibs," *Rio Grande Republican* (Las Cruces, NM), June 11, 1881, ABCLS.

[17] "Personal Prods." *Dolores News*, June 11, 1881, p. 3.

[18] "Ignacio's Indians," *Denver (CO) Republican*, August 11, 1881.

[19] L.F. Flood and Wm. Shea, "Fight on the Dolores," *Salt Lake Daily Tribune* (Salt Lake City, UT), June 30, 1881. Shea's name is spelled as both Shea and Shay in the letter.

[20] "The Trouble with the Utes," *Cimarron (NM) News and Press*, June 16, 1881.

[21] *Santa Fe Daily New Mexican*, June 19, 1881.

[22] "On the Eve of Battle," *Dolores News*, June 18, 1881, p. 2.

[23] "Personal Prods." *Dolores News*, June 18, 1881, p. 3.

[24] "Return of Rico's Reinforcements," *Dolores News*, July 9, 1881, p. 2.

[25] Mr. and Mrs. Jordon [sic] Bean, "Last Survivor Recounts 'Pinhook' Indian Fight," *Moab (UT) Times-Independent*, September 26, 1940.

[26] "Second Anniversary," *Dolores News*, June 16, 1883. The date of the first day of battle varies depending on the source. The actual memorial marker in the Pinhook Draw has the date of June 15, 1881. The *Dolores News* of June 16, 1883 says the final battle started on June 16th. The *Durango Weekly Record* in an article titled, "The Bad Break," on June 25, 1881 said the final battle started on June 16th and continued on the 17th. Flood and Shea in their letter of June 21, 1881 ("Fight on the Dolores,"), which was published in the *Salt Lake Daily Tribune* on June 30, 1881, put the date as June 14th. Frank Silvey in The *Moab (UT) Times-Independent* of September 5, 1940 in an article titled "The 'Pinhook' Indian Battle," says the Coloradoans finally caught up with the Indians "on or about June 15 1881."

[27] L.F. Flood and Wm. Shea, "Fight on the Dolores," *Salt Lake Daily Tribune*, June 30, 1881.

[28] "Ugly Utes," *Durango (CO) Herald*, July 7, 1881. The *Herald* may have been confused and not realized that Dawson was the captain.

[29] "Second Anniversary," *Dolores News*, June 16, 1883.

[30] "A Frontier Incident," *Deseret News* (Salt Lake City, UT), September 27, 1882; "Second Anniversary," *Dolores News*, June 16, 1883. The *News* says the Wilsons joined the Coloradoans at noon.

[31] Rusty Salmon and Robert S. McPherson, "Cowboys, Indians, and Conflict: The Pinhook Draw Fight, 1881," *Utah Historical Quarterly*, vol. 69, no. 1 (Winter 2001): p. 18.

[32] U.S.G.S. Map, *Warner Lake, Utah Quadrangle*, 2001.

³³ Silvey, "Rambling Thoughts Of A Rimrocker," *San Juan Record*, October 3, 1935. Exactly what happened on the expedition is not easily determined, due to conflicting reports. It seems unlikely that May and his followers would abandon their mission. The death of Billy May's brother along with Smith and Thurman was the reason for the expedition and he was the leading recruiter of volunteers. He despised the Indians and apparently the feeling was mutual. The men who went down the rim weren't exactly disoriented; they were simply not familiar with the local terrain. Whatever happened, May and the men with him missed the battle.

³⁴ "Second Anniversary," *Dolores News*, June 16, 1883. The *News* says there were thirty-eight men in all before the forces split. That figure does not include the Wilson brothers. The same article says seventeen Rico men pursued the Indians and then were joined by the two Wilson brothers.

³⁵ Ibid.

³⁶ Jordan Bean and Edgar C. McMechen, "Jordan Bean's Story and the Castle Valley Indian Fight," *The Colorado Magazine*, vol. 20, no. 1 (January 1943): p. 20.

³⁷ The battle location is evident, since the men were buried close to where they fell, which is now marked by the Pinhook monument.

³⁸ Silvey, "Rambling Thoughts Of A Rimrocker," *San Juan Record*, October 3, 1935.

³⁹ Silvey, "Rambling Thoughts Of A Rimrocker," *San Juan Record*, October 3, 1935. Silvey says that as the men advanced they came upon a ridge that was "covered with scrub oak, and large boulders." A fire in late August 2008 in the Pinhook valley exposed all of the boulders and there is no hillside on the southwest side of the valley that is covered with boulders. The Pinhook Battle Monument is the best evidence we have for the location of the most intense fighting. The monument marking where the men were buried is close to the southwestern side of the valley, directly across the valley from the only boulder strewn slope in the valley. The distance from the boulder covered slope to the monument is about five hundred yards, much too far away for an ambush and accurate rifle fire.

⁴⁰ Ibid. Eskridge and Hall were the only ones who survived the ravine. Silvey identifies them as "two of the Rico boys."

⁴¹ A.W. Bowen and Company, comp., *Progressive Men of Western Colorado* (Chicago: A.W. Bowen and Company, 1905), p. 862, http://archive.org/stream/progressivemenof00awborich#page/862/mode/1up/search/hall (accessed February 14, 2013). It does not appear that this James Hall was the same James Hall who was the Mancos school teacher.

⁴² Mr. and Mrs. Jordon [sic] Bean, "Last Survivor Recounts 'Pinhook' Indian Fight," *Moab (UT) Times-Independent*, September 26, 1940.

⁴³ "Second Anniversary," *Dolores News*, June 16, 1883.

⁴⁴ Silvey, "Rambling Thoughts Of A Rimrocker," *San Juan Record*, October 3, 1935.

⁴⁵ "Last Version of the Grand Valley Indian Battle," *Dolores News*, July 2, 1881 p. 2.

⁴⁶ Silvey, "Rambling Thoughts Of A Rimrocker," *San Juan Record*, October 3, 1935. The 1880 census for Utah shows Pat "McKenna," an Irish miner living in the eastern portion of Emery County close to the Wilson family. He is not mentioned elsewhere as being a member of the initial expedition or as a member of

the Moab rescue group, which arrived after the main battle was over. *U.S. Census 1880*, Emery County, UT, r. 1336, p. 322a, IA-ACPL. Also see F. Stanley, *Ike Stockton* (Denver: World Press, Inc., 1959), p. 108. Stanley says Tim Jenkins was the rescuer.

[47] "War! With the Indians!" *Dolores News,* June 25, 1881, p. 1.

[48] Silvey, "Rambling Thoughts Of A Rimrocker," *San Juan Record*, October 3 and October 10, 1935.

[49] L.F. Flood and Wm. Shea, "Fight on the Dolores," *Salt Lake Daily Tribune*, June 30, 1881. According to Flood and Shea's letter the rescue party from Moab included L.F. Flood, Walt Moore, L.B. Bartlett, William Shea, Frank Gains, A. Guyzer and his father, J. Fisher, William Miller, Joseph Burkholder, John Maloy and one other man whose name is illegible.

[50] "Second Anniversary," *Dolores News,* June 16, 1883.

[51] L.F. Flood and Wm. Shea, "Fight on the Dolores," *Salt Lake Daily Tribune*, June 30, 1881.

[52] Mr. and Mrs. Jordon [sic] Bean, "Last Survivor Recounts 'Pinhook' Indian Fight," *Moab (UT) Times-Independent,* September 26, 1940.

[53] L.F. Flood and Wm. Shea, "Fight on the Dolores," *Salt Lake Daily Tribune*, June 30, 1881.

[54] Faun McConkie, "A History of Moab," ch. 6, *Moab (UT) Times-Independent*, May 31, 1934.

[55] "The Fight With the Utes," *Denver Republican*, June 29, 1881. According to an account headlined "News from the Utes," in the *Santa Fe Daily New Mexican*, July 13, 1881, troops under Captain Carroll's command subsequently found the bodies of five dead Indians, one of them a woman.

[56] McConkie, "A History of Moab," ch. 6, *Moab (UT) Times-Independent*, May 31, 1934.

[57] L.F. Flood and Wm. Shea, "Fight on the Dolores," *Salt Lake Daily Tribune*, June 30, 1881.

[58] Mr and Mrs. Jordon [sic] Bean, "Last Survivor Recounts 'Pinhook' Indian Fight," *Moab (UT) Times-Independent,* September 26, 1940.

[59] L.F. Flood and Wm. Shea, "Fight on the Dolores," *Salt Lake Daily Tribune*, June 30, 1881.

[60] Silvey, "Rambling Thoughts Of A Rimrocker," *San Juan Record*, October 3 and October 10, 1935.

[61] "Latest Telegrams," *Salt Lake (UT) Herald*, June 26, 1881, from the *Durango Record*.

[62] "Return of Rico's Reinforcements," *Dolores News*, July 9, 1881, p. 2.

[63] Silvey, "Rambling Thoughts Of A Rimrocker," *San Juan Record*, October 10, 1935.

[64] U.S.G.S. Map, *Warner Lake, Utah Quadrangle*, 2001.

[65] L.F. Flood and Wm. Shea, "Fight on the Dolores," *Salt Lake Daily Tribune*, June 30, 1881.

[66] A.G. Wilson, R.H. Stewart and W.A. Peirce, "Correspondence," *Deseret News*, July 6, 1881.

[67] "Last Version of the Grand Valley Indian Battle," *Dolores News*, July 2, 1881, p. 2.

[68] "A Frontier Incident," *Deseret News*, September 27, 1882.

[69] "Last Version of the Grand Valley Indian Battle," *Dolores News*, July 2, 1881, p. 2.

[70] Bean and McMechen, "Jordan Bean's Story," p. 23.

[71] A.G. Wilson, R.H. Stewart and W.A. Peirce, "Correspondence," *Deseret News*, July 6, 1881.

[72] "Last Version of the Grand Valley Indian Battle," *Dolores News*, July 2, 1881 p. 2.

[73] "Neighborhood Notes," *Dolores News*, September 17, 1881 p. 1, from the *Ouray Times*.

[74] Salmon and McPherson, "The Pinhook Draw Fight," pp. 20 and 26. According to an article headlined, "A Frontier Incident" in the *Deseret News* of September 27, 1882, four months after the battle, Mrs. America J. Willis, the twenty-six-year-old mother of three and widow of Dave Willis, rode the 140 miles to the Wilson stock ranch. She was accompanied by two men and carried a Henry rifle and had two Colt revolvers hanging from her saddle. She asked Wilson for assistance and he provided seven men and himself to help procure the remains of her husband for reburial at their home. Relatives also removed the remains of Hi Melvin for reburial near Dolores. According to Hugo Weston four men traveled with Mrs. Willis on the journey to retrieve her husband's remains; H.M. Barber, Dalton Reynolds, Cal House and her brother Roy Weston. He reported that the group retrieved both the body of Willis and of Melvin. See the June 14, 1924 letter from Hugo Weston to Martin Rush, copy obtained by Florence Robison, March 27, 1934, Montezuma County, p. 184, CWA Pioneer Interviews, Special Collections, SHHLRC, HCC.

[75] "Latest Telegrams," *Salt Lake (UT) Herald*, June 26, 1881, from the *Durango Record; Dolores News*, June 25, 1881, pp. 2. See "extract from the *Durango Record* of June 22d."

[76] "WAR!" *Dolores News*, June 25, 1881, pp. 1.

[77] "The Trouble Between the Cattle Men and Pahutes," *Sacramento (CA) Daily Record-Union* June 25, 1881.

[78] "War With The Pah-Utes," *Denver Republican*, June 25, 1881.

[79] "The Indian Fight," *Saguache (CO) Chronicle*, July 1, 1881, p. 1.

[80] "The Ute War," *Cimarron (NM) News and Press*, June 30, 1881, from the *Durango Record*.

[81] "Latest Telegrams," *Salt Lake (UT) Herald*, June 26, 1881, from the *Durango Record*.

[82] "WAR!" *Dolores News*, June 25, 1881, p. 1.

[83] F.W. Raymond, *Ouray (CO) Times*, June 25, 1881.

[84] "War!" *Dolores News*, June 25, 1881, p. 1.

[85] "The Latest From The Utes," *Santa Fe Daily New Mexican*, June 29, 1881, from the *Denver Republican*.

[86] Charles Jones, "The Memoirs of Charles Adam Jones," n.d., p. 139, Clifford B. Jones Papers, 1814-1973 and undated, Accession Nos. 96-0122-B and 98-0001-B, Southwest Collection/Special Collections Library, Texas Tech University, Lubbock.

[87] "Return of Rico's Reinforcements," *Dolores News*, July 9, 1881, p. 2. According to the *News*, there were twenty-six members of the Pinhook Rescue Expedition at Piute Springs: L. Alderman, Al Bradley, John Carey, John Clark, Thomas Carroll,

Pat Cain, W.M. Eccles, Dison Eskridge, S.C. Grant, Worden Grigsby, Gus Hefferman, William Huntley, Charles A. Jones, W.H. Lilley, Mike Murphy, D. McIntyre, S.W. McCormack, Sam McCreary, H. Phillipi, L. Phillipi, George Perkins, A.M. Rogers, John Silvey, Frank Summers, Kid Thomas and D.G. Taylor. In his memoirs on p. 139, Jones also lists the name of Dee Breckenridge. *Dolores News*, October 2, 1880, p. 3, a blurb announcing Grigsby's appointment as a town trustee.

[88] Jones Adams [Charles Adam Jones], "In The Stronghold of the Piutes," *Overland Monthly*, vol. 22, issue 132 (December 1893): pp. 589-590, http://archive.org/stream/overlandmonthly221893sanf#page/583/mode/1up (accessed February 28, 2013).

[89] "Return of Rico's Reinforcements," *Dolores News*, July 9, 1881, p. 2.

[90] Adams, "In The Stronghold of the Piutes," p. 590.

[91] Jones, "The Memoirs of Charles Adam Jones," pp. 138-141; "Notes on the Indian Campaign," *Dolores News*, July 9, 1881, p. 2. This article identifies the Goshorn family and notes the return of Heaton's stallion. "Body of Victim of Famous Indian Fight at Pinhook, at Last Found," *Grand Valley Times* (Moab, UT), May 22, 1914.

[92] *Dolores News*, June 25, 1881, p. 2, from the *Durango Record*.

[93] Captain Carroll to Fort Lewis, June 20, 1881 and Captain Carroll to Fort Lewis, dated June 23, 1881, FLMP, Coll. M 118, box 2, series 4, folder 4, FLC-CSWS.

[94] "War With The Pah-Utes," *Denver Republican*, June 25, 1881.

[95] "Indians Punished in New Mexico," *Arizona Citizen* (Tucson), September 23, 1876, p. 3.

[96] "Miscellaneous," *Iola (KS) Register*, April 16, 1880, p. 2.

[97] Rusty Salmon, "The Little Castle Valley Fight," *Canyon Legacy*, Journal of the Dan O'Laurie Canyon Country Museum, vol. 41 (Spring 2001): pp. 23-24.

[98] Bean and McMechen, "Jordan Bean's Story," p. 23.

[99] *Dolores News*, July 23, 1881, p. 2, from the *Durango Record*.

[100] "Department of New Mexico," *Durango Weekly Record*, July 16, 1881.

[101] Duane A. Smith, *A Time for Peace: Fort Lewis, Colorado, 1878-1891* (Boulder: University Press of Colorado, 2006), p. 100. Smith places Byrne on the Ninth's foray into Utah. "Local Intelligence," *Dolores News*, July 9, 1881, p. 3.

[102] Jones, "The Memoirs of Charles Adam Jones," p. 143.

CHAPTER SIXTEEN – THE ALBUQUERQUE CAPTURE

[1] Herman Scheffauer, "Marta of Milrone," *Songs of the Cattle Trail and Cow Camp*, comp. by John A. Lomax (New York: The MacMillan Company, 1920), p. 48.

[2] Lew Wallace, *Lew Wallace: An Autobiography*, vol. 2 (New York and London: Harper and Brothers Publishers, 1906), p. 925, http://archive.org/stream/lewwallacevolii002480mbp#page/n3/mode/2up (accessed January 30, 2012).

[3] *Santa Fe Daily New Mexican*, June 1, 1881.

[4] "Governor Sheldon," *Santa Fe Daily New Mexican*, June 5, 1881.

[5] *Dolores News* (Rico, CO), May 14, 1881, p. 3, from the *Pueblo Chieftain*.

[6] "Trapped!" *Albuquerque Daily Journal*, June 17, 1881.

[7] "Disrupted Durango," *Denver Republican*, April 20, 1881.

⁸ "Trapped!" *Albuquerque Daily Journal*, June 17, 1881.

⁹ "Lodged in Limbo," *Denver (CO) Republican*, June 27, 1881.

¹⁰ "Allison's Gang," *Dolores News*, July 2, 1881, p. 1, from the *Santa Fe New Mexican*.

¹¹ Harry Jackson, "Harry Jackson and Mrs. Jackson," dictated to Ella Jackson Birkhimer, *Pioneers of the San Juan Country*, vol. 1, comp. and ed. Sarah Platt Decker Chapter D.A.R. (Durango, CO: Sarah Platt Decker Chapter D.A.R., 1942), p. 109.

¹² "Stage Robbery Near Pagosa," *Dolores News*, June 4, 1881, p. 2; "Another Stage Robbery," *La Plata Miner* (Silverton, CO), June 4, 1881, from the *Denver Republican*. According to the article titled "Hands Up!" in the *Saguache (CO) Chronicle*, June 10, 1881, p. 1, victims of the stage robbery included, A.L. Price of Pueblo, Moses Froelich of Denver, E.D. Kelly of Denver, J.E. Monroe of Leadville, G.N. Effinger of Omaha, Nebraska, J.K. Gash of Fort Lewis and the unnamed man who resided in Durango was Peter Keegan.

¹³ "Another Stage Robbery," *La Plata Miner*, June 4, 1881, from the *Denver Republican;* "More About the Late Stage Robbery," *Durango (CO) Daily Record*, May 30, 1881.

¹⁴ "Horses Stolen," *Durango Daily Record*, May 31, 1881

¹⁵ "Recovered!" *Durango (CO) Weekly Record*, June 4, 1881; "Horses Stolen," *Durango Daily Record*, May 31, 1881.

¹⁶ "The San Juan Desperadoes," *Cimarron (NM) News and Press*, June 9, 1881; Advertisement for Budweiser beer from C.L. Petherbridge of Chama, *Durango Daily Record*, June 1, 1881.

¹⁷ *Santa Fe Daily New Mexican*, June 2, 1881.

¹⁸ "The San Juan Desperadoes," *Cimarron (NM) News and Press*, June 9, 1881.

¹⁹ "Personal Prods," *Dolores News*, June 11, 1881, p. 3. The *News* contains the account of Schrock's losses. "Another stage Robbery," *Durango Weekly Record*, June 4, 1881.

²⁰ "Another Stage Robbery," *Durango Weekly Record*, June 4, 1881.

²¹ "Trouble in Conejos County," *Saguache (CO) Chronicle*, June 10, 1881, p. 5.

²² "Amargo Thieves," *La Plata Miner*, June 4, 1881.

²³ "Santa Fe Squibs," *Rio Grande Republican* (Las Cruces, NM), June 11, 1881.

²⁴ *Santa Fe Daily New Mexican*, June 14, 1881.

²⁵ "Colorado Taking a Turn," *Santa Fe New Mexican*, June 12, 1881, from the *Alamosa Independent*.

²⁶ Manuel Gonzales, letter to the editor, *Santa Daily New Mexican*, June 3, 1881; *Santa Fe Daily New Mexican*, June 2, 1881.

²⁷ "Can't Have Their Stock," *Dolores News*, June 4, 1881, p. 2, portions as reported by the *Durango Record* and *Trinidad News*.

²⁸ *Santa Fe Daily New Mexican*, June 14, 1881.

²⁹ "Personal," *Santa Fe Daily New Mexican*, June 15, 1881.

³⁰ *Santa Fe Daily New Mexican*, June 15, 1881.

³¹ "Stage Robbers Captured," *Denver Republican*, June 17, 1881.

³² "A Clever Capture," *Denver Republican*, June 24, 1881.

³³ General D.J. Cook, "Capture of the Allison Gang," *Hands Up, or, Thirty-Five Years of Detective Life in the Mountains and on the Plains*, comp., John W. Cook (Denver: D.J. and J.W. Cook, 1897), p. 37, http://www.archive.org/details/handsuporthirtyf00cook (accessed September 27, 2009).

[34] "A Clever Capture," *Denver Republican*, June 24, 1881; David F. Myrick, *New Mexico's Railroads - A Historical Survey*. Revised ed. (Albuquerque: University of New Mexico Press, 1990), p. 7. Myrick notes that the first train arrived in Santa Fe on February 9, 1880.

[35] Cook, "Capture of the Allison Gang," p. 37.

[36] "A Clever Capture," *Denver Republican*, June 24, 1881.

[37] Cook, "Capture of the Allison Gang," p. 38.

[38] Ibid.

[39] "A Clever Capture," *Denver Republican*, June 24, 1881.

[40] "Trapped!" *Albuquerque Daily Journal*, June 17, 1881.

[41] "A Clever Capture," *Denver Republican*, June 24, 1881.

[42] "Trapped!" *Albuquerque Daily Journal*, June 17, 1881.

[43] Ibid.

[44] "A Clever Capture," *Denver Republican*, June 24, 1881.

[45] "Allison's Arrest," *San Juan Herald* (Silverton, CO), June 30, 1881, from the *Santa Fe New Mexican*.

[46] "Stage Robbers Captured," *Denver Republican*, June 17, 1881.

[47] Criminal Complaint from Conejos County, Colorado, June 18, 1881, Requisitions for Extraditions from New Mexico, Governor Lionel Sheldon Papers, Records of the Territorial Governors, 1846-1912, TANM, NMSRCA.

[48] "Allison's Arrest," *San Juan Herald*, June 30, 1881, from the *Santa Fe New Mexican*.

[49] "A Clever Capture," *Denver Republican*, June 24, 1881.

[50] "Journal Jottings," *Albuquerque Daily Journal*, June 18, 1881.

[51] "The Prisoners," *Albuquerque Daily Journal*, June 20, 1881.

[52] "Allison's Arrest," *Saguache (CO) Chronicle*, June 24, 1881, from the *Denver News*; "The Allison Gang," *Denver Republican*, August 2, 1881. The *Republican* reported that Allison said he was an engineer and then went into mining and later sold his Arizona claims for $1700.

[53] "The Prisoners," *Albuquerque Daily Journal*, June 20, 1881; "Allison's Arrival," *Santa Fe Daily New Mexican*, June 21, 1881.

[54] Reward Certification Letter from Governor Sheldon, June 20, 1881, Governor Lionel Sheldon Papers, Records of the Territorial Governors, 1846-1912, Rewards for Wanted Men, TANM, NMSRCA.

[55] *Santa Fe Daily New Mexican*, June 24, 1881; Notice of Delivery of Prisoners, Santa Fe County Sheriff, July 5, 1881, Requisitions for Extraditions from New Mexico, Governor Lionel Sheldon Papers, Records of the Territorial Governors, 1846-1912, TANM, NMSRCA.

[56] *Santa Fe Daily New Mexican*, June 29, 1881.

[57] Cook, "Capture of the Allison Gang," pp. 41-42.

CHAPTER SEVENTEEN – THE CALM BEFORE THE STORM

[1] Glenn Norton and L.F. Post, "The Gila Monster Route," *Songs of the Cattle Trail and Cow Camp*, comp. by John A. Lomax (New York: The MacMillan Company, 1920), p. 170.

[2] "Local," *Durango (CO) Weekly Record*, July 9, 1881.

[3] "Local," *Durango Weekly Record*, September 3, 1881.

4 "Beginning of the End!" *San Juan Herald* (Silverton, CO), September 8, 1881.
5 "Home Affairs," and "Ugly Utes," *Durango (CO) Herald,* July 7, 1881.
6 "Local," *Durango Weekly Record,* July 9, 1881.
7 Ibid.
8 "Southwest Sayings," *Dolores News,* August 13, 1881, p. 1.
9 "A Cry From the Lower Animas," *San Juan Herald,* June 30, 1881.
10 W.B. Haines, "Letter From the Lower Animas," *San Juan Herald,* July 14, 1881.
11 "The Round Up," *Dolores News (*Rico, CO), July 9, 1881, p. 1, from the *Durango Record.*
12 "Personal," *Santa Fe Daily New Mexican,* June 30, 1881.
13 *Santa Fe Daily New Mexican,* July 12, 1881.
14 Governor Pitkin to Mrs. A.E. Stockton, November 8, 1881, Governor Frederick W. Pitkin, correspondence outgoing, Colorado State Archives.
15 "The Farmington Feud," *Denver (CO) Republican,* June 22, 1881.
16 "The Denver Republican Reporter Sold," *Dolores News,* July 2, 1881, p. 2, from the *Durango Democrat.*
17 *Dolores News,* July 2, 1881, p. 1.
18 "The Allison Gang," *Rocky Mountain News* (Denver, CO), June 26, 1881.
19 "Charles Allison," *Dolores News,* July 9, 1881, p. 1, from the *Denver News.*
20 *Dolores News,* July 16, 1881, p. 3, also, p. 2, an advertisement for Dr. A.J. McDonald and April 23, 1881, p. 1, an advertisement for C.H. Ashmeade, M.D and J.P. Landon, M.D.
21 "Gone the Way of All Killers," *Dolores News,* July 23, 1881, p. 2, from the *Denver Republican;* "Local Intelligence," *Dolores News,* July 23, 1881, 3.
22 *Dolores News,* August 6, 1881, p. 3.
23 *Dolores News,* July 23, 1881, p. 3.
24 *San Juan Herald,* July 7, 1881, from the *Durango Herald,* this is an article on the new terminus at Arboles; "Local Intelligence," *Dolores News,* July 30, 1881, p. 3.
25 "Local," *Durango Weekly Record,* July 30, 1881.
26 "Southwest Sayings," *Dolores News,* August 13, 1881, p. 1.
27 *Durango Weekly Record,* July 16, 1881.
28 *Durango Herald,* July 28, 1881, from the *Denver Tribune.*
29 "The Allison Gang," *Denver Republican,* August 2, 1881.
30 "Durango's First Telegram—A Gushy Greeting," *Santa Fe Daily New Mexican,* July 31, 1881.
31 "Late Locals," *Durango Herald,* July 28, 1881. The *Herald* noted that the silver spike had been fabricated by F.A. Foin of the firm, Foin & Boyle.
32 "Durango," *Denver Republican,* August 6, 1881.
33 "The Very Latest," "Reception of Gov. Pitkin," and "Governor Hunt's Visit," *Durango Herald,* August 5, 1881.
34 "Durango," *Denver Republican,* August 6, 1881.
35 "Programme of the Races," *Durango Herald,* August 5, 1881.
36 "Durango," *Denver Republican,* August 6, 1881.
37 "Full Particulars of the Shooting on F Street," and "The Shooting at 4 O'clock This Morning," *Durango Weekly Record,* August 6, 1881.
38 Governor Pitkin to Governor Sheldon, October 24, 1881, Governor Frederick W. Pitkin, correspondence outgoing, Colorado State Archives.
39 C.O. Ziegenfuss, "Ike Stockton," *Denver Republican,* August 12, 1881.

⁴⁰ C.O. Ziegenfuss, "Ike Stockton," *Dolores News*, August 20, 1881, p. 1, from the *Denver Republican*.

⁴¹ C.O. Ziegenfuss, "Ike Stockton," *Denver Republican*, August 12, 1881.

⁴² "Neighborhood Notes," *Dolores News*, August 20, 1881, p. 1, from the *Durango Record*.

⁴³ *Dolores News*, August 6, 1881, p. 3.

⁴⁴ "An Uncalled-For Slur On Our Governor," *Dolores News*, August 13, 1881, p. 2, portions as reported by the *Santa Fe New Mexican* and *Colorado Chieftain*. Newspapers of the time, especially those outside of New Mexico, sometimes referred to New Mexico as Mexico.

⁴⁵ "After Outlaws," *Denver Republican*, May 11, 1881.

⁴⁶ "A Sad Casualty," *Durango Weekly Record*, August 20, 1881.

⁴⁷ *Dolores News*, September 3, 1881, p. 1.

⁴⁸ *Dolores News*, September 24, 1881, p. 3.

CHAPTER EIGHTEEN – BLOOD IN SILVERTON

¹ Herman Scheffauer, "Marta of Milrone," *Songs of the Cattle Trail and Cow Camp*, comp. by John A. Lomax (New York: The MacMillan Company, 1920), p. 49.

² "Return of Rico's Reinforcements," *Dolores News*, July 9, 1881, p. 2.

³ Senator George E. West, "The Oldest Range Man," *Pioneers of the San Juan Country*, vol. 2, comp. and ed. Sarah Platt Decker Chapter D.A.R. (Durango, CO: Sarah Platt Decker Chapter D.A.R., 1946), pp. 117-118.

⁴ F. Stanley, *Ike Stockton* (Denver: World Press, Inc., 1959), p. 118.

⁵ From a photo courtesy of the Royal Gorge Regional Museum and History Center, Cañon City, Colorado.

⁶ "Blood in the San Juan," *Denver (CO) Republican*, August 29, 1881, from the *La Plata Miner* (Silverton, CO).

⁷ "No Train," *Rocky Mountain News* (Denver, CO), August 13, 1881.

⁸ "Stopped Half Way," *Rocky Mountain News*, August 17, 1881.

⁹ "General News," *Durango (CO) Weekly Record*, August 20, 1881.

¹⁰ *Dolores News* (Rico, CO), August 27, 1881, p. 2, from the *Durango Southwest*.

¹¹ "Blood in the San Juan," *Denver Republican*, August 29, 1881, from the *La Plata Miner*.

¹² "Midnight Murder!!!" *San Juan Herald* (Silverton, CO), August 25, 1881.

¹³ "Blood in the San Juan," *Denver Republican*, August 29, 1881, from the *La Plata Miner*; Allen G. Bird, *Bordellos of Blair Street*, rev. ed. (Pierson, MI: Advertising, Publications and Consultants, 1993), p. 15. Bird's book is an excellent history of early Silverton and its seamy side. It is outstanding for providing the locations of Silverton's oldest businesses, which are used here. It also contains an account of the murder of Clate Ogsbury and its aftermath.

¹⁴ "Midnight Murder!!!" *San Juan Herald*, August 25, 1881.

¹⁵ "Midnight Murder!!!" *San Juan Herald*, August 25, 1881; "Blood in the San Juan," *Denver Republican*, August 29, 1881, from the *La Plata Miner*.

¹⁶ "Midnight Murder!!!" *San Juan Herald*, August 25, 1881.

¹⁷ "On Their Track," *San Juan Herald*, September 1, 1881.

¹⁸ "Midnight Murder!!!" *San Juan Herald*, August 25, 1881; "Blood in the San Juan," *Denver Republican*, August 29, 1881, from the *La Plata Miner*.

[19] "Midnight Murder!!!" *San Juan Herald*, August 25, 1881.
[20] "Blood in the San Juan," *Denver Republican*, August 29, 1881, from the *La Plata Miner;* "Midnight Murder!!!" *San Juan Herald*, August 25, 1881.
[21] "On Their Track," *San Juan Herald*, September 1, 1881.
[22] "A Terrible Deed," *Dolores News*, August 27, 1881, p. 2.
[23] "Ordinance," *La Plata Miner*, April 2, 1881.
[24] "Blood in the San Juan," *Denver Republican*, August 29, 1881, from the *La Plata Miner*.
[25] "Notice," *Dolores News*, August 12, 1882, p. 4. By August 1882 an outfit named Berg and Sears was running the lodge at the lake and announced, "We have just refurnished an elegant house, at Trout Lake, formerly called Fish Lakes." "At Last," *Dolores News*, July 24, 1880, p. 1. This newspaper describes the Ophir route and other routes to Rico.
[26] "The Black Kid Lynched," *Denver Republican*, August 30, 1881; "The Lynching of the Kid," *Denver Republican*, August 31, 1881, from the *San Juan Herald*. The quotation is from the August 31st *Republican*.
[27] "A Few Necktie Socials," *Denver Republican*, August 27, 1881.
[28] Stephen J. Leonard, *Lynching in Colorado, 1859-1919* (Boulder: University Press of Colorado, 2002), p .117.
[29] "A Few Necktie Socials," *Denver Republican*, August 27, 1881.
[30] "Thirty-Seven Years in Jail," *Dolores News*, October 29, 1881, p. 2. Their sentences were later commuted.
[31] "Blood in the San Juan," *Denver Republican*, August 29, 1881, from the *La Plata Miner*.
[32] "The Summit House," *Dolores News*, August, 20 1881, p. 3; "Notice," *Dolores News*, August 12, 1882, p. 4.
[33] "Burt Wilkinson Captured," *Dolores News*, September 3, 1881, p. 1, from the *Durango Southwest* and the *Durango Record*.
[34] *Lake City (CO) Silver World*, September 3, 1881.
[35] "Wilkinson's Capture," *Dolores News*, September 10, 1881, p. 2, from the *La Plata Miner*.
[36] "The Silverton Tragedy," *Lake City (CO) Mining Register*, September 2, 1881.
[37] "On Their Track," *San Juan Herald*, September 1, 1881.
[38] "Blood in the San Juan," *Denver Republican*, August 29, 1881, from the *La Plata Miner*.
[39] "On Their Track," *San Juan Herald*, September 1, 1881.
[40] "Burt Wilkinson Captured by Marion Cook and Ike Stockton," *Dolores News*, September 3, 1881, p. 1, from the *Durango Southwest*.
[41] "Beginning of the End!" *San Juan Herald*, September 8, 1881.
[42] "Burt Wilkinson," and "Capture of Burt Wilkinson South of Durango," *Rocky Mountain News* (Denver, CO), September 1, 1881.
[43] U.S.G.S. Map, *Silverton, Colorado*, 30x60 minute Quad., 1982.
[44] "Wilkinson's Capture," *Dolores News*, September 10, 1881, p. 2. This article contains Flora Pyle's statement.
[45] "On Their Track," *San Juan Herald*, September 1, 1881.
[46] "Wilkinson's Capture," *Dolores News*, September 10, 1881, p. 2. Flora Pyle's statement.
[47] Ibid.

⁴⁸ Ibid. Some of the Farmington expatriates remained in Colorado and became permanent residents. Welfoot engendered much hatred in western Rio Arriba County. In late October or early November of 1881 he tried to return to his New Mexico home and was seen by one of the Coes. Reportedly a large group of armed men set out to meet him, but he escaped. See William Haines to Governor Sheldon, November 2, 1881, Campaign, TANM, NMSRCA. Welfoot would remain in Colorado for another two months.

⁴⁹ "Burt Wilkinson Captured by Marion Cook and Ike Stockton," *Dolores News*, September 3, 1881, p. 1, from the *Durango Southwest*. The *Southwest* refers to Cook as "Deputy Marshal M.C. Cook, of Durango." *Durango Weekly Record*, September 3, 1881. The *Record* refers to Cook as "Marshal Cook, of Animas City."

⁵⁰ "Wilkinson's Capture," *Dolores News*, September 10, 1881, p. 2. Flora Pyle's statement.

⁵¹ "Burt Wilkinson Captured," *Dolores News*, September 3, 1881, p. 1, from the *Durango Southwest*. The *Southwest* says they were captured on a mesa west of the Animas River and northeast of Animas City. "The Silverton Tragedy," *Lake City (CO) Mining Register*, September 2, 1881, says they were captured twelve miles north of Animas City as well as in the Needle Mountains; "The Murderer of Marshal Ogsbury Caught," *La Plata Miner*, September 3, 1881, says they were captured on a high mesa east of the Animas River seven miles above Animas City; "Beginning of the End!" *San Juan Herald*, September 8, 1881, says they were captured on a high bluff east of J.P. Lamb's ranch.

⁵² "Wilkinson's Capture," *Dolores News*, September 10, 1881, p. 2, contains Flora Pyle's statement; "Burt Wilkinson Captured," *Dolores News*, September 3, 1881, p. 1, from the *Durango Southwest*. The *Southwest* said the capture took place on Tuesday afternoon and reported Stockton's version, which involved no subterfuge on his part.

⁵³ Charles Jones, "The Memoirs of Charles Adam Jones," n.d., p. 102, Clifford B. Jones Papers, 1814-1973 and undated, Accession Nos. 96-0122-B and 98-0001-B, Southwest Collection/Special Collections Library, Texas Tech University, Lubbock.

⁵⁴ "Wilkinson's Capture," *Dolores News*, September 10, 1881, p. 2, contains Flora Pyle's statement. The quotes are from Flora's statement.

⁵⁵ "Beginning of the End!" *San Juan Herald*, September 8, 1881.

⁵⁶ "The Murderer of Marshal Ogsbury Caught," *La Plata Miner*, September 3, 1881. The *Miner* reported that Wilkinson was captured at 4:00 PM on Monday afternoon.

⁵⁷ "Burt Wilkinson's Captured," *San Juan Herald*, September 1, 1881, from the *Durango Record*.

⁵⁸ "Burt Wilkinson Captured," *Dolores News*, September 3, 1881, p. 1, from the *Durango Southwest* and the *Durango Record*.

⁵⁹ "Burt Wilkinson's Captured," *San Juan Herald*, September 1, 1881, from the *Durango Record*.

⁶⁰ "Burt Wilkinson Captured," *Dolores News*, September 3, 1881, p. 1, from the *Durango Southwest* and the *Durango Record;* Olive Frazier Cornelius, "Pioneer History and Reminiscences of the San Juan Basin," *Aztec (NM) Independent Review*, June 16, 1933. Cornelius identifies Mrs. Austin Puett as the first school teacher in Animas City.

⁶¹ "The Murderer of Marshal Ogsbury Caught," *Lake City (CO) Silver World*, September 3, 1881, from the *La Plata Miner*.
⁶² "The Murderer of Marshal Ogsbury Caught," *La Plata Miner*, September 3, 1881, portions as reported by the *Durango Southwest*.
⁶³ Ibid.
⁶⁴ Ibid.
⁶⁵ "Beginning of the End!" *San Juan Herald*, September 8, 1881.
⁶⁶ Ibid.; "Neighborhood Notes," *Dolores News*, August 20, 1881, p. 1, from the *Durango Record*. The *Record* reported on the progress of the D&RG grading.
⁶⁷ Allen Nossaman, *Rails Into Silverton*, vol. 3 of *Many More Mountains* (Denver: Sundance Publications, Ltd., 1998), p. 87, see footnote no. 27.
⁶⁸ "Beginning of the End!" *San Juan Herald*, September 8, 1881.
⁶⁹ "Wilkinson's Capture," *Dolores News*, September 10, 1881, p. 2; "Beginning of the End!" *San Juan Herald*, September 8, 1881.
⁷⁰ "Beginning of the End!" *San Juan Herald*, September 8, 1881.
⁷¹ "Wilkinson's Capture," *Dolores News*, September 10, 1881, p. 2.
⁷² "Beginning of the End!" *San Juan Herald*, September 8, 1881.
⁷³ "Wilkinson's Capture," *Dolores News*, September 10, 1881, p. 2.
⁷⁴ "Beginning of the End!" *San Juan Herald*, September 8, 1881.
⁷⁵ "Wilkinson's Capture," *Dolores News*, September 10, 1881, p. 2, portions as reported by the *La Plata Miner*.
⁷⁶ "Penalty Paid," *Durango (CO) Herald*, September 8, 1881.
⁷⁷ *Dolores, News*, November 19, 1881, p. 2.
⁷⁸ "Beginning of the End!" *San Juan Herald*, September 8, 1881.
⁷⁹ Interview with Frank and Sandra Pyle, December 14, 2009.
⁸⁰ "Beginning of the End!" *San Juan Herald*, September 8, 1881.
⁸¹ Nossaman, *Many More Mountains*, p. 88, see footnote no. 29.
⁸² "Beginning of the End!" *San Juan Herald*, September 8, 1881.
⁸³ "Burt Wilkinson," *Rocky Mountain News*, September 1, 1881.

CHAPTER NINETEEN – DURANGO'S JUDAS

¹ "The End of the Trail," *Songs of the Cattle Trail and Cow Camp*, comp. by John A. Lomax (New York: The MacMillan Company, 1920), p. 189. Lomax notes that the poem is "from Pocock's 'Curley.'"
² "On Their Track," *San Juan Herald* (Silverton, CO), September 1, 1881.
³ Ibid.
⁴ "Notes from Rico," *Durango (CO) Weekly Record*, September 17, 1881.
⁵ "Wilkinson's Capture," *Dolores News* (Rico, CO), September 10, 1881, p. 2.
⁶ "We Didn't Go to Do It, Isaac," *San Juan Herald* (Silverton, CO), September 15, 1881, portions as reported by the *Durango Southwest*.
⁷ *Durango (CO) Herald*, November 10, 1881.
⁸ "More Shooting at Durango," *Dolores News*, March 26, 1881, p. 1.
⁹ William B. Haines (signed W. Bullock Haines, Captain, San Juan Guards) to Governor Sheldon, September 22, 1881, Campaign, TANM, NMSRCA.
¹⁰ Governor Pitkin to Mrs. A.E. Stockton, November 8, 1881, Governor Frederick W. Pitkin, correspondence outgoing, Colorado State Archives.
¹¹ Haines to Sheldon, September 22, 1881, Campaign, TANM, NMSRCA.

¹² William B. Haines to Adjutant General Max Frost, September 27, 1881, LRRAGT, TANM, NMSRCA.

¹³ "Ike Stockton Killed," *Dolores News*, October 1, 1881, p. 1, from the *Durango Record*.

¹⁴ "State House Scraps," *Denver (CO) Republican*, September 28, 1881.

¹⁵ "Harg. Eskridge Arrested," *Dolores News*, October 1, 1881, p. 1, from the *Gunnison (CO) News-Democrat*.

¹⁶ *Ouray (CO) Times*, October 1, 1881, from the *Lake City (CO) Silver World*.

¹⁷ "Harg. Eskridge," *Durango Weekly Record*, October 1, 1881.

¹⁸ "Harg. Eskridge Arrested," *Dolores News*, October 1, 1881, p. 1, from the *Gunnison (CO) News-Democrat*.

¹⁹ "A Kid Gone," *Santa Fe Daily New Mexican*, May 19, 1881.

²⁰ "Eskridge Arrested," *Santa Fe Daily New Mexican*, September 24, 1881.

²¹ Requisition from New Mexico to Colorado, for Harge Eskridge, September 23, 1881, roll 1, microcopy 364, Coll. I 023, Interior Department, Territorial Papers, New Mexico, 1851-1914, RG 48, NARA, FLC-CSWS.

²² *Dolores News*, October 1, 1881, p. 3.

²³ "Eskridge Arrested," *Santa Fe Daily New Mexican*, September 24, 1881.

²⁴ *Dolores News*, October 1, 1881, p. 3.

²⁵ *Las Vegas (NM) Daily Gazette*, September 25, 1881.

²⁶ *Santa Fe Daily New Mexican*, October 2, 1881.

²⁷ "The Stockton-Eskridge Gang Broken Up," *Lake City (CO) Mining Register*, October 7, 1881.

²⁸ "Ike Stockton Killed," *Dolores News*, October 1, 1881, p. 1, from the *Durango Southwest*.

²⁹ Ibid.; "Gathered In," *Durango Herald*, September 29, 1881.

³⁰ "Ike Stockton Killed," *Dolores News*, October 1, 1881, p. 1, from the *Durango Southwest*.

³¹ "The Stockton-Eskridge Gang Broken Up," *Lake City (CO) Mining Register*, October 7, 1881.

³² Charles Jones, "The Memoirs of Charles Adam Jones," n.d., p. 104, Clifford B. Jones Papers, 1814-1973 and undated, Accession Nos. 96-0122-B and 98-0001-B, Southwest Collection/Special Collections Library, Texas Tech University, Lubbock.

³³ "Gathered In," *Durango Herald*, September 29, 1881.

³⁴ "John Gregory Bourke Diaries," September 27, 1881 to October 19, 1881, roll 3, vol. 48, p. 42, Coll. I 032, FLC-CSWS. Bourke's diaries enabled him to write extensively about his time on the frontier in the U.S. Army, including the classic book *On the Border With Crook*.

³⁵ "Important Arrest!" *Durango Weekly Record*, October 1, 1881.

³⁶ "State House Scraps," *Denver Republican*, September 28, 1881.

³⁷ "Ike Stockton Killed," *Dolores News*, October 1, 1881, p. 1, from the *Durango Southwest*.

³⁸ "Important Arrest!" *Durango Weekly Record*, October 1, 1881.

³⁹ Clifford R. Caldwell and Ron DeLord, *Texas Lawmen, 1835-1899: The Good and the Bad* (Charleston, SC: The History Press, 2011), pp. 28-29.

⁴⁰ "Ike Stockton Killed," *Dolores News*, October 1, 1881, p. 1, from the *Durango Southwest*.

⁴¹ "Gathered In," *Durango Herald*, September 29, 1881.

⁴² "The Stockton-Eskridge Gang Broken Up," *Lake City (CO) Mining Register*, October 7, 1881; "Ike Stockton Killed," *Dolores News*, October 1, 1881, p. 1, from the *Durango Southwest*.

⁴³ "Gathered In," *Durango Herald*, September 29, 1881.

⁴⁴ "Important Arrest!" *Durango Weekly Record*, October 1, 1881.

⁴⁵ "Ike Stockton Killed," *Dolores News*, October 1, 1881, p. 1, from the *Durango Southwest*; "Local," *Durango Weekly Record*, August 20, 1881. Folsom was new to Durango and that August he was setting up his dental office in the Windom block. "Woods Willing," *Durango Herald*, June 22, 1882. By the next year Dr. Folsom was also working as an undertaker.

⁴⁶ "Important Arrest!" and untitled article, *Durango Weekly Record*, October 1, 1881. Twenty-nine-year-old William Craig, evidently a friend of the family, was also present at the deathbed and provided the *Record* with an eyewitness account of the sad scene.

⁴⁷ *Durango Weekly Record*, October 1, 1881.

⁴⁸ "Gathered In," *Durango Herald*, September 29, 1881; *Dolores News*, October 1, 1881, p. 1, from the *Durango Record*. The *Record* places the funeral date and time as 2:00 PM on September 28th. On July 1, 1904 the first page of the *Durango (CO) Democrat* noted that Reverend C. Montgomery Hoge became overwrought when doctors told him they needed to remove his appendix. In a fit of temporary insanity and perhaps overcome by intense pain, Hoge committed suicide by shooting himself in the head at his home near Monterey, California. In latter day accounts, recollections of Parson Hoge by La Plata County's pioneers were universal in their praise of the bible-toting, trail-blazing minister.

⁴⁹ *Santa Fe Daily New Mexican*, October 5, 1881.

CHAPTER TWENTY - REFLECTION

¹ Charles B. Clark, Jr., "The Outlaw," *Songs of the Cattle Trail and Cow Camp*, comp. by John A. Lomax (New York: The MacMillan Company, 1920), p. 141.

² *Durango (CO) Herald*, September 29, 1881.

³ "To Those Contemplating Coming to Durango," *Durango (CO) Weekly Record*, April 16, 1881.

⁴ *Dolores News* (Rico, CO), October 1, 1881, from the *Pueblo Chieftain* (i.e. the *Colorado Chieftain* of Pueblo).

⁵ "Gathered In," *Durango Herald*, September 29, 1881.

⁶ "Important Arrest!" *Durango Weekly Record*, October 1, 1881.

⁷ *Iola (KS) Register*, October 7, 1881.

⁸ *Milan (TN) Exchange*, October 1, 1881; *Lancaster (PA) Daily Intelligencer*, September 28, 1881.

⁹ *Dodge City (KS) Times*, October 13, 1881, p. 1, from the *Las Vegas Optic*.

¹⁰ "Important Arrest!" *Durango Weekly Record*, October 1, 1881.

¹¹ *Santa Fe Daily New Mexican*, September 30, 1881.

¹² Requisition from New Mexico to Colorado, For Isaac Stockton and Others, September 27, 1881, roll 1, microcopy 364, Coll. I 023, Interior Department, Territorial Papers, New Mexico, 1851-1914, RG 48, NARA, FLC-CSWS.

¹³ *Santa Fe Daily New Mexican*, September 30, 1881.

AFTERWORD - LOOSE ENDS AND LATER LIVES

[1] Charles Badger Clark, Jr., "The Old Cowman," *Songs of the Cattle Trail and Cow Camp*, comp. by John A. Lomax (New York: The MacMillan Company, 1920), pp. 166-167.

[2] General D.J. Cook, "Capture of the Allison Gang," *Hands Up, or, Thirty-Five Years of Detective Life in the Mountains and on the Plains*, comp., John W. Cook (Denver: D.J. and J.W. Cook, 1897), p. 42, http://www.archive.org/details/handsuporthirtyf00cook (accessed September 27, 2009).

[3] "La Plata's Last," *Dolores News* (Rico, CO), August 12, 1882, p. 1, from the *Durango (CO) Herald*.

[4] "Deputy Sheriff Killed," *Dolores News*, October 28, 1882, p. 2, from the *Durango Herald*. Smith may have been fifty-year-old Robert L. Smith who was living in the Animas valley above Aztec in 1880. See *U.S. Census 1880*, Rio Arriba County, r. 803, p. 224b, NM, FLC-CSWS.

[5] Captain W.B. Haines to Governor Sheldon, "The Blancett Tragedy," *Albuquerque Review*, November 4, 1882.

[6] William B. Haines to Adjutant General Max Frost, September 27, 1881, LRRAGT, TANM, NMSRCA.

[7] Dispatch from Bean, "Blood at Bloomfield," *Santa Fe New Mexican*, October 31, 1882.

[8] Robert W Duke, "Political History of San Juan County, New Mexico 1876-1926" (master's thesis, University of New Mexico, June 1947), p. 44.

[9] "Lynching of Archuleta," *Dolores News*, November 4, 1882, p. 2, from the *Durango Herald*.

[10] Bernard James Byrne, M.D., *A Frontier Army Surgeon - Life In Colorado In The Eighties*, 2nd rev. and enlarged ed. (New York: Exposition Press, 1962), p. 36-37.

[11] "Settled the Trouble," *Albuquerque Review*, November 4, 1882.

[12] "Blood at Bloomfield," *Santa Fe New Mexican*, October 31, 1882.

[13] *Dolores News*, November 7, 1885, p. 4, from the *Durango Herald*.

[14] "Homicide at Tintic," *Deseret News* (Salt Lake City, UT), December 28, 1887.

[15] "First District Court," *Provo (UT) Daily Enquirer*, October 16, 1888. Utah Digital Newspapers operated by the University of Utah's J. Willard Marriott Library. *Daily Enquirer* courtesy of Brigham Young University.

[16] "The Rosita Row," *Colorado Daily Chieftain* (Pueblo), October 13, 1875, p. 4.

[17] "First District Court," *Provo (UT) Daily Enquirer*, October 16, 1888.

[18] "First District Court," *Provo (UT) Daily Enquirer*, October 12, 1888.

[19] "Homicide at Tintic," *Deseret News* (Salt Lake City, UT), December 28, 1887.

[20] "Cell Blancett Killed By Lightning," *San Juan County Index* (Aztec, NM), July 24, 1890.

[21] "The End," *San Juan County Index*, February 23, 1894, p. 2.

[22] C.V. Koogler and Virginia Koogler Whitney, *Aztec: Old Aztec From Anasazi to Statehood* (Fort Worth: American Reference Publishing Co., 1972), p. 28.

[23] "Socorro Justice" and "Another Account," *Santa Fe Daily New Mexican*, October 8, 1881; *Durango Herald*, October 13, 1881. The *Herald* identifies Clark as "Butch."

[24] *Dolores News*, November 19, 1881, p. 2.

25 "First Forced On Him," *Kansas City (MO) Journal*, September 17, 1899, p. 9, from the *Chicago Inter Ocean*.
26 Charles Valiton, "Forty-five Years in Colorado," *Silverton (CO) Standard*, June 12, 1926.
27 "Death of Catron," *Durango Herald*, May 13, 1882. The *Herald* said the shooting occurred on May 12th.
28 "Jim Catron's Cheek," *Aspen (CO) Weekly Times*, May 20, 1882, p. 1, from the *Pueblo News*. This account says Catron was shot on May 11th.
29 "Death of Catron," *Durango Herald*, May 13, 1882. On May 18, 1882, the *Richmond Democrat* of Ray County, Missouri reported that Catron's companion was a cowboy named Dick Rogers and that Rogers was killed and Catron fatally wounded. However, the *Leadville (CO) Daily Herald* cast doubt on Catron's fate when under "State Clippings" on May 16, 1882, they advised that Catron was "shot in the leg but not dangerously."
30 "Jim Catron's Cheek," *Aspen Weekly Times*, May 20, 1882, p. 1, from the *Pueblo News*.
31 "Death of Catron," *Durango Herald*, May 13, 1882.
32 "List of Proposals for Military Supplies at Fort Stanton," *Lincoln County Leader* (White Oaks, NM), May 3, 1890, p. 1.
33 "Roswell," *Albuquerque Daily Citizen*, October 13, 1898; *Albuquerque Daily Citizen*, March 27, 1900.
34 Smilydino, creator, Find A Grave, "Benjamin Franklin 'Frank' Coe," November 12, 2010, http://www.findagrave.com/cgi-bin/fg.cgi?page=gr&GScid=38008&GRid=61516825& (accessed May 25, 2012).
35 George Coe to J. Evetts Haley, August 12, 1927, p. 4, JEHC-HMLHC; "Death Claims Young Lady," *Carrizozo (NM) News*, June 14, 1918, p. 1.
36 "Former Pal Lauds 'Billy the Kid,' " *Douglas County Record Journal* (Castle Rock, CO), November 13, 1931, p. 7, a dispatch from Chicago.
37 Librarian, creator and maintained by Smilydino, Find A Grave, "George Washington Coe," October 27, 2009, http://www.findagrave.com/cgi-bin/fg.cgi?page=gr&GSln=coe&GSfn=george&GSby=1845&GSbyrel=after&GSdy=1938&GSdyrel=after&GSst=34&GScntry=4&GSob=n&GRid=43604695&df=all& (accessed May 25, 2012).
38 *New Mexico v. Louis W. Coe*, box 2, case no. 337, April 1883, Rio Arriba County District Court Records, NMSRCA.
39 *Santa Lulu Independent* (Aztec, NM), November 2, 1888.
40 "Ike Stockton Killed," *Dolores News*, October 1, 1881, p. 1, from the *Durango Record*.
41 "Bud Galbreth, alias Cook, at Large," *Dolores News*, October 15, 1881, p. 1, from the *Durango Record*.
42 *U.S. Census 1900*, Pottawatomie County, OK, r. 1342, p. 225b, IA-ACPL.
43 "Gathered In," *Durango Herald*, September 29, 1881. Determining the fate of the oldest child is complicated, since virtually the entire United States census for 1890 was destroyed by fire in 1921.
44 "Story of Lee of Tecumseh," *Wichita (KS) Daily Eagle*, March 6, 1898. See also, *Wichita (KS) Daily Eagle*, February 12, 1898, from the *Tecumseh Republican*.
45 *Wichita (KS) Daily Eagle*, November 27, 1897, from the *Tecumseh Republican*.
46 *Guthrie (OK) Daily Leader*, November 21, 1897.

47 "After Twenty Years," *Guthrie (OK) Daily Leader,* November 23, 1897.

48 *Wichita (KS) Daily Eagle,* November 27, 1897, from the *Tecumseh Republican.*

49 *Wichita (KS) Daily Eagle,* December 16, 1897, from the *Oklahoma City Oklahoman.*

50 *Texas v. M.H. Galbreath,* p. 329, case no. 1967, Criminal Minutes, Book D, January 18, 1898, Bosque County District Clerk Records.

51 "Story of Lee of Tecumseh," *Wichita (KS) Daily Eagle,* March 6, 1898.

52 *Texas v. M.H. Gilbreath [sic],* p. 12, case no. 101, State Docket, District Court, Bosque County District Clerk Records. This case from the June 1874 term of court is for "An assault with intent to commit a rape."

53 "Story of Lee of Tecumseh," *Wichita (KS) Daily Eagle,* March 6, 1898.

54 *U.S. Census 1860,* Erath County, TX. r. 1293, p. 118a, IA-ACPL; Randy Farrar, e-mail message to author, August 3, 2010. Farrar's research notes that James Galbreath's third wife was Elizabeth Ann Hickey. Farrar noted that more research was needed to confirm this information.

55 "After Twenty Years," *Guthrie (OK) Daily Leader,* November 23, 1897.

56 "Ike Stockton Killed," *Dolores News,* October 1, 1881, from the *Durango Southwest.*

57 *Texas v. M.H. Galbreath,* pp. 343 and 344, case no. 1967, Criminal Minutes, Book D, February 22, 1898, Bosque County District Clerk Records.

58 *U.S. Census 1900,* Pottawatomie County, OK, r. 1342, p. 225b, IA-ACPL.

59 "Sulphur, Okla. Directory," *Daily Ardmoreite* (Ardmore, OK) April 3, 1908.

60 *U.S. Census 1930,* Murray County, OK, r. 1914, p. 270a, IA-ACPL.

61 George B Anderson, comp., *History of New Mexico - Its Resources and People,* vol. 2 (Los Angeles, Chicago and New York: Pacific States Publishing Co., 1907), p. 863; S. Morgan Friedman, "The Inflation Calculator," *Ceci n'est pas une* homepage, n.d., http://www.westegg.com/inflation/infl.cgi (accessed December 5, 2008).

62 *Santa Lulu Independent* (Aztec, NM), November 2, 1888.

63 Olive Frazier Cornelius, "Pioneer History and Reminiscences of the San Juan Basin," *Aztec (NM) Independent Review,* April 21, 1933. According to Willie's headstone, he was born on February 25, 1872 and died on August 10, 1890.

64 Isaac Hiram Cox, "Tales," transcribed by Joeen Johnson Sutton, 1920s, courtesy of Les Sutton, p. 62; "Geo. Bauer Banker, and Wholesale and Retail Dealer in General Merchandise," *Mancos (CO) Times,* April 28, 1893, p. 4. Barb wire is listed prominently in Bauer's advertisement.

65 "Dead Pioneer," *Durango (CO) Democrat,* January 30, 1900, p. 3. This article about the death of Nancy Cox (the article calls her Mary) notes that H.W. Cox had previously died from cancer.

66 Edith Rhodes, "The H.W. Cox House," *Bulletins Pioneer Association San Juan County, New Mexico,* 1953 to 1976 (1963): p. 11, Farmington (NM) Public Library.

67 Stanley M. Cox, comp., *Joseph Cox, Ancestors and Descendants* (Kansas City, MO: 1955), p. 103.

68 *Durango (CO) Wage Earner,* December 22, 1898; "Dead Pioneer," *Durango Democrat,* January 30, 1900, p. 3.

69 *San Juan Democrat* (Aztec, NM), March 5, 1909.

70 *Aztec Independent Review,* May 13, 1932.

71 Phillip Craig, *The Cox-Truby Feud* (Flora Vista, NM: San Juan County Historical Society, 2002), pp. 1 and 7.

[72] Tweeti Walser Blancett and Kathy Summers Price, *Step Back Inn To Aztec's Roots* (Aztec, NM: Step Back Inn, 1994), p. 12.

[73] "Democratic Convention," *Dolores News*, October 22, 1881, p. 3; "In the Jug," *Dolores News*, January 21, 1882, p. 3.

[74] "After the Murderers," *Durango Herald*, June 10, 1882.

[75] "And Again," *Dolores News*, June 24, 1882, p. 4; "Murderers Captured," *Durango Herald*, June 17, 1882.

[76] Valiton, "Forty-five Years in Colorado," *Silverton (CO) Standard*, June 12, 1926.

[77] Dr. W.H.C. Folsom interviewed by A.L. Soens, March 20, 1934, La Plata County, p. 109, CWA Pioneer Interviews, Special Collections, SHHLRC, HCC.

[78] *Laws Passed at an Extra Session of the Thirteenth General Assembly of the State of Colorado* (Denver: The Smith-Brooks Printing Company, State Printers, 1902), p. 13, http://archive.org/stream/lawspassedatses10cologoog#page/n17/mode/2up (accessed March 2, 2013).

[79] "Passed Away," *San Juan Prospector* (Del Norte, CO), November 25, 1916, p. 4.

[80] "Harg. Eskridge Kills John Bennett," *Dolores News*, June 3, 1882, p. 1, portions as reported by the *Alamosa Independent*.

[81] Dr. W.H.C. Folsom interviewed by A.L. Soens, March 20, 1934, La Plata County, p. 109, CWA Pioneer Interviews, Special Collections, SHHLRC, HCC.

[82] Valiton, "Forty-five Years in Colorado," *Silverton (CO) Standard*, June 12, 1926.

[83] *U.S. Census 1910*, Los Angeles County, CA, r. 87, p. 32a, IA-ACPL. Joshua H. and Ella M. Eskridge had been married for twenty-four years in 1910.

[84] "Brief Mention," *The Columbian* (Bloomsburg, PA), April 30, 1896, p. 7.

[85] *U.S. Census 1900*, Centre County, PA, r. 1392, p. 86b, IA-ACPL.

[86] S.B. Row, *Illustrated Souvenir History of Philipsburg, Pennsylvania* (Williamsport, PA: Grit Publishing Company., 1909), p. 24, http://archive.org/details/illustratedsouve00phil (accessed December 15, 2012).

[87] *U.S. Census 1910*, Los Angeles County, CA, r. 87, p. 32a, IA-ACPL.

[88] San Diego Directory Co., comp., *San Diego City and County Directory* (San Diego: Ross and George Book Bindery, 1915), pp. 1239 and 1249, http://archive.org/stream/sandiegocitycoun00unkn#page/n0/mode/2up (accessed February 6, 2013).

[89] Charles Jones, "The Memoirs of Charles Adam Jones," n.d., p. 102, Clifford B. Jones Papers, 1814-1973 and undated, Accession Nos. 96-0122-B and 98-0001-B, Southwest Collection/Special Collections Library, Texas Tech University, Lubbock.

[90] *U.S. Census 1920*, Centre County, PA, r. 1549, p. 24b, IA-ACPL.

[91] "Indian Warfare and Mineralogy Topics at Rotary Meeting," *Clearfield (PA) Progress*, June 14, 1923, pp. 1 and 6, Pennsylvania State Library, Harrisburg, PA. Provided with special assistance by William T. Fee, Digital Collections Librarian.

[92] Collectiblesdelectables, Ebay.com.hk listing, 2011, http://www.ebay.com.hk/itm/1928-CARD-WIDOWS-RELIEF-FUND-JAFFA-TEMPLE-ALTOONA-PA-/150570639592 (accessed Nov. 30, 2011).

[93] Geringer Art Ltd., "Robert Lee Eskridge," 2009, http://www.geringerart.com/bios/eskridge.html (accessed November 30, 2011).

[94] *Wray (CO) Gazette*, March 18, 1910, p. 12.

[95] "Nature Exacts Final Tribute From Colonel Max. Frost," *Santa Fe New Mexican*, October 14, 1909.

96 "Another Chance for Frost," *Los Angeles Daily Herald*, March 10, 1888, p. 5.

97 Victor Westphall, *The Public Domain in New Mexico - 1854-1891* (Albuquerque: University of New Mexico Press, 1965), pp. 109-110.

98 "Nature Exacts Final Tribute From Colonel Max. Frost," *Santa Fe New Mexican*, October 14, 1909.

99 "Prominent New Mexican Editor Dead," *Fort Collins (CO) Weekly Courier*, October 20, 1909, p. 1.

100 "James W. Garrett Crosses the Dark River," *Creede (CO) Candle*, January 30, 1904, p. 1; *U.S. Census 1900*, Mineral County, CO, r. 127, p. 159b, IA-ACPL. The *Creede Candle* article says he was forty-eight, but the census says he was born in January 1857, making him forty-seven at the time of his death.

101 "Puget Sound Shrimpers," *San Juan Islander* (Friday Harbor, WA), November 16, 1907, p. 1. See also, *San Juan Islander*, July 29, 1905, p. 8 and *San Juan Islander*, July 15, 1905, p. 5. The last two articles confirm William B. Haines role in the oyster company as they mention Lula and Harry L. Haines, who lived in Bloomfield in 1880 with their parents.

102 Jones, "The Memoirs of Charles Adam Jones," p. 90.

103 "Farmington Republican Editor Frank Hartman Passes the Great Divide," *Farmington (NM) Times Hustler*, October 19, 1934.

104 Cornelius, "Pioneer History," *Aztec Independent Review*, June 30, 1933; *Santa Lulu Independent*, November 2, 1888.

105 "Durango's Newspaper Fight," *Alamosa (CO) Journal*, May 21, 1903, p. 2.

106 "Target Practice," *Durango Democrat*, August 31, 1906, p. 1.

107 "Local News," *Durango Wage Earner*, September 14, 1911, p. 4.

108 "Farmington Republican Editor Frank Hartman Passes the Great Divide," *Farmington Times Hustler*, October 19, 1934.

109 "Dan Howland," *Durango Weekly Record*, June 25, 1881.

110 "The 'Rustlers,' " *Durango Southwest*, March 15, 1884.

111 "Baptised in Blood," *Arizona Gazette* (Phoenix), December 13, 1883.

112 "The Robbers' Trail," *Arizona Weekly Citizen* (Tucson), December 22, 1883, p. 3.

113 *Durango Weekly Record*, May 14, 1881; "An Unauthorized Action," *Santa Fe Daily New Mexican*, May 27, 1881, portions as reported by the *Durango Record*.

114 " 'Big Dan' in the Prisoner's Dock," *Arizona Weekly Citizen* (Tucson), January 19, 1884, p. 4.

115 "Murder," *Tombstone (AZ) Daily Epitaph*, February 12, 1884.

116 "Five Felons," *Arizona Gazette* (Phoenix), April 3, 1884.

117 *Dolores News*, April 5, 1884, p. 2.

118 *Durango Herald*, May 17, 1882; *U.S. Census 1880*, La Plata County, CO, r. 91, p. 571a, IA-ACPL.

119 "Told in Town," *Durango Wage Earner*, October 24, 1901, p. 3; "Additional Local," *Durango Democrat*, December 8, 1901, p. 1, from the *Silverton Standard*; *Durango Democrat*, March 7, 1907, p. 4, May 16, 1908, p. 4 and May 6, 1909, p. 3.

120 *U.S. Census 1910*, San Juan County, CO, r. 125, p. 70a or 90a, IA-ACPL. Luke Hunter lived four miles up the Animas River from Silverton in Howardsville. *U.S. Census 1920*, San Diego County, CA, r. 132, p. 2b, IA-ACPL; *U.S. Census 1930*, San Diego County, CA, r. 193, p. 14a, IA-ACPL.

121 *Dolores News*, January 12, 1884, p. 2, from the *Ouray Solid Muldoon*.

122 Jones, "The Memoirs of Charles Adam Jones," pp. 195 and 200-202, 208, 230, 236.

123 George A. Wallis, "Cattle Kings!" *True West* vol. 11, no. 4 (March-April, 1964): p. 13.

124 Jones, "The Memoirs of Charles Adam Jones," pp. 285-288, 301, 323, 343, 345, 355.

125 Carl F. Mathews, "Rico, Colorado – Once a Roaring Camp," *The Colorado Magazine* vol. 28, no. 1 (January 1951): pp. 48-49.

126 Ira S. Freeman, *A History of Montezuma County Colorado – Land of Promise and Fulfillment* (Boulder: Johnson Publishing Co., 1958), p. 55 and 62.

127 "Mrs. H.C. Goodman Is Suddenly Called," *Moab (UT) Times-Independent*, March 13, 1941.

128 S.C. Lacy, "Dictation of the widow of I.W. Lacy," Western Americana Collection, The Bancroft Collection, Bancroft Library, University of California, Berkeley, CA, from microfilm archived at the Center for Southwest Research, University of New Mexico, Albuquerque, NM.

129 "Local Brevities," *Dolores News*, October 3, 1885, p. 3.

130 "A Cattle King's Son," *Los Angeles Herald*, October 24, 1895, p. 2.

131 Prof. J.M. Guinn, *History of the State of California and Biographical Record of the San Joaquin Valley, California*, (Chicago: Chapman Publishing Co., 1905), pp. 1314 and 1317 http://archive.org/details/cu31924028919375 (accessed August 2, 2013); "Almand Is Kept In Jail At Tulare," *San Francisco Call*, December 31, 1898, p. 3.

132 Ralph Emerson Twitchell, *The Leading Facts of New Mexican History*, vol. 4 (Cedar Rapids, IA: The Torch Press, 1917), pp. 174-175. Twitchell errs and says Sherman's last name was Hilton. In the 1880 Rio Arriba County census there was a large family named Helton living in the La Plata valley, which included seven boys born between 1854 and 1868. Sherman's full name was Frank Sherman Helton and he was named for his father who died in December 1880 and is buried in the La Plata, New Mexico cemetery. One of the boys, James, was a member of the San Juan Guards. For another account of the stereopticon show and the hoorawing of Hugh Griffin see Anderson, *History of New Mexico*, vol. 2, p. 867. The local cowboys delighted in hoorawing Reverend Griffin, even tricking him into holding a funeral service for a not quite dead man. See also "Parsons Hoge and Griffin," *Durango Wage Earner*, March 14, 1907, p. 4.

133 *St. Johns (AZ) Herald*, February 24, 1887.

134 *St. Johns (AZ) Herald*, February 17, 1887; *Annual Report of the Commissioner of Indian Affairs to the Secretary of the Interior* (Washington, DC, 1887), pp. 174-175, 177, http://archive.org/details/annualreportofco188700unitrich (accessed December 15, 2012). From the reports of agents of New Mexico, who advised that the shooting resulted in the death of three white men, one Indian and the severe wounding of another Indian. Navajo Indian Agent S.S. Patterson reported that the shootout took place on February 6th near Houck's Tank on the railroad. The agent believed that the trouble resulted when Lockhart attempted to arrest the wrong man, and not the one named in the warrant. In March, the agent refused to allow the sheriff of Apache County and a posse of about one hundred men entry to the reservation to search for an Indian who had committed a crime in the county. That same month a group of white men rode onto the reservation and stole over 150 horses. The Indians were able to recover the stolen animals.

[135] "Another Indian War," *Fort Worth (TX) Daily Gazette*, February 11, 1887, p. 6.

[136] *St. Johns (AZ) Herald*, February 17, 1887; April 26, 2013 interview with Wayne and Nona Dale and Priscilla Trummel. The Dales and Trummel report that family lore described the hatchet attack.

[137] "Another Indian War," *Fort Worth Daily Gazette*, February 11, 1887, p. 6.

[138] *St. Johns (AZ) Herald*, April 7, 1887. Captain Kerr reported that the posse was searching for Chee's hogan (not a tepee), but that the attack occurred at the home of Chee's brother-in-law Belto Manihogo.

[139] John Arrington, "William Henry Thomas," *Bulletins Pioneer Association San Juan County, New Mexico*, 1953 to 1976 (1963): pp. 8-9, Farmington (NM) Public Library.

[140] Lewis Publishing Company, comp., *History of Texas*, Central Texas ed. (Chicago: The Lewis Publishing Company, 1896), p. 801. http://archive.org/details/historyoftexassu00lewi (accessed March 1, 2013).

[141] "Bayfield Tragedy," *Durango Democrat*, April 20, 1899, p. 4. Bayfield was named for the family of Deputy Bay. He was kept busy in the little town. Less than a month after the killing of Sam Logan the *Durango Wage Earner* of May 11, 1899, p. 4, noted that Deputy Billie Bay arrested William Wieland at Arnold's Store for the killing of W.H. Brinkley.

[142] "He Surrenders," *Durango Democrat*, April 21, 1899, p. 4.

[143] "Local and Personal," *Durango Democrat*, April 22, 1899, p. 4.

[144] "Local and Personal," *Durango Democrat*, July 11, 1899, p. 4.

[145] "District Court," *Durango Democrat*, April 8, 1900, p. 1.

[146] "George Morrison Home," *Durango Democrat*, July 4, 1902, p. 1.

[147] "George Morrison Shot," *Durango Democrat*, June 19, 1907, p. 4.

[148] *Durango Wage Earner*, June 20, 1907, p. 1.

[149] *Durango Wage Earner*, March 12, 1908, p. 4.

[150] "Home Affairs," *Durango Herald*, June 2, 1882.

[151] "Rev. Ferguson's Words Over Remains of W.J. Thompson," *Durango Wage Earner*, January 11, 1906. Also see, Obituary for Doctor Alfred Thompson, n.d. provided to the author by George W. Thompson. These two items date the arrival of both William and his father, Doctor Thompson, in Durango as being 1882. William's brother, George, arrived before that and worked for the LC brand. He rode with the Farmington men at the Battle of Durango. It is clear that up until his death in May 1881, Irvin W. Lacy was the lead partner in charge of the San Juan operations of the Thompson and Lacy outfit. Immediately after his death it was their foreman, Henry Goodman, who took over the day to day management of the Thompson and Lacy herd.

[152] "Stabbing Affray at Durango," *La Plata Miner* (Silverton, CO), November 27, 1886, from the *Durango Herald*.

[153] "Stabbing Affray at Durango," *La Plata Miner*, November 27, 1886, from the *Durango Herald; The San Juan* (Silverton, CO), November 25, 1886.

[154] "Deplorable Tragedy Over Gambling Question," *Durango Wage Earner*, January 11, 1906, p. 1.

[155] *The San Juan* (Silverton, CO), January 20, 1887, from the *Durango Idea*.

[156] "First District Court Proceedings," *Salt Lake (UT) Herald*, March 16, 1888, p. 8.

[157] "The Several Courts," *Salt Lake (UT) Herald*, October 28, 1888, p. 8.

158 "Tom Nance Killed," *Coconino Weekly Sun* (Flagstaff, AZ), September 22, 1892; "One Cowboy Kills Another With a Blow From His Fist," *The Morning Call* (San Francisco, CA), September 20, 1892. This article identifies Mitchell as Ben and says Nance's neck was broken by Mitchell's punch. It also said that a month earlier Mitchell had his skull fractured during a fight.

159 Governor Pitkin to Governor Sheldon, October 24, 1881, Governor Frederick W. Pitkin, correspondence outgoing, Colorado State Archives.

160 *Colorado State Census 1885*, San Miguel County, r. 8, p. 7, ABCLS.

161 *U.S. Census 1900*, Eastland County, TX, r. 1629, p. 161a, IA-ACPL.

162 Mrs. George Langston, *History of Eastland County Texas* (Dallas, TX: A.D. Aldridge & Co., 1904), p. 75, http://www.archive.org/details/cu31924028801310 (accessed November 22, 2009).

163 "Home Stretch," *Durango Herald*, June 20, 1882; "Woods Willing," *Durango Herald*, June 22, 1882; *U.S. Census 1870*, Nevada County, CA, r. 75, p. 207a, IA-ACPL. George N. Wood (without the s) was living in Grass Valley with his father William D. and mother Elizabeth M. Wood.

164 "Durango's Killing," *Dolores News*, June 3, 1882, p. 1, from the *Durango Republican*. Quotations are from "Durango's Killing." "Murder at Durango," *Dolores News*, May 27, 1882, p. 2, from the *Durango Republican*. This article refers to the Estes and Buchanan cattle business.

165 Barry Cooper, "Coopers Were Early Pioneers Here," *Aztec (NM) Museum Association Newsletter*, September 1, 1988.

166 Muster Roll of the San Juan Guards, April 18, 1881, Campaign, TANM, NMSRCA.

167 "Durango's Killing," *Dolores News*, June 3, 1882, p. 1, from the *Durango Republican*.

168 Governor Pitkin to Mrs. A.E. Stockton, November 8, 1881 and Governor Pitkin to G.N. Woods, October 26, 1881, Governor Frederick W. Pitkin, correspondence outgoing, Colorado State Archives.

169 *Denver (CO) Republican*, September 28, 1881.

170 "Murder at Durango," *Dolores News*, May 27, 1882 p. 2, from the *Durango Republican*.

171 "Some of Woods' Last Letters," *Dolores News*, July 1, 1882, p. 1, from the *Durango Herald*.

172 Mary Alverda Estes Taylor interviewed by Anna Florence Robison, March 9, 1934, Montezuma County, pp. 98-99, CWA Pioneer Interviews, Special Collections, SHHLRC, HCC. Mrs. Taylor says that for a while her father, Joel Estes, Jr., raised cattle near Aztec, then left the area and returned in 1880. Upon their return to the San Juan country the Estes family lived about three miles east of Durango and later moved into Animas City. "Murder at Durango," *Dolores News*, May 27, 1882 p. 2, from the *Durango Republican*. In this article Joel Estes says he was aware that M.G. Buchanan left his pistol in Animas City on the morning he was killed. It seems likely that Estes knew this because the pistol was left at the Estes's residence.

173 "Murder!" *Durango Herald*, May 25, 1882.

174 "Home Affairs," *Durango Herald*, June 26, 1882.

175 "Durango's Killing," *Dolores News*, June 3, 1882, p. 1, from the *Durango Republican*.

[176] *U.S. Census 1860*, Erath County, TX, r. 1293, p. 123a, ABCLS; *U.S. Census 1870*, Erath County, TX, r. 1583, p. 455a, IA-ACPL; "Some of Woods' Last Letters," *Dolores News*, July 1, 1882, p. 1, from the *Durango Herald*. It does not appear that any of Angeline Tucker's older brothers were the father of George N. Woods, making his identification of her as Aunt Ange unclear, although there was an apparent relationship via the Wood/Woods line.

[177] "Murder!" *Durango Herald*, May 25, 1882. The *Durango Herald* was a daily paper, apparently published in the afternoon. Portions of the May 25th issue are difficult to read, but the *Herald* reported that the murder occurred "this morning." See also, "Murder at Durango," *Dolores News*, May 27, 1882 p. 2, from the *Durango Republican*.

[178] "Murder at Durango," *Dolores News*, May 27, 1882 p. 2, from the *Durango Republican*.

[179] "Murder!" *Durango Herald*, May 25, 1882. For an additional account see, "Durango's Killing," *Dolores News*, June 3, 1882, p. 1, from the *Durango Republican*.

[180] "Murder at Durango," *Dolores News*, May 27, 1882 p. 2, from the *Durango Republican*.

[181] *Dolores News*, July 1, 1882 p. 2.

[182] "Swift Justice," *La Plata Miner*, June 3, 1882.

[183] "Durango's Killing," *Dolores News*, June 3, 1882, p. 1, from the *Durango Republican*.

[184] "District Court," *Durango Herald*, June 3, 1882. Includes items from Saturday's and Monday's daily issues.

[185] "Swift Justice," *La Plata Miner*, June 3, 1882.

[186] "The Death Penalty," *Durango Herald*, June 2, 1882.

[187] "Some of Wood's Last Letters," *Dolores News*, July 1, 1882, p. 1, from the *Durango Herald*. In the same article in a letter to his friend, James Harris, he said his clothes could be found at Wilmers and Weller's Saloon and that he desired to be buried with his brother Harvey.

[188] "Home Stretch," *Durango Herald*, June 20, 1882; "Woods Willing," *Durango Herald*, June 22, 1882.

[189] "Home Affairs," and "Woods Willing," *Durango Herald*, June 22, 1882. Woods may not have been buried in California as he desired. Members of Durango's Victorian Aid Society, in a presentation at the Animas City Cemetery on April 21, 2012, pointed out a tiny, very worn grave stone bearing only the initials G, N and W, and said it marked Woods's grave.

[190] *Durango Herald*, June 21, 1882.

[191] "Gone to Join the Angels," *Tombstone (AZ) Weekly Epitaph*, June 24, 1882, p. 3.

[192] "Home Affairs," *Durango Herald*, June 26, 1882. The *Herald* says the wedding took place on the evening of the 25th. La Plata County, CO, Marriages, 1876-1889, La Plata County, CO, Government Records, Coll. M 028, series 3.2, FLC-CSWS. County records list the date as June 26th.

[193] *U.S. Census 1900*, Fresno County, California, r. 86, p. 30a, IA-ACPL.

[194] *U.S. Census 1900*, Fresno County, California, r. 86, p. 30a, IA-ACPL; *Colorado State Census* 1885, La Plata County, r. 5, p. 21, ABCLS; "In Trouble Again," *The Morning Call* (San Francisco, CA), April 26, 1890, p. 8.

[195] Bailey Millard, *History of The San Francisco Bay Region*, vol. 3 (Chicago, San Francisco, New York: The American Historical Society, Inc., 1924), p. 144,

http://archive.org/stream/historyofsanfran03mill#page/n7/mode/2up (accessed December 10, 2012).

[196] *U.S. Census 1900*, Fresno County, California, r. 86, p. 30a, IA-ACPL; *Colorado State Census* 1885, La Plata County, r. 5, p. 21, ABCLS.

[197] Millard, *History of The San Francisco Bay Region*, vol. 3, p. 144. In 2013, Durango's Coldwell Banker Real Estate Office was on the corner of Main Street and 8th Street. In 1881, 8th Street, then F Street, was home to the Tent Saloon owned by Ike Stockton and Hargo Eskridge.

[198] Colbert Nathaniel Coldwell, "Tales of Impetuous Romances with Clients," *El Paso Bar Journal* (February/March, 2010): p. 12, http://www.elpasobar.com/March2010.pdf (accessed May 18, 2010).

[199] *Colorado State Census 1885*, La Plata County, r. 5, p. 87, ABCLS.

[200] Wilma Crisp Bankston, *Where Eagles Winter - History and Legend of the Disappointment Country* (Cortez, CO: Mesa Verde Press, 1987), pp. 43 and 108.

[201] *Durango Herald*, April 22, 1893.

[202] *Dolores News*, September 30, 1882, p. 3; "News Summary," *Aspen Weekly Times*, September 30, 1882, p. 3.

[203] "San Juan Siftings," *San Juan Prospector* (Del Norte, CO), February 21, 1885, p. 3. The *Prospector* picked the article up from the *Durango Herald* which reported that their information came from the *Rico News* i.e. the *Dolores News*.

[204] "Ended Agony," *Durango Herald*, November 10, 1881.

[205] *Durango Herald*, November 17, 1881.

[206] "A Rapid Downfall," *Durango Daily Record*, April 21, 1882

[207] "Rates Restored," *Leadville Daily Herald*, January 12, 1884, p. 1.

[208] "Barney Watson's Trial," *Durango Southwest*, January 12, 1884.

[209] "Barney Watson Again in Limbo," *Dolores News*, May 24, 1884, p. 2.

[210] "State News," *Aspen Weekly Times*, May 31, 1884, p. 2.

[211] "The La Plata Contest," *Durango Southwest*, December 8, 1883.

[212] "Death of Seth Welfoot," *Dolores, News*, March 18, 1882, p. 3, from the *Durango Southwest;* Anderson, *History of New Mexico*, vol. 2, p. 876. Mrs. Vaughan's husband, James, died on August 11, 1879. He was the first interment in Farmington's cemetery.

[213] *Dolores News*, May 12, 1883, p. 3.

[214] *Durango Wage Earner*, February 2, 1899, p. 4.

[215] "Official Count," *Durango Wage Earner*, November 19, 1908, p. 2.

Bibliography

BOOKS

Adams, Andy. *The Log of a Cowboy: A Narrative of the Old Trail Days.* Boston and New York: Houghton Mifflin Company, 1903.
Adams, Ramon F. *The Cowman Says It Salty.* Tucson: The University of Arizona Press, 1971.
Anderson., George B., comp. *History of New Mexico - Its Resources and People.* Vol. 1. Los Angeles, Chicago and New York: Pacific States Publishing Co., 1907
-------. comp. *History of New Mexico - Its Resources and People.* Vol. 2. Los Angeles, Chicago and New York: Pacific States Publishing Co., 1907.
Armstrong, Ruth W. *The Chases of Cimarron.* Albuquerque: New Mexico Stockman, 1981.
Arrington, John B. and Eleanor D. MacDonald. *The San Juan Basin - My Kingdom Was A County.* Denver: Green Mountain Press, 1970.
Ball, Larry D. *The United States Marshals of New Mexico and Arizona Territories 1846-1912.* Albuquerque: University of New Mexico Press, 1978.
Bankston, Wilma Crisp. *Where Eagles Winter - History and Legend of the Disappointment Country.* Cortez, CO: Mesa Verde Press, 1987.
Bartholomew, Ed. *Wyatt Earp 1848-1880 The Untold Story.* Toyahvale, TX: Frontier Book Company, 1963.
Beckner, Raymond M. *Guns Along the Silvery San Juan.* Cañon City, CO: self-published, 1975.
-------. *Old Forts of Southern Colorado.* Cañon City, CO: self-published, 1975.
Bird, Allen G. *Bordellos of Blair Street.* Rev. ed. Pierson, MI: Advertising, Publications and Consultants, 1993.
Blancett, Tweeti Walser and Kathy Summers Price. *Step Back Inn To Aztec's Roots.* Aztec, NM: Step Back Inn, 1994.
Bryan, Howard. *Robbers, Rogues and Ruffians.* Santa Fe: Clear Light Publishers, 1991.
-------. *Wildest of the Wild West.* Santa Fe: Clear Light Publishers, 1988.
Burns, Walter Noble. *The Saga of Billy the Kid.* New York and Garden City, NY: Doubleday, Page and Company, 1926.
Burton-Cruber, Betty Ann, comp. *The Marriage Records of Itawamba County, Mississippi, 1837-1866, with Heads of Families, 1840 Federal Census.* Memphis: The Milestone Press, 1973.
Byrne, M.D., Bernard James. *A Frontier Army Surgeon - Life In Colorado In The Eighties.* 2nd Rev. and enlarged ed. New York: Exposition Press, 1962.
Caldwell, Clifford R. *Dead Right: The Lincoln County War.* Kerrville, TX: 2008.
Caldwell, Clifford R. and Ron DeLord. *Texas Lawmen, 1835-1899: The Good and the Bad.* Charleston, SC: The History Press, 2011.
Chapman, Arthur. *Out Where the West Begins and Other Western Verses.* Boston and New York: Houghton Mifflin Company, 1917.
Chesley, Hervey E. *Adventuring with the Old-Timers: Trails Travelled - Tales Told.* Midland, TX: Nita Stewart Haley Memorial Library, 1979.
City of Waco. *Fugitives From Justice - The Notebook of Texas Ranger Sergeant James B. Gillett.* With a foreword by Michael D. Morrison. Austin: State House Press, 1997.

Clark, O.S. "Clay Allison of the Washita," *Some Western Gun Fighters*. Compiled by Ed Bartholomew. Toyahvale, TX: Frontier Book Company, 1954.

Cleaveland, Norman and George Fitzpatrick. *The Morleys-Young Upsarts on the Southwest Frontier*. Albuquerque: Calvin Horn Publisher, Inc., 1971.

Coan, Ph.D., Charles F. *A History of New Mexico*. Vol. 1. Chicago and New York: The American Historical Society, Inc., 1925.

Coe, George W. *Frontier Fighter - The Autobiography of George W. Coe who fought and rode with Billy the Kid*. Boston and New York: Houghton and Mifflin Co., 1934; 2nd ed., Albuquerque: University of New Mexico Press, 1951; The Lakeside Classics ed., ed. by Doyce B. Nunis, Jr. with historical introduction by Doyce B. Nunis, Jr. Chicago: The Lakeside Press, R.R. Donnelly and Sons Co., 1984.

Conard, Howard L., *"Uncle Dick" Wootton*. Classics of the Old West ed. Chicago: W.E. Dibble and Co., 1890; reprint, n.p.: Time-Life Books, Inc., 1980.

Cox, James. *Historical and Biographical Record of the Cattle Industry and the Cattlemen of Texas and Adjacent Territory*. St. Louis: Woodward and Tiernan Printing Company, 1895.

Cox, Stanley M. comp. *Joseph Cox, Ancestors and Descendants*. Kansas City, MO: 1955.

Craig, Phillip. *The Cox-Truby Feud*. Flora Vista, NM: San Juan County Historical Society, 2002.

Curry, George. *George Curry 1861-1947 An Autobiography*. Edited by H.B. Hening. Albuquerque: University of New Mexico Press, 1958.

Delaney, Dr. Robert W. *Blue Coats, Red Skins and Black Gowns - 100 Years of Fort Lewis*. Durango, CO: Durango Herald, 1977.

Devere, William, "Tramp Poet of the West." *Jim Marshall's New Pianner - And Other Western Stories*. New York, Chicago and London: M. Witmark and Sons, 1908.

Dobie, J. Frank. *The Longhorns*. New York: Grosset and Dunlap, 1941.

Duke, Robert W. *San Juan County, New Mexico: The Early Years*. Farmington, NM: San Juan County Historical Society, 1999.

Erath County Genealogical Society, comp. *Erath County, Texas Marriage Record 1869-1891*. Vol. 1, Stephenville, TX: Erath County Genealogical Society, 1980.

Fernandez, Jose Emilio. *The Biography of Casimiro Barela*. Translated and annotated by Anthony Gabriel Melendez. Albuquerque: University of New Mexico Press, 2003.

Freeman, Ira S. *A History of Montezuma County Colorado – Land of Promise and Fulfillment*. Boulder: Johnson Publishing Co., 1958.

Frink, Maurice, W. Turrentine Jackson and Agnes Wright Spring. *When Grass Was King*. Boulder: University of Colorado Press, 1956.

Fulton, Maurice. G. *History of the Lincoln County War - A Classic Account of Billy the Kid*. Tucson: The University of Arizona, Press, 1968.

Furman, Agnes Miller. *Tohta - An Early Day History of the Settlement of Farmington And San Juan County, New Mexico 1875-1900*. Wichita Falls, TX: Nortex Press, 1977.

Garrett, Pat F. *The Authentic Life of Billy the Kid*. 1882. Western Frontier Library ed. Reprint, with an introduction by J.C. Dykes, Norman: University of Oklahoma Press, 1954.

Haley, J. Evetts. *Charles Goodnight - Cowman and Plainsman.*, New ed. Norman and London: University of Oklahoma Press, 1949.

-------. *The XIT Ranch of Texas*, Western Frontier Library ed. Norman: University of Oklahoma Press, 1953.

Hamner, Laura V. *Short Grass and Longhorns*. Norman: University of Oklahoma Press, 1943.

Hilton, Tom. *Nevermore, Cimarron, Nevermore*. Fort Worth: Western Heritage Press, 1970.

The History Committee of the Fort Lewis Mesa Reunion. *Pioneers of Southwest La Plata County Colorado*. Bountiful, UT: Family History Publishers, 1994.

Holden, Frances Mayhugh. *Lambshead Before Interwoven: A Texas Chronicle, 1848-1878*. College Station: Texas A&M University Press, 1982.

Hughes, Delbert Littrell and Lenore Harris Hughes. *Give Me Room!* El Paso: The Hughes Publishing Co., 1971.

Hunt, Frazier. *The Tragic Days of Billy the Kid*. New York: Hastings House, 1956.

Ingmire, Mrs. Frances Terry comp. *Marriage Records of Hopkins County, Texas, 1846-1880*. St. Louis, MO: 1979.

Keleher, William A. *The Maxwell Land Grant*. Santa Fe: Rydal Press, 1942; 2nd ed. New York: Argosy-Antiquarian, 1964; Reprint, with an introduction by John R. Van Ness, Albuquerque: University of New Mexico Press, 1984.

-------. *Violence in Lincoln County: 1869-1881*. Albuquerque: University of New Mexico Press, 1957.

Klasner, Lily. *My Girlhood Among Outlaws*. Edited by Eve Ball. Tucson: The University of Arizona Press, 1972.

Koogler, C.V. and Virgnia Koogler Whitney. *Aztec: Old Aztec From Anasazi to Statehood*. Fort Worth: American Reference Publishing Co., 1972.

Leckenby, Charles H. *The Tread of Pioneers*. Steamboat Spring, CO: The Pilot Press, 1945.

Leonard, Stephen J. *Lynching in Colorado, 1859-1919*. Boulder: University Press of Colorado, 2002.

Lomax, John A., comp. *Songs of the Cattle Trail and Cow Camp*. New York: The MacMillan Company, 1920.

Marriott, Barbara. *Outlaw Tales of New Mexico*. Guilford, CT: TwoDot/Globe Pequot Press, 2007.

McCoy, Joseph G. *Historic Sketches of the Cattle Trade of the West and Southwest*. Arthur H. Clark Company, 1966. Bison Book ed. Lincoln and London: University of Nebraska Press, 1985.

McKee, Irving. *"Ben-Hur" Wallace*. Berkeley and Los Angeles: University of California Press, 1947.

Myrick, David F. *New Mexico's Railroads - A Historical Survey*. Revised ed. Albuquerque: University of New Mexico Press, 1990.

Nolan, Frederick W. *The Life and Death of John Henry Tunstall*. Albuquerque: The University of New Mexico Press, 1965.

-------. *The Lincoln County War - A Documentary History*. Norman and London: University of Oklahoma Press, 1992.

-------. *The West of Billy the Kid*. Norman: University of Oklahoma Press, 1998.

Nossaman, Allen. *Rails Into Silverton*. Vol. 3 of *Many More Mountains*. Denver: Sundance Publications, Ltd., 1998.

O.L. Baskin and Co., comp. *History of the Arkansas Valley, Colorado*. Chicago: O.L. Baskin and Co., 1881.

O'Neal, Bill. *Encyclopedia of Western Gunfighters*. Norman: University of Oklahoma Press, 1979.
Otero, Miguel Antonio. *My Life On The Frontier 1864-1882*. New York: Press of the Pioneers, 1935; Reprint, with an introduction by Cynthia Secor-Welsh, Albuquerque: University of New Mexico Press, 1987.
Parsons, Chuck. *Clay Allison – Portrait of a Shootist,* Seagraves, TX: Pioneer Book Publishers, 1983.
Pearce, T.M., ed. *New Mexico Place Names – A Geographical Dictionary*. Albuquerque: University of New Mexico Press, 1965.
Rickards, Colin. *Mysterious Dave Mather*. Santa Fe: Press of the Territorian, 1968.
Roberts, Gary L. *Doc Holliday - The Life and Legend*. Hoboken: John Wiley and Sons, Inc., 2006.
Russell, Randy. *Billy the Kid – The Story The Trial*. Lincoln, NM: The Crystal Press, 1994.
Sarah Platt Decker Chapter N.S.D.A.R., comp. and ed. *Pioneers of the San Juan Country*. Vol. 1. Durango, CO: Sarah Platt Decker Chapter D.A.R., 1942.
-------. comp. and ed. *Pioneers of the San Juan Country*. Vol. 2. Durango, CO: Sarah Platt Decker Chapter D.A.R., 1946.
-------. comp. and ed. *Pioneers of the San Juan Country*. Vol. 4. Durango, CO: Sarah Platt Decker Chapter N.S.D.A.R., 1961.
Schweninger, Lee, ed. *The First We Can Remember*. Lincoln and London: University of Nebraska Press, 2011.
Smallwood, James M., Barry A. Crouch and Larry Peacock. *Murder and Mayhem – The War of Reconstruction in Texas*. College Station: Texas A&M University Press, 2003.
Smith, Cara Mae Coe Marable. *The Coe's Go West: From Billy the Kid Land to Movie and Other Entertainment Lands*. El Paso: C.M. Smith, 1988.
Smith, Duane A. *A Time for Peace: Fort Lewis, Colorado, 1878-1891*. Boulder: University Press of Colorado, 2006.
Speer, William S. and Hon. Johny Henry Brown, ed. *The Encyclopedia of the New West*. Marshall, TX: The United States Biographical Publishing Company, 1881; 2nd ed. Easley, SC: Southern Historical Press, The Rev. S. Emmett Lucas, Jr., 1978.
Stanley, F. *Desperadoes of New Mexico*. Denver: World Press, Inc., 1953.
-------. *The Grant That Maxwell Bought*. Denver: World Press, Inc., 1952.
-------. *Ike Stockton*. Denver: World Press, Inc., 1959.
Streeter, Floyd B. *Ben Thompson, Man With A Gun*. New York: Frederick Fell, Inc., 1957.
Taylor, Morris F. *Trinidad, Colorado Territory*. Pueblo: Trinidad State Junior College, 1966.
Twitchell, Ralph Emerson. *The Leading Facts of New Mexican History*. Vol. 4. Cedar Rapids, IA: The Torch Press, 1917.
Velarde Tiller, Veronica E. *The Jicarilla Apache Tribe - A History*. Rev. ed., Bison Book ed. Lincoln: University of Nebraska Press, 1992.
Ward, Margaret. *Cousins by the Dozens*. n.p.: 1966
Waybourn, Marilu and Vernetta Mickey. *Meet Me At The Fair*. Farmington, NM: San Juan County Fair Association, 1984.
Werner, Fred H. *Meeker – The Story of the Meeker Massacre and the Thornburgh Battle – September 29, 1879*. Greeley, CO: Werner Publications, 1985.

Westphall, Victor. *The Public Domain in New Mexico - 1854-1891*. Albuquerque: University of New Mexico Press, 1965.

-------. *Thomas Benton Catron and His Era*. Tucson: The University of Arizona Press, 1973.

Wilson, Delphine Dawson. *John Barkley Dawson – Pioneer, Cattleman, Rancher*. n.p.: Delphine Dawson Wilson, 1997.

Wilson, John P. *Merchants, Guns, and Money – The Story of Lincoln County and Its Wars*. Santa Fe: Museum of New Mexico Press, 1987.

Workers of the Writers' Program of the Work Projects Administration. *New Mexico – A Guide to the Colorful State –American Guide Series*. New York: Coronado Cuarto Centennial Commission, Hastings House, 1940.

Zamonski, Stanley W. "Rougher Than Hell." *1957 Brand Book of the Denver Westerners*. Vol. 13. Edited by Numa L. James. Boulder: Westerners, Inc., Johnson Publishing Company, 1958.

JOURNALS, MAGAZINES, PERIODICALS AND MAPS

Atwood, Mary, curator and editor. *Aztec (NM) Museum Association Newsletter*

Ayres, Mary C. "The Founding of Durango, Colorado." *The Colorado Magazine* Vol. 7, No. 3 (May 1930).

Bean, Jordan and Edgar C. McMechen. "Jordan Bean's Story and the Castle Valley Indian Fight." *The Colorado Magazine* Vol. 20, No. 1 (January 1943).

Benson, Maxine. "Port Stockton." *The Colorado Magazine* Vol. 43, No. 1 (Winter 1966).

Bowra, Bernice Gardner. "Cemeteries of San Juan County." *New Mexico Genealogist* Vol. 1, No. 1 (October 1962).

Bureau of Land Management Surface Management Status Map. *Farmington, New Mexico*. U.S. Dept. of the Interior, Bureau of Land Management (1991).

Cornelius, Olive Frazier. "Pioneer History and Reminiscences of the San Juan Basin." *Aztec (NM) Independent Review,* (February 24, 1933 – August 11, 1933).

Dalrymple Dick. "Henry Goodman: Moab's Forgotten Icon." *Canyon Legacy*. Journal of the Dan O'Laurie Canyon Country Museum. Vol. 45 (Summer 2002).

Fooshee, W.H. "Early Days in Stephenville." *Stephenville (TX) Tribune* (June 1923 – October 1923).

Kelsey, Harry, E., Jr. "Finis P. Ernest." *The Colorado Magazine* Vol. 31, No. 4 (October 1954).

Mathews, Carl F. "Rico, Colorado – Once a Roaring Camp." *The Colorado Magazine* Vol. 28, No. 1 (January 1951).

Moody, Marshall D. "The Meeker Massacre." *The Colorado Magazine* Vol. 30, No. 2 (April 1953).

Pioneer Association San Juan County, New Mexico. *Bulletins Pioneer Association San Juan County, New Mexico* (1953 to 1976), Farmington (NM) Public Library.

Rasch, Philip J. "Feuding at Farmington." *New Mexico Historical Review* Vol. 40, No. 3 (July 1965).

Salmon, Rusty. "The Little Castle Valley Fight." *Canyon Legacy*. Journal of the Dan O'Laurie Canyon Country Museum. Vol. 41 (Spring 2001).

Salmon, Rusty and Robert S. McPherson. "Cowboys, Indians, and Conflict: The Pinhook Draw Fight, 1881." *Utah Historical Quarterly* Vol. 69, No. 1 (Winter 2001).

Silvey, Frank. "Rambling Thoughts Of A Rimrocker." *San Juan Record* (Monticello, UT, October 3 and 10, 1935).
United States Geological Survey Map. *Silverton, Colorado*. 30x60 minute Quad. (1982).
------- Map. *Warner Lake, Utah Quadrangle* (2001).
Valiton, Charles L. "Forty-five Years in Colorado." *Silverton (CO) Standard* (December 19, 1925, March 13 and 20, 1926 and June 5 and 12, 1926).
Wallis, George A. "Cattle Kings!" *True West* Vol. 11, No. 4 (March-April 1964).

ARCHIVAL AND FAMILY RECORDS

Boettcher, Joe E. "Who Killed Porter Stockton?" n.d. Aztec (NM) Museum.
Cox, Isaac Hiram. "Tales." Transcribed by Joeen Johnson Sutton. 1920s. Courtesy of Les Sutton.
Duke, Robert W. "Political History of San Juan County, New Mexico 1876-1926." Master's Thesis, University of New Mexico, June 1947. San Juan County Archaeological Research Center and Library at the Salmon Ruins, Bloomfield, NM.
Johnson, Lillian Hartman. "In Memory of Orville D. Pyle." n.d. Courtesy of Frank and Sandra Pyle.
Jones, Charles. "The Memoirs of Charles Adam Jones." n.d. Clifford B. Jones Papers. 1814-1973 and undated. Accession Nos. 96-0122-B and 98-0001-B. Southwest Collection/Special Collections Library, Texas Tech University, Lubbock, TX.
Local History Project, comp. "Index Marriage Records, Colfax County, NM." Arthur Johnson Memorial Library, Raton, NM.
Nita Stewart Haley Memorial Library and J. Evetts Haley History Center, Midland TX, (HMLHC).
    J. Evetts Haley Collection. (JEHC)
        Bull, S.A. to J. Evetts Haley, February 27, 1927.
        Coe, Frank to J. Evetts Haley, August 14, 1927 and August 17, 1927.
        Coe, George to J. Evetts Haley, March 20, 1927, August 12, 1927 and August 18, 1927.
Thompson, George W.
    Obituary for Doctor Alfred Thompson, source unknown.
    Obituary for Martha Jane Thompson, source unknown.
    Thompson Family Tree
University of New Mexico, Center for Southwest Research, Albuquerque, NM.
    Lacy, S.C. "Dictation of the widow of I.W. Lacy." Vermejo, NM, 1885. Courtesy of the Western Americana Collection, The Bancroft Collection, Bancroft Library. University of California, Berkeley, CA.

ELECTRONIC DOCUMENTS AND SOURCES

Baker, Bonnie. "The Origins of the Posse Comitatus Act." *Air and Space Power Journal* (November 1, 1999), http://www.airpower.maxwell.af.mil/airchronicles/cc/baker1.html (accessed December 18, 2008).

Brinkerhoff, John R. "The Posse Comitatus Act and Homeland Security." *Journal of Homeland Security* (February 2002), http://www.homelandsecurity.org/journal/Articles/brinkerhoffpossecomitatus.htm (accessed February 2, 2009).

California Digital Newspaper Collection. The CDNC is a project of the Center for Bibliographical Studies and Research (CBSR) at the University of California, Riverside. The CDNC is supported in part by the U.S. Institute of Museum and Library Services under the provisions of the Library Services and Technology Act, administered in California by the State Librarian. Web portal at http://cdnc.ucr.edu/cdnc. 2008-2013. The following newspapers:

Los Angeles Daily Herald
Sacramento Daily Record-Union
Sacramento Daily Union

Chavez, Patti. "A Short History, 1876-2003." Research by Sergeant Dewayne Faverino. San Juan County Sheriff's Office [New Mexico]. n.d. http://www.sjcso.com/OfInterest/AgencyHistory/history.pdf (accessed March 2, 2009).

Coldwell, Colbert Nathaniel. "Tales of Impetuous Romances with Clients." *El Paso Bar Journal* (February/March, 2010), http://www.elpasobar.com/March2010.pdf (accessed May 18, 2010).

Colorado Historic Newspaper Collection. The collection is possible through the Collaborative Digitization Program (CDP), in partnership with the Colorado State Library and the Colorado Historical Society. Web portal at http://www.coloradohistoricnewspapers.org, 2003-2013. The following newspapers:

Alamosa Journal
Aspen Tribune
Aspen Weekly Times
Colorado Daily Chieftain (Pueblo)
Colorado Springs Gazette
Colorado Transcript (Golden)
Colorado Weekly Chieftain (Pueblo)
Creede Candle
Daily Colorado Miner (Georgetown)
Denver Daily Times
Denver Daily Tribune
Denver Mirror
Dolores News (Rico)
Douglas County Record Journal (Castle Rock)
Durango Democrat
Durango Wage Earner
Fairplay Flume
Fort Collins Weekly Courier
Las Animas Leader (West Las Animas)
Leadville Daily Herald

Leadville Daily and Evening Chronicle
Mancos Times
Mancos Times-Tribune
Rocky Mountain News (Denver)
Rocky Mountain Sun (Aspen)
Saguache Chronicle
San Juan Prospector (Del Norte)
Silverton Standard
Trinidad Enterprise
Wray Gazette

Ebay.com.hk. Listing by Collectiblesdelectables, 2011. http://www.ebay.com.hk/itm/1928-CARD-WIDOWS-RELIEF-FUND-JAFFA-TEMPLE-ALTOONA-PA-/150570639592 (accessed Nov. 30, 2011).

Find A Grave website at findagrave.com. The following grave listings:
- Librarian, creator and maintained by Smilydino. "George Washington Coe." October 27, 2009. http://www.findagrave.com/cgi-bin/fg.cgi?page=gr&GSln=coe&GSfn=george&GSby=1845&GSbyrel=after&GSdy=1938&GSdyrel=after&GSst=34&GScntry=4&GSob=n&GRid=43604695&df=all& (accessed May 25, 2012).
- Smilydino, creator. "Benjamin Franklin 'Frank' Coe." November 12, 2010, http://www.findagrave.com/cgi-bin/fg.cgi?page=gr&GScid=38008&GRid=61516825& (accessed May 25, 2012).

Fort Lewis College, Center of Southwest Studies.
- Animas City, CO Business Licenses Issued 1879-1896. Animas City, CO, Government Records, Collection M120, 2002 and 2004. http://swcenter.fortlewis.edu/inventory/AnimasCity.htm#licenses (accessed August 14, 2008).
- Durango, Colorado, Police Ledgers Index, List of Arrests, 1881-1885: by name. Durango, CO, City Government Records, Collection M 027, Series 6.6, 2003 and 2004. http://swcenter.fortlewis.edu/inventory/DgoArrests18811885.htm#1881-1885 (accessed May 12, 2009).
- "The Life of L.L. Nunn as recorded by the Western Colorado Power Company Collection." Collection M 002, http://swcenter.fortlewis.edu/inventory/Nunn.htm (accessed September 6, 2009).

Friedman, S. Morgan. "The Inflation Calculator." *Ceci n'est pas une* homepage, n.d. http://www.westegg.com/inflation/infl.cgi (accessed 2008-2010).

Geringer Art Ltd. "Robert Lee Eskridge." 2009. http://www.geringerart.com/bios/eskridge.html (accessed November 30, 2011).

Horn, Jonathon C. *Landscape Level History of the Canyons of the Ancients National Monument Montezuma and Dolores Counties, Colorado.* Dolores, CO: Bureau of Land Management, 2004. http://www.blm.gov/heritage/adventures/research/StatePages/PDFs/Colorado/Studies/Ancients%20Report.pdf. 2004 (accessed March 15, 2009).

BIBLIOGRAPHY

The Internet Archive at archive.org. The following books, articles and reports:

A.W. Bowen and Company, comp. *Progressive Men of Western Colorado*. Chicago: A.W. Bowen and Company, 1905. http://archive.org/stream/progressivemenof00awborich#page/862/mode/1up/search/hall (accessed February 14, 2013).

Adams, Jones. "In The Stronghold of the Piutes." *Overland Monthly* Vol. 22, Issue 132 (December 1893). http://archive.org/stream/overlandmonthly221893sanf#page/583/mode/1up (accessed February 28, 2013).

Annual Report of the Commissioner of Indian Affairs to the Secretary of the Interior. Washington, DC, 1875. http://archive.org/details/usindianaffairs75usdorich (accessed June 7, 2013).

Annual Report of the Commissioner of Indian Affairs to the Secretary of the Interior. Washington, DC, 1876. http://archive.org/details/usindianaffairs76usdorich (accessed June 7, 2013).

Annual Report of the Commissioner of Indian Affairs to the Secretary of the Interior. Washington, DC, 1887. http://archive.org/details/annualreportofco188700unitrich (accessed December 15, 2012).

Annual Report of the Secretary of War, Vol. 1. Washington, DC, 1879. http://archive.org/details/annualreportswa68deptgoog (accessed June 9, 2013).

Bradley, Glenn D. *Winning the Southwest – A Story of Conquest*. Chicago: A.C. McClurg and Co., 1912. http://archive.org/details/winningsouthwes02bradgoog (accessed September 8, 2013).

Buffa, Elizabeth Berry, comp. "Cox Family Outline." Pacific Palisades, CA, 1977. http://archive.org/stream/coxfamilyoutline00buff#page/n17/mode/2up (accessed February 25, 2013).

Chapman Publishing Company, comp. *Portrait and Biographical Record of the State of Colorado*. Chicago: Chapman Publishing Company, 1899. http://archive.org/stream/portraitbiograph00chaprich#page/193/mode/1up (accessed March 3, 2013).

Cook, General D.J. "Capture of the Allison Gang." *Hands Up, or, Thirty-Five Years of Detective Life in the Mountains and on the Plains*, comp., John W. Cook. Denver: D.J. and J.W. Cook, 1897. http://www.archive.org/details/handsuporthirtyf00cook (accessed September 27, 2009).

Crocker, George E. "Memories of Cimarron, New Mexico, 1871-1882." n.d. http://archive.org/details/memoriesofcimarr00croc, pdf version (accessed May 12, 2012).

Crooker, Lucien B., Henry S. Nourse, John G. Brown, and Milton L. Haney. *The Story of the Fifty-fifth Regiment Illinois Volunteer Infantry in the Civil War 1861-1865*. Clinton, MA: W.J. Coulter, 1887. http://archive.org/stream/ofthefiftyfifth00illirich#page/n0/mode/2up (accessed Feb. 4, 2013).

Darley, D.D., Rev. George M. *Pioneering in the San Juan*. Chicago, New York and Toronto: Fleming H. Revell Company, 1899. http://archive.org/details/pioneeringinsanj00darl (accessed June 9, 2013).

Guinn, Prof. J.M. *History of the State of California and Biographical Record of the San Joaquin Valley, California.* Chicago: Chapman Publishing Co., 1905. http://archive.org/details/cu31924028919375 (accessed August 2, 2013).

Hall, Frank. *History of the State of Colorado,* Vol. 4. Chicago: Rocky Mountain Historical Company, 1895. http://archive.org/stream/historyofstateof04hall#page/n9/mode/2up (accessed February 13, 2013).

Hinton Jr., Harwood P. "John Simpson Chisum, 1877-84." *New Mexico Historical Review* Vol. 31, No. 4 (October 1956). http://archive.org/details/newmexicohistori31univrich (accessed August 24, 2013).

Hough, Emerson. *The Story of the Outlaw: A Study of the Western Desperado.* New York: Grosset and Dunlap, 1907. https://archive.org/stream/storyofoutlawstu00houguoft#page/n5/mode/2up (accessed June 25, 2013).

Hunter, J. Marvin, comp. and ed. *The Trail Drivers of Texas.* Nashville: Cokesbury Press, 1925. http://archive.org/details/traildriversofte00hunt (accessed June 8, 2013).

Kenner, Charles L. "The Great New Mexico Cattle Raid - 1872." *New Mexico Historical Review* Vol. 37, No. 4 (October 1962). http://archive.org/details/newmexicohistori37univrich (accessed June 5, 2013).

Langston, Mrs. George. *History Eastland County Texas.* Dallas, TX: A.D. Aldridge & Co., 1904. http://www.archive.org/details/cu31924028801310 (accessed November 22, 2009).

Laws Passed at an Extra Session of the Thirteenth General Assembly of the State of Colorado. Denver: The Smith-Brooks Printing Company, State Printers, 1902. http://archive.org/stream/lawspassedatses10cologoog#page/n17/mode/2up (accessed March 2, 2013).

Lewis Publishing Company, comp. *History of Texas.* Central Texas ed. Chicago: Lewis Publishing Company, 1896. http://archive.org/details/historyoftexassu00lewi (accessed March 1, 2013).

Lewis Publishing Company, comp. *A Memorial and Biographical History of Johnson and Hill Counties, Texas.* Chicago: Lewis Publishing Company, 1892. http://archive.org/details/memorialbiograph01chic (accessed August 12, 2013).

Millard, Bailey. *History of The San Francisco Bay Region,* Vol. 3. Chicago, San Francisco, New York: The American Historical Society, Inc., 1924. http://archive.org/stream/historyofsanfran03mill#page/n7/mode/2up (accessed December 10, 2012).

Peterson, C.S., comp. *Representative New Mexicans.* Denver: C.S. Peterson, 1912. http://archive.org/details/representativene01denv (accessed August 10, 2013).

Poldervaart, Arie. "Black-Robed Justice in New Mexico, 1846-1912." *New Mexico Historical Review* Vol. 22, No. 4 (October 1947). http://archive.org/details/newmexicohistori22univrich (accessed September 1, 2013).

Row, S.B. *Illustrated Souvenir History of Philipsburg, Pennsylvania*. Williamsport, PA: Grit Publishing Company, 1909. http://archive.org/details/illustratedsouve00phil (accessed December 15, 2012).

Rye, Edgar. *The Quirt and The Spur – Vanishing Shadows of the Western Frontier*. Chicago: W.B. Conkey Company, 1909. http://archive.org/details/quirtandspurvan00ryegoog (accessed June 28, 2013).

San Diego Directory Co., comp. *San Diego City and County Directory*. San Diego: Ross and George Book Bindery, 1915. http://archive.org/stream/sandiegocitycoun00unkn#page/n0/mode/2up (accessed February 6, 2013).

Siringo, Charles A. *History of "Billy the Kid."* Santa Fe: 1920. http://archive.org/details/historyofbillyki00siririch (accessed June 25, 2013).

Wallace, Lew. *Lew Wallace: An Autobiography*. Vol. 2. New York and London: Harper and Brothers Publishers, 1906. http://archive.org/stream/lewwallacevolii002480mbp#page/n3/mode/2up (accessed January 30, 2012).

Wilbarger, J.W. *Indian Depredations in Texas*. Austin: Hutchings Printing House, 1890. http://archive.org/details/indiandepredatio00wilb (accessed August 24, 2013).

Library of Congress

Burleson, Mrs. Mary E. "Pioneer Story." Transcribed by Edith L. Crawford in Carrizozo, NM. U.S. Works Progress Administration, Federal Writer's Project, Folklore Project, Life Histories, 1936-1939, Manuscript Division. http://www.loc.gov/resource/wpalh1.19040404/seq-1#seq-1 (accessed September 18, 2013).

Chronicling America: Historic American Newspapers. Sponsored jointly by the National Endowment for the Humanities and the Library of Congress as part of the National Digital Newspaper Program (NDNP). Web portal at http://chroniclingamerica.loc.gov/

Albuquerque Citizen
Albuquerque Daily Citizen
Arizona Citizen (Tucson)
Arizona Weekly Citizen (Tucson)
Bisbee (AZ) Daily Review
Bismarck (ND) Tribune
Bolivar (TN) Bulletin
Brenham (TX) Weekly Banner
Carrizozo (NM) News
Coconino Sun (Flagstaff, AZ)
The Columbian (Bloomsburg, PA)
Daily Ardmoreite (Ardmore, OK)
Dallas (TX) Daily Herald

Dodge City (KS) Times
Edgefield (SC) Advertiser
Emporia (KS) News
Fort Worth Daily Gazette
Guthrie (OK) Daily Leader
Intermountain Catholic (Salt Lake City, UT)
Iola (KS) Register
Jasper (IN) Weekly Courier
Kansas City (MO) Journal
Lancaster (PA) Daily Intelligencer
Las Vegas (NM) Weekly Optic and Stock Grower
Leavenworth (KS) Weekly Times
Lincoln County Leader (White Oaks, NM)
Los Angeles Daily Herald
Los Angeles Herald
Memphis (TN) Daily Appeal
Milan (TN) Exchange
The Morning Call (San Francisco, CA)
National Republican (Washington, DC)
New York (NY) Sun
New York (NY) Tribune
Omaha (NE) Daily Bee
Richmond (MO) Democrat
Sacramento Daily Record-Union
St. Johns (AZ) Herald
St. Louis (MO) Republic
St. Paul (MN) Globe
Salt Lake (UT) Herald
San Francisco (CA) Call
San Juan Islander (Friday Harbor, WA)
Sedalia (MO) Weekly Bazoo
Smoky Hill and Republican Union (Junction City, KS)
State Journal (Jefferson City, MO)
Tombstone (AZ) Weekly Epitaph
Washington (DC) Evening Star
Weekly Arizona Miner (Prescott)
Weekly Kansas Chief (Troy)
Western Liberal (Lordsburg, NM)
Wichita (KS) Daily Eagle

McConnell, Joseph Carroll. *The West Texas Frontier.* Vol. 2. Palo Pinto, TX: Texas Legal Bank and Book Company, 1939. http://www.forttours.com/ pdf%20files/ Mcconnell%20MERGED.pdf (accessed December 1, 2009).

Meek, Christopher A. *The Meek/Meeks Family of Tennessee and Arkansas.* Revised draft. May 16, 2009. http://meekgenealogy.com/Articles/ The%20Meek%20Family%20TN_AR.pdf (accessed October 20, 2009).

National Park Service. Civil War Soldiers and Sailors System. http://www.nps.gov/civilwar/soldiers-and-sailors-database.htm (accessed November 30, 2012).

North Dakota Cowboy Hall of Fame. "Ranching – James William 'Bill' Follis." n.d. http://www.ndcowboy.com/Hall_of_Fame/Ranching/follis_james.asp (accessed January 3, 2011).

U.S Census Records

From the Internet Archive courtesy of the Genealogy Center of the Allen County (Indiana) Public Library (IA-ACPL). *Seventh Census, 1850. Eighth Census, 1860. Ninth Census, 1870. Tenth Census, 1880. Twelfth Census, 1900. Thirteenth Census, 1910. Fourteenth Census, 1920. Fifteenth Census, 1930.* Records of the United States Bureau of the Census. Washington, DC: National Archives and Records Administration (NARA). http://archive.org/details/us_census. Many of these same records were also accessed at the Albuquerque/Bernalillo County Library System, Special Collections Library and Genealogy Center and the Fort Lewis College Center of Southwest Studies, Collection I 002, for AZ, CO, NM, UT.

1850, Drew County, AR
1850, Hopkins County, TX
1850, Titus County, TX
1850, Upshur County, TX
1860, Buchanan County, TX
1860, Eastland County, TX
1860, Erath County, TX
1860, Fannin County, TX
1860, Hopkins County, TX
1860, Palo Pinto County, TX
1860, Schuyler County, MO
1860, Sussex County, DE
1870, Colfax County, NM
1870, Conejos County, CO
1870, Eastland County, TX
1870, Erath County, TX
1870, Gentry County, MO
1870, Harrison County, MO
1870, Henry County, IA
1870, Huerfano County, CO
1870, Johnson County, TX
1870, Knox County, IN
1870, Labette County, KS
1870, Lafayette County, MO
1870, Nevada County, CA
1870, Posey County, IN
1870, Schuyler County, MO
1870, Sussex County, DE
1870, Weld County, CO
1880, Chaffee County, CO

1880, Colfax County, NM
1880, Conejos County, CO
1880, Emery County, UT
1880, Erath County, TX
1880, Gunnison County, CO
1880, Johnson County, TX
1880, La Plata County, CO
1880, Las Animas County, CO
1880, Ouray County, CO
1880, Rio Arriba County, NM
1880, San Juan County, CO
1880, Santa Fe County, NM
1880, Sussex County, DE
1900, Centre County, PA
1900, Eastland County, TX
1900, Fresno County, CA
1900, Mineral County, CO
1900, Taylor County, TX
1910, Los Angeles County, CA
1910, San Juan County, CO
1920, Centre County, PA
1920, San Diego County, CA
1930, San Diego County, CA

Utah Digital Newspapers. University of Utah. Web portal at http://digitalnewspapers.org/. University of Utah, J. Willard Marriott Library. The following newspapers:

Ogden Standard Examiner, Collection of the Weber County Library
Provo Daily Enquirer, Collection of Brigham Young University

DOCUMENTARY RECORDS

Albuquerque/Bernalillo County Library System, Special Collections Library and Genealogy Center. *Colorado State Census, 1885 and New Mexico Territorial Census, 1885,* Records of the United States Bureau of the Census. Washington, DC.: National Archives and Records Administration (NARA).

1885, Dolores County, CO
1885, La Plata County, CO
1885, Rio Arriba County, NM
1885, San Miguel, County, CO

Bosque County District Clerk's Office. Meridian TX.
    Criminal Minutes, Book D.
    State Docket, District Court.
Colfax County Clerk's Office. Raton, NM.
    Marriage Record Book No. 1.

BIBLIOGRAPHY

Colorado State Archives. Governor Frederick W. Pitkin Collection. Correspondence outgoing. October 24 – November 8, 1881.
Erath County District Court boxed case records. District Clerk's Office. Stephenville, TX.
Fort Lewis College, Center of Southwest Studies (FLC-CSWS). Durango, CO.
- Animas City, CO, Government Records. Collection M 120
  - Board of Trustees Ordinance Book, December 24, 1878- March 13, 1888.
  - Business Licenses 1879-1896.
  - Police Magistrate Court Records, January 1879 – December 1883.
- Bourke, John Greg. "John Gregory Bourke Diaries." Volume 48, September 27, 1881 to October 19, 1881. Collection I 032.
- Justice of the Peace J.C. Craig, Docket Ledger, March 4, 1881 to December 29, 1881. Collection M 028, RG 17. Justice of the Peace Case Files. La Plata County, CO Government Records.
- La Plata County, CO, Marriages, 1876-1889. Collection M 028, Series 3.2. La Plata County, CO Government Records.
- Letters, correspondence, orders and Misc., 1878 -1891. Collection M 118. Fort Lewis Military Post Federal Records Inventory (FLMP).
- Territorial Papers, New Mexico, 1851-1914. Collection I 023. Microcopy 364, roll 1, RG 48, Interior Department, NARA.

History Colorado Center (HCC), Steven H. Hart Library and Research Center (SHHLRC), Special Collections, Civil Works Administration (CWA) Pioneer Interviews, 1933-34.
- Conejos, La Plata, Las Animas and Montezuma Counties.

Las Animas County Commissioner's Record Books No. 2 and No. 3, Trinidad, CO.
New Mexico State Records Center and Archives (NMSRCA), Territorial Archives of New Mexico, 1846-1912 (TANM) Collection 1959-293. On microfilm, 189 rolls.
- Colfax County Records, County Clerk. 1870-1890. Collection 1973-025, Subseries 1.3. Part of item 15.1.
  - Brand Record Book B.
- Colfax County Records, County Sheriff. 1869 to 1884. Collection 1973-025, Subseries 7.1, Box 4.
  - Outsize Record Books.
- Colfax County Records, Proceedings of Board of County Commissioners. 1876-1884, Collection 1973-025, Subseries 3.2, Box 4.
  - Outsize Record Books.
- Records of the Adjutant General of the Territory. 1847-1911, Series 7.
  - Campaign Records. Campaign Against Outlaws in Rio Arriba County, 1881. Roll 87 (Campaign).
  - Letters received by Max Frost, 1881. Roll 73 (LRRAGT)
  - Letters sent by Max Frost, 1881. Roll 78 (LSRAGT)
- Records of the Territorial Governors, 1846-1912, Series 11.
  - Governor Samuel Axtell Papers. Collection 1959-084.1875 to 1878. Roll 98.

Governor Lionel A. Sheldon Papers. Collection 1959-086. 1881 to 1885. Roll 100.
Governor Lew Wallace Papers. Collection 1959-085. 1878-1926. Roll 99 (GLWP).
Records of the United States Territorial and New Mexico District Courts for Colfax County.
Civil and Criminal Record Nos. 1, 2, 3 and 4, 1869-1884.
Criminal Case Files, Box 2, Case Nos. 3-700, 1869-1883.
Records of the United States Territorial and New Mexico District Courts for Lincoln County.
Criminal Cases Files, Box 2, Case Nos. 1-540, 1872-1883.
Records of the United States Territorial and New Mexico District Courts for Mora County.
Criminal Case Files, Case Nos. 1A-664, 1860-1881.
Records of the United States Territorial and New Mexico District Courts for Rio Arriba County.
Criminal Case Files, Case Nos. 115-428, 1874-1885.
Records of the United States Territorial and New Mexico District Courts for San Miguel County.
Criminal Case Files, Case Nos. 283-820, 1869-1876.
Palo Pinto County State Docket Book A. District Clerk's Office. Palo Pinto, TX.
San Juan County Book of Brands and Earmarks. County Clerk's Office. Aztec, NM.
Shackelford County Minutes District Court, Book A, 1875-1884. District Clerk's Office. Albany, TX.
Tarleton State University Dick Smith Library (TSU-DSL). Stephenville, TX.
Erath County Commissioners Court Minutes, Vol. A, 1867-1879.
Erath County District Court Minutes, Vol. A, 1866-1870; Vol. B, 1871-1874; Vol. C, 1874-1884.
Erath County Marriage Records, Vol. A, 1869-1877.
Record of Marks and Brands, Erath County, Texas (Under law of 1874).
Shackelford County District Court Minutes, Vol. A, 1875-1884.

OTHER NEWSPAPERS

Abilene Christian University, Brown Library (Abilene, TX)
Fort Griffin (TX) Echo
Frontier Echo (Jacksboro, TX)
Albuquerque/Bernalillo County Library System, Special Collections Library (ABCLS) (Albuquerque, NM)
Albuquerque Review
Rio Grande Republican (Las Cruces, NM)
Silver City (NM) Enterprise
Aztec Museum and Pioneer Village (Aztec, NM)
Aztec (NM) Independent Review
San Juan County Index (Aztec, NM)
San Juan Democrat (Aztec, NM)

BIBLIOGRAPHY

Carnegie Library of Trinidad (Trinidad, CO)
    Trinidad (CO) Daily News
    Trinidad (CO) Enterprise
Denver Public Library, Western History and Genealogy Department (Denver, CO)
    Colorado Springs Daily Gazette
Durango Public Library (Durango, CO)
    Durango (CO) Daily Record
    Durango (CO) Herald
    Durango (CO) Southwest
    Durango (CO) Weekly Record
Farmington Daily Times Community Center (Farmington, NM)
    Farmington (NM) Daily Times
Fort Lewis College, Center of Southwest Studies and Delaney Southwest Research Library (FLC-CSWS) (Durango, CO)
    Alamosa (CO) Empire
    Animas City (CO) Southwest
    Arizona Gazette (Phoenix, AZ)
    Cimarron (NM) News and Press
    Coconino Weekly Sun (Flagstaff, AZ)
    Denver Republican
    Deseret News (Salt Lake City, UT)
    Dolores News (Rico, CO)
    Durango (CO) Wage Earner
    Fairplay (CO) Flume
    Farmington (NM) Times Hustler
    Grand Valley Times (Moab, UT)
    La Plata Miner (Silverton, CO)
    Lake City (CO) Mining Register
    Lake City (CO) Silver World
    Las Vegas (NM) Daily Gazette
    Las Vegas (NM) Daily Optic
    Moab (UT) Times-Independent
    Ouray (CO) Times
    Rocky Mountain News (Denver, CO)
    Saguache (CO) Chronicle
    The San Juan (Silverton, CO)
    San Juan Herald (Silverton, CO)
    San Juan Record (Monticello, UT)
    Santa Fe Daily New Mexican
    Santa Fe Weekly New Mexican
    Silverton (CO) Standard
    Tombstone (AZ) Epitaph.
New Mexico Highlands University, Thomas C. Donnelly Library (Las Vegas, NM)
    Cimarron (NM) News
New Mexico State Library Southwest Collection (Santa Fe, NM)
    Raton (NM) Comet
    Raton (NM) Daily Range
    Santa Fe Daily New Mexican

San Juan College Library (Farmington, NM)
    Farmington (NM) Daily Times
    Farmington (NM) Times Hustler
    Santa Lulu Independent (Aztec, NM)
State Library of Pennsylvania (Harrisburg, PA)
    Clearfield (PA) Progress
Tarleton State University, Dick Smith Library (TSU-DSL) (Stephenville, TX)
    Stephenville (TX) Empire Tribune
    Stephenville (TX) Tribune
University of New Mexico, Zimmerman Library (Albuquerque, NM)
    Albuquerque Daily Journal
    Albuquerque Review
    Las Vegas (NM) Daily Gazette
    Las Vegas (NM) Daily Optic
    Raton (NM) Daily Range
    Rio Grande Republican (Las Cruces, NM)
    Santa Fe Daily New Mexican
    Santa Fe Weekly New Mexican
Weber State University, Stewart Library (Ogden, UT)
    Salt Lake (UT) Tribune
Western New Mexico University, J. Cloyd Miller Library (Silver City, NM)
    Cimarron (NM) News and Press

INTERVIEWS, PRESENTATIONS AND CORRESPONDENCE

Melba Arnold, October 1, 2009, in person.
Wayne Dale, Nona Dale and Priscilla Trummel, April 26, 2013, in person.
Lady E. Dalton, December 10, 11, and 12, 2012, email.
Randy Farrar, August 3, 2010, includes telephone and email correspondence.
Sandra Gwilliam, June 11 – June 16, 2009 and July 10, 2011, email.
Frank Pyle, November 18, 2009, telephone call.
Frank and Sandra Pyle, December 14, 2009, in person.
Ella Ann Spargo, July 5, 2008 and April 21, 2009, in person.
George W. Thompson, April 22, 2010, telephone call.
George W. Thompson and Lois Long and their families, May 15, 2010, in person.
Victorian Aid Society of Durango, April 21, 2012, presentation at Animas City Cemetery.

Index

Abiquiu, NM, 192
Acton, TX, 31
Adams, Alva, 297
Adams (Crouch), Mary Jane, 94, 110
Afton, Cy, 293
Agate (correspondent), 220-221
Airy, Sheriff Joseph P., 359
Alamosa, CO, 53, 86-89, 125, 137, 195, 247, 303, 313
   Allison Gang in, 291, 293, 295-297, 311, 343
   D&RG rails arrive, 122
Alarid, Trinidad, 296
Albany, NY, 314
Albany, TX, 70
Albuquerque, NM, 50, 52, 199, 285, 293-296, 332, 342-343
Alderson, Joshua H., 235-236, 240, 258, 270, 280, 298
Alexander, John, 42-44
Algodones, NM, 199
Allard, James, 7-8
Allen, Frank, 357
Allen, James W., 116-117; *see also, Smith, Thomas*
Allison, Charles, *287*, 303, 334, 343
   Allison Gang robberies, 284-291
   captured and held, 293-297, 301; *see also Allison Gang*
   Annis or Ennis, Charles, as, 170, 184-185, 291, 334
   Barker, Aaron, murder of, 170, 217
   description of, 185-186
   Guinan, Andy, shooting of, 184
   his fate, 340
   McCaffrey, Pat, shooting of, 185
   Stockton gang, blackballed from, 185-186, 293, 306-307
Allison, Robert Clay, 32, 72, 184
   Allison, John (brother), 31, 72
   birth, 29
   Burleson, Pete, 68
   Cimarron News, attacks, 39
   Colbert, Chunk, killing of, 37-39
   Cowley, John, lynching of, 37-38
   Cox, Wash, associate of, 44
   Griego, Pancho, kills, 46
   justifying his killings, 166,
   Lacy-Coleman partner, 30-31
      marries Coleman's sister, 40

Allison Gang, 284
   crime spree in Amargo, Chama and Pagosa Springs, 286-290
   Hyatt, Deputy Sheriff Frank, and, 293-297, 301, 311
   Albuquerque arrest, 294-296
   Denver, held in, 297, 301
   return to Conejos County, 309-311, 314-315
   members and formation, 284-285
      Allison, Charles, 284-291, 293-297, 301, 303, 309-311, 314-315, 340; *see also Allison, Charles*
      Perkins, Lew, the "Cross-eyed Kid," 285 *289,* 293, 296-297, 309-311, 314, 340
      Seely, Thomas "Little Tommy," 285, 293
      Watts, Henry, 285, *288,* 293, 296-297, 309-311, 314, 340
      Thomas, Kid, brother to, 310; *see also, Watts, Henry,*
   reward for, 290, 295, 296
   Stockton, Ike, impact on, 309-310; *see also Wilkinson, Bert; Stockton, Isaac T.*
Alma, CO, 88
Alsup, John, 16, 44
Alta (Cumbres Pass), 122
Amargo, NM
   Allison gang hideout, 285-288, 291,293
   Catron, Jimmy, rescues deputy, 194, 196, 359
   D&RG hell on wheels camp, 124, 180, 193-194, 196
   telegraph hub, 238-239, 245, 279
   White, Kid, murder of, 247-248, 331
Anderson, W.M. (Tex)
   accused of cattle/horse theft, 92, 94
   Anderson Allie, letter from, 95-96
   arrival in San Juan country, 88
   lynching of, 93-94, 102-106, 219
   Coe family's role, 92-96, 109-110
Andersonville Prison, 188
Andrette, Simon, 78
Angel, Frank Warner, 188
Animas City, CO, 101
   Battle of Durango, 209, 215-216
   cemetery, 207, 335-336, 368
   Coe, Frank, wedding, 162-163
   Cook, M.C., 297-298, 301, 319, 345, 347; *see also Galbreath, M.H. "Bud,"*

D&RG railroad, 111, 122, 125, 131, 194
early residents, 141
Elk Horn Club, 114, *115*
founding of, 55, 57-58, 60
Heffernan, James J., 163, 170, 181-182, 234, 244
Stockton, Ike, home in, 125, 131, 156, 167-168, 223, 246, 248, 252, 297-301, 307, 319, 323, 325, 329, 335
Stockton, Porter, in, 82, 105, 111, 118, 126
    Allen, J.W., assault on, 116-117, 166
    Hart, Cap, shooting of, 115-116, 126, 166, 412
    marshal of, 112-117, 152, 160-161
    Valliant and Hunter Saloon, 210
    Wilkinson, Bert, 298, 320-322
    Wilson, "One-Armed" Billy, in, 111-112, 132, 152
Animas River (valley), 1, 3, 19, 32, 51, 54-56, 61, 64, 83, 86, 88-89, 91-96, 98, 101, 104, 106-107, 109-111, 118, 121, 124-126, 129-132, 135-137, 139-141, 145, 147-148, 151, 153, 155, 157, 161-165, 167, 171-173, 178-179, 183, 186, 190, 192, 197, 201-202, 204-206, 208-210, 213, 219-222, 224, 226, 228-229, 232, 252-253, 259-260, 292, 298-300, 307, 311-312, 319-323, 326, 333, 336, 338, 343-345, 350, 353, 355, 362, 369-370
Baker Party of 1860, 45
Coe family moves to, 65-66
Cox/Graves families move to, 58-59
description of, 54, 58, 400
Eskridge/Garrett move to, 88
ferry on, 59, 120
Hendrickson brothers, explore, 60
homesteads in New Mexico, 90, 404, 414
livestock numbers in, 260
population in New Mexico, 90, 260
Stockton, Ike, move to, 78
Stockton, Porter move to, 103-105
home and grave location, 422
Annis, Charles; *see Allison, Charles*
Antonito, CO, 185, 190, *191*, 195, 290, 296, 315, 343, 351; *see also San Antonio, CO*
Antrim, William H., 64; *see Billy the Kid; Bonney, William*

Apache County, AZ, 150, 356
Apache Indians, 33, 42, 55, 57-58, 77, 133, 189-190, 281
Arapahoe County, CO, 310-311
Arboles, CO, 302-303
Arcade Ambo (correspondent), 257
Archuleta, Alvino, 72
Archuleta, Guadalupe, 340-342, 353, 371
Arcibia, Antonio, 46-47, 73, 77, 109, 165
Arellano, Guadalupe, 199, 222, 292
Armijo, Sheriff Perfecto, 295-296
Armour, Kirk, 355
Armstrong, Andrew J., 78
Arnold, Henry, 358
Arrington, Milton J. "Chuck," 26-27, 34, 72, 74
Ashmeade, Dr. C.H., 162
Atchison, Topeka and Santa Fe Railroad, 68, 74, 81, 249, 343
Avant, Taylor, 15-17, 44, 166, 379
Axtell, Governor Samuel B., 63, 188
Aztec, NM, 1, 79, 114-115, 121, 124, 151, 350
Aztec Land and Cattle Company (Arizona), 361
Aztec Ruins (National Monument), 60, 66, 78, 91, 114, 353

Baca, Sheriff Saturnino, 51, 78
Baker, Charles, 45
Baker, Doc, 354
Baker's Bridge, CO, 311
Bakewell, Charles "Tex," 35-37, 45
Bald Mesa, UT, 272, 277
Baldock, James, 128
Baldock, Reuben (Rube), 128, 241, 245, 415
Barela, Sheriff Casimiro, 47-48
Barker, Aaron, 425-426
    headstone, *172*
    murdered by Stockton-Eskridge gang, 170-175, 178, 204, 220-221, 230, 243, 250, 296, 302, 309, 425-426
    location, 427
    repercussions of murder, 179, 181, 187, 202, 224, 253, 261, 306
    indictments and requisitions, 216-217, 245, 291, 293, 330-331, 353, 435
Barlow and Sanderson Stage Line, 25, 193, 206, 217, 287, 289
Barnes, Governor Cassius, 345
Barrie, James, 179

INDEX 491

Bartol, Jerry, 144
Bassett, Deputy Sheriff Harry, 78-81
Battle of Durango, 208-214
  Farmington cowboys, names of, 208
  impetus for, 205
  Moorman lynching, impact of, 209
  Stockton, Ike, effect on support, 213-216
  Stockton-Eskridge gang involvement, 210-212
Battle of Monocacy, 188
Bauer, George, 268
Baughl's Station, NM, 81-83, 104, 154
Bayfield, CO, 118, 131, 133, 357-358
Beaumont, Lt. Col. A.B., 12
Becker, John, 52
Belen, NM, 52
Bellinger, Dr., 335, 360
Benavides, Santos, 199
Bennett, Harry, 315
Bennett, James, 195
Bennett, John, 351-352
Bennett, W.A., 234
Bennett's Store, 356-357
Benning, Henry, 178, 187, 371
Bernalillo, NM, 50, 52, 199, 292-295
Bernalillo County, NM, 199, 292, 295
Berry, James D., 15
Berry, Rena, 15
Bertram, Reuben, 194,
Bibb, Sarah Meek Hickey, 16, 18, 380
Bibb, William C., 16-17, 44-45
Big Thompson River, CO, 121
Billy the Kid, 63, 82, 166, 189, 229, 254
  Coe family, 62, 65, 165, 344
  Lincoln County War, 14, 64-65
  Mesilla jail, trip to, 226, 240, 242, 245
  Stockton, Ike, 64, 66, 78, 229, 301-302
Bisbee (Arizona) Massacre, 354-355
Blackmer, R.F., 305
Blain, Miles, 293
Blancett family
  Blancett, Enos (En), 218, 263, 306, 341-342, 361, 445
  Blancett, John, 218, 306, 340, 371
  Blancett, Linn, 152
  Blancett, Lucinda (Monie), 218, 306
  Blancett, Marcellus (Cell), 155, 218, 222, 342, 371
  Blancett, Moses, 199, 205, 216, 361, 435
    Archuleta, Guadalupe, lynching of, 340-342
    Blancett brand, *219*

    Rio Arriba County deputy sheriff, 218, 221-222, 227-229, 299, 306, 328-329, 338, 433
Blanco, NM, 199
Blankenship, A.J., 18-19
Blankenship, J.B., 18-19
Blazer's Mill Battle, 64-65
Bloomfield, NM, 58, 79, 127, 130, 135, 146, 157, 168, 180, 196, 198- 201, 218-219, 221, 261, 292, 341, 356, 370
Blue Mountain, UT, 86, 223, 231, 257-258, 265-266, 270-271, 370
Bohannon, Jake, 124-125, 129, 371
Bondad, CO, 132, 417
Bonney, William, 63-65; *see also Antrim, William H.; Billy the Kid*
Boren, Billy, 163
Bosque County, TX, 41, 248, 330, 332, 334, 345-346
Bosque River, North, 5-6, 15-18, 44-45, 57
Boucher, John S., 12, 15
Bowdre, Charlie, 51-52, 64-65
Bowen's Ferry (San Juan River), 200, 351
Bowers, Ed, 112
Bowman, Mason T. (Mace), 72, 74, 128
Bowman, T.E., 314
Boyle, O.F., 261
Brady, J.W., 315
Brady, Sheriff William, 64, 71, 78, 240
Brainard, Marshal J.T., 81
Brazos River, TX, 7-9
Breckenridge, CO, 37, 88
Brewer, Richard (Dick), 64-65
Brien, W.G., 321
Bristol, Judge Warren, 71, 78
Broad, Wilmot E., 289
Broad Creek Hundred, DE, 87
Broaddus, Dep. Sheriff, Robert, 112
Broadwell, Mayor D.P., 295, 297
Brown, Dr. James W., 176
Brown, George
  Eskridge, Dison, killed by, 135-140, 163, 175, 187, 217, 309, 317
  effect on settlers, 149, 156, 192
  headstone, *172*
  Eskridge brothers, dispute with, 105-106, 129
  see also Brown, John W. "Doc"
Brown, Henry, 65
Brown, Hoodoo (Hyman G. Neill), 71
Brown, John W. "Doc," 106, 141, 172, 186-187, 371
  Brown, Hattie (wife), 106, 172

492 INDEX

frontier "Doc," 140
peace maker, 159-160
Brown, West, 83, 401; *see also Stockton, Samuel*
Browne and Manzanares Store, 332, 342-343
Brumley, Delila Hickey, (Mrs. J.C.), 14, 245, 378
Brumley, Jefferson C., 14-15, 45, 245, 378
Brumley, Jim, 356
Brumley, John, 356
Brumley, William, 356
Brunot, Felix, 54-55
Brunswick Billiard Parlor, 211, 333
Bryant, Robert G., 281
Buchanan, M.G., 362-365
Buchanan County, TX, 8, 25, 31
Buckskin Charlie (Ute chief), *133*
Buell, Col. G.P., 88
Buena Vista, CO, 95, 206
Bull, Jake, 124
Bull, Solon A., 40, 124
Burleson, Peter, 80, 104
   Allison, Clay and, 44, 68
   Colfax County, sheriff of, 68, 74, 128, 252
      Morrison, George W., arrest of, 72-73
      Stockton, Ike, posse pursues, 104
      Stockton, Porter, posse pursues, 77, 79, 400
      Stokes, Deputy, killing of, 71-72
   Lacy, I.W., surety for, 20, 396
Burns, Thomas. D., 130, 196
   brand, *58*
   Burns National Bank, 57
   Frost, Adj. Gen. Max, assists, 201, 202
Burris, Judge William M., 365
Burroughs, Dillon R., 16
Bushnell, George A., 47
Byrne, Dr. Bernard James (Army surgeon), 128, 176, 258, 282

Caldwell, Joe, 148, 253, 360
Calhoun, J.M., 45
Camblin, Nick, 35-36, 71
Cameron, Robert A., 53
Cameron, Samuel, 37
Camp Henderson, TX, 4
Campbell, Bill, 66
Cambell, E.B., 15
Canada, John, 36, 71, 74, 78, 165-166
Canadian River, 22, 25, 31-32, 34, 37-38, 41-42, 58, 375, 382, 393
Cañon City, CO, 91, 315, 340
Cañon Largo, NM, 90, 198-199, 222, 261, 340; *see also Largo Canyon*
Cañon Largo Gang, 198-199, 222, 263, 291
Carey, Cornelius "Buck," 74
Carlisle's Livery (Silverton, CO), 313
Carmack, James, 18
Carney, Michael, 37
Carrizo Creek, CO, 99
Carroll, Captain Henry, 259, 281-282
Carroll, James, 91-93, 110, 121
Carson, Kit, 57
Carter, James H., 18
Cascade Creek, CO, 226
Cascade Hill, CO, 97, 116
Cascade Lakes, CO, 321
Castañeda Store (Bisbee, AZ), 354
Cates, P.J., 117
Caton, Jack, 74
Catron, Jimmy, 247, 309-310
   Allison, Charles, 296
   assaults and murders by, 194-195
   boyhood, 194
   Durango arrests, 303-305, 311-312, 315
   his fate, 343-344
   Johnson, deputy Charles, rescue of, 194-196
   robbery by, 311
Catron, Thomas Benton, 23, 63
Caviness, Henry and Nancy, 238
Caviness, Robert, 307
Cedar Hill, NM, 59, 91, 348, 350
Central City, CO, 207
Chabran, "French Frank," 114
Chaffee County, CO, 94-95
Chama, NM, 192,*193*, 200, *217*, 285, 315, 369-370
   Allison gang raid, 289
   D&RG's hell on wheels camp, 124, 192-194, 196, 216, 289, 359
Chama River, 3, 57, 293
Chandler, Zachariah, 39
Chapman, Huston, 66
Charleton, Thomas, 35-36
Chase, Manley, 11, 42, 77, 90
Chautauqua County, KS, 83
Chee, Hosteen, 356-357
Cheyenne Indians, 33, 41, 49, 69
Chickamauga, Battle of, 130, 237
Chicorica Creek, NM, 32; *see also Sugarite Creek (Canyon), NM*

INDEX

Chicoso, NM, 249
Childers, Hulda Ann Cox, 28, 383
Childers, Mart (Hugh Martin Childress, Jr.), 28-29, 383
Chilili, NM, 52
Chiricahua Apaches, 281
Chisholm Trail, 4, 6, 20-21, 375
Chisum, John, 256
Chittenden, Orson K., 27, 68
Cimarron, NM, 2, 27, 48, 70, 73, 77, 86, 154, 184, 247
  cattle thieves killed, 25-26
  Cowley, John, lynching of, 38
  Heffron and Crockett hooraw the town, 31, 47, 49-50, 74, 109, 281
  Morrison, George hooraws the town, 42-44
  Stockton, Porter, jail escape, 49-50, 68, 71, 73-74, 197
  Stockton, Porter, murders Antonio Arcibia, 46, 47
  Stokes, Deputy, killed, 71-72
Cimarron country (New Mexico), 23, 29, 45, 67, 78, 93
Cimarron River, 26, 39, 41
Civilian Punitive Expedition, 265, 271, 282; *see also Pinhook Indian fight*
Clark, Butch (Bush), 342-343
Clarke, George W., 369
Clay, Dr. H.A., 176, 309, 335, 340
Clay County, TX, 82-83
Clayton, E.A., 132, 168-169, 208, 338, 371
  brand, *168*
Clearfield, PA, 352
Cleburne, Gen. Patrick, 4
Cleburne, TX, 4-5, 14-15, 45, 245
Clifton, AZ, 354-355
Clifton House, 25, 36, 39, 45, 166
Cochran, Dr., 172
Cochran, John, 98
Coe, Benjamin Franklin (Frank), 184
  Anderson, Tex, lynching of, 93, 96
  Blazer's Mill Battle, 64-65
  Eskridge brothers, dispute with, 96, 106, 162-163
  later life, 344
  Lincoln County, in, 40, 62, 91
    vigilante acts in, 50-52
  reputation of, 96, 104, 109-111, 129, 141, 165, 220
  San Juan country, in, 65-66, 78, 91, 106, 124, 129, 182-183, 186-187, 307
  Stockton, Port, killing of, 148, 151
  Tully, Helena Anne, marriage to, 162-164
  see also Coe family
Coe, George, 40, 89, 164, 187
  Anderson, Tex, lynching of, 93, 96, 109
  Billy the Kid, 62, 165
  Blazer's Mill Battle, 64-65
  later life, 344
  San Juan country, in the, 66, 78, 91, 104, 106, 109, 220
    Navajos, chasing, 124
    Stockton, Porter, killing of, 148
  vigilante acts in Lincoln County, 51-52
  see also Coe family
Coe, Jasper (Jap), 40, 89, 92-93, 106, 124, 139, 165, 186, 371
  Barker, Aaron, describes murder of, 171, 426
  Hamblet home, shootout, 137
  Stockton, Porter, describes, 126
  Stockton-Eskridge gang, describes, 167-168, 170
  see also Coe family
Coe, Lew, 98-99, 125, 129, 151, 160, 173, 182, 186
  Anderson, Tex, lynching of, 92-95
  Battle of Durango, 208, 212
  Eskridge/Garrett, settle near, 88-89
  Frost, Max, assessment of, 220
  later life, 344-345
  Sugarite Canyon, settles in, 40, 65
  Virden claim, jumps, 66, 119
  see also Coe family
Coe family, 219, 318
  Anderson, Tex, lynching of, 93-96, 110
  Coe, Al, 40
  Colfax County, in, 40, 180
  Eskridge brothers, dispute with, 89, 105-107, 129, 136, 139-140, 162, 170, 175, 223-224, 227-228
  Hartman, Frank, dispute with, 99-100, 106-107, 110, 129, 174, 227
  reputation of, 51-52, 88-89, 103-106, 139, 154, 164-165, 174, 187, 204, 220
  San Juan country turmoil, 91-92, 121, 130, 140-141, 147-148, 179-180, 197, 227, 457

see also Coe, Benjamin Franklin (Frank);
  Coe, George; Coe, Jasper (Jap); Coe, Lew
Colbert, Chunk, 27, 34-39
Coldwell, Colbert, 368
Coldwell, N.C., 365-366, 368-369
Coldwell Banker Real Estate, 368, 470
Cole, D.C., 371, 438
Cole, Dr. A.L., 193
Cole School House, 222
Coleman, Lewis G. "Luke"
  Allison, Clay, and, 29-31, 40
  Colfax County, move to, 29
  herders, 22, 29, 31, 42, 47, 74, 108, 170
  Lacy, I.W., partnership with, 6, 11, 14, 20, 22, 43, 46-47, 85
Coleman County, TX, 44, 376
Colfax County, NM, 9-10, 26-27, 30, 32-33, 38, 51, 57, 85, 92, 118, 124, 128, 166, 180, 187-189, 249, 339
  cattle, cattlemen and cowboys, impact of, 23, 25-26, 28-29, 31, 37-43, 45, 47, 71
  open range, in, 84, 90
  stock association, organized, 40
  Cheyenne/Kiowa raid, 41-42
  County Commission, 46, 60
  County Fair, first, 40
  courts annexed to Taos County, 48, 390-391
  map, *24*
  Maxwell Land Grant, 39-40
  Stockton, Ike, in, 41, 47, 62, 66-68, 70-71, 104-105, 167, 197, 252
    indictments, 73-74, 78, 203, 391
  Stockton, Porter, in, 1, 20, 22-23, 25, 37, 39, 47, 53, 67-68, 77, 79, 81, 83, 105, 127, 146, 197, 252
    murder indictments, 36, 45, 48, 73-75, 374, 385, 390
Coliseum Theater (Durango), 144, 176, 206-207, 216, 261
Comanche Bill (Samuel Swinford), 144-145, 309, 325, 328-329
Comanche Indians, 4-5, 8, 28, 33, 42, 56, 112, 266
Comancheros, 28
Conejos, CO, 54, 57, 86-87, 139, 185, 191, 194-195, 290, 310, 318, 343, 351
Conejos County, CO, 137, 170, 185, 194-195, 225, 248, 287, 290-291, 293, 295-296, 309-311, 314-315, 334, 351, 369

Conejos River, CO, 87, 192
Coney Island, NY, 132
Cook, M.C.; *see* Galbreath, Marion H. "Bud"
Coon, Samuel, 144,
Cooper, E.H., 60
Cooper, Mrs. Thomas (Lucy), 120-121, 362
Cooper, Thomas, 120
Corona, NM, 82
Coronado Island, CA, 352
Corrumpa Creek, NM, 42
Cortez, CO, 231
Costiano (Navajo leader), 159-160, 200
Covert, Isaac Newlon, 135, 222, 371
Cowan, Elizabeth (Lizzie), 111, 363, 365
Cowan, Emily Jane (Mrs. Porter Stockton); *see* Stockton, William Porter
Cowan, John, 111, 118, 228, 363
Cowan, Sarah (Sally) Hickey, 16, 379-380
Cowan, William, 16, 379-380
Cowhouse Creek, TX, 8
Cowley, John, 37-38
Cowley County, KS, 83
Cox, Ed, 8
Hannah, Cox, 8
Cox, Hiram Washington (Wash), 14, 28, 33, 43, 68, 78, 84-85, 90-91, 132, 221, 286, *349,* 371, 376, 383, 435
  Allison, Clay, and, 32, 44
  Anderson, Tex, lynching of, 92-94, 96
  Animas valley, move to, 53, 55-60
  cattle herd, value of, 12, 86
  Colfax County, move to, 29, 32
  Cox, George Washington (son), 59, 93, 146, 371
    chasing horse thieves, 132
  Cox, Ike (son), 118, 125, 134, 178-179, 225, 350, 408, 417-418, 426
  Cox-Truby feud, 350
  Cox, James Allard (son), 93, 146, 178-179, *212,* 342, 371
    Animas valley, trailing cattle to, 57-58
    Morrison, George W., confrontation with, 118
  Cox, John Shriver (son), 91, 146, 186, 197, 357, 371
    Anderson, Tex, lynching of, 91-93
    Battle of Durango, 208-211
    chasing horse thieves, 132
  Cox, Nancy Allard (wife), 7-8, 178, 350, 376
  Cox (Graves), Nancy Belle, 57

INDEX 495

Cox, William A. (Willie), 350
Cox brand, 11, 78, *79,* 328
Cox's Crossing ferry, 60, 120
Erath County, in, 6-8, 11-12
Frost, Adj. Gen. Max, 198, 205, 216-218, 222
Indian fights, 8
later life, 348-350, 463
Morrison, George W., 43, 118, 412
reputation of, 7, 12, 31, 46, 90, 178, 204, 227, 229, 299, 354
San Juan country turmoil, 92-93, 179, 182, 186, 227-228
San Juan Guard militia, 222, 227, 371
Stockton, Ike, and, 1, 6, 167, 174, 182, 186-187, 196, 198, 204-205, 208, 211, 216, 222, 227-228, 299, 328, 348, 353
    Cox reward for Ike, ii, 197, 232, 338
    Ike threatens Cox family, 197
    see also Stockton, Isaac T.
Stockton, Porter, 1, 6, 132, 146-152, 167, 174
    Cox sanctions killing of Porter, 147
    see also Stockton, William Porter
trail drives of, 29, 31-32, 40-41, 59, 124, 388, 393
Crabtree, Ben, 45
Craig, J.C., 207-208
Craig, Sheriff, 83
Craig, William, 231
Creede, CO, 353
Crockett, David, 23, 31, 44, 47, 49-50, 74
Crockett, Robert, 31
Crofton, Col. Robert E.A.,
civilian discontent with, 260, 265
Farmington, reports of turmoil in, 160, 180-181, 199-200
Fort Lewis, establishment of, 102
Lacy, I.W. response to murder, 243-244
Ute Indian troubles, 233, 237-239, 258-259, 266
Cross Timbers (of Texas), 1, 5, 29, 112, 266, 337
Crotzer, Louis, 107
Cuba, NM, 222
Cuchara Valley, CO, 122
Culberson, Governor Charles, 345
Cumbres Pass, 57-58, 86-87, 122, 148, 190, 195, 248
Cummings, "Trinidad Charley," 350

Cunningham, George, 26-27
Current family, 414
Curry, George, 66
Curry, John R., 99
Curtis, Frank, 78
Curtis, J.C and W.S., 82
Curtis, Joel W., 8, 11, 22, 31-32, 39
Curtis, Richard A., 78
Curtis, Zenas, 31-32, 78, 80
Custer, George Armstrong, 55
Custer County, CO, 60
Cutler, Barney, 310

D&RG Railroad; *see Denver and Rio Grande Railroad*
Darley, Rev. George M., 97-98
Davies, 2nd Lt. W.S., 159, 258
Davis, Dr., 335
Davis, Theodore and E.L., 161
Dawson, Edwena Stockton, 25
Dawson, John B., 8, 11, 14, 22, 25, 32, 77, 90
Decatur County, Iowa, 98
DeGraffenried family, 11
Del Norte, CO, 53-54, 98, 291
Deluche, John, 200
Denison, TX, 345
Denver, CO, 9, 28, 31, 74, 85, 175, 185, 189, 204, 242, 308, 316-317, 328, 351
Allison Gang, 296-297, 301, 310-311
D&RG RR, 122, 190, 193, 240, 304
Denver and Rio Grande Railroad, 85, 102, *123,* 175, 180, 189-190, 201, 213-214, 216, 234, 245, 248, 251, *305,* 311, 322, 345, 430, 432
AT&SF RR, war with, 74, 343
Durango, rails enter, 302-304, 306-307
pierces San Juan country, 83, 122-123, 131, 302
turmoil, and, 124, 130, 175, 286, 308
in Amargo, NM, 193-194, 196, 291
in Chama, NM, 193-194, 196
in Conejos, CO, 195
Des Moines, NM, 42
Desdemona, TX, 5
Devere, William (Billy), 212, 215
Diamond Saloon (Silverton), 312-313
Dobie, J. Frank, 6, 14
Dodge City, KS, 21, 40-41, 165, 343
Dodson, James, 174
Dolan, James J., 63-66

Dolores, CO, 359
Dolores County, CO, 350
Dolores News (Rico, CO), *108*
   Hartman and Jones purchase, 98
   Hartman and Jones sell, 353, 355
   Stockton-Eskridge gang, support, 100, 105-107, 110, 129, 137, 155, 174, 226-227, 229-230, 247, 251-254, 263, 265, 282, 292, 298-299, 301, 307, 328, 351
Dolores River, CO, 86, 92, 96, 128, 239, 244, 259, 264, 271
   Big Bend of the Dolores, 97, 234-235, 237-238, 258, 266, 268, 270-272, 279, 356, 417
Dorris, H.C. (Hank), 293, 301
Dorsey, NM, 32
Doss, Sam, 34
Doughty, Anne, 195
Dowd, Big Dan; see *Howland, Big Dan*
Dry Cimarron River, NM, 42
Dudley, Will, 109
Duffau Creek TX, 6-8, 11-12
Dulaney, Henry, 44
Dunham, Alf, 369
Dunnsville, NY, 318
Dupuy, John, 248
Durango, CO, 1, 4, 54, 57-58, 96, 98, 111, 114, 121, 136, 152-153, 162, 185, 193, 198, 200, 217, 237-238, 243-244, 247-248, 250, 252-253, 257, 285-289, *290,* 291, 301, 308, 313, 315-317, 320-321, 331-332, 343-345, 350-351, 353-354, 358-361, *367,* 369
   Battle of Durango, 205, 208-213, 260-261, 325, 330
   Comanche Bill, murder of, 144-145, 309
   Denver and Rio Grande RR, 122-125, 130-131, 175, 193, 213, 260-261, 302-304, 325, 330
   first elections, 213, 226, 261
   founding and early days, 111, 125, 130-131, 136, 160-161, 163
   Greatorex, Thomas, murder of, 175-179
   Guinan, Thomas, shooting of, 184
   incorporation of, 226
   Moorman, H.R., lynching of, 206-210, 285
   New Mexico expatriates, 164-165, 181-183, 219, 317
   Stockton, Ike, killing of, 332-335, 338-339
   Stockton-Eskridge gang sanctuary, 137, 139, 144, 161, 168, 170, 172, 174, 182, 185, 190, 197, 200-205, 210, 213-216, 221-222, 224, 229-231, 241, 245, 247, 261, 299-300, 303, 306-307, 310-312, 316, 331
   Stockton-Eskridge gang support wavers, 212-215, 220-221, 224-226, 241, 260, 282, 299, 325, 328-330, 332, 342
   Ute Indian troubles, 237-238, 258, 268, 279, 282, 298
   Woods, George N., hanging, 362-368
Dustin, Almon E. (Al), 148, 151, 170, 208, 341-342
Dwyer, Robert, 160, 181, 241, *308,* 369
   description of, 206
   Durango, marshal of, 202, 204, 208
   Catron, Jimmy, arrests, 303
   notifies Eskridge, Garrett, others to leave, 214-215
   shot in head, 308-309
   homestead, 57, 141
Dyer, Leigh, 85

Eagle and Holstein sheep ranch, 82
Eagle Tail Mountain, NM, 32
Earp brothers, 77
Earp, Virgil, 112
Eastland County, TX, 5-6, 35, 362
Eclipse Hall (Durango), 139, 163, 206, 225, 260
Edwards, J.H., 20
Eizenstein, Hanna, 70
El Moro, CO, 85, 251
El Moro Saloon (Durango), 361
Eldridge family, 208
Elizabethtown, NM, 25-26, 92
Elkins, Stephen Benton, 23
Elko, NV, 184
Ellis, Mr., 71
Ellsworth, KS, 21, 165
Elmoreau, Frenchy, 342-343
Embudo, NM, 47
Engley, Eugene, 117-118, 132, 137, 215, 303
Enloe, Abraham and Nancy, 127
Ennis, Charles; see *Allison, Charles*
Epperson, Jacob A., 132

INDEX 497

Erath County, TX, 21, 23, 30-31, 35, 42, 45, 53, 56, 65, 71, 73- 74, 79, 85, 146, 170, 227
  cattle industry in, 9, 30, 227, 376
    cattle trails, 6, 20-21
    Cox, H.W., cattle drives from, 29, 40-41
    Cox, H.W., herd value, 12
    first brands registered, 11, 14
    Lacy/Coleman, herd value, 14
    mavericking regulated, 12
    thieves, 12, 18-19
  Colfax (NM)/Las Animas (CO) counties, residents bound for, 23, 29, 31, 35, 40, 42
  Cox, H.W., moves to, 7
  Indian attacks, 7-8, 56, 376-377
  Lacy, I.W., legal troubles, 14-15, 20
  Morrison, George, assaults in, 18
  population of, 5
  San Juan country, residents bound for, 6-7, 10, 18-19, 56, 118, 124, 167, 170, 201, 210, 217, 248, 358, 363
  Stockton, Ike, cattle theft in, 33
  Stockton, Ike, wedding, 33
  Stockton, Porter, assaults in, 15-17, 21, 44
  Stockton, Porter, wedding, 16
Ernest, Finis, 25-27, 37
Eskridge, Jeremiah, 86
Eskridge, Joshua Hargo, 86, 125, 161, 185-187, 202, 228, 261, *302,* 308-310, 334, 337, 343
  Bennett, John, murder of, 351
  Brown, George, dispute, 105-106, 129, 136-139
  cattle theft, accused of, 92, 225
  Coe, Frank attempted assault on, 162
  Coe family, dispute with, 96, 105-107, 110, 129, 140, 179
  description of, 223-224
  Durango, told to leave, 215-216, 224-225
  Eclipse Hall, owner of, 139, 163, 206, 225, 260
  Gunnison, arrested in, 330-332
  Halford, Judge, alliance with, 92, 105-106
  Hamblet home shootout, 136-140
  Hartman, Jones, Wilkinson, resides with, 107
  interview with "fake Hargo," 300-301
  marriage and children, 351-352
  Eskridge, Robert Lee, 352
  Pinhook Indian fight, 257, 263, 265-266, 268, 271-280, 282, 297
    ankle wound, 276, 279-280, 282, 301-302
  Pond, Johnny, attempts to shoot, 163
  Rico town marshal, 125, 264
  San Luis valley, moves to, 86-87
  shot twice, 330
  Stockton, Ike, joins with, 167
    Barker, Aaron, murder of, 168-175, 217
    Battle of Durango, 210-213, 226
    reward for, 229, 265
    Tent Saloon, opens, 190, 225, 260
    Wallace, Gov. Lew, letter to, 264-265
    White, Kid, murder of, 247-248
  Wilkinson, Bert, and, 101, 103, 107-108, 124-125, 131
Eskridge, Lorenzo Dow, 194, 343
  Animas valley, sends cattle to, 87-88
  attempts to recover herd, 192, 201-202, 219-220, 228-229, 292, 299
  Frost, Adj. Gen. Max, meets, 191-192
  later life, 351
  San Luis Valley, moves to, 86-87
Eskridge, Manlove Dison, 131, 161, 228, 297, 327, 332
  Animas valley, moves cattle to, 88-89
  Brown, George, dispute with, 105-106, 129
    Hamblet home killings, 131, 135-140, 145, 175, 219, 309, 317
    vigilantes pursue, 140, 145-146, 151
  cattle theft, accused of, 92, 225
  Coe family, dispute with, 96, 105-107, 129, 140, 162
  description of, 316
  Halford, Judge alliance with, 92, 105-106
  later life, 337, 343, 351
  Ogsbury, Marshal, murder of, 312-313, 325
    fleeing through the San Juans, 313-321, 323, 332
    reward for, 316
  Pinhook Rescue expedition, 272, 279-280, 301, 312
  Prindle, James K. Polk, murder of,

498 INDEX

206-209
San Luis valley, move to, 86-87
Stockton, Ike, joins with, 167
  Battle of Durango, 212, 226
  Durango, told to leave, 215-216, 224-225
Stockton, Porter, provides shelter, 139, 146
Thomas, Kid, and, 102-103, 312-313
Wilkinson, Bert, and, 101, 103, 312-320
Eskridge, Martha Marvel, 86
Eskridge, Permilia Garrett, 86-87
Eskridge, Sarah, 86
Estes, Joel, Jr.
  Animas city, residence, 121, 363-364, 369
  Cooper, Lucy, employs, 121, 362
  Estes, Cleve (son), 368
  Estes, Lev (son), 368
  Estes, Mary Alverda, 121
  Estes, Patsy (mother), 121
  Estes Park, CO, 121, 413
  marriage to Porter Stockton's widow, 121, 362, 365
  San Juan Guards, member of, 362, 371
  Woods, George N., conflict with, 362-364
Eureka, NV, 184, 235, 291
Eureka, UT, 342, 361
Everett, Matt, 200
Everingham, James, 324
Expectation Mountain, CO, 124-125, 263-264

Fannin County, TX, 127
Farmington, NM, 1, 3, 54, 97, 111, 129, 135, *143,* 151, 153, 163, 171-173, 175, 178, 197-198, 203, 221, 231, 241, 244, 250, 262, 282, 288, 300, 306, 309, 319, 344, 354, 356, 362, 369-370
  Battle of Durango, 208-209, 211-216, 221, 226, 241
  Durango seeks peace, 225, 338
  Brown, George murder repercussions, 140-141, 145, 149, 163, 170, 175
  Locke, William, forced out, 179-180
  McHenry, C.H., forced out, 181-183
  Pierce, Frank, forced out, 164-165
  Pyle family forced out, 317
  Welfoot, Seth, forced out, 156-157, 317

Farmington (Coe) Mob, 106-107, 129, 164, 170, 174, 179, 227, 230, 251-253, 261, 292
  first homesteaders, 60-61, 66, 88-91, 98, 100
  first school in, 140-141
  founding of, 60-61
  open to settlement, 55
  Raser and Meyers shoot Navajo, 157, 163, 199-200
  Navajos demand shooters, 159-160
Farrand, Charles, 27
Fassbinder, Peter, 130
Fenian Brotherhood, 181
Fife, C.R., 196
Fink, J.D., 55
Firbaugh, John, 186
Fish Lakes, CO, 314-315, 321; *see also* Trout Lake, CO
Fisher, George L., 214-215
Fisher, John, 27
Flagler, Griffin S., 114, 215, 305
Flora Vista, NM, 92-93, 120, 139, 362, 368
Florence, Co, 91, 164
Florida Mesa, CO, 2, 118
Florida Mountains, NM, 281
Florida River (valley), CO, 111, 118, 207, 358, 362
Foley, John, 261
Follis, William J. (Bill), 34-35
Folsom, Dr. W.H.C., 335, 351, 366
Fooshee, W.H., 6, 19
Fort Arbuckle, Indian Territory, 40
Fort Concho, TX, 264
Fort Flagler, 88, 102, 134
Fort Garland, CO, 52, 57, 344
Fort Griffin, TX, 70, 94
Fort Leavenworth, KS, 238
Fort Lewis, CO, 128, 134, 183
  beef contract, 101-102, 126, 129, 230
  civilian and Indian incidents, response to, 160, 180, 199, 257
  establishment of, 101-102,
  Farmington Indian troubles, 159-160, 199
  Lacy, I.W., murder of, 241, 245-247
  treatment of civilian casualties, 155, 171-172, 176, 282, 302
  Ute difficulties, 237-238, 241, 257, 259, 266, 281-282

INDEX 499

see also Crofton, Col. Robert E.A.
Fort Marcy, NM, 190
Fort Stanton, NM, 51
Fort Sumner, NM, 9, 112, 301
Fort Wingate, NM, 88
Foshay, John, 287
Four Corners region, 54, 83
  1888 map, *269*
Fox, Peter, 94
Frances, James, 19
Frank Leslie's Illustrated Newspaper, 198, 281
Freeport, TX, 356
Fremont County, CO, 91, 218
Fresno, CA, 368
Frey, J.A and William, 15
Frink, Charles A., 237, 271
Frost, Adjutant General Max, 260
  Allison Gang, and, 295-296
  Amargo and Chama report, 194, 196
  Archuleta, Guadalupe, lynching of, 341
  Cañon Largo Gang, 198-199, 223, 263, 291
  Eskridge, Dow, and, 191-192
  later life and death, 352-353
  Rio Arriba County (Stockton) investigation, 107, 160, 189-192, 196-201, 203, 205, 214, 217-220, 225
  Stockton, Porter, killing of, 147, 152, 155, 223
  San Juan Guards militia, 221-222
  Stockton, Ike, murder indictment, 216-217
  pursuing arrest of, 300, 329
Fulcher, John, 180
Fulcher, Tom, 89, 138, 180, 271

Gaines, C.C., 114
Gainesville, TX, 40
Galbreath, Elizabeth Ann Hickey, 19, 380
Galbreath, Green, 19-20
Galbreath, James M., 19
Galbreath, Madison, 248
Galbreath, Marion H. "Bud"
  Cook, M.C., as, 248
    Animas City town marshal, 298, 319
    arrested in Durango, 330, 332-335
    escape in Texas, 345
    Pinhook Indian fight, 257, 265-266, 268, 271-272, 297-298
    Wilkinson, Bert, arrest of, 319-322, 325, 329
    Lee, Marion, on the run as, 345-348
    Lee, Florence (wife), 345, 348
    Stockton, Ike, alliance with, 18-20, 249, 251, 261, 263, 298, 301, 348
    Pierson, Deputy Sheriff Jabez, murder of, 41, 248, 330, 334, 345-348
Gallegos Canyon, NM, 135
Gallup, NM, 356-357
Gannon, Bill, 141
Gannon, Den, 3, 134, 146, 152, 154, 165-166
Garrett, James W. (Jim), 106, 161
  Battle of Durango, 211
  Catron, Jimmy, and, 194
  cattle theft, 92
  Coe family, dispute with, 89, 129, 162
  Eskridge, Dow, Animas cattle herd, 87-89
    attempts to recover cattle, 202, 219-220, 228
  Eskridge family, relationship to, 86-87, 124
  Garrett, Cora (sister), 137, 139
  Garrett, Mancil (father), 87
  Garrett Eskridge, Permelia (sister), 86-87
  Hamblet home shootout, 110, 131, 135-140, 145, 175, 219, 226
  pursued by vigilantes, 146, 151, 163
  later life, 332, 353, 403
  runs man out of Durango, 161
  Stockton, Ike joins with, 163, 167, 170, 175, 187, 216
    Barker, Aaron, murder of and chase of Tom Nance, 170, 172-174, 217
    Durango, told to leave, 215-216, 224-225
  Stockton-Eskridge gang, 101, 211, 216, 224, 248
Garrett, Sheriff Pat, 62
Garvin County, OK, 40
Gash, T.K., 245, 247, 286
Gentle Anna, 83
Georgetown, CO, 207
Gilbreath, A.J., 11
Glen Rose, TX, 8

Glencoe, NM, 344
Glorieta, NM, 82, 105, 166
Gonzales, Juan, 50-52, 91, 165, 391
Gonzales, Manuel, 198-199, 222-223, 261-263, 291-292
Goode's Saloon (Silverton), 312-313, 327
Goodlet, Bill "Dutchy," 70-71, 74,
Goodman, Henry C., 31, 356, 369
  Howland, Big Dan, trails, 244
  Lacy, I.W., foreman for, 86, 109, 232, 241, 252, 298
  responds to Indian attacks, 237, 259
Goodnight, Charles, 1, 6, 8-10, 13, 22, 29, 82, 85, 112, 256
Goodnight-Loving Trail, 6, 9, *13,* 112, 128
Gordon, Henry, 72
Gordon, Mike, 77
Goshorn, Tom, 281
Gothic, CO, 184
Goudy, Frank C., 365
Graham, Major, 218, 342
Granbury, TX, 31
Granite, CO, 95
Grant, Jeff, 294
Grant, Ulysses S., 8, 55, 86, 130, 188, 284, 291
Graves, Alfred (Alf) Ulysses, 60, 92, 124, *153,* 186, *349*
  Anderson, Tex, lynching of, 92-93
  Animas valley, move to, 59
  Battle of Durango, 208
  Cox, Nancy Belle (wife), 57, *153,* 350, 385, 393
  death of, 350
  early life, 56-57
  Graves, John (son), *153,* 350
  Stockton, Ike, and, 174, 182, 186, 204, 208, 306, 328
    threatens Graves, 197
  Stockton, Porter,
    chasing rustlers with, 3, 132, 134
    conflict with, 134, 146-147
    killing of, 147, 151-152, 154-155, 166, 174, 306
      consequences of, 166, 174, 204, 371
Gravis, Perry, 17, 44, 166

Grayson County, TX, 334, 345
Greathouse, "Whiskey Jim," 82
Greatorex, Thomas, 175-178, 207
Greenhorn Mountains, CO, 132
Gregorio (Navajo Indian), 159
Griego, Francisco (Pancho), 46
Grierson, Col. Benjamin, 77
Griffin, Rev. Hugh, 356
Grigsby, Robert, 38
Grigsby, Worden (Ward), 280
Grout, I.E., 214
Guache, NM, 199
Guinan, Andy, 184, 290, 307
Gunnison, CO, 207, 268, 330-332, 351
Gunnison County, CO, 184, 331

Haines, William Bullock, 127, 130, 246, 266, 299
  Archuleta, Guadalupe, lynching of, 341
  Frost, Adj. Gen. Max meets with, 198, 205, 216, 219, 223
  Haines and Hughes Store, 125-126, 146, 154, 196, 263
  later life, 353
  San Juan Guard, captain of, 221- 222, 228-229, 244, 260-263, 329, 371
Hale, Josh, 132,
Halford, Hannibal H.
  Justice of the Peace, 91-93
    stormy tenure, 105-107, 109-110, 129, 344
Hall, James, 275-277, 279, 282, *302,* 352
Hamblet, Francis, Marion, 89
  Brown, George and Os Puett, killing of, 135-141, 154, 172, 175, 224, 226, 309, 317
  Hamblet, John (son), 138, 186, 371
  Hamblet, Lee (son), 137-138, 186, 371, 418
  Hamblet brand, *135*
  Stockton-Eskridge gang, foe of, 186, 253, 371
Hampton Columbus Evans, 118
Hansen, Christian, 113-114
Hansen, Lizzie, 113-114
Hansen's Elk Horn Club, *115*
Hanson, Otto Henry, 106-107, 186, 344
Hardeman County, TX, 82
Hardin, John Wesley, 248
Hardin County, TN, 85

INDEX

Hardscrabble mining district, CO, 218
Hargis, Pete, 124
Harlow, J.P., 331
Harris, James O., 365
Harris, Willis, 44
Harrison County, MO, 85, 128
Hart, Thomas B. "Cap," 114-116, 126, 147, 166, 218, 412, 417
Hartman, Frank, 128, *142,* 161, 179, 182, 266, 355
  Coe family, dispute with, 99-101, 106-107, 110-111, 129, 174, 227, 345
  Cox, H.W., opinion of, 7, 227, 345, 350
  Dolores News, purchase of, 98-99, 108
  early life, 98
  Eskridge and Wilkinson, resides with, 107, 110, 265
  Hartman, Lillie (sister), 129
  later life, 353-354
  Stockton-Eskridge gang, support of, 137, 154-155, 226-228, 247, 251, 254, 261, 280, 292, 299, 301, 315, 328
Harvey, Fred, 81
Hashknife outfit (Arizona), 361
Haskell, "Fat Alice," 176
Hatch, Col. Edward, 88, 190, 199, 259
Haverty and Eskridge Saloon, 139, 206
Hawley, Captain Charles A., 316, 323, 330
Hayes, Rutherford B., 188
Hays, S.D., 35-36, 386
Hazel Green, KY, 14
Head, Lafayette, 191, 304
Heathy, Marshal, 176, 184
Hefferman, Gus; *see Heffron, Gus*
Hefferman, James J., 163, 306
  Deputy U.S. Marshal, 170, 181
  Heffernan, Lilly, 258
  Heffernan, Mrs., 258, 309
  Stockton and Eskridge, support of, 181-182, 184, 186, 203, 209, 215
  Ute Indian troubles, 233-234, 244, 259, 266, 270
Heffron, Gus
  as Gus Hefferman, 50, 427
    Barker, Aaron, murder of, 170, 217
    Pinhook Rescue expedition, 280-281, 451
    Rico, CO, illicit cattle trade, 108-109, 176, 178, 207

  Cimarron, hoorawing of, 49-50, 74
  killing Buffalo Soldiers, 47, 108, 281
  Lacy, I.W., herder for, 31, 109
  Stockton, Porter, and, 47, 49, 109
Helling, Hugh, 37-38
Helton, Sherman, 356
Hendrickson, Ellen Puett Wilkinson,
  arrival in Colorado, 101
  Hendrickson, Simeon (husband), 60, 101, 144, 321, 407-408
  New Mexico residence, 98, 101
  troubles with son Bert, 101, 144, 321
  Wilkinson, Mahlon, death of, 101
Hendrickson, William
  Coe family, dispute with, 130, 299-300
  Farmington, founding of, 60-61
  Hamblet home shootout, 135, 140-141, 144, 155
  Navajo confrontation, account of, 159-160
  Stockton, Porter, describes, 126
Henrietta, TX, 83
Henry and Robinson's Saloon, 74
Hermosa, CO, 204
Herr, Hiram, 313-314
Hersey, Dona S., 204
Hickey family
  Hickey (Brumley), Delila, 14, 378
  Hickey (Galbreath), Elizabeth Ann, 19, 380
  Hickey (Stockton), Jane, 3, 14, 379-380
  Hickey, Mart, 44
  Hickey Cowan, Sarah (Sally), 16, 379
  Hickey (Bibb), Sarah Meek, 16, 380
  Hickey, West W., 12, 17, 20, 44, 379-380
  Hickey, William M., 44
Hickok, Wild Bill, 48
Hill, George, 19, 45, 71-73
Hill, Jim, 134
Hill, John, 72
Hilliker, Charles M., 184, 214
Hindman, George, 64
Hinton, Bill, 359
Hittson, John, 382
  New Mexico cattle raid, 27-29, 383
  Texas cattleman, 6, 25, 28, 31
Hodding, Henry, 72
Hodges, Charles W., 312-313
Hoehne, "Dutch Bill," 34
Hoffman, F.J., 200

INDEX

Hoffmire, James, 365, 369
Hoge, Rev. C. Montgomery, 97-98, 207, 212, 335, 406, 460
Holbrook, AZ, 361
Holbrook, Joe, 49, 74
Holliday, John Henry "Doc"
   Hurricane Bill Martin, and, 70, 74
   Las Vegas, NM, in, 71, 77
   witness to a Porter Stockton murder, 1, 75, 77-78
Hollis, John Durham "Bud," 8
Hopi Indians, 244
Hopkins County, TX, 4, 7-8, 52
Horn, William B., 222, 371
Horton, J.B., 264
Houck, AZ, 356-357
Howardsville, CO, 99, 355
Howe, Joseph, 66, 91
Howe, Samuel, 371
Howe, Sherman, 418
Howland, Big Dan, 128, 229
   Battle of Durango, 208, 435
   cattle detective, 202, 204-205, 229-230, 232, 241, 433,
   flees to Arizona (possibly as "Big Dan" Dowd), 354-355
   kills sheepherder, p. 204
   Lacy, I.W., murder of, 241, 243-246, 250-251, 292
      Stockton, Ike, response to, 246, 253-255
Hubbard, Clint, 155
Hubbard, Mrs., 110, 219
Hudson, A.W., 221
Hudson, "Spud," 258, 270-271, 282
Huerfano County, TX, 231, 237
Hughes, Levy A., 126, 146, 157, 196-197, 201, 219, 222, 229, 263, 292, 341, 371
Hughes, Wilson "Texas Jack," 170, 217
Hume, J.F., 272
Hunter, Bill "Tex," 170, 217, 261
Hunter, James, 215
Hunter, Luke
   La Plata County, sheriff of, 201, 216, 245, 300, 306, 322
   later life, 355
   Ogsbury, Marshal, murder of, 312-313, 323, 325, 327, 329
   Stockton-Eskridge gang, support of, 210, 213, 215, 241, 307-308, 316, 320, 327, 329-330, 363
Hurricane Bill Martin, 69-70, 74-77, 79
Hyatt, Deputy Frank, 290, 293-297, 301, 311
Hyatt, J.S., 18

Ilfled and Company, 126
Iliff, John Wesley, 9
Irminger, Rudolph, 42
Iron Gulch, CO, 110
Irvin, Samuel H. and William, 26
Itawamba County, Mississippi, 3
Ivy, Sarah, 5

JA (Goodnight) Ranch, TX, 82
Jacksboro, TX, 74
Jaquez, Juan N., 222, 262-263, 371
Jarrett, Lloyd, 82
Jefferson, TX, 9
Jenkins, Sheriff J.W., 345
Jessup, Alfred, Jr., 37
Jicarilla Apaches, 55, 133
Johnson, Amos, 101
Johnson, Charles (deputy and attorney), 194-196, 358-359
Johnson, Charles "Race Horse," 3, 131-133
   Johnson's Store, *133*
Johnson, E.M., 314
Johnson, Elihu, 27
Johnson County, TX, 4
Jones, Charles Adam, *100,* 128, 161-162, 179, 254, 355
   as Jones Adams, 233, 280
   Coe family, dispute with, 99-100, 107, 110-111, 174, 179, 227
   Dolores News, acquire, 98- 99, 108, 353
   early life, 98-99
   later life, 354-355
      Jones, Clifford B. (son), 355-356
      Jones, Hoyle, (son), 355
      Jones, Virginia Bartlett (wife), 355
      Spur Ranch manager, 355
   Pinhook Indian fight and rescue expedition, 265-266, 280-281
   Stockton-Eskridge gang, support of, 107-108, 137, 154-155, 174, 182, 226, 228, 247, 251, 261, 264-265, 280, 292, 299, 301, 315, 328, 352
      Eskridge and Wilkinson, reside with, 107, 110

INDEX 503

Lacy, I.W., murder of, 251-254
  Stockton, Ike, reassessment, 328
  Wallace, Gov. and Gov. Pitkin,
    letters to, 264-265
Jornada del Muerto, NM, 262
Junction Creek, CO, 57, 209, 234, 303

Kasserman, S.D., 53
Keegan, Peter, 234, 286
Keith, J.L., 12
Keith, M.L., 15
Keith, Thomas, 44
Keith, William, 18
Kelly, James, 40, 46
Kelsey, J.M., 215
Kerr, Capt. John Brown, 357
Kemp, John, 108
Kiffen, James, 124, 371
Kimbrell, Sheriff George, 71
Kingman, J.H., 74
Kiowa Indians, 5, 8, 28, 33, 41-42, 49, 56, 266
Kirkwood, Samuel J., 203
Kirtland, NM, 135
Knickerbocker, Peter, 132, 208, 371
Knowles, J.A., 78
Kreeger, Louis, 249
Kuch, Fred, 82
Kutz, Mr., 341
Kyle, Sheriff Matt, 334
Kylertown, PA, 352

L' Archeveque, Sostenes, 199
La Boa, Silva, 361
La Jara, CO, 87, 89, 351, 353
La Junta Station, NM, 68
La Plata, CO, 340
La Plata County, CO, 45, 57, 101, 118, 161, 176, 201-202, 210, 215-216, 226, 228, 245-246, 264, 303, 312, 319, 322, 325, 327, 329, 338, 350, 359, 361, 364, 366, 368, 370
  cattlemen's association, 224
  population of, 113
La Plata Mountains, CO, 60, 87, 97, 102, 336
La Plata River (valley), 54, 60, 66, 87, 178-179, 200, 221, 255, 338, 356-357, 466
  Barker, Aaron, murder of, 169, 172, 175, 184
  cattle herds in, 86, 127-128, 168-170,

224, 230-231, 241, 253, 302, 310
  Fort Lewis, 101-102, 126, 134, 155
  rustlers in, 93, 102, 125, 148, 222, 230, 312, 421-422
  San Juan Guards camp, 221, 244, 261
La Sal, UT, 278, 280
La Sal Mountains, UT, 258, 271-274, 278, 280-281, 292, 302
La Veta, CO, 315
La Veta Pass, CO, 122, *123*
Labette County, KS, 86
Laboeuf, Jean Baptiste, 308-309
Lacy, Irvin W.
  cattle business, 6, 11, 14, 84, 89-90
  Coleman, L.G., partnership with, 6, 14, 85
  Colfax County, in, 29, 32-33, 68
    chairman County Comm., 46
    chairman first Fair Board, 40
    chairman first Stock Assoc., 40
    Indians invade home, 33
  Erath County legal troubles, 14-16, 20
  estate of, 298, 302-303, 356
  Goodman, Henry, foreman for, 31, 86, 109, 232, 244, 298
  headstone, *255*
  his troublesome herders, 29, 42-43, 256
    Allison, Clay, 29-30, 46
    Crockett and Heffron, 31, 47, 74, 108-109, 170
    Howland, Big Dan, 128, 202-205, 229
    Dolores News fabrications, 251-255
    Lacy, I.W., murder of, 241, 243-256, 286, 292, 354
    Nance, Tom, 128, 147-148, 170, 178, 221, 250
Lacy, Mrs. Irvin W., 33, 45
  cousin to Stockton brothers, 14, 147
  later life, p. 356
  repudiation of Ike Stockton, 252, 254-255, 263
Lacy and Thompson Cattle outfit; see *Thompson and Lacy cattle outfit*
Lacy children, 251
  Lacy, Clay, 30, 251
  Lacy, Ecce Homo, 251
  Lacy, Irvin W. (Jr.), 33, 251
  Lacy, Lucy Fair, 251

INDEX

Montgomery, Ruth Norma Lacy, 251, 356
LC brands, 14, 30-31, 85, *232*
San Juan country, in the,
  cattle detective, hires, 202-203, 229, 251
  Fort Lewis beef contract, 230
  moves herd to, 85-86, 89-90
  reward for rustlers, 232
  size of herd, 231
  Ute troubles, 233, 241
Stockton family, relationship with, 1, 16, 45, 77, 81, 104, 182, 250-252
  early connections to, 6, 14, 22
  Lacy sanctions killing of Porter, 147-148,
  Stockton, Ike, attack on herders, 167, 170-171
  Stockton, Ike, reward for Big Dan Howland, 246-247, 253-255
  Stockton, Ike, stealing LC cattle, 202, 204, 217-218, 229-233
  Stockton, Porter, stealing LC cattle, 125-127, 147
Thompson, G.W., partnership with, 85-86, 249-250
Lafayette County, MO, 194
Lambert, Henri, 50
Lambert's Saloon (Cimarron), 47, 50
Lampasas, TX, 12
Lamy, NM, 82, 293, 332, 342
Lancaster, E.F., 76
Landon, Dr. J.P., 301
Langston, Mrs. George, 5, 362
Lant, David, 130
Largo Canyon, NM, 163; *see also Cañon Largo, NM*
Larn, John, 70
Las Animas County, CO, 22, 29, 35, 39, 47-48, 51, 85, 90, 112, 202, 231, 251
Las Cruces, NM, 262, 271, 281, 291
Las Vegas, NM, 29, 69, 81, 154, 249
  Dodge City Gang, 71, 254
  Holliday, Doc, 77
  Stockton, Sam, posse for, 82-83
Leadville, CO, 37, 304
Leavenworth, KS, 50
Leavenworth Mountain, CO, 207
Lee, Brownie, 98
Lee, Marion; *see Galbreath, Marion H. "Bud"*
Lee-Peacock feud, 127-128

Leggett, Wright, 91
Leigh, Robert, 72
Lemley Indian attack, 7, 56
Leslie, John, 120-121, 148, 156, 165
Leslie, Madam Cora, 369
Lesnett, Irvin, 344
Lightner Creek, CO, 230
Lincoln, Abraham, 127, 188
Lincoln, NM, 50-52, 62-63, 66, 70, 78
Lincoln, Robert Todd, 203
Lincoln County NM, 14, 189, 221, 229, 391
  Coe family, 40, 50-51, 62, 64-66, 91, 96, 104-105, 110, 139, 164-165, 182, 187, 344, 388
  Stockton, Ike, 52, 61-64, 66, 71, 78, 220, 252
Liner, Jerry, 218
Linton, Charles, 310-311
Littrell, Marion, 31-32, 80
Llano Estacado, 28, 82
Lobato, David, 199, 222, 291-292, 371
Locke, William, 105-106, 140-141, 164, 299-300, 419
  early life, 90-91
  forced out of Farmington, 165, 179-180, 182, 219-220
  Locke, Nettie Vaughan (wife), 91, 130, 164, 416,
Lockhart, George, *150,* 219, 338
  his killing, 150, 356-357
  kills José Marquez, 148
  Lockhart, Mary Ann (wife), 148, 155, 357
  Stockton, Porter, killing, 148, 151, 155
  Stockton brothers, foe of, 125, 140, 163, 169, 186, 208, 222
Logan, Sam, 358
Loma Parda, NM, 29
Lonesome Dove (Larry McMurtry novel), 112
Longwill, Robert H., 26, 37
Los Luceros, NM, 186, 197
Los Lunas, NM, 332.
Los Pinos River (valley), 111, 411; *see Pine River (valley)*
Loutsenhizer, Oliver D. "Lot," 233
Lovell, H.H., 194
Loving, Frank, 249
Loving, Oliver
  Comanches, killed by, 9, 112, 411

INDEX 505

first cattle drive to Colorado, 8, 31
Goodnight-Loving Trail, 6, 9, 128, map, *13*
Loving, Mrs. Oliver (Susan), 375
Lowe, William, 49-50
Lucero, Sheriff Juan, 186, 197
Luna, Antonia, 74
Luttrell, James, 122, 214
Lynch, Tom, 176, 208

MacVeagh, Wayne, 203
Mancos, CO, 244, 268
Mancos River (valley), 60, 86, 102, 126, 233, 259, 265, 277
Mansker, W.T., 18
Manzanares, Juan A., 222-223, 371
Manzano Mountains, NM, 52
Maori (of New Zealand), 116-117
Markley, W.G., 141, 223
Marquez, Jose, 148
Marshall, Charles W., 196
Marshall, E.J., 16
Marshall, Miles B. "Jim," 144-145, 176, 207, 212, 216, 261
Marshall, W.V., 74
Martin, David, 18
Martin, Elijah E., 18
Martin, J.D., 45
Martin, Jim, 134
Martin, William; *See Hurricane Bill Martin*
Martinez, Dolores; *see Steamboat (prostitute)*
Martinez, Martina, 192
Martinez, Sheriff Romulo, 296
Mason Spring, UT, 273-274
Masterson, Bat, 74, 249, 343
Masterson, James, 249
Mastin, Dave, 99
Mather, "Mysterious Dave," 71, 343
Mathews, J.B. (Billy), 64, 66, 71, 78
Maulding, Taylor, 11
maverick cattle, 12, 14, 20, 109, 227
Maxwell, Lucien, 11, 23, 43, 85
Maxwell, NM, 30
Maxwell Land Grant, 11, 22-23, 39-40, 45, 85, 119
May, George, 235, 237
May, Richard (Dick), 235
  killed by Indians, 235-238, 241, 244, 257-258

May, William (Billy), 235
  Pinhook Indian fight, 269-274, 277-279
  seeks vengeance against Indians, 237-238, 257, 259, 265, 446, 448
McBride, Curly, 131
McBride, Patrick A., 35-37
McCaffrey, Tom and Pat, 185
McClelland, John, 70
McCluer, Tim, 117, 132
McConnell, Milt, 356
McCook, Gov. Edward, 45
McCoy family, *214*
  McCoy, Angie Hart, 218
  McCoy, Charles, 208, 371
  McCoy, G.W. (Will), 208, *214*, 340, 371
  McCoy, Harvey, 208, *214*, 218, 371
  McCoy, James, *214*
  McCoy, Jennie, 218
  McCoy, Levi Allen, *214*, 371
  McCoy, Xuella, *214*
McCuiston, Thomas, 107, 125
McCullough, John B., 38, 49, 74
McDermott, John, 157
McDevitt, Marshal, 360
McDonald, Dr. A.J., 301
McGalliard, Mrs. Benajmin K. (Mary), 144, 159
McGee, Jim, 193
McHenry, Charles Holliday, 141, 220, 370
  Coe family, dispute with, 129-130, 182-183
  Heffernan, James J., influence on, 181-182
  Wallace, Gov. Lew, letter to, 93-94, 110, 140, 154, 405
  vigilantes, list of, 186-187
McHolland, J.H., 295
McKenney, Pat, 276-277
McMains, Rev. O.P., 46, 49
McMurtry, Larry, 112
McNab, Frank, 65-66
McPhee Reservoir, CO, 234
McSween, Alexander, 63-66
McSween, Susan, 66
McWilliams, James A. "Harry," 151
Meeker Massacre, 87-88, 102, 259-260
Mefferd, Leana, 57
Mefferd, William, 57
Meloche, Tony, 37, 42

506 INDEX

Melvin, Marion, 53
Meras, Nicas, 51
Meridian, TX, 6, 41, 330, 346
Mescalero Apaches, 281
Mesilla, NM, 226, 240, 242, 245
Meyers, Frank, 106, 156-157, 159-160, 165, 186, 199-200
Mezick, Edward F., 27, 36-37
Middaugh, Alice Snyder, 162
Middleton, John W., 12, 14, 65
Miera, Epimenio, 198
Miera, Pantaleon, 198-199
Mill Creek, UT, 272
Miller, Alison F., 159, 183-184, 198, 220
Miller, Fount, 40
Miller, Gad, 11, 40
Miller, M.J., 311
Miller, Richard D., 11
Milleson, Burr Hiram, 120, 147, *156, 212,* 357, 371
    Battle of Durango, 208, 211
    Stockton, Porter, killing of, 148, 151
Milleson, Henrietta, 120, 147, *156*
Milleson, John, 120, 147, *156,* 371
Mineral Creek, CO, 314
Missionary Ridge, CO, 319
Mitchell, Ernest and Henry L., 259
Mitchell, J.B. (Ben), 361
Moab, UT, 257, 271-272, 277-278, 281
Monero, NM, 288
Montague County, TX, 112
Montaño's Store, 62, *63,* 66
Montezuma Valley, 231, 244
Montgomery, P.J.S., 356
Monticello, UT, 257, 271
Moorman, Henry R., 206-210, 213, 285
Moqui (Hopi) Indians, 244
Moreland, Marshal Newt, 304-305, 308-309, 311
Moreno Valley, NM, 23
Morris, Charles, 27
Morrison, CO, 289
Morrison, George W., 45, 201, 439
    Bayfield, CO, murder in, 358-359
    Cimarron, hoorawing of, 42-44
    Colfax County arrest, 72-73
    Cox family, dispute with, 118, 412
    Erath County, troubles in, 17-18
    Morrison, Dudley (son), 358-359
    Morrison, Marinda O'Neal (wife), 18, 118
    Morrison, Sallie O'Neal (mother), 18
    Morrison, William (father), 18, 357
    prison and violent death, 359
    Stockton brothers, alliance with, 17-18, 118, 152, 169, 228, 319-320
Motheral, Green, 19
Motheral Gap, TX, 8
Mountz, Jim and George, 195
Murphy, L.G., 63
Murray, Dave, 132
Murray, Frank, 112
Myers and West Livery (Animas City, CO), 163, 215

Nachtrieb, Charles, 95
Nacimiento, NM, 199
Naegelin, Charles, 117
Nance, Thomas (Tom),
    hoorawing Seth Welfoot and Rev. Griffin, 156, 220, 356
    Lacy, I.W., murder of, 243, 251, 253
        letter from Nance, 250
    later life, 341-342, 356
        La Boa, Silva, assault on, 361
        Thompson, William, assault on, 359-360
        violent end, 361
    Lee-Peacock feud, 127-128
Nance, Dow, 128
Nance, Malinda Thompson (mother), 127
    Roberts, Jack, capture of, 178
    Stockton, Ike, testifying against, 205, 216
    Stockton, Porter, killing of, 147-148, 151-152, 155, 166, 173, 223, 292-293
    Stockton-Eskridge gang, chased by, 167, 169-171, 173-174, 179, 197-198, 202, 282, 302, 330
    Thompson and Lacy employee, 127-128, 221, 243, 251, 253, 293
        enforcer for, 128, 170, 178, 186
Nathrop, CO, 95
Navajo Indians, 54, 60, 89, 244, 257, 259, 351
    Bohannon, Jake attack on, 124, 129
    Hoffman, F.J., murder of, 200, 433
    Meyers and Raser assault by, 157, 159-

INDEX   507

160, 163, 165, 199
  Navajos respond, 159-160, 200
  Virden home, burning of, 66, 396
Navajo Reservation, 55, 101, 169, 357
Navajo Reservoir, 55
Needle Mountains, CO, 207, 210
Neill, Hyman G. (Hoodoo Brown), 71
Neis, Tony, *242*
  Billy the Kid, transport of, 226, 240
  Stockton, Ike requisition and warrant for, 226, 240-241, 245, 248, 308, 363
Nelson, E.F., 207, 247
Neumeyer, Mrs. A.W., 315
New Orleans, LA, 189, 369
New Orleans Exposition, 369
New York and San Juan Smelter, 130, 214, 304, *334*, 335
Newcomb, John, 64
Nichol, Thomas H., 199
Nichols, James, 195
Nicholson, Patrick, 42
Nowlin, Light, 19
Nunn, Al, 132-134
Nunn, Lucien, 215

O'Connor, Charley, 364
O'Connor, Judge George C., 185, 303
O'Donnell brothers, 236, 244, 266, 270
  O'Donnell, Mike, 236-237
  O'Donnell, Pat, 234, 236
O'Keefe, Georgia, 352
O'Neal, James, 117-118
O'Neal, John, 117-118, 228
O'Neal, John R.
  Lacy, I.W., surety for, 15,
  Stockton, Porter, surety for, 16, 44-45
  Stockton brothers, and, 17-18
Ogden, Bob, 354
Ogsbury, Marshal David Clayton, 312-314, 316-318, 320-321, 323, 325, 327, 352
Olinger, Robert, 229, *242*
Olio, NM, 135
Olympic Theatre (Trinidad, CO), 75, 399
Ophir, CO, 314
Ophir Pass, CO, 314
Osage County, MO, 91
Oschner Hospital, 359
Otero, Don Manuel A., 52
Otero, Miguel Antonio, 68
Otero, NM

description of, 68-69
fading away, 83
Holliday, Doc, in, 1, 70, 74, 77
Hurricane Bill Martin, marshal of, 69-70, 74, 77
Stockton, Ike, in, 70
Stockton, Porter, in, 73
  Bassett, Harry killing of, 79-81
  Withers, Ed, murder of, 1, 75-78, 83, 154, 399
Ouray, CO, 88, 231, 279
Ouray County, CO, 147, 161

Pagosa Springs, CO, 54, 101-102, 108-109, 121, 140, *286*, 287, 289-290, 293, 369
Pah-Ute Indians, 258-259; *see also Paiute Indians*
Painter, C.C., 6, 18
Painter, William (Bill)
  Barker, Aaron, murder of, 170, 217
  Erath County cattle thefts, 18-21
Paiute Indians, 1, 233
  Pinhook Indian fight, 274-279
  Thurman ranch killings, 235-238, 257
  response to, 258-259, 266, 270
Palen, Judge Joseph G., 26-27
Palmer, Ed, 357
Palmer, William Jackson, 131
Palo Pinto, TX, 6, 23, 25
Palo Pinto County, TX, 7, 12, 111, 382
  cattle industry in, 6, 9, 11, 23
  Goodnight, Charles, 6
  Hittson, John W., 6, 28
  Loving, Oliver, 6, 375
  Slaughter, G.W., 6, 9
Paquin, Louis, 265-266, 270
Pargin, Ben, 358
Parker, W.C. (Bill), 90, 105-107
Parker, William, 26
Parker County, TX, 31
Parral, Chihuahua, Mexico, 254
Parrish, Hank, 342
Parrott City, CO, 60, 164, 210, 243, 265, 340, 394
Parrott, Tiburcio, 60, 394
Pasadena, CA, 352
Patterson, James, 28
Peabody, William S., 333
Peacock and Lee feud, 127-128
Pearson, John and Charles, 102
Pease River, TX, 82

Pecos Mission, NM, 81
Pecos River, 9, 28, 58, 112
Pedgrift, Sam, 369
Pendleton, Jack, 315
Penitentes, 341
Pennington, Mrs., 258
Peppin, Dad, 64
Petherbridge, C.L., 289
Phelan, John, 296
Phelps, George, 237
Phelps, Orange, 180-181, 220
Phillipsburg, PA, 352
Pi-Ute Indians, 259; see also Paiute Indians
Piedra River, CO, 108
Pierce, Franklin M., 160
 Pierce, Sara Vaughan, 164
 run out of Farmington, 164-165, 180-181, 220, 345
Pierson, Jabez Deputy, 41, 334, 345-348
Pike's Peak, CO, 189
Pike's Peak Gold Rush, 85, 91
Pine River (valley), 108, 111, 113, 117-118, 131-133, 169, 201, 410-411, 417, 439
Pinhook Indian fight
 Alderson, Joshua H., 280, 298
 Bean, Jordan, 272, 274-279
 Brown, Bob, 280, 282
 Bullock, Charles, 275
 Castle Valley, 273, *274*, 278
  Little Castle Valley, 350
 Cook, M.C., 257, 265-266, 268, 271-272, 297; *see also Galbreath, Marion H. "Bud"*
 Curtis, Richard (Dick), 274-275, 281
 Dawson, William H. (Bill), 269-282, 350-351, 446-447
 Eskridge, Hargo, 265-266, 268, 271-272, 274-277, 279-280, 282, 297
 Flood, L.F., 272, 277, 447
 Hall, James, 275-277, 279, 282, *302*, 352
 Jenkins, Tim, 275-276, 446, 449
 killed in battle, 278
  Click, Tom, 278
  Galloway, John B. "Tarheel Jack," 278, 280
  Heaton, James A., 278, 280-281, 451
  Melvin, Hiram, 278, 450
  Pinhook Monument, *283*
  Tartar, Hard, 274-275, 278, 280
  Tartar, Wiley, 278, 280

 Taylor, T.C., 278, 281
 Willis, Dave, 265, 277-279, 450
 Wilson, Alfred E., 272-274, 277-279, 447-448
 Wilson, Isadore D., 272-274, 277-279, 447-448
 Mancos Jim (Ute Indian), 279
 May, Billy, 265, 269-274, 277-279, 448; *see also May, William (Billy)*
 McCarty, George, 280
 McCarty family, 278
 McKenney, Pat, 276-277, 448
 Moab men, list of, 449
 Parks, Billy, 274-275
 Pepper, Tom, 277, 279, 446
 Pinhook Rescue Expedition, 280-282, 301
  members of, 450-451
 Pinhook valley, *274*
 Porcupine Rim, 273-274, 278
 Shea, William, 272, 277
 Silvey, Frank, 273, 275
 Stockton, Ike, 265-266, 268, 270-272, 274-275, 279, 282, 284, 297-298; *see also Stockton, Isaac T.*
 Wilson, Alfred, 272, 278, 450
Pinkerton detective, 334-335
Pinkerton ranch, 311
Pinkerton trail, 96
Pitkin, Gov. Frederick W.,
 Allison Gang, and, 290-291, 295-296, 334
 Durango, trip to, 304-305
  meeting with Ike, 307
  meeting with law officers, 306
 Eskridge, Hargo requisition and warrant, 331-332, 334
 Heffernan, James, letter from, 181-182, 186
 Radigan, Tommy, warrant, 361
 Stockton, Amanda, letter, 362-363
 Stockton, Ike, letter, 264
 Stockton, Ike, requisition and warrant, 224, 226, 240-242, 261, 300, 307-308, 329, 334, 339
 Ute Indian troubles, 87, 238-239, 268
 Wallace, Gov. Lew, 203, 261-262
 Wilkinson/Eskridge, reward for, 316, 322, 325
 Woods, George, letter, 362-363
Piute County, UT, 264
Piute Indians, 244; *see also Paiute Indians*

INDEX 509

Plumb, Dr., 176, 184
Plumto, Mr., 354
Poncha Pass, CO, 95
Poncha Springs, CO, 315
Pond, Johnny, 127, 148, 160, 163, 169
Ponil Creek, NM, 43, 72
Pope, General John, 102, 127, 199, 238
Posey County, IN, 210
Posse Comitatus, 180, 221
Prescott, AZ, 112
Prevost, Medick E., 26
Price, Col. Sterling, 192
Price, Mrs. Shadrick (Flora Ellen), 87
Prince, Justice L. Bradford, 68, 71, 73, 78, 189, 198, 203, 218
Prindle, James Knox Polk, 207, 285
Proles, Edward, 200
prostitution, 50, 70, 110, 131, 144, 195, 325
Provo, UT, 361
Pueblo, CO, 8, 37, 57, 85, 112, 304, 311, 315, 325, 338
Puett family
   center of the San Juan turmoil, 101, 140, 144-145, 156, 325
   Puett, A.M, Jr., 109-110
   Puett, Al, 109, 140-141, 144, 154, 186, 320, 408, 410
     founding of Farmington, 60, 101
     hostile Utes, 235, 237, 244
   Puett Austin, 101, 109, 144, 320, 410
   Puett, Mrs. Austin (Maria), 109, 320, 410, 457
   Puett, Oscar (Os), 109, 154, 410
     burial of, 140-141, 144, 155
     Eskridge and Garrett, friendship with, 110, 131, 317
     murdered at the Hamblet's, 135-139, 156, 163, 175, 186, 219, 309, 317, 418
     Wilkinson, Bert, cousin to, 101, 109, 131, 144
Puget Sound, WA, 353
Pulvermiller, Conrad, 211
Pyle, Flora Wilkinson, 144, *324*, 419-420
   Puett, Os (cousin), 140-141
   Pyle, Orville (husband), 141, 317, 319, 323, *324*
   Wilkinson, Bert (brother)
     assisting escape, 317-319
     lynching of, 321, 323, 325, 351

Quick, Benny, 237
Quinlan, Mr., 70
Quintana, Juan Andres, 197

Radigan, Tom, *302*
   Barker, Aaron, murder of, 170
   indictment and reward for, 217, 229
   later life, 361
   shot in leg, 171-173
Rambo, W.M., 200
Randal, Frank, 71
Raser family
   Raser, Cal (son), 147, 186
     Stockton, Porter, killing of, 147, 151, 220
   Raser, James (father), 147, 186, 220, 438
   Raser, James H. (son), 147, 186
     shooting of Navajo man, 157, 159-160, 165, 199
     Stockton, Porter, killing of, 147, 151, 220
     Welfoot, Seth, hoorawing of, 156
   Raser, Jane (mother), 147
Rash, Charles W., 222, 340, 371
Ratliff, James, 60
Raton, NM, founding of, 68, 83
Raton Mountains, 42
Raton Pass, 34-35, 48, 68
Ray, Ed, 186
Raymond, F.W., 280
Razier, Bill, 58
Red (Canadian) River, NM, 22, 25-26, 31-32, 34-35, 37-38, 41-42, 57- 58, 382, 393
Red River (Texas/Oklahoma), 3, 40
Reed, James, 261
Reed, Syl, 8
Reid, John, 86, 224, 353
Reid, M.W., 237
Reilly, J.J., 198, 281
Reynolds, Lark
   Barker, Aaron, murder of, 170, 217
   Stockton-Eskridge gang member, 170, 243, 251, 263
Ricard, Charles, 108
Richland, KS, 86
Rico, CO, 117, 160-161, 221, 247, 290, 312, 350-351, 359, 422
   cattle thieves in, 92, 108-109, 170, 176, 207, 210

description of, 96-98
Dolores News of, 98-100, 106, 108, 128-129, 137, 142, 154, 174, 179, 226, 228, 261, 328, 353, 355, 369
Indian trouble, 233, 235, 237, 239
  Pinhook Indian fight, 265-266, 271, 275, 277, 279
  Pinhook Rescue Expedition, 280-282, 301
Stockton-Eskridge gang refuge, 96, 107-110, 124-125, 131, 162, 170, 182, 245, 251-252, 261, 263-265, 291, 297, 302, 307, 314-315, 317, 328, 330-331, 361
Sullivan, Jim, marshal in, 161-162, 302
Riley, John, 63
Riley, Rees, 96
Rincon, NM, 240
Rinehart, Sheriff Isaiah, 48-49, 74
Rio Arriba County, NM, 79, 86, 118-119, 141, 147, 155, 195, 199, 216, 226, 228, 260-261, 263, 265-266, 291-292, 299, 329, 361, 369
  deputy sheriffs appointed, 218, 222
  elections in, 129-130, 182
  law enforcement challenges, 91-92, 102, 104-105, 130, 160, 164-165, 181-182, 186, 188-190, 192, 194, 196, 199, 201, 203, 218-219, 223
  map, *158*
  San Juan County, NM created from, 148, 158, 263, 345
  San Juan Guards militia, 221-222, 227, 262, 271, 362,
    muster roll of, 371-372
  San Juan portion annexed, 90
  Stockton, Ike, grand jury, 189, 205, 330, 332
Rio Bonito, NM, 64
Rio Grande (River), 45, 54, 199, 293, 332, 342
Rio Grande County, CO, 175
Rio Grande Gorge, NM, 394
Rio Ruidoso, NM, 91
Rissler, Dave, 195
Ritch, William Gillet, 48, 190, 203
Riverside, NM, 179
Roberson, Nathan, 124
Roberts, Buckshot, 64-65
Roberts, Gov. Oran Milo, 83
Roberts, J.H., 330

Roberts, Jack
  Greatorex, Thomas, murder of, 176
  lynching of, 178-179, 209
  Nance, Tom, captured by, 178,
Roberts, James (killed by Indians), 42
Roberts, James (jail guard), 49
Roberts, James H., 18
Roberts, John H., 18
Roberts, Leonard F., 8, 18, 20
Roberts, Rev. Harlan P., 97, 317-318
Robinson, Green, 258, 270
Robinson, Isaac (family), 16, 379-380
  Robinson, Amanda Ellen (Mrs. Ike Stockton), 16, 33, 380, 385; *see also Stockton, Isaac T.*
  Robinson, Polly, 111, 379
  Robinson, Sarah (Sally), 16, 111, 379
Rocky Mountain Detective Association, 241, 314, 316, 330
Rocky Mountains, 8-9, 39, 86, 91, 314
Rogers, Captain Benjamin H., 159-160, 199, 257, 259, 266, 270
Romney, Caroline W., 136, 172-174, 208, 211, 213, 225, 258
Rosita, CO, 218, 342
Ross, W.W., 314
Rouse, Mr., 211
Routt, Gov. John L., 48
Routt County, CO, 130
Ruby Hill, NV, 184
Rudabaugh, "Dirty Dave," 71, 254
Russell, James L., 114, 320, 359, 365
Ryan, Bud, 74
Rye, CO, 132
Rynerson, William L., 65

Saguache, CO, 315
Salyer, Martin Van Buren, 20, 90, 358
  Salyer, Mrs. M.V.B. (P.J. Lacy), 358, 381
San Andres Mountains, NM, 281
San Antonio, CO, 185, 190-192, 195, 197, 430; *see also Antonito, CO*
San Diego, CA, 351-352, 355
San Joaquin Valley, CA, 356, 366
San Juan Basin, 350
San Juan County, CO, 54, 175, 312, 316-317, 321-323, 327
San Juan County, NM, 7, 40, 54, 59, 148, 263, 342, 345, 350
San Juan County, UT, 54, 257, 272

INDEX

San Juan Guards (militia), 190, 196, 221-223, 227-228, 244, 261-263, 271, 299, 341, 362, 430, 438, 445, 466
   muster roll of, 371-372
San Juan Mountains, 60, 66, 97, 103, 110, 122, 208, 314, 317, 320, 400
   opened to settlement, 54-55
San Juan River (valley), 55, 60, 66, 89-90, 94-95, 126, 135, 140-141, 171, 175, 186, 190, 192, 197, 200, 205, 223, 261, 299, 342-343, 351
   description of, 54
San Miguel County, CO, 361
San Miguel County, NM, 29, 81, 399
   1889 map, *24*
San Saba, TX, 31
Sanderson, Harley, 285, 287
Sanderson, J.L., 285
Sandoval (Alcalde), 223, 262-263
Sandoval, Placido, 332
Sanftenberg, H., 200
Sangamon County, IL, 127
Sangre de Cristo Mountains, 9, 11, 26, 28-29, 58
Santa Fe, NM, 34, 45-46, 48, 57, 64, 66, 81, 89-90, 106, 114, 126, 154, 164, 175, 179, 186, 188-190, 192, 198, 203, 229, 240, 242, 246, 248, 259, 262-263, 284, 293, 295-296, 299, 331-332, 339, 341, 352-353, 369-370
Santa Fe County, NM, 295-296
Santa Fe Ring, 46, 63, 390
Santa Fe Trail, 22, 25, 34
Santa Lulu, NM, 353-354
Saratoga Springs, NY, 131
Saunders, Ab, 40, 51-52, 62, 388
Scherrer, Fred, 330-331
Schiffer, Ed, 137
Schneider, J., 90
Schrock, Mr., 289
Schuyler County, MO, 89
Schwenk, Henry, 49
Scotch Creek, CO, 96
Scott, Andrew, 26-27, 36
Scott, Pete, 208
Scurlock, Doc, 51-52, 64-65
Seely, Thomas "Little Tommy," 285, 293
Selles, John, 35-36, 78, 386
Shackelford County, TX, 45, 70
Shane, William, 169, 222-223
Shannon, Mark, 321
Sharp, Ollie, *156*

Shaw, Charles, 215
Shaw, D.J., 97
Shaw, John W., 162, 215
Shea, Pat, 342
Shea, William, 272, 277
Sheepshead Bay, NY, 131
Sheldon, Governor Lionel A., 190
   Allison gang and, 293, 295-296
   appointed governor, 284
   Archuleta, Guadalupe, lynching, 341
   Eskridge, Hargo, requisition, 332
   Locke and Hendrickson meeting, 299-300
   Pitkin, Gov., letter, 306
   Radigan, Tom, requisition, 361
   Stockton, Ike, requisition, 329
Sheridan, Gen. Phil, 101, 162
Sheridan, Walter C., 218
Sherman, John, Jr., 189
Sherman, TX, 345, 347
Shoe Bar Ranch, TX, 85
Shoemaker, J.R., 335
Shreveport, LA, 9
Sierra Abajo, 257
Silverton, CO, 52, 54, 87, 96-97, 99, 106, 114, 130, 136, 145, 160, 175-176, 231, 264, 291, 299, 304, 355, 369
   Ogsbury, Marshal Clayton, murder of, 312-314, 317-318, 327
   Thomas, Kid, lynching of, 314
   Wilkinson, Bert, lynching of, 320-326, 328-329
   Wilkinson and Eskridge, pursuit of, 314-318, 330, 332
Simmons, Frank, 407
Simms, "Broke Nose" Dick, 98, 312-313, 327
Skaggs, R.B., 14
Slaughter, George Webb, 6, 9
Sloan, Judge W.B. (correspondent Agate), 221
Sloan, Robert, 12
Smith, Byron, 235, 237-238, 241, 257, 259
Smith, George, 350
Smith, Robert, 344
Smith, Sheriff Joseph, 185, 290, 311, 314
Smith, Thomas, 116-117; *see also Allen, James W.*
Smith, W.H., 82
Snowden, Francis M., 324
Socorro, NM, 342-343

Sourdough Sam, 98
South, Wilson L., 74, 90, 249, 399
Spiller, James, 42-44
Spore, Cass, 195
Springfield, IL, 127
Spur, TX, 355-356
Spur Ranch, TX, 100, 355
Squatter's rights
  Coe, Lew, jumps claim, 66
  Maxwell Land Grant, 22-23, 40, 85
  Rio Arriba County, 91, 119, 141, 413
  Stockton, Porter jumps claim, 118-121
St. James Hotel (Cimarron), 43, 46, 50
St. Joseph's Academy (Trinidad, CO), 251
St. Mark's Episcopal Church (Durango), 98, 207; *see also Hoge, Rev. C. Montgomery*
Standefer, Wiley, 112
Stanley, Patrick "Cap," 130, 178, 209, 214
Stansel, Jesse, 361
Starr, Bill, 354
Starriett, Josiah, 180-181, 220
Steamboat (prostitute), 69
Steele, Richard, 44
Steffey, Perry, 207
Stephens, John M., 5
Stephens County, TX, 8, 11, 376
Stephensport, KY, 210
Stephenville, TX, 8, 10-12, 14-16, 18-19, 31, 35, 40-41, 44, 56, 72, 111, 248, 346, 358; *see also Erath County, TX*
  description of, 5-7
  Galbreath meat market, 19-20
  Lacy, I.W., shoots attorney, 15
Stephenville Museum, 15
Sterrit, Ben, 52-53; *see Walters, Charles*
Stevens, Steve, 65
Stevens and Worsham Ranch, 82
Steward, Frank, 82
Stockton, Isaac T. (Ike)
  cattle and horse theft, 19, 33, 47, 202, 204, 210-211, 230-232
  cattle trails, 6, 22, 41
  Coe family, and, 51, 62, 78, 105, 167-168, 174, 179-180, 186-187, 223
  Colfax County, in, 22, 41, 197
    in Otero, 70-71
    Stockton, Porter, jail break, 49-50, 78, 104, 203
  Cox and Graves families, and, 7, 182, 186, 204, 228, 338, 348
    Cox assists Adj. General Frost, 198, 217-218, 222, 227
    Cox family, threats to, 196-197
    Cox plan to "get" Ike, 205, 208; *see Battle of Durango*
    Cox reward for Ike, ii, 197, 232, 338
    Cox seeks Ike's indictment, 198, 205
    Ike seeks vengeance, 167, 174, 186-187
    paths converge with Ike, 1, 6, 53, 55-56, 78
    see also Cox, Hiram Washington (Wash)
  description of, 168, 223-224, 306
  early life, 4-5, 7, 9, 17-19, 35
    birth, 3
    marriage, 33
  Galbreath, Marion H. "Bud" (aka M.C. Cook), and, 19, 41, 248, 261, 263, 332-335, 345, 347-348
  genealogy, 3-4, 374-375, 379-380
  his children, 111
  his headstone, *336*
  Lacy, I.W., and, 45, 249-250
    cattle detective and spies, 202-203, 230
    Ike, family relationship with, 14
    Ike and Lacy's murder, 246-247, 251-254
    Ike stealing LC cattle, 202, 230
    Lacy puts pressure on Ike, 230-233, 241, 245
    Lacy's widow repudiates Ike, 254-255, 302
    see also Lacy, Irvin W.
  Lincoln County, in, 51-53, 66
    Billy the Kid, 62, 64, 229, 301-302
    Brady, Sheriff William, murder of, 64, 71, 78, 240
    Ike's saloon building, *63*
  Pinhook Indian fight, 234, 257, 265-266, 268, 270-275, 279, 282, 298
  reputation, 17, 105, 200-201, 204, 220
  reward notice and image of Ike, *ii*
  San Juan country, in, 1, 61, 78-79, 98, 104-105, 118, 131, 146, 264
    Allison, Charles, 184-186, 284, 291, 293, 297, 306-307, 309-310
    Animas City, moves to, 125
    Battle of Durango, 209-212

INDEX 513

    Dolores News, support by, 100, 108, 174, 228-229, 251-254, 265, 292, 299, 328
    Durango support, 181-182, 186, 203, 210, 215-216, 260-261, 307
    Durango support erodes, 212, 214-216, 220, 224-225, 260, 299-300, 303, 327-328
    Eskridge brothers, alliance with, 102-103, 151, 163, 167, 187, 190, 229, 292, 301
    Ike's killing, 329-330, 332-339
    Porter's killing, impact of, 155-156, 163, 167, 197, 223
        Barker, Aaron, murder of and chase of Tom Nance, 168-175, 292, 306
        Ike's murder indictment, 216-217
        requisitions, reward, warrants for, 229, 240, 245, 307-308
    racing horses, 304, 307
    Tent Saloon (Durango), 190, 225, 260
    Wallace, Gov. Lew, letter, 264-265
    Wilkinson, Bert, betrayal of, 316-329
Stockton, Jane Hickey (mother), 3
Stockton, Mrs. Ike (Amanda Ellen Robinson), 16, 33, 302, 347
    Coldwell, N.C., marriage to, 366
    Coldwell Banker Real Estate, 368
    death of, 368
    more children, 368
    Woods, George, role in hanging of, 362-366
Stockton, Samuel (father), 3-4, 17
Stockton, Samuel (younger brother to Porter and Ike)
    Eastland County, TX, in, 5
    horse theft, 19, 47, 71, 82-83, 104
    later life, 362
Stockton, Thomas L. (Tom), 35
  cattle thieves, killing of, 25-27
  Clifton House, 25
  early life, 25,
  Hittson's raid, 27-29
  Stockton, Mathias (brother), 11, 25
  Texas cattleman, 11, 22
  witness to murder by Porter Stockton, 36
Stockton, William Porter (Port)
  Allison, Clay, and, 39

  as a braggart, 3, 17, 126, 147, 152, 165-166
  Black Book description, 17
  cattle trails and industry, 6, 9, 20-23
    a "cow boy," 76
    stealing cattle, 20, 125-127, 146, 231
  Colfax and Las Animas Counties, in, 22-23, 25, 67, 73, 83, 197
    Arcibia, Antonio, murder of, 46-47, 73, 109
    Bassett, Harry, killing of, 79-81
    Burleson, Sheriff Peter, 20, 68, 71, 73, 77
    Canada, John, murder of, 33-36, 45, 71, 74, 78
    capture and escape, 47-49, 197, 252
    Colbert, Chunk, chasing, 27, 33-37, 39
    Holliday, Doc, 1, 70, 75, 77
    Hurricane Bill Martin, 75-77
    Withers, Ed, murder of, 75-78
  Cox and Graves families, 134, 146-147
    chasing rustlers with, 3, 132-134
    paths converge with Porter, 1, 6, 55, 105
    role in Stockton's killing, 151-152, 154-155, 166, 174, 306
    see also Cox, Hiram Washington (Wash); Graves, Alfred (Alf) U.
  early life, 3-5
  Erath County, in
    attempted murder, 17, 19, 44-45, 71
    Avant, Taylor, assault, 15-17, 44
    Gravis, Perry, hoorawing, 17, 44
  Fort Garland trouble, 52-53
  genealogy, 3-4, 12, 14, 16, 374-375, 379-380
  Gonzales, Juan, killing of, 50-52
  his assaults and murders, 165-166
  his first murder, 4
  Lacy, I. W., 1, 6, 16, 22, 45, 68, 77, 253
    family relationship, 14
    Porter stealing his cattle, 125-127
    sanctions Porter's killing, 147-148
    see also, Lacy, Irvin W.
  marriage and children, 16, 21-22, 104, 118
  San Juan country, in, 10, 103-105, 197
    Allen, J.W. (barber), assault on, 116-117, 166
    Animas City, marshal of, 113-115
    Eskridge/Garrett assists, 139, 146

Gannon, Den, killing of, 3, 132-134
Hart, Cap, shooting of, 114-116, 126, 166, 412
Leslie, John, assault on, 120-121, 148, 165, 413
Porter's killing, 147-156, 173-174, 197, 220, 223, 228, 253, 292, 306, 309, 362
Porter's killing and Ike, 167, 170-171, 186
Rio Arriba County, move to, 118-119
San Miguel County, NM, assault in, 81-82, 105
Stockton, Jane Hickey (mother), 3
Stockton, Mrs. Porter (Emily Jane Cowan), 16, 21, 118, 379
  death, 369
  Estes, Joel, Jr., marriage to and children, 121, 228, 362, 368
  shot when Porter is killed, 151 152, 154-155, 220, 228, 318
  Woods, George, hanging of, 362, 364-365
Stockton, Samuel (father), 3-4
Wilson, "One-Armed" Billy, and, 111-112
Stokes, Deputy, murder of, 71-72
Stollsteimer, Charles, 54
Stowe, Ike, 82-83
Strater's Drug Store, 360
Stump, Alfred F., 186, 222, 371
Sugarite Creek (Canyon), NM, 40, 65; *see also Chicorica Creek, NM*
Sullivan, Dan, 263
Sullivan, Daniel J., 294-296
Sullivan, Jim (Marshal/Deputy), 362
  description of, 131, 160-161, 264
  Galbreath, Bud, extradition, 345
  Rico, CO, marshal of, 161, 264
  stealing cattle, 369
  Stockton-Eskridge gang supporter, 144, 161, 302
    Coe, Frank, attempted assault on, 162
    Eskridge, Hargo, friend of, 162-163
    Stockton, Ike, killing of, 329, 332-333, 338, 362
    Wilkinson, Bert, assisting, 144, 329
Sullivan, John, 184
Sulphur, OK, 348
Sulphur Springs, TX, 4

Summit County, CO, 37
Sussex County, DE, 87
Sutherland, James, 132
Swenson, E.P., 355-356
Swenson, S.A., 355-356
Swinford, Samuel; *see Comanche Bill*
Swope and Cronk (freighters), 190

Tabor, Sadie, 195
Tabor and Wasson Stage Line, 288-289, 291
Tafoya, Sheriff Juan, 85, 112
Taft, B.A., 314
Taos, NM, 48, 90, 93, 192, 405
Taos County, NM, 48, 73-74, 90, 93, 186, 390
  1889 map, *158*
Taos Pueblo, NM, 34
  Taos Rebellion, 34, 192
Taylor, D.C., 78
Taylor, D.G., 277, 279-281
Taylor, E.A., 287
Taylor, E.C., 82
Taylor, John, Jr. "Doc," 261, 303
Tecumseh, OK, 345-346, 348
Telluride, CO, 215, 231, 361
Tesor, Albert, 47
Texas Panhandle, 82, 85, 100, 167, 355, 382, 388
Texas Ranger's fugitives Black Book
  Galbreath, Marion H. "Bud," 248
  Hurricane Bill Martin, 70
  Morrison, George W., 18
  Stockton, Porter, 17
  Stockton, Samuel, 82
Thomas, Kid
  headstone, *316*
  lynching of, 314-315, 321, 333, 343
  Ogsbury, Marshal Clayton, murder of, 310-315
  Pinhook Rescue Expedition, 272, 279-280, 451
  Stockton-Eskridge gang member, 102-103, 309
Thompson, George W., 167, 174, 208, 232, 252-253, 292, 384, 402
  Lacy, I.W., partnership, 85, 230
  Lacy's estate, 302-303, 356; *see also Lacy, Irvin W.; Thompson and Lacy cattle outfit*
  land grant dealings, 231
  Las Vegas incident, 249-250

INDEX 515

Lincoln, Abraham, 127
Nance, Malinda Thompson, 127
Nance, Tom (nephew), 127, 293
Stockton, Porter, sanctions killing of, 147
Thompson, Doctor Alfred, 360
Thompson, Dow, 127
Thompson, George W. (nephew), 186, 232, 359-360, 384, 402, 421
  Battle of Durango, 208, 435, 467
  foreman of San Juan herd, 359-360
Thompson, Guadalupe Bent (wife), 85
Thompson, Martha Jane, 127
Thompson, William, 358, 421
  cut up by Tom Nance, 360-361
  foreman San Juan herd, 359-360
Thompson, John, 132
Thompson and Lacy cattle outfit
  foreman and herders for, 86, 127-128, 148, 178, 232, 253,
  rustlers, impact of, 109, 127-128, 170, 178, 218, 230-231
  San Juan herd, 86, 89, 147, 170, 230-231, 241, 245, 250
Thornburgh, Major Thomas, 87
Thorniley, Sheriff George, 312, 315, 317, 320, 322-323, 325; *see also, Ogsbury, Marshal David Clayton; Wilkinson, Bert*
Throckmorton County, TX, 82
Thurman, John, 235-237, 241, 244, 257-258, 265, 441
Tierra Amarilla, NM, 57-58, 86, 90 130, 133, 160, 186, 190, 196-201, 203, 205, 216, 218, 222, 262-263, 332, 341
Tinley, Deputy H., 44
Titus County, TX, 16
Tolby, Rev. Franklin J., 46
Toltec Gorge, *305*
Tombstone, AZ, 75, 77, 221, 355
Tomlinson, Samuel, 4
Totah (Farmington), NM, 54
Townsend, Fred W., 371
Tracy, Dr., 335
Tracy, Harry, 130
Trauer, Maurice, 43
Trimble, Frank, 311
Trimble, John T., 307
Trinidad, CO, 37, 39, 51, 57, 68, 75, 86, 89, 170, 174, 188, 203, 231, 249, 254, 340, 363

Colbert, Chunk, posse for, 34-36, 45, 78
  description of, 35
  Howland, Big Dan, 202, 292
  Lacy, I.W., burial of, 245-246, 251, 253
    headstone, *255*
  Lacy, Widow, home of, 356
  Radigan, Tom, 170
  Stockton, Porter, arrest of, 47-48
  Tafoya, Sheriff, murder of, 85, 112
  Thompson and Lacy herders, 127-128, 202, 292-293
Triplet, Wash, 344
Trout Lake, CO, 314; *see also Fish Lakes, CO*
Truby (feud with Cox family), 350
Trujillo, Jose C., 262-263, 371
Tucker, Angeline, 363
Tulare County, CA, 356
Tull, Elizabeth, 95
Tully, Fred, 187, 371
Tully, Helena Anne, 162
Tully, James, 187, 371
Tunstall, John Henry, 63, 65, 78
  murder of, 64
Tunstall Store, 62, 64, 66
Turner, John Charles (Jack)
  Baker Party, member of, 45, 53
  Colfax County Sheriff, 37, 39, 45
    Cowley, John, lynching of, 37-38
    Morrison, George, standoff with, 43-44
  La Plata County, Sheriff of, 45
Turner, W.R., 82

U.S. Army, 1, 70, 77, 86-88, 101, 180, 189, 192, 200, 218, 266, 357, 369, 372; *see also Fort Lewis, CO; Crofton, Col. Robert E.A.*
Uncompahgre Valley, 233-234, 238
Upshur County, TX, 3
Upton's Siding, NM, 262
Urraca Mesa, NM, 49
Ute Creek, NM, 26
Ute Indians, 1, 4, 42, 57, 60, 200, 240
  Buckskin Charlie (Ute Chief), *133*
  cattle herds, harassment of, 89, 233, 238, 244, 258
  Ignacio (Ute chief), 160, *234, 239*, 244
  Mariano (Ute leader), 235, 244
  Narraguinnep (Ute leader), 235, 244,

516 INDEX

257
Paiute Indians, and, 233, 236, 238, 244, 257-259
Pinhook Indian fight, 272-278; *see also Pinhook Indian fight*
Poca (Poco) Narraguinnep, 259
San Juan country, cession of, 54-55
Southern Utes, 157, 160, 233, 239, 271
Tabeguache Utes, 192
threats and attacks of, 114, 147, 157, 200, 235, 238, 257, 266
　Meeker Massacre, 87-88, 259-260
　Thurman Ranch raid, 236, 238, 244, 263
　U.S. Army involvement, 259, 266, 270, 281
Uncompahgre Utes, 233, 238
Weeminuche Utes, 233-234
White River Utes, 259

Valencia County, NM, 52
Valiton, Charles, 343, 351, 354
Valliant, William, 210
Valser, Leonidas Van, killing of, 26-27
Vaughan family
　Coe family, dispute with, 165, 180
　Vaughan, Boyd, 130, 223, 416
　　forced to leave, 180, 220
　Vaughan, Eliza, 370, 470
　Vaughan (Locke), Henrietta, 91
　Vaughan (Pierce), Sarah, 164
Vega, Cruz, 46, 49
Vermejo River (valley), 37, 40, 42-43, 57, 124
　Dawson, John B., ranch of, 11, 22
　Lacy, I.W., ranch of, 31, 33, 46, 231, 245-246, 356, 385
Vermillion, Dakota Territory, 101
Victorio (Apache leader), 77
Vigil and St. Vrain Grant, 231
vigilantes, 26-27, 38, 70, 76, 92, 94, 134, 146, 148-151, 154-156, 163-165, 174, 179, 181, 195-196, 208-209, 213, 219, 228, 303, 315, 320-321, 323-324, 343, 351, 368
　list of New Mexicans, 186-187
Virden family, 396
　Coe, Lew, jumps claim, 66, 119
　founding of Farmington, 60-61
　Virden, Charles, 371

Virden, Milton, 60
Virden, Thomas, 60-61
Virginia and Truckee Railroad, 185
Voorhees, James, 287, 296

Waldo, Henry L., 71-73
Wall, Tom, lynching of, 350
Wall and Witter Stage Line, 193
Wallace, Gov. Lew, 183, 223, 248, 284, 295
　appointed governor, 188
　Billy the Kid, meeting with, 66
　Frost, Adj. Gen. dispatched, 189-190
　Frost reports to Wallace, 147, 152, 155, 197-198, 200-201, 203, 214, 217, 260
　Haines, William, letters from, 229, 244, 261-262
　letter from other citizens, 186-187
　McHenry, C.H., letter from, 154, 186-187, 220
　Pitkin, Gov. letter, 261-262
　San Juan Guard militia, calls for, 221-222
　Secretary of Interior, 203
　Stockton and Eskridge letter, 265
　Stockton-Eskridge Gang
　　indictments, requisitions and rewards, 217, 224-226, 229, 240, 242, 307, 331, 363
　U.S. Marshal, 189
Wallace, Lieutenant (outlaw), 42-44
Waller, George, murder of, 34-35, 37-38
Waller, William G., 12, 19, 44
Walsen and Levy (contractors), 81
Walsenburg, CO, 81, 122
Walters, Charles, 53; *see Sterritt, Ben*
Wasson, Perly, 289
Watson, Sheriff Barney, 210, 264, 350-351
　later life, 369
　Stockton, Ike, shooting of, 329-330, 332-334, 338, 362-363
　Woods, George, hanging of, 365-366
Watts, Henry, *288*
　after prison, 340
　Allison Gang member, 285, 293, 296-297, 309-311, 314
　Eskridge, Dison, associate, 207, 208
　Thomas, Kid, brother of, 310
Weatherford, TX, 31, 82, 112

INDEX

Weatherwax, W.H., 88
Webb, George, 108
Webb, J.J., 71, 254
Webber, Phil, 114, 117
Webster, Judge S.T., 160
Weidner, Marshal Cicero, 53
Welch, William, 35-36
Welfoot, Seth, 180, 219, 318, 404, 457
   early death, 369-370
   forced out of Farmington, 165, 317, 319
   hoorawing of, 156-157
   Puett, Os, burying of, 141
West, George, 102, 126, 243-244, 272, 310, 370, 408
Westcliffe, CO, 101
Wet Mountain Valley, CO, 61, 101
Whigham, Harry, 47
White Oaks, NM, 82
Wickline, Billy, 114
Wilburn, Frank, 25
Wilcox, P.P., 304
Wildcat Canyon, CO, 179
Wilkinson, Bert, 110, *326*, 333, 337, 342-343
   chased by Silverton posse, 314-318
   Comanche Bill, killing of, 144, 309, 325, 329
   Hartman, Frank, lived with, 107-109, 265
   his family, 98, 101
   lynched in Silverton, 323-325
   Ogsbury, Marshal Clayton, murder of, 310-313
   Puett cousins, lives with, 109-110
   Pyle, Flora (sister) assists, 317-318
   reward for, 316-317, 322-323
   robbery by, 311
   Stockton, Ike, captured by, 316-323
      repercussions for Ike, 326-330
   Stockton-Eskridge gang, 101-103, 107, 131, 167, 298, 309, 328
      mining interests with Stockton and Eskridge, 124-125, 263
Will, Laura, 258
Williams, C.M., 214
Williams, D.D., 235, 238, 258, 266
Williams, Frank, 96, 320, 322
Williams, P.K., 371
Williams, R.W., 222, 371
Williams, Sandy, 379
Willow Springs, NM, 68, 83

Wilson, Alfred and sons; *see Pinhook Indian fight*
Wilson, Col. H.B., 365
Wilson, Henry, 211
Wilson, Jack
   Battle of Durango, 211
   Stockton-Eskridge gang, associate of, 207, 211, 215-216, 333, 434
Wilson, "One-Armed" Billy (William J.), 132
   Animas City, in, 111
   Barker, Aaron, his herder, 170, 173, 425
   Loving, Oliver and Comanche attack, 111-112
   Stockton brothers, and, 111, 152, 174
   Tafoya, Sheriff Juan, killing of, 112
   Wilson, Fayette (brother), 112
   Wilson, George (brother), 112
   Wilson Gulch, named for, 111
Wilson Gulch, CO, 111, 113
Windsor Hotel (Denver), 240
Winkfield, Jacob W. "Wink," 48
Winkle, Pete, 171, 421
Winters, Dr., 360
Wirz, Captain Henry, 188
Withers, Ed
   Hurricane Bill, associate of, 69, 77
   Stockton Porter, murdered by, 1, 75-80, 154, 165-166
Wood, D.W., 210
Wood, Eugene, 17, 45, 166
Wood, Lucinda, 7
Woodburn, John K., 72
Woods, George N., 362-366
   his hanging, *367*
   his headstone, *368*
Woods, Henry, 60, 363
Woodworth, Major, 81
Wootton, R.L., Jr., 75, 90, 399-400
Wootton, "Uncle Dick," 33-36
Wootton, William (Bill), 75, 78, 399
Wright, Coroner, 207
Wright, Joseph, 101

Yavapai County, AZ, 112
Yuma, AZ, 351

Ziegenfuss, C.O., 306-307
Zuni (correspondent), 129

www.ingramcontent.com/pod-product-compliance
Lightning Source LLC
Chambersburg PA
CBHW050157240426
43671CB00013B/2160